A history of the peoples of Siberia is the first ethnohistory of Siberia to appear in English, analysing ethnographic and linguistic features of the native peoples and tracing their history from the Russian conquest onwards. James Forsyth assesses the impact of Russian exploration and settlement, and looks at Siberian relations with Kazakstan, Mongolia and China. He shows how Russian occupation generated warfare, tribute-exaction and exploitation to such an extent that many doubted the capacity of the Siberian peoples to survive.

After the 1917 Revolution and the vicissitudes of civil war (not to mention the growth of Altai, Buryat and Yakut separatist movements) the new Soviet regime brought 'autonomy', medical services and education. However, the policies of the Stalinist era – collectivisation, denomadisation, amalgamation of settlements, Russification and the destructive environmental effects of Russian industrial development – further undermined the native communities, as did conscription during the Second World War. Their critical situation in the post-war period, revealed to outsiders as a result of Gorbachev's policy of *glasnost*, is viewed as the inevitable outcome of Leninist 'nationalities policy', and gave rise in the 1980s to a notable 'native rights' movement. James Forsyth compares the Siberian experience with those of Indians and Eskimos in Canada and the USA, and the book as a whole will provide anglophone readers with a vast corpus of ethnographic information previously inaccessible to Western scholars.

A HISTORY OF THE PEOPLES OF SIBERIA

Symbols of colonial empire from the atlas of Siberia compiled for Peter the Great by S. Remezov, showing, below the double-headed eagle of the Russian Empire with allegorical figures, angels supporting the arms of Siberia: two sables trapped in a bow, and two crossed arrows. The kneeling figures are a Russian Siberian (*sibirets*) with an anchor, representing the river-borne exploration of Siberia, and three submissive natives offering fur tribute: a Tatar (here *tartarinets*) identifiable by his bow-case and quiver, a Samoyed with characteristic knife, and an *obdarinets* or Ostyak of the river Ob in typical head-dress.

A HISTORY OF THE
PEOPLES OF SIBERIA

RUSSIA'S NORTH ASIAN COLONY
1581–1990

JAMES FORSYTH

Reader in and Head of the
Department of Russian, University of Aberdeen

CAMBRIDGE
UNIVERSITY PRESS

Published by the Press Syndicate of the University of Cambridge
The Pitt Building, Trumpington Street, Cambridge CB2 1RP
40 West 20th Street, New York, NY 10011–4211, USA
10 Stamford Road, Oakleigh, Melbourne 3166, Australia

First published 1992
First paperback edition 1994

Printed in Great Britain at the University Press, Cambridge

A catalogue record for this book is available from the British Library

Library of Congress cataloguing in publication data
Forsyth, James, 1928–
A history of the peoples of Siberia: Russia's north
Asian colony.
1581–1990/James Forsyth.
p.   cm.
Includes bibliographical references (p.   ) and index.
ISBN 0 521 40311 1
1. Ethnology – Russian S.F.S.R. –Siberia.
2. Siberia (RSFSR) – Social life and customs.
3. Siberia (RSFSR) – Discovery and exploration.
4. Siberia (RSFSR) – History. I. Title.
DK758.F67   1992
957'.004–dc20 91–8137 CIP

ISBN 0 521 40311 1 hardback
ISBN 0 521 47771 9 paperback

To Jo and Marion

CONTENTS

CONTENTS

ILLUSTRATIONS

Acknowledgements for illustrations: *frontis.* by permission of the Houghton
Library, Harvard University; 3, 8 by courtesy of Department Library Services, American Museum of Natural History; 2 Library of the Academy of
Sciences of the USSR; 5 Hamburgisches Museum für Völkerkunde; 7, 11
Izdatelstvo 'Khudozhnik RSFSR'; 9 Izdatelstvo 'Russkiy yazyk'. Every effort
has been made to contact copyright holders, but if any have been overlooked
the publishers will be pleased to make the necessary arrangement at the first
opportunity.

MAPS

PREFACE

MY reason for writing this book was that, as a consumer of histories of Russia (although not a professional historian) I could find no book in English which narrated and interpreted the stages in the conquest and exploitation of Siberia and the place of this process in Russian and world history. As Siberia, which is another name for northern Asia (roughly everything lying east of 60°E and north of 50°N) occupies almost one-third of the land mass of Asia – an area larger than the United States or Australia – this seems hardly a negligible matter. Quite a number of books and articles in European languages have been published in recent years dealing with Siberia as one of the regions of the Soviet Union occupying an important place in the state economy, and its relationship to other parts of the world in terms of strategy and economic resources to be developed in the service of a late twentieth-century style of prosperity. From this point of view Siberia is usually considered to be simply an extension and integral part of Russia – her eastern treasure-house of mineral wealth awaiting exploitation. And of course it is true that the great majority of Siberia's inhabitants are now Russians, just as the overwhelming majority of people in North and South America are the descendants of settlers from Europe. Up to the eighteenth century, however, this was not the case. As in the Americas, the colonists shared the territory with a large number of native tribes whose presence long predated theirs.

This is the aspect which has attracted least attention – the role of the native peoples: who they are, how they lived before the Russian invasion, the effects of the latter on their lives, their present state and future prospects. As the indigenous peoples of Siberia – Buryat Mongols, Yakuts, Tatars, Samoyeds, Tunguses, Chukchis and others – have been under Russian rule for 350 years or more (Yermak's expedition beyond the Urals began in 1581) several obvious questions arise. In the first place – have they been as well treated by the Russians as the picture presented by Soviet propaganda would have us believe? Their numbers are small: in 1989 some 1.6 million among the total of 32 million inhabitants of Siberia. Are they therefore so insignificant numerically as to warrant no more than a footnote in the history of Russia? Have they now lost their cultural identity, swallowed up by the great mass of Russian and other incomers? Are the thirty or so indigenous communities of Siberia – the largest numbering only 350,000, the smallest 350 – destined to disappear altogether? In considering these questions it is natural to think also of the aboriginal inhabitants of the Americas. Has the fate of the Siberian natives been similar to that of the Indians and Eskimos of North America? Is there a parallel with the Indians of the South American forest who face extinction as a result of the ruthless commercialism of the dominant whites? This question leads inevitably to the related problem of the natural environment, as the original habitat of the native peoples is threatened by the inexorable destruction of forest and tundra.

Such were the general concerns underlying my investigation of what has been written, mainly in Russian, about the past and present of Siberia. The literature is enormous, if not always revealing, and the sources I have used are diverse, including: printed collections of early documents, scholarly surveys based on unpublished documents, Russian-language histories of Siberia, both nineteenth-century and Soviet, works on aspects of Siberian history published in the West, ethnographic accounts of native peoples, their traditions and religion, works about the ethnic history of northern Asia, recent Soviet sociological studies, books on the languages of Siberia, censuses of the USSR, geographical descriptions, travellers' accounts, literary works by Siberian authors, and popular propagandist narratives – material which has been utilised only to a relatively small extent in English-language publications. What I have put together from these sources has, I hope, resulted in a many-sided account of the peoples who live in Siberia – not entirely neglecting the Russians – and what happened to them in the course of the four centuries of their recorded history. (Archaeological evidence goes back much farther than this, but the speculation about the prehistory of Siberia which arises from it falls beyond the scope of this book.)

My aim has in fact been to write in the genre that some recent North American writers have called ethnohistory – 'a common-law marriage of history and anthropology' (J. Axtell, *The European and the Indian: Essays in the Ethnohistory of Colonial North America*, Oxford, 1981, p. vii) – in which an account of the way of life of the different aboriginal communities is presented in its changing (and reciprocal) relationship with the society and national history of the Russian incomers. My book does not set out to be a history of Russian Siberia as such – the visitors and settlers of many kinds who carried Russian life and culture eastward into northern Asia and established this as the dominant element in the colony. That would require a study of the military conquerors and administrators, the growth of towns, of agriculture and of trade, the origins of the rank-and-file settlers, the exile and prison system, and so on. None of this – which has been and no doubt will be the subject of works by other writers – can be more than sketched in a book which concentrates on the indigenous peoples and their problems as the subjects of their Russian rulers. My venturing into this field of historical and ethnographic specialisms is perhaps somewhat rash, but as the time is ripe for a general history of the peoples of Siberia to be attempted, I take the risk in the hope that what I have written may be a useful contribution to the study of a vast area of human activity which has been largely neglected by historians willing to dismiss pre-conquest Siberia as an 'empty land' inhabited by only 'thinly scattered natives'.

As any work on Siberian history must take into account the many works published in Russia between the 1920s and the 1980s, the Soviet Marxist formulations continually repeated therein offer the main body of historical interpretation which the investigator has to confront. It is with reference to such ideological commonplaces, and their echoes in some Western works, that at various points I focus attention on some of the larger misconceptions which have been presented as unquestioned dogma in the Soviet Union until very recently. Such are, for instance, the assertions that the occupation of Siberia by the Russians was on the whole a peaceful process, that incorporation into Russia was of more benefit than harm to the native peoples because it brought them into contact with a 'higher culture', and that there was no resemblance between Russian rule and other colonial régimes under which native peoples were cruelly exploited. Distortion and the hushing-up of facts reached a preposterous level in Soviet writings about the post-revolutionary period: while on the one hand it is asserted that 'Leninist nationalities policy' led the world in humanity and justice in dealing with minority peoples, including those of Siberia, the facts of the actual suffering they underwent during enforced acculturation to Soviet Russian social and political institutions – in particular collectivisation, denomadisation and the destruction of traditional cultures and occupations – have been almost totally suppressed. *Glasnost* under the aegis of Mikhail Gorbachev has begun to open up such questions, but much of the truth about the twentieth-century history of the peoples of Siberia still has to be revealed before a comprehensive account can be written.

My own, far from complete, account will inevitably be superficial or inaccurate in places, either through shortcomings in the sources I have used or through my own errors, and I take full responsibility for them.

ACKNOWLEDGEMENTS

THE writing of this book has left me greatly indebted to many friends who have helped me with materials, criticism and encouragement. These include colleagues at the University of Aberdeen – in the first place Paul Dukes – and David Capitanchik, James Thrower, and David Scrivener, now at the University of Keele; farther afield, Alan Wood of the University of Lancaster and the British Universities Siberian Seminar, Martin Dewhirst of Glasgow University, Terence Armstrong and Frances Cooley of the Scott Polar Research Institute, Cambridge, Kitty Inglis of the Library of the University of East Anglia, Andrey Terentyev of the Buddhist Board of the USSR, Moscow, Boris Chichlo of the Centre d'Études Sibériennes, Paris, John Stephan of the Center for the Soviet Union in the Pacific-Asian Region, University of Hawaii, and Phyllis DeMuth of the Alaska Historical Library, Juneau. Thanks also to Judith Thrower for helpful comments on the typescript. Without the resources of Aberdeen University Library and the excellent service of the Inter-Library Loans scheme which allowed me to draw upon the stock of many other libraries, I could not have undertaken this task. Nor could the typescript have been prepared for publication without the skills of Elizabeth Weir, Joan Scrivener, Doreen Davidson, Jennie Albiston, Gillian Silver, Chris Anderson, and especially during the final fraught stages of revision, Lorna Cardnow.

In a category of its own is my gratitude to my wife Josephine Newcombe not only for constant support and advice, but for putting up with my internal exile to Siberia for so long.

NOTE ON SPELLINGS AND TERMS

RUSSIAN words and names are transliterated according to the widely accepted British system, with *ya*, *yu* for я, ю (i.e. Yakut, Iya not Iakut, Iia) and *ye*, *yo* for е, ё initially and after vowels, but *e* after consonants (i.e. Yenisey, Khrushchev not Enisey, Khrushchov). The essential difference between the vowel и and the semivowel й is conveyed by *i* and *y* respectively (e.g. *moy* 'my' singular and *moi* 'my' plural), and y is also used for ы (pronounced approximately as *i* in 'give'), e.g. Irtysh. The soft sign ь, often rendered by ', is ignored throughout as its occurrence is obvious to those who speak Russian and it adds little for those who do not (e.g. Ob, Ilmen not Ob', Il'men').

In the case of many names which are not Russian but belong to other languages of Siberia or to Mongolian, Tatar, Arabic, etc., spelling conventions appropriate to these are used. Thus such spellings as Altai, Baikal (not Altay, Baykal) are used, as are *yasak*, *yasyr* (not *iasak*, *iasyr*). Russified spellings such as *dzh* for *j* as in 'jar' have been eschewed (e.g. not Selemdzha, Dzhugdzhur but Selemja, Jugjur), as has the Russian obsession with palatalisation which gives to e.g. Vilui, Korak the unnecessarily clumsy appearance Vilyuy, Koryak. In, for example, Turkic names the Russian spellings я, ю, е have been rendered as *ä*, *ü*, *ö* where appropriate. As English has the bilabial consonant *w* which Russian lacks, it has been used in names which contain it in the original language, e.g. Ewen, Ewenki. Other Russian, as opposed to indigenous, spellings have been avoided in e.g. Ulaan-Üde, Örgöö (in Russian Ulan-Uda, Urgu). Similarly, Polish names retain their native form: Czersky not Cherskiy. For Chinese words traditional spellings or the Wade-Giles romanisation is used, not Pinyin, e.g. Sinkiang, Ch'ing, Hsing-an.

In naming administrative territories the following equivalents have been used: *guberniya*, *oblast* – 'province', *kray* – 'territory', *okrug* – 'region', *rayon* – 'district'.

I

SIBERIA 'DISCOVERED'

SIXTEENTH-CENTURY RUSSIA AND THE ADVANCE TO THE URALS

BY the middle of the sixteenth century the colonial expansion of European states was well under way. Tempted by dreams of trade, the merchant-adventurers of Western Europe had set out to explore unknown parts of the world, and the bases they established in various foreign lands became bridgeheads for the conquest of colonies, the introduction of settlers from the metropolis, and economic exploitation at the expense of the native inhabitants. In the Americas the empires of Spain, Portugal, England, Holland and France embraced vast territories by the middle of the seventeenth century, and bases for later European conquests existed in Africa, India and the East Indies.

Muscovite Russia, using similar means of conquest and colonisation, participated in this European expansionism by annexing the largest continuous territory of any empire – the whole of northern Asia, which came to be called Siberia. The only basic difference between Russia's colonial expansion and that of the West European states was that it was not dependent upon fleets of sailing-ships plying long distances across the ocean, but on an advance overland (or rather, by river) into 'unexplored' regions of the same Eurasian continent. Otherwise the Russian explorer–conquerors shared with their West European contemporaries the developments in state and military organisation and technology – above all, firearms – which gave them a powerful advantage over the less 'advanced' native inhabitants of the lands they seized.

Russia in the sixteenth century had become one of the most formidable states in Europe. The yoke of Tatar domination imposed by the Mongol invasion in the thirteenth century had gradually weakened and was eventually thrown off by successive grand princes of Moscow. Thereafter the Moscow grand princes succeeded in building up their own power during the fifteenth century as the Golden Horde disintegrated into the separate khanates of Crimea, Astrakhan, Kazan, Nogai and Siberia. This process culminated in the subjugation of the other Russian principalities by Ivan III, called the Great (1462–1505). The universal role first claimed for Russia by this grand prince was symbolised by his assumption of the imperial insignia of the double-headed eagle and the title Caesar (i.e. Tsar). At the same time he adopted the nationalist doctrine of Moscow as the 'Third Rome', the centre of Christendom which, unlike Rome itself and Constantinople, was destined never to fall to heathen invaders.

However, the Tatar khans continued to consider the grand princes of Moscow to be their vassals, and from time to time they still raided the territory of Moscow and indeed the city itself. Moreover, the Kazan Tatars controlled the middle Volga, frustrating the ambitions of Russia's rulers to extend their trading activities to the east. In 1552, therefore, Ivan IV, 'the Terrible', sent a large army to attack Kazan, and, in the words of the chronicler, 'by the help of our Lord Jesus Christ and the prayers of our Sovereign Lady and Mother of God and the intervention of the Archangel Michael'[1] the city was captured, the khan cast down from his throne, and a large territory from the Volga to the Ural mountains was claimed for Russia. The Russians, who on the one hand were unable to defeat the Crimean Tatars for another 200 years, and on the other were being hard pressed in the west by Sweden and Poland, found scope for expansion in the east. Before them lay a whole continent of practically 'unknown land' – northern Asia. Of its inhabitants the Russians had had contact only with the 'Yugrians' of the northern Urals, some of whom were nominally subjugated first by Novgorod and later by Moscow.

Novgorod, which long before the emergence of the principality of Moscow was one of the two main centres of early cultural development among the eastern Slavs (the other being Kiev), lived by trade, deriving its wealth from furs and other products to be found in the northern forests and the Arctic shore. Its merchant boyars had begun extending their activities in that direction as early as the tenth century, the main routes for their ships being the great rivers of the north, such as the Sukhona, which flows 300 miles to the north-east before joining the Vychegda to form the Northern Dvina. Because the low watershed at White Lake (Beloye ozero) was the door to the whole north-western region, the Novgoroders' name for these lands was Zavolochye – 'beyond the portage', from the Russian word *vólok* (portage) – and its Komi inhabitants were 'the Chud beyond the portage'. Expeditions 'beyond the portage', instead of taking the northward course of the Dvina to the White Sea, could sail along a 1,000 mile waterway from the Sukhona up the river Vychegda to the north-east, where other low water-

---

[1] *Lvovskaya letopis (Polnoye sobraniye russkikh letopisey*, t. 20), St Petersburg, 1910, vol. II, p. 530.

2

sheds made it possible to cross to the northward-flowing river Pechora, one of whose tributaries, the Usa, led upstream as far as the Ural mountains, or to the Kama, which flows in a great clockwise arc first north, then south to join the Volga. All this land lies within the *taiga* or northern coniferous forest, with spruce and fir predominating.

The Novgoroders had penetrated far into Zavolochye by the eleventh century, setting up their posts on river banks and forcing the Komi people to bring in furs as tribute. Official Soviet historians gloss over the facts of colonial exploitation with such bland statements as: 'As in most of the subordinated lands the political dependence of Komi territory on Novgorod was expressed merely by the regular payment of tribute: the Novgoroders did not interfere in the internal life of the territory.'[2] In fact the violent methods used in subjugating the natives of the northern European forest west of the Urals were typical of those used by the Russians throughout their subsequent campaigns in quest of wealth from furs. Their subjection of the peoples of Zavolochye proved to be only the first stage in their conquest of the whole of northern Eurasia – a drive to the east which would develop a powerful momentum of its own, although the Russians in the twelfth century could not be aware of the magnitude of the enterprise they had initiated.

If the Komi living in the basin of the Vychegda (whose land was known as Perm) submitted to the Novgorod Russians without any recorded resistance at this time, people living farther east and north, near the Ural mountains, inflicted sufficiently serious blows on the invaders to warrant the attention of the monastic chronicler: the Pechora (presumably Samoyeds) living in the basin of the river of that name, and the Yugra (probably ancestors of the present-day Khantys) in the vicinity of the Urals, killed the Novgorod marauders who came to extort tribute in 1187. A few years later:

they set out from Novgorod to the Yugra with an army led by Yadreyko, and . . . came to another town. And [the Yugrians] barricaded themselves up in the town, and it was besieged for five weeks. And they sent out false word [to the Russians] that 'we are gathering silver and sable-skins and other treasure, so do not destroy us your serfs or your tribute', but all the time they were assembling an army. And when they had gathered warriors they send out word to the commander: 'come into the town with twelve men'. And they entered the town . . . and they slew them.

Similar events are recorded 150 years later, and another century after that, when in 1445 two Novgorod commanders took an army of 3,000 into Yugra-land, again meeting disaster after demonstrating their methods of coercion: 'they seized many Yugrian people and their women and children, who were terrified. But the Yugrians succeeded in deceiving them, saying "we shall give you tribute . . .", but meanwhile they gathered together and struck at

---

[2] B.N. Ponomarev, ed., *Istoriya SSSR s drevneyshikh vremen do nashikh dney*, Moscow, 1966–, vol. II, p. 24.

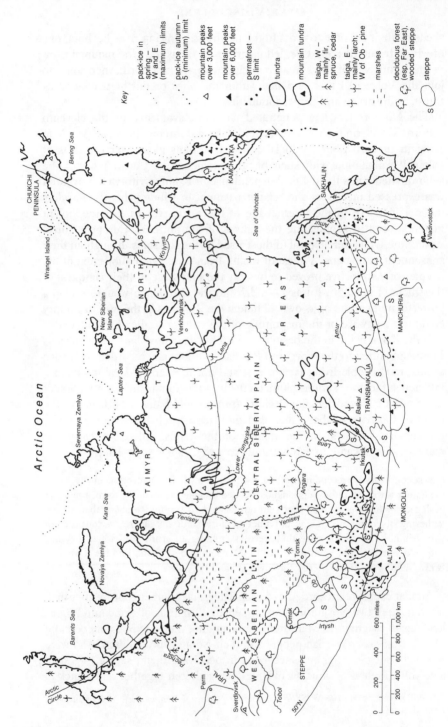

Key

pack-ice in
spring –
W and E
(maximum) limits

pack-ice autumn –
5 (minimum) limit

△ mountain peaks
over 3,000 feet

▲ mountain peaks
over 6,000 feet

permafrost –
S limit

T tundra

▲ mountain tundra

⋌ taiga, W –
mainly fir,
spruce, cedar

⋋ taiga, E –
mainly larch;
W of Ob - pine

- - marshes

deciduous forest
(esp. Far East),
wooded steppe

S steppe

Map 1 Natural features of Siberia

Vasiliy's fort, and they killed as many as eighty good [Russian] people, of boyar line and gallant people, and it was pitiful to hear the slaughter.'[3] The mention of boyars is a reminder that the Novgorod colonisation of Zavolochye was essentially a private enterprise undertaken by the great magnates of the city for commercial ends. Some boyars, having dug themselves in and established a retinue of workers and warriors around them, began to act as land-owners in their own right and to forget the interests of the mother city.

The rulers of Novgorod had to cope not only with insubordination among their own people, but also with the growing rivalry of the princes of Moscow. During the first century of Tatar domination of the Volga–Oka region its princes had little time for skirmishing with the Novgoroders, but in the fourteenth century the raiding on both sides intensified, with ever-increasing anger on the part of the Moscow princes at the refusal of Novgorod to recognise their suzerainty. The outcome was scarcely in doubt, considering the Muscovites' determination to crush all rivals, but during the last century of its independent existence Novgorod defended its lands valiantly in a long series of wars for the possession of Zavolochye.

An important development in Moscow's intrusion into 'the land beyond the portage' was the part played by the Christian church. There had been a great upsurge in monastic activity in the Moscow lands during the fourteenth and fifteenth centuries, emanating from the Trinity-Sergiev monastery, founded by St Sergiy of Radonezh. It was this expansion of the field of activity of the Orthodox church from Muscovy which made the first inroads upon the traditional life and beliefs of the Komi or Permian people (the northern group of which was called by the Russians 'Zyrians'). In 1383 the monk Stefan Khrap, a native of Ustyug, decided to go to preach the Christian religion among them. The missionary, later known as St Stefan of Perm, sailed up the Vychegda to the mouth of the river Vym, where he built his church and set about learning the Komi language and creating an alphabet in order to write translations of religious texts. The account of his life tells of the hostility of the people of Perm and of Stefan's profanation of their shrines and religious images ('and he struck the idols on the head with the back of an axe, and chopped their legs, and felled them . . . and smashed them to pieces', etc.). His frenzied zeal triumphs in the final theological debate against the head shaman, Pan, when the latter sensibly refuses either to jump into a fire or into a hole in the ice, hand-in-hand with Stefan, to prove whose god is the stronger.[4] Stefan of Perm's proselytising was followed sixty years later by the baptism of the Komi on the river Kama by the Moscow bishop Ioan – an event which required reaffirmation by military

---

[3] *Novgorodskaya pervaya letopis*, Moscow, 1950, pp. 232, 425.
[4] Yepifaniy Premudryy, *Zhitiye Svyatago Stefana, yepiskopa Permskago*, St Petersburg, 1897, pp. 8, 17–19, 22–3, 27, 35–40, 50–6.

means in 1472, when prince Fyodor Pestryy was sent from Moscow to subdue the Komi prince of Great Perm.[5]

The religion Stefan of Perm found among the Komi combined animism with the cult of ancestors. All natural phenomena were endowed with soul, and each clan had a sacred grove in the forest in which they congregated from time to time to invoke the spirits and make sacrifices to them. One of Stefan's acts was to cut down a tall birch-tree near his settlement, which was revered and used as a sacrificial site by the Komi people. The rituals performed by the shamans or priests included propitiatory sacrifices of animals in the fields, and rain-making. There was a variety of gods, both great and small, such as the sky-god, the mother of the sun, or the mother of water.

Christianity was imposed upon the Finnic peoples, but for many it never fully replaced their old religion. Despite campaigns organised by the Russian state from the seventeenth to the nineteenth centuries, in which shrines and sacred groves were destroyed, paganism persisted as the real religion, especially in places most isolated from the attention of the authorities.[6]

To the south and east of the territory of Moscow and Novgorod the native inhabitants of the Urals came within the orbit of the Tatar khanate of Sibir. Like the Russians, the Turco-Tatar rulers of Sibir had forced some of their immediate neighbours in the Ural region – the Khantys and Mansis – into subjection, and thus obtained from them as tribute the furs in which the virgin forest was so rich. As furs were much in demand in the countries of Central Asia and the Middle East, some awareness of the dark northern land was carried across the steppes and desert of what is now Kazakstan to such centres of Islamic civilisation as Bukhara, Samarkand and Baghdad. Similarly, in the Far East the people of China had from the beginning of their civilisation known something of the distant forests which lay beyond their immediate 'barbarian' neighbours, the Mongolian, Tungus and Turkic nomads of Inner Asia. The earliest accounts of some of the peoples inhabiting the southern fringe of Siberia are therefore preserved in Chinese chronicles.[7] Little of this, however, was known to the Russian adventurers who set out to explore and conquer Siberia in the late sixteenth century.

THE GEOGRAPHICAL BACKGROUND

The land of northern Asia which lay before them stretches for some 2,800 miles from the Urals to the shores of the Pacific Ocean (roughly the distance

---

[5] S.M. Solovyov, *Istoriya Rossii s drevneyshikh vremen*, Moscow, 1962–6, vol. III, p. 73.
[6] *Narody yevropeyskoy chasti SSSR*, V.N. Belitser et al., eds., vol. II, Moscow, 1964, pp. 401–3, 431–2, 444–6, 455, 472–9, 491–3, 499–502.
[7] e.g. N.Ya. Bichurin (Iakinf), *Sobraniye svedeniy o narodakh, obitavshikh v Sredney Azii v drevniye vremena*, St Petersburg, 1851, revised and reprinted, Moscow, 1950; A.G. Malyavkin, *Istoricheskaya geografiya Tsentralnoy Azii: materialy i issledovaniya*, Novosibirsk, 1981.

across North America from coast to coast at the latitude of the Great Lakes), while in its most northerly, arctic latitudes, it extends for a further 950 miles eastward to the tip of Chukchi-land (in Russian *Chukotka*) where the 50-mile-wide Bering Strait separates Asia from Alaska. As nearly all of Siberia lies north of the fiftieth parallel of latitude, its position on the earth is comparable with that of northern Europe or Canada.

It is also to Canada that Siberia must be compared with regard to climate. The range of temperatures over the seasons is similar, but Siberia, because of the huge land-mass of Eurasia, is even more extreme than Canada, with average winter temperatures over much of its territory between $-30°$ and $-40°C$. In some parts of the north-east, such as Verkhoyansk and Oymyakon – the coldest places in the northern hemisphere – the temperatures can fall as low as $-71°C$, although in summer it may rise to $+34°C$.

Despite the severity of its climate, every part of Siberia had had its human inhabitants for thousands of years before the Russians came in the seventeenth century. The very earliest signs of habitation in Siberia during the Stone Age occur in the more southerly regions and the upper Lena valley, but by about 3500 BC several different Neolithic cultures existed which, however sparsely distributed their population may have been, extended over the whole of Northern Asia, including the shores of the Arctic Ocean.[8] The ethnic and linguistic composition of these cultures as they developed during the course of many centuries can only be surmised from scant relics of material culture and the evidence of languages, and in practice it was not until the seventeenth century that the recorded history of most of the native peoples of Siberia began. The ethnic pattern was already complex by that time, and Siberia was certainly not an 'empty', uninhabited land.

The vast territory of Siberia falls into three sections from west to east. From the Ural mountains the land descends to the wide plain of Western Siberia which forms the basin of the great river Ob and its equally majestic tributary the Irtysh. These rivers carry the abundant waters of the Altai mountains northward across the low-lying plain into the sub-arctic region where the ground is permanently frozen and the surface of the Arctic Ocean is icebound for many months in the year. Over most of their course the Irtysh and Ob have a relatively slight gradient, so that they flow slowly. The watersheds between their many tributaries are low, and as their exit to the sea is blocked by northern ice, large areas of the plain are flooded in spring when the snow begins to melt, and numerous lakes and marshes are a permanent feature of much of Western Siberia. South of the Arctic Circle

[8] V.N. Chernetsov and W. Moszyńska, *Prehistory of Western Siberia*, ed. H.N. Michael, Montreal and London, 1974; I.S. Gurvich, ed., *Etnogenez narodov Severa*, Moscow, 1980; *Istoriya Sibiri*, A.P. Okladnikov, ed., Leningrad, 1968–9, vol. I, pp. 39–44, 94–6; A.P. Okladnikov, *Yakutia before its Incorporation into the Russian State*, ed. H.N. Michael, Montreal 1970.

the vegetation is rather sparse forest of pine, cedar, larch and spruce inter-spersed with peaty bogs of moss and lichen. This coniferous forest, generally known in Russian by its Turkic name *taiga*, is the home of wild animals which occur throughout Siberia – brown bear, wolf, elk, reindeer, lynx and many smaller fur-bearing animals such as squirrel, chipmunk, polecat, ermine and sable. Towards the south, about the latitude of Tomsk, the land gets drier and the coniferous forest gives way to aspen and birch woods, which thin out first into wooded steppe and then the open steppe-land where grasses form the predominant vegetation. This transitional fringe between forest and steppe is the only natural boundary which Western Siberia has in the south. From here the plains of Turkestan stretch away for 1,000 miles, in the direction of Afghanistan and Iran.

East of the Western Siberian plain the uplands of Central Siberia rise to an average height of about 2,000 feet, with the river Yenisey running north-ward along their western edge. The Yenisey contrasts strongly with the Ob-Irtysh: all its main tributaries, such as the Lower Tunguska, Mountain Tunguska and Angara, flow into it from the east, falling rapidly from sources at over 1,300 feet. East of the Yenisey the zone of permanently frozen sub-soil (permafrost) extends much farther south to embrace practically the whole of Central and Eastern Siberia. However, because of more broken relief and better drainage, the *taiga* in this central part of Siberia is more dense and continuous, the most typical tree being the larch. In the south-east the Central Siberian uplands come to an end on the shores of Lake Baikal, which is over 400 miles long and 30 wide and is the deepest lake in the world. Fed by over 300 rivers, Baikal has only one outlet, the Angara, one of the tributaries of the Yenisey. The Yenisey itself rises in the Sayan mountains amid snow-clad peaks of up to 9,800 feet. These mountains along with the Altai originally formed the natural southern limit of Central Siberia, separating it from the plateau of Mongolia. The western shore of Lake Baikal rises in a steep wall of mountains, just beyond whose crest, a mere 6 miles from the lake, is the source of the third great river of Siberia – the Lena. Like the others it flows northward, making its way through Yakutia towards the Arctic Ocean.

East of Baikal and the Lena lie the larch-clad mountains and plateaux of the Far East. From Lake Baikal the Yablonovyy and Stanovoy mountain ranges run out towards the Okhotsk Sea, with summits as high as 10,000 feet. To the south of these the dominant larch, cedar and pine forests give way to areas of grassy steppe in the basins of the rivers Selenga, Onon (or Shilka) and Argun, all of which rise in Mongolia or Manchuria. The Shilka and Argun combine to form the largest river of south-eastern Siberia, the Amur, which flows in a great S-bend for 1,790 miles to reach the sea opposite the island of Sakhalin. Most of this territory shares the same kind of climate and vegetation as Central Siberia. Beyond the middle reaches of the

Amur, however, from the point where it is joined by the river Ussuri near the present-day city of Khabarovsk, a very different region begins. The climate of this maritime region (called *Primorye* in Russian) has warmer summers and is affected by monsoon winds from the Pacific which bring much rain. As a result the vegetation differs from that of Siberia proper, the coniferous forests of the mountains giving way at lower levels to such deciduous trees as oak, maple, walnut, ash and lilac. Among these forests and the high grasses and cane-brakes of the river-valleys live spotted deer, black Himalayan bears and tigers.

In the northern part of Eastern Siberia, beyond the lower reaches of the Lena, rise the austere Verkhoyansk, Suntar-Khayat and Cherskiy mountains, with peaks exceeding 10,000 feet. Here, in the coldest region of the earth outside the Antarctic, the rivers Yana, Indigirka and Kolyma rise and flow north to the Arctic Ocean. Despite the extremely low temperatures of the north-east, its somewhat dry climate gives relatively favourable conditions for human life. The forest is sparser than that of the *taiga* to the west of the Lena, and towards the Pacific coast the prevailing tall larch is replaced by impenetrable thickets of low, recumbent cedar-pine clothing the lower slopes of the mountains. Towards the shores of the northern Pacific or Bering Sea, the climate becomes somewhat less extreme than in the interior of Eastern Siberia, but the summer monsoon brings much rain and mist. As a result, the maritime region of the north-east is in some ways more inhospitable to human beings than Central Siberia. The Kamchatka peninsula, which projects south-westward into the Pacific Ocean, has a high ridge of mountains with peaks up to 15,586 feet. This is a 'young' mountain system with many active volcanoes located along a line which continues southward from Kamchatka into the Kuril Islands and Japan. Thanks to the abundance of moisture in Kamchatka its vegetation is luxuriant, with deciduous forests and tall grasses.

Right across the far north of Siberia stretches the tundra, which forms a fringe along the shores of the Arctic Ocean, mainly about 200 miles wide, but in many places much more extensive than this. Between the mouths of the Yenisey and the Lena the Taimyr peninsula takes the tundra 750 miles north of the Arctic Circle, while in the Putoran plateau and in Eastern Siberia large expanses of mountain tundra extend far south beyond the Arctic Circle. In the tundra the average day temperature rises above $-10°C$ on no more than half of the days in the year, the 'summer' of frost-free days lasts no more than two-and-a-half months, and although the total snowfall is not great, the ground is snow covered for at least 240 days in the year. In such conditions the only plants which can grow are mosses, lichens and stunted woody shrubs, with a brief flowering of small herbaceous plants in the summer. Animal life in the tundra is restricted to small rodents, fox, reindeer, snowy owls and other birds of prey, and the hosts of aquatic birds which congregate along the shore in summer. The Arctic coast, islands and offshore ice also provide a home for seals, walrus and Polar bears.

Despite the climatic rigours of its relatively featureless coniferous forests and its treeless tundra, Siberia offered a variety of environments for human habitation, and these gave rise to the different ways of life of the numerous indigenous peoples who populated it before the advent of the Russians. The number of aboriginal nationalities is less obvious than present-day administrative divisions or lists of the peoples and languages of the USSR might suggest. Some thirty-five indigenous languages are recognised in Siberia today,[9] but many of these fall into several dialects which are more or less unintelligible to each other – two in the case of Selkup, four in Buryat, eight or even twelve in Khanty, and so on. (It is by no means easy to define 'dialects' and 'languages' in a consistent way.)[10] Moreover, it is known that at least nine languages or dialects of the Samoyed and Ket families, such as Kamas and Arin, have died out since the seventeenth century. Thus it is likely that the number of different language communities encountered by the Russians in their penetration of Northern Asia was about 120. This is a more probable degree of complexity, comparable with the linguistic situation in other parts of Asia as well as in North America, where between 200 and 300 native languages are known to have existed.

THE KHANTYS AND MANSIS OF WESTERN SIBERIA

In the sixteenth century the territory lying to the north-east of the Grand Princedom of Moscow was inhabited by Finno-Ugrian peoples: the Komi in the basins of the Vychegda, Pechora and Kama rivers west of the Ural mountain range, and the Samoyed (Nenets) in the tundra both west and east of the Urals. The Muscovite state had already encroached upon these peoples and founded outlying towns at Ust-Vym, Pustozersk, Cherdyn and Solikamsk, and Russian expeditions had even penetrated beyond the northern end of the Urals and established nominal suzerainty over the Khanty and Samoyed inhabitants of the region around the mouth of the Ob. On this basis the phrase 'ruler of Obdor, Konda and all Siberian lands' was added to the title of the Tsar of Muscovy in the middle of the sixteenth century.

Up until that time the Russians were restrained in their advance to the east by a double barrier: the Ural mountains themselves, and their native inhabitants the Ostyaks (Khanty), Voguls (Mansi) and Siberian Tatars. Although the Urals are not particularly high mountains, rising to occasional peaks up to 6,000 feet, they constitute an obstacle to movement at least as serious as the highlands of Scotland or the Appalachians. At the latitudes

---

[9] *Yazyki narodov SSSR*, 5 vols., V.V. Vinogradov, ed., Moscow, 1966–8 – see appropriate sections in vols. II, III and V.

[10] B. Comrie, *The Languages of the Soviet Union*, Cambridge, 1981, pp. 6–8.

where the Russians approached them they were thickly covered with forest, and their deep valleys led for the most part into densely forested dead-ends, so that even in the nineteenth century, settlements in the northern Urals were isolated and remote.

The Khantys and Mansis, who may have numbered altogether about 16,000 people[11] at a time when the population of Muscovite Russia was perhaps about 10 million, were not nations with a single ruler or a sense of common identity, but belonged to many separate clans, each with its own hereditary chieftain. Among the most important Mansi clans were those inhabiting the valleys of the rivers Vishera, Southern Sosva, Lozva and Tavda, and for a time groups of clans cohered sufficiently under one ruler to act as principalities or kingdoms, such as those of Pelym and Konda. Similarly, the Khantys living in the basins of the lower Ob and Irtysh had their principalities, such as Koda, Lapin, Kazym and Kunowat. Conflicts between clans arose from such causes as blood vengeance or plundering the property of a neighbouring clan. In the north, sporadic warfare went on between the Ob Khantys and the Samoyeds of the tundra. For the time the armaments of the Khantys and Mansis were quite advanced: longbows and arrows, spears, coats of mail and helmets made of iron which they themselves extracted and forged. The chiefs of the Khanty and Mansi clans wielded considerable power over their subjects and were surrounded by a certain degree of wealth and barbaric splendour, including silver ornaments and vessels and large quantities of sable, fox and other furs. Their residences were forts surrounded by stockades and earth ramparts. Irrespective of tribal allegiance, the whole Khanty–Mansi people was divided into two moieties, the members of which had to take marriage partners from the other group, so that strict exogamy was observed. 'Bride-price' was paid by the husband's family in the form of horses, reindeer, furs, clothing, domestic utensils, etc., and a man could have as many wives as he could pay for.[12]

The territory occupied by the Khantys extended from the mouth of the Ob and the northern Urals for 400 miles up the Ob to the confluence of the Irtysh, and from there a further 400 miles eastward into the heart of Siberia. The territory of the Mansis lay to the south-west of the Khantys and extended westward across the Urals at their lowest part around the Chosva (in Russian, *Chusováya*) river. Formerly it was believed that in earlier times the Mansi, Khanty and other Ugrian tribes had lived entirely to the west of the Urals near the Volga, where the migrations of peoples from Eastern Eurasia impinged upon them. As a result, some of the Ugrians were pushed

[11] B.O. Dolgikh, *Rodovoy i plemennoy sostav narodov Sibiri v XVIIv.*, Moscow, 1960, p. 616.
[12] S.V. Bakhrushin, *Ostyatskiye i vogulskiye knyazhestva v XVI–XVII vekakh*, Leningrad, 1935, pp. 13–15, 23, 37, 55, 78–9; I.N. Gemuyev, A.M. Sagalayev, A.I. Solovyov, *Legendy i byli tayozhnogo kraya*, Novosibirsk, 1989, pp. 47–57, 107–34; *Narody Sibiri*, M. G. Levin and L. P. Potapov, eds., Moscow–Leningrad, 1956, pp. 591–3; A.I. Solovyov, *Voyennoye delo korennogo naseleniya zapadnoy Sibiri: epokha srednevekovya*, Novosibirsk, 1987.

north-eastward, while others – the Magyars – moved south beyond the forest edge, adopting a horse-riding, pastoral way of life. A more recent view of the origins of the Ugrians is that about 1000 BC they lived east of the Urals in the wooded steppes around the Irtysh, from where some of them gradually pushed north into the forest. In either case it was from the wooded steppe south of the Urals that the Ugrian tribe of Magyars set out in the ninth century AD on the long westward migration which eventually brought them to Central Europe as the founders of the Hungarian nation. It is possible that the Bashkirs of the southern Urals are descended from those Magyars who remained behind.[13]

The language of the Hungarians belongs to the Finno-Ugrian family, which includes Finnish, Estonian, Mari, Udmurt, Komi and several other languages of northern Europe. While these languages as a whole have many common features of vocabulary and grammar, it is with Mansi and Khanty that Hungarian has the greatest affinity, as table I suggests. Differences between Hungarian and the Khanty–Mansi language group are also considerable, however, and indeed the latter two languages themselves are not only mutually unintelligible, but each of them falls into a number of strongly marked dialects. This makes communication between speakers from different regions difficult, and the standardisation of a single Khanty or Mansi language problematic. Despite this, the two peoples have lived for so long in close proximity to each other that, apart from language, it is difficult to differentiate between them. In way of life, clothing, dwellings, religious and social customs the Mansis and Khantys are very similar to each other and indeed are often bracketed together as one ethnic group.[14]

In the sixteenth century the Mansis and Khantys lived chiefly by hunting and fishing, and they were semi-nomadic. Log huts, or lodges made of branches covered with earth, served as permanent winter quarters, but in spring many of them moved out from their villages to the hunting and fishing grounds, where they put up light rectangular shelters of poles and birch-bark. In a land where a heavy covering of snow persists for half of the year, skis were an essential means of movement in winter, while canoes – either dug-out or built of birch-bark – were important when the spring thaw transformed much of their territory into a vast network of rivers, lakes and marshes. Those of the Khanty who lived in the Far North, and some of the Mansi living close to the mountains, had adopted from their neighbours, the Nenets Samoyeds, the nomadic reindeer culture, keeping small herds near their homes in the forest, and following them in their summer migration up

---

[13] P. Hajdu, *Finno-Ugrian Languages and Peoples*, London, 1975, pp. 124, 127; *Istoriya Sibiri*, vol. I, pp. 234, 303–5; *Narody Sibiri*, pp. 493–3, 572; *Narody yevropeyskoy chasti SSSR*, vol. II, pp. 685, 687; S.A. Tokarev, *Etnografiya narodov SSSR*, Moscow, 1958, pp. 482–3.
[14] *Narody Sibiri*, pp. 570–1; Z.P. Sokolova, *Puteshestviye v Yugru*, Moscow, 1982, pp. 52–3; *Yazyki narodov SSSR*, vol. III, pp. 316–21, 359.

Table 1

	Khanty	Mansi	Hungarian	Finnish
one	ii, it	akw	egy	yksi
two	kat	kit	két	kaksi
three	khutem	khurum	három	kolme
four	nyate	nila	négy	neljä
five	wet	at	öt	viisi
six	khut	khot	hat	kuusi
twenty	khus	khus	húsz	kaksikymmentä
woman	ne	ne	nö	nainen
ice	yenk	yank	jég	jää
eye	sem	sam	szem	silmä
horse	tow	luw	ló	hevonen
good	yam	yomas	jó	hyvä

the mountain slopes or towards the sea-shore. Only in the southern part of their range was it possible for the Mansis to carry on agriculture, growing mainly barley and keeping cattle and horses. In this region of mixed forest, bee husbandry was also an important part of the economy. Hives of wild bees in trees would be located and marked with the family symbol, and the honeycombs later harvested to be stored in wooden vessels for the winter. The principal items of food were fish and animals, the flesh of which was boiled, dried in the sun or smoked. Fish and the more tender parts of animal flesh – kidneys, liver, marrow, eyes etc. – were eaten raw, and the blood was either drunk fresh or mixed with other food. The only vegetables in their diet were those which could be gathered in the forest – berries, wild onions, bird-cherries and cedar nuts. Dried and powdered flesh was carried on hunting trips and boiled over the camp fire.

Animals also provided the Khantys and Mansis with most items of clothing. Thigh-length hose of soft reindeer-skin were attached to a waist-belt, and on their feet they wore moccasins of deer or elk-skin with the hair on the soles lying so as to provide a grip on snow. Outer garments – wrap-over coats in the south, and pull-over hooded parkas in the north – were made from various furs and lined with hare or squirrel-skins. The skins of fish and birds were also used for clothing by the northern Khantys. In southern areas the Mansis and Khantys wove cloth from nettle or hemp fibres and made shirts which, in the case of women, were decorated with rich embroidery designs in coloured wool, and with glass beads and tin ornaments. As the primitive looms they used, and many of their weaving terms, were the same as those of their Tatar neighbours, it is probable that weaving was one of the contributions made by Turkic culture to the life of the Ugrian peoples. Not only clothing, but the various boxes, vessels and babies' cradles made by the Mansis and Khantys from wood and bark were decorated with simple but

1 Khantys (Ostyaks) of the North, wearing fur-trimmed reindeer-skin winter clothing similar to that of the Nenets (Samoyeds). The man has a belt with knife and pouch attached; the woman carries a birch-bark pitcher. From a nineteenth-century drawing.

striking designs of stylised animal or plant forms, some of which had religious significance as tribal totems. Another form of decoration was tattooing – using a pike's jawbone or other needle-like instrument and soot to apply geometrical designs to the face and body. Sometimes this was performed by the shaman, who used the clan symbol as a tattoo to heal sickness.

The tribal religion of the Khantys and Mansis resembled that of all the native peoples of northern Eurasia. They had a pantheon of nature gods headed by the supreme god Num Torem, and believed that spirits dwelt in all natural phenomena – rocks, rivers, lakes, trees, thunder, animals etc. Some of these spirits belonged to the family or clan and took the form of its totem animal, such as goose, beaver, elk, eagle or swan, from which the clan was supposed to be descended. Effigies of spirits were kept in sanctuaries in the forest where from time to time all the men of the clan congregated for such special ritual ceremonies as averting epidemic diseases or preparing to go to war. The tribal priests or shamans presided over religious rites in these sacred places, sacrificing horses, reindeer or other animals under a tree and smearing the mouths of the spirit effigies with blood to 'feed' them. In early times human beings were sometimes sacrificed in this way. Sacrificial rites were also performed in cemeteries, where the dead were laid to rest in wooden boxes on the ground, accompanied by weapons, implements, spoons and sometimes silver vessels for use in the next world.

The prosaic necessity of killing animals for food was combined with an attitude of reverence for nature and a particular prohibition on killing one's totem animal. For the Khantys and Mansis, as for all Siberian (and North American) native peoples, the brown bear occupied a unique position among animals. It was considered to be the embodiment of justice on earth and, as 'master of the forest', was held in such awe that various nicknames and circumlocutions were used to avoid naming it, such as 'the old man with claws'. Nevertheless bears were sometimes killed and their flesh eaten as a rare delicacy. In order to justify this, the bear spirit had to be propitiated by a special ceremony to ensure that it would not take vengeance on its killer and that there would always be more bears. This custom was shared by all the peoples of Siberia, but the 'bear feast' was particularly developed among the Mansis and Khantys, where it was performed up till the early twentieth century. The dead animal was welcomed by the villagers, who performed a ritual dance around it. Inside the successful hunter's house the bear's skin was spread out on the table with its head, decorated with a red cloth, lying between its paws, and food and drink set before it. The bear was the 'guest' during a feast at which the village people, wearing masks of birch-bark, pantomimed the bear hunt, touched the bear while making vows, told tales and sang songs. (The Khanty and Mansi had a very rich tradition of oral poetry and were the only people in northern Siberia to have stringed musical instruments, a swan-necked harp and a kind of psaltery.) After several days

15

of celebration the bear's flesh was cooked and eaten. The skulls of bears treated in this way were impaled on a post in the village.

Other religious rituals of the Khanty and Mansi people also involved dancing, such as preparation for a hunting expedition, when men dressed up as animals imitated the movements of the hunter and his quarry. Ritual war-dances were also performed at the tribal gathering place, to which the men of the two moieties into which the tribe was divided took separate paths. To summon the tribe for a war a 'magic' arrow was sent around the settlements, and oaths of loyalty were sworn by kissing a sword sprinkled with blood.[15]

THE SAMOYEDS OF THE TUNDRA

To the north of Khanty territory, the Arctic tundra was the home of the Samoyeds.[16] Within this nationality three groups are distinguished according to linguistic and cultural features. Between the Lena and the Yenisey, the Taimyr peninsula was the home of the Tavgi and other Samoyed tribes which are now officially known by the name Nganasan – which simply means 'people'. Their neighbours to the west, the Samadu and other tribes, from whose word for 'man' – *enete* – the modern ethnonym Enets is derived, lived around the lower Yenisey and Taz rivers. The third group, the western Samoyeds or Yuraks, occupied a large territory on both sides of the Urals, roaming between the forest edge and the Arctic coast and into the Kanin, Gydan and Yamal peninsulas. This western group now forms the largest community of Samoyed people, to which the official name Nenets (also meaning 'man') has been given. Linguistically the Samoyeds belong to the Uralic family, which is rather distantly related to the languages of the Finno-Ugrian family. Obvious correspondences in vocabulary between Nenets and these languages are few, however (e.g. *pää* 'tree' – Finnish *puu*; *tuu* 'fire' – Finnish *tuli*; *min-* 'to come' – Finnish *mene-*), and the numerals are quite different. Anthropologically the Samoyeds, like the Ugrians, differ considerably from Finnic peoples in having the stocky build and straight black hair which is a typical feature of Northern Asia.

Although many of the Samoyed clans lived north of the Arctic circle, a considerable number, belonging to the Aivasida, Pyak and Pebai clans,

---

[15] *Aziatskaya Rossiya*, G.V. Glinka, ed., St Petersburg, 1914, vol. I, pp. 111–12; Bakhrushin, *Ostyatskiye i vogulskiye knyazhestva*, pp. 9, 12–18, 26–33, 78; N.N. Grevens, 'Kultovyye predmety khantov' in *Yezhegodnik Muzeya istorii religii i ateizma*, vol. IV, Moscow, 1960, pp. 434–5; I.S. Gurvich, ed., *Etnicheskaya istoriya narodov Severa*, Moscow, 1982, p. 38; U. Holmberg, *The Mythology of All Races, Finno-Ugric, Siberian*, Boston, 1927, pp. 83–99; *Narody Sibiri*, pp. 580–91; W. Moszyńska, 'An ancient sacrificial site in the Lower Ob region', and Z.P. Sokolova, 'The representation of a female spirit from the Kazym river', in V. Diószegi and M. Hoppál, *Shamanism in Siberia*, Budapest, 1978, pp. 469–79, 491–501.

[16] The name Samoyed has been variously interpreted and misinterpreted; most probably it comes from the name Samadu given to the Enets tribe of the Yenisey by its neighbours; cf. L. V. Khomich, *Nentsy: istoriko-etnograficheskiye ocherki*, Moscow, 1966, p. 27.

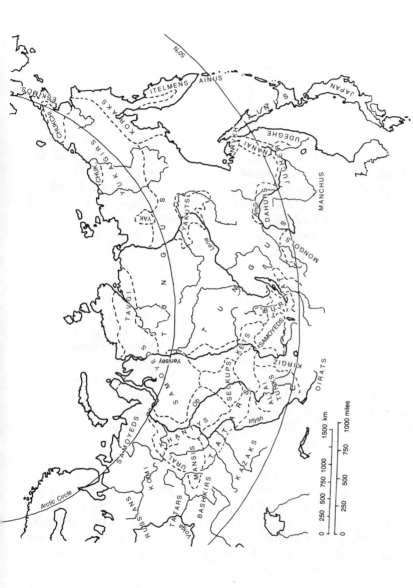

Map 2 Peoples of northern Asia c. 1600 AD (approximate territories)

inhabited the swampy forests almost as far south as the middle Ob, following a way of life as hunters and fishers similar to that of the Khanty. It is in fact widely accepted that the Arctic Samoyeds originated in a homeland lying even farther to the south. The evidence for this is that at the beginning of recorded history a large Samoyedic population existed in southern Siberia. Among these peoples speaking languages akin to Samoyed were the Selkups on the middle Ob, and a number of tribes living among the Eastern Sayan mountains, of whom only a few Kamasins preserved their own language into the twentieth century.[17]

Because of similarities in their natural environment, the tundra Samoyeds share many features of material culture with the peoples of the north-eastern regions of Siberia – the Yukagir, Chukchi and others – above all their dependence on reindeer, both wild and domesticated. As people of the tundra, the Nenets did not ride their reindeer but harnessed them to wooden sledges, which were of a very light and efficient design. To control their reindeer herds they used dogs of the sturdy breed which has made the name Samoyed known all over the world. In addition to reindeer herding, many Samoyeds lived by fishing and hunting seals and walrus in the long sea inlets at the mouths of the rivers Pechora, Ob, Yenisey and Khatanga.

Samoyed clothing consisted of double deerskin trousers tucked into boots made out of the leg-skins of reindeer, and a top garment of the same material. These upper garments with their attached hoods and mittens were decorated with appliqué patterns and stripes of deer-skin (or later, cloth), fringes and collars of fur, and coloured sashes and ribbons on the sleeves. All Samoyeds lived in deerskin-covered conical pole-tents (up to 30 feet in diameter), which were transported on sledges during their frequent migrations. The way of life of the more easterly Nganasan Samoyeds was somewhat more primitive than that of the Nenets: their reindeer were only semi-domesticated, sledges were less commonly used, and much of their travelling was done on foot.[18]

The Samoyeds belonged to a number of clans with names such as Solander, Khudya and Ngokateta, which played an important part in social matters such as the choice of marriage partners (exogamy), the control of hunting, fishing and grazing grounds, mutual assistance, blood vengeance etc. The most usual way of disposing of the dead was to lay them on the surface of the earth or in shallow graves under wooden boxes, accompanied by requisites for the other world, all of which, including the sledge on which the body had been brought to burial, were broken. Reindeer were sacrificed at the grave, as well as on the occasion of other rites of passage. The

---

[17] Dolgikh, *Rodovoy i plemennoy sostav*, pp. 77–93, 178, 239–41, 260–4, 272–3; Hajdu, *Finno-Ugrian*, p. 217; Khomich, *Nentsy*, pp. 29–41; *Narody Sibiri*, pp. 109–10, 379, 383, 493–5.
[18] Khomich, *Nentsy*, pp. 114–32; *Narody Sibiri*, pp. 613–18, 650–3.

Samoyeds had sacred sites on elevated ground where effigies of gods were placed and bones, skulls and antlers from sacrificed animals accumulated.[19]

As among most other peoples of the tundra and taiga, the Samoyeds had no permanent clan chiefs, but for special purposes, such as a communal hunt or warfare, a particularly experienced and trusted man would be chosen to lead operations. Like civilised nations, the Samoyed clans from time to time came into conflict with each other or with their neighbours – west of the Urals this meant the Russians and their vassals the Komis, east of the Urals the Khantys, Selkups or Tungus. Oral legends suggest that preparations for war were not haphazard, but rather ceremonious and conventional, involving a chosen leader and shamans. The place and conditions of the battle were negotiated beforehand, so that, as has been said of Canadian Indians, fighting was in the nature of a blood sport rather than the highly organised campaigns of destruction which characterised the wars of the more 'advanced' contemporary states of Europe and Asia.[20]

The practice of warfare, among other features of the life of the 'primitive' peoples of Northern Asia, shows that, while their economy was on a simple level, their lives were far from being merely wretched or cowed in the face of a harsh natural environment, which from time to time brought famine. Left alone without alien interference, such primitive communities achieved a balance with their environment in which, over and above the bare minimum of necessities to support life, a certain surplus was available for ornament, display and ceremonial, and their social and religious institutions made their life as meaningful as that of people in more complex and sophisticated societies.

THE SELKUPS AND KETS

The south-eastern part of Western Siberia was the home of two further peoples. Beyond the Khanty, farther up the Ob towards present day Tomsk, lived tribes speaking Samoyedic languages. These people, formerly called by the Russians 'Ostyak–Samoyeds', now go under the official name Selkup (Sölkup). At the beginning of the seventeenth century they may have numbered about 3,200 people, living in the basins of the Ob tributaries Tym, Parabel, Ket and Chulym. Farther east in the Yenisey valley lived the people whose few surviving modern descendants, so far as language is concerned, are called Kets. Their tribes included the Inbak, Zemshak, Kott, Asan, Arin and Baikot, strung out along the Yenisey from the confluence of the Moun-

---

[19] *Narody Sibiri*, pp. 623–8; A.E. Nordenskiöld, *The Voyage of the Vega round Asia and Europe*, London, 1881, vol. I, pp. 93–4, 206–7.
[20] W.J. Eccles, *The Canadian Frontier 1534–1760*, New York, 1969, p. 6; Khomich, *Nentsy*, pp. 144–6.

tain Tunguska up-river for some 700 miles to present-day Minusinsk. The total number of the Ket people was about 5,500.[21]

The Kets speak one of northern Asia's isolated languages which appear to be unrelated to any other known languages. For instance, the first five numerals in Ket are: *kogd, inyang, dong, sing, kang*; 'father' is *op*, 'water' *ul* and 'tree' *oks*. Unlike any other Siberian language Ket distinguishes masculine and feminine gender, and its structure possesses other unique features for which explanations have been sought in possible links with Tibetan or the North Caucasian languages.[22] Physically too, the Kets stand out somewhat among other northern Asiatic peoples. It was long believed that they were fair-skinned, with blue-grey eyes lacking the marked epicanthus of most Siberian peoples, brown hair, and straight or aquiline noses, and these features led to some rather far-reaching comparisons with West Europeans or even North American Indians. Recent anthropological studies have shown, however, that where fair pigmentation occurs among the Kets it is the result of miscegenation with Russians, and that basically the Kets have the dark hair, slight build and 'Mongoloid' facial features characteristic of many Asian peoples, although their origins lie farther to the south.[23]

In their way of life based on fishing and hunting, both the Kets and the Selkups were very similar to the Khantys and Mansis. Their clothing – wrap-over coats, soft deerskin boots, and head-cloths as the only headgear even in cold weather – was characteristic of southern Siberia, and it was only those Selkups and Kets who lived farther north, in the neighbourhood of the forest Samoyeds, who kept reindeer. Both Selkups and Kets were skilled boatmen, at home on the rivers in their dug-out canoes, and sometimes the Kets lived on house-boats similar in appearance to Chinese sampans. Their winter dwellings were log-cabins with primitive stoves, partly dug into the ground and covered with earth, while summers were spent in conical tents covered with birch-bark. In the seventeenth century those Kets who lived in southern areas carried on some agriculture, possessed horses and cattle, and could smelt iron ore.

Among both Kets and Selkups (like their Samoyed and Ugrian neighbours) tribes were divided into two moieties for purposes of exogamy. Selkup clans bore animal, bird, or fish names – bear, raven, swan, capercaillie, perch etc. – and their practice of taming birds, including eagles, and keeping them in captivity is taken as evidence of their totemic significance.

The religious beliefs of the Selkups and Kets, involving the propitiation of nature-spirits, were typical of Siberian shamanism. Among them the special

[21] Dolgikh, *Rodovoy i plemennoy sostav*, pp. 85, 89, 93, 101, 178, 219, 272.
[22] Comrie, *Languages of the Soviet Union*, pp. 261–6; *Yazyki narodov SSSR*, vol. V, pp. 453–73.
[23] Ye.A. Alekseyenko, ed., *Ketskiy sbornik: antropologiya, etnografiya, mifologiya, lingvistika*, Leningrad, 1982, pp. 7–15, 77–8, 197–235; *Narody Sibiri*, p. 110; Tokarev, *Etnografiya*, pp. 496, 498.

costume of the shaman was highly developed, consisting of a long coat ornamented with trailing ribbons and well-wrought metallic objects representing the bones of the skeleton, sun-discs and birds (often two-headed), and an iron-framed open crown formed like wings or antlers. The shaman's drum bore designs representing the 'upper', 'middle' and 'under' worlds.[24]

THE SIBERIAN TURKS

If in the sixteenth century the forests of Western Siberia were the home of Ugrian, Samoyed and Ket tribes, there were also, along their southern edge, Turkic peoples whose ancestors may have come from the steppe-lands, but who cannot be considered any less native to the region than their more northerly neighbours. Their descendants at the present day include the Bashkirs of the southern Urals, the Tatars of Tyumen, Tobolsk, the Irtysh, Baraba, Tomsk and Chulym, the Khakas, Altaian and Tuva peoples of the Altai-Sayan mountains, and the Kazak[25] nomads of the steppes. A few typical words of their vocabulary suggest the close linguistic affinity which exists between these peoples, uniting them in one language family along with the Kazan Tatars of the Volga, the Uzbeks and other peoples of Central Asia, the Azerbaijanis of the Caucasus, and the Turks of Turkey. In all of these Turkic languages, for instance, the word for 'horse' is *at*, 'to take' is *al-*, and many other words and grammatical constructions show close similarities: see Table 2.

Turkic peoples had been present in south-western Siberia since at least the second century BC, when the Huns extended their empire westward from Inner Asia. Before then the open wooded land between the steppe and the *taiga* may have been inhabited by Ugrians and Samoyeds, while the steppe itself provided pastures for the Iranian-speaking Scythians whose migrating grounds stretched from the Altai mountains to the Black Sea.

At their eastern end the zones of grass steppe and wooded steppe abut against the Altai mountains with their different vegetation of pine, larch and spruce at lower altitudes and cedars on the heights, which rise to many rocky peaks over 6,500 feet, the highest summit, Belukha, reaching 14,800 feet. Although these and the other mountain ranges to the east – the Sayan and Tannu Ola – form very considerable natural barriers, the fertile valleys between them are not entirely cut off from each other. Passes from the Inner

---

[24] Ye.A. Alekseyenko, 'Categories of Ket shamans', and A.J. Joki, 'Notes on Selkup shamanism', in V. Diószegi and M. Hoppál, *Shamanism in Siberia*, pp. 255–64, 373–86; Holmberg, *Finno-Ugric, Siberian*, pp. 335, 476, 513, 517–18, 520; *Narody Sibiri*, pp. 665, 671–7, 679, 691–7.

[25] Sometimes spelt Qazaq to render the back velar consonants. The spelling *Kazakh* is a purely Russian convention to distinguish this name from *Kazak*, which in Russian means 'Cossack'.

Table 2

	Volga Tatar, Bashkir	Baraba, Chulym	Altai, Kazak	Tuva
one	ber	pir	bir	bir
two	ike	iki/igi	eki	iyi
three	öch/ös	üts/üs	üch/üsh	üsh
four	dürt	tört	tört	dört
five	bish	pesh/pis	besh/bes	besh
ten	un	on	on	on
son	ul	oghyl/ool	ool/ul	ool/oglu
head	bash	pash/pas	bash/bas	bash
lake	kül	köl	köl	khöl
water	hyw/su	su/sugh	suu/suw	sugh
black	kara	kara/khara	kara	kara
to give	bir-	per-/pir-	ber-	ber-

Asian plateau of Mongolia allowed pastoral nomads to reach the upper course of the Yenisey in the region which is now called Tuva, and from there cross over into the steppe-land near present-day Minusinsk, which lies farther down the Yenisey to the north. In addition to mountain passes, nomadic pastoralists from Inner Asia had easy access south of the Altai to the plains of present-day Kazakstan either by way of the Dzungarian gap near Lake Balkhash or along the course of the upper Irtysh. From there they could reach not only wide areas of wooded steppe and grassland in the basins of the upper Ob and the Tom, but also the Minusinsk steppe and the pocket of wooded steppe near present-day Krasnoyarsk.

It was in this region of lofty mountain peaks and tracts of steppe that the most advanced cultures of ancient Siberia flourished. Living in approximately the sixth to fourth centuries BC, the creators of the Altai-Sayan culture buried the bodies of their chiefs (and the women and horses which were slaughtered to accompany them) in tombs covered over with mounds of earth and stones. Along with the bodies they placed in the tombs carved wooden furniture, leatherwork, woven textiles – some of native manufacture, some brought from Persia and China – appliqué decorations made of felt, silver mirrors, and in one case, at Pazyryk, a chariot. In the same period in the Minusinsk basin, people of the Tagar culture were constructing megalithic barrows, which also contained bronze weapons, clothing, ornaments and pottery. Thanks to its black earth soil and the fact that it is free from permafrost, the Minusinsk basin was one of the cradles of agriculture in northern Asia, and the contents of vessels left with the dead show that the Tagar people cultivated crops. The most distinctive feature of the sophisticated decorative art of these early Siberian cultures is the stylised representation of animals – the 'Scythian animal style' – which was used by the nomadic pastoralists. Beautifully finished gold belt-plaques and other articles of costume with tigers, wolves, elk, horses, swans, eagles etc. have been found all over 'Scythian' territory from the Sayan to the northern Caucasus and the Crimea.[26] It is generally assumed that the creators of these cultures were of Indo-European origin.

By the first century AD the Sayan region had become the seat of the Turkic Kirgiz people whose name dominated it for the next 1,800 years. The state formed by these Yenisey Kirgizes reached its zenith in the ninth century AD, when its power extended from Lake Baikal to the Altai. Later it came into conflict with the powerful East Turkic and Uighur khanates of Inner Asia, and the Kirgiz, being at least nominally vassals of China, collaborated with the Chinese in breaking the power of the Uighurs. Like the Scythians, the Kirgiz exploited both the forest for hunting and the fertile valleys for agriculture, for which they built irrigation channels. The occurrence of metal ores here also made this a region of advanced metallurgy for its time: copper, iron, tin and gold were mined, smelted and forged into implements and weapons. The Yenisey Kirgiz traded with other countries, exporting iron weapons, furs and other animal products to China and Persia. In exchange they obtained silks and other luxury wares. At this period the Kirgiz, like the Uighur and other Turkic tribes of Inner Asia, had a form of writing which they used on gravestones and inscriptions on rock faces. The way of life of the Kirgiz remained semi-nomadic, and although they built some towns, they were less advanced in this respect than the Uighurs, who built several towns in Tuva during their occupation of it in the eighth and ninth centuries AD.[27]

While the Kirgiz ruling class were of Turkic origin, their subjects, the hunters, reindeer-herders and sedentary farmers who formed the original population of the Sayan region, probably belonged to Samoyed and Ket tribes. Ethnic mixing over a prolonged period of time led to the assimilation of some of these peoples by the Kirgiz and the adoption of Turkic speech by the local tribes – the ancestors of the present-day Khakas, Shor and Altaian peoples. The ethnic composition of the Altai-Sayan lands was further complicated when they were invaded in the thirteenth century by Chingis Khan's horde led by his son Jöchi, thus falling within the influence of Mongolia for several centuries. After the initial destructive period of subjugation, and the division of Chingis Khan's empire among his sons, the khans of the Great Horde in the east settled down to a more civilised way of life. Under this

---

[26] British Museum, *Frozen Tombs: the Culture and Art of the Ancient Tribes of Siberia*, London, 1978; *Istoriya Sibiri*, vol. I, pp. 227–33; E.D. Phillips, *The Royal Hordes, Nomad Peoples of the Steppes*, London, 1965.

[27] W. Barthold, *Histoire des Turcs d'Asie Centrale*, Paris, 1945, p. 27; B.D. Grekov, ed., *Ocherki istorii SSSR. Period feodalizma*, Moscow, 1953, vol. I, pp. 740–4; *Istoriya Sibiri*, vol. I, pp. 253–61, 266–87, 296–302; *Narody Sibiri*, pp. 378–80, 422–3.

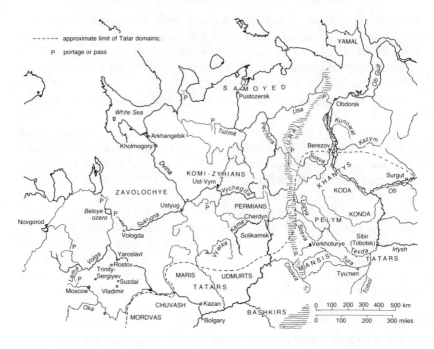

Map 3 Russia and Siberia in the sixteenth century

régime the land of the Yenisey Kirgiz became one of the frontier provinces of the Chinese Empire and, as in every part of Yüan China, the native inhabitants of the fertile Tuva and Minusinsk basins were organised as agricultural colonies to support the local Mongol-Chinese army garrison, and a new religious element was introduced to Tuva in the form of Tibetan Buddhism.

When, late in the fourteenth century, the Mongol dynasty in China came to an end, Mongolia itself was not only pushed back on its own resources again, but fell into disunity and internal strife. It was the chieftains of western Mongolia, the Oirat (including the Dzungar and Dörböd tribes) who first succeeded in imposing their rule over much of Inner Asia including the Kirgiz lands, which they dominated until the early part of the eighteenth century. Mongolian influence left its mark on the physical features of the inhabitants of the Altai-Sayan region, and on the Turkic languages spoken there, so that the present-day Tuva, Khakas, Altai and Shor languages all contain a substantial amount of Mongol vocabulary.[28]

[28] J. Deny et al., eds., *Philologiae Turkicae Fundamenta*, Wiesbaden, 1959, vol. I, pp. 568–670; *Istoriya Sibiri*, vol. I, pp. 374–6; *Narody Sibiri*, pp. 111, 330–1, 379–83, 423, 492–6; *Yazyki narodov SSSR*, vol. II, pp. 387, 400, 442, 480, 502–3, 520–1.

24

THE TATAR KHANATE OF SIBIR

West of the Altai, along the open transitional zone beyond steppe and forest which stretched to the southern Urals, a similar pattern of penetration by Turkic peoples occurred. In the eleventh century AD the Kipchak Turks who occupied the steppes of present-day Kazakstan impinged upon the wooded steppe of south-western Siberia and the Urals. Their gradual movement into the forest pushed the Selkup, Mansi, Khanty and Bashkir people northwards or resulted in the assimilation of those who remained in their old territories.

In the thirteenth century the Kipchak steppe and south-western Siberia were overrun by the Mongols and formed part of the Khanate of the Golden Horde under Batu. The subsequent disintegration of the Golden Horde during the fourteenth and fifteenth centuries resulted in a triple division of the Mongol–Tatar possessions in the region between the Volga and the Altai; the Nogai horde under Edigü and his descendants occupied the territory from the southern Urals west to the Volga, the Uzbek horde of the descendants of Shiban had the steppe to the east of the Urals, and the clan which claimed descent from Taibuga held the forest lands of Western Siberia. The Taibugas had their capital at Chimgi-Tura (or Tümen) on the river Tura.[29] Later the seat of the khan of Siberia was moved to Kashlyk (also known as Isker or Sibir) at the confluence of the Irtysh and its tributary the Tobol. As a result of the Turkicisation of the aboriginal peoples of the wooded steppe between the southern Urals and the Ob, various groups of 'Tatars' were formed, such as the Bashkirs in the west and the Baraba, Chat, Eushtin and Chulym Tatars in the east, all of whom came under the rule of the khanate of Sibir to a greater or lesser extent.

The Siberian Tatar khanate was involved in the inter-tribal wars of the various khans of the Kipchak steppe. About 1400 AD the deposed khan of the Golden Horde Tokhtamysh, fleeing from the emir Edigü, found refuge in Siberia until his death. Twenty years later, one of the Shiban faction, Abu-'l-Khair, gathered much of the northern steppe into his hands to form the Uzbek confederation. He deposed and killed the reigning khan of Sibir after a battle on the Tobol. After Abu-'l-Khair's death in 1468 a rival Shibanid khan, Ibak, seized power in Chimgi-Tura with the help of the Nogai, who wanted to bring about a union between the khanates of Sibir and Kazan. Meanwhile, the more easterly territories on the Irtysh came under the rule of the Taibuga clan, and it was one of their leaders, Muhammad, who at the end of the fifteenth century united the Irtysh and Tobol ter-

---

[29] The name Chimgi-Tura probably meant 'Chingis Khan's town'; Tümen, the Mongolian word for '10,000', no doubt referring to a whole region, was Russianised in the form Tyumen. A.K. Matveyev, *Geograficheskiye nazvaniya Urala*, 2nd edn, Sverdlovsk, 1987, pp. 172–4.

ritories, and made his capital at the fortress of Sibir, from which Siberia subsequently took its name.

The West Siberian khanate, like that of Kazan, was one of many examples of Turkic peoples of the steppe who had previously been nomadic forsaking their pastoral way of life in favour of a settled or semi-settled existence in a predominantly forest environment. They had several towns in the khanate in addition to Chimgi-Tura and Sibir, such as Kyzyl-Tura and Tashatkan on the Irtysh. From these towns the khan and his *mirzas* ruled their subjects – not only the Tatars, but also the local Bashkirs, Mansis, Khantys and Selkups – from whom they extorted tribute, known by the Turkic name *yasak*, in the form of furs and other forest products. The economic importance of Sibir was considerable enough to make it not only a bone of contention between rival khans, but also an enticement to the Russians. Its importance was particularly enhanced by its location on a long-established caravan route linking Kazan with Central Asia by way of Perm, Chimgi-Tura, the Irtysh, and the Kipchak steppe. Thus Sibir was connected with Bukhara, Khiva and other important centres of trade and civilisation in Islamic Central Asia, and Bukharan merchants were always present in the Siberian Tatar towns.

The Russian conquest of the Kazan khanate in 1552 brought a new threat to the Turkic peoples beyond the Volga and the Urals, which the leaders of various groups met in different ways. In Sibir the Taibuga rulers Yediger and Bek-bulat sent a message of congratulation to Ivan the Terrible along with gifts which the Tsar chose to interpret as tokens of submission to his suzerainty. Attitudes towards Moscow varied among the peoples of the steppe – the Nogai horde in the Volga–Ural region, and the Uzbek horde east of the Urals. Some of the latter under Muhammad Shaibani had by then moved south and conquered the Central Asian khanates, while the main body which remained in the northern steppes came to be known as Kazaks. In 1563 one of the latter, the Shibanid Kuchum, with the support of the Nogais, deposed and killed Yediger and Bek-bulat and made himself khan of Sibir. Kuchum not only adopted a defiant attitude towards the Russians, but initiated a campaign of conversion to Islam among his Tatar and other subjects, receiving support in his endeavour from the Uzbek khan of Bukhara, Abdallah II. The anti-Russian position of Kuchum thus had a religious dimension which no doubt also found sympathy among those Muslims from Kazan who had fled from Russian persecution to take refuge among the Bashkirs and Siberian Tatars. Kuchum also hoped to obtain military assistance from the Crimean Tatars and the Sultan of Turkey for his fight against the infidels of Moscow.

Up till then Islam had not taken root deeply either among the Siberian Tatars or the Kazaks. Their khans and *mirzas* may have been educated in Bukhara or Samarkand, but the mass of ordinary people living at the northern extremities of Turkestan, separated by wide tracts of desert from these religious centres, adhered to their old shamanist religion with its nature spirits, ancestor cult and animal sacrifice. In fact this pre-Islamic religion persisted among all the Siberian 'Tatar' peoples from the Urals to the Altai right up until the twentieth century, even if, as in the case of the Kazaks and Tobolsk Tatars, it was interwoven with elements of Islam. In the khanate of Sibir the non-Turkic subjects – the shamanist Mansis, Khantys and Selkups – were even less inclined towards Islam and indeed may have been alienated from Kuchum by attempts to convert them. In Moscow the war against the Kazan Tatars could be rationalised as a Christian crusade against Islam. If Kuchum hoped to rally the Muslim faithful in a like spirit against the Russians he was not in a strong position because of the weakness of Islam beyond the Urals, not to mention the continual inter-tribal feuds which divided the various Turkic communities from within.[30]

[30] *Aziatskaya Rossiya*, vol. I, p. 6; Barthold, *Histoire des Turcs*, pp. 88–91; *Entsiklopedicheskiy slovar*, St Petersburg, 1890–1907, vol. III, pp. 227; vol. XXIX, p. 797; vol. XXXII, p. 672; Grekov, *Ocherki istorii SSSR. Period feodalizma*, vol. II, pp. 463–7; *Istoriya Sibiri*, vol. I, pp. 234, 239, 305, 360–1, 364–7, 371–2; vol. II, p. 26; *Narody Sibiri*, pp. 332–3, 349–50, 391–9, 474–5, 484, 516; *Narody yevropeyskoy chastri SSSR*, vol. II, pp. 685–8; A.N. Nusupbekov et al., eds., *Istoriya Kazakhskoy SSR v pyati tomakh*, Alma-Ata, 1979, vol. II, pp. 109–12, 150, 176–7, 183–7, 236, 252–5, 260–3, 275–8, 280–1, 291–3, 356, 360–2.

2

SIBERIA INVADED: THE SEVENTEENTH CENTURY

UNTIL the middle of the sixteenth century, Russian excursions beyond the Urals had taken place exclusively by northern routes. The rivalry between Moscow and Novgorod for possession of the lands between the Northern Dvina and the Urals, with their native population of Komi-Zyrians and Samoyeds, was resolved in 1456 by a treaty in Moscow's favour. Under Grand Prince Ivan III the Muscovites consolidated their position in these north-eastern lands, on the route by which large quantities of valuable furs were regularly brought from beyond the Urals. Exploiting the antagonism which existed between the Komi people of the Pechora region and their easterly neighbours the 'Yugra', i.e. the Mansi and Khanty, Moscow recruited Komi men as auxiliary soldiers in the campaigns which were mounted against the Yugrians. As a result of one raid by Russians from Ustyug in 1465, two Yugrian chiefs, Kalpik and Techik, were forced to submit to Moscow and promised to deliver tribute in furs gathered from their people. Muscovite campaigns on a much larger scale were sent to subjugate the people living beyond the Urals in 1483 and 1499. Lands along the rivers Pelym, Northern Sosva, Ob and Irtysh were raided and hostages taken, so that various communities of Khanty, Mansi and Samoyeds made tactical (and temporary) agreements to become tribute-paying vassals of Russia. By the early sixteenth century Russians were also venturing on to the waters of the Arctic Ocean, so that in addition to land and river routes to the north-east, a sea-route was established from the White Sea region to the mouth of the Ob.[1]

Although a distance of some 750 miles by river lay between the mouth of

---

[1] *Istoriya Sibiri*, vol. I, pp. 368–70.

the Ob and the centre of the Khanate of Sibir (near present-day Tobolsk), the political influence of the Siberian Tatars extended far beyond the Mansi-Khanty tribes in their immediate vicinity, to the Koda and Obdor Khanty on the lower Ob.[2]

Clearly the Russians could not with impunity extend their colonisation of northern Siberia farther to the east so long as the whole Ob region on their right flank, as well as the Volga–Kama region, was held by hostile Tatars. This situation was changing, however. At the same time as they were infiltrating into Siberia by northern routes the Muscovite Russians were pushing forward towards the Urals in a south-easterly direction, beyond the salt-trade centre of Solikamsk. The conquest of the land of Perm, inhabited by Komi people, in 1472, and of the independent Novgorodian settlement on the river Vyatka in 1489, brought Muscovite power up against the northern marches of the Kazan and Sibir Tatar khanates. Half a century later Kazan fell to the armies of Ivan IV, and the Khan of Sibir found the Russians on his doorstep. It was therefore at these more southerly latitudes, where the Ural range offered a conveniently low pass through the valley of the Chosva, and the power of the Siberian khan and his vassals the Mansi extended west of the mountains, that direct conflict between the Russians and the Siberian Tatars first occurred.

After the extinction of the Kazan khanate, the land of Perm was opened up to a flood of Russian settlers and prospectors. Opportunities for private initiative were great, and it was in connection with the discovery and exploitation of minerals that a new power in the land appeared in the form of the Stroganovs, a Novgorod merchant family long established in the Dvina region. In 1558 Grigoriy Stroganov received from Ivan the Terrible a charter allowing him to colonise 'empty lands' on the Kama, where 'till now no fields have been ploughed, no homesteads have stood and no tax has accrued to the Tsar's treasury'. Here he would fell trees and clear farming land, bring in peasants, and extract any mineral 'salts' which were found. Inevitably the Komi natives of the region became serfs of the Russians.

Like other pioneers in frontier lands where the state wanted to establish a Russian population, the Stroganovs were granted immunity from taxes and customs dues for twenty years. On the other hand, they accepted responsibility for the defence of Russian settlements and the frontier of Muscovy against attack by 'Nogai and other hordes'. For this purpose they were permitted to erect fortified towns and maintain soldiers with fire-arms. The rights and privileges which Stroganov was granted made him practically the governor of the Kama region, and soon provided him with the opportunity to extend his private enterprise, and the frontier of the Tsar's realm, beyond the Urals into Siberia. Stroganov domains on the rivers Chosva and Sylva

---

[2] Bakhrushin, *Ostyatskiye i vogulskiye knyazhestva*, p. 38.

encroached upon Mansi territory, and the influx of Russian settlers caused just resentment, as did the building of new towns. The Siberian Tatars had long considered that this region belonged to them, but when Kazan was conquered Ivan the Terrible anticipated further conquests by adding to his many titles that of 'emperor of Siberia'. There was therefore cause for tension in the Kama region, and the threat of Tatar raids on Russian settlements and travellers was ever present.[3]

In 1572 Kuchum, having established himself as Khan of Sibir, decided to attack the Russian intruders in his territory. Lulling their suspicions by sending an embassy to Moscow to offer his submission to the Tsar, Kuchum also sent an army consisting of his Mansi, Khanty, Bashkir and Mari vassals to carry out a reconnaissance into the Stroganov lands on the Chosva. Russian settlements were devastated, and the region remained in turmoil during subsequent years as Tatar raids and anti-Russian revolts continued, reaching a culmination in 1581, when not only the Chosva settlements were again plundered by the Mansi prince Begbeli Agtai, but the towns of Cherdyn and Solikamsk were raided and villages burned by the Pelym Mansi prince Kikhek.[4]

During this war the Stroganovs relied heavily on Cossacks whom they had hired in their traditional function as frontier warriors, and when Ivan IV authorised the Stroganovs' proposal to seize land beyond the Urals, it was Cossack mercenaries who were entrusted with the mission. A certain Yermak Timofeyevich, presumably a Don Cossack, had made a name for himself as leader of a band of freebooters who lived by robbing caravans crossing the steppes – irrespective of whether they consisted of Tatars or Russians. Yermak's band established themselves on the Volga – now open to Russian navigation since the fall of Kazan – where they made piratical assaults on the shipping which carried rich cargoes between Moscow, Bukhara and Persia.[5] These were the men who offered their services to the Stroganovs for the invasion of the khanate of Siberia.

In the autumn of 1581[6] Yermak set out at the head of an army of some 800 men on the long campaign which took them by way of the rivers Chosva, Tura, Tavda and Tobol as far as the Tatar capital Sibir. Along the way the Russian invading force plundered Mansi and Khanty villages and fought several victorious battles against the Tatars. In October 1582, after a battle on the Irtysh, Kuchum fled with an entourage of about 1,000 Tatars, and Sibir was occupied by Yermak.

The Russians spent the next three years marauding along the Ob north-

[3] *Sibirskiya letopisi*, St Petersburg, 1907, pp. 2–7; Solovyov, *Istoriya Rossii*, vol. III, pp. 688–91.
[4] *Istoriya Sibiri*, vol. II, pp. 26–7; *Sibirskiya letopisi*, pp. 9–12; Solovyov, *Istoriya Rossii*, vol. III, pp. 691–2, 697.
[5] *Sibirskiya letopisi*, pp. 7–8, 367–8.
[6] According to R.G. Skrynnikov it was 1582, *Sibirskaya ekspeditsiya Yermaka*, 2nd edn, Novosibirsk, 1986, pp. 168–9, 249–50.

ward from Sibir and up the Irtysh to the south-east. They enjoyed the enormous advantage of having fire-arms, whereas the Tatars and other natives had only bows and arrows, and their task was made easier by the disintegration of the Tatars into rival groups and the defection of many of their Khanty, Mansi and Bashkir vassals. Nevertheless, the Russian force was isolated among a more numerous and highly mobile enemy, and short of supplies, especially in winter. As a result the Tatars wore them down by a series of stratagems, and in August 1585 Yermak and most of his men were killed. Russian occupation temporarily came to an end, and the territory of the khanate was once again in the hands of the Tatars, but as a political entity it was beyond repair. Kuchum had taken refuge among the Nogai Tatars in the steppe and from there his son Ali led an army to reoccupy Sibir. There, however, he found himself under attack by Seid-Ahmet of the Taibuga clan who for many years carried on the old rivalry against the Shibanids. Muscovite control over the territory of the khanate in the wooded steppe was not secure until further expeditions under the command of a series of military commanders (*voyevody*) took place during 1586–98. Even then Kuchum and his descendants did not give up the struggle to regain their patrimony until the 1670s, and the Russians had to fight a long and bitter war on the southern steppe frontier in order to retain their hold on their new colony.[7]

The part played by Yermak in opening up Western Siberia to further Russian colonial expansion has made him a great hero in the eyes of Russian nationalists. One near-contemporary eulogy described him in these terms: 'Let us recall, brothers, the most worthy and valiant soldier, the admirable, wise and excellent warrior Yermak Timofeyev, Cossack ataman of the Volga, and his most admirable, valiant and single-minded fighting men, and let us render to him our admiring praise, for the Lord God has glorified him and made him a wonder by so many miracles . . .'[8] His exploits were celebrated in folk-songs and chronicles, with an admixture of miracles,[9] and the legend of Yermak was maintained by various means. For instance, an Orthodox banner depicting St Dimitri, which ostensibly belonged to Yermak, was preserved in the cathedral in Omsk; a monument to him was erected in Tobolsk in 1839; he was made the subject of a famous ballad by the Romantic poet Ryleyev; and his (Christian) victory over the 'pagans' is celebrated in a vast painting made by V.I. Surikov in 1895 which hangs in the Russian Museum in Leningrad. In pre-revolutionary Russia it was possible to see

---

[7] *Entsiklopedicheskiy slovar*, vol. XXIX, pp. 27–31, 35–6; *Istoriya Sibiri*, vol. II, pp. 27–31, 35–6; *Sibirskiya letopisi*, pp. 8–11, 16–21, 26–43; Solovyov, *Istoriya Rossii*, vol. III, pp. 279–82, 374, 692–701.

[8] *Sibirskiya letopisi*, p. 93.

[9] T. Armstrong, ed., *Yermak's Campaign in Siberia: a Selection of Documents Translated from the Russian*, Hakluyt Society 2nd ser., vol. 146, London, 1975, especially pp. 13–18, 112–16, 131, 137–40, 157, 163, 196, 211–16.

2 Yermak defeats Kuchum's Tatars on the river Tobol in 1581. The Tatars, on the right, have only spears, swords, slings and arrows; the Russians win not only by having fire-arms, but through the intervention of the Archangel Michael. In other encounters recorded in S. Remezov's Chronicle (c. 1700) the Russians are helped by St Nicholas, by the banner of Christ and by the apparition of Christ himself.

Yermak as 'not only a valiant conqueror but also a wise, far-sighted organizer',[10] a man who showed 'skill, resourcefulness and statesmanship' in carrying out his 'glorious task'.[11] Official Communist Party history maintains

[10] *Entsiklopedicheskiy slovar*, vol. XXIX, p. 798.
[11] *Aziatskaya Rossiya*, vol. I, pp. 10–11.

the same attitude to Yermak: he was 'a man of heroic power, bold, courageous, well-versed in the art of war',[12] and his expedition earns especial
praise because ostensibly it was carried out not by government troops but 'by
men thrown up by the common people – Don and Volga Cossacks led by
Yermak, who liberated the Khantys, Mansis, Bashkirs, West Siberian Tatars
and others from the yoke of Chingis Khan's descendants . . .'[13] The 'unofficial' nature not only of Yermak's expedition but of the conquest of Siberia as
a whole is a commonplace of both pre-1917 and communist historiography,
but it would be wrong to suppose that the Tsars and their governments
looked on idly while 'the Russian people' took over half a continent by
unaided private enterprise. It was Ivan IV who in 1572 *ordered* the Stroganovs to find a Cossack *ataman* to lead an expedition against rebellious
natives and force them into submission to Moscow; and the Tsar readily
agreed to the Stroganovs' proposal for an invasion of Siberia and authorised
the use of guns and the making of gunpowder for this purpose. Nor did the
Tsar show any hesitation in welcoming the news of Yermak's conquests and
rewarding the Cossacks with money and rich textiles, and the Stroganovs
with further commercial immunities. If Ivan IV was content to leave such an
important military matter as the conquest of a neighbouring state to the
initiative of the Stroganovs and their Cossacks, the government of Ivan's son
Fyodor, who succeeded to the throne in 1584, adopted a new policy.
Immediately a whole stream of *voyevodas* (military governors), men of service,
and soldiers were sent to reinforce Yermak's conquests and to put the
annexation of Sibir on a thoroughly official footing only three years after its
inception.[14]

Even less convincing is the attempt made by Russian communist
historians to idealise the Cossacks who played a large part in the whole
process of subjugating the Siberian peoples and occupying their territory.
Such 'free Cossacks' as Yermak's band were notoriously irresponsible and
uncivilised, and their contemporaries knew well that they 'did many vile
things to Russian people of all callings, plundering and hindering travellers
by their lawless activities'.[15] To apply to sixteenth and seventeenth-century
brigands the twentieth-century concept of 'liberating subject peoples' is
particularly inappropriate. In frontier regions and newly conquered colonies,
where conditions were particularly rough and hazardous for Russian pioneers – many of them near-outlaws – they were even less likely to act with
benevolence and humanity, and the record of the doings of the mercenary

[12] A.M. Pankratova, ed., *Istoriya SSSR: uchebnik*, 3 vols., Moscow, 1957, vol. I, p. 124.
[13] *Istoriya Sibiri*, vol. II, p. 31. In the same spirit the native inhabitants of Western Siberia are
said to have seen the Russian invaders as allies against the 'Tatar feudal lords' – B.N.
Ponomarev, *Istoriya SSSR*, vol. II, p. 340.
[14] *Sibirskiya letopisi*, pp. 13–14; Solovyov, *Istoriya Rossii*, vol. III, pp. 691–2, 697–9, 701; vol. IV,
pp. 279–81.
[15] *Sibirskiya letopisi*, p. 367.

soldiers usually described as Cossacks in the conquest of Siberia was in reality one of ruthlessness and arbitrary violence. In this context the word 'Cossack' is often used to cover not only Cossacks proper, but also regular soldiers of the state (*streltsy*) and 'men of service' (*sluzhilye lyudi* and *deti boyarskiye*). Both of these categories, like the Cossacks, expected to supplement their income with plunder.[16]

Another factor which tended towards oppressive and dishonest practices in Russian colonial possessions was the system of 'feeding' (*kormleniye*), by which provincial governors appointed by the Moscow government received no salary, but were expected to 'nourish themselves' from the taxes and dues which they exacted in excess of the rates required by the treasury. Although this system was abolished in Russia proper in 1555, among the ranks of the gentry eligible for appointment as military governors of the newly conquered Siberian territories the view persisted that such a post carried with it the perquisite of requiring personal 'gifts' from local chiefs and of diverting fiscal revenues to their own pockets.[17]

The Russian conquerors of all classes treated the native peoples of Siberia as enemies so inferior to themselves in way of life and military potential that they could be disposed of callously and unceremoniously, and exploited for the enrichment of the invaders. It was quite usual for armed bands of Russians to kill natives whom they encountered and divide the booty, and it has been said that in the first stages of the conquest the natives were hunted like animals.[18]

In the lands of the Siberian khanate the Russians consolidated their conquests by building forts where garrisons of Cossacks, *streltsy* and men of service were stationed. The sites of old Tatar towns were obvious locations for new Russian towns, the first of which, Tyumen, was built near the ruins of Chimgi-tura in 1586, followed by Tobolsk near the site of Sibir in 1587. Tura was founded up-river from Tyumen in 1600, and farther east on the Irtysh, Tara was established as the headquarters for the subjugation of the Baraba steppe and for defence against Kuchum, who had the support of the Chagat (Chat) Tatars in this region.[19] It was typical of Russian practice that Tatar *mirzas* who offered to become vassals of the Tsar were permitted to retain their position and continue to rule their people in semi-independence in exchange for providing armies of their own men to assist in Russian campaigns against other native communities. This category of collaborators

---

[16] For an account of the misconduct of Russian troops passing through their own country see G.V. Lantzeff, *Siberia in the Seventeenth Century: A Study of the Colonial Administration*, Berkeley, 1943, pp. 73–4.

[17] V.I. Ogorodnikov, *Ocherk istorii Sibiri do nachala XIX stoletiya*, Irkutsk, 1920, vol. I, p. 5; Lantzeff, *Siberia*, pp. 19–24.

[18] N.M. Yadrintsev, *Sibir kak koloniya. K yubileyu trekhsotletiya: sovremennaya Sibir, yeya nuzhdy i potrebnosti, yeya proshloye i budushcheye*, St Petersburg, 1882, p. 280.

[19] *Istoriya Sibiri*, vol. II, pp. 34–5; Dolgikh, *Rodovoy i plemennoy sostav*, p. 49.

was called 'service Tatars' (*sluzhilye tatary*).[20] Tatar collaborators from Tobolsk and Tyumen were among the Russian armies which inflicted the final defeat on the ageing Kuchum in the Baraba steppe in 1598.[21]

Among those who continued to resist Russian occupation of the lands immediately to the east of the Urals were not only Siberian Tatars but other native peoples. Some of the Mansi and Khanty kingdoms which had been strongly influenced by the Tatars and to some extent Islamicised, to judge by the names of their leaders – Yusup, Al-Seit etc. – put up a determined opposition. The Mansi prince of Pelym, Ablegirim (Abu-l-Kerim?), who commanded a strategic position on the most-used route across the Urals, refused to submit until a Russian fort was built on the Lozva in 1590 and his warriors were overwhelmed. Ablegirim and his family were taken to Moscow as hostages, and a Russian town was built on the site of his fort to keep the Pelym land in subjection. In a similar expedition sent in the following year to crush the Konda Mansi, the Russians made use of the Khanty kingdom of Koda, whose prince Alach's submission to vassal status had earned him the right to maintain his own government and military organisation. These 'service Ostyaks', like the service Tatars, were permitted to exist as semi-independent vassal states only as long as this suited Moscow. In the case of the Koda Khanty this continued until 1643, when they were reduced to the same level of subjection as their neighbours whom they had helped the Russians to conquer.[22]

The subjugation of the most southerly groups of Mansi, along with some of their Bashkir neighbours, was marked in 1598 by the establishment of the Russian town of Verkhoturye on the upper reaches of the river Tura, commanding the road across the Urals from Solikamsk.[23]

RUSSIAN PENETRATION INTO WESTERN SIBERIA

Farther north, towards the mouth of the Ob, where the first intrusion of Russians in search of furs had occurred perhaps as early as the eleventh century, their grip was now consolidated by the founding of the town of Berezov near the mouth of the Northern Sosva in 1593, and Obdorsk at the mouth of the Ob itself two years later. The earliest route to this region lay along a series of rivers and portages linking the Dvina and Pechora, west of the Urals, with the Sosva and the Ob. In the late fifteenth century men from northern Russia also began to approach the trans-Ural region by sea. Using navigational skills they had developed for sailing in Arctic waters, they

---

[20] S.V. Bakhrushin, 'Sibirskiye sluzhilye tatary v XVII v.', in his *Nauchnye trudy*, vol. III, pt. 2, pp. 153–75; Dolgikh, *Rodovoy i plemennoy sostav*, p. 39; Lantzeff, *Siberia*, pp. 69–70, 91–2.
[21] *Istoriya Sibiri*, vol. II, pp. 35–6, 94, 130–1, 309.
[22] Bakhrushin, *Ostyatskiye i vogulskiye knyazhesteva*, pp. 40–1, 46–62, 75–6.
[23] *Istoriya Sibiri*, vol. I, p. 357.

ventured out from Kholmogory by way of the White Sea during the brief summers and sailed eastward, skirting the coast as far as the Yamal peninsula. Here rivers and lakes linked by portages allowed them to take their ships across to the wide estuary of the Ob. Exploring the waters of this huge gulf and its eastern arm into which the rivers Pur and Taz flow, these Russian adventurers traded with the Samoyeds, exchanging coloured glass beads and metal wares for sable, marten and beaver pelts. It was here that the very first Russian settlements in Siberia were probably founded early in the sixteenth century, several decades before Yermak's invasion of the khanate of Sibir.[24]

As in the case of the Stroganov–Yermak venture, although the first Russian visitors and settlers in the Gulf of Ob came by private enterprise, towards the end of the sixteenth century the Russian state became actively interested in the acquisition of territory and tribute, and armed expeditions consisting of Cossacks and Komi-Zyrian auxiliaries were sent from Tobolsk and Berezov with the purpose of exploring the region and setting up forts. Their efforts were at first hampered by the resistance of the natives – Nenets Samoyeds. In 1601, however, a Russian fort was successfully established on the river Taz about a hundred miles from its mouth, and this came to be known, after the name of the local Samoyed tribe Mongkansi, as Mangazeya. This quickly grew into a typical Russian town, with its stockaded fort containing the governor's residence, church, prison, barracks etc., and the trading quarter (*posad*) outside the walls, with its commercial buildings, customs house, several churches, and houses.[25]

With Mangazeya as their base, the Russian colonisers penetrated the surrounding Arctic lands and set up a network of out-posts or 'winter quarters' (*zimovya*) for the collection of fur tribute from the native tribes, at first chiefly Samoyeds. Pressing farther and farther east they reached the Yenisey, on whose banks were established the outposts of Turukhansk (1604) and Khantaysk (1620). For seventy years after its foundation Mangazeya was the metropolis of a vast province of Central Siberia embracing the Yenisey and its tributaries as far south as the Mountain (*Podkamennaya*) Tunguska and as far east as the watershed of the Lena basin.[26]

Meanwhile the advance of the Russian conquerors had also continued in more southerly latitudes. The subjugation of the Khanty people east of the Ob-Irtysh confluence was marked by the building of the town of Surgut in 1594. Although Russian historians mention the 'voluntary' submission of the

---

[24] S.V. Bakhrushin, 'Puti v Sibir v XVI–XVII vv.', in his *Nauchnye trudy*, vol. III, pt. 1, pp. 72–111; R.H. Fisher, *The Russian Fur Trade 1550–1700*, Berkeley, 1943, pp. 11–13, 159, 163; M.I. Belov et al., *Mangazeya. Mangazeyskiy morskoy khod*, Leningrad, 1980, pt. 1, pp. 33–5, 67, 109–12, 116–23.

[25] Belov, *Mangazeya*, pt. 1, pp. 35–6, 132.

[26] Dolgikh, *Rodovoy i plemennoy sostav*, pp. 18, 119–20.

Khanty prince Bardak here, resistance to the foreign occupiers continued for some time, and rebellions of various Khanty tribes on the middle Ob took place for instance in 1606, 1608 and 1616.[27] Beyond Surgut the Russians entered the territory of the Selkups, where they encountered a tribal confederation known in Russian as the 'skewbald horde' (*pegaya orda*). Its prince, Vonya, was in alliance with Kuchum and offered stubborn resistance to the invaders, but was eventually overcome. In 1596 the town of Narym was founded, and six years later another Russian fort in Selkup land – Ketskiy ostrog – was established on the river Ket, a tributary farther up the Ob. The Ket itself became an important route for further Russian penetration of Siberia, since it led eastward through swampy lowlands to within 100 miles of the Yenisey. On its upper reaches, in the heart of country inhabited by Ket tribes, the fort-town of Makovskiy ostrog was founded in 1618 at a point where a portage gave access to one of the tributaries of the Yenisey. Among the troops who took part in this operation were Koda Khanty auxiliaries. On the Yenisey itself, north of the confluence of the Angara, the important fort of Yeniseysk was founded in 1619.[28]

Pushing on southward beyond Ketsk, the Russians' advance up the Ob eventually brought them out of the coniferous forest at the edge of the wooded steppe of Baraba. Here for the time being Russian interest ceased, since no more fur-bearing animals were to be found in that direction. In any case the steppe-land to the south-east, beyond the territory of the Chat Tatars, was occupied by Turkic tribes of the Altai – the Teleut, who were vassals of the formidable West Mongolian khanate known as the Oirat. As a result, the frontier of the Russian Empire established in the early seventeenth century on the Ob and Irtysh did not advance further in this direction for a hundred years.

However, within the shelter of the outlying ranges of the Altai mountains the Muscovites did extend their conquests southward into the fertile valley of the river Tom. Here the local Turkic tribes, including the Eushta, the Chat, and the 'Blacksmith Turks' (known in Russian from the word *kuznets* 'blacksmith' as *Kuznetskiye Tatary*) who stood out among the peoples of Western Siberia for their skill in forging iron, were gradually subjugated after the foundation of the towns of Tomsk in 1604 and Kuznetsk in 1618. The Eushta Tatars, whose leader Toyan accepted Russian rule voluntarily, were at first not subjected to the exaction of *yasak*, as a reward for collaborating with the Russians in the subjugation of other tribes. In the foundation of Tomsk itself Russian soldiers had been reinforced by Tatars from Tobolsk and Khantys from Koda.[29]

[27] *Istoriya Sibiri*, vol. II, p. 34; P.A. Slovtsov, *Istoricheskoye obozreniye Sibiri*, St Petersburg, 1886, p. 35.

[28] *Istoriya Sibiri*, vol. II, p. 34; *Narody Sibiri*, p. 573.

[29] Dolgikh, *Rodovoy i plemennoy sostav*, pp. 94, 101–2, 116; *Istoriya Sibiri*, vol. II, p. 36.

During the seventeenth century the most antagonistic neighbours of Tomsk and Kuznetsk districts were the Teleuts, who alternately submitted to their Oirat overlords and raided the Russian settlements, or made temporary alliances with the Russians for campaigns against the Yenisey Kirgiz – a powerful and warlike people who continued to hold the Russians at bay for a century.[30] At the same time the Chulym, another tributary of the Ob, was being explored. Here too the Russians came up against serious opposition, since the local Turkic tribes were also vassals of the Yenisey Kirgiz.

By 1620 Russian possessions were established in the Tomsk–Kuznetsk region in a 250-mile long tongue of mountainous land extending south between the upper Ob and the Yenisey. Exposed on either side to hostile Turkic peoples, this Russian enclave was subjected to many raids throughout the seventeenth and early eighteenth centuries. As a result, the isolated town of Kuznetsk, linked to the rest of Russia only by the Tom valley, remained a fortified garrison outpost with few pretensions to urban culture.[31]

THE FUR TRADE AND TRIBUTE

By 1620 the annexation of Western Siberia was complete and the Muscovite colonial régime in full swing, with the Russians dominating all the territory from the Urals eastward to the Yenisey valley, and from the Arctic Ocean to the steppe frontier and Altai Mountains in the south. Some 1.25 million square miles of land had been added to Muscovy, more than doubling its territorial extent, and a network of fortified towns had been set up to extend the Tsar's government to the native peoples and administer the system of tribute which was the principal reason for the Russians' presence among them.

Furs provided the Russian state with an enormous source of wealth during the sixteenth and seventeenth centuries. Indeed for hundreds of years before then the pelts of fur-bearing animals had been of great importance to the trading economy of the East Slavonic principalities. In Kievan Rus furs probably constituted the biggest single item of export, except perhaps slaves, and in the pre-coinage economy they were used as the standard medium of exchange, the basic unit being the marten (*kuna*). At that time furs were most in demand in countries lying to the south of Rus – the Byzantine Empire and the Islamic Middle East. Other European countries were able to obtain furs from their own local forests, which survived without serious denudation until about the twelfth century. As hunting and forest clearance became more intensive, however, the most prized animals – in that period squirrel and

[30] A.P. Umanskiy, *Teleuty i russkiye v XVII–XVIII vv.*, Novosibirsk, 1980.
[31] *Istoriya Sibiri*, vol. II, pp. 269–70.

○ Russian forts, winter-posts, towns
main transport routes
→ sea route
cataracts
marsh

Map 4 Western Siberia in the seventeenth century

ermine – became scarce at the same time as the developing medieval societies of Europe were making an ever increasing demand for furs both for warmth and for display in dress.[32]

From the middle of the fifteenth century onward the prosperity and pomp of Renaissance Europe created a great demand for luxury goods, including furs (no longer the humble squirrel, but costly sable and marten). It was the ability of Muscovite Rus to engage in this trade, especially after it had crushed and enveloped Novgorod, that gave it its principal commodity of foreign exchange, and provided the means for purchasing goods from abroad which Russia lacked, such as precious metals, textiles, fire-arms, lead, sulphur, tin etc. Russia's eastern trade was always at least as important as that with European countries, and this continued to be the case in the sixteenth and seventeenth centuries, when Ottoman Turkey replaced the Byzantine Empire as a trading partner in the Black Sea area, and direct trade with Persia became possible after the destruction of the Tatar khanates of Kazan and Astrakhan. In this Middle Eastern trade Russia imported silk and other textiles, dried fruits, spices etc. in exchange for arms, leather, furs and other traditional forest products such as beeswax.[33] It was also in terms of furs that the Tsars of the sixteenth and seventeenth centuries were able to display their munificence in relations with other countries. For instance, in 1595 Moscow sent to the German Emperor Rudolf II, as a contribution to the war against the Ottoman Turks, a huge gift of West Siberian furs which caused wonderment and was valued at 400,000 roubles.[34]

Of all furs it was the sable, with its dark colour and luxurious texture, which commanded the highest price, followed by the black fox and the marten. Because of the extreme market value of sable, the possession of a few pelts from a single hunting or trading trip could make a man in Russia prosperous for the rest of his life. As a result, the opening up of Siberia to the Russians led to a veritable 'fur fever' comparable with the gold rush of the nineteenth century.[35] In the period 1585 to 1680 the total number of sables and other valuable skins obtained in Siberia amounted to tens of thousands per year, reaching a peak of over a hundred thousand. Their value in Moscow (which was considerably less than the prices they fetched on the foreign markets for which many of them were destined) constituted about 10 per cent of the total income of the state.[36] Because of the resources of the *taiga*, Russia was unrivalled as a supplier of furs to European and Asian markets until the eighteenth century. Compared with the only potential

---

[32] Fisher, *Russian Fur Trade*, pp. 1–4, 8–9; E.M. Veale, *The English Fur Trade in the Later Middle Ages*, Oxford, 1966, pp. 1–7, 57–63, 134–7.

[33] Fisher, *Russian Fur Trade*, pp. 9–16, 21–2, 210–17; Ponomarev, *Istoriya SSSR*, vol. II, pp. 118–19, 146, 318; Veale, *English Fur Trade*, pp. 136, 140–6, 156, 160.

[34] Solovyov, *Istoriya Rossii*, vol. IV, p. 248.

[35] Fisher, *Russian Fur Trade*, p. 29.

[36] *Ibid.*, pp. 109–19, 122.

competitor in the trade, that other great northern colonial territory exploited by Europeans – North America – Russia enjoyed the advantage of overland communication with its hunting grounds. Even when Canadian furs did begin to reach European markets in large numbers, the absence of the sable in North America left this exclusively Siberian product in its supreme position, and it was the pelts of beaver (by then hunted to extinction in Europe) that were the most valuable commodity brought from Canada. Any newly discovered hunting ground for sable was quickly exhausted by the Russians, who then moved on inexorably to the next region, and it is to this process of extermination of animals more than anything that the rapidity of the Russian conquest of Siberia can be attributed.[37]

The methods used by the Russian state in pursuit of wealth from furs resemble those of the Spanish conquerors in Peru and Mexico: the natives were coerced into submission and then directly exploited as producers of wealth. Wherever the Muscovites extended their territory in northern Eurasia they used armed force to exact regular tribute – *yasak* – from the natives, and this was the principal means of obtaining sable and other furs for the treasury. Once a year a fixed number of sables or their equivalent (varying according to the locality between one pelt and twelve) for each male member of the tribe from the age of fifteen, had to be handed over to Russian officials. The submission of native peoples to this system was enforced by oaths administered to clan chiefs and by taking hostages – for whom the Russians used the Tatar term *amanat* (a word of Arabic origin). The hostages, usually chiefs or members of their families, were held in the local Russian fort until their kinsmen brought in the required number of pelts. Although this was a system of extortion by the threat of force, it was accompanied by government regulations which were intended to prevent arbitrary violence towards *yasak*-paying natives so that their usefulness as a source of furs should not suffer and they should not be tempted to rebel. On paper such regulations made by a European power on behalf of its colonial subjects may appear quite humane and progressive, but in practice it was almost impossible to enforce them, and the natives were subjected to much exploitation and cruelty.[38]

While the Muscovite state aimed at a high degree of monopoly in the fur trade, it could not exclude private trading entirely. Hunting and trapping for furs had long been a way of life for many Russians of the north, and private enterprisers, usually operating on behalf of a merchant in European Russia, always found their way to new hunting grounds in advance of the agents of

[37] Eccles, *Canadian Frontier 1534–1760*, p. 26; H.A. Innis, *The Fur Trade in Canada: an Introduction to Canadian Economic History*, Newhaven, 1930, pp. 33–4, 77; Fisher, *Russian Fur Trade*, pp. 33–4.

[38] S.V. Bakhrushin, 'Yasak v Sibiri v XVII v.', in his *Nauchnye trudy*, vol. III, pt. 2, pp. 49–85; Fisher, *Russian Fur Trade*, pp. 28, 59, 72–9, 116–18.

the state. Violence was not a feature of such initial contacts between Russians and the natives they encountered, because the latter, not valuing sable skins, and being ignorant of the value they represented in Russia, were eager to exchange them for cooking-pots, beads or other trinkets. If the Russians were delighted to receive for a cooking-pot as many sable pelts as could be stuffed into it, or to barter an iron axehead for eighteen skins, the natives were no less pleased, and indeed often laughed at the apparent naïveté of the incomers in making such unequal bargains.[39]

Just as in the Americas and other parts of the European colonial empires, however, the simplicity of the natives laid them open to cheating, and soon fair barter was replaced by demands backed up with force.

Given the harsh climate, difficult terrain, and long distances involved, the administration of the huge Siberian territories would have made severe demands on the best organised government, but in the politically and culturally backward Muscovite state this was a formula for inefficiency and abuse. However consistent and reasonable the rules and regulations drawn up in the capital might be, the low standards of civic responsibility and the disregard for human rights which prevailed in Muscovite Russia resulted in ubiquitous corruption among all ranks of state officials. In Siberia the military governors, to whom, as we have seen, no salary was allocated, were absolutely forbidden to take part in the fur trade, as were their subordinates, and penalties for infringement of the laws were severe. Nevertheless, practically all governors did acquire valuable furs for their own profit by a variety of illegal means, including bribing customs officials, and extortion from natives and Russian private enterprisers. Men of service acted similarly on a smaller scale, and sometimes had to pay the *voyevoda* a bribe for the right to collect *yasak* – and additional exactions – from the natives of a given region. So great was the cupidity of Russian *yasak*-collectors that they squeezed the natives mercilessly, sometimes returning after a *yasak* collection to demand a second or even a third tribute. Men of neighbouring districts also came into conflict with each other over their jurisdiction over *yasak* regions, so that the native inhabitants sometimes found themselves subjected to the extortion of tribute first by a gang from one district, and then from another.[40]

RUSSIAN COLONIAL SETTLERS IN WESTERN SIBERIA

The influx of Russians into Siberia did not consist only of soldiers, officials and trappers. The functions of the Russian towns required the presence of a variety of craftsmen; churches needed priests; merchants came and went; and so on. From the start the Russian authorities were therefore faced with

---

[39] *Kolonialnaya politika tsarizma na Kamchatke i Chukotke v XVIII veke*, compiled by S.V. Okun, Leningrad, 1935, p. 4.
[40] Fisher, *Russian Fur Trade*, pp. 81–93; *Istoriya Sibiri*, vol. II, pp. 131–2.

the problem of food supplies. Since the cost of sending grain to Siberia from European Russia was so high, and the time it took to reach its destination so long, the government conceived the idea of making the Russian settlements beyond the Urals self-supporting in agricultural produce.

The introduction of agriculture initiated a movement of peasants from Russia into Siberia which later became a mass migration. It is this process of settlement by the 'peaceful working people' of Russia – rather than the subjugation of the natives to fur tribute – which is emphasised by Communist Party historians in order to present the Russian annexation of Northern Asia as a progressive phenomenon which brought benefits to primitive Siberia. Thus an ostensible justification is provided for the fact that the 'empty' land cleared of forest and ploughed up by the new settlers was taken from the native peoples. All 'empty' land in fact supported the existence of some natives, and was all the more vital to their survival precisely because it was sparsely populated and permitted them to roam freely in search of prey and pastures for their reindeer. The attitude of the Russian peasants, whether those officially imported to supply the needs of towns and monasteries, or individual pioneers seeking land of their own initiative, was like that of European colonisers in other parts of the world. To paraphrase words written about the British in North America: the average colonist was a farmer, and to him the [Siberian] native was either a nuisance or a menace, who did not go away and who indeed resisted the encroachments of the newcomers. So far as rights to the land were concerned, in practice 'if the whites needed the land, they took it'.[41] Moreover, as the frontier of settlement created by axe and plough moved steadily forward at the expense of the forest, the animal and human life it sustained was killed or driven farther to the east and north, so that the frontiersman, in Siberia as in Canada, was 'the enemy and destroyer of the frontier forestland and its denizens'.[42]

Apart from soldiers, trappers, merchants and peasants, another category of persons who from the earliest stages of the conquest played a part in the Russian settlement of Siberia were those sent into punitive exile by the government. These included convicted criminals, political prisoners and prisoners-of-war taken in every conflict from the Livonian War onward, including Poles and Ukrainian Cossacks (who, along with other natives of lands on the western border of Muscovy, were generally called 'Lithuanians'), Germans, Swedes, Mordva and others. By the time of Tsar Aleksey (1645–76) exile to Siberia was well established as a punishment for a number of offences. These ranged from suspicion of treasonable intent on the part of courtiers if they behaved with insufficient respect towards the Tsar, to common crimes such as robbery or forging coins. Some of those sent into Siberian exile were put to work on the land as state peasants, or employed as

---

[41] W.T. Hagan, *American Indians*, Chicago, 1961, pp. 8–9.
[42] Eccles, *Canadian Frontier*, pp. 3–4.

craftsmen in towns, but the majority were drafted into the ranks of the Cossacks.[43] Settlement by deportation to Siberia was naturally resented by many of the exiles, who took the first opportunity to run away from their enforced place of residence, either with the intention of returning to European Russia or of seeking a free life in some unsettled frontier region. As a result of such illegal flight the vagabond element appeared in Siberia. Living as outlaws in the wilds, vagabonds were a potential menace to other inhabitants of the colony.[44]

One very specific group of Russian settlers in Siberia were the 'Old Believers' – people who refused to accept changes in the Orthodox Church ritual introduced in 1654. They were subjected to harsh persecution by the state, and many fled beyond the Urals, especially from Archangel province where the Old Believer movement was very strong as a result of the imprisonment and martyrdom of its leader, Archpriest Avvakum, at Pustozersk in the land of the Nenets Samoyeds. In Siberia the largest communities of Old Believer refugees congregated in the Altai mountains and among the Buryats east of Lake Baikal. They shunned contact with the rest of the population and were extremely conservative in their social customs and in their dress, in which many old-fashioned features originating in the European North were preserved up to the twentieth century.[45]

The conquest of Western Siberia was on the one hand a systematic operation on the part of the state, which imposed its system of towns, garrisons, and *yasak* administration, and sought to control the lives of native peoples and Russian settlers alike. On the other hand, it set in motion a spontaneous, uncontrollable flow of Russian citizens to the east, which partly contributed to the aims of the state but often conflicted with them. In later stages of the occupation of Siberia the degree of control from the capital was even less and the undisciplined movement more marked, so that somewhat different conditions came to prevail beyond the Yenisey in the remote central and eastern regions of the colony. Western Siberia remained a distinct region with its own characteristics imposed by natural conditions and its relative proximity to Central Russia. As parts of it offered good soil and a reasonably favourable climate, it was here that the majority of Russian peasant farmers came to settle. As a result, up till the twentieth century the

---

[43] *Aziatskaya Rossiya*, vol. I, pp. 180, 202; G.K. Kotoshikhin, *O Rossii v carstvovanie Alekseja Mixajloviča: text and commentary*, A.E. Pennington, ed., Oxford, 1980, pp. 43–4, 57–8, 68, 106, 109, 111, 116, 129; V.I. Shunkov, *Voprosy agrarnoy istorii Rossii*, Moscow 1974, pp. 33–7; Solovyov, *Istoriya Rossii*, vol. IV, pp. 301–2, 374; vol. V, pp. 19, 125, 152, 171–2, 481, 509, 567; vol. VI, p. 162; vol. VII, pp. 111, 240.

[44] A. Wood, 'Crime and punishment in Imperial Russia', in O. Crisp and L. Edmondson, eds., *Civil Rights in Imperial Russia*, Oxford, 1989, pp. 215–33; A. Wood, 'Sex and violence in Siberia: aspects of the tsarist exile system', in J.M. Stewart and A. Wood, *Siberia: Two Historical Perspectives*, London, 1984, pp. 23–42.

[45] *Narody Sibiri*, pp. 138, 167, 177, 182.

region between the Urals and the Yenisey was not only by far the most populous part of Siberia, with a larger number of towns than the rest of the colony, but it was the only part with a significant peasant population, which was concentrated in two main agricultural regions: near the Urals in Tobolsk district, and on the upper Ob around Tomsk. By 1670 the former region already had at least 7,586 Russian homesteads, with a population of some 34,000 peasants.[46]

From the very beginning, the native inhabitants of Western Siberia showed considerable opposition to the intrusion of the Russian conquerors into their territories. Leaving aside the protracted warfare in the southern region of the Siberian Tatar khanate, we find the Samoyeds of the Arctic staunchly pitting their spears and arrows against the Russians' guns on many occasions from the seventeenth to the nineteenth centuries. In 1600 the first expeditionary party of Cossacks and Komi-Zyrians, led beyond the Ob into Samoyed country by Prince M. Shakhovskoy, suffered heavy casualties and was put to flight. The subsequent foundation of Mangazeya among the Samoyeds was supported by an army of *streltsy*, Cossacks and 'Lithuanians', and their commander received orders from the Tsar to seize the Samoyeds' chiefs as hostages and keep them imprisoned in the fort. In case of defiance, troops were to be sent out 'to make war on the unsubmissive districts' until their chiefs submitted.[47] The sequel to pacification was a régime of plunder in the name of the Tsar's *yasak*. One of the Samoyed chiefs, Ledereiko, wrote of this in a petition to Tsar Aleksey: 'for five years . . . they have been robbing and abusing us in every way, taking from us . . . with violence and all manner of threats our sable and beaver furs, our deerskin bedding and clothing, our ropes and all kinds of footwear, our geese, ducks and reindeer-flesh . . .'[48] Theft of the laboriously hand-made garments and stores of food on which survival in the Arctic depended was tantamount to murder by starvation and cold, so that Ledereiko's protestation that 'we are left naked and barefoot and shall perish completely' may be taken quite literally.

West of the Urals the town of Pustozersk was repeatedly attacked by Nenets tribes during the seventeenth and first half of the eighteenth century. Its counterpart in the east, Mangazeya, was similarly besieged by Samoyeds in 1604 and 1606, and at least four times in the 1640s. In the second half of the seventeenth century, despite frequent reinforcement of the military garrison sent from Tobolsk, uprisings of various groups of Samoyed tribes flared up one after the other on the Taz, Yenisey and Lower Tunguska. Such rebellions were not always isolated local affairs: the Samoyeds, whom Bakhrushin calls 'the archetypal nomads', were extremely mobile, so that, despite the great distances involved, their various tribes from the Pechora in

---

[46] *Istoriya Sibiri*, vol. II, p. 38.
[47] G.F. Mueller, *Istoriya Sibiri*, Moscow, 1937–41, vol. I, pp. 398–9.
[48] Belov, *Mangazeya*, pt. I, pp. 89–90.

the west to the Yenisey in the east were in communication with each other and could act in concert. One of the biggest Samoyed wars, embracing the whole of their homeland, took place in the winter of 1662–3, when Pustozersk, Obdorsk and Mangazeya all came under attack. Pustozersk was burned down and the *voyevoda* and all his men put to death, while in Mangazeya many *yasak*-collectors and trappers met the same fate. The Russians restored order in the usual manner, by carrying out punitive expeditions and hanging rebel leaders. As each year from 1666 to 1669 brought renewed assaults by the Samoyeds on Mangazeya – the concrete manifestation of the alien power among them – the position of the Russians in the town became untenable. It was therefore abandoned in 1672 and the Russian administrative and garrison base for the north was transferred to Turukhansk (at first called 'New Mangazeya') on the Yenisey. The Samoyeds on the Taz were still held to their *yasak* obligations, but their resentment continued to be shown in numerous rebellions. In 1679, for instance, a clash occurred at the old Mangazeya fort between a *yasak* gang and a defiant Samoyed chief, Nyla. After a three-day siege the Russians were saved only by the treachery of other Samoyed chiefs who attacked their assailants. As these events show, the annexation of the northern part of Western Siberia was by no means a peaceful or voluntary matter, but a campaign as violent and ruthless on the part of the conquerors as those carried out in any other colonial empire.[49]

In Soviet Russian historical writing such conflict is played down as far as possible. Where mention of it cannot be avoided, as in the case of major uprisings of the native peoples, the aggressive force is said to be the Russian ruling class and its corrupt agents, but not the Russian people in general. Thus, for instance, the activities of Russian private trappers and traders are said to have been welcomed by the Samoyeds, since by bartering furs they would obtain from the Russians those products which were highly desired by native peoples all over Siberia – iron axes, knives and cooking-pots, fishing-nets and coloured glass beads for ornament. The unscrupulous behaviour of the *voyevodas*, on the other hand, was also a truth of life in the Siberian colony, and Mangazeya provided one of the most glaring examples of this. *Voyevodas* were often appointed by the Tsar in pairs, the intention being that they should control each other. The two *voyevodas* sent to Mangazeya in 1630, Kokorev and Palitsyn, were so antagonistic to each other that they carried on an armed feud there for over two years. The result of this conflict was the destruction of much of the commercial quarter, and considerable

---

[49] Ibid., pp. 31–2, 35, 51, 67, 83, 89–92; Bakhrushin, 'Samoyedy v XVII v.', in his *Nauchnye trudy*, vol. III, pt. 2, pp. 5–12; Mueller, *Istoriya Sibiri*, vol. I, pp. 310, 398–9; Solovyov, *Istoriya Rossii*, vol. VI, p. 582; vol. VII, p. 235; *Istoriya Sibiri*, vol. II, pp. 42, 140 (in this large-scale work references to Samoyed resistance or rebellions are almost entirely absent, and the initiative for the 1600 Mangazeya revolt is attributed not to the natives but to the Russian trappers, in terms of a popular protest against 'feudal power').

damage to the fort. These two *voyevodas*, whose quarrel was no doubt over means for administering their vast district for their own profit, were not unique in the irresponsibility with which they abused their power in Mangazeya. In the 1640s Prince P. Ukhtomskiy distinguished himself by his 'unbridled robbery' and peculation, which included smuggling dishonestly obtained sables out of Siberia by having them sewn into the linings of coats. Even this scoundrel, however, is said to have differed little from other seventeenth-century *voyevodas* such as N. Boryatinskiy or Ya. Tukhachevskiy.[50]

While some admission may be made by Soviet historians of the misdemeanours of these high-ranking representatives of Russian power in north-western Siberia, no blame for the destruction of the life of the native peoples is attributed to the Russian peasantry who moved in in the wake of the trappers and state officials. On the contrary, and in disregard of the realities of Russian peasant life and character, and of the social relations of the times, the seventeenth-century peasant settler is depicted as the bearer of humane attitudes and a higher culture to the primitive Siberian natives. Thus, where some pre-revolutionary Russian writers wrote with shame about the low cultural level of the Russian peasant, the exploitation of the native peoples and the destruction of their way of life,[51] official Soviet history writes only with pride about the Russian people's titanic labour in the opening up and appropriation (*osvoyeniye*) of a sparsely populated region, about the Russian plough cutting a furrow all the way from the Urals to Kamchatka, and about the function of 'peaceful' agricultural development in laying the foundation for the growth of Siberia's productive forces.[52] So far from being detrimental to the native peoples, the coming of the Russians supposedly brought them great material and social benefits, as contact with Russian cultural centres 'overcame their isolation'. The interests of natives and settlers are said to have been reconciled in their struggle against their common class enemies.[53] With the exception of this last idea, the official Soviet view of the settlement of Siberia by the Russian people echoes many Russian nationalist writers of tsarist times, as does the most frequently repeated political assertion of all: that the annexation of Siberia was 'the logical continuation of a natural historical process', and Siberia itself 'a natural extension' of the territory of the Russian state and 'an organic part' of it.[54]

---

[50] Belov, *Mangazeya*, pt. 1, pp. 31, 51, 53, 55, 89; Lantzeff, *Siberia*, p. 54.

[51] E.g. Yadrintsev, *Sibir kak koloniya*, pp. 46–7, 99–100.

[52] *Istoriya Sibiri*, vol. II, pp. 18–19, 25, 38, 72, etc.; A.P. Okladnikov's popular work *Otkrytiye Sibiri*, Moscow, 1979, pp. 164–5, etc.

[53] *Istoriya Sibiri*, vol. II, pp. 50, 108; Ponomarev, ed., *Istoriya SSSR*, vol. II, p. 351 and passim.

[54] Ponomarev, *Istoriya SSSR*, vol. II, p. 351; *Narody Sibiri*, p. 118; *Istoriya Sibiri*, vol. II, p. 55; and many others.

3

CENTRAL AND NORTH-EAST SIBERIA IN THE SEVENTEENTH CENTURY

THE TUNGUS

THE main highways of Russian penetration into Central Siberia were the rivers flowing into the Yenisey from the east – the Lower Tunguska, the Mountain Tunguska,[1] and the Upper Tunguska or Angara – and the river system of the Lena which was reached either by portages from the Ilim, a tributary of the Angara, or from the Lower Tunguska by way of a large tributary of the Lena, the Vilui. Most of this region was occupied by the Tungus people, whose territory – larger than that of any other nationality in Siberia – extended eastward beyond the Lena as far as the shores of the Pacific. Beyond the Lena and Lake Baikal, Tungus territory embraced the whole of south-eastern Siberia as well as northern Mongolia and Manchuria. The Tungus, who may have numbered about 36,000 in the seventeenth century,[2] shared this vast territory of over 2 million square miles with two other more compact ethnic communities – the Yakuts on the Lena and the Buryat Mongols around Lake Baikal. The distinctness of the languages of these three peoples is evident when a few common words in each are compared: see Table 3.

The Ewenki language of Central Siberia is one of a family which includes Manchurian and other languages of the Amur region, Yakut is a Turkic language, and Buryat is Mongolian. Despite the obvious differences between the languages of these families in respect of vocabulary, there are many other features which they have in common, such as vowel-harmony and agglutinative structure, which has led some linguists to group the Tungus–Manchurian, Turkic and Mongolian languages together into a larger 'Altaic' family. Some go farther and include nearly all the languages of northern

[1] *Podkamennaya Tunguska* – frequently mistranslated as 'Stony Tunguska': *kamen* here means 'mountain', as it did frequently from the Urals eastward.
[2] Dolgikh, *Rodovoy i plemennoy sostav*, p. 617.

48

Table 3

	Tungus (Ewenki)	Yakut	Buryat
one	umun	biir	negeng
two	dyur	ikki	khoyor
three	ilan	üs	gurwang
ten	dyan	uon	arwang
father	amin	agha	esege
son	omolgi	uol	khüwüüng
head	dil	bas	tolgoy
house	dyu	die	ger
houses	dyul	dieler	gernüüd
good	aya	üchügey	hayng
give	bu-	bier-	üge-
take	ga-	yl-	awa-

Eurasia, including Finnic and Ugrian, under the heading of the 'Uralo-Altaic' family.[3]

The name by which the Siberian Tungus call themselves is Ewenki west and south-east of the Lena, and Ewen to the east, and these terms are now used as official designations in Soviet Russian writings, in the forms *Evenk* and *Even*. However, the old, and etymologically unexplained, name Tungus has much to commend it as a unifying term for the widely distributed groups belonging to this nation.

The Tungus were essentially forest dwellers, highly adapted to the nomadic life of hunters. Lightly built and agile, with acute powers of observation, they were adept at merging with their surroundings, moving swiftly and silently, and stalking and killing the animals and fish which provided their principal food.[4] Like the Samoyeds, they lived in easily transportable conical tents consisting of a few larch poles and a covering of reindeer-skins or sheets of birch-bark. Here, within a diameter of some fifteen feet, they disposed their fire, their sleeping places, and their meagre accoutrements. The characteristic Tungus costume was adapted to the cold but rather dry climate of Central Siberia and to a life of mobility, whether on foot or on skis. Like North American Indians, they wore brief garments of soft reindeer or elk skin around their hips, along with leggings and moccasins, or else long supple boots reaching to the thigh. The upper part of the body was covered by a very characteristic close-fitting deerskin coat, rather short at the front and longer at the back where it came to a point. This coat did not meet in front, the gap being closed by an apron or breast-piece

[3] Cf. N.A. Baskakov, *Altayskaya semya yazykov i yeye izucheniye*, Moscow, 1981, pp. 5–28; Comrie, *Languages*, pp. 10–14, 39, 59–85.

[4] S.M. Shirokogorov, *Social Organization of the Northern Tungus*, Shanghai, 1929, pp. 310–11, 335.

which, like the coat itself, was decorated with fringes of goat-hair and geometrical designs worked in different shades of deerskin and embroidered with coloured glass beads. On their heads the Tungus wore close-fitting caps made from the head-skin of reindeer, sometimes retaining the animal's ears, and some had designs tattooed on their faces.[5]

The Tungus, unlike some of the Samoyeds and peoples of north-eastern Siberia, had domesticated their reindeer completely, using them as beasts of burden for carrying their equipment and their young children when moving camp. They had also developed saddles and bridles so that they could ride on reindeer-back, and they were among the few Siberian peoples who milked their does. On the other hand, the Tungus did not originally possess riding-sledges, but only small ones on which a person on snow-shoes could drag a load behind him. While domestic reindeer were almost never killed for food, the wild herds which roamed the *taiga* constituted, along with elk, the main quarry of the Tungus.[6]

For much of the time the Tungus lived in small bands consisting of a couple of families in one or two tents, but in summer families of the same clan would congregate in camps of about a dozen tents, which among other things were convenient for the protection of the reindeer herds from insect pests by means of smoky fires. As in all North Asian societies, the communal spirit was strong, so that the spoils of hunting belonged not to the hunter who had killed them but to the whole band, among whom they were shared – a custom which the Tungus called *nimat*. Reindeer were the property of the clan as a whole, and the concept of mutual assistance, essential in primitive conditions in a hostile environment, included free access to the store-houses which were set up on posts at various points in the forest. Clans looked upon certain territories as their hunting-grounds, but as the earth was considered to belong by nature to all people and animals, it is said that they did not claim exclusive rights and were prepared to share territory with others if necessary.[7]

There were over twenty tribes of forest Tungus, each made up of a number of clans, and marriage partners had to be found within one's own tribe, but outside the clan. The Tungus language has many dialects, and there were local variations in the social customs of different tribes, so that many obstacles existed to prevent inter-marriage even with neighbouring Tungus groups. Because of constant migrations, clans became very scattered, and it was sometimes difficult for a man to find a wife within the permitted categories unless he made a long journey to an appropriately related band. Usually, however, marriages were arranged by parents while

[5] *Entsiklopedicheskiy slovar*, vol. XXXIV, p. 67; *Narody Sibiri*, p. 721.
[6] *Narody Sibiri*, pp. 707–17.
[7] Shirokogorov, *Social Organization*, pp. 194–6, 295–8; V.A. Tugolukov, *Sledopyty verkhom na olenyakh*, Moscow, 1969, pp. 120–4.

their children were quite young, and although pre-marital virginity was not expected, various customary conditions had to be fulfilled before the union could be formalised, including service by the husband in the bride's family and the exchange of 'bride-price' and dowry. Outside of marriage, which was polygynous, sexual relations were subject to a fixed system of rules and prohibitions which only permitted intercourse between a woman and any of the men of her husband's or mother's clan who counted as 'junior'.[8] As in many primitive societies, a woman in childbirth was put into a separate small tent in the forest, where she either delivered the baby entirely unaided or with the assistance of an older woman. The child was named according to the season or some other circumstance, such as the first person encountered after the birth, e.g. Garpalak 'sun-ray', Innaksa 'dog-skin'. Superstition forbade Ewenkis to tell others their own names or those of others. At the age of maturity this name would be supplemented by another appropriate name.[9]

Tungus clans had no hereditary or permanent chiefs, but from time to time meetings of the whole clan took place to decide such matters as divorce or punishment for serious crimes. In these meetings the opinions of the elders and shamans carried much weight. The question of going to war was also a matter for clan meetings, and it was mainly for this purpose that temporary leaders were chosen. As the Tungus accumulated few personal possessions, conflicts did not arise on this score, but other causes of fighting did occur, such as the abduction of women and children, the belief that all natural deaths were caused by magic spells put on by another clan, and the operation of the custom of blood vengeance. For such reasons war parties would set out, some men wearing simple armour of wooden or bone plates, and armed with bows and arrows, swords and glaives (knife-blades mounted on long wooden shafts, known as *palma*). Warfare was a matter of raiding the enemy camp or ambushing their hunting parties in the forest. Sometimes confrontations took place between two war-parties which might proceed to fighting until all on one side had been put out of action, or be decided by single combat between two champions. In some cases conflicts were settled peacefully by parleys in which the clan shamans played an important part. Like other aspects of the life of Siberian native peoples, this style of warfare suggests similarities with the North American Indians.[10]

Like all other Siberian peoples, the Tungus had a coherent religious cosmology. They believed that there were three worlds – middle-earth where people normally live, the upper world of the supreme god and other divinities, and the underworld inhabited by the spirits of the dead. These

[8] *Istoriya Sibiri*, vol. I, p. 398; Shirokogorov, *Social Organization*, pp. 206–9, 214–19, 224–8, 366–7; Tugolukov, *Sledopyty*, pp. 127–42.

[9] *Entsiklopedicheskiy slovar*, vol. XXXIV, p. 66; Shirokogorov, *Social Organization*, pp. 259–61, 274–6; Tugolukov, *Sledopyty*, pp. 146–8.

[10] *Istoriya Sibiri*, vol. I, pp. 396–9; *Narody Sibiri*, pp. 717, 724; Shirokogorov, *Social Organization*, pp. 70, 192, 197–8, 220, 222, 316–17, 336.

three worlds were linked by a river. The whole of nature was animate with occult force which took the form of 'masters' of the forest, of mountains, rivers, animals, fish etc. One of the functions of the shaman (which is in origin a Tungus word) was to perform religious rites involving the sacrifice of white or dappled reindeer reared specially for this purpose, on such occasions as weddings, funerals, the start of the hunting season or divisions of the clan. The shaman's great power lay in his or her supposed ability to establish contact with spirits and control them by projecting his own soul and flying into the spirit world. By this means it was believed that people could be cured of disease. For the trance-inducing dance and song by which the shaman performed his arduous task he or she wore a special costume, the general form of which represented the shaman's familiar or animal 'helper' – a deer, a bear or a bird. An association was recognised between the black-smith's ability to forge iron and the possession of magical powers, and this was reflected in the variety of iron objects – some of them beautifully formed abstract representations of birds or antlers – which were attached to the shaman's costume.[11]

In disposing of their dead the Tungus did not bury them in the earth, but employed 'aerial burial': the body, placed in a coffin made from a hollowed-out log or simply laid on a board, was placed above the ground on posts or tree-trunks. For life in the other world the deceased was accompanied by his weapons and other possessions.[12] The Tungus considered that the killing of animals or trees was permitted by nature if necessary for human survival, but the unnecessary infliction of pain, death or destruction was wrong. They therefore showed a certain reverence towards the animals they hunted and, in common with all the peoples of northern Eurasia (as well as North America) particularly respected the bear, observing strict rituals of propitiation when one had to be killed, including the scrupulous dissection of its body, and the burial of its bones.[13]

While the central Siberian larch forest was the classical setting of Tungus life, their mobility in search of hunting grounds had taken them in every direction from their presumed place of origin east of Lake Baikal. In the region of the middle Angara the Ewenkis went naked in summer apart from a fringed deerskin loin-cloth, painted their faces with various colours, sacrificed dogs, and used birch-bark canoes in which they knelt to wield their two-bladed paddles. These features, which are atypical of the Tungus, have been attributed to their predecessors in this region, the Asans and Kotts,

[11] A.F. Anisimov, *Religiya Evenkov v istoriko-geneticheskom izuchenii*, Moscow, 1958; Holmberg, *Finno-Ugric, Siberian*, pp. 496–523; H.N. Michael, ed., *Studies in Siberian Shamanism*, Toronto, 1963, pp. 46–123; Tugolukov, *Sledopyty*, pp. 165–74, 179–83.
[12] I.S. Gurvich, ed., *Semeynaya obryadnost narodov Sibiri*, Moscow, 1980, pp. 165–76; Tugolukov, *Sledopyty*, pp. 175–8.
[13] Diószegi and Hoppál, *Shamanism*, pp. 420–3; Tugolukov, *Sledopyty*, pp. 143–6, 148–64.

who were related to the Kets, and whom the Ewenkis presumably assimilated or drove out to the west, beyond the Yenisey.[14]

In the north, several Tungus tribes, including the Edyan and Vanadir, had moved beyond the edge of the forest, into the even less hospitable environment of the tundra. Here they ousted or absorbed the local Samoyed people (the Tavgi or Nganasan) and adopted elements of their Arctic culture, such as the use of reindeer to draw sledges and of dogs to control herds. Subsequently these far northern Tungus, who are generally known as Dolgans, were themselves subjected to the influence of the Yakuts, as the latter spread out from their base on the middle Lena.[15]

Another area of Tungus colonisation lay to the east of the Lena, reaching as far as the shores of the Okhotsk Sea, where they came into contact with the Yukagirs in the north and the Koraks in the east. These north-eastern Tungus or Ewens (formerly known in Russian as Lamuts) resembled their Korak neighbours in falling into two types of economic community. The majority were nomadic reindeer-herders and hunters among the mountains and valleys of the interior, but others, having reached the sea-coast, had adopted a semi-sedentary way of life based on hunting sea-mammals and catching fish, especially salmon. While the nomadic Ewens used the typical portable conical tent of the Tungus, the shore-dwellers had adopted the more permanent large tent of the Korak and Chukchi, or in winter made semi-subterranean lodges with a central smoke-hole which also served as the entrance. The use of dog-sledges was also taken over by the Pacific coast Tungus from their neighbours. However, even here on the wet and stormy Pacific seaboard the Ewen preserved the traditional Tungus costume with its cut-away, open-fronted deerskin coat.[16]

A Tungus culture of quite a different type developed in the region of upland steppes to the south-east of Lake Baikal, where the predominant population was Mongolian. Here, and farther south in Mongolia and Manchuria, the Tungus had gone over to the cattle-rearing and horse-riding life of the Mongols. These 'Horse-Tungus' of the Solon, Manyagir, Birar and other clans adopted the typical dwelling of the steppe-nomads – the felt-covered *yurt* or *ger* – and even foresook their Tungus costume in favour of the quilted wrap-over coat with an asymmetrical band of ornament along its collar, which reflects the dominance of Mongolian influence among all the peoples of the Baikal–Amur region.[17]

The westward limit of Tungus territory in the seventeenth century was long considered to have been the Yenisey, beyond which only individual

[14] V.A. Tugolukov, *Tungusy (evenki i eveny) Sredney i Zapadnoy Sibiri*, Moscow, 1985, pp. 42–4, 62–5, 94–5.

[15] Gurvich, *Etnicheskaya istoriya*, pp. 81–115; *Narody Sibiri*, pp. 742–54.

[16] *Narody Sibiri*, pp. 760–75.

[17] Ibid., pp. 701–2, 718–23; *Istoriya Sibiri*, vol. I, pp. 401–2; Shirokogorov, *Social Organization*, pp. 62–5.

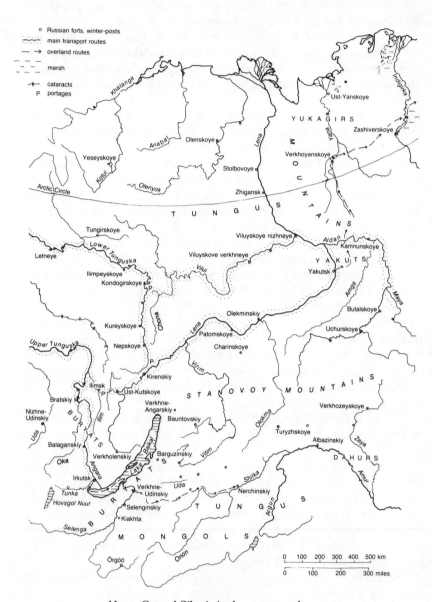

Map 5 Central Siberia in the seventeenth century

Tungus hunters penetrated. A more recent study suggests, however, that groups of Tungus had found their way to Western Siberia as early as the eleventh century, and some of their clans may have been in the service of the Tatar khanate.[18]

THE YAKUT NATION OF THE LENA

The most remarkable case of the intrusion of Turkic peoples of Inner Asia into the northern forests is that of the Yakuts, who live on the river Lena among the Tungus, some 800 miles distant from the nearest open steppe-land. (The Yakuts call themselves Sakha, but as it was from the Tungus that the Russians first heard of them, the Tungus name for them – Yeket – became established in Russian.) In the seventeenth century the Yakuts were well established in the lowlands around the northward bend of the Lena and the lower reaches of its eastern tributary the Aldan, where amid the larch forests were areas of meadowland providing grazing and hay for their horses and oxen. Although it appears obvious that the Yakuts must have come from a steppe environment south of the Siberian forest, no convincing explanation exists of the reason for this or the time when it occurred.[19] Their language, while unambiguously Turkic in its vocabulary and grammar (see pp. 22, 49), shows the influence of both Tungus and Mongolian.[20]

In summer several families congregated in one glade in the forest, where they set up very large and solid conical dwellings called uraha, consisting of poles leaning inward to a peak, covered with double sheets of birch-bark. Along with sheds for cattle, such a summer house was the centre of an area of pasture surrounded by a pole fence.

For the winter, Yakuts moved to a different type of settlement scattered more widely where only one or two family homes were grouped together. The dwellings here were cabins or lodges consisting of a rectangular framework of logs clad with lean-to poles. The roof was covered with tree-bark and earth, and the walls plastered with a mixture of clay and cow-dung. Windows were made of mica, animal bladders or sheets of ice, and the door was made of boards covered with leather. The Yakut dwelling was more advanced than that of most other Siberian peoples in having a fireplace with a chimney, which provided both heat and light.

Only during the summer did the cows and mares yield much milk, and this formed the basis of much of the Yakuts' diet. Cow's milk was drunk fresh or curdled, and as cold weather set in it was frozen, with an admixture of berries and roots, into large slabs, and thus stored for consumption in winter. More highly prized than cattle products, however, were horse-meat

---

[18] Dolgikh, *Rodovoy i plemennoy sostav*, pp. 177–9; Tugolukov, *Tungusy*, pp. 72, 237–45, 267–8.
[19] *Narody Sibiri*, pp. 268–70.
[20] *Yazyki narodov SSSR*, vol. II, pp. 403, 424.

and mare's milk. In common with all equestrian Turkic peoples the Yakuts used mare's milk in fermented form to make the drink known as *kumys*. This was the focus of their summer festival *yhyakh* in honour of the gods of nature and fertility, for which the whole clan congregated and drank *kumys* ceremonially out of carved wooden chalices. Competitive games, wrestling and horsemanship were also a part of these clan gatherings.[21]

The costume and decorative arts of the Yakuts also differed from those of other Siberian peoples. In winter they wore long fur coats richly ornamented with appliqué designs and fur trimmings, and fur hats with long ear-flaps, which sometimes assumed an exaggerated height and were elaborately decorated with silver or other metal ornaments. Other costume details – belts, necklaces, gorgets, earrings etc. – tended to be of rather massive design, as were saddles and other horse accoutrements.

The Yakuts were more advanced than most other Siberian peoples in their use of iron. Several other native peoples, such as the Tungus, knew how to forge articles out of iron bars, but only the Yakuts and Shors ('Blacksmith Tatars') had the skill of smelting iron from ore. So greatly was this skill respected among the Yakuts that smiths were believed to possess magical powers which made them 'powerful' as shamans. The weapons of hunting and war made by the Yakuts were, like those of the Tungus, glaives, bows and arrows, helmets and coats of mail.[22]

The Yakuts were energetic and adaptable colonisers who since the seventeenth century have expanded their territory towards the north, west and east. During this process they assimilated many Tungus, Samoyeds and Yukagirs, so that eventually Yakut language and culture came to dominate very large areas of Central and Eastern Siberia. This led to the formation in the Far North, around the river Khatanga, of the Dolgan people, whose ancestors, belonging to Tungus clans, are believed to have received a strong admixture of Yakuts as the latter moved north-westward from the lower Lena. The language of the Dolgan people is a dialect of Yakut strongly influenced by Tungus.[23]

In the original area of Yakut settlement on the Lena their language was very uniform, so that they can be considered to have belonged to a single tribe. The many clans which composed this tribe, such as the Kangalas, Nam, Megin, Gorogon, Betun and Baturus, were, however, independent of each other. Within each clan, rights over pastures, meadows and hunting and fishing-grounds were communal, and all members were bound by obligations of mutual assistance. Clan chiefs, called *toyons*, wielded considerable

[21] M.V. Khabarova, *Narodnoye iskusstvo Yakutii*, Leningrad, 1981, pp. 2, 6–13, 35–41 and passim; *Narody Sibiri*, pp. 284–91, 302; Tokarev, *Etnografiya*, pp. 462–4, 469.

[22] *Istoriya Sibiri*, vol. I, pp. 388–91; Khabarova, *Narodnoye iskusstvo Yakutii*, pp. 82–91, 94–117; *Narody Sibiri*, pp. 273, 280, 283, 288, 301.

[23] *Narody Sibiri*, pp. 742–54; *Yazyki narodov SSSR*, vol. II, p. 404.

authority, and may have occupied their position by election, with the blessing of the shaman, or by heredity.[24]

For religious observances the Yakuts had shamans, whose costume, tambourines and practices were very similar to those of the Tungus. Unlike the Tungus, the Yakuts believed not only in ubiquitous spirits of natural phenomena, but also in a pantheon of gods with *Uluu-toyon* ('great chief') at their head. In this they showed their affinity with the Turkic peoples of the Altai-Sayan region. In common with other Siberian peoples the Yakuts revered wild animals, in particular the bear, the eagle and the raven, and as an equestrian people it was natural that they used horses as victims for sacrificial offerings to the spirits of the 'upper world'.[25] The Yakuts, like nearly all Siberian peoples, had no musical instruments, but songs and recitations played an important part in their social life. Eloquent speechmaking was a highly valued talent, and the tribal traditions were preserved in long epics and heroic songs which were proclaimed by gifted story-tellers at clan assemblies.

THE CONQUEST OF CENTRAL SIBERIA

Russians made their way into Central Siberia from two widely separated bases: Mangazeya in the north, and Yeniseysk in the south, the northerly route being the earlier. Trappers and *yasak* gangs pressed on beyond Mangazeya from the very beginning of the seventeenth century, and a number of outposts were established east of the Yenisey among the Samoyeds in the Taimyr peninsula, and among the northernmost clans of Tungus who inhabited the forests in the basins of the Kotui, Anabar and Olenyok rivers. Other Mangazeya men who advanced southward up the first large tributary of the Yenisey, the Lower Tunguska, or found further tributaries between there and the Mountain Tunguska, also came into Tungus country.

Due to the difficulty of the terrain, with its narrow, rocky valleys and many rapids, penetration into the heart of Central Siberia was relatively difficult and slow. The Tungus, once alerted to the intentions of the Russians, offered resistance everywhere, so that by the 1620s few of them had been forced to submit to *yasak*. However, by 1640 sables were being brought in regularly by all the northern Tungus clans, from the Vanadir who lived north of the Arctic Circle, to the Chapogir and Kondogir on the Lower Tunguska

---

[24] Russian Marxist historians are much concerned with the question of whether 'feudalism' had developed among the Yakuts before the Russian conquest, or whether they still had a patriarchal system of tribal communism which only later degenerated into class divisions and 'feudal' exploitation under the effect of Russian government; cf. I.M. Trotskiy, 'Nekotorye problemy istorii Yakutii XVII veka' in *Kolonialnaya politika Moskovskogo gosudarstva v Yakutii XVII v.*, Ya.P. Alkor and B.D. Grekov, eds., Leningrad, 1936, pp. xx–xxvii; *Istoriya Sibiri*, vol. I, pp. 390–2, 394; vol. II, p. 101; Tokarev, *Etnografiya*, pp. 466–7.

[25] *Narody Sibiri*, pp. 299–301.

and the Katanga or Mountain Tunguska. Around the confluence of the latter river with the Yenisey the natives encountered by the Russians were not Tungus but Kets. The latter were under pressure from Tungus clans who were moving into this region from the beginning of the seventeenth century, having in their turn been pushed north and west by the expansion of the Buryat Mongols around Lake Baikal. Thus territorial conflicts were taking place on the Yenisey between Kets and Tungus – a local conflict which the Russians were able to exploit by enlisting some of the Kets as auxiliary forces to assist in the subjection of the Tungus. Culturally, however, the Kets were dominated by the Tungus, so that by the 1680s they were much reduced as a distinct ethnic group. Another factor in the sharp reduction in numbers of the Kets was no doubt the incidence of epidemic diseases, especially smallpox, which had been unknown in Siberia before the advent of the Russians. The first outbreak in 1630–1 carried away many of the Khanty, Mansi, Samoyed, Selkup and Ket peoples of Western Siberia. The Tungus of Central Siberia were affected by smallpox twenty years later, and the Kets and Selkups suffered virulent epidemics again in the 1660s.

On the more southerly route into Central Siberia, Russian *yasak* bands moved east on to the Yenisey before 1610. Here the Tungus under their leader Danul resisted and fought fiercely. However, the Ket tribes Dyukan and Pumpokol quickly submitted to the Russians and promised *yasak*, thus incurring the wrath of Danul, whose Tungus warriors inflicted punitive raids on them. The Tungus–Russian war on the Yenisey continued for several years as a sequence of ambushes and skirmishes between Cossack gangs and Tungus war parties. In order to crush the resistance of the Tungus, reinforcements, including men of the Koda Khanty, were sent from Surgut in 1617. The Tungus, however, kept up their attacks during 1618–20 in a brave but vain attempt to prevent the establishment of the new Russian forts of Makovsk and Yeniseysk. With the foundation of the latter as a Russian base the conquest of Central Siberia gathered momentum. Within two years the Asan Kets on the river Chuna were giving *yasak* to Yeniseysk, and the leader of a local Tungus clan, Iltik, also submitted in 1621–2. By 1633 most of the opposition was crushed, and the Russians were receiving sables regularly from all the Tungus clans on the lower Angara and Taseyev.

To the south of Yeniseysk the Russians did not have such a free hand, because the forest tribes on the upper Yenisey and Angara were already vassals of other overlords – either the Kirgiz or the Buryat Mongols and, more distantly, the khans of Mongolia itself. The Russians were therefore directly challenging the authority of established rulers when in 1628 men from Yeniseysk erected the forts of Krasnoyarsk and Kansk in order to exact fur-tribute from the Kets and Samoyeds who had long been *yasak*-paying subjects of the Kirgiz. Throughout the seventeenth century the latter continued to assert their rights over these tribes and to enlist their cooperation against the Russian invaders, so that an intermittent war went on along the frontier to the south and west of Krasnoyarsk.

To the south-east, on the upper Angara near Lake Baikal, it was the Buryat Mongols whose right to obtain *yasak* from the local Tungus, Samoyeds and Kets the Russians now sought to usurp. In this conflict the Buryats, with the assistance of their Tungus vassals, were able to hold out against the Russians on the Angara until 1655, despite their disadvantage in not possessing fire-arms. Thus in the Yenisey and Angara regions, like the Irtysh region farther to the west, the frontier was far from being an 'open' one, and the southern marches of the Russian empire moved forward very slowly against stiff resistance.[26]

While the Russians were gradually establishing themselves south of Yeniseysk, other less-well-defended routes of advance into Central and Eastern Siberia had been found. In the 1620s men from Mangazeya moved up the Lower Tunguska, setting up outposts among the Goragir, Nyuril, Kondogir and Shilagir Tungus clans. At the same time Mangazeya Cossacks and trappers were also exploring the Mountain Tunguska river, and fortified *yasak*-posts were established among the Vargagan, Chapogir and Chemdal clans. It was after following the Lower Tunguska upstream for some 1,500 miles that Russians crossed a narrow neck of land and found themselves on the bank of another great river – the Lena. Venturing down the Lena from there, Cossacks in their boats emerged from the rocky highlands of the upper course of the river on to the broader waters and more open valley of its middle course, and passed from the territory of the Tungus into that of the Yakuts. Another route also pioneered in the 1620s led from the middle course of the Lower Tunguska by way of portages on to the Chona, which flows into the principal western tributary of the Lena, the Vilui. The Yakuts living around the confluence of the Vilui and Lena were subjected to *yasak* by men from Mangazeya in 1630.

The trappers and Cossacks of Yeniseysk district also pioneered a new route to the east, striking off up the Ilim tributary of the Angara into the territory of the Nalagir Tungus, where they established the fort of Ilimsk in 1630. From there they also found a convenient portage which led to the Lena, where they began to demand *yasak* from the same Tungus natives that had been visited by Mangazeya men. Sailing on down the Lena, the Russians from Yeniseysk also made their way into Yakut territory.

When the Russians began to demand *yasak* from the Yakuts in the early 1630s, they met resistance which continued sporadically for the next fifty years. However, there was little tribal unity among the Yakuts, and the

[26] Dolgikh, *Rodovoy i plemennoy sostav*, pp. 87, 97, 119–23, 148, 161, 164, 183–7, 192–5, 204–9, 222–3, 234, 241–2, 443; Fisher, *Russian Fur Trade*, pp. 475–6; *Istoriya Sibiri*, vol. I, pp. 378, 387, 401; vol. II, pp. 43, 50, 58; Mueller, *Istoriya Sibiri*, vol. II, pp. 24, 41, 43, 45, 87, 208, 221, 239, 439–40.

antagonism which existed between the separate clans, and also between the Yakuts and their Tungus neighbours, made it difficult to achieve an effective combination of forces against the invaders. Nevertheless many of the Yakuts recognised the danger when in 1632 Cossacks from Yeniseysk erected the first fort of Lensk (later renamed Yakutsk) in the land of the Kangalas clan. During the following two years the latter combined with neighbouring clans under the *toyon* Mymak in an unsuccessful attempt to destroy the fort and drive the Russians out. In 1636 the Kangalas and Betun clans again besieged the fort but were repulsed by the Russians. As the stranglehold of Russian colonialism tightened and demands for *yasak* became more ruinous, resentment among the Yakuts and Tungus on the Lena rose to a pitch. A census of the population and their cattle carried out by the Russians in 1641 with a view to increased exactions led to the biggest of the Yakut rebellions, involving many clans. They killed a number of Russian soldiers and trappers and besieged Yakutsk, but because of inter-clan dissension the attack failed and the movement against the colonial régime fell apart. Russian retaliation for this so-called 'treason' took the form of punitive raids by Cossack bands on Yakut villages, where defensive stockades had been set up.

The remarkable momentum and energy of the Russian conquerors, set in motion by greed (governmental and private) for sables, took their vanguard on swiftly beyond the Lena into Eastern Siberia. Four hundred and fifty miles further down the Lena the fort of Zhigansk was established in the same year as Yakutsk, and in the following year, 1633, a Russian expedition sailed north to the delta of the Lena and from there south-westwards up the river Olenyok, where a fort was set up among the Edyan Tungus. To east and west of the Lena, on the Vilui and Aldan tributaries, forts were built among the Tungus and Yakuts in 1634–8, and the commitment to pay *yasak* was forced from the natives by the usual combination of threats and the seizure of hostages.[27]

A typical feature of the Russian conquest of Central and Eastern Siberia was active rivalry between the various colonial districts under their *voyevodas*. As each district pushed the frontier forward, disagreements arose over the limits of their territories and their 'rights' to exact tribute or obtain furs by trade with the natives. So in the 1610s armed bands from both Ketsk and Mangazeya were extorting *yasak* from the Kets on the Sym and Kas rivers in a spirit of ruthless competition, and somewhat later the interests of Mangazeya and Yeniseysk came into conflict over tribute from the Pit and Vargagan Tungus. In the 1630s, after the foundation of Krasnoyarsk on the upper Yenisey, its Cossacks clashed with those sent from Yeniseysk over fur tribute from the Kets of the Kan river and the Tungus of the upper Angara. On the Lena, bloody conflicts took place between Cossack bands from

---

[27] *Istoriya Sibiri*, vol. II, pp. 47–8, 143–4; Mueller, *Istoriya Sibiri*, vol. II, p. 85; Solovyov, *Istoriya Rossii*, vol. VI, pp. 588–9.

Tomsk and Yeniseysk, each of which had enlisted the support of different Yakut clans. The conflict between Yeniseysk and Mangazeya over *yasak* from the Tungus and Yakuts of the Lena regions may have been resolved by the creation in 1639 of a new district of Yakutsk with its own *voyevodas*, but fourteen years later the Far North was still a turbulent area. Here confused and bloody fighting between Tungus of the Vanadir and Edyan clans was induced by the rival activities of Russian *yasak* gangs from Mangazeya and Yakutsk operating on the river Anabar, where double exaction of tribute was a recurrent problem.[28]

Once they had established themselves on the Lena, in one of the few parts of Siberia where they could obtain fodder for their horses, and other supplies, including cattle, the Russians were in command of a relatively secure base for further operations. The fort, and later town, of Yakutsk became a Russian administrative centre of great importance for the further annexation of Eastern Siberia – the 'capital' of a vast district which soon extended all the way to the shores of the Pacific Ocean. Yakutsk also became a flourishing centre of trade, as wealthy fur merchants from European Russia moved in to establish trapping and trading businesses. Eastern Siberia was the source of vast numbers of sable and other furs from 1630 onwards, and by 1650 the district of Yakutsk had almost 2,000 Russian inhabitants.[29]

YAKUTS AND TUNGUS UNDER RUSSIAN RULE

It has sometimes been stated that in recently acquired territories the Russians did not really interfere in the tribal life of the natives, but were content to allow this to go on as before, provided the tribe, clan or territorial unit (*volost*) produced the required amount of tribute each year.[30] Certainly traditional customs, laws and religious practices were not interfered with in the first stages of colonial rule, but nevertheless the *yasak* system put immediate strains upon the social organisation of the native communities and set off changes which inevitably had far-reaching effects. In practice it meant that the chief of the clan or tribe was designated as the person responsible for organising the collection and delivery of pelts, with the sanction of hostages to force members of the clan to do as required. The Russian authorities, with their own hierarchical view of social relations, sought out the leaders or 'best people' (*luchshiye lyudi*) of the given community to parley with, or dictate to. If, as in the case of the small hunting bands of the Tungus and other northern peoples, no real chief existed, a man was chosen arbitrarily in

---

[28] Mueller, *Istoriya Sibiri*, vol. II, pp. 23, 216, 222; Dolgikh, *Rodovoy i plemennoy sostav*, pp. 191, 248–9, 295, 298; *Kolonialnaya politika ... v Yakutii*, pp. xi, 18–20, 53–55; Slovtsov, *Istoricheskoye obozreniye*, pp. 41–3.

[29] *Istoriya Sibiri*, vol. II, p. 48.

[30] e.g. Fisher, *Russian Fur Trade*, p. 18; *Istoriya Sibiri*, vol. II, p. 99.

this capacity. The designated chiefs were referred to by the condescending Russian term 'princeling' (*knyazets* or *knyazyok* as distinct from *knyaz* 'prince'). As the Yakuts already had a social hierarchy, it was normally the *toyon* of each clan who was made responsible for collecting *yasak* on behalf of the Russians.

In the first stages of Russian occupation it was also the *toyons* who, as war leaders, led resistance movements against the invaders. After some forty years of Russian rule, however, when local resistance had been crushed with an iron hand, when wars and exactions had taken their toll, and tribal customs and morale had been undermined by the colonial régime, the native rulers allowed themselves to be coerced or bought over, and came to terms with the occupying power. Their status as native lords was therefore enhanced by Russian laws of 1677–8 which defined their responsibilities in respect of *yasak* collection, the preservation of order and the administration of justice. This elevation of the Yakut clan chiefs to the status of a hereditary aristocracy was accompanied by a corresponding abasement of the ordinary members of the clan to the status of serfs – a process which Soviet Russian historians refer to as the feudalisation of Yakut society.[31] The *toyons*, with the example of Russian social inequality and maladministration before them, all too often succumbed to the temptations of greed and used their position as agents for their imperial masters both to squeeze wealth, in the form of furs, out of their compatriots, and to exploit their labour. Since recognition as the 'princeling' responsible for *yasak* collection carried with it not only personal status but exemption from paying *yasak* themselves, Yakut chiefs sometimes offered bribes to the *voyevoda* in order to obtain the coveted title – a procedure which was in full conformity with Russian practice.[32]

Adjustment to Russian rule did not only affect the chiefs, however. It appears that, whether through astuteness or weakness, the Yakuts in general were quick to adapt to the ways of their conquerors. For instance, a class of Yakut traders emerged to play a part in the commerce of Eastern Siberia similar to that of the Komi-Zyrians in the Urals and Western Siberia. As a result of much inter-breeding a local blending of the Yakuts and Russians took place relatively painlessly. One indicator of this was the facility with which even in the seventeenth century most Yakuts adopted the Russian system of forename and patronymic, such as Turenei Kologuyev, and later the native Yakut names were completely ousted by Russian ones. In contrast, the Tungus kept themselves apart from the Russians and preserved their own names for longer.[33]

If the Russian colonial régime in Siberia led directly to the disintegration

---

[31] *Istoriya Sibiri*, vol. II, pp. 99–101, 130; *Kolonialnaya politika . . . v Yakutii*, pp. xxi–xxvi.

[32] *Istoriya Sibiri*, vol. II, p. 132.

[33] *Kolonialnaya politika . . . v Yakutii*, p. xxvii n.; A.V. Superanskaya, ed., *Spravochnik lichnykh imen narodov RSFSR*, 2nd edn, Moscow, 1979, pp. 200–1.

of the social system of the Yakuts, it also brought disaster to the fur-bearing animals of the forest, and as a result of this contributed further to the impoverishment of the native peoples. Under conditions of intensive and uninterrupted hunting, the sables, black foxes and other highly prized animals were simply hunted to extinction. By 1650 the supply of sable pelts was failing in parts of Western Siberia, so that towards the end of the century the natives there were being permitted to pay half the value of *yasak* in money instead of furs. This dearth of furs had spread to the Yenisey by the 1670s, and even the virgin forests of Central Siberia and Yakutia, which had been a fabulous source of furs between the 1630s and the 1670s, were almost exhausted within fifty years of their discovery. In 1684 the Moscow government acknowledged this fact in a decree forbidding the hunting of sable by Russian trappers in the Yeniseysk and Yakutsk provinces – a decree which is unlikely to have had much effect, in view of the large volume of private trade still carried on by the fur merchants in these provinces in the following decade.[34]

By the second half of the seventeenth century many Yakuts had attempted to escape from Russian oppression by moving away from central Yakutia to the north, where they adopted the Tungus way of life, relying for a livelihood on fishing and hunting wild reindeer. As the taiga and wooded tundra of the region west of the Lena supported huge numbers of reindeer as well as a multitude of water-fowl and fish, migrant Tungus and Yakuts were drawn to the banks of rivers in the basins of the Olenyok, Anabar and Kotui. Even here, however, they were not safe from the Tsar's Cossacks and the *yasak* system, which pressed on them inexorably, irrespective of the fact that sable and fox had already become scarce. In order to avoid imprisonment and torture for non-fulfilment of Russian demands, many people were driven to the expedient of buying furs from Russian trappers and passing these on to the *yasak*-gatherers. The price of the furs was paid in other hard-won necessities of life, mainly reindeer meat and skins.[35]

While sable or fox furs were intrinsically of little importance to the natives of Siberia, they had been forced to adjust, or revolutionise, their way of life by the Russian government's insatiable demand for *yasak* and the tempting prospects of private trade, which so often ended in the natives being cheated or robbed. Much of their energies had perforce been diverted from the essential activity of herding reindeer (and, in the case of the Yakuts, horses and cattle) to sable-hunting, so that they lost their economic self-sufficiency. Russian, and especially Marxist, writers are quick to assert that these bad effects of colonialism on the native Siberian peoples were far outweighed by the positive benefits of their being brought out of their isolation into the

---

[34] Fisher, *Russian Fur Trade*, pp. 179–82; *Istoriya Sibiri*, vol. II, pp. 48, 78, 130; Belov, *Mangazeya*, p. 32.

[35] *Kolonialnaya politika . . . v Yakutii*, pp. 121–2; Gurvich, ed., *Etnicheskaya istoriya*, p. 183.

Russian market network and into contact with the higher culture of the Russians. The reality was, however, that the native communities had been forced into dependence upon a single commodity – the furs prized highly by Europeans – which they themselves were obliged to destroy around them systematically. By the time that commodity had run out they had been brought to economic and social ruin.[36]

Another factor in the process of the Russian annexation of Central Siberia which led to conflicts with the native peoples was the influx of Russian peasants. Agricultural settlement began near Yeniseysk in the 1620s, and areas of black earth around Krasnoyarsk attracted many peasants from Russia in the thirties. In the upper Lena and Angara basins, although the soil was less fertile and the problems of supply beyond Yeniseysk were great, the need for grain led to the importation of peasants in the middle of the century. As a result, pockets of Russian agriculture developed at various places on the Angara and Ilim, where the felling of trees and burning of undergrowth allowed crops (mainly rye, oats and barley) to be planted in the clearings.[37]

Because of their encroachment on the territories of the indigenous population, Russian peasant settlers were frequently attacked by Buryats, Tungus and Yakuts, who had to learn to match the complaints sent to Moscow by the Russians, by making similar petitions to put their own case. In 1680, for instance, a petition was written in the name of a Tungus, Murgucha, who had been beaten by a Russian peasant, 'the said Murgucha having lived in his clan territory on the River Uda for many years and now he is being driven out of it by the peasants of Ilimsk'.[38] Similarly, in Ilimsk district a Buryat clan led by Zayaikaiko Burlai and Fetka Kamnagadai procured the removal from their territory of a Russian farm for which one of the Yakutsk 'boyar's sons' had taken land. So seriously, in the end, did the Moscow government take the loss of *yasak* caused by peasants ploughing up native hunting grounds that in 1683 the Siberian Office sent to the Yakutsk *voyevodas* 'a firm prohibition on pain of death that henceforth in sable hunting grounds no forest whatever is to be cut or burned, in order that the animals be not exterminated nor flee to distant parts'.[39]

The evidence which such official documents contain of attempts by the native peoples to defend their way of life from the invaders can represent only a fraction of the land-grabbing which occurred wherever the Russians went. With such causes, and the inter-tribal strife which the quest for *yasak* encouraged, warfare was frequent in Central Siberia in the second half of the seventeenth century. One incident occurred in 1675–6 on the Vilui,

[36] Fisher, *Russian Fur Trade*, pp. 90–1; *Istoriya Sibiri*, vol. II, pp. 44–5, 50, 53, 108 and passim.
[37] *Istoriya Sibiri*, vol. II, pp. 44, 46, 50; *Kolonialnaya politika . . . v Yakutii*, pp. 47, 156.
[38] Dolgikh, *Rodovoy i plemennoy sostav*, p. 210.
[39] *Kolonialnaya politika . . . v Yakutii*, pp. 47, 156–7, 170–1, 194, 201–7.

3 Ewen (Lamut) family of the lower Kolyma, early twentieth century, wearing deerskin leggings, boots, aprons and coats decorated with the fine glass-bead embroidery which was particularly characteristic of the Tungus and Dolgans. AMNH neg. no. 22410 Bogoras.

when a fight between Russians and Yakuts over hunting grounds resulted in the death of a Cossack and several Russian trappers. When a punitive detachment consisting of Russians and Yakut collaborators was sent out to bring the Yakut chief Baltuga to heel, he met them with a war-party of fifty Yakuts and Tungus. Defeated by the Russians, Baltuga was taken to Yakutsk, imprisoned and tortured, but in conformity with Moscow's expressed policy of conquering by 'kindness' rather than coercion, he was not executed. In response to a petition drawn up by a number of Yakut *toyons*, Baltuga was 'pardoned' and released. No doubt this was not an isolated incident of desperate resistance to the depredations of the *yasak*-gatherers and trappers, since in 1680 the Yakutsk *voyevodas* were aware of much unrest among the natives and feared a general uprising. Yakut revolts did in fact occur in 1681–2 under the leadership of Jenik of the Kangalas, and in 1684, when a dispute between clans developed into an uprising directed against the Russians and collaborationist *toyons*. The Yakut leaders Oryukan and Dachig mustered a considerable army of Yakuts and Tungus, but their struggle against the heavily armed Russians was hopeless, and in this case the leaders of the rebellion were hanged and quartered as an example to other potential rebels against the colonial régime.[40]

The Tungus continued to be the most resolute of the Central Siberian peoples in their opposition to the Russians. Their small social units and lack of class differentiation made them more difficult to control than the sedentary Yakuts. As a result of the imposition of *yasak*, difficulties in obtaining furs to pay their dues in bad years, the corruption of the Russian administration, and frequent epidemics of smallpox, the Tungus, whose way of life was in any case highly mobile, became even more prone to migration. From about 1630 many Ewenki Tungus from the Angara, Vilui and Lena rivers moved south-east to the Chinese–Manchurian border area on the river Amur. About the same time some of the Ewenki Tungus clans on the Lower Tunguska moved away northward into the basin of the Kotui. Such migrations often led to wars between Tungus clans, which were sometimes provoked by Russian officials for their own ends. Tungus attacks on trappers and *yasak*-gatherers were frequent, and the biggest uprising of the second half of the seventeenth century took place in the Far North near the Kotui where, because of the extortion and cruelty of the Russian garrison at the Lake Yesei outpost, the Tungus killed them and attempted to cover their traces by migrating eastward to the Olenyok and Lena valleys.[41]

In the seventeenth century the journey from Moscow to Yakutsk took more than a year, travelling by the only feasible means – river boats – and with an interruption of several months during the winter. The round trip required anything from three to four years.[42] This was indeed a remote region where the effect of decrees made in Moscow was long delayed, and the consequences of actions performed in Yakutia need not reach the ears of the Tsar, or even the head *voyevoda* in Tobolsk, for many months – if ever. Such remoteness, combined with the general cumbersomeness and corruption of Russian colonial administration, made the huge district of Yakutia the most lawless of all the Siberian provinces – a field for arbitrary actions, injustice and self-enrichment at the expense of all those of inferior status who could be exploited, whether they were natives or Russian peasants, trappers or rank-and-file Cossacks.

---

[40] Ibid., pp. xvi–xviii, 87–90.
[41] Dolgikh, *Rodovoy i plemennoy sostav*, pp. 161, 443–86; Gurvich, *Etnicheskaya istoriya*, pp. 135–7, 185.
[42] Fisher, *Russian Fur Trade*, pp. 174–7.

An inevitable factor in sending out detachments of men to explore and subjugate distant lands and remain as long-term forces of occupation has always been an acute need for women. In 1630, when the Russian frontier had advanced half-way across Siberia, the Moscow government attempted to cope with this problem by decree. It ordered 150 girls to be recruited voluntarily from the north-eastern provinces of European Russia and sent to Siberia, and seven years later a further consignment of 150 girls was dispatched 'for marriage to Cossacks'.[43] Long before this, however, Russian men of all ranks in Siberia had found their own way to get women. In the anodyne words of a Soviet Russian historian: 'settlers eagerly entered into marriage with local girls'.[44] Certainly mixed marriages did take place in Siberia, and as the women concerned were not Christians but 'pagans' this caused the Orthodox Church authorities some concern. But it was the prevalence of much more serious sexual irregularities that evoked a diatribe from Patriarch Filaret and led to the appointment of the first archbishop of Siberia in Tobolsk in 1621. Because of the lack of women, said Filaret, Russian men in Siberia were given to incestuous relations with their sisters, mothers or daughters, while those men of service who had wives resorted to mortgaging them to other men when they were sent away on expeditions.[45] Widows and spinsters and wives of poor men were taken by force, and the women thus procured were passed on to others and even 'married' to them with the cooperation of the complaisant Orthodox clergy. The *voyevodas* did little or nothing to discourage such practices, in which they themselves were often involved.

If women brought from Russia provided sexual partners for some of the invaders of Siberia, the majority obtained their women from the native peoples. At the time of Archbishop Kiprian's appointment it was the Khanty and Mansi women of Western Siberia who were most liable to abduction, but wherever the Russian invaders went, it was women and girls that they seized first of all in their assaults upon the native inhabitants.[46] No doubt the Cossacks drew some justification for their abduction of women from the customs prevailing among the native peoples themselves, according to which women and children were part of the natural spoils of war, while payment of 'bride-price' as a ubiquitous feature of marriage in Siberia may have appeared to Europeans as the purchase of wives. In any case the Russians were not slow to adopt such practices, no doubt applying them with greater thoroughness and irresponsibility, by killing native men in order to take their womenfolk, and by buying and selling 'wives'. Not only were female captives exploited in this way, but, once the Russian régime of occupation was

---

[43] Mueller, *Istoriya Sibiri*, vol. II, pp. 87, 374–5.
[44] Ponomarev, *Istoriya SSSR*, vol. II, p. 352.
[45] Solovyov, *Istoriya Rossii*, vol. V, pp. 323–4; Yadrintsev, *Sibir kak koloniya*, pp. 12–14.
[46] *Istoriya Sibiri*, vol. II, pp. 86–7.

established, it became a regular custom that detachments of men of service on their journeys had to be provided with women wherever they stayed, and this practice, which continued in Eastern Siberia until the middle of the nineteenth century, was looked upon as one of the obligations required of native communities.[47]

Keeping women captives as concubines was but one element of the more general phenomenon of slavery in Northern Asia under Russian rule. From the earliest stages of the conquest of Siberia captured natives were made an object of trade, and 'even the enslavement of native women for concubinage and marriage served the purpose not only of satisfying sexual instincts, but also of commercial profit'.[48] Slavery on a small scale had existed among some Siberian peoples, notably the Yakuts and Buryats, before the advent of the Russians. The latter, who in serfdom had their own systematised form of slavery, recognised and accepted the phenomenon, and in Yakutia the governor frequently had to deal with petitions from native slave-owners who, like serf-owners in Russia itself, claimed back slaves who had run away or been abducted by other Yakuts.[49] In Siberia the term used by the Russians to describe captives taken in military operations (the most common means of enslavement) was *yasyr* – a word of Arabic origin taken over, like *yasak* and other terms, from Tatar vocabulary and practice. Such captives were exploited by their Russian owners for service and physical labour in the household, agriculture and hunting.[50]

Examples of the Russian slave trade in the seventeenth century include a petition by a merchant asking permission to take back with him to Russia a Yakut boy for whom he had paid 10 roubles to the Cossack who had captured him during a raid. Cases involving women were frequent. For instance, in 1642 a Cossack departing on service mortgaged his Yakut wife to a Russian trapper for $13\frac{1}{2}$ roubles but when he returned to redeem his pledge the trapper refused to give the woman back to him. One of the most complicated cases of this traffic in women involved a certain Mynik of the Betun clan who was first sold by her Yakut family to a Russian trapper for 50 kopeks, a cooking-pot and ten strings of beads. She was then passed on for 1 rouble to another trapper, who sold her to an Orthodox priest for 2 roubles. The petition presented by the latter after his 'wife' had been taken away by a Yakut, resulted in the priest's possession of her being legalised in a deed of purchase, and the woman's declaration that she did not want to go back to live among the Yakuts, but to be baptised as a Christian.[51]

Permission for baptism of a Yakut – usually a wife or a child – was the

[47] *Entsiklopedicheskiy slovar*, vol. xxix, p. 810.
[48] Yadrintsev, *Sibir kak koloniya*, p. 280.
[49] *Kolonialnaya politika . . . v Yakutii*, pp. 205–6, 209–10, 215 and passim.
[50] Yadrintsev, *Sibir kak koloniya*, pp. 281–2.
[51] *Kolonialnaya politika . . . v Yakutii*, pp. 152, 154–6.

subject of numerous petitions by Russian men. The authorities of Yakutsk, far from seeking the wholesale conversion of natives to Christianity in the seventeenth century, looked upon this as a favour to be granted only in specific cases. The reason for this was that natives who were admitted to the Orthodox Church qualified as Russians and were no longer liable to pay *yasak*. On the other hand, the owners of native slaves wanted to have them baptised because of the government decrees directed against slavery (as a depletion of the *yasak*-paying population) which ordered the release of non-Christian slaves but permitted Russians to keep native slaves who had been baptised.[52] It was indeed the rule that any native who was baptised became bound as a serf to the person who effected the conversion – whether a representative of the Orthodox church or a layman. As a result, Cossacks and traders strove to make 'converts' – often by force – for the purely material reason of obtaining slaves who could thereafter be sold for cash. A *voyevoda's* report of 1712 makes unambiguous reference to the slave-trade: 'Those [natives] who are poorest and have no means of livelihood are handed over to Cossacks for winter labour in lieu of yasak ... And their wives and children have been taken from many of them – so many have been taken that there is hardly a Cossack in Yakutsk who does not have natives as slaves.'[53]

NORTH-EASTERN SIBERIA: ESKIMOS, CHUKCHIS AND YUKAGIRS

When the Russians had established themselves among the Yakuts on the Lena in the mid-1630s they were more than two-thirds of the way across Siberia at the latitude of Yakutsk. The third stage of conquest up to mid-century took them in two main directions. Travelling some 450 miles south-east from Yakutsk through mountainous country, they reached that part of the Pacific Ocean known as the Sea of Okhotsk, where the population was mainly Ewen Tungus (or 'Lamuts'). Taking the north-east direction from Yakutsk, they entered a region of forest, tundra and high mountains stretching for over 1,500 miles, where the inhabitants were principally Yukagirs. Beyond these lived the Chukchis, Koraks and Eskimos, who were only partially subjugated by the end of the seventeenth century, while the 800-mile long peninsula of Kamchatka with its Korak, Itelmen and Ainu population was not conquered until the eighteenth century. Like the rest of Siberia, the extreme north-east was by no means an 'empty' land when it was first 'discovered' by the Russians, but had been inhabited for many thousands of years. In terms of cultural development, however, this was the most primitive region of Siberia, where none of the native inhabitants knew the use of

---

[52] *Entsiklopedicheskiy slovar*, vol. xxix, p. 810.
[53] *Kolonialnaya politika ... na Kamchatke*, pp. 8–10.

metals, so that the Russians, with their relatively sophisticated equipment and arms, found themselves in a stone-age environment. As we shall see, this did not mean that the invaders had an easy victory.

In the seventeenth century the promontory forming the farthest part of north-eastern Siberia was, like the neighbouring land of Alaska, the home of the Eskimos. For them the narrow Bering Strait was no more of an obstacle to movement than other waters that separated the mainland of Canada from the Arctic islands and Greenland, and their culture was more or less uniform over the whole vast territory of northern America and Asia, although they spoke several different languages.[54] Some typical works in the language of the Asiatic Eskimos are: 'friend' *ila*, 'ice' *siku*, 'knife' *sawik*, 'house' *guygu*. The structure of the language is polysynthetic, i.e. many elements of meaning are put together to form one long word which corresponds to a whole sentence in English.[55]

The Asiatic Eskimos, who call themselves Yugit or Yupigit – 'people' – were exclusively a coastal people whose whole way of life was bound up with the hunting of sea-mammals – seals, walrus and whales. The hazardous task of killing such huge beasts as whales on the open sea and bringing their carcases to land was performed by means of the most primitive equipment – open boats constructed of wooden frames covered with walrus hide, and spears and harpoons with bone tips.

In winter the Eskimos lived in villages of semi-subterranean huts, the walls of which were made of slabs of stone and whale ribs or jaw-bones, with a covering of earth and snow. Some of these earth-houses were large enough to accommodate several families or to serve as places for communal meetings and religious ceremonies. In summer the families comprising the village community moved out into large tents of reindeer-skin or seal-skin, which were scattered over a wider area than the village. The hunting of walrus and whales was a community activity requiring the collaboration of several families as boat crews, and in the division of the catch the communal principle of mutual help resulted in the distribution of equal shares not only to members of the successful boat crew but to all who happened to be present.

Seals, walrus and whales provided almost every item of everyday requirements: the flesh was eaten either raw or cooked, or preserved in meat-holes in the ground for future use; the blubber made not only nourishing food but also oil for use in stone lamps to heat and give light in the dwelling; baleen and walrus tusks were used to make many objects; and the skins were processed for a variety of uses ranging from boat-hulls to footwear. Clothing consisted partly of sealskin, partly of reindeer-skin, and strips of walrus

---

[54] I.I. Krupnik, *Arkticheskaya etnoekologiya: modeli traditsionnogo prirodopolzovaniya morskikh okhotnikov i olenevodov Severnoy Yevrazii*, Moscow, 1989.

[55] *Yazyki narodov SSSR*, vol. V, pp. 357–85; Comrie, *Languages*, pp. 252–7.

intestine were sewn together to make waterproof hooded parkas for wearing during rainy weather or at sea in boats. Eskimo women wore their straight black hair in two plaits, while men cut their hair short all round. Designs of lines and circles were tattooed on their faces, forearms and hands, and men wore labrets – round plugs of bone inserted in their lips at the corners of their mouths.

The shamanist beliefs of the Eskimos involved the propitiation of the ubiquitous spirits of Nature, especially the austere sea goddess Migim Agna and her assistant the grampus. Since the large Greenland whale played such an important part in their lives, the Asiatic Eskimos performed religious rites to celebrate the beginning of the whale-hunting season early in November and the end of the season in late November or December. Dramatic re-enactments of the hunt, and ritual dances, formed part of these ceremonies, as well as the 'feeding' of the dead whale to ensure similar catches in future seasons.[56]

Before the seventeenth century the settlements of Asiatic Eskimos probably extended along the Arctic coast from the easternmost cape as far as the mouth of the Kolyma, and south-west along the Pacific coast to the Anadyr river.[57] Their immediate neighbours, who now occupy most of these coastal settlements as well as the interior of the north-eastern peninsula, were the Chukchi people (whose name has been applied to the peninsula in its Russian form *Chukotka*). A number of other peoples related to the Chukchi occupied the land along the north-western part of the Pacific Ocean, the Bering Sea. From the Gulf of Anadyr south to the neck of the Kamchatka peninsula and around the northern shore of the Okhotsk Sea lived the ancestors of the present-day Koraks (in Russian *Koryaki*), while most of the main part of the peninsula was the home of the Itenmen (known in Russian as *Itelmen* or *Kamchadaly*). The southern extremity of Kamchatka, as well as the Kuril Islands and Sakhalin, were at that time inhabited by the Ainus, who now survive mainly on the Japanese island of Hokkaido.

The Chukchi and Korak languages are quite unrelated to that of the Eskimo, but are very close to each other in structure and vocabulary. In both, for instance, the word for 'friend' is *tumget*, 'ice' is *gilgil*, and 'knife' is *wala*, and the Chukchi and Korak words for 'house' are respectively *yaranga* and *yayanga*. The Chukchi for the first five numbers is *ennen, ngirek, ngerok, ngerak, metlengen*, and they are very similar in Korak. Similarities with the Itelmen language are less obvious, but it clearly belongs to the same family of languages as Korak and Chukchi – a family which has no affinities with any other known languages.[58]

[56] *Narody Sibiri*, pp. 940–3; S.A. Arutyunov et al., '*Kitovaya alleya': drevnosti ostrovov proliva Senyavina*, Moscow, 1982, pp. 85, 100–1, 107–11.
[57] *Narody Sibiri*, pp. 934–5.
[58] *Yazyki narodov SSSR*, vol. V, pp. 236–43.

Despite the ethnic and linguistic differences between the Eskimos and the Chukchis and Koraks, the most significant factor in the identity of communities was the way of life dictated by their environment. Thus both the Korak and the Chukchi fell into two groups depending on whether they lived on the sea-shore or inland. Those who lived in more or less permanent settlements on the coast fed and equipped themselves chiefly by killing sea-mammals: their way of life and clothing was identical with that of the Eskimos. The maritime Chukchi called themselves *angkalit* or *ramaglat* 'sea' or 'coastal people', while the Korak of the coast called themselves *nimilu* 'village people'. Inland, however, the Chukchi and Korak led a nomadic life, accompanying the herds of reindeer which made seasonal migrations between mountain or forest pastures and the coastal tundra. Those who lived in this way called themselves 'rich in reindeer', irrespective of whether they were Chukchi – *chawchuwat*, or Korak – *chawchiwaw*.[59] The name Korak itself derives from the word for 'reindeer' – *koranga* in Chukchi and *koyanga* in Korak. Unlike other Siberian peoples, they had not succeeded in domesticating completely the reindeer on which their livelihood depended. Although the coast-dwellers in particular kept dogs – the well-known Siberian husky breed – for dragging their sledges, they had not trained them as herd-dogs, so that it was the herdsmen themselves who had to guard the deer against predators and round them up when required.

For the reindeer-Chukchi and Korak their beasts provided nearly all of the requirements of life – traction for sledges, meat for the pot, skins and sewing-thread (sinews) for clothing and tents. Other needs were supplied by barter with their coastal brethren (including the Eskimos). In exchange for reindeer products they obtained whale-oil for heat and light, straps and thongs of sealskin, and sealskin clothing and boots. The winter clothing of all Koraks and Chukchis consisted of reindeer skin. Men wore brief breeches of fine, soft skin, two pairs of long trousers, one worn with the hair-side to the skin, the other with the hair-side out, and a pull-over jacket also of two thicknesses of deerskin. Women's clothing was of the same materials, but made up into a single capacious combination garment. Out of doors in summer, and in the warmth of the hut or tent, they often went naked, and even on cold winter days women working out of doors frequently bared their arms and upper parts of their bodies. Like the Eskimos, Koraks and Chukchis rarely covered their heads even in the lowest temperatures, and their way of wearing their hair, and their body decorations, including tattoo marks, were also similar to those of the Eskimos.

Chukchi and Korak dwellings were of two kinds. Some coast-dwellers lived in huts dug down three or four feet into the earth, similar to those of the Eskimos, but the typical dwelling of the reindeer-Chukchis and Koraks

[59] V.G. Bogoraz, *The Chukchee (Memoirs of the American Museum of Natural History)*, vol. XI, Leiden, 1904–9, pp. 11, 72.

was a tent of large proportions – up to twenty-five feet in diameter. This had vertical sides and a conical top, the apex of which, around the crossed poles, was open to let out smoke from the central hearth. At night the temperature became quite low in the large tent, but part of it was partitioned off as a rectangular inner chamber of skins or bear-furs on a frame, and it was in this low chamber, warmed by whale-oil burning in a stone lamp, that the family slept together.[60]

The Chukchi, Korak and Itelmen lived in groups of related families, but unlike most other Siberian communities these peoples of the far north-east were not bound to marry outside their own clan, and cousin-marriages were common. Marriages were arranged by parents, usually when the future mates were still infants, but this early betrothal was no obstacle to freedom of sexual intercourse among young unmarried people. The Chukchis had no word for 'virgin' and gladly accepted the birth of children out of wedlock.

Polygamy was quite common, as was divorce. Nor was the sexual relationship of man and wife exclusive: group marriage existed in the sense that several men – usually second or third cousins, but not brothers, and usually not members of the same band or camp – were 'wife-friends' with a right to sexual intercourse with each other's wives. As among the Eskimos, it was also a normal practice of hospitality that a man visiting another settlement should be offered one of his host's wives to sleep with. These sexual relationships, as in all primitive societies, were regulated by custom and provided a degree of social cohesion and a basis for mutual assistance in peaceful or warlike activities. In a society which had no tribal chiefs and no concept of authority or collective responsibility for punishing those who offended against the established rules of conduct, these family links were of considerable importance. Freedom of sexual relations within the permitted limits did not mean unregulated promiscuity, although it was readily misunderstood – and often exploited – in this sense by incomers with European and Christian social prejudices.[61]

The cosmology and religion of the Chukchis and Koraks was very close to that of the Eskimos, and as in all other parts of northern Siberia the most regular religious observance was the anointment of the mouths of simple wooden or stone spirit effigies with blood and fat from sacrificed animals – most commonly reindeer or dogs. Fear of malicious spirits or *kelet* was a pervasive feature of their life.[62]

The harsh environment of the tundra gave little scope for sentimentality,

---

[60] *Narody Sibiri*, pp. 902, 908–13, 954, 962–3. The material culture of the North-east is described and illustrated in W.W. Fitzhugh and A. Crowell, eds., *Crossroads of Continents: Cultures of Siberia and Alaska*, Washington, 1988, and N.V. Kocheshkov, *Etnicheskiye traditsii v dekorativnom iskusstve narodov Kraynego Severo-Vostoka SSSR (XVIII–XX vv.)*, Leningrad, 1989.

[61] Bogoraz, *The Chukchee*, pp. 537–43, 571–9, 598–607.

[62] Ibid., pp. 277–93, 330–48.

and the social institutions of the Chukchi, Korak and Eskimo peoples showed a realism which must be understood within this context. Violent personal quarrels could arise, especially over women, and killings were not uncommon.[63] Chukchi and Korak people not only accepted violent death as a probability, but if they became old and infirm or suffered from a disease, they would choose to be killed by spear or strangulation rather than die miserably, and it was the moral duty of a friend or relative to fulfil the request for voluntary death. With this tradition of a courageous acceptance of death behind them, the Chukchis and Koraks made formidable warriors who, when necessary, donned armour of bone-plated seal-hide, helmets and shields, and took up their bone-tipped arrows and hunting spears against an enemy.[64]

To the west of the Chukchis and Koraks a large territory of arctic and sub-arctic Siberia, reaching as far as the Lena, was originally occupied by the people known to the Russians as Yukagirs. They speak a language unrelated to any other known languages, in which, for instance, the first five numerals are *morkon*, *kiyon*, *yalon*, *yalaklan*, *imdaldan*. So different are the two main dialects of the Yukagir language that their speakers had great difficulty in understanding each other, and even in accepting that they belonged to the same nationality.[65] The many groups of Yukagirs had no general name for their nation (except such terms as *odul* 'mighty') and were known to the Russians by tribal or locality names, such as Chuwan, Khodin, Omok, Khoromo, Lawren etc. The Yukagirs had, like the Chukchi and Korak, developed two ways of life. Some led a sedentary existence on the lower reaches of rivers and on the coast, where they lived by fishing and hunting elk. These 'settled Yukagirs' used dogs to pull sledges. The 'reindeer-Yukagirs', on the other hand, roamed over the tundra from the Arctic coast to the sparse larch forest in the basins of the rivers Yana, Indigirka and Kolyma, and in the high mountains of the interior. While some groups of Yukagirs had learned to domesticate reindeer, and used them to pull sledges, the basis of existence for the reindeer-Yukagirs was the more primitive device of hunting the wild herds. This required them to follow the deer in their migrations from the forest towards the coastal or mountain tundra in May, and back again towards the forests from August onwards, when mating took place and huge herds congregated. Mass slaughter of reindeer was organised communally at places where the migrant herds had to swim across rivers, and in other places by driving them into corrals where they could be approached and killed. Yukagir dwellings were conical tents

---

[63] In American Eskimo communities in recent times it was found that every man over thirty was likely to have killed at least one man during his lifetime. Driver, *Indians of North America*, p. 355.
[64] Bogoraz, *The Chukchee*, pp. 516–33.
[65] Tokarev, *Etnografiya*, pp. 522–3; *Yazyki narodov SSSR*, vol. V, pp. 451–2.

covered with reindeer-skins or sheets of larch-bark, such as were used by many Siberian peoples; in winter they lived in log cabins or lodges covered with bark and earth.[66]

In seventeenth-century Yukagir society clans were a social reality, dictating restrictions in the choice of marriage partners. One of the features of their clan system was that each clan had its priest or shaman who presided over the cult of the ancestor after whom the clan was named. Among the Yukagirs each priest himself found a place in the clan's religious cult after his death – his body was cut into pieces, the flesh and bones being distributed among members of the clan as sacred relics, while the skull was placed on a wooden body as a spirit effigy.[67] The Yukagirs were unique among the peoples of Siberia in the degree to which the cult of the clan shaman was developed. Other religious beliefs which they shared with many peoples concerned the guardians or 'master' spirits of natural phenomena, of which the most specific in their case was the guardian of the elk and the reindeer.[68] Among the relatively few surviving relics of the original culture of the Yukagir people was a system of pictographs by means of which simple messages could be conveyed.[69] By the seventeenth century the Yukagirs were already succumbing to the influence of their neighbours the Tungus and Yakuts, and the next two centuries saw them being so rapidly assimilated that their numbers became reduced to the point of near extinction. (In the 1970 census only 600 people gave Yukagir as their nationality.) The fact that this decline coincided with the period of Russian conquest inevitably suggests that the latter was the prime cause of the rapid decline of the Yukagirs.

How many inhabitants north-east Siberia as a whole had before the Russian conquest is impossible to establish, but it has been estimated that the number of Yukagirs, Chukchis, Koraks, Itelmens, Eskimos and Ainus together may have been about 40,000 (out of a total native population in Siberia of some 220,000).[70] This sparse population of about one person to every 28 square miles was no doubt about the natural maximum which the territory could support given the climatic conditions and the technology available to the natives.

THE RUSSIAN CONQUEST OF NORTH-EASTERN SIBERIA BEGINS

'The Yakutsk authorities, drawn to yasak as surely as a magnet to the pole, went on sending out their scouts to track down any human retreat which had not yet been subjected to yasak.'[71]

[66] *Narody Sibiri*, pp. 885–91. [67] Gurvich, *Semeynaya obryadnost*, pp. 199–202.
[68] *Narody Sibiri*, p. 893. [69] Tokarev, *Etnografiya*, pp. 524–5.
[70] Dolgikh, *Rodovoy i plemennoy sostav*, pp. 616–17.
[71] Slovtsov, *Istoricheskoye obozreniye*, p. 56.

The first reconnaissance of north-eastern Siberia was carried out by boat during 1633–8, when men of service from Yakutsk sailed down-river to the mouth of the Lena, explored the Arctic coast to west and east, and sailed up the rivers Olenyok, Yana and Indigirka. Meanwhile, other Russians, travelling overland, had reached the upper courses of these same rivers. *Yasak* was first obtained from Yukagir settlements about 1635, and between then and the 1650s Russian forts were established at Verkhoyansk ('upper Yana'), Podshiversk and Zashiversk ('below' and 'beyond' the rapids on the Indigirka) and a dozen other places, forming a network of outposts as far east as the rivers Kolyma and Anadyr. In 1644 on the Kolyma the Russians first encountered the Chukchis, and subsequently they met with vigorous resistance from this indomitable people, against whom they waged a sanguinary war for 120 years without subduing them.

In the region beyond the Lena the Russians faced even worse rigours of climate than in previously occupied parts of Siberia. The relatively level or hilly terrain of Central Siberia now gave way to high mountain ranges; between these and the Arctic coast lay an expanse of rather flat larch forest and tundra containing a huge number of lakes. Here the summer was shorter and the winter colder than in Central Siberia, although snowfalls were quite light. The Arctic Ocean offered the Russians another route for exploring the north-east during the brief summer period when its waters were free from floating ice, and in the 1630s and 1640s many voyages were undertaken with the aim of obtaining walrus ivory. Ice and changing winds made this sea treacherous, however, and it was not unusual for the Russians' sailing-ships to be caught in the ice and crushed.[72]

The exaction of *yasak* from the Yukagirs was accompanied by the usual violence: their encampments and settlements were raided and *amanats* taken. So, in 1639 a Cossack gang seized hostages, including the clan shaman, from the Khoromo clan at the mouth of the Yana and sent them into custody at Yakutsk. In view of the great respect in which shamans were held by the Yukagirs, such an event must have been a severe blow to the morale of the community. But, as one Russian historian put it – 'The savages of north-eastern Siberia were as unwilling to bear the domination of the newcomers as were the savages of western Siberia, and they rebelled at the first opportunity.'[73] In 1641, for instance, the Yana Yukagirs led by Yandarak killed the men of a Russian *yasak* gang.[74] A few years later on the Indigirka the Yukagirs under their leader Peleva attacked and killed the Cossacks at an outpost and freed their comrades who were being held there as hostages. They quickly learned how relentless the Russian colonialists were, however, when a punitive force sent from Yakutsk killed Peleva and seized new

[72] Bogoraz, *The Chukchee*, pp. 686–7.
[73] Solovyov, *Istoriya Rossii*, vol. VI, p. 588.
[74] Dolgikh, *Rodovoy i plemennoy sostav*, pp. 382–3.

hostages. A similar expedition used their guns against a large war-party of Yukagir 'traitors' on the Alazeya in 1650.[75] (Native rebels were always called 'traitors' by the Russians because they broke the oath of submission which they had been forced to take.) As in other parts of Siberia, Russian soldiers were quite callous in destroying the natives' winter clothing and equipment, such as fishing nets, on which they relied for laying in a store of food for the winter.[76] In 1653 Russian armed men carried out an unprovoked surprise attack on Yukagirs of the Uyandin clan on the Indigirka, killing many men, sharing out their reindeer as booty, and taking their women and children as slaves. The result of such destructive raids on sedentary Yukagir clans was that, robbed of their reindeer and other possessions, the men were forced to take to the nomadic life of the reindeer-Yukagirs in order to survive.[77] The Russians also exploited conflicts existing between clans, as for instance, in 1656 and 1658, when the Khoromo clan helped the Cossacks to oppress the Yandins. Despite savage punitive measures by the Russians, sporadic uprisings of Yukagir bands continued up to the 1670s.

Extortion and oppression were rife beyond the Lena, where Russians in high office enriched themselves by farming out *yasak* collection – that is, the right to plunder the natives – to men of service. Once out in the tundra the soldiers felt no restraint or compunction in terrorising the Yukagirs in order to extort sable or fox furs in quantities far in excess of the *yasak* rates laid down by law. Here, too, Cossack gangs competed with each other in exploiting the natives, as for instance, in 1650 when rival detachments came to blows over the 'right' to extort tribute from the Yandin clan.[78] One particular piece of gangsterism came to light in the 1660s, when it was reported that the boyar's son Dunay and the man of service Tatarin, after receiving the *yasak* due from the local Yukagirs, were having them locked up and beaten to force them to buy ironware at extortionate prices to be paid in sable skins.[79] (These iron goods – knife-blades, axe-heads, and rods for forging – were in fact supplied by the state as 'gifts' to be distributed to the natives in exchange for *yasak*.)[80] If the 'debts' thus recorded in a book were not redeemed, the Russians seized the Yukagirs' womenfolk and sold them as slaves to Russian trappers in exchange for furs. The trappers or hunters in Eastern Siberia were themselves often enrolled as 'half-Cossacks' who were authorised to maraud native settlements. In these operations the trappers (who are presented in official Communist Party history as true and honest representatives of the Russian toiling masses, sympathising and making common cause with the oppressed natives) could be even more savage than the soldiers in seizing

[75] Solovyov, *Istoriya Rossii*, vol. VI, p. 588.
[76] *Kolonialnaya politika . . . v Yakutii*, p. 56.
[77] Gurvich, *Etnicheskaya istoriya*, p. 171.
[78] Dolgikh, *Rodovoy i plemennoy sostav*, pp. 383, 413.
[79] *Kolonialnaya politika . . . v Yakutii*, pp. 106–9.
[80] Fisher, *Russian Fur Trade*, pp. 60, 77.

the Yukagirs' winter clothing and tent-skins, and carrying off all their chattels.

The enormous number of sables obtained by these illegal means not only ruined the Yukagirs, but led to the rapid extermination of these animals in north-eastern Siberia. Some of the victims of this rampant colonial exploitation complained that if the official *yasak* payment which they were required to hand over for the Tsar's treasury was, for instance, 40 sable-skins per year, the trappers and men of service forced them to give 200 more. There is abundant evidence in the many petitions sent to the Yakutsk governor by oppressed Yukagirs that such criminal activities were the rule rather than the exception.

By the 1670s these methods of exploitation had brought many Yukagir bands to ruin. Since sable had become almost impossible to find between the Lena and the Kolyma, some Yukagirs were reduced to the ultimate desperate expedient: in order to fulfil the *yasak* demands put upon them they gave away their transport reindeer and other essential possessions to buy from Russian or Yakut traders sable furs which they then handed over to the authorities as *yasak*.[81]

Of all the Siberian peoples, the sedentary Yukagirs seem to have been the least able to defend themselves from the Russian invaders. Once their previous way of life had been disrupted and they had been made destitute by ruthless depredation, they were simply absorbed by the Russians – the women as concubines, the men as auxiliary soldiers. It has been estimated that at any given time in the middle of the seventeenth century about 6 per cent of adult Yukagir men were removed from useful life in their communities and held as hostages in Russian forts – where the mortality rate was high – and 10 per cent of the women were taken away by Russian soldiers and trappers. The degree of racial mixing between Russian men and Yukagir women was particularly high, so that a population of halfbreeds was established – one of many local mixed strains which were subsequently absorbed into the Russian population of Siberia. Smallpox, apparently unknown before the advent of the Russians, also took a particularly heavy toll among the Yukagirs in several epidemics between 1657 and 1694.[82] By the end of the seventeenth century the total number of Yukagirs had been reduced by 44 per cent to only some 2,500 people.[83]

Although this region was populated chiefly by Yukagirs before the Russians came, they were not the only inhabitants. Several groups of Yakuts had established themselves on the Yana, and from there gradually spread eastward to the Indigirka and Kolyma. Inevitably they were also subjected to *yasak*, and suffered the same kinds of coercion and abuse as other natives. As

[81] *Kolonialnaya politika . . . v Yakutii*, pp. 98–9, 105–16.
[82] Dolgikh, *Rodovoy i plemennoy sostav*, pp. 388, 392, 398, 408, 415, 439–40.
[83] Gurvich, *Etnicheskaya istoriya*, p. 172.

in the land to the west of the lower Lena, here also the Yakuts were successful colonisers. Their numbers increased as those of the Yukagirs declined, so that by the 1660s there were some 1,120 Yakuts living in the Yana-Kolyma region.

At the same time, Tungus people were also moving into Yukagir territory. These were the north-eastern Tungus, formerly known to the Russians as the Lamuts, and today called Ewen. When the Russians first appeared in north-eastern Siberia the reindeer-Lamuts inhabited the mountains of the Verkhoyansk, Suntar-Khayat and Cherskiy ranges, and only descended to the valleys of the northern rivers to trade in summer. During the second half of the seventeenth century, however, many of them moved north among the Yukagirs. As the latter were also on the move, trying to escape the Russian occupation forces, they came into conflict with the Lamuts near Zashiversk fort. The Lamuts themselves resisted Russian oppression actively, besieging Zashiversk in 1666–7 and once almost succeeding in storming it in a surprise attack before guns were deployed against them. In the same years Lamuts of the Kukugir clan attacked parties of Cossacks on their way from the Yana to Zashiversk, killing twenty Russians in one battle. Lamut attacks on the Russians in the Yana-Kolyma region continued until 1692, but like all the others, they were unable to throw off the Russian yoke and were forced into submission. By 1700 the resistance of the Yukagirs and Lamuts had come to an end, as had fighting between them. In the 1730s the Yukagirs were in a minority throughout what had been their territory, and some two-thirds of its *yasak*-paying natives were Lamuts and Yakuts.[84]

In the most easterly part of Yukagir territory, beyond the river Kolyma, the advance of the Russian conquerors stirred up other conflicts in which the Korak and Chukchi peoples were involved. It was in 1649 that bands of Cossacks and trappers from Kolyma fort set off in search of plunder up the river Anyui. Near its source in the Kolyma plateau they found a portage to the river Anadyr, and some 350 miles downstream, where the river left the mountains behind and flowed through a broad and relatively hospitable valley, the fort of Anadyrsk was founded. The native inhabitants here were Yukagirs: the Anaul clan in the immediate vicinity of the fort, and the Khodin and Chuwan to south and north respectively. Some nomadic Koraks also roamed in the neighbourhood.[85]

The Anadyr fort, which was more than 1,800 miles distant from Yakutsk, and took about six months to reach overland,[86] became the military base for the Russian conquest of the extreme north-eastern part of Siberia. An

---

[84] Dolgikh, *Rodovoy i plemennoy sostav*, pp. 390, 403, 532, 544; Gurvich, *Etnicheskaya istoriya*, p. 172; *Kolonialnaya politika … v Yakutii*, pp. 64, 125, 213–14, 239–41; Solovyov, *Istoriya Rossii*, vol. VI, p. 590.

[85] Solovyov, *Istoriya Rossii*, vol. VI, pp. 588–9.

[86] *Kolonialnaya politika … na Kamchatke*, p. 6.

indication of its sphere of operations is given by a document of 1681 listing the persons of non-Russian origin, chiefly *yasyrs* (i.e. war captives) who lived in the fort as the property of the Cossacks and trappers of its garrison. Beginning with the commander, the 'boyar's son' Kobelev, who owned one unbaptised Korak woman and two Chukchi boys, one of whom was baptised, the Russians owned altogether thirty-seven slaves, mainly women, including fifteen Yukagirs, sixteen Koraks and five Chukchis.[87] These were quite separate from the hostages who were held in the fort.

The Anaul Yukagirs living around the fort resisted the invaders but were quickly crushed, their women and children being taken captive, and the men seeking refuge in Korak territory to the south. It was in this direction too that some Yukagirs of the Khodin clan tried to escape from subjugation, and their migration to the south brought them into conflict with the Koraks, who attacked the newcomers and seized their women and children and reindeer. Fighting between the Yukagirs and Koraks continued till the end of the century, and was greatly exacerbated after the 1697–9 expedition led by the Cossack officer Atlasov from Anadyrsk, who passed through Korak territory to reach Kamchatka. This instituted a prolonged war between the native inhabitants of the peninsula and the Russian invaders.[88]

The Chuwan Yukagirs, whose migration grounds lay to the north of Anadyrsk, were neighbours of the Chukchis, with whom the Russians had few direct contacts in the seventeenth century. However, the subjection of the Chuwans to Russian rule inevitably led to conflicts here too. On the one hand, the long-standing barter trade between the Chukchis and Yukagirs was disrupted once the latter were forced into the *yasak* relationship with the Russians; on the other hand, the ironware and other objects obtained by the Yukagirs from the Russians in exchange for furs were coveted by the Chukchis, who did not hesitate to raid Yukagir communities in order to steal them. Some of the Chuwans had evaded Russian oppression by keeping away as far as possible from Anadyrsk, and correspondingly closer to Chukchi territory. In the 1670s, however, Chukchi pressure caused these Yukagirs to move south and west into the orbit of the Russian forts. By this time the Chukchis were beginning to manifest their warlike spirit, so that both at Anadyrsk and at Lower Kolyma fort the local Yukagirs put themselves under the protection of the Russians. As usual, the European colonisers benefited from inter-tribal antagonisms. In 1681, for instance, when Cossacks on the Anyui were attacked and besieged for four weeks by a large war-party of Khodin Yukagirs, it was Chuwan Yukagirs who came to the rescue and drove the Khodins off.[89]

[87] *Kolonialnaya politika . . . v Yakutii*, p. 193.
[88] Dolgikh, *Rodovoy i plemennoy sostav*, pp. 428–32; Gurvich, *Etnicheskaya istoriya*, pp. 201, 210.
[89] Gurvich, *Etnicheskaya istoriya*, p. 201; Dolgikh, *Rodovy i plemennoy sostav*, pp. 427, 432; *Kolonialnaya politika . . . v Yakutii*, p. 238.

Direct Russian action against the Chukchis began in 1701 when, in response to Yukagir complaints, the commander at Anadyrsk sent out a force consisting of 24 Russian Cossacks and trappers and 100 Yukagir and Korak auxiliaries to subdue the Chukchis who lived along the coast near the mouth of the Anadyr. In the first Chukchi settlement they reached, the inhabitants were called upon to submit to 'the Tsar's high hand' and pay *yasak*. When they refused, the Russians attacked, killing 10 men and capturing the women and children. In a second fight 200 of the 300 Chukchi warriors were said to have been killed. The renewal of the battle on a third occasion, when over 3,000 Chukchis assembled, resulted in the death of many Chukchis, but also caused heavy casualties among the Russian raiders and their native auxiliaries, who were pinned down by the Chukchis for five days before they escaped and fled to Anadyrsk. Other expeditions were sent out to try to subjugate the Chukchis in 1708, 1709 and 1711, but thereafter the Russian government gave up attempts to conquer them for some twenty years. This was no doubt because Chukchi-land had no sables, and the Russian government was concentrating its attention during these years on the conquest of the rich hunting grounds of Kamchatka. As a result of this lull in Russian activity beyond the Anadyr and Kolyma, the Chukchis were able to expand to the west and south, occupying the lands of the Chuwan Yukagirs and assimilating them by intermarriage. The people known today as Chuvantsy are taken to be the Chukchi-speaking or Russian-speaking descendants of the Chuwans.[90]

At the same time as Russians from Yakutsk were establishing themselves in the land of the Yukagir along the northern fringe of Eastern Siberia, they were also advancing due east. The highway for penetration beyond the Lena in this direction was its tributary the Aldan. Some 500 miles up-river from its confluence with the Lena the Aldan is joined by the river Maya, the upper reaches of which gave access by portage to the Ulya which flows out to the Sea of Okhotsk. In the 1630s Russian forts were set up on the Aldan at Kamnunsk and Butalsk for the exaction of *yasak* from the Yakuts and Tungus of the region, and in 1638 a band of Cossacks commanded by Moskvitin set out up the Maya and reached the Pacific coast. An outpost was established at the mouth of the Ulya to collect fur-tribute from the Lamuts who lived there, and a few years later the fort of Okhotsk (so named from the Lamut word *okat* 'river') was founded some fifty miles farther north along the coast. This became the main Russian base on the Pacific seaboard for the next 200 years.

In this new region of the Far East the familiar pattern of extortion, plunder and embezzlement by Russian officials quickly manifested itself, as

[90] Gurvich, *Etnicheskaya istoriya*, pp. 201–3, 208; *Kolonialnaya politika . . . na Kamchatke*, pp. 155–8; A.I. Timofeyev, ed., *Pamyatniki Sibirskoy istorii XVIII veka*, St Petersburg, 1882–5, vol. I, pp. 405–6, 435–6, 457–8; vol. II, pp. 524–5; Tokarev, *Etnografiya*, p. 525.

did desperate attempts by the natives to preserve their liberty. Tungus (Lamut) opposition to the establishment of Okhotsk was considerable, and they massed large bodies of warriors – over 1,000 at a time – to fight the Russians. In 1654 under the leadership of Komka Boyash they stormed the fort, released the hostages held there, and burned down the buildings. These were soon rebuilt, however, the resistance of the local Lamuts was crushed, and hostages for *yasak* again taken. A few years after this the first epidemic of smallpox carried away many of the Okhotsk Lamuts. Another mass uprising took place in 1665 when the Lamut leader Zelemei exhorted them to destroy all Russians along the coast and the river Maya and then call in the Chinese to be their overlords. After initial success, when fifty Cossacks and trappers were annihilated, the rebellion fizzled out. Some of the Lamuts taken prisoner were hanged, the fortifications of Okhotsk were strengthened, and *yasak* was again imposed. Twelve years later the depredations of the Okhotsk commander and his men led to a third big rebellion, led again by Zelemei. The fort was again besieged by 1,000 native warriors armed only with bows and bone-tipped arrows. Although the chief officials concerned were removed from their posts and flogged for their misrule and embezzlement, the commander who succeeded in Okhotsk adopted the same cruel and dishonest practices as his predecessor, torturing and hanging Lamuts in order to extort furs for his own profit. Once again the natives took the law into their own hands and in 1680 ambushed and killed him and his detachment of Cossack marauders.[91]

From their forts in the Far East the Russians pushed their tribute frontier forward both to the south-west, into the territory of the Lalagir Tungus, beyond which lay the watershed between the Aldan and Amur basins, and also to the east and north-east from Okhotsk into the territory of the Uyagan and Dolgan clans of the Lamuts. In the latter region the invaders came up against the southern limits of settlement of the Koraks, who annihilated one of the first Cossack detachments on the river Taui (near present-day Magadan) in 1669. Just as the Russians pressed the Yukagirs into service as auxiliary troops against the Koraks in the more northerly Anadyr region, so in the Okhotsk region they used Lamuts of the Dolgan clan in this capacity, with the same consequence of inter-tribal slaughter. In retaliation for a raid on the Koraks by a combined force of Russians and Dolgans in 1684, the Koraks attacked the Lamuts at their grazing grounds in the following year. This act in its turn brought swift retribution from the Russians in the form of a raid on the nearest Korak villages. Because the Koraks would never give themselves up alive, and refused to be coerced by the Russian practice of seizing hostages, none were taken prisoner, but it may be assumed that the Russians as usual killed as many of the Korak men as possible and carried

[91] Dolgikh, *Rodovoy i plemennoy sostav*, pp. 369, 494–5, 520, 525–6; Solovyov, *Istoriya Rossii*, vol. VI, pp. 590–1; vol. VII, pp. 237–8; *Kolonialnaya politika . . . v Yakutii*, pp. 119, 241–4.

off the women and children.[92] The end of the seventeenth century thus saw the Koraks under attack by the Russians from two directions – from Anadyrsk in the north and Okhotsk in the south-west. Few Koraks submitted at this time, and the main military campaigns against them, as against the Chukchis, did not take place until the middle of the eighteenth century.

[92] *Kolonialnaya politika* . . . *v Yakutii*, pp. 114–15, 149, 246–7; Dolgikh, *Rodovoy i plemennoy sostav*, pp. 531, 555.

4

THE MONGOLIAN AND CHINESE FRONTIER IN
THE SEVENTEENTH CENTURY

LAKE BAIKAL AND THE BURYAT MONGOLS

WHILE the Russian advance beyond the Lena into north-eastern Siberia faced opposition from no enemy more formidable than the valiant but ill-organised primitive tribes of Koraks and Chukchis, their expansion to the south and south-east brought them ever closer to the frontiers of Mongolia and China, where more sophisticated and powerful forces opposed them.

The natural frontier of the high grass steppes of Mongolia lies today within the Soviet Union: the landscape in the basins of the rivers Onon and Argun, which flow out of Mongolia to combine as the Amur, is mainly grass-steppe, and a broad tongue of similar terrain forms the valley of the Selenga, which flows into Lake Baikal. These grasslands east of the lake were the home of pastoral nomads from time immemorial, and indeed it was on the Onon, just south of the present-day Russian border, that Chingis Khan was born. There was therefore some justification for the Buryats who lived to the east of Baikal considering themselves to be 'pure Mongols'. These tribes included the Tabunut, Atagan and Khori – the latter living also on the western shore of the lake and on the large island Oikhon (known in Russian as Olkhon). Other Mongol tribes – the Bulagat, Ekherit and Khongodor – had made their way across or around Lake Baikal to the valley of the Angara which flows out of the south end of the lake. Here and in neighbouring valleys, extending as far as the upper reaches of the Lena, they found areas of meadow-steppe suitable as pastures for their horses and cattle. It was these Mongols, settling among the Tungus and other inhabitants of the forests, who became the western Buryats.

The Buryats east of Baikal preserved the traditional Mongol way of life based on horses and herds of cattle, migrating between pastures and living in portable felt-covered tents. West of the lake, however, some of them adopted a more sedentary way of life and learned to build wooden cabins – octagonal, with a smoke-hole in the centre of the pyramidal roof – and to cultivate hay-grass and crops such as millet, barley and buckwheat. Hunting played a significant part in the life of all Mongols, and the Buryats are known to have organised big communal hunts involving several clans. In the relatively advanced culture of the Buryats the use of iron was an important feature from ancient times, and, as in other Siberian communities, the blacksmiths who forged weapons, axes, knives, pots, harness and silver ornaments, enjoyed an almost supernatural status.[1]

Like all Mongols up to the sixteenth century, the Buryats believed in the shamanist religion. However, this took a more elaborate form than in most Siberian communities, since they not only revered spirits of natural phenomena (to whom they raised cairns, called *oboo*, in sacred places) but also had a complex pantheon consisting of ninety-nine divinities as well as their numerous ancestors and offspring. Within this highly developed mythology fire was particularly revered. The shamans themselves – mainly a hereditary caste – were of two kinds: 'white' ones who served the heavenly divinities, and 'black' ones who served the gods of the underworld. Buryat shamans differed from those of the Tungus or Kets in not accompanying their ecstatic dance with a tambourine, but using as accessories in their rituals a small bell and a hobby-horse. A central ritual in the religious practice of the Buryats, as of all shamanist Mongols, was blood-sacrifice to the sky god Tengri, in which a horse (usually white) was killed and its skin hung on a high pole. Shamanism, which was the religion Chingis Khan knew, persisted until the late sixteenth century, when Buddhism from Tibet spread rapidly among the Mongols. The Buryats, however, did not abandon their tribal religion until a century later, and indeed it was mainly those living east of Lake Baikal who then adopted Buddhism, while the forest Buryats to the west remained true to shamanism.[2]

The language of the Buryats (see p. 49) is one of the Mongolian family, which also includes the language of the Kalmyks (i.e. the Oirat or Western Mongols) and that of Mongolia itself, which is nowadays based on the Khalkha dialect. Many words are identical in Buryat and Khalkha, such as *gar* 'hand', *ger*, 'house', *ulaan* 'red' and *khoyor* 'two', but there are some regular sound differences. For instance, Buryat has *uha* 'water' for Mongolian *us*, *hara* 'month' for *sar*, *seseg* 'flower' for *tsetseg*, *morin* 'horse' for *mor*, *üder* 'day' for *ödör*. In its grammar Buryat preserves personal endings in the verb, e.g. *bi yabanab*, *shi yabanash*, *tere yabna* 'I go/you go/he goes' whereas Mongolian has only the single form *yabna* for 'I/you/he goes'.

[1] *Aziatskaya Rossiya*, vol. I, p. 133; Dolgikh, *Rodovoy i plemennoy sostav*, pp. 208–20; Holmberg, *Finno-Ugric, Siberian*, p. 464; *Istoriya Sibiri*, vol. I, pp. 379, 385–6; *Narody Sibiri*, pp. 230–4.
[2] *Aziatskaya Rossiya*, vol. I, pp. 132–8; Holmberg, *Finno-Ugric, Siberian*, pp. 308–11, 318–20, 323–7, 391–7, 441–9, 460–6, 472–9, 481–2, 488–9, 496–522, plates XLVII, L–LII, LIV, LVII; *Narody Sibiri*, pp. 240–1; Tokarev, *Etnografiya*, p. 454.

Because of prolonged contact with the Turkic peoples of Inner Asia and southern Siberia, the Buryat language contains many Turkic words, as well as borrowings from Chinese, Sanskrit, Tibetan, Manchurian and other languages. Since before the time of Chingis Khan the Mongols have had a written language, which was used by all Mongolian tribes up till the twentieth century. This Classical Mongolian language was written vertically in an alphabet derived from that of the Uighur Turks. Even after their conquest by the Russians in the seventeenth century, the eastern Buryats maintained their contacts with Mongolia and used the Mongolian literary language, whereas the western Buryats, living in relative isolation from the main body of Mongols, were mainly illiterate. However, the western Buryats had a strong oral tradition of folk poetry, including epics about Geser Khan, a legendary Tibetan hero, and a wealth of tales.[3]

Living as they did on the boundary between the northern forest and the steppes of Inner Asia, the Buryat Mongols acted as intermediaries in barter-trade, exchanging their own cattle, ironware and grain for furs from the Tungus and other forest peoples, which in turn they exchanged with traders from China for textiles, jewels and silver. The participation of the Buryats and other Mongols in the general cultural complex of Inner Asia was shown by their traditional costume – a wrap-over coat with a decorated facing on the right side and around the neck, made of skins or imported woven materials, and soft leather boots with thick felt soles.

The Buryats were a more numerous people than most of the natives of Siberia, with a total of at least 30,000 in the seventeenth century. Their social organisation was also more highly developed. Clan chiefs (*khans* or *taishis*) formed a hereditary aristocracy who wielded considerable power over ordinary members of the clan, and a class of rich herd-owners (*noyons*) existed, especially in eastern Buryatia. Nevertheless, rights to pastures and meadows were considered to be communal, and within the clan a system of mutual assistance operated (which Russian Marxist writers assert to have been merely a pretext for the exploitation of the poor by the rich). In the seventeenth century, differences had already developed between the social structure of the western Buryats, which retained many traditional tribal features, and that of the Buryats living east of Baikal, whose closer links with central Mongolia had taken them farther along the road towards a kind of feudalism. Even in the west, however, chieftains used their power to subjugate neighbouring tribes and extort tribute from them. The Buryat chiefs also called upon such vassals to provide armed men for war. Thus, before the Russians came, many of the Tungus, Samoyed and Ket tribes living between Lake Baikal and the Yenisey were in the position of subject peoples, dominated either by the Buryat Mongols or by the Kirgiz Turks.

[3] Tokarev, *Etnografiya*, pp. 455–7; *Yazyki narodov SSSR*, vol. V, pp. 7–11, 24, 31; Z.K. Kazyanenko, *Sovremennyy mongolskiy yazyk*, Leningrad, 1968, pp. 14–22.

As Mongolian tribes, the Buryats fell within Chingis Khan's empire in the thirteenth century, but historians disagree as to whether they took part in the campaigns of Chingis's armies.[4] Clearly, however, they shared the Mongol tradition of military organisation, effective equestrian tactics and the deadly use of the bow and arrow. As a result, they were a much more formidable enemy for the Russians to overcome than the primitive tribes of Central Siberia. At one point during the Russian wars against the Buryats, the men of service at Verkholensk fort were so hard pressed that they wrote to Tsar Mikhail:

> Spare us, your slaves, lord, and command that in the ... fort two hundred mounted men be garrisoned ... and that for these men of service two hundred carabines, two hundred coats of armour, and three hundred muskets for the foot soldiers be sent from your majesty's armoury in Moscow, because, lord, the Buryats have many mounted warriors who fight in armour ... and helmets, while we, lord, your slaves, are ill-clad, having no armour, and our poor hand-guns cannot pierce their armour ...[5]

THE RUSSIAN CONQUEST OF THE WESTERN BURYATS

The Russians first heard rumours of the Buryats in 1609, when an expedition sent from Tomsk to subjugate the tribes east of the Yenisey was told by the Ket and Samoyed of the Kan and Kizir basins that they already paid tribute to the Buryats. The latter lived beyond the mountains in the Uda valley and only crossed over occasionally to reassert the mutual relationship between vassals who paid tribute and provided armed warriors, and overlords who 'protected' them from other potential raiders. As a result, the Russians did not encounter the Uda Buryats directly until almost twenty years later.[6]

The main pastures of the western Buryats lay in the valley of the Angara, from the point where it flows out of Lake Baikal as far as the sharp double bend in the river at the great rapids where Bratsk now stands. In 1625 Russians from Yeniseysk taking *yasak* from the Tungus on the lower stretches of the Angara first heard of the Buryat Mongols in this region and

---

[4] M. N. Bogdanov, *Ocherki istorii Buryat-mongolskogo naroda*, Verkhneudinsk, 1926, pp. 96–106; Dolgikh, *Rodovoy i plemennoy sostav*, pp. 184, 208–9, 213, 220, 248–9, 273, 293, 324, 354, 616; *Istoriya Sibiri*, vol. I, pp. 384–6; T.M. Mikhaylov, 'Yugo-vostochnaya Sibir v otnosheniyakh s Tsentralnoy Aziyey v XIII–XVII vv.', in T.M. Mikhaylov, ed., *Etnokulturnye protsessy v yugo-vostochnoy Sibiri v Sredniye veka*, Novosibirsk, 1989, pp. 85–98; *Narody Sibiri*, pp. 220–1, 236–8; S.B. Okun, 'K istorii Buryatii v XVII v.' *Krasnyy arkhiv*, Moscow, 1936, vol. LXXVI, no. 3, p. 157; Tokarev, *Etnografiya*, pp. 451–4; B. Zoriktuyev, 'Bylo li vtorzheniye voyska Chingis-khana v Pribaykalye?', *Baykal*, 1990, no. 2, pp. 98–101.

[5] *Kolonialnaya politika ... v Yakutii*, p. 232.

[6] Bogdanov, *Ocherki istorii*, pp. 28–30; Ye.M. Zalkind, *Prisoyedineniye Buryatii k Rossii*, Ulan-Ude, 1958, p. 16.

4 Buryat Mongols inside their felt-covered tent (*ger*) with its lattice-work lower frame. The man's shaven head, pigtail, his bow-case, quiver and thick-soled boots, are typically Mongolian. From a nineteenth-century drawing by Ye. M. Korneyev.

resolved to explore and conquer their land as well.[7] In order to do so they had to overcome not only the power of a people accustomed to dominating neighbouring tribes, but also some very difficult terrain. At many places the Angara poured its waters down towards them in a swift and powerful torrent over a series of high cataracts where granite outcrops cut across the valley, making navigation impossible. On either side rose steep rocky banks covered by dense forests which provided ideal conditions for the Buryats and Tungus to lie in ambush. Particularly hazardous were the rapids near the confluence of the Ilim in the territory of the Shamagir Tungus, from whose name the Russians called them the Shaman rapids, and those south of the sharp U-loop at the confluence of the Oka. Here a 45-mile stretch of river was intersected by seven major cataracts, the largest of which, named by the Russians *Padun*, 'the Faller', thundered between rocky islands for a mile or more. Although the Russians depended greatly upon river transport, they were not to be turned aside by such obstacles, even if it took them some thirty years to win through to the upper end of the river and gain direct access to Lake Baikal. What took place during that time could be called the Buryat wars – a series of campaigns, raids and counter-attacks in which the blood of many Buryats, Tungus and Russians was shed.[8]

One of the aims of the Russians in invading Buryat territory was to find the silver-mines which were rumoured to be there. The earliest expeditions sent out from Yeniseysk did not succeed in reaching the Buryats, although 'new' clans of Tungus around the Angara were subjected to *yasak*. It was in 1628 that the first encounter took place at the mouth of the Oka river. The Russians got no tribute from the Buryats on this occasion, but they defeated them and carried off their women and children as prisoners. In the following year the Cossack commander P. Beketov also penetrated as far as the Oka and succeeded in extorting tribute from the Buryats he met there.[9] By the end of the invasion of the Angara valley a series of Russian forts had been established – Bratsk (so named from the 'Brat', i.e. Buryat people among whom it was built) just below the Padun rapids, Balagansk and Idinsk among the main Buryat pastures, and Irkutsk, founded as a *yasak* outpost in 1652, toward the upper end of the river.

The route to Yakutsk by way of the river Ilim also led to Buryat territories on the upper Lena. Here again it was Beketov who led the first expedition in 1631, using Tungus pathfinders to guide him through the forest. Dissatisfied with the few pelts brought by the Buryats from the nearest settlement, the Cossack upbraided and threatened them in the name of the Tsar. The sixty Buryats, who had dismounted and been disarmed of their bows and arrows before entering the Russian stockade to parley, reacted to

---

[7] Dolgikh, *Rodovoy i plemennoy sostav*, p. 209; *Istoriya Sibiri*, vol. I, p. 387; vol. II, p. 50.
[8] Okun, 'K istorii Buryatii', pp. 156, 158.
[9] Bogdanov, *Ocherki istorii*, pp. 30–2.

Beketov's arrogance by attacking the Russians with their daggers. Forty of the Buryats were then massacred on the spot and the rest left wounded, while the Russian soldiers made their escape on the Buryats' horses. Another raid on the Buryats of the upper Lena was described in 1641 in a report written by its commander Vasilyev. Again using Tungus as guides to betray the Buryats, the Russians made a surprise attack at night on a settlement of twenty huts. Thirty Buryats were killed, and none would surrender, the lead being given by their chief Chepchugui, who defied the attackers and continued to shoot arrows at them from his cabin until it was set on fire by the Russians. 'And prisoners (*yasyr*) were taken – old and young and infants to a total of twenty-eight ... The prisoners were shot and killed in their cabins.' By the time this massacre was accomplished some 200 Buryat and Tungus warriors came on the scene and a battle ensued. The natives, as always put at a disadvantage in the face of Russian guns, were defeated, and the remnants of Chepchugui's clan were forced to submit and hand over *yasak* to the Russian raiders.[10] After much fighting in this region, the fort of Verkholensk was established in 1641, and the local Nalagir Tungus and Ekherit Buryats subjected to *yasak*.[11]

Southward from Yakutsk, penetration of the mountainous country round the northern end of Lake Baikal during the 1630s and 1640s resulted in the establishment of several Russian outposts, including Tungursk in the Olokma basin, Bauntovsk on the Vitim and Barguzinsk in the vicinity of the great lake itself. Many Tungus (Ewenki) clans such as the Kindigir, Pochegor and Chilchagir, were thus subjected to *yasak*. Beyond them, however, the Russians again encountered the Buryats and a situation involving the powerful military forces of Mongols and Manchu-Chinese, in which the Russians met their match. The conflict which arose here will be outlined in a later section.

The Russians' other main campaign against the Buryats emanated from Krasnoyarsk on the Yenisey. Here, on the forested northern slopes of the Sayan mountains, lived Tungus, Ket and Samoyed clans from whom tribute was exacted either by the Yenisey Kirgiz, by the western Mongols from south of the Sayan, or by the Buryats of the Bulagat tribe who were based in the valleys of the Iya and Uda. Penetrating into this region from 1628 onward, the Russians gradually subjected the forest tribes to tribute, thus arousing the anger of the Mongols and Kirgiz, who looked upon the Samoyeds and Kets as their vassals. In 1633 Cossacks from Krasnoyarsk encountered and fought Buryats on the Biryusa, and when warfare again broke out in 1645, the Bulagat prince Oilan was defeated and temporarily forced into submission. A Russian fort was set up on the Uda in 1647

---

[10] Ibid., pp. 30–1, 44–5.
[11] Dolgikh, *Rodovoy i plemennoy sostav*, pp. 276, 280; *Kolonialnaya politika . . . v Yakutii*, pp. 219, 229–38.

(known as Udinsk or later Nizhneudinsk) as a base for further operations against the Buryats, but also partly in response to a request by them for protection from the Mongols. The reason for this was that while the Buryat chiefs carried out raids on their former Tungus, Ket or Samoyed vassals to deter them from paying tribute to the Russians, the Buryats themselves were subjected to punitive raids by Mongol chiefs with the same purpose. Only after many battles did the Russians succeed in imposing their rule on the Buryats of the Uda-Iya-Oka region in 1652.[12]

Meanwhile, resistance by the Buryats continued in other areas. On the Angara, major anti-Russian campaigns occurred in 1634, when Bratsk fort was burned, and during the period 1638–41. By the middle of the 1640s the Buryats were driven to desperation by the endless depredations of the Russian conquerors. One of these, the Cossack ataman Kolyosnikov of Yeniseysk, became particularly notorious for his marauding operations, both on the Angara and beyond Baikal. Bent upon self-enrichment, he did not scruple to extort booty from Buryat and Tungus clans which were already subject to the garrison of Verkholensk. It was as a result of this merciless plundering that the biggest series of Buryat uprisings took place in 1644–6. In this war the Bulagat tribe of the Angara and the Ekherit of the Lena cooperated with each other, at times putting as many as 2,000 warriors in the field. They attacked and killed Russians in their scattered settlements and besieged Verkholensk three times in 1645. Once again, however, the more deadly weapons of the Russians ensured the eventual suppression of resistance.[13] In the course of this war the following threat was conveyed to the Buryat leaders in a letter from the *voyevoda* in Yakutsk calling on them to submit:

But if in future you rebels betray the Tsar and do not hand over the Tsar's yasak annually, and if you come to attack our fort and our peasant farmers, then for your treachery . . . the voyevodas . . . will send many of the Tsar's soldiers with fire-arms to attack you, and they will command that not only you and your cattle, but your wives and children and all your people be killed and destroyed and your homes burned down mercilessly, and that none be taken prisoner for ransom, but those of you that are captured shall be hanged and executed, just as was done to the Yakut traitors, and you yourselves will be the cause of your destruction.[14]

Despite such naked threats couched in terms worthy of Chingis Khan himself, resistance to the Russian occupation continued, and a big revolt occurred throughout Buryat territory in 1695–6, when the town of Irkutsk was besieged.[15]

---

[12] Bogdanov, *Ocherki istorii*, pp. 50–1; Dolgikh, *Rodovoy i plemennoy sostav*, pp. 241–2, 247–8.
[13] Bogdanov, *Ocherki istorii*, pp. 45–50; *Kolonialnaya politika . . . v Yakutii*, pp. 219–38.
[14] *Kolonialnaya politika . . . v Yakutii*, p. 231.
[15] Bogdanov, *Ocherki istorii*, pp. 50–1; Dolgikh, *Rodovoy i plemennoy sostav*, pp. 212–15, 249; *Entsiklopedicheskiy slovar*, vol. XIII, p. 330; Solovyov, *Istoriya Rossii*, vol. VI, pp. 544–6, 587.

No small part in the complex story of the Buryat wars was played by that recurrent phenomenon in the history of the conquest of Siberia – rivalry between different Russian colonial headquarters. In 1653–4 there was conflict over *yasak* from the natives on the Uda between Krasnoyarsk and Yeniseysk gangs, and the foundation of Balagansk on the Angara by men from the latter district was calculated to block further advance in this direction by forces from Krasnoyarsk. The new forts established in the region themselves came into competition, for instance in 1661 when both Irkutsk and Ilimsk claimed rights over the Buryats on the Angara.[16]

One of the habitual means of coercion used by the Russian colonists to bring about the submission of native tribes – the capture of their leaders to be held as hostages against tribute payments – was less successful in the case of the Buryats. In order to fight the Russians, their clans abandoned their homes, combined in large armies to give battle against the invaders, withdrew to strongholds in the forest and carried on guerrilla warfare; but once all efforts proved vain in face of the Russian's guns, the Buryat chiefs still had one last resort – to lead their people in mass migration away from the yoke of the conqueror into the steppes of Mongolia.[17] (In Soviet Russian accounts, based on the simplistic dogma of universal class conflict, the normal role of the *taishis* and other Buryat Mongol tribal leaders is considered to have been collaboration with the forces of 'imperialism' in order to preserve their power over the masses. If, on the other hand, tribes followed their chiefs in fleeing from the Russian colonial system, this could only be because their princes, acting in their own class interests, supposedly forced their subjects to migrate!) As hopes of expelling the Russians faded in the 1640s, some of the Ekherit Buryats left their homes in the upper Lena region, crossed the ice of Lake Baikal and went south into Mongolia. Similarly, the defeat of the Ashekhabat Buryat tribe on the river Oka by men from Krasnoyarsk caused them to migrate southward out of Russian occupied territory in 1658, and in the same year the cruelty and extortion employed by the Yeniseysk Russians in crushing an uprising of the Angara Buryats was followed by the exodus of a large part of the Bulagat tribe in the same direction. Unfortunately for the Buryats, Mongolia became a less hospitable refuge in the latter part of the century.[18]

MONGOLIA AND MANCHURIA IN THE SEVENTEENTH CENTURY

At the beginning of the seventeenth century the Muscovite Russians knew little about Mongolia, from whence their overlords of the Golden Horde had

---

[16] Dolgikh, *Rodovoy i plemennoy sostav*, pp. 248–9, 295; *Kolonialnaya politika ... v Yakutii*, p. 225; Solovyov, *Istoriya Rossii*, vol. VI, pp. 587–8; Zalkind, *Prisoyedineniye Buryatii*, pp. 30–1.
[17] Bogdanov, *Ocherki istorii*, pp. 26, 33.
[18] Ibid., pp. 37, 52–4; Dolgikh, *Rodovoy i plemennoy sostav*, pp. 212–15, 249, 296.

come 400 years before. But now their advance southwards from Krasnoyarsk and Yeniseysk brought them ever nearer to its borders, and their annexation of the lands of the Buryat Mongols took them over that border into Mongolian territory. Thus the Russians in southern Siberia became involved in the politics of Mongolia, which in the seventeenth century was passing through a crisis leading to its eclipse as an independent country for over two centuries.

In 1368 the Mongol dynasty in China, known as Yüan, had fallen and the Chinese dynasty of Ming followed. The Mongols who were expelled from China at that time returned to their tribes in the steppes, and although Mongolia was nominally ruled thereafter by a supreme khan belonging to the Chingis line, in practice what ensued was a long period of inter-tribal warfare during which every chieftain called himself 'khan'. The main political division was between the western Mongols or Oirat, whose base was near the head-waters of the Yenisey south of present-day Tuva, and the eastern Mongols, principally the Khalkha, who lived around Chingis Khan's capital Karakorum. Mongol raids on the Chinese border provinces became a common event in the fifteenth century, and in 1550 the Mongolian chief Altan Khan invaded China and besieged Peking. As a result the emperor was persuaded to open markets on the border, where the Mongols exchanged horses and cattle for textiles and other manufactured goods. Altan Khan had a city built as his capital, and he was the first Mongol khan to be converted to Buddhism in its Tibetan form. With the discovery of a 'Living Buddha' in Örgöö (in Russian 'Urga') Lamaist Buddhism became established as the national religion of the Mongols. In the end, the 'Living Buddha' became not only the head of the Buddhist Church but also practically the political ruler of the Khalkha Mongols.[19]

While the late sixteenth and early seventeenth centuries saw a certain regeneration of Mongolian culture, and relatively peaceful relations between China and the Mongols, China itself was in the throes of another dynastic transition, as the Ming dynasty in its turn degenerated. In the far north-eastern part of the empire, beyond the Great Wall, lived the Juchen or Jurchid people, who were related to the Tungus and later adopted the name Manchu. The Jurchen had played an important part in Far Eastern history between the sixth and thirteenth centuries AD, but thereafter lapsed into obscurity until their divided tribes were united late in the sixteenth century by an ambitious leader, Nurhachi. So great became the power of Nurhachi's successor Abahai that in 1636 he proclaimed himself Manchu Emperor and proceeded to conquer Korea and the whole of the Amur region. Three years after Abahai's death in 1643, the Manchu army invaded China and occupied

---

[19] C.R. Bawden, *The Modern History of Mongolia*, London, 1968, pp. 24–5, 28–38, 50–8, 68–70; R. Dawson, *Imperial China*, London, 1972, pp. 204, 208–9, 239, 247–9, 254; *Istoriya Mongolskoy Narodnoy Respubliki*, A.P. Okladnikov et al., eds., 3rd edn, Moscow, 1983, pp. 180–86, 190, 193.

Peking. The last Ming emperor committed suicide, and a Manchu boy-prince was installed as the first Chinese emperor of the Ch'ing dynasty, which lasted until the early twentieth century.[20]

The Ch'ing rulers were ambitious to extend the bounds of their empire in all directions, and in the north this was facilitated by the dissension which existed between various Mongol factions. At the time when the Manchus subjugated the Chahar tribes of what became known as 'Inner Mongolia', the Khalkha tribe of the north had given no support to their compatriots, and again in the 1630s, when Khan Bator-Khuntaiji of the Oirats in the west sought to unite the remaining independent Mongol communities against the Manchus, the Khalkhas refused to cooperate. By the middle of the century the Khalkhas too were being forced into the position of tributaries of the Chinese emperor. In 1688 the Oirat Mongols, now constituting the khanate of Dzungaria (Dzüngaar) under Galdan Khan, launched a campaign against the Khalkhas, who were so thoroughly routed that their chiefs fled into Inner Mongolia and there submitted to Peking. Galdan then turned to attack the Manchus in the extreme eastern region of Mongolia, where his Oirat horde was annihilated by the Chinese army. Now, with the Oirats out of the way, the Emperor K'ang-hsi called a convention of Khalkha chiefs at Dolon-nor in 1691, at which the Khans made their peace and Khalkha became 'Outer' Mongolia – a mere borderland of the Ch'ing empire, its inhabitants being used as soldiers to guard the northern frontier.[21]

Russians in Siberia came into contact with the Mongols at a time when the process of their political subjection to China was just beginning. In the first decades of the seventeenth century men of service from Tomsk made several expeditions up the Yenisey and across the Sayan mountains, thus finding their way into the lands of the Oirats and of the Khalkha chief Sholoi Ubashi, whose adopted title of 'Altan Khan' was used also by his successors. His territory stretched from near Krasnoyarsk on the Yenisey to the Selenga.

After the power of the Altan Khan dynasty waned, their lands (including Tuva) with their mixed vassal population of Turkic, Samoyedic and Ket peoples whom the Mongols called Uriyangkhai ('original inhabitants'), became part of the Oirat khanate of Dzungaria. In 1647 an agreement was reached between the Tsar and the Oirat Khan Bator-Khuntaiji whereby the Mongols were permitted to trade duty-free in Siberia. This led to a large-scale traffic by way of Tomsk in which the Mongols exchanged horses, cattle, sheep, furs and rhubarb for textiles, leather, metalware, etc. from Russia.

In the region of the Sayan and upper Yenisey the Kirgiz and west Mongol

[20] Dawson, *Imperial China*, pp. 253–72; *Istoriya Sibiri*, vol. I, pp. 308–43; *Istoriya Mongolskoy Narodnoy Respubliki*, pp. 192–4.
[21] Bawden, *Modern History of Mongolia*, pp. 58–9, 75–80; Bogdanov, *Ocherki istorii*, p. 210; *Istoriya Mongolskoy Narodnoy Respubliki*, pp. 193–7, 211–15.

overlords frequently fought over the fealty of the native inhabitants, and at times the Kirgiz themselves were subjugated by the Mongol khans, who encouraged their raiding of the Krasnoyarsk, Tomsk and Kuznetsk Russian settlements. As a result of this dual suzerainty, some of the native tribes in the upper Yenisey basin were forced to pay tribute to both the Kirgiz and the Oirat. Russian intrusion into the region added further complications, but it may, as Soviet Russian historians assert, have come as a relief to some of the natives when the supremacy of the Russians was established, even if they were now obliged to give *yasak* to new overlords in the name of the Tsar. While the Yenisey valley was the route by which Cossacks from Krasnoyarsk penetrated north-western Mongolia in the 1630s, their later conquest of the Angara region allowed them to approach the land of the Uriyangkhai from the east as well. In 1661, for instance, Russians under Yakov Pokhabov, led by Tungus guides, went up the Irkut valley and crossed the Great Sayan range to Lake Hovsgol (Khubsu-gul). Here they encountered people of Tuva, forced them to submit to *yasak* and abducted one of their princes as a hostage. In the course of Russian raids into eastern Tuva, *yasak* bands from Krasnoyarsk came into conflict with those from Irkutsk, and the jurisdiction of the latter over this region was marked by the establishment of Tunka fort in 1675. However, Russian suzerainty over the Turkic and Samoyedic inhabitants of Tuva was no more absolute than that of various Mongol khans had been, and in 1727, according to the Treaty of Kiakhta between Russia and China, the whole of the upper Yenisey region south of the Sayan mountains was acknowledged to be part of Outer Mongolia within the Chinese Empire.[22]

THE EASTERN BURYATS AND MONGOLS BETWEEN RUSSIA AND CHINA

The first Russian contact with eastern Mongolia occurred in 1647 when a Cossack expedition under Ivan Pokhabov crossed Lake Baikal and encountered Buryat Mongols on the Selenga. From there they were taken to the Tsetsen Khan's headquarters, where Pokhabov proposed to the Khan that he should submit to the Tsar. In the following year an envoy from the Tsetsen Khan travelled to Moscow. The fate of the next Russian party sent to the Khalkha Mongols illustrates the hazards of such contacts: having reached the Selenga they were awaiting horses to take them to the Khan when Buryats attacked and killed most of them.[23]

Russian hunters and Cossacks had begun to probe into the lands beyond

[22] Bogdanov, *Ocherki istorii*, pp. 52–3; Dolgikh, *Rodovoy i plemennoy sostav*, pp. 233–4, 242–3, 257, 260, 263–4, 294, 297–8; *Narody Sibiri*, pp. 124, 128, 333, 382–3, 420, 423.
[23] J.F. Baddeley, *Russia, Mongolia, China*, New York, 1919, vol. II, pp. 128–9; Bawden, *Modern History of Mongolia*, p. 62.

Lake Baikal soon after they established themselves on the Lena in the 1630s, making expeditions southward up the Vitim and Olokma rivers. From there they reached the eastern shore of Lake Baikal, where one of the first Russian bands was annihilated in 1643 by the local Tungus. Two years after this a group of Russians for the first time succeeded in entering the western end of the great lake from the Angara. Once the Russians had found their way to the east of Baikal they proceeded to set up a cordon of forts from its north-eastern end to the mouth of the Selenga in the south.

Russian occupation of the Transbaikal lands had the usual effect of driving out those of the native inhabitants who refused to submit to the extortion of *yasak*. So in the 1640s many of the Namyasin Tungus of the Barguzin valley moved away east towards Manchuria. Their neighbours, the numerous Khori tribe of Buryat Mongols, after fighting the Russian *yasak* gangs for several years, withdrew from their homeland on both shores of Lake Baikal in the early 1650s and moved south across the Yablonov mountains into northern Mongolia.

Pushing on farther to the south-east, the Russians founded more forts in the basins of the Khilok and Shilka rivers, the most important of which was Nerchinsk (1654). Here, among a fairly dense population of Tungus of the Kindigir, Pochegor, Lunikir, Dulikagir and Bayagir clans, the Cossacks faced a long campaign against determined opposition, in the course of which their forts were frequently besieged and sometimes burned down. The Russian invasion also exacerbated inter-clan warfare, in which free Tungus bands inflicted punitive raids on clans which had submitted to the payment of *yasak*. Out of such conflicts arose the recruitment of 'friendly' Tungus and Buryat clans as auxiliary troops to assist the Russians in subjugating other, unsubmissive clans. Subsequently, in the eighteenth century, such auxiliaries became the Tungus and Buryat Cossack regiments of the Transbaikal region.[24]

One of the most turbulent areas lay southward from the western end of Lake Baikal, in the valley of the Selenga, where despite the establishment of several forts, Russian control was insecure until the 1690s. The native peoples here were Tungus of the Kumkagir, Chelkagir, Poinkir and Chemchagir clans, and Mongols of the Tabunut and other tribes, all of whom were subjects of the khans of Mongolia. Far from 'not standing in the way' of the Russians in their annexation of the Transbaikalia, as the official Soviet Russian version has it,[25] the Mongols were greatly concerned about the Russian advance and interfered against it as much as they could. The reason for their intervention was that the Russian occupation of the northern fringe of Mongolia deprived them of tribute-paying subjects and thereby of com-

---

[24] Dolgikh, *Rodovoy i plemennoy sostav*, pp. 305, 307, 310, 314, 318, 324, 326–7, 335, 342, 345–6; *Istoriya Sibiri*, vol. II, pp. 51–4, 58; Solovyvov, *Istoriya Rossii*, vol. VI, pp. 591–2.
[25] *Istoriya Sibiri*, vol. II, pp. 52–3.

modities for trade with China. So, in 1652, the chief of the Tushetu Khalkhas to whom a Russian delegation was sent, spoke of the Buryats of the Angara and Baikal as former vassals who must now be considered lost to the Russians, but he expressed the determination that the Transbaikal Buryats and Tungus who paid tribute to him and other Mongol princes would not be relinquished. Even in the case of the Angara region, particularly the rather isolated Russian outpost in the Tunka mountains to the west of Irkutsk, messengers from the Mongol khans frequently infiltrated among the local Buryats, trying to obtain tribute. In 1684 a Mongol delegation from the Tushetu Khan pursuing this aim was received by the *voyevoda* in Irkutsk. As this meeting led to nothing more than their being conducted out of Russian occupied territory, the Mongols came to besiege the Tunka, Upper Uda, Selenga and Nerchinsk forts in the following year. One result of the Mongolian incursions into these lands of their former vassals was that some of the latter voluntarily submitted to Russian rule in order to obtain protection from the Mongols, as did, for instance, the Tungus in the neighbourhood of Nerchinsk in 1664.[26]

In the late 1660s the whole of northern Mongolia, including the Buryat borderlands, was in turmoil as the Altan, Dzasagtu and Tushetu Khans fought each other over the possession of *yasak*-paying subjects. As a result of this many of the Buryats who had taken refuge from the Russian colonial régime by decamping to Mongolia in the 1640s and 1650s, began to move back into the zone of Russian occupation. In fact mass migrations within the Transbaikal region and from there into Mongolia and back again, were one of the most significant features of this period when the Khalkhas were being squeezed between the Russians and the Manchu-Chinese. In the early stages of this process plenty of space had been available in the Selenga and Onon steppes, so that the Buryat tribes of Transbaikalia could simply move away southward from areas occupied by the Russians. In this they had an advantage over the Angara Buryats, for whom flight involved a much more difficult journey. On the other hand the very fluidity of nomadic life east of Baikal, and the absence of fixed tribal territories, made it easier for the Russians to subdue the Buryat-Mongol groups here one by one, and they never put up such a concerted opposition as the western Buryats did. It was at this time that the Tabunut Mongols of the Selenga began to move eastward into the Uda and Khilok valleys, where they clashed with Tungus who were subject to the Russian fort of Irgensk. The Russians retaliated by attacking the Tabunut in the 1670s. Meanwhile, the Manchu-Chinese subjugation of the Khalkha Mongols had begun, as had the assault upon them by Galdan Khan's Oirats. This caused some of the Khalkhas to flee into the Selenga region, where they joined forces with the Tabunut in raiding not

[26] Bogdanov, *Ocherki istorii*, pp. 51, 56–8, 63, 65, 208, 210; *Kolonialnaya politika ... v Yakutii*, p. 66.

only the Russians, but also those Khori Buryats and Tungus clans who had established themselves in the mountainous forests south of the river Khilok. From this base they harried the Russian Cossacks and hunters and their *yasak*-paying subjects in the region of Nerchinsk fort. As a result of these disturbances the whole region of Russian occupation from the Selenga to Nerchinsk was in a state of siege from the late 1670s to the end of the century.[27]

The local representatives of the Russian imperial régime did not distinguish themselves by tact or humanity in these complicated circumstances. Particularly notorious for his irresponsible actions was the commander of Nerchinsk, Pavel Shulgin, who persecuted those unfortunate Buryats who attempted to cross back into Russian occupied territory and return to their native lands. Like other Russian fort commanders, Shulgin considered such fugitives – who had already run the gauntlet of Mongol frontier patrols – to be fair game for plunder. So in 1675 when the Khori prince Zerbo appeared at Nerchinsk with his clan, prepared to submit to the Tsar, Shulgin first extorted bribes from him and then turned him back with Cossacks in pursuit. Brought back to the fort as a prisoner, Zerbo was forced to give further large bribes. After such treatment the Khori chief, instead of paying *yasak* to the Russians, returned to Mongolia, carrying off with him such Russian horses and cattle as he could seize.[28]

The Chinese, who now considered that all of 'Outer' Mongolia was within the bounds of their empire, played some part in fomenting the anti-Russian activities of the Mongols, Tungus and Buryats. In 1689 the Manchu-Chinese government asserted its interest in the region by sending an embassy to Nerchinsk to settle the border problems caused by Russian intrusion. The treaty which resulted, although it required the Russians to relinquish the Amur region to China, at least secured for the Tsar the north-eastern corner of Mongolia – the steppe-lands of the Onon basin. Among the Mongol tribes who lived there were many of the Khori Buryats who had lived near Lake Baikal before the Russian invasion, and subsequently this became the territory of one of the largest Buryat communities east of Baikal.[29]

Amid the chaos of the final stages of the Manchu and Russian conquest of the northern fringe of Mongolia, movements of large groups of Mongols and Tungus out of and into Russian-held territory continued in response to changing circumstances. A Russian victory over the Tabunut in 1688 resulted in the transfer of the allegiance of some to the Russian side. The

[27] Bogdanov, *Ocherki istorii*, pp. 55–9, 66–8, 211; Dolgikh, *Rodovoy i plemennoy sostav*, pp. 249, 296, 317, 320–1, 325, 327–8, 335, 339, 345–7, 350; *Istoriya Mongolskoy Narodnoy Respubliki*, pp. 196, 215.

[28] Bogdanov, *Ocherki istorii*, pp. 59–61; Zalkind, *Prisoyedineniye Buryatii*, p. 68.

[29] Solovyov, *Istoriya Rossii*, vol. VII, p. 420.

chiefs (*taishis*) were to become 'eternal subjects of the Russian throne' and abjure allegiance to the khans of Mongolia, but they retained their position as tribal chiefs so long as they ensured delivery of *yasak* and provided auxiliary troops for the Russian army. Feeling that none of their rights had been guaranteed, and resenting the encroachment on their lands by Russian settlers, some of the Tabunut and Khoris 'turned traitor' in 1691 and decamped into Mongolia. A contemporary Russian document allocates the blame for this defection: 'the [Russian] men of service drove away these ... tribes by their offensive behaviour and impositions ... After this, those whom the *taishas* left behind in Selenginsk, Udinsk, Ilyinsk and Kabansk forts were all put to death [by the Russians] and thrown into the Selenga, and their wives and children and possessions were shared out and sold off.'[30] In the same year, many of the Ashekhabat Buryats on the Angara defied their chiefs and the Russians, and migrated south to the Selenga.

In the eighteenth century the Sino-Russian border remained a problem for the Mongols, since the imperial authorities on both sides were equally committed to fixed frontiers and to the belief that nomadic peoples must be made to abandon their itinerant way of life which recognised no state frontiers. The Treaty of Kiakhta in 1727 effectively closed the Russo-Chinese frontier except for the permitted trade route through Kiakhta, so that for the first time in history, movement between northern Mongolia and the southern edge of the Siberian forest was arrested by the phenomenon of a closed border. As a result of this, following the many migrations of the previous century, a considerable number of Khalkha Mongols remained within Russian territory to be absorbed among the Buryats, while almost half of the Khori Buryats were left living in Mongolia.[31] In view of this ethnic mixing, it is not surprising that the differences between the Transbaikal Buryats and Mongols are hard to define.[32]

The constant intercourse between the Buryat Mongols and their cousins in Mongolia had an important social consequence during the seventeenth century, as Buddhism spread among them. It was, for instance, a visit to the Tabunut and Khoris by an emissary from the Mongolian 'Living Buddha' in 1691 which persuaded some chiefs to remove their clans from Russian territory into Mongolia. The first Lamaist monastery-temple (*datsan*) was founded among the Transbaikal Buryats in 1710, but until the middle of the eighteenth century the great majority remained, like their brethren to the

---

[30] Bogdanov, *Ocherki istorii*, p. 70.

[31] Ibid., pp. 37, 64–75, 211, 215; Dolgikh, *Rodovoy i plemennoy sostav*, pp. 315–16, 321, 328–31, 346.

[32] Bogdanov, *Ocherki istorii*, pp. 215–16. Soviet Russian writers have been obliged to emphasise the distinctiveness of the Buryats as a nationality separate from the Mongols, and the use of the term 'Buryat-Mongol', attributed to 'Buryat bourgeois nationalists' such as M.N. Bogdanov, was abolished in 1958 and replaced by simple 'Buryat' – cf. Tokarev, *Etnografiya*, p. 455; Zalkind, *Prisoyedineniye Buryatii*, pp. 146–59.

west of the lake, true to their shamanist beliefs. By 1740 there were eleven *datsans* among the Buryats, and in the second half of the eighteenth century Buddhism made great strides and became the dominant religion of the eastern Buryats, with Tibetan as its ecclesiastical language. This was a Mongolised form of Buddhism, which incorporated many elements of the old Shamanist beliefs, such as blood sacrifice. Only the eastern Buryats were converted to Buddhism in the eighteenth century, while their compatriots living west of Lake Baikal kept their shamanist religion.[33]

While the role of Buddhism and of the native ruling class in Buryatia is presented in an exclusively negative light in Soviet Russian works, that of the Russian conquerors (who are never so called) is said to have been, as ever, beneficial. A typical quotation in this spirit of Marxist equivocation speaks for itself in the light of the events narrated above:

The voluntary union with the Russian state of various tribes and peoples of Siberia languishing under the oppression of the warring feudal nomadic lords of Asia answered the vital interests of the popular masses, including the Buryats. It delivered them from devastating feudal conflicts and the violence of the Manchurian feudal lords under whose yoke other Mongolian peoples had fallen, and acquainted them with higher forms of economy, everyday life and culture. It was for this reason that the Russian detachments advancing swiftly into the regions inhabited by the Buryats did not encounter any serious resistance from them.[34]

The last sentence in particular is, as we have seen, very far from the truth.

THE RUSSIANS REACH THE AMUR

It is generally agreed by Russian historians that by the end of the seventeenth century in the territory of northern Asia held by the Russians there were at least as many Russians as native inhabitants – roughly 150,000 to 200,000 of each. It is impossible to discover exactly how many natives there were, since the only written records are the Russians' official registers of tribute exacted, which show only how many adult males fell within the *yasak* net.[35]

Russian colonisation was not spread evenly over the whole of Siberia. There was a big contrast between the western and eastern halves, separated approximately by the rivers Yenisey and Angara. As we have seen, it was the southern districts of Western Siberia that became the main centre of agriculture and therefore of Russian settlement, and there were objective reasons for this situation to persist. The Yenisey was also a frontier, to the

---

[33] *Aziatskaya Rossiya*, vol. I, pp. 133–7; Dolgikh, *Rodovoy i plemennoy sostav*, p. 329; Tokarev, *Etnografiya*, p. 454; *Narody Sibiri*, pp. 240–2, 261–3.

[34] *Narody Sibiri*, p. 219. Similar sentiments may be found in *Istoriya Sibiri*, vol. II, p. 50.

[35] Dolgikh, *Rodovoy i plemennoy sostav*, pp. 616–17; omitting the 'north-eastern Palaeoasiatics', Eskimos, Ainus and the population of the Albazin region, the number of Siberian natives arrived at here is 151,210; *Narody Sibiri*, pp. 123–4; *Istoriya Sibiri*, vol. II, p. 56.

east of which began the permafrost where cultivation of crops was impossible except in a few places enjoying favourable conditions. So, while in Western Siberia the Russians' avid quest for sable furs could be succeeded by the opening up of land for cultivation, beyond the Yenisey there was little scope for such a shift of activity. On the whole, when the fur supplies were exhausted the trappers simply moved on in search of new hunting grounds.

As a result, by 1710 there were only some 66,000 Russians living in Eastern Siberia as compared with 247,000 in the west.[36] (During the next 200 years there was to be little change in these proportions, despite the large increase in the total population of Siberia: in 1897 the huge territory of Irkutsk, Yakutsk and Transbaikal provinces had 909,000 Russian inhabitants – less than one third of the number in the western provinces of Tobolsk and Tomsk.)[37] Thus the number of native people in Eastern Siberia at the beginning of the eighteenth century – 106,000 (or 139,700 if the unsubdued peoples of the north-east and those of the Manchu-Chinese Amur lands are included) – was considerably greater than that of the Russian population, which here consisted almost exclusively of soldiers and hunters.[38]

The main historical justification put forward by Soviet Russian writers for the annexation of Siberia is the introduction of agriculture 'as the principal economic activity, which subsequently had a decisive influence on the economy and way of life of the local native peoples'. In more eloquent phrases: 'in one century the Russian plough had cut a furrow from the Urals to Kamchatka', and the credit for this 'heroic feat of enormous historical significance' was entirely due to the Russian peasant.[39] This somewhat dubious view is certainly untrue so far as Eastern Siberia is concerned. Since the number of Russian peasants in Eastern Siberia up to 1700 was so small, the impact of agriculture can only have been very slight, compared with that of the most conspicuous examples of Russian civilisation seen by the native peoples, namely: guns, forts, the *yasak* system, exiles and later mines. Far from welcoming the Russian peasants, the Siberian natives had every reason to hate them, since they stole their land. Their use of this land also had disastrous effects, since the peasants cleared areas of forest for cultivation by starting fires which swept through the natives' hunting-grounds, killing or driving out the animals. This crude 'slash and burn' technique was used wherever Russian peasants moved in, and was still a curse to the natives in the twentieth century.[40]

In view of the unsuitability of most of Central and Eastern Siberia for

[36] *Istoriya Sibiri*, vol. II, p. 55.
[37] *Entsiklopedicheskiy slovar*, vol. XXIX, p. 759.
[38] Dolgikh, *Rodovoy i plemennoy sostav*, pp. 616–17; Shunkov, *Vosprosy agrarnoy istorii*, p. 26.
[39] *Istoriya Sibiri*, vol. II, pp. 19, 62, 72, 75.
[40] *Narody Sibiri*, p. 136; Shirokogorov, *Social Organization*, pp. 17–18.

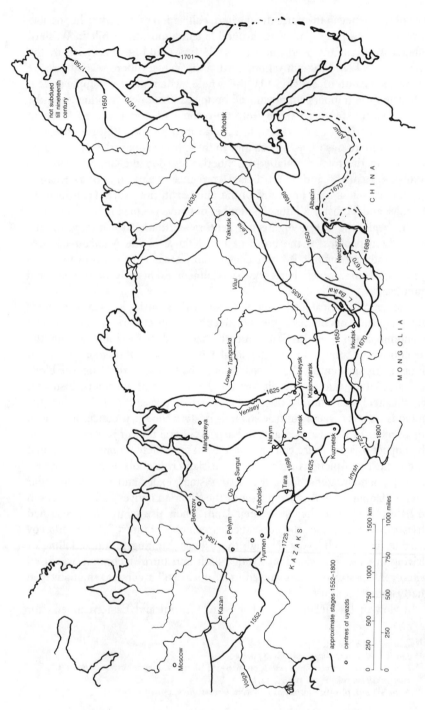

Map 6 The Russian conquest of Siberia

cultivation, and the chronic problems of victualling the Russian settlements there, the discovery of large tracts of fertile land beyond Nerchinsk could not but act as a magnet on the Russians. The river Amur, from the point where it is formed by the confluence of the Shilka and Argun, curves away southward out of the mountainous taiga and the permafrost into a region of deciduous forest. To the north of the Amur, in the valleys of its left tributaries the Zeya and Bureya, lies a plain with oak woodlands on black-earth soil. With its mild summers and adequate rainfall, the Amur region was a paradise compared with the harsh conditions prevailing elsewhere in Siberia.

In the seventeenth century the Amur valley as far as the Zeya was inhabited and cultivated by people known as Dahurs, who spoke a Mongolian language. Below the confluence of the Zeya lived the Juchers, whose language was related to those of the Tungus and Manchus, while on the lower part of the Amur, beyond the confluence of the Ussuri and between it and the Sikhote Alin mountains, lived other Manchu-Tungus peoples, the ancestors of the present-day Nanais, Ulchis, Udeghes and Oroches. Around the mouth of the Amur and along the north-western coast of Sakhalin island lived the Nivkhs or Gilyaks. The Amur valley, particularly in its middle and lower reaches, was quite densely populated, with almost 9,000 Dahurs, over 14,000 Juchers and other Manchurians, and several thousands of Tungus and Nivkhs.[41]

It appears that this region was never fully subjugated by the Chinese, although they sent military expeditions there in the fourteenth century. Northern Manchuria, however, lying between the Amur and Argun rivers, had been incorporated into the Chinese state between the tenth and twelfth centuries during the existence of the Northern Liao and Chin states with their Mongol and Tungus–Manchu dynasties. By the beginning of the seventeenth century the Dahurs (who have been described as 'Mongolised Tungus') were established on the upper Amur and Zeya, where they practised agriculture and built fortified towns. The fact that the Tungus Manegir and Birar clans were tribute-paying vassals of the Dahurs suggests that the latter were a people of some power and influence. Indeed they extended their trading contacts as far north as the Yakuts of the Aldan, and it is possible that either the Dahurs or the Juchers exercised hunting rights over a large territory in the upper reaches of the Aldan and Amga, some 400 miles north of the Amur. To the west of the Dahurs, in the highlands around the river Argun, lived people known as 'Solons' or 'Horse-Tungus'. In the early seventeenth century they were subject to the Manchus, to whom they were obliged to supply mounted troops. Thus there was no doubt that the Argun–Amur region was within the long-established sphere of interest of the Manchus both historically and in terms of current political strength. Aba-

---

[41] Dolgikh, *Rodovoy i plemennoy sostav*, pp. 611–13; *Narody Sibiri*, pp. 705–6, 785, 862; *Yazyki narodov SSSR*, vol. V, pp. 407–8.

hai's armies had made the whole of this region subject to the Manchus by 1643, but it was not until the 1650s, after Russian incursions into it had begun, that it was brought under their direct rule and its native population of Solons, Dahurs and Juchers organised into banner armies.[42]

Russians received the first reports of populous and fertile lands on the Amur in the late 1630s, and within a few years expeditions were despatched from Yakutsk by way of the river Aldan. The first successful expedition of 133 men was led by Vasiliy Poyarkov, who in 1643–6 found a portage through the Stanovoy mountains from the Aldan basin to that of the Zeya. After spending the winter among the Dahurs, he sailed down the Amur through the land of the Juchers, wintered among the Nivkh (or Gilyak) people, and returned to Yakutsk by way of the Okhotsk coast. Like other Russian commanders in these remote regions, Poyarkov saw his venture in terms of plunder – he brought back a large tribute of sables – and of natives to be subjugated 'in perpetual servitude' to the Tsar. He also confirmed that the Amur valley could be a source of grain for the Tsar's soldiers in Eastern Siberia. His own detachment was ill supplied with victuals, and Poyarkov manifested the contemptuous brutality typical of Siberian commanders in dealing with their men: he beat them mercilessly, killing some with his own hands, and deprived them of due rations. So began the episodic Russian adventure on the Amur.[43]

Its second episode began in 1650 when one of the most experienced and wealthy Siberian colonialists, Yerofey Khabarov, set off to reconnoitre another route by way of the Olokma river and emerged on the upper Amur. Puzzled but encouraged to find all the Dahur settlements there deserted by their inhabitants – who no doubt knew what to expect from the Russians – Khabarov returned to Yakutsk to muster a larger army of mercenaries. Whereas on his first visit the Dahur chiefs had only parleyed and shunned contact with the Russians, now they gave fight. With their guns the Russians had little difficulty in killing hundreds of the Dahurs, but could not induce them to accept the subjugation of their land to the Tsar, as they already owed allegiance to the 'Bogdo-khan' (celestial ruler), as the Mongolian peoples called the emperor of China. Continuing their path of plunder down the Amur, Khabarov's band raided the settlements of the Juchers and other natives. Even when a Manchu army with guns appeared in order to assert the territorial rights of the Chinese emperor, the Russians, calling on the aid of 'the Saviour and the All-Pure Lady Mother of God and Christ's blessed Saint Nicholas the Wonderworker', gained the victory and 'killed many of

[42] Bichurin, *Sobraniye svedeniy*, vol. I, pp. 376–80; Dolgikh, *Rodovoy i plemennoy sostav*, pp. 495, 498, 510, 583; *Istoriya Sibiri*, vol. I, pp. 307–9, 403–8; R.H.G. Lee, *The Manchurian Frontier in Ch'ing History*, Cambridge (Mass.), 1970, pp. 3–4, 34, 41, 50–1, 112; *Narody Sibiri*, pp. 704–5, 789.

[43] *Istoriya Sibiri*, vol. II, pp. 52–3; Solovyov, *Istoriya Rossii*, vol. VI, pp. 591–2.

those dogs' – 676 Manchus, as against 10 Cossack dead, if Khabarov's report is to be believed. With this victory behind him, Khabarov continued to rove up and down the Amur with his fleet of ships, raiding settlements to extort *yasak*, and losing over one-third of his Cossacks who, satisfied with the booty so far collected, mutinied and sailed off down-river in defiance of their commander.[44] Khabarov's operations in the land the Russians called Dauria, i.e. Dahuria, figure in Soviet Russian history as 'the official annexation' of the Amur region to Russia.[45]

Meanwhile, Manchu-Chinese armies were sent to put an end to the Russians' intrusion into the northern marches of the empire. Since grain was one of the main reasons for Russian raids on the native settlements, the Chinese went so far as to forbid the Dahur and Jucher population to continue the cultivation of crops, and deported them all from the Amur to the valley of the river Nun. As a result, the Russians found themselves in a region of ghost towns surrounded by abandoned fields. Nevertheless, Khabarov's successor, O. Stepanov, continued to defy the Chinese and to maraud up and down the Amur for several years until a large Chinese fleet caught up with him in 1658 and he and more than half of his 300 Cossacks were killed. So ended some fifteen years of officially encouraged Russian buccaneering on the Amur. From then onward the Russians consolidated their positions farther to the west at Nerchinsk on the Shilka. Despite this tacit drawing back of the Russian frontier, however, some Russian hunters and fugitive peasants stayed on in the Amur valley, taking advantage of the conveniently deserted villages, and when active settlement on a considerable scale was renewed in the 1660s, it was on the private initiative of similar outlaws in revolt against the Russian colonial administration.

While the main thrust of Russian conquest in the Far East during the 1650s had been towards the fertile lands of the Amur basin, the mountainous forest lands to the north of this were also subject to penetration. Here the native inhabitants were Tungus and, around the mouth of the Amur, Gilyaks. The latter, like the Tungus, did not submit lightly to the Russian invaders, and there was much fighting before they were compelled to hand over *yasak* in 1652. The Manchus also claimed tribute from the natives of the Okhotsk coast, and in the 1670s sent expeditions to assert their sovereignty. They penetrated as far as the upper reaches of the Maya river, to Tungus (Lamut) clans who were already subject to the Russians, and tried to persuade some Yakuts to move south to the Zeya. Armies were sent to clear the Russians out, and their three forts on the Zeya, Selemja and Tugur

[44] Dolgikh, *Rodovoy i plemennoy sostav*, pp. 579–80; Solovyov, *Istoriya Rossii*, vol. VI, pp. 592–5.
[45] E.g. *Istoriya Sibiri*, vol. II, p. 53. The most nationalistic Soviet Russian publications imply that Russia thereby gained not only all the land lying to the east of the Amur as far as the ocean, but also northern Mongolia eastward of the river Argun to the Great Hsing-an mountains. V.F. Buturlinov et al., *O Sovetsko-kitayskoy granitse: pravda i Pekinskiye vymysly*, Moscow, Military Publishing House, 1982, p. 17.

were demolished in 1683–4.[46] Having dealt with the Russian threat in the maritime region, the Chinese were able to return to the main thorn in their flesh – the Russian settlements at Albazin on the Amur.

The mutiny which disrupted Khabarov's Amur campaign in 1652 was no isolated occurrence. Since the beginning of the conquest of Siberia the lower ranks in the colonial armies – in any case an unruly collection of mercenaries of very varied origin – were frequently placed under such oppressive conditions by their superiors that they came out in revolt against them. Since the Cossacks did not receive regular wages direct from the state, but were paid by the district *voyevodas* at such times as the latter saw fit, this was another field in which the higher officials could enrich themselves at the expense of their subordinates. In northern and eastern districts where no crops could be grown, the *voyevodas* were also responsible for distributing to the soldiers an allowance of grain for bread. One of the most profitable rackets open to governors was the illicit brewing and distilling of alcohol, which was a valuable commodity for trading with the natives – and also, frequently, a means of getting them drunk and fleecing them. Vodka could not be produced without grain, and grain could only be obtained from the state's granaries. Thus what was intended to supply the needs of the men of service and others was frequently diverted to the purpose of producing alcohol for the *voyevoda*'s personal profit.

A less concrete but equally potent cause of rebellion by the Siberian Cossacks was conflict between the authority of the state, in the person of the *voyevoda*, and Cossack traditions of equality, self-government, and the election of officers from their own ranks. In Siberia there was frequent cause for Cossacks to believe that their rights were being curtailed, and accordingly to rise up in their defence. The traditional Cossack remedy sanctified by long practice on the plains of Europe was to throw off oppressive authority, move to some distant borderland, and there set up their own community free from the authority of any government. Krasnoyarsk experienced several such mutinies, and was the centre of one of the biggest and most prolonged revolts, which during 1695–8 ran through all of the south-east Siberian districts from the Yenisey to Nerchinsk. It was such a revolt of Cossacks in Yakutsk which led to the final episode of Russian settlement on the Amur. By the 1650s the reputation of 'Dauria' as a promised land was widespread among the Russians in Siberia, so that settlement on the Amur was the aim of three rebellions which took place in the Lena region. The third of these occurred in 1655 as a result of the usual abuses of power by the *voyevodas* of Yakutsk, Verkholensk and Ilimsk. The Cossacks of the region, having congregated and sworn on the cross to be free of their oppressors, equipped themselves for the long journey by raiding warehouses and requisitioning

[46] *Aziatskaya Rossiya*, vol. I, p. 514; Dolgikh, *Rodovoy i plemennoy sostav*, pp. 513–14, 581, 611; *Kolonialnaya politika . . . v Yakutii*, p. xi.

boats, and with M. Sorokin as their *ataman* some 300 men set out for the Amur. A decade later, in 1665, similar events took place at Ilimsk, whence the rebels, having killed the *voyevoda* Obukhov, set off for the Amur under the leadership of the Ukrainian exile, N. Chernihovskyy. It was this group that occupied the abandoned Dahur town of Albazin and made it the centre of their unofficial, independent colony.[47]

Although the Muscovite authorities rightly considered the Albazin fort under Chernihovskyy to be mutinous, the latter acted like any other colonial commander by exacting tribute from the Tungus who lived in the vicinity, and sending the furs received to the treasury in Moscow. As a result, in 1672 the Albazin Cossacks received the Tsar's pardon for their rebellion, and Chernihovskyy was recognised as the official commander of the fort. Cossack privileges were even tolerated, so that in Albazin they continued to elect their own *ataman* until 1684, when the district was subordinated to the Tsar's command and, under a *voyevoda* appointed by Moscow, became officially part of the Russian Empire. Agriculture had been developed around Albazin sufficiently to provide regular supplies of grain to Nerchinsk district, but its continued existence in land claimed by China was highly insecure. The Manchu army in fact attacked the fort in 1670 and again in 1685. Despite these campaigns the scattered Russian settlements of Albazin district succeeded in existing until 1689, having been a reality for some fourteen years.[48]

THE RUSSO-CHINESE BORDER, 1689

If the Russians knew little about China at the beginning of the seventeenth century, they came to realise by mid-century that in China, for the first time in the course of their conquest of Northern Asia, they faced a political power and a civilisation which not only opposed their advance, but even assumed the right to dictate to them as inferiors. The arrogance of the 'Great Lord, Tsar and Grand Duke of All Russia' who called upon each Siberian people in turn to submit and come under his 'high hand' was more than matched by the arrogance of the 'son of Heaven', the Celestial Emperor of the Middle Kingdom. Until then the Russian invaders in Siberia had had no need to consider frontiers. All along the southern edge of their conquests, as far east as Lake Baikal, there was only the open and unstable frontier of the steppes with their nomadic inhabitants, while the native peoples encountered and subjugated by the Russians elsewhere were too weak to assert their right to territories. Beyond Baikal, however, the Chinese were fully aware of fron-

---

[47] *Aziatskaya Rossiya*, vol. I, p. 513; Lantzeff, *Siberia*, pp. 79, 81–4; *Istoriya Sibiri*, vol. II, pp. 54, 141–51; *Narody Sibiri*, pp. 127–8.

[48] Dolgikh, *Rodovoy i plemennoy sostav*, pp. 580–1.

tiers, both in concept and in practice, so that the question of recognising territorial claims could not be ignored.

In 1670, when the Cossack mutineers from Yakutsk were already installed in Albazin, Tsar Aleksey sent an official embassy to China. Ignoring the Russians' usual offer to take China under the Tsar's high hand, the Emperor proposed that if the Tsar's men in future refrained from attacking 'our borderlands', the two monarchs could live in peace and harmony. Apart from the Emperor's demand that Russians in Siberia should refrain from attacking his subjects, one of the issues most strongly emphasised by K'ang-hsi was that of Gantimur – a Tungus chief who in 1667 had defected from Chinese service with his clan. Gantimur was baptised into the Orthodox Church and became a Russian citizen and a member of the nobility. Although the Manchus continued to demand his repatriation to China, the services of his Tungus in south-eastern Siberia were so valuable to the Russians as auxiliary troops that they would not give him up, and the 'Gantimurov' family, like many members of the Tatar nobility in earlier centuries, gained considerable wealth and fame in Russia.[49]

The Chinese again warned the Russians off the Amur in 1682, and then renewed their military campaign, using as a base the newly constructed town of Aihun (in Russian Aygun). Albazin was attacked and came under continuous siege by a Manchu army. In 1689, when an embassy arrived from Moscow, the Chinese demonstrated their dominance in the region by advancing right up to Nerchinsk with a large army, which grew daily in size as more and more Mongols and Buryats from the frontier area went over to the Chinese. The latter drove a hard bargain, to which the Russians had no alternative but to agree. Albazin was to be demolished and the Russians excluded from the Amur. The frontier was fixed along the Argun to the Shilka confluence and from there along the tops of the Stanovoy mountain range – the northern watershed of the Amur basin – to the sea. Thus the Russians were obliged to relinquish the whole province north of the Amur, and to abandon their desire to annexe it for 150 years.[50]

---

[49] Solovyov, *Istoriya Rossii*, vol. VI, pp. 599–604.
[50] *Aziatskaya Rossiya*, vol. I, p. 514; Buturlinov, *O Sovetsko-kitayskoy granitse*, pp. 24–9; Solovyov, *Istoriya Rossii*, vol. VI, pp. 413–20.

5

RUSSIA'S NORTH ASIAN COLONY

THE CONQUEST OF SIBERIA IN RUSSIAN HISTORY

THE Russian conquest of Siberia was an event of epic proportions, yet it passed almost unnoticed in the world, apart from its impingement upon China, and has found little or no place in general histories of Russia written in English ever since. To West Europeans, Muscovy itself seemed a remote enough land; geographical knowledge of the world beyond the Baltic Sea and the Carpathians was very limited and inaccurate; and the untamed nature of Siberia itself did not invite travellers. It is no doubt for such reasons that most histories of Russia in the English language have almost entirely disregarded this vast and immensely important process of Russian empire-building, and that where this has been mentioned, certain bland commonplaces have been the norm. Among these are the simple vindicatory view that Siberia consisted of nothing but 'great waste spaces' having only thinly scattered native inhabitants. Consequently 'the road was open' before the Russian advance to the east, and there was supposedly almost no armed resistance to it, so that it took the form of assimilation 'by sheer force of flowing'. This process was 'the work of the Russian people' with but little help from the government, but even Moscovite government policy towards the natives 'can be considered enlightened'.[1] These oft-repeated misconceptions about the conquest of Siberia derive from Russian historians, who have laboured to convince readers that it is incorrect to call this a 'conquest' (*zavoyevaniye*). Instead of this word, or even 'annexation'; (*prisoyedineniye*), Russian Marxist historians prefer the word equivalent to 'assimilation, making one's own' (*osvoyeniye*), which emphasises the exploration and economic utilisation or development of the land.[2] As we have seen,

---

[1] Bernard Pares, *A History of Russia*, rev. edn, 1947, pp. 134, 198; N.V. Riasanovsky, *A History of Russia*, New York, 1963, pp. 213, 215.

[2] A. I. Alekseyev, *Osvoyeniye russkimi lyudmi Dalnego Vostoka i Russkoy Ameriki do kontsa XIX veka*, Moscow, 1982, p. 3.

the 'correct' view of the colonisation of Siberia arrived at by Soviet historians is that the real basis of the development of the 'productive forces' of Siberia was the settlement and opening up of the land to agriculture by simple peasant folk. One of the main benefits this brought to the native peoples was the inclusion of their isolated and backward communities in the 'growing Russian national market'. Hand in hand with these theoretical formulations goes a systematic minimisation of the role of the Russian state and especially of its military representatives in Siberia – the boyars' sons, men of service, *streltsy* and Cossacks, who are said to have been very few in number.

So far as the native peoples are concerned, the view propagated by the Communist Party, at least in works for popular consumption, is based on the concept of 'absence of conflict' (*beskonfliktnost*) which came to dominate all writing in the Soviet Union during Stalin's reign. In the context of Siberian history this means the denial or minimisation of armed conflict between the native inhabitants (unless misguided by their 'ruling cliques') and the Russian bringers of a higher culture. The natives and the lower-class Russian settlers are said to have understood that they had more in common with each other than they had with their respective rulers, and in particular racial hatred is said to have been alien to 'ordinary Russian people'. The 'correct' picture of the annexation of Siberia which emerges from the carefully woven tissue of Soviet Russian doctrine is almost idyllic:

The Russians settled in expanses ... which had previously lain vacant or were occupied by a few groups of hunters. The settlement of Siberia took place not by the expulsion of the aboriginals, much less their extermination, but by the assimilation of vacant expanses by newcomers 'flowing around' the dwelling-places of the indigenous peoples, or sprinkling their settlements among the compact mass of aborigines. Peaceful colonization helped to create an atmosphere of good-neighbourliness and mutual enrichment of cultures.

According to this view there is a fundamental difference between this 'peaceful' settlement of Siberia by the Russians and the violent and destructive colonisation of other parts of the world by West European countries, which resulted in the annihilation of whole peoples and their cultures:

Nothing of this kind occurred during the assimilation of Northern Asia by the Russians. Even under the yoke of Tsarism and the corruption and arbitrary rule of the local administration, the Russian people and the aboriginal peoples of Siberia drew together in friendship.[3]

While the Russian peasantry serves as the generalised hero of this supposedly non-exploitative colonisation, the need for more identifiable heroic personages is filled by the commanders of Siberian expeditions of discovery. Far from condemning these representatives of the Russian state's aggressive

---

[3] *Opisaniye Tobolskogo namestnichestva*, A.D. Kolesnikov, ed., Novosibirsk, 1982, pp. 6–7, preface by A.P. Okladnikov.

thrust to the east, Communist Party writers subscribe to the spirit of Russian nationalism by adulation of the explorer–conquerors. Yermak occupies first place as the trail-blazer, and after him a whole pantheon of similar men (Penda, Moskvitin, Poyarkov, Dezhnyov, Khabarov and others) are celebrated as discoverers whose achievements are placed – with some justification – on a par with those of Columbus, Cabot, Magellan or Cortes. The official Soviet Russian view presents the rough and ready explorers of Siberia as upright men who aroused 'a sympathetic attitude among the local population'. So the 'great tasks of the state' associated with the 'economic assimilation' of the vast colony were carried out by

the simple, unassuming representatives of the working Russian people – the first discoverers of Siberia, our seventeenth-century explorers. The Russian state owes much to their energy and valour, to their wisdom and persistence, their noble patriotism based upon an understanding of the significance to the state of the annexation of Siberia, for without the active efforts of these representatives of the Russian people the incorporation of Siberia in such a short time and with such success would have been impossible.[4]

The truth is, however, that if these men were fired with a spirit of enterprise similar to that of their Portuguese, Spanish, Dutch or English counterparts, so also were they essentially adventurers of the same type – courageous but ruthless men-of-action, mainly belonging to the petty nobility. As such they sought above all fame and fortune, being drawn as irresistibly by the quest for sable furs as the Spanish conquistadores were by gold, and they and their crews were no better in their treatment of the native inhabitants of lands they discovered than were the voyagers from Western Europe in the Americas.[5]

RUSSIAN ADMINISTRATORS AND MERCHANTS

The Russia which Peter the Great inherited at the end of the seventeenth century was vastly greater than it had been a century before, having more than doubled its territory by expansion into northern Asia. The young Tsar, mobilising everyone and everything in Russia for his military ventures, appreciated the importance of Siberia and its resources – in the first place its fur tribute, which was essential for state finances. Knowing that this source of revenue, like all others, was subject to much depletion through the dishonesty of officials and merchants, Peter sought ways of preventing this. In his desire to overcome the inertia and obstructivism inherent in the old

---

[4] *Narody Sibiri*, pp. 120, 129.
[5] For an account of various Russian views of the conquest of Siberia, including recent studies which are more objective than those quoted here, see D.N. Collins, 'Russia's conquest of Siberia: evolving Russian and Soviet historical interpretations', *European Studies Review*, 1982, vol. XII, no. 1, pp. 18–43.

administrative system, the Tsar pinned his hopes on a structure of provinces and districts based on the modernised government system of Sweden.[6]

Unfortunately, the introduction of new institutions in itself could not alter radically the traditions of Russian officials, and the actual behaviour of governors and other officials in colonial Siberia during the eighteenth century was no different from that of *voyevodas* in the seventeenth century. The first governor of the new province, Prince M. Gagarin, was hanged in 1721 for a catalogue of crimes which included defrauding the government of profits from the China trade, nepotism, and the selling of offices and promotions to his subordinates for bribes. The division of Siberia into two provinces in 1736, with Irkutsk as the seat of the vice-governor of Eastern Siberia, offered further scope for peculation. The first Irkutsk vice-governor, Zholobov, amassed a huge fortune from bribes extorted from natives, Russian peasants and gentry alike, from contraband trade, and from withholding pay from the Cossacks, and his methods of extortion included torture. Zholobov was beheaded for his crimes. The lawlessness of Siberian officials went so far as armed resistance to government agents sent to arrest them, and in one case at least rival officials waged open war on each other. This happened in Irkutsk province in the 1760s, when the governor, Nemtsov, a notorious bribe-taker, quarrelled with the director of the Nerchinsk silver mines, Naryshkin.[7]

Agents sent from distant Petersburg to investigate such crimes themselves abused their special powers, as in the case of Krylov, an official with rank equivalent to major, who was sent to Irkutsk in 1758 to look into the suspected misappropriation by merchants of the tax on alcohol. Having cast seventy-four merchants into prison and subjected some of them to torture, Krylov extorted from them on his own account bribes on at least as large a scale as the loss sustained by the Treasury in the first place. Thereafter he assaulted the vice-governor, a major-general, and affixed his own name to the imperial double-headed eagle above the city tower to proclaim that he himself was now the ruler of Irkutsk province. Half a century later the nadir of corrupt administration in Siberia was reached under the governor-generalship of I.B. Pestel. Preferring to live in St Petersburg rather than Tobolsk, he left the conduct of Siberian affairs to the vice-governor Treskin – a man who earned the utmost notoriety not only for his vicious abuse of power, but for his ruthless suppression of any protests which the inhabitants of Siberia might try to send to the capital. When a petition against the gross injustice of this regime did eventually reach St Petersburg in 1818, the

---

[6] Klyuchevskiy, *Sochineniya*, vol. IV, pp. 187, 197–9; Timofeyev, *Pamyatniki*, vol. I, pp. 78, 196; Yadrintsev, *Sibir kak koloniya*, p. 300.
[7] *Istoriya Sibiri*, vol. II, pp. 137, 302, 308, 311; Solovyov, *Istoriya Rossii*, vol. VIII, pp. 494–6; vol. X, pp. 608–9; vol. XIV, pp. 22–3.

subsequent investigation carried out by M.M. Speranskiy resulted in the dismissal of Pestel and Treskin and the trial and punishment of the latter and forty-eight other officials. Over 300 others were charged with complicity in misrule, which was estimated to have cost the state over 2.8 million roubles.[8]

Whatever the Russian inhabitants of Siberia suffered from the misrule of Pestel and Treskin, its effects upon the inarticulate native peoples were as always incalculable. For instance, those living in the north, whose primitive economy had been so undermined by colonial rule that they were now dependent upon Russian grain, were starving because Treskin controlled and used for his own profit the grain provided by the government for distribution in time of need. Nearer the vice-governor's seat in Irkutsk, pressure brought to bear upon the chiefs of the Buryat Mongols in the collection of *yasak* resulted in Treskin's receiving 'gifts' of furs amounting to almost 86,000 roubles, which inevitably had been extorted from the rank-and-file Buryats.[9]

It was not only the official class who extracted great profit from the Siberian colony. From the very earliest days of Russian occupation private traders had played a large part in the penetration of Siberia and the exploitation of its natural resources. Profits extracted from the colony during the early part of the eighteenth century went mainly to the merchants of Moscow and Ustyug, such as the Grebenshchikovs, 'the scourge of the northern Ob region', who in the 1730s enjoyed a monopoly of trade in elk-skins with the Khanty and Nentsy. The abolition of internal customs barriers in 1753, however, led to a big development of private trade and manufacturing, and the merchant class – including the Pokhodyashins of Verkhoturye and Tobolsk, the Perevalovs of Tyumen, and the Sibiryakovs of Irkutsk – became a power in the land.[10]

Another milestone in Siberian commercial development was the ending of the Russian government's monopoly on trade with China in 1762. The organisation of China trade caravans by the Russian government ceased, and the transportation of goods between Siberian towns and Kiakhta (the only transit point on the Chinese border where trade was permitted) was thereafter carried out by private enterprise. The Chinese maintained their demand for furs, and it was the flourishing of this trade with China between the 1760s and 1820s which led Russian merchants to look further afield for

---

[8] *Entsiklopedicheskiy slovar*, vol. XXIX, pp. 810–11; *Istoriya Sibiri*, vol. II, pp. 306, 451–3, 457–60; Solovyov, *Istoriya Rossii*, vol. XII, pp. 592–3, 647; Yadrintsev, *Sibir kak koloniya*, pp. 301–15.

[9] Okun, 'K istorii Buryatii', p. 160; Yadrintsev, *Sibir kak koloniya*, pp. 305–15.

[10] *Entsiklopedicheskiy slovar*, vol. XXXIII, pp. 572, 578; *Istoriya Sibiri*, vol. II, pp. 93, 254–77, 305; vol. III, pp. 69–70.

new sources of pelts – an enterprise which eventually led to the extension of Russian colonialism into North America.[11]

The Asiatic connections of Russian Siberian merchants were not limited to China: as in the past, caravans from Bukhara, Khiva and Samarkand brought silk, brocade, spices, oil and carpets from Central Asia, Persia and India, and the inhabitants of Russian towns situated near the edge of the 'Kirgiz steppe', such as Tara, Tobolsk, Tyumen and Tomsk, included considerable numbers of 'Bukharans', as the Russians called all merchants from Central Asia. Until the eighteenth century the caravan routes had been made hazardous by wars between the nomadic peoples of the plains – the Nogais, Bashkirs, Oirat Mongols (Kalmyks), Kazaks and Kirgizes. The removal of the Kirgiz to Dzungaria in 1703, the establishment of friendly relations between the Russians and the Kazaks from 1731, the crushing of the Bashkirs in the 1730s to 1740s, and the defeat of the Oirats by the Chinese in the 1750s, all helped to make these routes safer, so that commerce with Central Asia developed considerably in the latter half of the century. The Kazak and Kalmyk nomads themselves played an important part in the economy of Siberia, since they provided the Russians with horses and cattle. The Kazaks were also instrumental in providing the human wares for the slave trade which existed in Siberia throughout the eighteenth century. The main centres of this trade were Tomsk, Tyumen and Tobolsk, and in Eastern Siberia, Yakutsk. Although the St Petersburg government from time to time decreed that the trade in 'boys and girls' must cease, this was contradicted by other decrees, such as that of 1757, which stated that 'The acquisition of purchase or barter ... of people of various nationalities brought by the Kirgiz [i.e. Kazaks], and their subsequent baptism as Christians, should not only not be prohibited but must be encouraged in view of the shortage of people in Siberia, and because greater efforts should be made to bring Mohammedans and idolators to the Orthodox Christian religion.'[12] Attempts made by officials to deprive slave-owners of their legal property evoked indignant protests as late as 1825, and although the final prohibition of slavery (as distinct from serfdom) was proclaimed in that year, the government found it difficult to eradicate deeply ingrained attitudes, especially among Russians of the commercial class, who continued to find ways of enslaving Siberian natives. Even at this period official policy was confused, and a law of 1825 ordered local authorities, because of the chronic lack of women in Siberia, to purchase girls from the native peoples as a means of providing wives for Russian settlers.[13]

[11] Entsiklopedicheskiy slovar, vol. XXX, p. 232; vol. XXXIII, p. 579; Istoriya Sibiri, vol. II, pp. 277–82. [12] Kolonialnaya politika ... na Kamchatke, pp. 8–9.
[13] Aziatskaya Rossiya, vol. I, p. 185; Entsiklopedicheskiy slovar, vol. XXIX, p. 810; vol. XXXIII, pp. 570, 578; Istoriya Sibiri, vol. II, pp. 259, 264–8, 273; S.S. Shashkov, Istoricheskiye etyudy, St Petersburg, 1872, vol. II, pp. 122–66; Yadrintsev, Sibir kak koloniya, pp. 12–13, 21, 280–1.

RUSSIAN PEASANTS AND INDUSTRIAL SERFS

The number of Russians living in Siberia increased from some 300,000 at the beginning of the eighteenth century to perhaps 900,000 at the end of the century. By the middle of the nineteenth century it had soared to about 2.7 million, and this figure was almost doubled by 1900. In 1911 the Russian inhabitants of the colony totalled almost 8 million. As the number of incomers increased, the relative proportion of indigenous people fell. Over Siberia as a whole the natives were already outnumbered by the immigrants at the end of the seventeenth century, and the ratio of natives to Russians remained approximately 1:3 throughout the eighteenth century.[14] Thereafter, however, the indigenous peoples fell to 21.5 per cent at the middle of the nineteenth century, and by 1911 only about 11.5 per cent of the inhabitants of Siberia belonged to the aboriginal peoples.[15]

Thus from about 1700 onward the population of Northern Asia included a large number of people originating in European Russia who, like the British, French and Spanish incomers in the Americas, settled and established families, and after a few generations considered the land in which they lived to be their home, and themselves to be native to it. The 'old Siberian' Russians, chiefly peasants, came to be known in Russia as *starozhily* – 'old inhabitants'. As a result of freedom from exploitation by *pomeshchiki*, many Russian peasants in Siberia attained a standard of living which was beyond the dreams of peasants in the central provinces of European Russia.

The 'old Siberians' evolved into a somewhat specific race of people with a reputation for toughness, independence of mind, self-reliance and initiative. Indeed, they have been compared with Americans, in that after a history of unremitting struggle with nature and aboriginal peoples, and the insecurity of frontier life, they enjoyed a similar sense of scope and freedom, the opportunity to prosper, and more democratic social relations than those who they had left behind in their countries of origin. By the same token, Siberian old settler society also provided opportunities for rapacious and callous individuals to exploit their poorer neighbours by involving them in debt.[16]

---

[14] Figures for the population of Siberia before the twentieth century vary considerably in different sources. In *Istoriya Sibiri*, vol II, pp. 55, 183–4, numbers are of male adults only ('souls' for taxation purposes), which must be multiplied by a factor of perhaps 4 to give the following approximate totals for men, women and children in 1795: natives 732,000 (31 per cent of total); Russians 1,648,000 (69 per cent of total); total 2,380,000. In official statistical accounts of Western and Eastern Siberia prepared about 1790 the numbers of inhabitants recorded are considerably less: natives 303,395 (32 per cent of total); Russians, etc. 639,966 (68 per cent of total); total 943,361. *Opisaniye Tobolskogo namestnichestva*, pp. 28, 34–5; *Opisaniye Irkutskogo namestnichestva 1792 goda*, O.N. Vilkov, A.D. Kolesnikov, M.P. Malysheva, eds., Novosibirsk, 1988, pp. 48–9.

[15] *Aziatskaya Rossiya*, vol. I, pp. 88–5; *Istoriya Sibiri*, vol. II, pp. 183–4, 363.

[16] *Aziatskaya Rossiya*, vol. I, p. 186; *Istoriya Sibiri*, vol. II, pp. 304, 315–16, 375, 435–9; vol. III, p. 151; Yadrintsev, *Sibir kak koloniya*, vol. I, pp. 59, 64–72.

An economic factor which had a significant effect on the Russian settlement of Siberia was the stimulus given to metallurgy by Peter the Great's demand for weapons of war. In Siberia this led to a switch of emphasis from furs to minerals. Iron and copper ores had been discovered in the Ural region as early as 1630, but it was not until 1696, when Peter received samples of high-quality ore from the basin of the river Neyva north of present-day Sverdlovsk, that the exploitation of the mineral resources of the Urals began in earnest. The initiative for this was provided in the first place by N. Demidov, a gunsmith from Tula, and by the 1730s the land on the south-eastern flank of the Ural mountains had become the biggest mining and metallurgy region in the Russian Empire, with the newly founded city of Yekaterinburg as its administrative centre. It was also on Demidov's initiative that another important metal-working region was opened up in the 1720s – the Kolyvan district in the northern foothills of the Altai mountains, where not only iron and copper but also lead and zinc ores were found. As further mining concessions were granted to Demidov at Barnaul on the river Ob, and on the coal seams of Kuznetsk on the Tom, he eventually became virtual ruler of a huge area measuring some 250 miles from north to south and 130 miles from east to west, lying on the recently conquered southern frontier of Siberia, in territory inhabited by the Turkic tribes of the Altai such as Teleuts and Shors.[17]

The scale of Demidov's mining enterprise, and the discovery of silver and gold in his vast domains, eventually caused the government concern, and in 1744 the Altai works were taken over by the Treasury as the preserve of the Royal Family – the 'Lands of His/Her Imperial Majesty's Cabinet' – in which no private enterprise was permitted. Under royal management the territory of the Cabinet lands was greatly extended, so that by the end of the eighteenth century it embraced the whole southern half of Tomsk province – an area larger than Spain or France.

In 1786 another region of Siberia was made the personal preserve of the reigning monarch – the silver mines near Nerchinsk east of Lake Baikal. Here silver and lead-bearing ores were first discovered about 1700 and mining engineers were sent by Peter the Great to exploit them. In order to provide labour for them, Russian peasant families were forcibly settled at the mines, and from 1722 onward convicts from the prisons of European Russia were sent, so that thenceforth the labour force of the Nerchinsk mines consisted partly of convicts and partly of industrial serfs. The Nerchinsk mines became notorious in the last decades of the nineteenth century, when they came to be used as hard-labour prisons for political prisoners.[18]

---

[17] *Istoriya Sibiri*, vol. II, p. 228; Kalesnik, *Sovetskiy Soyuz. Ural*, pp. 75–6; Klyuchevskiy, *Sochineniya*, vol. IV, pp. 120–1.

[18] *Aziatskaya Rossiya*, vol. I, pp. 407–8; L.M. Goryushkin, ed., *Ssylka i katorga v Sibiri (XVII–nachalo XX v.)*, Novosibirsk, 1975, pp. 40–5; *Istoriya Sibiri*, vol. II, pp. 228–52; G. Kennan, *Siberia and the Exile System*, New York, 1891, vol. II, pp. 279–80.

6

THE EIGHTEENTH CENTURY

AS the Russians continued their take-over of Northern Asia during the eighteenth century, the life of the native peoples was gradually, but irrevocably, altered without regard for their wishes or rights.

The most persistent opposition to the invaders was maintained in the region where the Russian conquest began – the southern Urals. In the almost continuous wars which went on in this region during the seventeenth and eighteenth centuries the Russians were opposed by three main ethnic communities: The Bashkirs, the Kazaks and the Oirats.

In order to get away from the Russians after the fall of Kazan in 1552, many Bashkirs had migrated eastward beyond the Urals. As Russian peasants also increasingly came to settle in the forests and wooded steppe of what they considered to be Tobolsk province, they encroached more and more on the Bashkirs' grazing and hunting lands, and many conflicts developed. Moreover, as mines and metallurgical works were established, and the towns of Yekaterinburg and Chelyabinsk were founded, the survival of the Bashkirs and their Islamic religion were threatened by the ever-growing Russian presence in their midst. In their struggle to preserve their independence the Bashkirs frequently received help from the Kazaks – the large and powerful nomadic conglomeration of Turkic clans which dominated the steppe between the Urals and the river Ob.

Typical incidents included a petition sent to the Tsar in 1700 by Bashkirs complaining about Russian peasants who were poaching fish and beavers from their rivers and lakes, cutting down their trees, along with the wild bee-hives on which they depended for honey, and killing game of all kinds. Another typical complaint was that Russians had established a new village among the Bashkirs and then sought to drive them out by terror and murder. In retaliation for such acts Bashkirs often attacked Russian settlements as, for instance, in 1709 when their horsemen besieged a Russian district near

Tyumen, drove away all the cattle, killed many of the Russian settlers and burned their dwellings. In another similar incident Bashkir warriors with guns and bows and arrows, after plundering a Russian village spared one of the peasants to carry back to the nearest Russian fort the message that it would soon be attacked by a large horde of Kazaks. Whether this threat came to anything or not, such rumours of imminent attack by the Kazaks and their allies the Karakalpaks were frequently put about by the Bashkirs, as was the story that Khan Kuchum himself was returning to reconquer the Siberian khanate which he had lost to the Russians more than a century before.[1]

The Russians on their side mounted many punitive expeditions against the Bashkirs, in which their settlements were destroyed, many men killed, and women and children captured as slaves. For the suppression of Bashkir revolts the Russians sometimes enlisted the help of another nomadic tribe of the steppes – the Kalmyks. These were a part of the West Mongolian Torgut tribe which had broken away from the Oirats in 1618 and migrated westward to pastures on the Yaik and Volga. For over a hundred years the Kalmyks alternately raided the southern borderlands of Russia and volunteered to be peaceful vassals of the Tsar. The presence of the Buddhist Kalmyks south of the Urals sometimes provided the Russian government with a useful buffer against the raiding Kazaks, but on many occasions the Kalmyks themselves proved to be unreliable allies. Nevertheless, in 1708 the khan of the Kalmyks, Ayuka, was persuaded to provide 2000 warriors to help the Russians crush a large Bashkir rebellion proclaimed as a holy war of Islam. On another occasion, after the flight of 50,000 Bashkir insurgents to the steppe in 1755, it was the Kazaks who were invited by the Russian governor to deal with them by hunting them down and enslaving those whom they did not kill.[2]

Despite such drastic operations against the Bashkirs they continued to rebel at frequent intervals, making the southern Urals insecure for Russian settlers and mine-workers during most of the eighteenth century. But the advance of Russian colonisation, both official and unofficial, was inexorable, and the strength of its Muslim opponents on the south-western edge of Siberia was steadily eroded. A significant stage in the suppression of resistance to the Russians was the creation during 1733–44 of a double line of forts which stretched from the Volga to the new fortress of Orenburg on the river Yaik and ran along the eastern side of the Urals. The effect of this was to put a barrier between the Bashkirs and their old allies the Kazaks, so that the former were deprived of assistance from the steppe in their struggle

[1] Timofeyev, *Pamyatniki*, vol. I, pp. 75, 78–80, 150, 327–65, 368, 393.
[2] Shashkov, *Istoricheskiye etyudy*, vol. II, pp. 126–7; Solovyov, *Istoriya Rossii*, vol. VIII, pp. 173–5.

against the Russian colonisation of their territory during the second half of the eighteenth century.[3]

The eighteenth century also saw the Russians consolidating and pushing forward their steppe frontier in the face of the Kazaks. The numerous Kazak clans fell into three large groups. The Great or Elder Horde had its base between the river Irtysh and the T'ien-Shan mountains, bordering on the territory of the Oirats of Western Mongolia – Dzungaria; while the Middle Horde occupied territory to the west of this as far as the Aral Sea, and the Lesser or Younger Horde inhabited pastures which stretched from there to the river Yaik, beyond which lived the Kalmyks. The migration routes and pastures of the Kazaks, however vast, were thus limited both on the west and east by Oirat Mongol territories, and conflicts with these were frequent. During the seventeenth century the power of the Kazak khans was waning because of disunity among them, at the same time as that of the Oirats of Dzungaria was growing. As a result, early in the eighteenth century the Elder Horde was forced to acknowledge the suzerainty of the Dzungarian Khan while the Middle and Younger Hordes were pushed farther to the north and west, thus increasing the turmoil in the southern Urals. Seeking support from another quarter against the onslaught of the Oirats, the Kazak khans in 1717 offered to become subjects of the Tsar. Peter The Great did not respond to this approach, but in 1732 the Younger Horde swore allegiance to the Empress Anna, and two years later the Middle Horde did the same. The principal gain for Russia from these agreements was peace to push the frontier of their Empire forward into the steppe. In the 1730s forts were built to form a west–east line of defences from the upper Yaik to Omsk, and this line was pushed farther south in the 1750s. Behind this line the Russians began to colonise the fertile northern stretches of the Kazak steppe[4] in relative safety. At the same time a degree of security was obtained for traffic on the caravan routes connecting Russia with the Islamic khanates of Central Asia.[5]

THE TATARS OF WESTERN SIBERIA

In the eighteenth century those descendants of the Tatars of the Sibir khanate who had made their home within the southern margin of the taiga or in the wooded steppe, formed several social and geographical communities. A relatively small number of Tatars who entered the service of the Tsar at the time of the Russian conquest in a military or administrative capacity were

---

[3] *Entsiklopedicheskiy slovar*, vol. III, pp. 228–9; vol. XV, pp. 745–6.
[4] It is confusing that until the early twentieth century the Russians used the name Kirgiz for the Kazaks and called this region the Kirgiz steppe.
[5] *Entsiklopedicheskiy slovar*, vol. XV, p. 96; Nusupbekov, *Istoriya Kazakhskoy SSR*, vol. II, pp. 264, 287.

classed as 'service Tatars' and were paid accordingly, whereas the majority who remained separate from their conquerors were subjected to *yasak* and labour obligations in conformity with Russian colonial practice. As in all cases of 'service' status for native peoples, this ceased to exist once their military function became unimportant to the Russian state. Thereafter the rank and file fell into the same fiscal category as other Tatars, while a handful of the native leaders – *mirzas* – were absorbed into the Russian gentry class. While conversion to Orthodox Christianity was not at first made a condition for the *mirzas'* retention of their privileges, the fact that Muslim land-owners possessed Orthodox Russian serfs was not acceptable to Peter the Great, who therefore decreed in 1715 that unless such Tatar lords renounced Islam their estates and peasants would be confiscated by the state. Within the Siberian Tatar community two groups were looked upon as incomers with special status. One of these was the Bukharis – merchants and craftsmen living chiefly in Tyumen and Tara who maintained trading links between the Russian Empire and the khanates of Central Asia. The Bukharis, who stood out among the Siberian Tatars for their urbanity, relative loyalty to the Russian government, and literacy in Arabic and Persian, not only formed the nucleus of a business middle class, but also helped to maintain cultural contacts with Bukhara and other centres of Islamic culture. The other special group among the Siberian Tatars were those who moved from Kazan and the Volga region during the eighteenth and nineteenth centuries in order to escape the social and religious pressures exerted on that region by the Russians.[6]

Geographically the Siberian Tatars fell into several communities. Around the old Tatar towns of Tyumen, Yalutor and Tobolsk in the eighteenth century lived some 15,000 Tatars, including over 300 'service men' and over 800 Bukharis. The city of Tobolsk itself had contained a considerable Tatar and Bukhari community until the period of intensive persecution of Islam in the reign of the Empress Elizabeth. At that time Metropolitan Silvestr, as well as coercing Tatars to renounce Islam by imprisonment and beatings, had a new church built in close proximity to the Tatar quarter in Tobolsk. As a result, most of the Muslims moved out, so that in the late eighteenth century no Tatars resided in the Russian – and Orthodox Christian – capital of Siberia. A distinctive community who lived near Tobolsk were the 'swamp Tatars' (in Russian *zabolotnyye*). These were the descendants of Tatars of the Siberian khanate who after its conquest in the sixteenth century took refuge in the swampy region lying just to the north-west of Tobolsk. Here they lived chiefly by catching fish and waterfowl in the numerous rivers and lakes, although they also engaged in some agriculture and hunted elk and other forest animals. The Tatars who lived along the Irtysh upstream from

[6] *Istoriya Sibiri*, vol. II, p. 94; *Opisaniye Tobolskogo namestnichestva*, pp. 113–14, 297; Solovyov, *Istoriya Rossii*, vol. VIII, pp. 568–9.

Tobolsk had a similar way of life. Here in the city of Tara, the chief point of communication between Russian Siberia and Central Asia, with its large Bukhari population, conflict between Russians and Muslims was greatly exacerbated by Peter the Great's decree of 1722 requiring all subjects to swear an oath of allegiance to the Tsar. In the rebellion which broke out because of this some 500 houses were destroyed in Tara, and the Russians used the most savage punishments such as decapitation and impalement, in order to 'pacify' their Asiatic subjects.[7]

Farther east, from the Irtysh to the upper Ob at Novosibirsk, stretches the wooded steppe of Baraba with its hundreds of lakes and marshes. Here the Tatars preserved their independence throughout the seventeenth century, maintaining contacts with the Kalmyks and migrating to more southerly pastures whenever the Russians attempted to subjugate them. In the eighteenth century most were nomadic pastoralists with herds of cattle, sheep and horses, and although many of them were later obliged to abandon their old way of life and settle down to agriculture, seasonal migrations required the Baraba Tatars to preserve a certain degree of nomadism even in the early days of the twentieth century. In the south the woods of Baraba gave way to the open grasslands of the Kulunda steppe lying between the Irtysh and the Altai mountains. The ostensible reason for the construction of a line of military outposts in this region by the Russians – Tara, Omsk, Kainsk and other forts – was to protect the Baraba Tatars from the Kazaks.[8]

While it is undeniable that in the seventeenth and eighteenth centuries the Kazaks were not above raiding vulnerable prey, it is also true that, being as dependent as any other nomadic people upon trade with settled communities, the Kazaks normally had a working relationship with the Tatars as their source of furs and other forest products. A traditional pattern of trade and tribute existed which was destroyed by the intrusion of the Russians into this region. In the early eighteenth century, moreover, the Kazaks found themselves under pressure from the Oirat Mongols of Dzungaria, who laid claim to the Irtysh steppe-lands of Kulunda and Baraba, and indeed subjected the Baraba Tatars to tribute in addition to that demanded of them by the Russians. The advances of the Russians and the Oirats could not but stir up unrest in Kazakstan, and it is not altogether surprising that the Kazaks attempted to reassert their rights in the Baraba steppe by attacking Russian settlements there. The line of forts built by the Russians in the 1730s made Russian settlement in the wooded steppe zone safer, but did so little to cut off Baraba from steppe influences that it was only after this, in the 1740s, at the very time when Russian persecution of Muslims was being intensified,

---

[7] *Opisaniye Tobolskogo namestnichestva*, pp. 39–40, 68; *Narody Sibiri*, pp. 475–8; Solovyov, *Istoriya Rossii*, vol. XII, pp. 120–1.

[8] S.V. Bakhrushin, 'Sibirskiye sluzhilye tatary v XVIII v.', in his *Nauchnye trudy*, vol. III, pt. 2, p. 175; *Narody Sibiri*, p. 478.

that the Baraba Tatars were converted from shamanist religion to Islam. The Bashkir uprisings and Pugachov rebellion of the 1770s also had their repercussions in the Baraba steppe, where unrest among the Tatars did not subside for several years.[9]

Less accessible to contacts with the Kazak steppe were the 'Tatar' communities of the small areas of steppe-land to the east of the Ob, between the edge of the taiga and the Altai-Sayan mountain ranges. Here many of the Tatar clans in the vicinity of Tomsk – the Chat and Eushta – had entered Russian service as auxiliaries, and assisted in the conquest of neighbouring territories situated to the east and south which were inhabited by the Teleuts, the Yenisey Kirgiz and their vassals. The Tomsk Tatars were augmented by refugees from Kuchum's khanate, who brought Islamic religion with them. Further east, among the Turkic tribes living in the valleys of the Kiya and Chulym, the prevailing ethnic element was probably Samoyed or Ket, and Islam never ousted shamanism here. The way of life of the Chulym Tatars also differed from that of the Baraba and Tomsk Tatars in being based not on nomadism but on the forest occupations of hunting, fishing and gathering cedar-pine nuts, and during the eighteenth century the Chulym Tatars began to practise agriculture under the influence of Russian peasant settlers.[10]

Although Russian military forces made their presence felt in the southern frontier zone of Western Siberia during most of the eighteenth century, and the strong arm of colonial administration reached out to exact *yasak* and to oppress the Muslims in the towns, there was little colonisation by Russian settlers beyond the forest margin. Most of the Tatars were left largely to their own devices, except for those who lived in the valleys of the big rivers, which remained for long the only highways of practical value to the Russians in their comings and goings in Siberia. However, the south–north alignment of the navigable rivers of Siberia limited their usefulness, and in the eighteenth century the Russian imperial government conceived the need for easier and swifter east–west communications across Siberia. A system of post-stations set up in the 1740s to link the line of forts across the Baraba steppe was the prelude to the creation in the 1760s of the Moscow–Siberian highroad, known as the *trakt* – which was a great achievement for the Russian colonists, but a disaster for the Tatars and other peoples of south-western Siberia. It was through their territory that the new land route was driven from Tyumen by way of Ishim and Tukalinsk to the Irtysh and thence

[9] *Entsiklopedicheskiy slovar*, vol. XIII, p. 940; *Istoriya Sibiri*, vol. II, p. 321; *Narody Sibiri*, p. 478; Nusupbekov, *Istoriya Kazakhskoy SSR*, vol. II, pp. 184–280; *Opisaniye Tobolskogo namestnichestva*, pp. 67, 84, 191, 298; Solovyov, *Istoriya Rossii*, vol. XII, pp. 120–1; Timofeyev, *Pamyatniki*, vols. I, pp. 516–17, 522; II, pp. 66–7, 148; Yadrintsev, *Sibir kak koloniya*, p. 113.

[10] *Narody Sibiri*, pp. 393–5, 475; V.V. Radlov, *Aus Sibirien*, Leipzig, 1884, vol. I, pp. 180–1; Timofeyev, *Pamyatniki*, vol. I, pp. 18, 108, 137 and passim.

across the Baraba steppe via Kainsk to the Ob. From there, by-passing Tomsk, the *trakt* cut across the Chulym steppe by way of Mariinsk and Achinsk to reach Krasnoyarsk on the Yenisey. The effects of this major development – the first trans-Siberian highway – were quickly felt. Russian posts and villages appeared all along the *trakt*, and the forest and steppe lands lying to either side became accessible to the operations of Russian officials, clergymen, merchants and peasants. In the Baraba steppe in particular the government took the first step in Russian colonisation by setting up villages along the highway for people exiled from European Russia. By the end of the eighteenth century the Tatars, who numbered about 39,000, were outnumbered ten to one by some 400,000 Russians living in the Tatar territories of Western Siberia.[11]

THE ALTAI-SAYAN BORDERLANDS OF MONGOLIA

While the Siberian Tatars who lived on the northern edge of the Kazak steppe had come under Russian occupation from the end of the sixteenth century, the Turkic peoples of the Altai-Sayan region were not conquered for at least another hundred years, and some of them very much more recently. It was only in the reign of Peter the Great that the Russian Empire, whose frontier in the vicinity of Tomsk, Kuznetsk and Krasnoyarsk had been more or less static for almost a hundred years, was able to push forward again towards the south, tempted principally by the mineral wealth of the Altai.[12]

The indigenous peoples of the Altai-Sayan region were referred to by the Mongols as *Uriyangkhai*, and in the eighteenth century the Russians adopted this term, especially with regard to the natives of Tuva.[13] The Altai-Sayan peoples fell into two groups according to their way of life. Those whose home was the taiga of the mountain ranges lived chiefly by hunting and fishing, and their dwellings ranged from primitive lean-to shelters or bark-covered wigwams to simple log cabins. At the time of the Russian conquest most of those living east of the Yenisey – the Asans, Baikots, Kotts, Kamasins, Motors, Karagas and others – still spoke dialects of Ket or Samoyed. The Altai region to the west of the Yenisey, however, had for long been subject to Turkic influence, so that, despite their Samoyedic ethnic origins the Kumandin, Chelkan, Tubalar, Shor and other communities had already adopted Turkic speech. The other way of life followed in the Altai-Sayan region was nomadic pastoralism, combined in some places with

---

[11] Figures derived from *Opisaniye Tobolskogo namestnichestva*; *Istoriya Sibiri*, vol. II, pp. 191, 268–9, 273; Yadrintsev, *Sibir kak koloniya*, p. 132.
[12] *Istoriya Sibiri*, vol. II, pp. 44–6.
[13] B.P. Gurevich, *Mezhdunarodnye otnosheniya v Tsentralnoy Azii v XVII – pervoy polovine XIX v.*, Moscow, 1979, p. 66; M. Vasmer, *Russisches etymologisches Wörterbuch*, Heidelberg, 1953–8, vol. III, p. 189.

rudimentary agriculture. These nomads with their herds of cattle, sheep and horses roamed the open grasslands, and lived in the felt-covered yurts which were used throughout Turkestan and Mongolia. Once again some of these communities, such as the Chats, Eushta, Kyzyl, Kachin, Arin and Koibal were probably of Samoyed or Ket origin, but by the seventeenth century they were entirely Turkicised in language and way of life. A kind of aristocracy among these nomadic tribes was formed by the Kirgiz in the Yenisey valley and the Teleuts of the Kulunda steppe and Altai, each of which acted as tribute-gatherers on behalf of their Mongol overlords.

Culturally, one community stood out among the inhabitants of the Altai. These were the 'Blacksmith Tatars', in whose territory on the middle course of the river Tom the Russian fort of Kuznetsk was founded in 1608. They had no general name for themselves until after 1917, when the name of one clan, Shor, was adopted for the whole people. With facial features said to be most reminiscent of the Khanty-Mansi of north-west Siberia, the Shors also showed their Siberian affinities in one particular feature of their shamanist religion – the bear cult. The climate of the whole Altai-Sayan region is influenced by its position close to the very centre of Asia (which is in Tuva). It therefore has very cold winters and quite warm summers, and rain and snow-fall is heavy, so that movement about the dense forest is very difficult in winter. Under these conditions the agricultural methods of the Shors were very primitive. On the other hand, they were famed for their skill in metal-working, and they relied on trading their iron products – swords, spear and arrow-heads, armour, harness, cooking pots etc. – for the cattle, horses and other necessities of life which the pastoral nomads could provide. To the Yenisey Kirgiz, the Shors were very useful vassals.[14]

When the Russians first entered the Altai-Sayan region, the Kirgiz, consisting of the Altysary, Yezer, Altyr and Tuba clans, occupied the steppe-lands of the upper Yenisey valley, particularly to the west of the river, as far as the Alatau and Abakan mountains. From their capital, a stone-built town on the upper Chulym, the Kirgiz khans imposed their rule over an area as large as Poland, requiring allegiance and tribute from vassals who ranged from the Samoyedic Motors in the Sayan foothills to the Arin and Asan Kets who lived as far north as the Angara confluence, and the Shors and other peoples of the Altai. Conflict with the Russians began in the first decade of the seventeenth century, when the latter began to probe southward from Tomsk and Yeniseysk, also demanding tribute from the local tribes. The Achin and Kyzyl tribes on the middle Chulym, following the example of the Eushta and Chat Tatars, submitted to the invaders in 1623. As the Russians established themselves on the Yenisey and began the construction of

[14] *Istoriya Sibiri*, vol. I, p. 362; *Narody Sibiri*, pp. 492–517; L.P. Potapov, *Ocherki po istorii altaytsev*, 2nd edn, Moscow, 1953, p. 172; L.P. Potapov, *Ocherki po istorii Shorii*, Moscow, 1936, p. 12; Radlov, *Aus Sibirien*, vol. I, pp. 188, 346, 358.

Krasnoyarsk fort among the Kachas and Arins, the Kirgiz tried to prevent the defection of these tribes by forcing many of them to move away to the south. Nevertheless the Arins and Kachas returned to their home pastures and submitted to Russian *yasak*. As a result of this defiance of their former masters these tribes were subjected to punitive raids by the Kirgiz and, like their neighbours the Kyzyls, were sometimes forced to provide them with warriors. The Russians were therefore unable to extort regular tribute from the Arins and Kachas until the 1650s, and even as late as 1678 the latter were again forced to move from their pastures when the Kirgiz made one of their not infrequent attacks on Krasnoyarsk.[15]

In another direction, Russian incursions up the river Kan in 1630 in quest of fur tribute from the Kets, Kamasins and Motors, led to war on a significant scale, since they came up against not only the Tuba Kirgiz, but also *yasak*-collectors sent into the Sayan region by two rival Mongol rulers – the Altan Khan and the Taiji of the Oirats.

DZUNGARIA

The political forces at work in this region of Inner Asia were complex. At its western end, Inner Asia is divided into three lobes by high mountain ranges which bound it in the west. The middle lobe lying between the T'ien Shan and the Mongolian Altai is relatively open towards the west, with gaps between the mountains affording access to the steppes of Kazakstan in the vicinity of Lake Balkhash. It was this middle lobe that provided pastures for the West Mongolian tribes known collectively as the Oirats, and later as the Dzungarians. Despite the subjugation of the Khalkhas of Eastern Mongolia by the Manchu-Chinese at the end of the seventeenth century, the Oirats not only succeeded in holding out against China for more than a hundred years, but extended their own empire for a time into Eastern Turkestan and Central Asia, and even as far as Tibet. At the same time they had to face the advance of the Russian Empire from the north. In that direction the Oirats claimed that their territory extended far down the Irtysh into the Baraba steppe, while in the Ob–Yenisey region their boundaries embraced the whole mountainous land of the Altai and Sayan.[16]

Although north-western Mongolia was clearly the domain of the Altan Khan, from the 1630s its borderlands were subjected to infiltration by Russians who attempted to subjugate the eastern extremity of what is now called Tuva. A Russian *yasak* gang operating 'beyond the Mongol moun-

[15] S.V. Bakhrushin, 'Yeniseyskiye kirgizy v XVII v.', in his *Nauchnye trudy*, vol. III, pt. 2, pp. 176–205; Dolgikh, *Rodovoy i plemennoy sostav*, pp. 223–47; Timofeyev, *Pamyatniki*, vol. I, p. 12.

[16] *Entsiklopedicheskiy slovar*, vol. XXXVIII, p. 808; Gurevich, *Mezhdunarodnye otnosheniya*, pp. 17, 20, 48, 57, 60; *Narody Sibiri*, p. 423; *Istoriya Mongolskoy Narodnoy Respubliki*, pp. 180, 586–7.

5 A shaman of the Tuva people, with feather head-dress, coat decked with dangling straps and chains, and large drum which is beaten with a fur-covered stick. The tent is a typical *ger* of felt over a wooden frame, of the kind used by the Mongols and all other nomadic peoples of Inner Asia. (c. 1900).

tains' was annihilated in 1663 by Tuva people, and the official limit of Russian expansion between the Yenisey and Lake Baikal until the twentieth century did not move beyond the northern slopes of the Sayan range.

During the seventeenth century the recurrent warfare between the Mongol khans had its repercussions upon the native peoples of the Sayan and Altai. The Altan Khan Ombo Erdene claimed suzerainty over the Sayan and the Yenisey valley with their Turkic population, and in the early 1620s he made an alliance with the Khalka Mongols and the Kazaks in an attempt to restrain the growing power of the Oirats in this region. It was when the latter united in 1635 as the Dzungarian khanate, that the Altan Khan offered allegiance to the Tsar. However, this was only a temporary move. Russians had been trading with the Oirats on the Irtysh since 1613, and it was in fact they who were favoured by the Russians in 1647, when they were permitted to trade with the towns of Siberia. At mid-century some of the native peoples of the upper Yenisey and Altai, including the Shors, were being subjected to demands for *yasak* from three overlords – the Altan Khan, the Oirats and the Russians. Even some of the Kirgiz, who were vassals of the Oirats, were forced to pay tribute to the Altan Khan at this time. Others chose rather to submit (temporarily) to the Russians, while many of the Tuba clan withdrew into the relative safety of the upper Abakan valley or across the Sayan mountains. The turmoil caused by the rivalry between these two groups of Mongols was resolved in 1667 when the last Altan Khan was annihilated by the Oirats, who then, with the assistance of the Kirgiz, went on to besiege Krasnoyarsk. The Oirats also turned their attention to the former vassals of the Altan Khan in the western part of Tuva – the Baikot and Motor – whom they subjected in 1670.

Meanwhile the Kirgiz under Yerenyak resumed their struggle against the Russians and carried it on vigorously throughout the last three decades of the century. It required a large Russian army (including Kacha auxiliaries) to defeat the Kirgiz prince Shandychka in a war on the River Kan in 1690–2, during which the Tuba clan was practically wiped out. To mark the success of this operation the Russian commander had Shandychka's head carried back to Tomsk on a spear. As raids on the Tomsk district continued nevertheless, another Russian assault was launched against Yerenyak in 1700, and in the following year the Russians inflicted a decisive defeat on the Kirgiz in their main stronghold in the Abakan steppe. As a result, the Kirgiz called for a truce and made a promise (which remained unfulfilled) to give hostages and pay *yasak* to the Russians.

In 1703 the Kirgiz, who had played a vital part in holding the Russians at bay on the upper Yenisey, suddenly ceased to exist as a political force. Already weakened by Russian attacks, they were now denied the support of the Oirats, whose Khan, Tseven Rabdan, was preoccupied with rebuilding the strength of Dzungaria after the disastrous eastern campaign of his predecessor Galdan, so that he could renew the fight against the Manchu-Chinese. In order to avoid conflict with Russia at this time, Tseven Rabdan forced most of his Kirgiz vassals to migrate out of the Yenisey valley and establish themselves in Dzungaria south of Lake Balkhash on the river Ili.[17]

The departure of the Kirgiz gave the Russian government the freedom of movement in the Altai-Sayan region which it had long desired. Its isolated outpost of Kuznetsk was made secure, and further forts were built at Biysk (1709), Kolyvan (1713), and Barnaul (1739), in order to consolidate Russian rule over the northern Altai with its Turkic population and its valuable mines. However, the Dzungarians had not intended to relinquish their rights over the Altai-Sayan territories permanently. Tseven Rabdan, inspired by the seductive memory of the world empire of Chingis Khan, was bent upon the territorial aggrandisement of his realm. He therefore indulged recklessly in wars against China, the Central Asian khanates and Russia. Laying claim to all the land in the Sayan, Altai and Irtysh regions which the Russians had seized during the preceding century, the Dzungars raided Kuznetsk district

[17] Bakhrushin, 'Yeniseyskiye kirgizy', pp. 207–24; Bawden, *Modern History of Mongolia*, pp. 49–50, 63; Dolgikh, *Rodovoy i plemennoy sostav*, pp. 223, 233–4, 237, 241–2, 264–7, 298; Gurevich, *Mezhdunarodnye otnosheniya*, pp. 31–2, 35, 52–55; *Istoriya Sibiri*, vol. II, pp. 37–8, 44–6; *Istoriya Mongolskoy Narodnoy Respubliki*, p. 199; *Narody Sibiri*, pp. 383, 423–4; Nusupbekov, *Istoriya Kazakhskoy SSR*, vol. II, pp. 287–9; Potapov, *Ocherki po istorii Shorii*, p. 16; Solovyov, *Istoriya Rossii*, vol. VI, pp. 584–5; Timofeyev, *Pamyatniki*, vol. I, pp. 3, 5–6, 9–23, 52–4, 69–72, 136–42, 190, 233–4, 237–8, 243–5.

in 1709. Despite this, the imperious material needs of Tseven's western counterpart, Peter the Great, led to a provocative intrusion into Dzungarian territory on the Irtysh by a large Russian military expedition in search of gold. No gold was found, but it was as a result of this expedition and the Oirats' armed opposition to it that the Russian forts of Omsk, Pavlodar, Semipalatinsk and Ust-Kamenogorsk were founded along the Irtysh between 1716 and 1720. By installing themselves on the banks of the Irtysh, the Russians began their annexation of the Teleuts' territory lying between it and the Ob. Tseven Rabdan, hard-pressed by the Chinese, was unable to offer a serious challenge to Russian aggression at this time. However, in order not to lose vassals, the Dzungarians again resorted to deportation. Some Teleuts were forced to move from their home pastures on the Ob to Dzungarian territory south of the Irtysh, while others chose to submit to the Russians. This split in the allegiance of the Teleuts led to a cultural division which persisted until the nineteenth century.

The Oirats' long drawn-out fight against the Ch'ing Empire reached its tragic culmination in mid-century. The death in 1745 of the last powerful ruler of the Oirats, Galdan Tseren, left the country a prey to civil war, and in 1756, with the self-interested collaboration of the Dzungarian renegade Amursana, the Manchu-Chinese launched a decisive campaign to subdue this remote and insubordinate corner of their empire. The punishment inflicted upon the Dzungarians for their former defiance of the Manchus was genocide: during 1755–6 about 1 million of the Mongol and Turkic inhabitants of Dzungaria – the majority of its population – were slaughtered by the Chinese. To escape this fate thousands of Dzungarians fled south towards Kashgaria and Tibet, or north towards Russian Siberia. In the latter case their lot was far from enviable, since, like any other 'heathens', they were considered by Russian officials in the frontier districts to be fair game for extortion. Those Oirats who consented to become Christians were allowed to enter Russian territory and were sent to join the Kalmyks on the Volga, but those who would not abandon their Buddhist religion were abused and robbed by the Russians and then sent back destitute to survive or perish as they might in the steppe. The Kazaks frequently played a part in the harassment of the Oirat refugees by raiding them during their flight and capturing women and children for delivery to the slave-markets of Siberia.[18]

---

[18] Bawden, *Modern History of Mongolia*, pp. 113–16; Dolgikh, *Rodovoy i plemennoy sostav*, p. 115; *Entsiklopedicheskiy slovar*, vol. XXXVIII, p. 809; Gurevich, *Mezhdunarodnye otnosheniya*, pp. 66, 70–1, 77–8, 85, 98–100, 102–19, 122, 126–8; *Istoriya Mongolskoy Narodnoy Respubliki*, pp. 216–17; *Istoriya Sibiri*, vol. II, pp. 40–1, 182, 185; Shashkov, *Istoricheskiye etyudy*, vol. II, pp. 127–46; Solovyov, *Istoriya Rossii*, vol. XII, p. 389; Yadrintsev, *Sibir kak koloniya*, p. 89.

RUSSO-CHINESE CONFRONTATION IN THE ALTAI

The destruction of the Oirat Khanate of Dzungaria by the Manchus, and the annexation of its territory to the Chinese Empire, was matched by a further Russian advance into north-western Mongolia. In 1756 the Empress Elizabeth's government seized the opportunity presented by the turmoil in the Altai to decree the annexation to the Russian Empire of its southern, mountainous region, including the headwaters of the Ob in the basins of the Katun-Chuya and Biya-Chulyshman rivers, with its native population of Altaians, Telengits and Tölös. At the same time a further stretch of the upper Yenisey gorge and the valley of its right tributary, the Us, were also occupied by the Russians. Thus, as a result of their respective territorial conquests in the Altai-Sayan region, the Chinese and Russian Empires now faced each other directly across a frontier which stretched continuously for almost 3,000 miles from the Irtysh to the Sea of Okhotsk. Most of this frontier had been clearly established by treaty, but at its western end in the Altai, the frontier markers stopped at the river Abakan. As the Manchu-Chinese proceeded with their annihilation of the Dzungarians, the Russian government was careful to maintain a stance of non-intervention, while in fact accepting the allegiance of an increasing number of Altaian *zaisangs* as they fled from Chinese oppression. More of these Teleuts – wrongly called 'White Kalmyks' by the Russians – would have submitted to the latter if they had not imposed the severe condition that they must go to join the Kalmyks on the Volga – a Mongolian people with whom the Teleuts and other Turkic peoples of the Altai had nothing in common. The Chinese on their part considered that the Altai and all of its native inhabitants, as a former vassal territory of the Oirats, belonged by right of conquest to them. Accordingly, between 1753 and 1758 detachments of Chinese troops repeatedly made raids across the mountains into the valleys of the Chulyshman, Bashkaus and Chuya rivers, while others advanced down the Irtysh to the Bukhtarma. The aim of these campaigns was to terrorise the Altai tribes into submission to the Manchus, but in fact they reacted by withdrawing towards the Russian lines or into remote mountain areas, and by combining to oppose the invaders. Five years of Chinese ravaging left the southern Altai devastated and largely depopulated. Some 15,000 Altaians had fled north to seek refuge near Russian forts such as Biysk, while many others were forced to move from their homeland into Chinese territory.

So far as relations between China and Russia were concerned, the destruction of Dzungaria did not bring an end to tension between the two imperialist powers in north-western Mongolia. The Russian government rejected the Chinese claim to the Altai region while the Chinese, carried forward by the momentum of their punitive campaign and lusting for the blood of Amursana and other Dzungarians, frequently advanced in forces several thousand strong up to the ramparts of the Russian forts at Ust-Kamenogorsk and Semipalatinsk.[19]

The ambiguity arising from the undefined border between Russia and China in the Altai was reflected in the status of the native peoples in relation to their conquerors. After the wars of the 1750s those tribes which had departed from their homes returned to their former pastures and resumed their previous way of life in the steppes or mountain valleys and, as subjects of the Russian Empress, paid *yasak*. Some of them – the Teleut, Telengit and Tölös, having been forced by the Dzungarians or the Manchus to move into Dzungarian territory, were still considered by the Ch'ing authorities to be their subjects even though they had gone back to Russian-controlled areas. As a result, such clans were obliged to pay *yasak* not only to the Russians but also to the Chinese. This category of 'dual tribute-payers' (*dvoyedantsy* in Russian) continued to exist for a century and was abolished only in 1864 at a time when China's weakness allowed the Russian government to force upon it the Protocol of Chuguchak, by which Russia gained the southern Altai.[20]

---

[19] Bawden, *Modern History of Mongolia*, pp. 110–32; Fu, Lo-shu, *A Documentary Chronicle of Sino-Western Relations*, Tucson, 1966, vol. I, pp. 209, 228–9, 239–40; Gurevich, *Mezhdunarodnye otnosheniya*, pp. 75, 82, 91–2, 105, 116, 120–30, 144, 149, 152, 199, 202–6, 218–22; *Istoriya Mongolskoy Narodnoy Respubliki*, p. 216; *Istoriya Sibiri*, vol. II, pp. 182, 185; Potapov, *Ocherki po istorii altaytsev*, pp. 180–1; D. Twitchett and J.K. Fairbank, *The Cambridge History of China*, vol. 10, pt. 1, Cambridge, 1978, pp. 55, 320–6.

[20] Bai Shouyi, ed., *An Outline History of China*, Peking, 1982, p. 447; D.J. Doolin, *Territorial Claims in the Sino-Soviet Conflict: Documents and Analysis*, Stanford, 1965, pp. 16–17; *Entsiklopedicheskiy slovar*, vol. XXXIII, p. 487, vol. XXXVIII, p. 809; Radlov, *Aus Sibirien*, vol. I, pp. 215, 250–1, 256–7; Twitchett and Fairbank, *Cambridge History of China*, vol. 10, pt. 1, p. 348.

7

EXPANSION IN THE NORTH PACIFIC

KAMCHATKA AND THE RUSSIAN CONQUEST

BEFORE the eighteenth century the geography of the northern Pacific Ocean was almost completely unknown to the Europeans of various nations whose seafaring explorers had established the map of most of the world's continents. Only the Russian Cossacks Dezhnyov and Alekseyev, setting out from the mouth of the Kolyma on the Arctic coast, may have strayed beyond the easternmost tip of Eurasia and been cast ashore near the river Anadyr in 1648. At any rate, this voyage is celebrated in official Russian history as the 'discovery' of the straits between Asia and America, although these men can have had little idea at that time what land, if any, lay to the east as they hugged the coast of the Chukchi peninsula. The Russian explorers of Siberia were unskilled in cartography, and only the most primitive and inaccurate maps of Siberia and its coastline were available until the late eighteenth century.[1]

Chukchi-land itself, being devoid of forest and unproductive of valuable animal skins, offered few incentives to the Russian colonialists, but the impetus to find new sources of furs did not abate as the sables of Eastern Siberia were hunted to the point of extinction in the late seventeenth century. Peter the Great, avid for all sources of revenue to pay for his wars in the West, in 1697 decreed a complete state monopoly on sable furs, and at the same time sent explicit orders to the military governors of Siberia to discover 'new lands' as further sources of sable.

In any case the next stage of Russian conquest had already begun. In 1697 the Cossack officer V. Atlasov set out southward from the Anadyrsk fort in

---

[1] R.H. Fisher, 'Dezhnev's voyage of 1648 in the light of Soviet scholarship', *Terrae incognitae*, vol. V, pp. 7–26, Amsterdam, 1973; F.A. Golder, *Russian Expansion on the Pacific, 1641–1850*, Cleveland (Ohio), 1914, pp. 67–95, 118–31; S.U. Remezov, *The Atlas of Siberia (Imago Mundi: a Review of Early Cartography. Supplement I)*, The Hague, 1958; A.V. Yefimov, ed., *Atlas geograficheskikh otkrytiy v Sibiri i v severo-zapadnoy Amerike XVII–XVIII vv.*, Moscow, 1964, maps 45–7, 157 and passim.

quest of new tribute, with a detachment of sixty Russians and sixty Yukagir auxiliaries. Some sedentary Korak communities on Penzhina Gulf – the northern end of the Sea of Okhotsk – were induced 'by kindness and goodwill' (*laskoy i privetom* – the standard formula) to submit to the 'high hand of the lord-autocrat', and *yasak* in the form of red-fox skins was taken in exchange for iron knives and axe-heads. Hearing from these Koraks of the existence of the Kamchatka peninsula, Atlasov pressed on to the south, making a foray into the territory of the Koraks of the Olutor tribe on the Pacific coast before following the western side of the isthmus of Kamchatka. This was wild and extraordinarily remote country, and from the first the Russian adventurers who explored it manifested a brutal lust for booty and a contemptuous disregard for the natives. The latter could not but respond with equal violence, and the reindeer Koraks who roamed the tundra with their herds made the overland journey to Kamchatka an extremely hazardous undertaking for the Russians. Reaching the Tigil river, Atlasov took some of his men up into the mountains which form the backbone of the peninsula and, below the towering peak of Alnei, found a pass leading down to the valley of the Kamchatka river, which flows north between two volcanic massifs, forming a broad, marshy flood-plain before it cuts through the coastal range to flow into the Pacific. Here the Cossacks saw an awe-inspiring sight – the snow-capped smoking cone of the active volcano now known as *Klyuchevskaya sopka* which rises from the valley floor to a height of 15,583 feet.

This land of birch and larch forest supported quite a large population of Itelmens[2] or Kamchadals as the Russians called them – a people who spoke a language related to Korak and Chukchi. Like the other tribes of north-east Siberia, the Itelmens had no hereditary chiefs, and their social equality was modified only in so far as the opinion of a particularly brave or intelligent man would be listened to at clan gatherings. They lived in quite large villages surrounded by palisades as a protection against raids by neighbouring clans. In summer their dwellings were leaf-covered tent-like shelters standing on platforms raised well above the ground on posts. Although the temperature in summer does not rise much above 14°C, the Itelmens usually wore nothing but a leather loin-cloth when engaged in fishing or hunting or making war. As a protection against the frequent rains they wore capes woven from leaves. Their winter homes were lodges half-sunk into the ground, with a timber frame covered with earth and a smoke-hole used as the main entrance. Winter clothing consisted of the skins of reindeer, dogs, seals or sometimes birds, made into breeches, boots and pull-over coats, similar to those worn by the Koraks and Chukchis. Like them too, they used implements and weapons of bone and stone, knowing iron only from the rare

[2] Dolgikh, *Rodovoy i plemennoy sostav*, pp. 568–9, 577, estimates an Itelmen population of only 12,680, but quotes other conjectures of as many as 25,000.

objects which found their way to Kamchatka from Japan via the Kuril Islands, and even an occasional visit to the shores of Kamchatka by Japanese ships. Their bows were made of whalebone, their arrows were tipped with bone or stone, and they used slings to hurl stones.

Summer was a season of plenty for the Itelmens, as the Pacific salmon rushed up the rivers to their spawning grounds, and they could be taken in great quantities at the expense of little trouble. Salmon flesh and roe, and the flesh and blubber of seals, were prepared for the winter by drying in the sun or smoking in pits, and they were stored on the platforms of the summer homes, beyond the reach of wild animals, and of the dogs which were the Itelmens' only domestic animals. Thanks to the wet and relatively mild climate, various edible plants grow freely in Kamchatka, and these were gathered by the women for food. According to the earliest Russian observers of Itelmen life, they not only raided each other's villages frequently, with the aim of carrying off women and slaves, but were more sadistic than most Siberian natives in their treatment of captives. Like the Koraks and Chukchis, the Itelmens scorned death, so that when losing a battle they would kill their own wives and children and court death for themselves in a suicidal way rather than fall into enemy hands alive.[3]

The Kamchatka peninsula and its prolongation in the Kuril Islands and Japan forms one of the most unstable regions of the earth's crust. Kamchatka itself has twelve active volcanoes forming a secondary range of mountains along its eastern side, while the main central range consists of extinct volcanic peaks. The earthquakes and tidal waves associated with eruptions inspired in the Itelmens the belief that evil spirits had their homes on the mountains. To climb these or enter areas of hot springs and geysers was therefore considered to be dangerous and sinful. Unlike most Siberian peoples, the natives of Kamchatka had no specific category of shamans, and the old men and women who performed religious rites neither wore special costume nor beat a drum. They attributed great importance to dreams, and as an element in their feasts they shared with the Koraks the habit of consuming fly agaric mushrooms as a means of inducing hallucinations.

The Itelmens had neither chiefs nor tribal organisation so that it was easy for Atlasov's Cossack bands with their guns to exploit local dissension and subdue the clans one by one. Where the inhabitants refused to submit to the invaders, the latter 'attacked them, killing some and setting fire to their villages in order to terrorize them and make them submit to the Tsar'.[4] The Cossacks continued their exploration southward, subduing the natives by force wherever they were encountered, but shortage of gunpowder and lead obliged them to abandon their attempt to reach the southern tip of the peninsula. They therefore retraced their steps over the 1,100 mile journey

[3] S.P. Krasheninnikov, *Opisaniye zemli Kamchatki*, Moscow–Leningrad, 1949, pp. 402–3.
[4] *Kolonialnaya politika . . . na Kamchatke*, pp. 27–8.

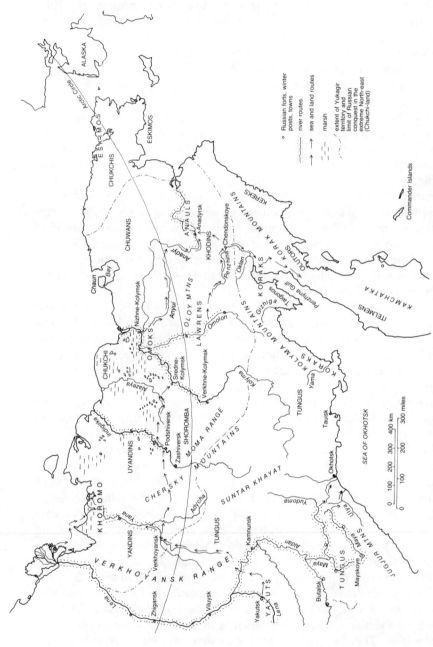

Map 7 North-east Siberia in the seventeenth century

back to Anadyrsk fort, which they reached two years after their departure, bringing with them considerable booty in the form of sable, fox and sea-otter pelts. From the Russian point of view, Kamchatka sables were extremely valuable, being not only very plentiful, but bigger than those of other regions. Atlasov therefore brought important news when he made his report in St Petersburg, and he was promoted to chief of the Cossacks in Yakutsk district.

Despite the rich promise of Kamchatka, however, it provided the Tsar's treasury with little regular tribute during the first two decades of occupation of the colony. It was one thing to force the Itelmens to bring in sables, but quite another to ensure the safe transportation of bales of furs by boats and sledge through unsubdued Korak territory to Anadyrsk fort and thence to Yakutsk. During the first decades of Russian operations in this region, shipments of tribute were frequently lost, and hundreds of soldiers and officials were killed. As in all other parts of Siberia, the conquest of the naive and ill-armed natives of Kamchatka was accompanied by arbitrary violence, cruelty and extortion. Peter the Great's decree of 1697 on the conquest of new lands forbade the Russian colonialists to abuse or enslave the natives, but this seemingly humane instruction was as much disregarded in Kamchatka as previous orders in the same vein had been everywhere else. From the start Itelmen women and girls were easily procured by trade or capture, while boys and men were also forced to serve the Russians. Later, the Cossacks would accept in lieu of fur tribute boy and girl slaves, who could be sold in Yakutsk. In 1724 the Russians in the Upper Kamchatka and Big River forts possessed between them 209 slaves (*kholopy*).[5]

Not until 1706 did the indignation of the Itelmens express itself in a mass rebellion against the invaders. In that year the clans in the south-west attacked the Russian fort on Big River – Bolsheretsk – killing many of the Cossacks, while those on the east coast also killed a *yasak* gang. It was the original explorer of Kamchatka, Atlasov, who was sent to the peninsula in the following year to mount a punitive expedition against the Itelmen 'traitors' in the vicinity of Avacha Bay. Crude and ill-disciplined as the Cossack adventurers were, they had a worthy commander in Atlasov. Like that other brigand of Russian Far Eastern exploration, Khabarov, he was 'greedy, selfish, despotic and cruel',[6] and within a few months of his arrival in Kamchatka he had provoked a mutiny among the Cossacks by withholding their provisions, by conducting underhand dealings with the natives, and by his generally unscrupulous actions. These were the years of Peter the

---

[5] Ibid., pp. 7–8; Timofeyev, *Pamyatniki*, vol. I, pp. 434–5, 441–51.

[6] *Istoriya Sibiri*, vol. II, p. 151. Even Soviet historians find little to say in favour of Atlasov as a man, although this 'Yermak of Kamchatka' or 'Pizarro of Kamchatka' has been presented in a heroic light by some Russians with nationalistic leanings, cf. *Kolonialnaya politika ... na Kamchatke*, pp. 18–20.

Great's biggest campaigns against Charles XII of Sweden, when the Tsar was desperately in need of income, including that from Siberian furs, but the combination of the hazards of travel through Korak territory and the turmoil in Kamchatka itself prevented the *yasak* system from operating, so that in fact no fur shipments got through to Yakutsk between 1707 and 1714. New commanders continued to be sent, however, and by 1709 there were three of these officials in the peninsula. In 1711 all three, including Atlasov, were killed by the Cossack mutineers, who then elected two of their own men as ataman and *yesaul*, and set out to rob the Itelmens on their own account. A chaotic situation, in which groups of rebel Cossacks were at each other's throats, prevailed until 1713, when a new commander, Kolesov, succeeded in suppressing the Cossack revolt.[7]

During these disorders among the Russians, the Itelmens availed themselves of the opportunities which occurred to attack their oppressors. In 1709, for instance, the natives on Big River were able to kill eight Cossacks, and in 1712 a similar number were killed on the Avacha, and over twenty on Big River. Even the rebel Cossacks, however, continued to raid Itelmen villages in the hope that their zeal in getting tribute would earn them a pardon from the Tsar. In 1711 they launched a big sortie in the south-west and slaughtered so many natives that Big River was said to have been strewn with corpses. A still larger toll of Itelmen lives was taken after the suppression of the Cossack revolt, when Kolesov's successor led a combined force of Cossacks and Itelmen collaborators against the clans at Avacha. After a two-week siege the Itelmens were burned out of their defensive positions and only those who promised to submit to *yasak* were allowed to live. It was not only the indigenous human population of Kamchatka that suffered from the Russian onslaught in these years: between 1707 and 1715 some 24,000 sables, as well as over 5,000 foxes and some 460 sea otters were gathered in. Indiscriminate hunting on this scale was obviously as short-sighted as it had been in the rest of Siberia, and the sable population of Kamchatka became sadly depleted before the end of the eighteenth century.[8]

RUSSIAN VOYAGES OF DISCOVERY

Until 1716 the only practicable route between Yakutsk and Kamchatka lay overland by way of Anadyrsk and from there south to Kamchatka by land or in boats – a journey of over 2,000 miles. This was almost double the distance

---

[7] *Kolonialnaya politika . . . na Kamchatke*, pp. 39–42, 194n.10; Timofeyev, *Pamyatniki*, vol. I, pp. 537–41.

[8] *Kolonialnaya politika . . . na Kamchatke*, p. 5; Krasheninnikov, *Opisaniye*, pp. 487–8; Timofeyev, *Pamyatniki*, vol. I, pp. 503–8. Despite the freedom of speech of the late 1980s a new book – 'the first all-round work' on the Itelmens – still makes no mention of Russian violence and resorts to the standard clichés of Communist Party distortion: N.V. Kocheshkov, ed., *Istoriya i kultura itelmenov: istoriko-etnograficheskiye ocherki*, Leningrad, 1990, pp. 4–5, 35–9.

between Yakutsk and Kamchatka's Big River as the crow flies, but the use of a more direct route was impossible because the Russians there had neither the ships nor the nautical knowledge to make the 700 mile crossing of the Sea of Okhotsk. In 1714, however, Peter the Great, concerned about delays in getting sable furs from Kamchatka, commanded that a party of men be sent urgently to Okhotsk to build ships, and soon it became possible to establish a regular sea route and abandon the hazardous journey through Korak territory.[9]

This modest beginning to sea-faring on the Sea of Okhotsk was the forerunner of more ambitious ventures. Since Atlasov's first incursion into Kamchatka, some knowledge had been obtained about the Kurils – an archipelago consisting of more than thirty islands which stretches from the southern tip of Kamchatka to Hokkaido in Japan. These islands, the largest of which are between 60 and 110 miles long, and many of which rise to several thousand feet, are of volcanic origin, ten of them having been active at intervals from the seventeenth century to the twentieth. Their aboriginal inhabitants were the Ainus, a race of fair-skinned people unusual among northern Asiatic peoples in having luxuriant, wavy dark hair, and speaking a language unrelated to any others. The way of life of the Ainus was generally similar to that of the Itelmens, with whom a considerable degree of inter-marriage took place in the northernmost islands of the chain and on the southern point of Kamchatka. The cult of the bear was highly developed among the Ainus, the regular practice being that a cub obtained when a she-bear was killed was kept in a cage till it was two or three years old. Then it was killed ceremonially and eaten at a ritual feast for the whole village. Scattered as they were over many islands, the Ainus depended upon boats to carry them from one community to another for such social purposes as weddings. This, along with their custom of ritualised warlike behaviour in greeting visitors, was more typical of a Pacific archipelago than of the continental Siberian peoples.[10] Russian intrusion into Ainu territory began in 1713, when a band of Cossacks went to take over the islands lying nearest to Kamchatka. A new species of prey was the main attraction for the *yasak*-takers: the sea-otter, with its luxuriant, soft fur, which was so abundant in the coastal waters of Kamchatka and the adjacent islands that the first

---

[9] J.R. Gibson, *Feeding the Russian Fur Trade: Provisioning of the Okhotsk Seaboard and the Kamchatka Peninsula 1639–1856*, Madison, 1969, pp. 113–40; Golder, *Russian Expansion*, pp. 107–9; Timofeyev, *Pamyatniki*, vol. II, pp. 37–40; S. Waxell, *The American Expedition*, London, 1952, pp. 66–9.

[10] J. Batchelor, *The Ainu of Japan: The Religion, Superstitions, and General History of the Hairy Aborigines of Japan*, London, 1892, pp. 13–33, 158–78; Krasheninnikov, *Opisaniye*, pp. 165–74, 467–9; B. Pilsudski, 'Das Bärenfest der Ajnen auf Sachalin', *Globus*, 1909, vol. XCVI, pp. 37–41, 53–60; 'Der Schamanismus bei den Ainu-Stämmen von Sachalin', *Globus*, 1909, vol. XCV, pp. 72–8, and 'Die Urbewohner von Sachalin', *Globus*, 1909, vol. XCVI, pp. 325–30; J.J. Stephan, *The Kuril Islands: Russo-Japanese Frontier in the Pacific*, Oxford, 1974, pp. 22–8.

Russian name for the Pacific Ocean was the Beaver Sea. This first Russian exploration of the Kurils was a raid carried out in typical Cossack fashion by the mutineers who had murdered Atlasov. Two hostages were abducted and taken back to Kamchatka with other booty. So far as potential *yasak* was concerned, there were neither sables nor foxes on the islands, but subsequently the Kuril natives were pressed into service to catch sea-otters for their Russian masters.[11]

This brief excursion to the Kurils was a modest contribution to geographical knowledge, which merely whetted the curiosity of Peter the Great, who shared the intense interest of early eighteenth-century scholars in the question whether North America and north-eastern Asia were joined, and if not, what land or ocean lay between them. Peter therefore conceived the idea of a large-scale expedition to the Far East to discover America, with a view to extending the territory of the Russian Empire in that direction, and shortly before his death he designated a Danish sea-captain, Vitus Bering, to be its commander. In 1727, two years after setting out from St Petersburg, Bering arrived in Okhotsk, and the first ship was built to carry the party over to Kamchatka, where the construction of a second ship, the *St Gabriel*, was carried out. In this vessel Bering sailed north-eastward up the Siberian coast, past the point of Chukchi-land and into the Arctic Ocean (thus 'discovering' the passage which is now called the Bering Straits) but he made no landfall on the American side, and in September 1728 arrived back in Kamchatka.[12]

The opening of navigation on the Sea of Okhotsk had allowed the Russians to consolidate their position as the rulers of Kamchatka, and to organise the shipping of furs out of the colony on a regular basis. This regularity, however, depended upon the imposition of a severe régime of exploitation which from time to time drove the Itelmens beyond endurance. In 1731 uprisings broke out all over Kamchatka, and for the first time the names of individual Itelmen war-chiefs emerge, such as Harchin and Golgoch. Another new development was that the Itelmens, like the Koraks, had learned to use firearms which had fallen into their hands, so that they were able to hold the Russians at bay and inflict considerable casualties on them until cannon brought from the *St Gabriel* drove them from their positions.[13] Here and at other centres of revolt, especially Avacha valley, the Russians crushed the uprising with great severity, and large numbers of Itelmens were massacred by punitive expeditions. Their much depleted communities were also removed by force from their homes to new sites in

---

[11] Alekseyev, *Osvoyeniye*, p. 66; Stephan, *The Kuril Islands*, pp. 45–50.
[12] R.H. Fisher, *Bering's Voyages: Whither and Why*, Seattle, 1977, pp. 20, 23–4, 152, 157, 173–4; Golder, *Russian Expansion*, pp. 114, 133–62; *Kolonialnaya politika . . . na Kamchatke*, p. 194n.15.
[13] *Kolonialnaya politika . . . na Kamchatke*, pp. 50–81.

other parts of the peninsula.[14] As a result of military action and epidemics of diseases unknown before the coming of the Russians, it has been estimated that between 1697 and 1715 the number of Itelmens was reduced from about 12,700 to 9,800, and the following twenty-three years saw a further decrease to 7,000 – a total reduction of 45 per cent between 1697 and 1738.[15]

An investigation by the Imperial authorities into the causes of the 1731–2 Kamchadal rebellion revealed gross abuses of power by all ranks of the military-administrative régime. Commanders appointed by the *voyevoda* in Yakutsk to bring *yasak* out of Kamchatka had to pay him a large bribe, amounting to hundreds of sable and fox pelts, for the opportunity to enrich themselves in the colony. In order to ensure this, a commander needed to extort from the natives double the official quantity of tribute, for which purpose he licensed the Cossacks – a privilege for which they in turn had to pay him a bribe – to go out into the villages on their own account and compel the natives to hunt fur-bearing animals regardless of their other needs. Refusal or inability to produce furs resulted in the abduction of the Itelmens' wives and children as slaves for the Cossacks' own use or for sale at a profit, or, not infrequently, as chattels to be lost or won in card-playing. Firearms and military organisation rendered the Itelmens almost entirely helpless against the foreign marauders who flogged and massacred the 'savages' ruthlessly and robbed them of all they possessed. As a result of an investigation into the uprising, the Empress Anna piously decreed that the Itelmens' possessions must be returned to them, that those who had been enslaved must be released and returned to their families (unless they had been converted to Christianity) and that the perpetrators of the worst acts of oppression be executed.[16]

The last large-scale rebellion of the Itelmens coincided with the second Pacific Ocean expedition under Bering's command, and was indeed partly a consequence of the extra demands placed upon the native population by such an elaborate operation. The 'Great Northern Expedition' received the approval of the Senate in 1733, but it was not until 1740 that two new ships – *St Peter* and *St Paul* – were completed at Okhotsk and sailed to the newly created port of Petropavlovsk at Avacha Bay in south-eastern Kamchatka. In the following year Bering's ships left port on the voyages of discovery which put the Aleutian Islands on the map and initiated the exploration of the Alaskan coast. The voyage of the *St Peter* took Bering and his crew into the Gulf of Alaska, where a landing was made on Kayak Island, and on to the south-west, past Kodiak and the Alaskan Peninsula. Contrary winds and

---

[14] *Narody Sibiri*, p. 982.

[15] Dolgikh, *Rodovoy i plemennoy sostav*, pp. 568–71, 577.

[16] *Kolonialnaya politika . . . na Kamchatke*, pp. 8, 47–81, 85–86; Krasheninnikov, *Opisaniye*, pp. 493–500, especially footnotes, pp. 498–500.

storms along with a shortage of supplies and water made the homeward voyage disastrous, and Bering himself died of scurvy on an uninhabited island relatively close to Kamchatka, on which the ship found refuge. In honour of the explorer, Bering Island, where he was buried, and its neighbour Copper Island, were later called the Commander Islands (Komandorskiye).[17]

ITELMENS AND AINUS UNDER THE RUSSIAN YOKE

While the Russian Imperial authorities and their frequently Danish or Swedish employees were responsible for the organisation of the numerous expeditions which explored the geography and resources of Siberia, it was the local native population that had to provide the labour. The transportation of Bering's second expedition from Yakutsk to Okhotsk required over 500 porters and drivers – a burden which fell upon the Yakuts. In the middle of the eighteenth century some 4,000–5,000 Yakut horses were required each year for this route, and by the end of the century its annual demands had risen to 1,200–1,600 men and 6,000–10,000 horses.[18]

The Itelmens too were subjected to the obligation of transporting Russian officials and goods in Kamchatka, which disrupted the essential fishing and hunting activities on which their survival depended. The year 1728 brought a special burden of forced labour in connection with Bering's first voyage. The absence of transport ships capable of sailing from Okhotsk round to the eastern side of Kamchatka, forced Bering to the expedient of exploiting the Itelmens. Men were herded in from all the native villages, along with their canoes and dog-sleds, to carry the supplies for the expedition from Big River across the peninsula to the Lower Kamchatka fort – a distance of some 500 miles. Apart from the loss of the crucial hunting season, most of the dogs died from excessive work, and the Itelmens themselves were given no recompense for their labour and privations except money, which was useless to them. No doubt the indignation they felt at this heartless treatment contributed to the rebellious mood which erupted in the uprising in 1731. On Bering's second visit to Kamchatka in 1740 the captain-commander – who assumed control of all administrative matters in the peninsula – once again pressed the Itelmens and their dogs into service. The distance from Big River to Petropavlovsk harbour on Avacha Bay was considerably less, but the natives remembered the disastrous effects of their earlier experience, and rebellion broke out in May 1741. It fell to Bering and his fellow officers to organise the suppression of the Itelmen revolt by military action, and they did not stop short of using hand-grenades against the 'savages' and their

---

[17] Golder, *Russian Expansion*, pp. 165–231; Waxell, *American Expedition*, p. 43.
[18] Golder, *Russian Expansion*, pp. 177–8; *Istoriya Sibiri*, vol. II, p. 281; Lantzeff, *Siberia*, pp. 104–5; Waxell, *The American Expedition*, pp. 67–8.

families, and flogging their leaders.[19] Thus the years of Bering's second voyage were for the natives of Kamchatka 'one of the worst episodes in the whole period of Russian domination. Although Bering did condemn the arbitrary extortion of *yasak* and the abuses perpetrated by the *prikazchiks*, it was none other than he himself who undermined the economic prosperity of the natives – doing this indeed to such a degree that it could never again be restored.'[20]

Another consequence of the 'pacification' of southern Kamchatka and the exploratory voyages of Bering's ships was the exploitation of the Kuril Islands, whose Ainu inhabitants were gradually subjected to *yasak* and converted, at least nominally, to Christianity. Russian private traders found their way to the Kurils from 1743 onward, and some of these made very great profits from sea-otter skins, which came to dominate the Far Eastern fur market just as the supply of sables from Kamchatka was beginning to dwindle. As the Russians gradually increased their hold on the Kuril Islands, some of the Ainus migrated to islands lying farther south in order to avoid subjection and enslavement. Meanwhile Japanese merchants were also showing an increasing interest in the Kurils, to which ships came every year from Yezo (Hokkaido), the most northerly island of Japan. Thus the Ainu inhabitants of the islands found themselves squeezed between Russian encroachment from the north and pressure from Japan in the south. So far as contacts with Japan itself were concerned, Russian advances met the wall of isolationism which excluded from Japan all foreigners except a limited number of Chinese and Dutch ships. Russian embassies were received courteously, but were told firmly that trade with foreigners was permitted only at Nagasaki. Thus relations between the two countries remained distant, and their rival claims to the Kurils were unresolved until the twentieth century.[21]

The conquest of Kamchatka's Itelmen inhabitants was practically made complete by the crushing of the 1741–2 uprising, leaving the southern and eastern parts of the peninsula firmly under the control of the Russian authorities, and open to settlement by incomers from Russia who were brought to Okhotsk and Kamchatka from the 1730s onward in an attempt, largely unsuccessful, to develop agriculture.[22] The Russian state's activities were also represented by the Orthodox Church, which sent a missionary to

---

[19] *Kolonialnaya politika ... na Kamchatke*, pp. 83–6; A.S. Sgibnev, *Istoricheskiy ocherk glavneyshikh sobytiy v Kamchatke s 1650 po 1856*, St Petersburg, 1869, pt. 1, pp. 49, 76–7; pt. 2, p. 10; Waxell, *The American Expedition*, pp. 97–100, 187.

[20] *Kolonialnaya politika ... na Kamchatke*, pp. 194n.15, 195n.28.

[21] *Istoriya Sibiri*, vol. II, p. 196; Stephan, *The Kuril Islands*, pp. 50–72; Alekseyev, *Osvoyenie*, pp. 64–73. Among other fabrications the latter writer states that the mission of Russian representatives here in the 1780s was 'to secure Russia's right to the Kuril Islands, which had belonged to it since time immemorial (*iskoni yey prinadlezhashchiye*)' p. 71.

[22] Gibson, *Feeding the Russian Fur Trade*, pp. 160–208.

Kamchatka as early as 1705. Both he and his successors played an ambiguous role in its subjugation, since they combined their Christian mission with participation in Cossack mutinies, and received their share in the booty, including child slaves. No less deplorable traits were exhibited by the abbot Khotuntsevskiy who was sent at the behest of the Empress Elizabeth in 1745 as head of an Orthodox mission to convert the natives of Kamchatka. He appears to have been a violent bigot who believed in the efficacy of the whip as a means of stamping out native religious rites and punishing Itelmens and Russians alike for the sins he attributed to them. Nor did he hesitate to interfere in secular matters, especially during the native uprising of 1745, when he helped to organise the defence of Nizhnekamchatsk fort and subsequently participated in the interrogation of those involved. One aspect of the mission was the foundation of twenty elementary schools in Kamchatka and the Kuril Islands – a unique phenomenon in Siberia at that time. These functioned as a means of Russification until the 1760s, when they began a decline towards their demise in the 1780s.[23]

After the establishment of the sea-route from Okhotsk, for all practical purposes Kamchatka was treated as an island (as indeed it still is in the late twentieth century because of the absence of roads),[24] and although it was not separated from the political metropolis by vast oceans, nevertheless it was an overseas possession of the Russian Empire where an unbridled colonial régime developed to the full. As even an official Soviet Russian historian says – 'Here in remote Kamchatka, where even that minimal degree of control over the actions of the local administration which existed in Western and Eastern Siberia was lacking, the arbitrariness and extortions of the administration were particularly scandalous.'[25]

One corrupt nonentity succeeded another as commander of Kamchatka, to lord it over not only the natives but the Cossacks and Russian traders, and return to Russia with his pockets well lined. For a time in the 1770s a man of rare integrity, Captain Magnus Karl von Böhm, attempted to restrain the Russian soldiers and make them treat the Itelmens as human beings, and to introduce justice and honesty into the administration of Kamchatka, according to lengthy instructions issued by Catherine the Great. After his departure, however, things went back to their former state, and in the 1780s the governor of Okhotsk, under whose jurisdiction the colony came at the time, surpassed his predecessors in depravity. In order to make a tour of his dominions in vice-regal style he forced hundreds of Itelmen slaves to haul his elaborate barges in summer, and commandeered them and their dogs for long winter journeys far beyond their native land. The Itelmens sent a

---

[23] *Istoriya Sibiri*, vol. II, p. 324; *Kolonialnaya politika . . . na Kamchatke*, pp. 16, 96–9, 196–7n.2; Sgibnev, *Istoricheskiy ocherk*, pt. 2, pp. 3–5, 14.
[24] Kalesnik, *Dalniy Vostok*, p. 294.
[25] *Istoriya Sibiri*, vol. II, p. 293.

deputation to the East Siberian governor in Irkutsk, but got no redress for their wrongs, and ruthless exploitation continued into the nineteenth century.[26]

Kamchatka, above all other Russian possessions, gives the lie to the bland myth propagated in Russian Communist Party literature that, unlike other European colonial powers, Russia did not conquer its subject peoples by force or subject them to a régime of exploitation and extirpation. In fact, war and epidemics took a fearful toll of the Itelmens, whose numbers continued to decline in the second half of the eighteenth century. In the thirty years between 1737 and 1767 the Itelmen population fell from over 7,000 to 6,000, and was further reduced by the smallpox epidemic of 1768–9 and other causes, to about 3,000 in 1781. Moreover, the Itelmen stock which survived was much diluted with Russian blood. It was an inescapable fact of conquest by force that more male than female natives were killed, and that many of the women were raped by Cossacks and officials, so that quite soon after the initial invasion of the peninsula a population of mixed blood developed. Many of the Russian peasants who were brought in also took local wives and went native, except that they continued to speak Russian. As a result, the name 'Kamchadal', which was originally applied to the Itelmen, came to mean in addition a half-Russian or indeed a fully Russian inhabitant of Kamchatka.

By the beginning of the nineteenth century it was hard to find any Kamchadals of purely Itelmen descent. The native population had suffered further great losses through epidemics, and by 1820 they numbered only 1,900. During the nineteenth century the way of life of the Itelmens and of the Russian and creole inhabitants of the peninsula became so close that it was practically impossible to distinguish between them. All lived in log cabins, wore similar clothing, used the same implements, to some extent cultivated kitchen-gardens but lived mainly on dried fish, and were nominally Orthodox Christians. At the end of the nineteenth century a large percentage of the Kamchadals were bilingual, while no more than 58 per cent claimed to speak only Itelmen, and on the lower reaches of the Kamchatka and around Avacha Bay – originally the areas of concentrated Itelmen population – many of the natives had already gone over entirely to the Russian language.[27]

THE KORAKS AND CHUKCHIS UNDER ATTACK

The other important native community in Kamchatka were the Koraks. Although the Russians controlled most of Itelmen Kamchatka by 1742, they

---

[26] Sgibnev, *Istoricheskiy ocherk*, pt. 2, pp. 24–6, 30–1; pt. 3, pp. 7–8; pt. 4, pp. 1–21, 33–8.
[27] Gurvich, *Etnicheskaya istoriya*, pp. 219–20; *Narody Sibiri*, pp. 978, 984; Sgibnev, *Istoricheskiy ocherk*, pt. 4, pp. 45–6.

had to maintain a constant state of vigilance against possible attacks by the natives. It was now the Koraks from whom they had most to fear, since they were intensely hostile towards the Russian occupiers of their territory, and were in a strong position, controlling the northern approaches to the isthmus and roaming its mountain tundra.[28]

In their earliest operations against them, the Russians had learned that the Koraks' intelligence, in every sense, was good, that they were fierce fighters, and that their clans were capable of forgetting their own differences in order to combine against the invaders. Perfectly at home in subarctic conditions, the Koraks developed tactics which put the Russians at a disadvantage; they quickly learned to use the firearms which they captured, and made such deadly use of their own more primitive weapons that a Russian commander in 1708 sent an urgent request to Yakutsk for armour and skilled bowmen to provide defence against the Korak archers.[29]

Because of frequent attacks on Anadyrsk fort and its outposts, and ambushes on caravans carrying *yasak* from Kamchatka, the Russians launched the first phase of their war against the Koraks in the years 1708– 15. Their settlements on the river Penzhina were ravaged, and forts were built at Oklan and Chendon. At the same time the Koraks living farther to the south-west in the coastal region of Taui and Yama, who had been harassing the *yasak*-paying Ewen Tungus, were attacked by Russian troops from Okhotsk. In all these battles the Koraks demonstrated their readiness to defend their homes to the death, even when the Russians set fire to them, and many of them speared their own wives and children before killing themselves or making a final desperate sally against the enemy. During Russian campaigns in Kamchatka itself the reindeer-Koraks of the uplands were attacked and partly subjugated. The eastern side of the isthmus, inhabited by the Olutor tribe, constituted one of the main centres of resistance to the Russians. Here too some Koraks submitted to *yasak*, but the fort built among them in 1714 to house hostages and receive tribute did not survive long, since the whole region was soon in turmoil again. In this phase of the war the Koraks found allies in the Yukagirs. As we have seen, the Yukagirs had long been forced into the role of collaborators and were used by the Russians as auxiliary troops against the Koraks and Chukchis. Their Russian commanders, ruthless as they often were in dealing with their own Cossacks, also treated their native auxiliaries harshly, with the result that in 1714 the Yukagirs in the Kamchatka isthmus rebelled against their commander and killed over seventy Cossacks. The Koraks in the area joined the Yukagirs for a combined assault on Oklan fort, where two other Kamchatka commanders and their Cossacks were killed, and the Olutor fort was also besieged. The losses suffered by the Russians in this incessant warfare left

[28] *Kolonialnaya politika . . . na Kamchatke*, p. 99.
[29] Timofeyev, *Pamyatniki*, vol. II, pp. 425, 476–8, 487–8.

the garrison of Anadyrsk, and of Yakutsk district as a whole, severely depleted, and Yakutsk officials appealed desperately to the governor of Siberia for reinforcements and more gunpowder. Thus the whole Anadyr operation, essential to the maintenance of communications with Kamchatka, had become very precarious by 1715, and might have had to be abandoned altogether even if the opening of the sea passage from Okhotsk to Kamchatka had not provided a respite by reducing the importance of the land route.[30]

When the war in north-east Siberia was renewed in 1729 it was the Chukchi who were the first target. For many years the reindeer-Chukchi in the vicinity of Anadyrsk fort had been a menace to the Russians, abducting them and their children, frequently besieging the fort itself, and harassing the foraging parties of Cossacks who, in order to get food, had to go downriver to the fishing-grounds and points where migrating reindeer crossed the Anadyr. A secure base in the far north-east could only be found if the natives were brought into subjection, and for this purpose a Cossack expedition, including Tungus, Yakut and Korak auxiliaries, set out from Okhotsk in 1729. It came to grief on the shores of Penzhina Bay, where it encountered a large Chukchi war-party which had come there to raid the Koraks. The Chukchis inflicted a severe defeat on the Russian army, and killed its commander. Thenceforth command of the Russian forces in the Chukchi wars was taken by Major Pavlutskiy, a man who became notorious in Chukchi folklore for his ferocious cruelty. The Russians' intention in their war on the Chukchi was to kill as many of them as possible, as the (perhaps exaggerated) statistics reported by Pavlutskiy show. On his first campaign from Anadyrsk in 1730–1 his band, consisting of some 225 Russians and 280 Korak and Yukagir auxiliaries, killed 450 Chukchis in one battle, 300 in the next, and 40 in the third, while every small Chukchi camp or settlement they encountered was destroyed. Their reindeer herds were driven off and their women and children taken prisoner, to be sold as slaves in Yakutsk if they did not die on the journey there. Since Eskimo coastal settlements were interspersed with those of the Chukchis, and the Russians scarcely distinguished one from the other, no doubt many Eskimos also perished.[31]

Compared with eighteenth-century wars in Europe, these Chukchi and Korak wars were small-scale affairs which attracted no attention in the outside world, but so far as the indigenous inhabitants of this remote corner of Asia were concerned they were of crucial importance. As desperate struggles to preserve the freedom, territory and way of life of the Koraks,

[30] Krashenninikov, *Opisaniye*, p. 489; Timofeyev, *Pamyatniki*, vol. I, pp. 403–10, 425–6, 432, 435; vol. II, pp. 53–7, 73–5, 110–20, 475–92, 507–16, 532–3.
[31] Bogoraz, *The Chukchee*, pp. 650–4, 694; Golder, *Russian Expansion*, pp. 153–7; Gurvich, *Etnicheskaya istoriya*, p. 207; *Kolonialnaya politika ... na Kamchatke*, pp. 158–9, 162–6; Timofeyev, *Pamyatniki*, vol. I, pp. 403–6; vol. II, pp. 482, 524–5.

Chukchis and Eskimos against alien conquerors, they are clearly comparable with the resistance of the North American Indians to the forces of the white men in their land. So far as their effect upon the Chukchis is concerned, Pavlutskiy's savage attacks were counter-productive, since they served merely to arouse their warlike spirit against their would-be conquerors. It was unfortunate for both the Chukchis and the Koraks, however, that even in the face of the Russian menace these neighbouring peoples continued to fight amongst themselves, for instance in 1738, when a war-party of 2,000 Chukchis came to raid the Koraks near Anadyrsk and drove off their reindeer herds.[32]

A decade after Pavlutskiy's Chukchi campaign the Russian government decided once again to return to the attack in north-east Siberia. European interest in the North Pacific was now intense, and the plans for the second series of expeditions under Bering's command included the exploration and mapping of the whole of the northern Asian coastline. In 1742 the Senate of Empress Elizabeth ordered that the Chukchis and Koraks be attacked and 'totally extirpated' (iskorenit vovse). This was to be a genocidal war, since even those Chukchis and Koraks who submitted to yasak were to be driven from their homes and dispersed in various parts of Yakutsk province so that they would 'forget their restless way of life and be loyal subjects'.[33] (It is noticeable that by now in the vocabulary of Russian officialdom not only was 'unreliability' attributed to the Siberian peoples, but 'Asiatic' had come into use as a self-explanatory pejorative term.)[34] Pavlutskiy, by then promoted to be voyevoda in Yakutsk, was again put in command of operations on the Anadyr, and the Chukchi War of 1744–7 began. In their raids Pavlutskiy's troops hunted down bands of Chukchis and destroyed them 'with the help of Almighty God and to the good fortune of Her Imperial Highness', and once again the principal subject of report was the number of men killed and of women and children captured and shared among the Cossacks. Like the Koraks, the Chukchis frequently killed their families and themselves rather than surrender. This phase of the war came to an inconclusive end when Pavlutskiy was killed. It was said that after this victory the Chukchi kept his head as a trophy for many years.[35]

While the Russians were engaged in their assault on the Chukchis in the Anadyr region, they were not allowed to forget the hostile presence of the Koraks all around the northern end of the Sea of Okhotsk. Scarcely a year passed without a Korak raid on one or other of the Russian forts, and the

---

[32] Golder, Russian Expansion, pp. 163–4; Gurvich, Etnicheskaya istoriya, p. 203; Sgibnev, Istoricheskiy ocherk, pt. 2, p. 5.

[33] Kolonialnaya politika . . . na Kamchatke, pp. 12, 162–3.

[34] Ibid., pp. 116, 124, 132, where the phrase po ikh aziatskomu nepostoyanstvu 'because of their Asiatic unreliability' occurs in official documents of the time.

[35] Golder, Russian Expansion, p. 164; Kolonialnaya politika . . . na Kamchatke, pp. 12, 162–9; Krashenninikov, Opisaniye, p. 151; Sgibnev, Istoricheskiy ocherk, pt. 2, p. 5.

land routes from Anadyrsk and Okhotsk to Kamchatka were as hazardous as ever. The Koraks on their part found no improvement in the attitude of the occupying forces. Defiance towards a *yasak* gang by the Korak chief Tuina in the Taui-Yama region in 1744 brought a punitive expedition from Okhotsk, which succeeded in capturing Tuina and other warriors alive and taking them to Okhotsk. There they were shackled to the wall of the prison, which for people so proud as the Koraks was a great offence to their honour. The Korak leaders languished in prison for eight years, until in 1752 plans were laid for an attack on the Okhotsk garrison by Korak slaves employed there, to coincide with an uprising of those held in the fort. However, prompt action by the Russian soldiers frustrated this conspiracy. The gaol, which the prisoners had taken over, was bombarded by cannon, and the Koraks chose to remain in it and perish by fire. Their comrades outside the fort had meanwhile been apprehended. Over 600 Tungus had assembled at the fort to hand over tribute-furs at this time. Fearing trouble from them, the small Russian garrison publicly executed the Korak slaves as an example to others. To press home the message of Russian supremacy, further punitive expeditions were sent out from Okhotsk during 1753–4 to kill the Koraks in the Gizhiga-Taigonos region.[36]

In the 1740s a new development took place which must have caused the Russians some concern: in their determination to rid the north-east of Russians, not only did the Chukchis and Koraks make a truce, but they also got the support of the Yukagirs on the Kolyma and the Itelmens of north-eastern Kamchatka. In 1746 a concerted attack was made on Nizhnekamchatsk fort, the centre of Russian power in the peninsula, and almost all the natives there rebelled. One reason for this attempted confederation was the Russian campaign of forcible conversion to Christianity, which had reached a pitch under Khotuntsevskiy. While the Kamchadal uprising was on a much smaller scale than previous ones, and the multi-national confederation did not last for long, the Koraks in Kamchatka and the Penzhina region were in a state of war with the Russians for a whole decade (1745–56). During this time the latter again pursued a ruthlessly genocidal policy against all the Korak communities. In 1751, for instance, some 400 Koraks were forced to take part in building a new fort on the Gizhiga river, where a fierce anti-Russian campaign had been led by the war-chief Alyk, and a force of Russians and Tungus had killed 300 Koraks. As the fort neared completion and the Russian commander no longer required so much slave-labour, he had half of the Koraks killed in the forest and took their women 'for fornication'. When the fort was finished forty more slaves were killed and the surviving Korak families were handed over as slaves to the Russians' Tungus collaborators. In addition to this fort, three others were constructed among

---

[36] *Kolonialnaya politika . . . na Kamchatke*, pp. 113, 123–31; Sgibnev, *Istoricheskiy ocherk*, pt. 2, p. 10; Solovyov, *Istoriya Rossii*, vol. XII, p. 121.

6 Chukchi couple wearing pull-over reindeer-skin clothing trimmed with dog or wolverine fur, for snowy weather. Usually they wore hoodless parkas and, like Eskimos, seldom covered their heads, even in cold weather. Behind them is a *yaranga*, a large tent covered with reindeer or walrus-skin. From a nineteenth-century drawing.

the Koraks of the Okhotsk coast at this time. Worn down by ceaseless Russian attacks, which had reduced their population by more than 60 per cent (from 12,910 in 1698 to about 4,880 in the 1760s) the valiant Koraks were brought to their knees in 1757–8, and at last submitted to their conquerors as *yasak*-paying subjects of the Empress Elizabeth.[37]

The war against the Chukchis also continued in the 1750s. In 1752, for instance, the commander of Anadyrsk fort reported to the governor in Irkutsk about his recent raiding activities, in terms which reveal that he considered Chukchi people to be of no greater significance than animals: 'During this campaign were captured two children of male sex, ten females old and young, twenty-six red fox-skins including three with half their tails missing and two with tails missing altogether . . .'[38] One of the last episodes in the Chukchi Wars demonstrated once again the great mobility of the Chukchis. In 1759 a party of 200 of them appeared on the north-east coast of Kamchatka, some 650 miles from their home base, where they captured 14 Cossacks, killed several Koraks and carried away their wives, children and reindeer. Making their way northward they joined with another Chukchi party in subjecting Anadyrsk fort to yet another siege. By 1762, when Catherine II came to the throne in Russia, it had become clear to some Siberian officials that the prolonged attempt to beat the Chukchis into submission had failed, and that the profit accruing to the state from Anadyrsk over the previous half-century – some 29,150 roubles – was only one forty-seventh of the costs of maintaining the fort and its beleaguered garrison – some 1,380,000 roubles. Accordingly, it was decided that the pointless war in north-east Siberia should be stopped, and Anadyrsk was abandoned in 1764.[39]

The defeat of the Koraks and cessation of attacks on the Chukchis allowed new patterns of relationships between ethnic groups in north-east Siberia to develop in the latter part of the eighteenth century. Some of them were changing their territories quite radically. Ewen Tungus clans were moving into Korak reindeer grounds around the northern shores of the Sea of Okhotsk, while the Chukchis were extending their grazing-grounds southwards towards Kamchatka and westward to the Kolyma river and eventually beyond it. In the 1780s the Chukchis stopped their raids on the Koraks, and even came to the aid of the latter when they made a last stand against the re-establishment of a Russian fort within their territory on the Penzhina. The Chukchis were aware of the material benefits to be derived

[37] Bogoraz, *The Chukchee*, p. 694; Gurvich, *Etnicheskaya istoriya*, pp. 211–13; *Kolonialnaya politika . . . na Kamchatke*, pp. 14, 97, 108, 113–14, 196n.32; Sgibnev, *Istoricheskiy ocherk*, pt. 2, pp. 2–5, 9, 13–18, 21, 32.

[38] *Kolonialnaya politika . . . na Kamchatke*, p. 177.

[39] Ibid., p. 191; Bogoraz, *The Chukchee*, p. 698; *Entsiklopedicheskiy slovar*, vol. XLI, p. 628; Gurvich, *Etnicheskaya istoriya*, pp. 202–5; Sgibnev, *Istoricheskiy ocherk*, pt. 2, p. 32, pt. 3, pp. 4–5.

from trade with the Russians, especially ironware and firearms, and they themselves initiated contacts with the Russians after 1764, some groups even being willing to give *yasak* on condition that no hostages were taken. To facilitate trade the Yakutsk authorities from 1788 onward organised an annual market on the river Anyui near Lower Kolymsk. In the same year iron coats-of-arms with the imperial double-headed eagle were erected on the coast around Chukchi-land to assert Russian sovereignty, although the Chukchis and Eskimos were officially recognised as 'peoples not completely subdued'. They continued to live according to their own customs and laws, and the Russian authorities limited themselves to peaceful methods of inducing the warlike Chukchis to become Russian citizens, mainly by providing useful 'gifts' to be exchanged for furs, and by singling out respected members of Chukchi communities as 'chiefs' to be favoured by gifts of official coats and swords. The Chukchis' right to their territory was confirmed by various treaties, e.g. that of 1837, which prohibited the establishment of any Russian settlements or posts among them. Unlike the Koraks and other neighbours, the Chukchis increased in numbers during the eighteenth century, from about 6,000 to 8,000 or 9,000. The reason for this, apart from their success in repelling the Russians and thus never being subjected to the colonial régime of exploitation, was no doubt that because of their isolation the Chukchis were saved from the diseases brought by the Russians. For instance, a smallpox epidemic in 1769 killed more than half of the Korak and Itelmen population of Kamchatka, and typhus introduced to Kamchatka by a shipload of soldiers in 1799 again took a toll of 30 per cent of the inhabitants of the peninsula.[40]

One aspect of Russian life to which Chukchi-land had not been subjected before the nineteenth century was Orthodox Christianity. Thanks to the religious tolerance of Catherine the Great there was little missionary activity in the Russian Empire in the late eighteenth century, and it was not until Alexander I forsook freedom of thought after 1815 that the government began to foster organised campaigns of Christianisation. The first Russian missionaries to the Kolyma region did not enter Chukchi territory, and when their successors did begin to go among the Chukchis, the response of the latter to the overtures of the Russian Church was not enthusiastic. The answer given by one old Chukchi to a priest's proposal of baptism was that conversion to the Russian religion brought no good to his people: 'They are getting poorer, their herds are declining . . . there are almost no old men left, and many have died without human dignity. No, I want to die according to our customs, like a human being.'[41] In fact Christianity made little headway

[40] Bogoraz, *The Chukchee*, pp. 699–706, 724; Gurvich, *Etnicheskaya istoriya*, pp. 198, 202–8, 213–15; *Istoriya Sibiri*, vol. II, pp. 281, 289, 429–30; Sgibnev, *Istoricheskiy ocherk*, pt. 3, pp. 10–14, pt. 4, pp. 28–31, 45–6.
[41] Yadrintsev, *Sibir kak koloniya*, p. 117.

among the Chukchis, almost all of whom still adhered entirely to their shamanist religion in the early twentieth century.[42]

THE ALEUTIAN ISLANDS AND ALASKA

At the same time as the final stages of the Russian occupation of north-east Siberia were taking place, the Russians were reaching out from the mainland of Asia towards the North Pacific islands and eventually North America. This colonisation movement began soon after Bering's second voyage, when hunter-trappers, hearing of the abundance of sea-otters in the region, rushed to exploit this new easy source of wealth, first in the uninhabited Commander Islands and then the Aleutians. The latter – a 1,500 mile long string of over 150 islands – were first discovered and inhabited by people speaking a language akin to Eskimo, whom the Russians called Aleuts, although they called themselves Unangan. Under severe climate conditions similar to those of north-east Siberia, the Aleuts lived in semi-subterranean lodges large enough in some cases to house as many as forty families. They fed themselves by hunting seals and walrus, fishing, and collecting birds' eggs. Like the Eskimos, they travelled on the sea in sealskin-covered kayaks and canoes, some big enough to hold a dozen men.[43] Before the Russians came, the Aleuts probably numbered between 19,000 and 25,000.

In their first encounters with the islanders, the Russian fur-seekers, like Viking raiders, were utterly ruthless in killing the men in order to possess the women. The resistance and retaliation offered by the Aleuts, scattered as their communities were along the archipelago, was easily crushed by the Russian sailors and hunters, and the usual colonial régime was established. Hostages (mainly children and women) were seized as a means of forcing the Aleuts to hunt on behalf of the Russians, and sea-otter and fox pelts were amassed, some as tribute for the treasury in St Petersburg, but most as profit for the piratical hunters and their Siberian merchant sponsors. One of the most effective measures used by the Russians to prevent any cooperation between various Aleutian communities in defence of their liberty was the prohibition of canoes capable of carrying more than two men.[44] Only after two decades of enslavement, atrocity and genocide did considerations of humanity begin to prevail, when Catherine the Great issued various instructions, in the pious hope that barbaric treatment of the Aleuts would cease. As time went on, indeed, the few surviving Aleuts were spared and received

[42] *Aziatskaya Rossiya*, vol. I, p. 237; Bogoraz, *The Chukchee*, pp. 723–30.
[43] Fitzhugh and Crowell, *Crossroads of Continents*, pp. 53–7, 199–20; *Narody Sibiri*, p. 986; *Yazyki narodov SSSR*, vol. V, pp. 353, 386.
[44] H.H. Bancroft, *History of Alaska* (*Works*, vol. XXXIII), San Francisco, 1886, pp. 102–5, 115, 121–40, 150–4, 161–8, 235–6; *Entsiklopedicheskiy slovar*, vol. I, p. 426; Innokentiy, mitropolit (I.E. Venyaminov), *Zapiski ob ostrovakh Unalashkinskogo otdela*, St Petersburg, 1840, vol. I, pp. 119–31; vol. II, pp. 182–94; *Istoriya Sibiri*, vol. I, pp. 425–6.

somewhat less cruel treatment, because they had become essential to the Russians for hunting sea-otters. During the last decade of the eighteenth century some 100,000 sea-otters were killed for their skins which, as the most highly prized furs among the Manchu rulers of China, were an extremely profitable commodity. This wholesale slaughter of a species which did not breed quickly, however, led to their rapid depletion, so that the Russians were led into longer expeditions to more distant islands, and eventually, in 1763, to the large island of Kodiak in the Gulf of Alaska.[45]

Here and on the neighbouring mainland the native inhabitants were not Aleuts but Eskimos of the Konyaga and Chugach communities, while the long inlet later named after Cook was inhabited by Kenai Indians of the Tanaina tribe. While these, like the Aleuts, defended themselves from the Russians as far as possible, or withdrew into the interior of Alaska to avoid them, it was farther east, in the maritime region of Alexander Archipelago, that fierce and sustained opposition was eventually encountered in the form of the Tlingit (or Kolosh) Indians, who were scarcely ever induced to collaborate with the colonialists. Constant conflict with the Tlingits led to the Russians' use of Aleuts as auxiliary troops. As in the case of the Yukagirs who had been similarly exploited in north-east Siberia, the Aleuts' military services to the Russians evoked the hatred of those against whom they were used, and the warlike Indians avenged themselves by massacring Aleuts whenever opportunity occurred. By the 1790s only about 2,500 Aleuts had escaped extermination, and these survivors were all subjected to systematic exploitation. The men were forced to hunt sea-otters, often at a great distance from their homes, while the women and children left at home on the islands had to work for the Russians in other ways. In effect this was a form of slavery, since the Aleuts and the ever-growing number of half-breeds were driven hard, received practically no pay, and had no redress against their masters. This ruthless régime continued as long as the Russians' sea-otter and seal-hunting activities remained profitable, and Aleut hunters were transported to any location where sea-otters could be found. Some were taken to California during the existence of a Russian settlement there in the first half of the nineteenth century, while others were settled on the previously uninhabited Commander Islands, where their descendants live to this day.[46]

Russian America – the colonial outposts which existed in Alaska for a hundred years – was a venture which could not be sustained, because of

[45] Bancroft, *History of Alaska*, pp. 126, 140–8, 168, 224–9, 241–6, 297, 310–11; Sgibnev, *Istoricheskiy ocherk*, pt. 4, p. 15.

[46] Alekseyev, *Osvoyeniye*, p. 124; Bancroft, *History of Alaska*, pp. 188–91, 228, 238–41, 290–1, 325–7, 339; J.R. Gibson, *Imperial Russia in Frontier America*, New York, 1976, p. 8; Innokentiy, *Zapiski*, vol. II, pp. 194–6; K.T. Khlebnikov, *Russkaya Amerika v neopublikovannykh zapiskakh*, 2 vols., Moscow–Leningrad, 1979–85; V.I. Iokhelson, *Peoples of Asiatic Russia*, New York, 1928, pp. 62–4; Yadrintsev, *Sibir kak koloniya*, p. 88.

enormous problems of communication and victualling, and it ended in 1867 with the sale of Alaska to the United States of America.[47]

[47] The history of Russian America is traced in Alekseyev, *Osvoyeniye*, pp. 86–135; Bancroft, *History of Alaska*; Gibson, *Imperial Russia*; Khlebnikov, *Russkaya Amerika*.

8

SIBERIA IN THE RUSSIAN EMPIRE: THE NINETEENTH CENTURY

RUSSIAN RELIGIOUS AND ADMINISTRATIVE POLICIES

AFTER a century of Russian domination, the native peoples of Western Siberia had mainly submitted to the *yasak* system. They had little reason, however, to respect those who had imposed this alien yoke upon them, and their distaste for things Russian was increased in the early years of the eighteenth century by an intensive campaign to convert them to Russian religion by force.

The Orthodox Church in Siberia had been stirred into further activity in 1702, when Peter the Great sent his protégé Filofey Leszczyński, an energetic Ukrainian churchman, to be bishop of Tobolsk. Twenty-five years later a second Siberian bishopric was established at Irkutsk, where another Kievan ecclesiastic, Innokentiy Kulchitskiy, was installed as bishop of Eastern Siberia. Through the activities of these two 'apostles of Siberia' the network of Orthodox Church institutions was extended by the foundation of new churches and monasteries.

The native peoples were not forgotten in this process of consolidation of Russian religion throughout Siberia. Bishop Leszczyński sent out missionaries first to the Khantys and Mansis of Western Siberia, and subsequent imperial decrees of 1706 and 1710 required the conversion of all natives (*inorodtsy*) to Orthodoxy, threatening the death penalty to any who opposed this campaign. Officials were sent out along the northern tributaries of the Ob in search of 'idols' and 'sacrilegious temples', with orders to burn them and bring the natives to baptism. As an inducement to converts, gifts of cloth and some remission of *yasak* payments were offered. Many of the Khanty and Mansi rejected this and moved away as far as they could from Russian settlements, carrying their sacred effigies of wood or stone with them into secret places in the depths of the forests. In some localities the desecration of their sanctuaries aroused the Ob Ugrians to active retaliation, as for instance in 1717 when the Orthodox official put in charge of new converts in the Konda region was killed by the Mansis. The Khantys who rejected Christian baptism moved either to the north of the Ob or farther to the south-east in the direction of the Irtysh, where they mixed with the Selkup and Tatar population. Meanwhile the Mansis who similarly withdrew to the east frequently occupied land which the Khantys had moved out of. But migration to remote places could not in the end ensure immunity from the unwanted attentions of either *yasak*-collectors or Orthodox zealots. In 1748, for instance, the Russian authorities carried out an intensive search for an 'idol' which the Khantys were believed to have concealed in the dense Vasyugan forest region south of Surgut. Nothing could induce these 'heathens' to reveal the whereabouts of their sacred image, and the Khantys fought the soldiers sent to rob them of it, thereby incurring the punishment of severe flogging. Naturally such brutal methods of Christianisation were largely counter-productive, so that while most of the Mansis and Khantys had been forced to adopt the semblance of Christianity – proudly displaying crosses around their necks and styling themselves 'Russians' – in fact they continued to practise their shamanist religion in secret throughout the nineteenth century.[1]

Crude attempts at mass conversion to Orthodox Christianity in other parts of Siberia bore the same fruits as in the case of the Ob Ugrians. In 1731, for instance, missionaries were sent from Irkutsk to convert the Yakuts, many of whom, tempted by gifts and a five-year remission of *yasak*, were happy to swell the numbers of nominal Christians while continuing the observance of their old nature religion.[2]

The cultural level of many Russian peasants who settled in Siberia in the eighteenth and nineteenth centuries was little higher than that of the native people among whom they lived. Many Russian Siberians of the north were as ignorant and savage in their ways as the Khantys and Nenets, eating raw flesh (which was anathema to the Orthodox Church) and not infrequently adopting shamanist beliefs. So far as Christian theology was concerned, the Russian settlers had only the most rudimentary knowledge of their own religion, and if asked who were the three persons of the Trinity, might well reply that they were, of course, Jesus, the Virgin Mary, and St Nicholas. The latter was indeed so highly revered by the Russian peasantry of the north that it was natural for native converts to Orthodoxy to adopt his cult. The Khantys placed St Nicholas among the pantheon of their own gods to whom blood sacrifices were made; the shamanist western Buryats similarly adopted

[1] *Aziatskaya Rossiya*, vol. I, pp. 205–15; Gurvich, *Etnicheskaya istoriya*, pp. 11, 26–7, 34, 44; *Istoriya Sibiri*, vol. II, pp. 96, 107, 287–8, 324; Sokolova, *Puteshestviye v Yugru*, pp. 31–2, 49, 54; Solovyov, *Istoriya Rossii*, vol. VIII, pp. 568–9, vol. XII, pp. 120–1; Timofeyev, *Pamyatniki*, vol. I, pp. 320–3, 413–14, vol. II, pp. 179, 210; Yadrintsev, *Sibir kak koloniya*, pp. 13, 114.
[2] *Istoriya Sibiri*, vol. II, p. 296.

'the white-haired old man'; and the Yakuts elevated him to supreme status, saying, 'there are many gods, but the chief one is Nicholas'.[3]

During the reign of Catherine the Great a more tolerant attitude prevailed in religious matters, and in general she attempted to introduce greater humanity and rationality into the administration of the Siberian population. The almost uncontrolled exaction of furs from the native peoples had brought many of them near to destitution, as well as practically wiping out the sable and other fur-bearing animals in Western Siberia. For this reason payment of *yasak* in money instead of pelts had been permitted there since the end of the seventeenth century, and now, in 1763, new instructions on tribute were drawn up for the whole of Siberia. The pernicious hostage system was abolished, and in its stead the whole clan was made responsible for producing the requisite tribute, the clan chief being entrusted with the task of collecting it and handing it over to the state officials, as well as the dispensation of justice according to traditional tribal law. Although the aim of this reform was to moderate *yasak* demands, its effects were quite the opposite. Clan chiefs quickly learned to exploit their rank-and-file compatriots as mercilessly as did the Russian officials, while the latter continued to utilise their power in order to squeeze profit out of the native communities. As a result, the native hunters were never able to produce their full quota of pelts, and their arrears of unpaid tax grew ever larger.[4]

For the majority of the native peoples of Siberia the nineteenth century was the time of their deepest decline and degradation. The iniquities involved in exacting tribute had long been obvious, and in 1822 another reform was brought in under the governor-generalship of the famous statesman M.M. Speranskiy. Once again the intention – to moderate and regularise the taxation of the Siberian natives according to an up-to-date assessment of their numbers and actual way of life – was good, but the new 'Regulations for the administration of the natives' (*Ustav ob upravlenii inorodtsev*) merely increased the burdens put upon them. All native communities were allotted in an arbitrary way to one of three newly created categories: the 'settled' (*osedlye*) – who had permanent homes in villages, the 'nomadic' (*kochevye*) – who migrated regularly between summer and winter quarters, and the 'wandering' (*brodyachiye*) – who supposedly had no regular territory but continuously roamed the forests or tundra in small bands. Typical representatives of the nomadic category were the Yakuts, Buryat Mongols, Khakas and other peoples of the steppes, while the 'wanderers' included the

---

[3] *Aziatskaya Rossiya*, vol. I, pp. 228, 233; *Entsiklopedicheskiy slovar*, vol. V, p. 61; vol. XLI, p. 633; Gurvich, *Etnicheskaya istoriya*, p. 113; E. Reclus, *The Earth and Its Inhabitants: (Asia)*, vol. I, *Asiatic Russia*, London, 1876–94, p. 342; Shashkov, *Istoricheskiye etyudy*, vol. II, p. 237; Yadrintsev, *Sibir kak koloniya*, pp. 33–4, 46–8.

[4] *Istoriya Sibiri*, vol. II, pp. 289, 310–11; M. Raeff, *Siberia and the Reforms of 1822*, Seattle, 1956, pp. 117, 127–8; Shashkov, *Istoricheskiye etyudy*, vol. II, p. 171; Solovyov, *Istoriya Rossii*, vol. XIII, p. 237; Yadrintsev, *Sibir kak koliniya*, pp. 106–7, 287.

Ewens, Yukagirs, Kets and Samoyeds. These two categories were as before subject to *yasak*, but the amount demanded per capita was increased, with the result that many of them fell into arrears which could never be made up, and many were reduced to a state of abject pauperism.

So far as the 'settled' category was concerned, all native Siberian peoples had been nomadic to a greater or lesser extent before Russian occupation, only the Bukharis and some Tatars being fully sedentary. Until 1822 even such communities as the Mansi-Khanty and West Siberian Tatars who did live in villages were subject to the same laws as the nomads – principally the obligation to pay fur tribute. Under the new regulations thousands of such people were arbitrarily classified as 'settled' and placed under the same laws and obligations as Russian state peasants – which meant subjection to village communes and the payment of poll-tax. This was a disaster for most of the natives, since they were immediately liable to pay taxes at a much higher rate – sometimes ten times as much as the *yasak* previously required of them – which they were quite incapable of producing, especially as local officials and Cossacks continued as before to extort additional 'gifts' from them. Once again the only possibility of escape lay in flight to the forest. Even those who were at first placed in the nomadic category lived in fear of arbitrary transfer to that of the settled, and in order to avoid this calamity went so far as to buy furs which they then handed over in fulfilment of the *yasak* obligation which was now their only guarantee of nomadic status.

As regards administration, the new rules provided for 'self-government' of native communities through 'clan directorates' (*rodovye upravleniya*) and 'steppe councils' (*stepnye dumy*), which further confirmed the privileges of the native chiefs. One of the most outrageous features of the 1822 'constitution' was its assumption that all land was the property of the Russian state, which graciously allowed the natives to use it according to its own rules. The general tendency and intention of the reform in fact was to encourage, and if necessary force, nomadic peoples to abandon their traditional way of life and settle down as peasants. The effect of restricting and ultimately preventing nomadism, in order to make pasture-land available for cultivation, was once again to reduce many ex-nomads to penury.[5]

In general the Russian government's decrees on the 'native question' in the nineteenth century led contemporary observers to pessimistic conclusions:

The old self-government system was disappearing, the old social union was crumbling; no new one was being created, and the natives were like a herd terrorised by the local police ... neither the monarch's decrees, nor legislation, nor Speranskiy's

[5] *Aziatskaya Rossiya*, vol. I, pp. 52–5; *Entsiklopedicheskiy slovar*, vol. XXIX, pp. 745–6, 773; Shashkov, *Istoricheskiye etyudy*, vol. II, pp. 190–2; Yadrintsev, *Sibir kak koloniya*, pp. 104–5, 110–12.

humane constitution, nor fear of the law, nor the stirrings of human conscience have succeeded in protecting the native and enforcing respect for his human rights.[6]

THE SIBERIAN NATIVES IN DECLINE

When the Siberian natives had satisfied the demands of state officials, another more insidious form of oppression still awaited them: financial contracts made with Russian merchants or peasants, into which they entered voluntarily but with such naive trust and ignorance of commercial agreements that they could not suspect that they were thereby bringing about their own downfall. Russian traders had always been active in the Siberian colony, but they enjoyed even greater scope after the abolition of the government's monopoly of the fur trade in 1762. One notorious case in the late eighteenth century was the merchant Saltanov of Turukhansk who oppressed the Samoyeds and Tungus, meting out punishments and selling them into slavery at will. Russian Marxist historians present the process whereby the natives were sucked into commercial relationships and thus into the 'all-Russian market', as essentially a progressive phenomenon, however much suffering it may have caused at the time.[7] Yadrintsev, a historian of the old school, however, saw the involvement of the natives of Siberia in a money economy in the light of morality and common humanity:

All that the Englishman needed to do was to cast a piece of red cloth from Europe into the backwoods of Asia or America, and the fate of the savage was sealed. A demand developed and with it dependence was created – a dependence more powerful than that based upon force of arms . . . The Siberian savage, surrounded by even cruder and more unceremonious traders, shared the same fate. Having been introduced to the use of bread, vodka, tobacco, gunpowder and iron, they manifest a continual demand for them, and in order to procure these things at exorbitant prices they exhaust all their means and hand over all their produce. Yet the demand remains unsatisfied, so that they are left in the situation of the expiring Tantalus.[8]

Apart from being simply cheated in barter transactions, the native Siberians were often more formally enmeshed by leases. Much land was simply grabbed by the Russian incomers without the least concern as to its previous ownership or economic use, but in some cases, such as hay-meadows and fishing-grounds on rivers and lakes, where some habitual rights could not be ignored, a form of lease against a loan was used. Having no concept of debt, such people as the Khantys readily accepted cash loans, but were incapable of repaying the money when it became due. Thus they forfeited the leased land for ever, and in addition were frequently held to their debt – ever increasing through interest – so that eventually they could

---

[6] Yadrintsev, *Sibir kak koloniya*, p. 108.
[7] *Istoriya Sibiri*, vol. II, p. 278.
[8] Yadrintsev, *Sibir kak koloniya*, pp. 102, 282.

be deprived entirely of rights to use land for essential purposes of hunting, fishing and gathering. Destitute and helpless in the hands of their Russian creditors, they could pay their debts only with their own person, working as slaves for those who had robbed them. As a result of this insidious type of bargain, many native debtors in the nineteenth century were the victims of mortgages contracted by their ancestors 200 years before.

Similarly, natives became the victims of the usury which was widely practised by the Russians in Siberia. Interest at rates as high as 300 per cent for goods unwisely bought in advance mounted up enormously, so that, for instance, the purchase price of an axe or a pair of worn boots bought by a tribesman in the Altai region would amount after four years to the cost of a horse, and eventually to the value of a whole herd of horses, which the rapacious creditor would drive away without compunction. Russian peasants and traders also brought into Siberia for the first time the commercial exploitation of forest produce. Wherever cedar-pines (*pinus sibirica*) grew, the 'nuts' from their cones were gathered by the local people as an essential part of their winter diet. The honey made by wild bees was also valuable to them. In the nineteenth century the Russian colonisers began to covet these free resources for their market value, and they obtained them by giving the natives advance loans against the value of the crop in future years, imposing iniquitous rates of interest, and taking full possession of the given area of forest when the debt, inevitably, remained unpaid. The spirit of unscrupulous commercialism which inspired this process can be praised blandly as a progressive phenomenon by Marxist apologists: 'In the old days cedar-nuts were gathered in insignificant quantities [by the Shors] to satisfy their own needs. The penetration of Russian commerce into the taiga made the nut crop a marketable commodity and promoted its development.'[9] The reality was that while the astute Russian entrepreneur could make large profits out of the natural resources which formerly were used freely by the native communities, the latter were thus frequently deprived of their last means of subsistence. Not only was the forest crop removed wholesale before their eyes, but the carefully preserved breeding-grounds of animals on which they relied for food and furs were unceremoniously ravaged by the Russian settlers as they felled trees to clear fields and provide wood for house-building and fuel. In such circumstances the natives could be reduced to the status of beggars and scavengers roaming the forest in search of roots, carrion or edible tree-bark.[10]

The St Petersburg government was not blind to the havoc being created among the Siberian natives, and laws were introduced in the first half of the nineteenth century with the aim of preventing usury in dealings with the

---

[9] *Narody Sibiri*, p. 500.
[10] Shashkov, *Istoricheskiye etyudy*, vol. II, pp. 177–9, 252–7; Yadrintsev, *Sibir kak koloniya*, pp. 93, 97–8, 282–3.

non-Russian population and restricting or even prohibiting the entry of Russian traders into native territories. Unfortunately, like the laws forbidding slavery or the sale of alcohol to the natives, these government measures had little effect, and the destruction of the way of life of the non-Russian peoples – which ultimately meant the undermining of their self-sufficiency and human dignity – continued without check.[11]

In the complex process of erosion of traditional patterns of native life in Siberia a significant part was played by the food which formed the staple diet of the Russians – bread. As the constant pressure on the forest peoples to hunt sables and foxes in order to pay *yasak* and trading debts disrupted their natural economy, their vulnerability to the caprices of the severe climate was greatly increased, so that they gradually became dependent on this new, but not cheap, form of food. Apart from sheer necessity, a taste for bread quickly developed, and as grain and flour became ever more essential to the survival of the hunting peoples, the Russian traders were provided with yet another way of fleecing them. It was in an attempt to protect the *yasak*-paying natives from this form of exploitation that the government, as part of Speranskiy's reform, set up grain stores from which they could buy grain and flour at fixed prices. In times of great need these prices were to be lowered substantially in order to save nomadic and 'wandering' natives from starvation. Once again the Tsar's government showed a humane intention which was, however, completely perverted by those who put it into practice. Even within the limits of legality Ewenki or Khanty people could be ruined by the ease with which they could run up debts for goods obtained from the grain stores, if officials were merciless in the exaction of payment by the confiscation of such chattels as they possessed. The possibilities of illegal exploitation were much greater. By entering into dishonest arrangements with the merchants who supplied the grain, and selling it to the natives at exorbitant prices, many storekeepers made considerable fortunes and became known in their localities as 'kings of the tundra', since in times of famine they had the power of life or death over the natives who were already in debt to them for grain consumed in advance of payment.[12]

Whatever the social status of the Russian traders, the norm in Siberian commerce in the nineteenth century was still, as it had been for 200 years, self-enrichment at the expense of the indigenous population. What the Russians had imported into Siberia was a hierarchy of power in which there were practically no effective laws and no ethical imperatives. At the bottom of the pyramid, the natives were subject to arbitrary treatment by Russians of

[11] *Istoriya Sibiri*, vol. II, pp. 410, 439, 453. In this Marxist work it is asserted that the government's attempts to prevent the intrusion of capitalist relations into Siberian life was 'objectively reactionary', since they merely amounted to conservation of the old ways.

[12] Shashkov, *Istoricheskiye etyudy*, vol. II, pp. 266–74; Yadrintsev, *Sibir kak koloniya*, pp. 102–3, 113, 283, 287.

all classes, as well as by their own chiefs who had been appointed or bought over by the Russian authorities. In the words of a nineteenth-century Russian historian, there was no class or institution in Siberia which did not exploit the natives, and trade in conformity with normal concepts of fair exchange and honest dealing simply did not exist.[13]

All observers of the Siberian native peoples in the late nineteenth century agree that, with the exception of the Buryats, Yakuts, and the semi-independent Chukchis, most had reached a state of demoralisation and near-destitution. Factors contributing to this decline included alcohol addiction, which was exploited by the traders, and epidemic diseases. Smallpox, measles, influenza and typhus were responsible for deaths in numbers which were large in proportion to the small populations concerned. To what extent these were endemic diseases or had been introduced to Siberia by the Russians, in the same way as diseases are believed to have been introduced to America by Europeans, seems unclear. In this connection nineteenth-century writers also paid much attention to the prevalence of syphilis, particularly among the Samoyeds, Khantys and Yukagirs. Diagnosis at that time was generally inaccurate, so that syphilis and leprosy (which was also prevalent, for instance among the Yakuts) were often confused with each other. Moralising writers with an imperfect knowledge of medical and anthropological facts therefore attributed the high incidence of 'the incurable malady of impurity' – from which, it was said, not a single person in Beryozov district was free – to the 'excessive concupiscence of the Ostyaks' on the one hand, and on the other to the Russian conquerors, exiles and vagabonds who had supposedly introduced the disease by their promiscuous intercourse with native women. Whatever the truth of this, it appears that a non-venereal form of syphilis was widespread in northern Siberia, where bodies, clothing, and shared food vessels were not washed and many people lived together in close proximity in cramped tents.[14]

All in all, the view of the Siberian native peoples presented by Russian writers of the late nineteenth and early twentieth centuries is a gloomy one. The universal conclusion was that economic, moral and pathological influences bearing on them had brought about racial 'degeneration' (a stock concept of racialist doctrine at the time) and would inevitably lead to the extinction (*vymiraniye*) of nearly all of the Siberian peoples. Historians found support for this idea in the supposed disappearance of numerous names of clans which had previously existed in various parts of the colony. However, more recent research suggests that in fact the total number of Siberian

---

[13] Yadrintsev, *Sibir kak koloniya*, pp. 102, 280.
[14] E.H. Ackerknecht, *History and Geography of the Most Important Diseases*, New York, 1965, pp. 117–20; *Entsiklopedicheskiy slovar*, vol. XXXIII, p. 378; *Istoriya Sibiri*, vol. II, pp. 339, 429, 431; *Istoriya Yakutskoy ASSR*, Moscow, 1957, vol. II, p. 219; Shashkov, *Istoricheskiye etyudy*, vol. II, pp. 279–83; Yadrintsev, *Sibir kak koloniya*, pp. 6, 56, 80, 92, 206.

natives increased steadily from about 200,000 in 1700 to about 800,000 at the beginning of the twentieth century. A large decline in numbers during this period is indeed recorded for some nationalities – notably the Yukagirs, Itelmens and Koraks in the north-east, and some groups of Kets, Nenets and Nganasans in the north-west. In the case of the Kets, Selkups and Tungus (Ewenki and Ewen) the apparent decline in numbers was due in part to changes in geographical location and assimilation by other peoples. But for most Siberian peoples the demographic trend followed the overall world pattern of growth over these two centuries. The most spectacular increase was that of the Buryat Mongols, who increased tenfold to 289,000, while the Yakuts grew by almost eight times to 227,000. In Western Siberia the Khantys and Mansis almost doubled to 23,277, as did the northern Samoyeds (Nenets and Enets) who reached about 15,000. None of these were in danger of dying out, despite the immense changes which had occurred in their way of life, and the many vicissitudes they had gone through, since the Russian conquest.[15]

Even a substantial increase in the absolute numbers of an ethnic group, however, did not necessarily guarantee its survival as a distinct cultural entity, as the fate of the West Siberian Tatars shows. They grew from about 12,500 in the seventeenth century to 68,000 at the end of the nineteenth, but this increase occurred within the context of a much greater expansion of the Russian element in the regions of Siberia which the Tatars inhabited. The Tatars, who lived in small settlements scattered among the predominantly Russian population, inevitably began to fall under the influence of the way of life of the latter and to lose their own national culture. This took place most swiftly in non-Islamic areas isolated from other Tatar communities. In the more westerly region between Tyumen and the Ob the Tatars in general enjoyed a certain respite during the eighteenth and nineteenth centuries, under conditions of strict segregation of Muslims and Christians. After the Bashkir revolt of 1755 the Russian government permitted the building of mosques in villages having exclusively Muslim populations, and by 1851 there were 188 mosques in Western Siberia, with 237 mullahs. The great majority of these outposts of Islam were in Tobolsk province, and there were only a few in the region of Tomsk, but even here the few thousand Tom Tatars still preserved their religion and national culture to a considerable degree at the beginning of the twentieth century. East of Tomsk, however, in the lower valley of the river Chulym the Tatars were already almost completely Russified, to the extent of losing their native language. The Baraba steppe with its many lakes, marshes and attendant noxious insect life did not attract so many peasant settlers from European Russia, but the *trakt* did

---

[15] *Aziatskaya Rossiya*, vol. I, pp. 81–4; Dolgikh, *Rodovoy i plemennoy sostav*, pp. 4, 293, 324, 351, 542–4, 618–21; Gurvich, *Etnicheskaya istoriya*, passim; Shashkov, *Istoricheskiye etyudy*, vol. II, p. 291; Yadrintsev, *Sibir kak koloniya*, p. 88.

bring Russian villages to Baraba, and most of the Tatars were pushed northward out of the more fertile ground into the marshy woods, where they began to cultivate crops, as well as keeping herds of horses, cows and sheep. In the 1890s there were about 5,000 Baraba Tatars, all Muslim, and it was not until the great wave of immigration in the early twentieth century that they became subject to intensive Russian influence.

More and more of the forest was cut down to provide land for agriculture and villages, forest fires caused by slash and burn techniques became frequent, and the Tatars lost their hunting grounds and cedar-nut groves to Russian peasants and traders. Consequently, the Siberian Tatars, who had been relatively prosperous, became very poor in the nineteenth century, and they were forced to become hired labourers, either felling trees to provide fuel for river steamships or working on gold-placers. By the 1880s one Russian observer wrote of the West Siberian Tatars as a completely impoverished people reduced to the state of an apathetic, semi-savage pro-letariat.[16] They differed little from the Russian peasants except in some details of their costume, and as their Islamic beliefs became eroded they entered into many mixed marriages with Christians, so that a considerable proportion of the 'Russian' population in these districts was of mixed Slav and Tatar blood.[17]

THE YAKUTS, 1700–1907

The geographically isolated Turkic community of Yakuts developed during the eighteenth and nineteenth centuries in a way that was unique among Siberian peoples. In many respects the structure of native Yakut society seems to have adapted with relatively little trouble to the social relations prevailing among their Russian conquerors, since it already possessed class divisions, ranging from rich and powerful chiefs (*toyons*) to landless poor and rightless bondsmen or slaves. The latter, being bound to the farms of their masters, no longer functioned as hunters and providers of furs for *yasak*, and so represented a depletion of income for the Russian state. In order to increase revenue, therefore, the government of Empress Anna decreed in 1733 that all slaves in Yakutia must be freed. To compensate the *toyons* for their loss, their role as local administrators and judges was confirmed, and in 1752 they were empowered to administer corporal punishment and to imprison their subjects for crimes. In fact the Yakut chiefs enjoyed almost

[16] Yadrintsev, *Sibir kak koloniya*, p. 97.
[17] *Entsiklopedicheskiy slovar*, vol. XIII, pp. 939–40; vol. XVIII, p. 629; vol. XXXIII, pp. 486–90; vol. XXXIV, pp. 348–9; *Istoriya Sibiri*, vol. II, p. 414; vol. III, pp. 82, 305; *Narody Sibiri*, pp. 476–85; Radlov, *Aus Sibirien*, vol. I, p. 241; Shashkov, *Istoricheskiy etyudy*, vol. II, pp. 190, 228, 291; Solovyov, *Istoriya Rossii*, vol. XII, p. 386; Tokarev, *Etnografiya*, p. 429; D.G. Tumasheva, *Dialekty sibirskikh tatar: opyt sravnitelnogo issledovaniya*, Kazan, 1977, pp. 16–19; Yadrintsev, *Sibir kak koloniya*, pp. 91, 97–8, 110–11, 132.

absolute power over their compatriots, since the latter were specifically deprived of the right to complain to the Russian authorities in cases of unfair judgments. The privileges of the *toyons* were further extended to new tribute regulations introduced in the second half of the eighteenth century, which divided the Yakut population into five categories, the amount of hay-meadow distributed to each family for its use being dependent upon the amount of *yasak* produced. This system allowed the *toyons* to take over the best meadows for themselves and in many cases to treat the rank-and-file members of the administrative clan (*nasleg*) as serfs. To complete the parallel with Russian serfdom, no Yakut was allowed to travel beyond the confines of his district without a permit. However, even Soviet Russian accounts cannot claim that this worst extreme of class exploitation was universal throughout Yakutia. In fact during the eighteenth century the great majority of Yakuts retained their individual farms as freemen, and the norms of the old clan system of communal land-use and mutual aid still prevailed.

The Yakut *toyons* were almost unique in Siberia in aspiring to join the ranks of the Russian gentry. Showing their customary enterprise, the Yakut chiefs obtained representation at meetings of Catherine the Great's Legislative Commission in 1767, and followed this up with more specific requests in 1789. While these included further extension of the *toyon*'s privileges, other proposals showed the chiefs' justifiable concern for the preservation of Yakut national culture as a whole by requesting the appointment as police inspectors of people familiar with Yakut customs and language – i.e. not the normal run of Russian colonial officials, who had no interest in the native people except as a means of self-enrichment. These proposals were not accepted in St Petersburg, but it is remarkable that the Yakuts in their remote homeland amid the *taiga* anticipated the kind of demands for the recognition of their own culture which nationalities in other parts of the Russian Empire would make during the nineteenth century.

As a result of Speranskiy's 'Regulations' of 1822 the Yakuts, being classified as a nomadic people, were placed under the control of a steppe council (*stepnaya duma*) composed of clan chiefs. Thus invested with unregulated authority within their clan territories, the *toyons* proceeded to abuse it in order to extort personal profit from such activities as allocation of land to their subjects, and illicit trading with the Tungus. Eventually an investigation of extortion and embezzlement led to the dismissal from their posts of all the Yakut clan chiefs, and the steppe duma itself was abolished in 1838. However, the continued existence of the subordinate institutions of self-government – the 'clan directorates' and 'native offices' still left the *toyons* wide scope for exploitation of their compatriots.[18]

Despite the entrenched power and privilege of the Russian colonial

---

[18] *Istoriya Yakutskoy ASSR*, vol. II, pp. 141–8, 168–78, 191.

administrators, Yakutia succeeded in asserting its individuality in unexpected ways. Yakut was the only Siberian native language which gained a foothold in Russian town society. In other Siberian towns the local natives had no place except as servants, or at best craftsmen and petty traders, but in Yakutsk many Russians adopted the Yakut language and it was said that even at the governor's evening parties it was heard among the Russian guests. Thus, in the words of a nineteenth-century observer: 'The Yakuts present the remarkable phenomenon of a subjugated people which has imposed its customs and language on its conquerors – a people which had not only not submitted to the influence of its conquerors but on the contrary had drawn them into its own sphere.'[19] In fact all over Eastern Siberia Yakut became in the nineteenth century a lingua franca indispensable for communication with the Tungus, Yukagir and other northern peoples from the Yenisey to Sakhalin. The extensive currency of their language reflected the wide-ranging activities of the Yakuts as traders – an occupation in which they came to rival the Russians themselves.[20]

In religion too the Yakuts preserved their national physiognomy as shamanists. Few were converted to Christianity in the eighteenth century, and although the bishop of Irkutsk headed an Orthodox mission to Yakutia in the 1840s and 1850s, when he was reputed to have converted 200,000 – or practically the whole Yakut population – to the Russian faith, in fact most Yakuts thereafter were only Christian in name, their attendance at church being enforced by a fine of 5 kopeks for absence. Meanwhile they continued to invoke the services of the shamans for healing the sick and for the rituals performed at sacred sites. Here horses were sacrificed to the spirits of the underworld, while the substances used for libations to the sky-spirits were melted butter and *kumys*. One result of the superficial Christianisation of the Yakuts was their adoption of Russian names to the exclusion of the original Turkic ones. The Russian names, however, were so thoroughly adapted to their own tongue by the Yakuts that it is difficult to recognise in a Suöder Bahylaiabys Mapyaiap or a Biere Uibaanabyna Kereekine the original Fyodor Vasilyevich Matveyev and Vera Ivanovna Koryakina.

During the nineteenth century, conditions in central Yakutia deteriorated considerably and many of its inhabitants were reduced to poverty. In a land with a severe climate, where in any case subsistence as cattle-rearers or hunters was only marginal and famine was an annual occurrence, the presence of colonial exploitation coupled with the decay of the old clan system made it almost impossible for many of the poorer Yakuts to survive. Sometimes poor Yakuts banded together to rob rich clan officials and take their cattle. The most renowned leader of such a band of outlaws was Vasiliy

---

[19] Quoted in Yadrintsev, *Sibir kak koloniya*, p. 39.
[20] *Entsiklopedicheskiy slovar*, vol. XLI, pp. 633–4; *Istoriya Sibiri*, vol. II, pp. 294–6.

7 A Yakut driving to the *kumys* festival (*yhyakh*) with his bullock-cart loaded with the typical Turkic triangular leather vessel and pestle for churning mare's milk into *kumys*, large birch-bark buckets, and ceremonial drinking vessels (*choron*) made of wood. Yakut ivory-carving by D.I. Ilyin (1946).

Manchary who, after several arrests and escapes from prison was sentenced in 1847 to be shackled to the prison wall for ten years.

By the end of the nineteenth century as many as one-third of all Yakuts were in such a state of destitution, having fallen into perpetual debt to their own *toyons* or to Russian or Tatar traders, that they were entirely without cattle or rights to hay-meadows and so had nothing to live on. As the protection of the extended family and communal cooperation had been lost, the only hope of survival lay in becoming a hired labourer to a rich Yakut (who was in fact only very moderately rich himself by Russian standards). Despite such widespread pauperism, as the Polish political exile Sieroszewski observed, the very hazards presented by their environment seemed to give the Yakuts an optimistic outlook on life:

Yakuts are loath to enter the service of others, and they return to an independent way of life as soon as the slightest opportunity occurs. Often destitute families who lack even a roof over their heads live for years as lodgers with people as poor as themselves, scraping a living by casual labour, or begging and going hungry . . . in the expectation that there will come an opportunity to set themselves up with their own cattle. And not infrequently they succeed. All that is required is a succession of years with good harvests for the small beginnings of future fortunes to spring up. No young

Yakut doubts that one day he will be rich – and indeed this hope is not entirely groundless. The enormous effort and suffering that such a transformation costs makes nonsense of the opinion that the Yakut savage lacks self-discipline and is given to gluttony, idleness and levity.[21]

Indeed, the Yakuts emerge as a vigorous, enterprising people with a gift for accommodating themselves to adversity and overcoming it.[22]

In the eyes of the Russian government the remoteness of Yakutia from the main west–east lines of communication in Siberia made it a suitable place for the isolation of political 'criminals'. However, the resulting concentration of exiles meant that Yakutsk and its outlying regions became a hotbed of radical political ideas, which spread among the local Russian and Yakut inhabitants alike. This was demonstrated during the 1905 Revolution, when the first Yakut national movement emerged. News of events in European Russia took some time to reach Eastern Siberia, but the concessions made by Tsar Nicholas II in his October Manifesto, the introduction of local councils (*zemstva*) to Siberia, and the promise of an elected State Duma, encouraged educated members of the Yakut community to conceive the possibility of national autonomy. As a result a Yakut Union was formed under the leadership of Vasiliy Nikiforov, a Yakut lawyer and city councillor (and later author of the play *Manchary* and other works) with the collaboration of Russian political exiles. Among the most irksome features of Russian colonial rule were the interference of the police in the affairs of the Yakut community, the taxes and labour obligations (including the provision of horses for transportation of Russian officials) which the Yakuts were made to fulfil, and the arbitrary appropriation of land by the state for reallocation to Russian settlers. It was in protest against these impositions that the Yakut national movement voiced its demands: all land in Yakutia must belong to the Yakut people; they must govern their own affairs free from the tutelage of the Russian police; they must enjoy civil rights, and be represented as a nation in the Duma in St Petersburg. To support these demands the Yakut peasants used the only means they possessed of bringing pressure to bear on the Russian government, namely, the withholding of taxes and labour. It was reported, perhaps falsely, that Nikiforov had tried to obtain guns, and the local police were worried by the challenging manner in which the usually cowed-looking natives now looked at them. When in Yakutsk itself the Union acted directly to make the city council stand down, and many thousands of Yakuts in the surrounding region joined the movement, the

[21] W.L. Sieroszewski, *Yakuty: opyt etnograficheskogo izsledovaniya*, St Petersburg, 1896, vol. I, pp. 422–3.

[22] *Aziatskaya Rossiya*, vol. I, pp. 145, 222; M.A. Czaplicka, *Aboriginal Siberia, A Study in Social Anthropology*, Oxford, 1914, pp. 277–8, 297–8; *Istoriya Yakutskoy ASSR*, vol. II, pp. 172–9, 193, 209; Sieroszewski, *Yakuty*, vol. I, pp. 422–7; Superanskaya, *Spravochnik lichnykh imen*, pp. 200–7.

governor, in a panic, requested the Ministry of the Interior to supply troops and a machine-gun. Luckily these reinforcements could not be supplied, since the authorities in Irkutsk and other towns were fully occupied with revolutionary events in their own areas, but the governor of Yakutia did succeed in arresting the leaders of the Yakut Union, and the movement fizzled out by April 1906. The request for a Yakut representative in the first Duma was, however, granted, and the leaders of the Union were released from prison quite quickly. The events of 1905–6 had shown that a sense of national identity existed among the Yakuts, and this continued to develop in the ensuing years.[23]

THE BURYAT MONGOLS, 1700–1907

Local autonomy was granted to the Buryats as early as 1728 in connection with the Russians' use of the Buryats and Horse Tungus east of Lake Baikal as Cossacks to guard the frontier with Chinese Outer Mongolia. The interference of the Russian authorities in the domestic matters of the Buryats was to be minimal, while their clan aristocracy, called in Mongolian *noyons*, were confirmed in their status as chiefs. They retained their traditional judicial powers in all except capital crimes, and were made responsible for the exaction of taxes from their subjects. A hierarchy of chiefs existed, bearing such Mongol titles as *taishi* and *zaisang*, but under Russian rule many chiefs of relatively low social standing were given preference over the princes of the old nobility, in conformity with the Muscovite tradition of nurturing a service gentry owing allegiance only to the monarch. The eastern Buryats preserved till the nineteenth century the old social system in which groups of tents belonging to extended families stood near each other, forming a clan community whose members were committed to mutual assistance in the work of herding and hunting, and in supporting orphans and poor relatives. Slavery did not exist among the Buryats before the Russian conquest, but as the officially appointed chiefs came to own herds numbering thousands of horses, cattle, sheep and camels, the ordinary members of the clan were often exploited as herdsmen whose only payment was the right to use the milk of the animals which were put into their care. Some of the Buryat *noyons* were granted the status of gentry by the Russian government and, having the example of Russian administrative corruption before them, many became petty despots in the image of their imperial masters. Such was the *taishi* Dymbyl Galsan of the Khori clan, whose greedy appropriation of land in the first decades of the nineteenth century evoked open protests from his subjects. Although he was deprived of his chieftainship for a time, the *taishi* gained favour in St Petersburg by his conversion to Christianity, and was

---

[23] *Istoriya Sibiri*, vol. III, pp. 296, 433; M. Konstantinov, ed., 'K istorii "Soyuza Yakutov"', *Krasnyy arkhiv*, Moscow, 1936, vol. LXXVI, pp. 67–82.

reinstated, until continuing unrest among his clansmen and further financial crimes led to his imprisonment. The Russian government's eagerness to gain converts from Buddhism allowed a successor of Dymbyl – a godson of Nicholas I himself – to conceal his gross abuse of power for many years before the authorities discovered his guilt and he was condemned to hard labour. At the time of Speranskiy's investigation of misrule in Siberia some 255 Buryat *noyons* were found guilty of administrative abuses and punished accordingly.

For over a century the Buryats and Tungus served the Russian Empire as auxiliary troops on the Mongolian frontier from the river Selenga to the Argun. The Sartol clan on the Selenga were first brought into service in 1727, and thirty-five years later frontier Cossack regiments were formed: one of Tungus (based on the clan ruled by the princes Gantimurov) and four of Buryats. For long these Buryat and Tungus Cossack regiments were the principal guardians of the Russian frontier east of Lake Baikal, and they defended it willingly against the Manchu-Chinese who had subjugated their compatriots in Outer Mongolia. Early in the nineteenth century, however, more Russian Cossacks were sent to this frontier, and in 1851, when the Transbaikal Cossack Host was formed, the Buryat and Tungus regiments were incorporated into it. Since the seventeenth century the Horse Tungus of the Argun area had been increasingly assimilated to the Buryat Mongols or, later, the Russians, so that by the late nineteenth century they were a rapidly dwindling ethnic group. As the numbers of Russians east of Lake Baikal increased, the Buryats themselves were ousted from the actual border area, which came to be inhabited entirely by Russians, so that an alien frontier zone devoid of native population was created, corresponding to the empty zone formed by the Manchus on their side of the frontier. Direct communication between the Mongols of Buryatia and those of Outer Mongolia was thus made more difficult. By the 1890s the Tungus and Buryats, numbering some 170,000, constituted less than one-third of the total population of Transbaikalia, which they now had to share with roughly the same number of Russian peasant colonists and an even larger number of Cossacks and their families.[24]

The most significant new development among the Buryats in the eighteenth century was their adoption of Tibetan Buddhism, which was not opposed by the Russian government, thanks to the new religious policy of Catherine the Great. In conformity with her rationalist leanings, the Empress wished to make conversion to Orthodox Christianity less of a

---

[24] *Aziatskaya Rossiya*, vol. I, pp. 367–9; M.N. Bogdanov, *Ocherki istorii Buryat-mongolskogo naroda*, Verkhneudinsk, 1926, pp. 96–7, 106; *Entsiklopedicheskiy slovar*, vol. V, p. 62; vol. XII, pp. 83–4; vol. XIII, p. 889; vol. XXXIV, p. 66; *Istoriya Sibiri*, vol. II, pp. 58, 288, 296–7, 310, 422–4, 445–6; Shashkov, *Istoricheskiye etyudy*, vol. II, p. 246; Zalkind, *Prisoyedineniye Buryatii*, pp. 255, 294–7.

mockery than it had been till then, and expressed this desire in her Edict of Toleration in 1773. Catherine's lack of religious prejudice provided a respite for the non-Christian peoples of Siberia, but this was granted not entirely without ulterior motives. It was potentially dangerous that religious communities within the Russian Empire should look towards centres of authority in other countries. In the case of Islam there was no possibility of establishing a Russian substitute for Bukhara – far less Mecca – but it was politic to stop the persecution of Muslims in Siberia and elsewhere, and even to pay salaries to mullahs and pay the costs of building mosques in the Kazak steppe, rather than to continue to antagonise the faithful both within Russia and abroad.

Some Mongol chiefs in the region east of Lake Baikal already had Buddhist shrines in the middle of the seventeenth century, but the first big stimulus to the spread of Buddhism there was given by the arrival in 1712 of 150 lamas who had fled from oppression in Mongolia. In 1741 the Russian government acknowledged the role of lamas in Buryat society, and freed them from *yasak* and other state impositions, but decreed that their number must not exceed 150. About 1750 the first wooden monasteries, known as *datsans*, were built among the Tsongol Buryats in the vicinity of Kiakhta and Goose Lake (*Galuuta Nuur* in Buryat). It was the strategic importance of eastern Buryatia, rather than a high-minded spirit of tolerance, that motivated Catherine the Great to give active encouragement to the Lamaist church there. So long as the spiritual focus of Buryat Buddhism was the Khutukhtu of Örgöö in Mongolia or the Dalai Lama in Tibet – both within the Ch'ing Empire – the allegiance of the Buryats to St Petersburg would be in doubt. In order to secure the Russian grip on the Buryats it was therefore desirable to cultivate the favour of their clan rulers by creating an independent Lamaist church in Russian-occupied territory. In 1764 the chief lama of the Tsongols, Damba Darja Zayai was given the title of Supreme Lama of the Buryats (*Bandida Khambo-lama*). Despite various Russian laws aimed at the limitation of the number of *datsans* and lamas, their numbers grew rapidly. In 1774 there were 617 lamas in Buryatia, in 1822 there were 2,502, and by 1831 there were 4,637 lamas (out of a total eastern Buryat population of some 150,000).

Up to 1825 little attempt had been made to convert the Buryats to Christianity, except by a handful of Protestant missionaries from the London Missionary Society who worked in Transbaikalia from 1820 under the patronage of Alexander I and M.M. Speranskiy. The latter is said to have been particularly well disposed towards Buddhism as a religion with ethical principles close to those of Christianity, and this idea accorded well with the Emperor's religious eclecticism. Under Nicholas I, however, the Orthodox Church, jealous of its monopoly in the empire, had the activities of foreign missionaries stopped, and intensified its own attempts to convert the

Buryats.[25] The Russian government disapproved of the ever-growing number of lamas because, as clergy, they were exempted from payment of taxes and from Cossack service. As a result, in the middle of the nineteenth century, the governor-general of Siberia, N.N. Muravyov-Amurskiy, drew up regulations limiting the number of Buryat lamas to 255 and forbidding the foundation of new monasteries. Whatever were the reasons of state for these restrictions upon the Buddhists, they arose partly from racial and religious prejudice: most nineteenth-century Russians saw lamas simply as ignorant charlatans and idle parasites reputedly given to sexual excesses with their numerous concubines – a view which is perpetuated in Soviet Russian accounts. In fact, thanks to their adoption of Buddhism the Buryats participated in a highly developed international religious culture, and they were the only Siberian native people to have a written language before 1917. They shared with their cousins in Mongolia a common heritage of religious, astrological and medical books written or printed by wood-blocks, mainly in Tibetan, but partly in the Mongol language. Art work also had an important place in the Tibetan Buddhist ritual of the Buryats, and dramatic performances and dances were an essential part of various religious festivals. In Mongolian Lamaism, including that of the Buryats, the symbolic and philosophical doctrines of Buddhism did not entirely displace the old shamanist beliefs and practices – despite persecution of the shamans and in some cases their being burned to death – but absorbed them and became mixed with them as the new faith gradually spread.

West of Lake Baikal Buddhism came somewhat later to the Buryats, and as this was not a vulnerable frontier region, the Russian colonial authorities did not offer it encouragement as they had done in the Transbaikal region. Instead, the Orthodox missionaries based in Irkutsk were given a free rein, and were able to claim some 20,000 Buryat converts from shamanism during the 1840s, and a further 16,000 during the 1870s – much larger numbers than were converted to the east of Lake Baikal. Nevertheless Buddhism did begin to gain ground among the western Buryats as well (the first *datsan* was built in the Angara region in 1814) and despite Alexander III's campaign of Russification and enforced conversion to Orthodoxy, during which some Buddhist temples were burned down and people were birched by the police, there were some 14,210 Buddhists in Irkutsk province in 1892. Naturally the Christianity imposed by such means was only skin deep, so that during the 1905 Revolution many Buryats, especially in the Tunka region, renounced the new religion again. A relaxation of the discriminatory laws after 1905 allowed Buddhism to spread farther among the Western Buryats at the expense of shamanism and Christianity, so that several new *datsans* were

---

[25] C.R. Bawden, *Shamans, Lamas and Evangelicals: the English Missionaries in Siberia*, London, 1985, pp. 14–15, 61, 72, 108–16, 322–30, 346; Raeff, *Siberia and the Reforms of 1822*, pp. 112–16.

founded in the Angara and upper Lena regions during the early years of the twentieth century and especially after the February Revolution of 1917.[26]

In works written in Russia before 1917 it was possible to acknowledge the moral benefits received by the Mongols from Buddhist teachings, which had 'subdued the savage proclivities of the nomads',[27] and the eastern Buryats, in contrast with their shamanist cousins west of Lake Baikal, were said to be milder, more peaceable and restrained in character. 'As regards moral improvement the Transbaikal Buryats owe much to Buddhism ... the numerous monasteries ... are still for them centres of education and culture.'[28] In Communist Party writings, however, the spread of Buddhism, like that of any religion, can only be presented as an evil plot imposed on the masses by their scheming – and apparently omniscient – rulers. For example:

In order to consolidate their power the feudal lords required more refined means of ideological influence over the tribesmen than shamanism provided ... the Mongol feudal lords ... calculated on using Lamaism for the subjection of the wide mass of the people ... it is beyond doubt that Lamaism, as the ideological buttress of the feudal system, strengthened the power of the feudal lords by helping to increase feudal exploitation and social oppression.[29]

Within the Russian Empire the government in the eighteenth century is said to have been similarly calculating in the ambiguous policy it adopted towards the Buddhist religion:

On the one hand it fostered the spread of Orthodox Christianity among the Buryats, but on the other it legalised Lamaism in order to make use of the feudal ruling class of the adherents of Lamaism for its own political purposes ... The exploiting class in the person of the feudal lords and senior lamas used Lamaism with its doctrine of non-resistance to evil in its own ends for the enslavement of the labouring masses.[30]

The early years of the twentieth century produced political movements among the Buryat Mongols, who were goaded into activity by profound changes introduced by the Russian government. Their autonomy was reduced by the abolition of the 'steppe councils' presided over by native leaders, and the substitution of the same *volost* system of rural government as applied to Russian peasant communities. At the same time a blow was struck at the traditional nomadic way of life of the Buryat cattle-rearers by the appropriation of their land to the Russian state and its redistribution to the Buryats and new Russian settlers in allotments of 40.5 acres per adult male. At

[26] V.V. Mantatov, ed., *Lamaizm v Buryatii, XVIII – nachala XX veka*, Novosibirsk, 1983, pp. 16–24, 26–9, 32–3, 44–5, 74–9, 107–14.
[27] *Entsiklopedicheskiy slovar*, vol. XIX, p. 750.
[28] *Aziatskaya Rossiya*, vol. I, p. 133.
[29] *Istoriya Mongolskoy Narodnoy Respubliki*, pp. 190–1. Here within twenty-one lines, the word 'feudal' is used ten times, and phrases equivalent to 'consolidating their power' four times!
[30] *Narody Sibiri*, pp. 241–2.

meetings held during 1905, particularly at Chita, demands were made for democratic self-government and the opening of schools with instruction in the Buryat–Mongolian language. An interest in education was by no means a new thing in Buryat society: apart from the monasteries with their Buddhist learning, it was possible, thanks to Speranskiy's legislation of 1822, for native children to attend Russian schools, and also for native communities to open their own schools. In the late nineteenth century a particularly successful Buryat school existed near Balagansk on the Angara, and the total number of Buryat children (almost exclusively boys) attending Russian schools in west and east Buryatia was over 600. While the literacy rate of 8.4 per cent at the end of the nineteenth century was not high, this took no account of a knowledge of languages other than Russian, and even the Russians, who tended to have the same arrogant prejudices concerning the educability of their native subjects as other European colonialists, were obliged to acknowledge the educational potential of the Buryat Mongols. During the nineteenth century several Buryats had graduated from Russian universities, and two at least had emerged as considerable scholars – Galsan Gombo (known as Gomboyev in Russian) who translated many Mongolian chronicles and tales into Russian, and Dorzho Banzar (in Russian Dorzhi Banzarov) who, as the son of an officer, received his primary education in the Cossack school at Kiakhta, graduated from Kazan university and thereafter devoted himself to ethnographic studies of his own people.

The Buryat Mongols were a thriving community at the beginning of the twentieth century. In 1911 those in Irkutsk province totalled about 128,000 and those in the region east of Lake Baikal roughly 204,000. However, over the same period the number of Russians living in these Buryat homelands had increased at a much greater rate, so that the Buryats in Transbaikalia were outnumbered almost three to one, while those to the west of the lake were swamped by almost five times as many Russians. It is not surprising, therefore, that while only about 5 per cent of Transbaikalian Buryats were Russified in language and culture, in Irkutsk province, where the unifying factor of Buddhist religion was weak, as many as 13 per cent of Buryats were Russified in language and about 50 per cent belonged nominally to the Orthodox Church. These differences between eastern and western Buryats are reflected in the names they give to their children: east of Lake Baikal the old Mongol, Tibetan and in a few cases Sanskrit names persist, such as Baatar 'hero', Seseg 'flower', Altan 'gold', Damba 'highest', Dorzho and Bazar 'diamond', Garma 'Karma, action', whereas the western Buryats have mainly lost the traditional names and now use Russian ones, often in strongly Buryatised forms, e.g. Bashiila for Vasiliy or Armaan for Roman. From the economic point of view the main difference between the two communities at the beginning of the twentieth century was that many of the western Buryats had been induced to abandon nomadic pastoralism and turn to farming, while those beyond the great lake were still chiefly engaged in cattle-rearing, although pressure was already being brought to bear upon them by the state to settle and take up agriculture.[31]

NORTHERN AND EASTERN SIBERIA: MOVEMENTS OF PEOPLES

The ethnic geography of Siberia was altered radically by Russian occupation, as it proceeded first along the river routes, then by the *trakt* driven from west to east across the southern fringe of the *taiga*, and finally by the railway. Finding themselves at best disregarded, but frequently exploited and abused by the Russian invaders of their territory, the native Siberians living to the north of the *trakt* could only seek escape from the destruction of their way of life by retreating in one general direction – northward.

The Khanty and Mansi people of the Urals were among the first Siberians who thus abandoned their homelands and migrated deeper into the basin of the Ob and its tributaries. As a result, the Selkups and the Kets, pressed upon by Russians, Khanty, and Ewenki Tungus, began to migrate northwards towards the Arctic, so that by the end of the seventeenth century several Selkup clans had moved into the northern fringe of the taiga on the upper reaches of the river Taz, while some Kets reached the same latitudes near the confluence of the Lower Tunguska and the Yenisey. The vicissitudes experienced during this migration, including epidemics of smallpox and influenza, had a severe effect upon the numbers and clan organisation of these two peoples. Epidemics also took a heavy toll of the Kets in the nineteenth century, reducing them from over 1,000 in 1839 to 667 in 1844. Because of the persistence of exogamic institutions within both tribes, the difficulty of finding permissible marriage partners among their own people led to many mixed marriages between Kets and Selkups, and eventually to shifts in the ethnic affiliation of some clans. On the Taz, some clans eventually came to speak Selkup dialects irrespective of their ethnic origins, while similar groups on the Yenisey became linguistically Kets and in many cases forgot their Selkup origins. Those Kets who remained farther south in the Yenisey basin, where contact with Russian settlers was unavoidable, became some of the most cruelly oppressed and destitute people of the Russian Empire in the nineteenth century. Wherever possible they shunned personal relations with Russians and held to their traditional culture, so that even at the beginning of the twentieth century they maintained a lively awareness of

---

[31] *Aziatskaya Rossiya*, vol. I, pp. 82, 84, 132–3, 212, 220, 233; *Entsiklopedicheskiy slovar*, vol. V, pp. 61–2; vol. XIII, pp. 324–5; vol. XXIX, pp. 745–6; *Istoriya Sibiri*, vol. II, p. 461; *Narody Sibiri*, pp. 223–4, 242–4, 258, 261–3; Shashkov, *Istoricheskiye etyudy*, vol. II, pp. 222–3, 225–8, 232, 234; Superanskaya, *Spravochnik lichnykh imen*, pp. 208–12; Tokarev, *Etnografiya*, pp. 453, 457; Yadrintsev, *Sibir kak koloniya*, p. 114.

their Ket nationhood. By that time, with the exception of a few small Ket settlements, only Russians lived in the valley of the Yenisey itself, the land they occupied forming a long narrow corridor running from south to north. This Russian corridor separated the Selkups, Kets and Ewenkis of Western Siberia from the population of Central Siberia, which consisted chiefly of Ewenkis, apart from two areas of Ket territory around the mouths of the Mountain Tunguska and Lower Tunguska.[32]

In Central and Eastern Siberia also, Russian expansion created complex ethnic movements directed mainly towards the south-east and the north-east. Colonisation to north and south of Krasnoyarsk, combined with the construction of the *trakt* from that town to Irkutsk, drove out all the native people from a huge area and gave the Russians a strong base in the Yenisey–Angara basin as far as the south end of Lake Baikal. From there one tentacle of Russian settlement extended down the Lena valley as far as Yakutsk, while another reached out eastward towards the Amur. Until the late eighteenth century the Russian population of the Lena was in fact limited to only four post-stations, but after the laying of the *trakt* from Irkutsk to Yakutsk the pace of settlement increased, so that by the 1860s over sixty Russian villages lined the Lena valley. Increasing colonisation by Russians caused a general movement of Ewenki Tungus towards the north, away from the Angara and Lena. Other Ewenkis, Kets and Samoyeds who lived in the line of the Krasnoyarsk–Irkutsk *trakt* withdrew southward towards the Sayan mountains or into the territory of the Buryat Mongols, among whom they became assimilated. The Buryats themselves were the one nation in southern Siberia numerous enough to retain their homeland and a strong sense of ethnic identity in the face of Russian occupation. Nevertheless, even they did not succeed in keeping their territory intact. After the wars of the seventeenth century those Buryats who lived to the west of Lake Baikal were pushed back from Irkutsk and the eastern bank of the Angara, while those on its western bank moved farther west to find new homes among the Ewenkis and Soyots of the Irkut, Kitoi and Oka rivers and the Tunka mountains near the Mongolian frontier. To the south of Baikal the area of Buryat habitation in the basin of the Selenga was more extensive, but here too a wedge of Russian settlement running along the Ingoda-Shilka river separated the Khori and Barguzin Buryats near the great lake from the Aga clans who lived farther south. By the end of the nineteenth century most of the Tungus clans in the region lying between Lake Baikal and the Chinese–Mongolian border had lost their separate identity and become assimilated either to the Buryats or to the Russians. The general effect of Russian colonisation was to reduce

---

[32] Alekseyenko, *Ketskiy sbornik*, pp. 15–16, 84–7, 114–15, 121–31; Gurvich, *Etnicheskaya istoriya*, pp. 99–129; F. Nansen, *Through Siberia: the Land of the Future*, London, 1914, pp. 149, 170–3, 189, 198–202, 212–26.

the area of predominantly Buryat population to four separate areas divided from each other by Russian settlements.[33]

The most remarkable development among the native inhabitants of Central and Eastern Siberia in the eighteenth and nineteenth centuries was the expansion of the Yakuts who, in order to evade the Russian colonial régime, spread far and wide beyond their homeland on the Lena. Many moved to the north-east, continuing a migration which began with the establishment of Yakut settlements in the basin of the Yana as early as the sixteenth century. From there they drifted eastward into the valleys of the Indigirka and Kolyma at the same time as the Lamuts or Ewen Tungus were moving in from the south. Thus in north-eastern Siberia, in a vast territory which until the seventeenth century had been the homeland of the Yukagirs, a new population was formed among which the survivors of the latter became a small minority, while the Yakuts and their language became the dominant element. Similarly the Yakuts also moved westward into the basin of the Vilui, driving out or assimilating the Ewenkis whose territory this had been. Towards the north-west the Yakuts pushed far into the Olenyok and Anabar basins – land formerly occupied by Ewenkis of the Adyan, Sinigir and Vanadir clans – until they occupied the northern part of the forest and reached the edge of the tundra. Within this subarctic forest region there was much intermarriage between Yakuts and Ewenkis, and a culture developed which combined elements from both peoples. Yakut became the dominant language here also, but, unlike their cattle and horse-rearing forebears on the middle Lena, these northern Yakuts were reindeer-herders, living in conical pole-tents. Their costume was a compromise between the open-fronted deerskin coats of the Ewenkis and the fur-lined coats favoured by the Yakuts. The Yakut element also became dominant in the rites of passage of the northern Yakuts, even where their clan affiliations were originally with the Tungus. By 1900 the population of the whole belt of forest and tundra between the Anabar and the border of Chukchi land consisted of about 13,000 Yakuts, 4,760 Tungus (Ewens and Ewenkis) and 760 Yukagirs, among whom lived some 1,590 Russians who were largely occupied in trading with the natives.

The shifting of Tungus and Yakut people towards the north-west continued beyond the Anabar and Kheta (the lower reaches of which are known as the Khatanga) into the treeless tundra of Taimyr. During the seventeenth century the depredations of Russian *yasak*-collectors had led to much fighting in this Arctic region, not only against the Russian invaders but also between various Samoyed clans. The result was a general movement of the Samoyeds farther to the north. The Tavgi appear to have vacated a band of

---

[33] Gurvich, *Etnicheskaya istoriya*, pp. 130, 140, 147–51; F.G. Safronov, *Russkiye na severo-vostoke Azii v XVII – seredine XIX v.*, Moscow, 1978, pp. 117–21; Shirokogorov, *Social Organization*, pp. 60–2, 87, 108–11.

lowland stretching from the Anabar river almost to the Yenisey. Into this territory along the Kheta, flanked on the south by the inhospitable mountains of Anabar and Putoran, came Ewenki and Yakut migrants from the south and, as in the Olenyok region, an ethnically mixed new culture developed. Here in Taimyr, however, it was the Tungus influence which predominated, and the name of a Tungus clan – Dolgan – came to be used for the new community which emerged in the early years of the nineteenth century. Combining Ewenki use of reindeer for riding and pack-carrying with the Samoyed technique of harnessing reindeer to sleighs, and the use of herd-dogs, the Dolgans lived chiefly in conical Tungus wigwams, although some built earth-covered lodges of the Yakut type or even Russian log-cabins. Their costume was basically Ewenki, but they adopted on the one hand pullover winter hooded parkas such as the Arctic Samoyeds wear, and on the other hand women's fur coats of the Yakut kind. The most characteristic Tungus feature of all Dolgan garments – in contrast with the rather plain clothing of the northern Yakuts – was its colourful decoration with strips and geometric designs made of cloth appliqué and glass beads. Despite the strong Ewenki influence in the material culture of the Dolgans, their language is essentially Yakut, but its lexis is very mixed, including many Ewenki words.[34]

In Western and Central Siberia north of the Arctic Circle the Samoyed peoples had more chance of resisting or evading interference in their lives than did more southerly peoples, so that many remained free from the Russian yoke even in the eighteenth century.

The most remote from Russian settlements were the Tavgi Samoyeds, now known as Nganasan, who inhabited the Taimyr tundra. Like other aboriginal peoples of the extreme north, the Nganasans lived mainly by hunting wild reindeer and waterfowl, and they used domesticated reindeer for drawing sledges. The remoteness of their territory and lack of goods to be plundered left them relatively free from direct interference by the Russians, so that they preserved their distinctive culture and social structure of exogamic clans until the twentieth century. However, during the seventeenth century the Russians had carried their wars of conquest even into this northern realm and compiled registers of the population for the exaction of *yasak*. According to such records the Nganasans numbered only some 600 in the seventeenth century, and about 800 in the 1790s. By that time their ethnic composition included not only a hypothetical pre-Samoyed substratum, but also a considerable element of Ewenki Tungus who had become assimilated with them through migration and inter-marriage. Like other Siberian peoples, the Nganasans were subject to devastating epidemics of such diseases as smallpox and 'rotting fever', which in the 1830s reduced

---

[34] *Entsiklopedicheskiy slovar*, vol. XLI, p. 622; Gurvich, *Etnicheskaya istoriya*, pp. 131–2, 140–3, 180–96; *Narody Sibiri*, pp. 742–54; *Yazyki narodov SSSR*, vol. II, p. 404.

their numbers by half. Unlike their neighbours – the Enets to the west and the Dolgans to the south – who had become nominal converts to Christianity, the Nganasans with few exceptions preserved their tribal, shamanist religion intact throughout the nineteenth century. They attributed life even to man-made objects such as sledges, and recognised master spirits not only of rivers, hills, fire and sky, but also of the austere phenomena of hunger and smallpox (the latter being a Russian spirit). Their biggest annual ritual took place when the sun reappeared in February. A new 'clean' tent was then built in which the shaman performed his rites while the young people danced outside. The Nganasans had a rich folklore, including epic accounts of wars against the Nenets and Ewenkis, and they held contests in which men vied with each other in eloquent speech.[35]

Essentially a people who lived by hunting wild reindeer and waterfowl, the Nenets on both sides of the Urals were forced by the exaction of *yasak* and the hostage system to spend much time trapping sables or, after the extinction of the latter in north-west Siberia, foxes, in order to satisfy the demands of Russian officials and traders. In the early eighteenth century, Bishop Leszczyński's efforts to convert the Siberian natives to Orthodox Christianity evoked resolute opposition on the part of the Nenets. In 1714–18, for instance, they made several attacks on Pustozersk on the European side of the Urals, and threatened to attack Berezov and Surgut, the main *yasak* centres on the lower Ob. They also made punitive raids on Khanty clans who had submitted to *yasak* and the Russian religion. Nenets raids on Pustozersk continued until 1746. East of the Urals the presence of Russian authorities in Berezov and Obdorsk caused many of the Nenets to migrate to more remote areas. Some moved across the Urals to the western side, while some went north into the tundra of the Yamal peninsula, and others migrated farther east. The latter, moving from the Ob towards the Yenisey, came into conflict with the Enets of the Somatu, Muggadi and other clans, who inhabited the Taz basin, and who were at the same time coming under pressure from the Selkups and Kets in their northward retreat from Russian colonisation. After two wars between the Nenets and the Enets, most of the latter were obliged to withdraw beyond the Yenisey, so that by the nineteenth century the main body of the Enets occupied the tundra along the eastern shore of its estuary. Some Enets, however, retained their territory on the west bank of the Yenisey, and when in the middle of the nineteenth century the Nenets once again attempted to push them back, it was the Enets who won the battle and held on to their territory. By then, however, the Enets were dwindling as an ethnic community because of epidemics and assimilation by the Selkups, Nenets and later, Dolgans.

The continuous unrest among the Nenets during the first half of the

---

[35] Diószegi, ed., *Popular Beliefs*, p. 137; Dolgikh, *Rodovoy i plemennoy sostav*, pp. 120–3, 178; Gurvich, *Etnicheskaya istoriya*, pp. 81–99; *Narody Sibiri*, pp. 648–57.

nineteenth century arose from several causes. Military subjugation, arbitrary exaction of fur-tribute, and the influence of a money economy undermined their primitive system of exogamic clans and communal ownership of pastures. The clans broke down into small roaming bands, each possessing small numbers of reindeer, and these formed an easy prey for the more ruthless individuals in the community, who in some cases succeeded in building up large herds at the expense of their poorer brethren. Not only the activities of the Russian officials, traders and peasants impinged upon the Nenets at this time, however: two other native peoples of the north, the Khanty and the Komi-Zyrians, also began to play a significant part in their lives. The direct involvement in Nenets affairs of the Khanty was the result of Speranskiy's administrative reform. The Ob Nenets, having been categorised as 'roaming' (*brodyachiye*) and lacking acknowledged chiefs of their own, were ascribed to Khanty districts and thus, for purposes of tribute and justice, subordinated to their traditional enemies. Naturally this caused considerable resentment among the Nenets. In other regions the Russians arbitrarily designated one of the Nenets in a given territory as chief for administrative purposes. The assault on Nenets tribal religion was renewed in 1824, when Orthodox missionaries were sent out to convert the western Nenets and burn the spirit effigies which they kept at their clan sanctuaries. It was rumours of a campaign to force the Siberian Nenets to adopt Christianity, with its concomitants of subjugation to the Russian state officials and ensuing ruination, that caused them to revolt in 1828. By this time a rebel leader had appeared among the eastern Nenets – Vavlo Nenyang or Vauli Piettomin – who is presented in Soviet Russian accounts as a kind of Samoyed Robin Hood, robbing the rich of their reindeer in order to distribute them to the poor. After fourteen years of such activities (1825–39) Vavlo was caught, flogged and imprisoned in Surgut. Within a year he had escaped and returned to the tundra where, styling himself 'great chief' of the nomadic clans, he gathered men from 400 tents, both Nenets and Khanty, for an attack on the town of Obdorsk. His intention was to depose the Khanty prince who controlled Nenets affairs, and obtain a reduction in *yasak*. However, the Russian authorities succeeded in capturing Vavlo Nenyang and he was sent to hard labour in Eastern Siberia. The remnants of his band of outlaws were not finally suppressed until the 1850s.

Economically, the life of the Nenets became dominated not only by the Russians, but also by the Komi-Zyrians from the European side of the Urals. The Komi-Zyrians exhibited considerable business initiative, and during the eighteenth century a merchant class emerged among them who emulated the methods of their Russian counterparts in ensnaring the more naive Nenets and Khanty with irredeemable debts and thus depriving them of their reindeer. Komi-Zyrian entrepreneurs thus made themselves masters of the tundra, owning huge herds which they utilised cleverly for commercial profit by selective breeding, judicious culling and the sale of meat and skins at the Izhma market. The concentration of ever larger herds and pastures in the hands of Komi and Russian owners continued throughout the nineteenth century, so that by 1895 in the tundra west of the Urals only about 17 per cent of all reindeer (which numbered some 280,000) were left in the possession of the Nenets. It was only towards the end of the century that Komi reindeer-farmers began to operate east of the Urals, but here too they were acquiring large herds by 1910. The result was that many Nenets families were left without any reindeer, or with too few of them to provide the essential skins for clothing and tent-covers. Their only hope of survival then lay in receiving short-term assistance from the state grain stores and being hired as poorly paid herdsmen by big herd-owners, whether Komi-Zyrian or Enets, or as fishermen in the employ of Russian entrepreneurs, who built up a profitable fishing industry on the Ob in the late nineteenth century.

Like most Siberian peoples, the Nenets were subject to devastating epidemics of influenza and smallpox, as well as endemic syphilis. Famine due to severe winters or failure of reindeer migration was also a recurrent hazard, which was increased by epidemics of anthrax and foot-and-mouth disease that decimated the herds. Rather than these natural hazards, however, it was the general degeneration of their traditional society and ruthless exploitation by Russians and Komi-Zyrians that reduced the once prosperous and brave Nenets people to a state of destitution and apathy and an attitude of timidity and inferiority in relation to their colonial rulers.[36]

SOUTH-WESTERN SIBERIA AND THE ALTAI, 1800–1860

In the mountainous Altai-Sayan region the Turkic-speaking people with their shamanist religion survived the onslaught of Russian colonisation better than their Islamic cousins who lived farther north along the line of the *trakt*. Although their territories were also greatly encroached upon by the Russians, the effect of this was to drive the various Turkic tribes inward towards each other, so that they formed a compact block in the Altai mountain region and its northern outliers, the Abakan and Kuznetsk ranges.

Originally most of the Turkic inhabitants of the upper Yenisey basin, lying to the east of the Kuznetsk Alatau range – the Kyzyl, Kacha, Sagai, Koibal and Beltir tribes – had been pastoral nomads. But, after the departure of the Kirgiz, the black-earth soil of their steppes attracted an ever-growing num-

---

[36] *Aziatskaya Rossiya*, vol. I, pp. 122–3; vol. II, pp. 326–7; *Entsiklopedicheskiy slovar*, vol. XXXIII, p. 378; vol. XXXVIII, p. 244; vol. XLI, p. 408; G.P. Gunn, *Po nizhney Pechore*, Moscow, 1979, p. 127; Gurvich, *Etnicheskaya istoriya*, pp. 48–81; *Istoriya Sibiri*, vol. II, pp. 98–9, 418, 443–4; Khomich, *Nentsy*, pp. 46–8, 59–74; *Narody Sibiri*, pp. 612–13, 661–5; Nansen, *Through Siberia*, pp. 104–5, 124–6; Nordenskiöld, *The Voyage of the Vega*, vol. I, p. 92; Shashkov, *Istoricheskiye etyudy*, vol. II, pp. 229, 256; Timofeyev, *Pamyatniki*, vol. II, pp. 33–4, 106–9, 170–1, 181–2; Yadrintsev, *Sibir kak koloniya*, p. 92.

ber of Russian peasant colonisers, and in the late eighteenth century the Russian town of Minusinsk was founded on the east bank of the great river opposite the mouth of its tributary the Abakan. Thus the indigenous people were gradually pushed southward and westward. Some of them found a home in the forested upper valleys of the Chulym and Abakan and their tributaries, where they adhered to their semi-nomadic way of life, their homes being conical pole-tents or polygonal huts covered with bark. But most of the 'Minusinsk (or Abakan) Tatars', as the Russians called them, remained in the steppe where, surrounded by Russian peasant settlements, many of them went over to a more sedentary existence, adopting log cabins of the Russian type, and turning increasingly to the cultivation of crops. While the main occupation of these Yenisey Turks remained cattle-rearing, under the conditions imposed by the Russian colonial régime communal possession of herds broke down, to be replaced by private ownership of large herds by clan nobles who employed the poorer members of their clan as herdsmen. Tribesmen deprived of their place in the old clan society were among the first Siberian natives to be employed in the Russian gold-mining industry, which began in the Minusink region in the 1820s.

The Yenisey Turks, like most of the indigenous peoples of Siberia, were nominally Christian by the end of the nineteenth century. One large mass conversion to Orthodox Christianity took place in the region of Askiz in 1876 when a congregation of 3,000, under duress, was collectively baptised by the bishop of Krasnoyarsk – all the men, it is said, being given the name Vladimir, and all the women Maria. Despite such triumphs of Orthodoxy the Turks retained their animist religion; the beating of the shaman's drum was frequently heard at night, and communal gatherings were held to sacrifice lambs and pray to the spirits of the sky, the mountains or the water. It was thanks to the activities of the Altai religious mission in the 1890s that literacy in their own language was first spread among the Yenisey Turk, using the Russian alphabet. By this time the various tribes had adapted themselves to the Russian way of life in varying degrees. Russian costume was adopted during the nineteenth century by some communities, notably the Kyzyls of the north, although traditional Tatar costume also survived, especially among the Kacha, into the early twentieth century.

Until the early twentieth century the Yenisey Turks, as a nomadic people, were governed by steppe councils consisting of clan elders. The ordinary clan members were subject to *yasak* and other types of obligation imposed by the Russian state, but, like all non-Russian natives of Asia, they were not conscripted for military service. After 1900, in order to provide land for new Russian settlers, large areas in the Yenisey–Abakan basin were taken over by the imperial authorities. Under this dispensation the native inhabitants, who had already been deprived of much land by Russian peasants, felt cheated because they themselves received poorer land, and less of it, than the standard allotment made to Russian colonists, while at the same time state confiscation of forests prevented the Turks from using them, except for hunting. Following upon this 'land-settlement' the Russian government abolished the Yenisey Turks' organs of self-government which had existed since 1822, replacing them by territorial units (*volosti*) administered in the same way as those of the Russian peasants.[37]

Numerically the largest intrusion of Russian settlers into old Turkic territory in Siberia occurred in the steppes of Kulunda and the northern Altai. Until the 1860s the Russian population of the Altai consisted almost exclusively of Old Believers, whose ancestors had been deported to the region in order to provide labour and agricultural support for the Kolyvan mines and metallurgical works of the Imperial Cabinet. The original nomadic inhabitants of these steppes were the Teleuts. Having been caught up in the wars between Dzungaria and China, they were either forced by the Manchus to move south, or themselves withdrew northward into the Baraba steppe, westward into Kazakstan, or eastward into the territory of the Shors – in each case becoming assimilated to their hosts. As a result, relatively few Teleuts remained, chiefly in the eastern part of their homeland near Kuznetsk, but also in the foothills of the Altai south of Biysk. By the middle of the nineteenth century the northern remnants of the Teleuts were isolated among the villages of Russian peasants, and subject to the arbitrary rule of Russian officials. Believing that this land belonged by right to them, they submitted unwillingly to the imperious conquerors who took their land wholesale and then allocated it to its original owners in lots no larger than those handed out to immigrants from Russia. Not surprisingly, the Russian ethnographer Radlov, who visited the Teleuts in the 1860s found them obtuse to the logic of Russian imperialism: 'It was in vain that I sought to explain to them that this was Crown land, so that the Crown had the right to dispose of it, and moreover, that until now most of their land had lain unused.'[38] Radlov was gratified to observe, however, that in these circumstances the Teleuts on the Bachat, having no forests or hills to withdraw into, had been forced by necessity to abandon nomadism and settle to the life of tillers of the soil. In this pursuit he foresaw that they would soon attain the same level of civilisation as that of the Russian peasantry. Indeed by then the northern Teleuts had already adopted Russian costume, although they remained shamanist in religion and made sacrifice of horses to the sky-god.[39]

The other Turkic language community of the northern Altai, the Shors,

---

[37] J. Deny et al., *Philologiae Turcicae Fundamenta*, vol. I, p. 602; *Entsiklopedicheskiy slovar*, vol. XIV, p. 811; vol. XXVIII, p. 43; vol. XXXIV, p. 348; *Istoriya Sibiri*, vol. II, p. 394; vol. III, p. 84; Kennan, *Siberia and the Exile System*, vol. II, pp. 397–403; *Narody Sibiri*, pp. 384–405; Radlov, *Aus Sibirien*, vol. I, pp. 374–9; Timofeyev, *Pamyatniki*, vol. II, p. 282.

[38] Radlov, *Aus Sibirien*, vol. I, p. 334.

[39] *Aziatskaya Rossiya*, vol. I, pp. 392–3, 408; *Entsiklopedicheskiy slovar*, vol. XXIX, p. 807; *Narody Sibiri*, p. 496; Radlov, *Aus Sibirien*, vol. I, pp. 215, 330–3.

were similarly affected by the expansion of Russian settlement on the upper Tom after the whole region had been secured for the Russian Empire in the eighteenth century. Formerly suppliers of ironware to the Oirats, Kirgiz and Teleuts, the Shors now found their function undermined by the competition of Russian traders offering more sophisticated products. At the same time they were subjected to the Russian officials' demand for *yasak* in the form of furs. As a result, most of the Shors abandoned their former occupations and withdrew from their homeland near the Russian town of Kuznetsk, to take up hunting for sable, squirrel and other animals in the taiga. Here, in the upper valleys of the Tom, Mras and Kondoma, the small community of Shors, numbering some 11,000 in the 1860s, lived very poorly. Clothing made from nettle-fibre or wild hemp persisted among them into the twentieth century, and their implements and techniques were very primitive. In their remote, mountainous environment the Shors preserved until the middle of the nineteenth century many features of ancient clan society, such as exogamy, relics of matrilocal marriage, a classificatory system of kinship terms, and various taboos associated with this. Hunting territories belonged to the clan, which organised communal hunts and divided the spoils equally among its members. Later the clan system broke down into separate families; under Russian influence a money economy, involving usury and cheating, developed to the detriment of old ways, and differentiation according to wealth appeared in Shor society. As Russian occupation of their country had brought only the destruction of their culture and interference from officials, traders, peasant settlers and Orthodox missionaries, the Shors, like the Teleuts, harboured feelings of enmity towards their conquerors. Only those relatively few Shors who remained in the vicinity of Kuznetsk went over completely to the Russian way of life, costume and dwellings.

The living conditions of the Chelkan, Kumandi and Tubalar tribes who lived to south and west of the Shors in the lower valley of the Biya, were very similar. In addition to hunting, they cultivated forest clearings with the mattock, growing principally barley and oats. They also gathered edible roots and bulbs, as well as cedar-nuts, which became the object of commercial exploitation by Russian peasant-traders and a source of inextricable debt for the 'black-forest Tatars', as they were called by the Russians. They staunchly maintained their shamanist religion despite the efforts of the Orthodox mission, and as far as possible they avoided the Russians by withdrawing deeper into the forest.[40]

In the Altai proper – the mountainous region lying to the south of Biysk (where the twin sources of the Ob unite) – Russian influence penetrated more slowly, since not only was it conquered later than the north (in the

---

[40] *Istoriya Sibiri*, vol. III, p. 84; *Narody Sibiri*, pp. 338, 342, 497–517; Radlov, *Aus Sibirien*, vol. I, pp. 343–9, 358–68.

second half of the eighteenth century) but its rugged terrain made it much less accessible to colonisers. Consequently its native inhabitants – the Telengit, Tölös and Altai-kizhi tribes who are nowadays grouped together under the name Altaians – preserved their way of life, traditional nomadic culture and Turkic language more completely than the northern Teleuts and Shors. Those clans of Tölös and Telengits who lived farthest up the valleys of the Chuya, Bashkaus and Chulyshman near the Chinese border were known in Russian as *dvoyedantsy*, i.e. 'dual tributaries', because they were subject to the exaction of tribute by both the Russian and the Chinese imperial governments until 1865. At that time, when Russia was pressing various territorial claims against a powerless China, the dual-tribute Altaians, presented with the alternative of belonging fully to the Russian Empire or moving from their homes into Chinese Mongolia, chose the former course. Intercourse with Mongolia, however, continued to be an essential feature of life in the high valleys of Altai, whose inhabitants wore clothing in the Mongolian style. One of the most specific customs of all Altaian men was to shave the head entirely except for a small patch on the crown, from which a long tuft of hair grew. Girls wore their hair in a great number of plaits heavily bedecked with metallic ornaments.

In general those Altaians who lived nearer to Russian settlements in the basins of the Katun and Biya retained less of their native culture and lived more poorly than those of the high valleys. The latter were still semi-nomadic at the beginning of the twentieth century, having herds of sheep, goats, cattle, yaks, and camels, and living in felt-covered yurts. The down-river Altaians, on the other hand, like the Tubalar, Kumandis and Chelkans, had log huts, wore clothing similar to that of Russian peasants, and lived by hunting fur-bearing animals, gathering cedar-nuts and various tubers, and by primitive agriculture. Under Russian rule the clans or territorial group-ings of Altaians were governed by native rulers having the Mongol title *zaisang*. These, like all chiefs of administrative clans in Siberia, were under the general supervision of the Russian police, but enjoyed considerable power within their clans. So far as moral qualities are concerned, Radlov's opinion of the Altaian Turks in their primitive state was very positive, as their behaviour was honest, dignified and restrained.

The native culture of the Altaians was based upon their nature religion. Shamans presided over communal prayers to the gods of the underworld and overworld, to whom horses were sacrificed, their skins thereafter being hung on poles beside sacrificial birch trees. No doubt it was because the persistence of this paganism on the territory of the Orthodox Tsar's private domain was considered to be intolerable, that in 1830 a Christian mission to the Altai was founded by the St Petersburg Synod. From its headquarters at Ulalu (now Gorno-Altaysk) a network of mission-stations was established, at which Orthodox priests preached Christianity to the Altaians, Teleuts, black-forest Tatars and Shors, and eventually a considerable number of them accepted the new religion – if only because of the material benefits offered. Perhaps the most positive achievement of the Altai Christian mission was in education: by 1913 it had established seventy-four schools at which not only Russian but Altaian children were receiving basic education, including reading and writing in their own language, resulting in a higher level of literacy than was general among Siberian natives. It was gratifying for contemporary Russian empire-builders to see religious conversion as a part of the general national mission of bringing Russian civilisation to the so-called savages, some of whom, along with shamanism, now abandoned their nomadic life and settled as peasant farmers. As in other parts of Siberia, the conversion of the Altaians to the Orthodox Church in most cases did not go far beneath the skin. Moreover, with greater penetration by Russians into Altaian communities, that other powerful element in Russian civilisation – vodka – began to take its toll, reducing many of the natives to poverty. Other vices previously almost unknown among the Altaians, such as theft and deceit, also became common, while the shortcomings so often attributed by outsiders to the Siberian native peoples – 'idleness' and lack of cleanliness – did not disappear.[41]

RUSSIAN COLONISATION AND ALTAI NATIONALISM

The Altai lands appropriated by the Royal Cabinet were the first region beyond the Urals to which a mass migration of peasants from European Russia took place in the second half of the nineteenth century. In the same year as the emancipation of the serfs (1861) the industrial serfs and ascribed peasants of the Altai were freed from obligatory labour and became state peasants paying rent to the state treasury. These, largely Old Believer, Russians constituted the 'Old Siberian' peasants (*starozhily*) of the region, whose farms and villages were relatively well-established and prosperous. The importance of agricultural land as a potential source of income to the Crown increased as the value of mineral production fell, and in 1865 it was decided to open up the Cabinet land to peasant settlers from European Russia. In the course of the next twenty years some 200,000 people from the west poured into the Altai, where they obtained plots chiefly by the age-old lawless method of seizure by force (*zakhvat*) from the natives, a method which was encouraged by a decree of 1879 which permitted Russian peasants to settle in the very territories occupied by semi-nomadic natives. In some cases the Russians simply ploughed up the land directly surrounding

[41] *Aziatskaya Rossiya*, vol. I, p. 215; D.N. Collins, 'Colonialism and Siberian development: a case-study of the Orthodox Mission to the Altay, 1830–1913', in A. Wood and R.A. French, eds., *The Development of Siberia: People and Resources*, London, 1989, pp. 50–71; *Narody Sibiri*, pp. 334–50; Radlov, *Aus Sibirien*, vol. I, pp. 215, 250–9, 304–10, 321–5.

the *yurt* of an Altaian family, cut down their hay and destroyed their hurdles, leaving them no alternative but to remove themselves from what was now a Russian's field.

The building of the Trans-Siberian railway greatly facilitated peasant migration to the east, and as the flood of new settlers into the Altai region continued unabated in the 1890s, more and more 'empty' land, mostly in the lowland areas, was distributed. By 1912 about 2 million people from European Russia had availed themselves of the land generously handed out by the St Petersburg government (which totalled some 105,000 square miles). As a result the Altai became the region of Siberia with the most dense concentration of Russian inhabitants. On the eve of the First World War it had become clear that the reserve of so-called free land in the Altai suitable for agricultural purposes was almost exhausted. 'What remained in the possession of His Majesty's Cabinet consisted principally of inaccessible mountain areas and tracts of forest which were in a completely wild state and unprepared for utilization.'[42] These were precisely the regions of the east and south which provided a last refuge for the native peoples of the Altai. Under the land division project of 1899 the Shors, Teleuts, Tölös, Telengits and black-forest Tatars were to receive land on the same basis as the Russian settlers, without regard for the needs of nomadism and communal clan ownership. This provoked so much opposition from the Altaians that its implementation was postponed until 1912. A bone of contention for native inhabitants and Russian incomers alike was the Imperial Cabinet's conservation of forests for its own purposes, which restricted the rights of the population to fell timber.

As the Altaians of the lowlands were constrained within ever-diminishing tracts of free territory scattered among Russian villages, more and more of them were obliged to settle down as farmers, and the Russian authorities were once again able to see this as the march of civilisation against nomadism. In the high Altai, on the other hand, cattle-rearing was still the main occupation, and some of the native owners of large herds were in the forefront of modern cattle-breeding and commercial production, taking their share in competition with Russian farmers in the development of the Siberian butter-exporting industry.[43]

The cultural contacts of the Altaians were not limited to Russia, since an important trade route linking the Russian town of Biysk with Mongolia ran through their territory in the Chuya valley. Intercourse with Mongolia along

---

[42] *Aziatskaya Rossiya*, vol. I, p. 391.

[43] Ibid., pp. 389–93, 406–17, 426–7; *Istoriya Sibiri*, vol. III, pp. 96–9, 206, 251–73, 289–90, 303; *Narody Sibiri*, pp. 334, 344–8; A.P. Okladnikov, ed., *Itogi i zadachi izucheniya istorii Sibiri dosovetskogo perioda*, Novosibirsk, 1971, p. 157; Potapov, *Ocherki po istorii altaytsev*, pp. 233–5; Potapov, *Ocherki po istorii Shorii*, pp. 253–4, end map.

this road contributed to a significant socio-political development in the Altai in the early years of the twentieth century – a new national religion based on Buddhism. The conversion of the Altaians to Christianity had been superficial. While some were baptised with Russian Christian names, these were scarcely ever used and tended to be forgotten, while the native Turkic names persisted. (These names referred to everyday objects, such as *malta* 'axe', *koi* 'sheep' or *tyt* 'larch', and various taboos existed, such as giving children born in the year of the pig unpleasant or indecent names – dog's ear, dung, pus etc. – in order to repel evil spirits. A wife was prohibited from ever using words which entered into the names of her husband or any elder male relatives.) In the spring of 1904 news went round the Altai mountain region that God had revealed to a herdsman, Chet Chelpan, a new religion – the 'white faith' (*ak chang*) as opposed to shamanism which Russian priests had dubbed the 'black faith'. Some of the most important elements of this religion came from folk traditions about the Oirat empire of Dzungaria to which the Altai had once belonged. The Messiah of the Altaians, who would come to lead his people to liberty, bore the names of seventeenth and eighteenth-century Oirat leaders, such as Galdan and Amursana, but was usually called simply Oirot. Another of his names, Yapon-kan, 'Japanese Emperor' shows that news of the success of the Japanese in the Russo-Japanese War was welcomed in the Altai. The political content of Chet's revelation was essentially anti-Russian, as the following excerpt from a song indicates: 'Nothing is worse than the red-bearded Russians. The wind will blow and the bleached grass disappear . . . Russian matches are bad fire. The shaggy Russian priest is a bad man . . . If six bows are bent there will be fire throughout Altai. Golden Oirot will come – Russia will be no more.'[44] Not only matches, but many other things used by Russians were to be rejected, including kerosene lamps, textiles, bath-houses and potatoes – all symbols of the Russian occupation of the land of the Altaians.

Clearly this gave the Russian settlers cause for concern, especially when in May 1904, in response to Chet's message, some 3,000 Altaians congregated at Derem, about a hundred miles south of Biysk. To deal with these signs of insurrection the Russian police organised a volunteer militia of local peasants armed with guns. In a morning raid on the Altaians' camp many were cudgelled and one killed by the Russian peasants, who also stole their cattle and other possessions. Chet and his entourage were arrested, but given a fair trial and acquitted, no doubt because the Russian authorities saw little danger in such a primitive religious movement.

As recently as 1895 it had been possible to say that the Altaians knew

---

[44] A.G. Danilin, 'Burkhanizm na Altae i ego kontr-revolyutsionnaya rol', *Sovetskaya etnografiya*, 1932, no. 1, p. 79.

nothing of Buddhism, which had not reached them even when their eighteenth-century Oirat overlords were persecuting shamans and establishing monasteries on the very edge of the Altai. However, in the nineteenth century the nearest town in Chinese Sinkiang, Burultokai, was a centre of Tibetan Buddhism from which lamas penetrated the mountain region, and Chet himself spent some time in Mongolia. Because of their reverence of Buddhist images, called *burkhans* 'gods' in Mongolian, the adherents of Chet's 'white faith' were called 'Burkhanists' by the Russians. Like the early Buddhists in Mongolia itself, Chet's followers tried to stamp out the old nature religion by burning the shaman's drums and the ribbons and horse-hides hung on trees; they beat the shamans themselves and trampled their fields. Blood sacrifice was abolished. However, just as among the Mongols, many shamanist beliefs and practices in fact survived along with imported elements of Buddhism. The followers of the new religion still observed the cult of fire and of various nature spirits, and they made libations to the sky-god by sprinkling milk towards the sun and the mountains, and by burning sprigs of heather in a fire.

Whereas Orthodox Christianity, being associated in the minds of the Altaians with colonialism, the exaction of tribute, and above all eviction from the land of their forefathers, had earned little respect, the new 'white faith' flourished rapidly. Thus, on the eve of the first Russian revolution, Chet's religion gave organised expression for the first time to the national self-awareness of the Altaian Turks, under their preferred title of Oirots. This movement for national independence existed not only at the level of the common herdsman, but also involved the emergent native intelligentsia, represented by the prosperous owners of large herds such as Argamai Kuljin. A similar national movement appeared during 1905 on the other side of the Kuznetsk Alatau, among the Yenisey Turks. Here, as in the Altai, the main forms of active protest against the Russian authorities during 1905 were the non-payment of taxes and the cutting of timber in state forests. A further sign of the awakening of political consciousness among the peoples of southern Siberia was the fact that a congress of Yenisey Turks in November 1905 adopted the same project for national autonomy, education in the native language, and preservation of national territory which had been formulated by Buryat conferences earlier in the year. At the same time the idea of a 'Union of Siberian natives' to protect and further the interests of the indigenous peoples was mooted. The institution of the State Duma in St Petersburg in 1906 gave some opportunity for the expression of the aspirations of the subject peoples of the Empire, which the Altaians took up by sending two delegates to petition for the preservation of their land rights.

The spontaneous anti-colonialist movement which had sprung up in the Altai-Yenisey region among one of the most populous groups of native Siberians (totalling about 109,000 people in 1897) was contained by the

Russian imperial régime in the early years of the twentieth century, but it did not disappear and was bound to grow stronger, since its causes had not been removed.[45]

[45] Ibid., pp. 63–91; *Aziatskaya Rossiya*, vol. I, p. 420; *Entsiklopedicheskiy slovar*, vol. XIV, p. 58; *Istoriya Sibiri*, vol. III, pp. 78, 294–5; W. Kolarz, *The Peoples of the Soviet Far East*, London, 1954, p. 172; *Narody Sibiri*, pp. 233, 262; Superanskaya, *Spravochnik lichnykh imen*, pp. 45–6; *Yazyki narodov SSSR*, vol. II, p. 54.

9

COLONIAL SETTLERS IN SIBERIA: THE NINETEENTH CENTURY

THE OPENING OF SIBERIA TO MASS SETTLEMENT

THE Russian population of Siberia was unevenly distributed. It was natural for immigrants to settle along the routes by which they entered the colony from the west – in the first place along the roads through the Ural mountains, the courses of the big rivers and the valleys of the region east of Lake Baikal. Because of the increasing distance from Russia and the severity of the climate in the east, it never became as densely settled as Western Siberia. As a result, in the 1760s the western provinces of Tobolsk and Tomsk had about 196,000 Russian (male) settlers, while Irkutsk province – the whole vast territory beyond the Yenisey – only had 62,000.[1] The disproportion was even more marked by the end of the nineteenth century, when Western Siberia had a Russian population of 3,567,000, and Eastern only 850,000.[2]

An event of great importance for the opening up of Siberia to Russian penetration on a large scale was the creation of a continuous land route from the Urals to Irkutsk and beyond – an operation begun in 1763 which required the clearance of a wide swathe of forest and the provision of a surface regular enough to carry wheeled vehicles or sledges. The 'Great Moscow *trakt*' was an enormous achievement, little sung in Russian history, the construction of which had far-reaching effects. For one thing, this dryland road to a great extent superseded the use of river routes with their

---

[1] *Istoriya Sibiri*, vol. II, pp. 183–4. Multiplying by four for approximate family size gives a total 'Russian' population (both sexes) in Siberia in the 1760s of: 784,000 (western provinces)+248,000 (eastern)=1,032,000. Siberian natives numbered c. 528,000. For 1795 the figures in the same source give a total 'Russian' population of 1,336,000 (western) +312,000 (eastern) =1,648,000; natives totalled 732,000. The statistical accounts of the two governor-generalships prepared c. 1790 give lower figures: 'Russians' 504,650 (western)+135,316 (eastern)=639,966, with natives totalling 303,395. *Opisaniye Irkutskogo namestnichestva*, pp. 48–9; *Opisaniye Tobolskogo namestnichestva*, pp. 28, 34–5.

[2] *Aziatskaya Rossiya*, vol. I, p. 82.

seasonal hazards and the high cost of maintaining boats and barges. Caravans of carts or sledges now took over the transportation of goods between European Russia and Siberia, many having as their destination Kiakhta on the Chinese border. The *trakt* also opened up new land for peasant settlers and greatly stimulated the growth of those towns which lay on or near its course, such as Tyumen, Tomsk, Yeniseysk and Irkutsk. On the other hand, towns which were by-passed by the new highway suffered a decline. So Tobolsk, whose position far to the north of the *trakt* at the confluence of the Irtysh and the Ob had formerly ensured its supreme importance as a river-port, now gradually lost its commercial significance. It continued to be the seat of the governor-general of Siberia until 1824, when it was superseded in this function by Omsk, a town founded in 1716 on the Irtysh on the edge of the Kazak steppe frontier. One further aspect of the Siberian *trakt* was its detrimental effect on both the wild life of the forest and the nomadic hunting peoples. This first gross intrusion of European technology marked the beginning of the process – slow in its initial stages – of exploitation and irreversible alteration of the natural environment of northern Asia which, as in other parts of the world, would accelerate to breakneck speed in the second half of the twentieth century.[3]

The Siberian *trakt* was the highroad by which multitudes of immigrants from European Russia came to swell the population of Siberia, particularly from the middle of the nineteenth century up to 1914. In Russia the basis of the old agricultural régime – serfdom – had always prevented large-scale peasant migration, and even the decree abolishing it in 1861 did not remove the principal legal obstacle to freedom of movement, because peasants were still bound to the village commune, and it was not until 1906 that the reforms introduced by P.A. Stolypin made peasants legally free to move as they wished. Nevertheless, large numbers of people were driven by poverty to disregard the law and set out on the long journey to Siberia or the steppes of Kazakstan in search of a new life. In the 1880s there were about 35,000 such migrants per year, but this rose to approximately 96,000 per year in the late 1890s, and between 1906 and 1914 emigration from European Russia to Siberia became a flood. This reached its peak in the year 1908, during which 759,000 people crossed the Siberian boundary.

Another event of enormous significance for emigrants from European Russia was the construction of the Trans-Siberian railway, which began in 1891. By 1900 the line extended to Irkutsk, but it was interrupted by Lake Baikal and continued from the eastern shore to Chita and Sretensk, near Nerchinsk, where it ended. After the Russo-Japanese War (1904–5) the Russian government became actively interested in increasing the Russian population of Siberia in order to counterbalance the influence of Japan and

[3] *Istoriya Sibiri*, vol. II, p. 500; Kennan, *Siberia and the Exile System*, vol. I, p. 49; Yadrintsev, *Sibir kak koloniya*, p. 132.

other foreign powers in the Far East. Consequently, financial assistance to settlers was greatly increased. The period up to the beginning of the First World War saw the completion of the Trans-Siberian railway around Lake Baikal and from Sretensk to Khabarovsk and Vladivostok, which opened up the Far East for further settlement. Between 1896 and 1912 almost 1.8 million Russians left the provinces west of the Urals to go to Asiatic Russia, along with more than the same number of Ukrainians and half a million Belorussians. The predominance of Ukrainians increased during the three years immediately preceding the First World War, when they made up 60 per cent of all migrants to Asiatic Russia. Migrants from a given district tended to gravitate towards their fellow-countrymen, so that in many parts of south-west Siberia, the Altai and northern Kazakstan, more or less homogeneous colonies grew up which maintain their identity even today. Among Ukrainian settlements, for instance, there are at least four towns or villages called Poltavka, four Chernigovkas, two Ukrainkas, a Kharkovka, a Kievka and a Kievskiy. Poles and Lithuanians who joined the mass migration to the east (totalling about 90,000 by 1911) also formed compact communities in south-west Siberia and Yenisey province, while the peoples of the Volga chose sites on the edge of wooded steppe and taiga: by 1911 there were almost 54,000 Mordva, mainly in the Altai region, and settlements of at least as many Chuvash were scattered from Tobolsk to Krasnoyarsk. Estonians and Latvians migrated to Siberia in smaller numbers (some 27,000 altogether) but they earned a particularly high reputation as cultured and energetic settlers using modern farming methods.

The type of 'new Siberian' settler produced by the post-1905 wave of migration was generally of a higher calibre than his predecessors. Escaping from the cramping conditions of traditional village life in European Russia, they found in Western Siberia – a land which had never known Russian serfdom – new scope for their initiative. Many responded by developing a keen interest in agricultural innovation, including the latest machinery, so that Siberia before the First World War, far from being a backward region, was a shining example to the rest of the Russian Empire.

The most popular region for settlement remained the black-earth steppe of Tomsk province between the Irtysh, the Ob and the Altai mountains, where over 800,000 new settlers obtained land between 1893 and 1912. Altogether, from 1870 and 1914 a total of 5 million people moved from western Russia to Siberia and Kazakstan. By 1911 the population of Siberia had reached 9.4 million, of whom the unassimilated native peoples, numbering 1,073,154, now constituted only 11.5 per cent of the total, while Russians, Ukrainians and Belorussians accounted for 85 per cent.[4]

[4] *Aziatskaya Rossiya*, vol. I, pp. 188–98, 205, 214, 236, 450–99; vol. II, pp. 331–8; *Entsiklopedicheskiy slovar*, vol. XXIII, pp. 265–81; vol. XXIX, pp. 763, 769; *Istoriya Sibiri*, vol. III, pp. 199–203; Kalesnik, *Zapadnaya Sibir*, pp. 185, 393; Kennan, *Siberia and the Exile System*, vol. I, p. 33; D.W. Treadgold, *The Great Siberian Migration: Government and Peasant in Resettlement from Emancipation to the First World War*, Princeton, 1957, p. 9.

EXILES AND POLITICAL PRISONERS IN SIBERIA

Although the overwhelming majority of immigrants to Siberia in the nineteenth century were peasants, it was settlers of another kind that for long drew the attention of most visitors to the colony – the exiles and convicts who were sentenced to enforced residence there. The Russian government had almost completely abolished physical mutilation as a punishment in the late seventeenth century, and the death sentence in 1744, substituting deportation to Siberia as the punishment for an ever-expanding repertoire of crimes. (This practice was in line with the use of transportation to penal settlements in overseas colonies introduced at this period by other European states such as Britain and France.) The towns and villages of European Russia rid themselves of criminals, vagabonds and 'undesirable' elements by deporting them to Siberia, but once they reached their journey's end the question of what to do with them became a problem for the local population. Exiles were supposed to be attached to the households of 'Old Siberian' peasants, but the latter seldom welcomed them. Nor would the peasant communities allocate land to exiles as they were supposed to do, so that, in order to live, the latter were often obliged to sell themselves into a kind of bondage to the 'Old Siberians', who did not scruple to exploit their unfortunate brethren. Towns and industrial sites offered some opportunities for casual employment, but here too exiles were usually unwelcome and received very little recompense for their labour. As a result of these circumstances, many peasant exiles turned to begging and to vagabondage, and by the end of the nineteenth century this, with the associated evils of criminality and alcoholism, was one of the biggest social problems in Siberia, which aroused protest from the municipal authorities against the exile system.[5]

One possible refuge for runaway exiles and other uprooted people which opened up during the nineteenth century was gold-mining. Apart from the Urals, where some underground lodes were mined, most of the discoveries were of alluvial gold in river beds (placers) – first in the Altai and Tomsk regions, then the Angara and Yenisey valleys. Later the main gold field was on the river Vitim in the Lena basin in Eastern Siberia. For the laborious work of shifting earth and sand and feeding the separating machines, large numbers of workers were required, and the drifting hordes of exiles and landless peasants provided managers with an inexhaustible supply of cheap labour. In the 1850s over 30,000 workers were employed in the Yenisey gold-fields alone.[6]

Apart from criminals, many different catagories of people were subject to punitive exile. Thousands of religious non-conformists, particularly Old

[5] *Entsiklopedicheskiy slovar*, vol. XXXI, pp. 379–83; Wood, 'Sex and violence in Siberia'; Yadrintsev, *Sibir kak koloniya*, pp. 179–205.

[6] *Aziatskaya Rossiya*, vol. I, pp. 291, 399, 425, 431–4; vol. II, pp. 85, 485; *Istoriya Sibiri*, vol. II, pp. 362, 393–401, 440–3; vol. III, pp. 54–6; Kalesnik, *Ural*, p. 81, 124; Kennan, *Siberia and the Exile System*, vol. I, pp. 41–2; vol. II, pp. 164–5; Yadrintsev, *Sibir kak koloniya*, pp. 68, 182.

Believers, were banished to Siberia in the eighteenth century, so that settlements consisting predominantly of 'schismatics' grew up in certain localities. Other sects sent to Siberia for 'religious crimes' included the self-castrators (*skoptsy*) who, despite the especially harsh conditions in which they were obliged to found their settlements in Yakutia, achieved considerable prosperity as farmers, and so encouraged the development of agricultural techniques among the Yakuts. 'Religious crimes' were singled out for punishment on a level with political offences as late as 1900, when it was decreed, for instance, that Jews or Muslims who let baptised children lapse into their original faith, or non-Orthodox Christians who attempted to convert Orthodox believers to another religion, were to be deported to permanent residence in the most remote and primitive province of Yakutia. A special category of non-Russian exiles were people from Daghestan, Circassia and Trans-Caucasia, convicted for killing enemies in blood-feuds, or for participation in revolts against the Russian authorities and other political activities.[7]

The practice of sending prisoners-of-war to Siberia, which grew up in the seventeenth century, continued in the eighteenth, when about 1,100 Swedish officers, soldiers and sailors captured during the Great Northern War found themselves living beyond the Urals. Polish prisoners were also sent to Siberia, especially at the time of the Partitions of Poland (1772–95), and of subsequent insurrections against Russian rule in the nineteenth century, when as many as 100,000 Poles, largely members of the gentry, were deported. Many of them continued to defy their oppressors even under the most severe prison conditions, and from time to time tried to organise uprisings. This Polish element in the settler population of Siberia made a significant contribution to its cultural life as craftsmen, teachers, doctors and scholars, including J. Czerski, a geologist whose name is perpetuated in two Cherskiy mountain ranges in Eastern Siberia, A. Czekanowski, the explorer of northern regions of Central Siberia, W. Sieroszewski who described the life of the Yakuts among whom he was obliged to live in exile and B. Pilsudski the ethnographer of Sakhalin.[8]

The most notorious aspect of exile to Siberia was its application to 'political crimes'. This practice, which began in the seventeenth century, was continued up to the twentieth. Among the political exiles sent to Eastern Siberia were numerous Ukrainian Cossack leaders and Peter the Great's

[7] *Entsiklopedicheskiy slovar*, vol. XXXI, pp. 380; *Istoriya Dagestana*, ed. G.D. Daniyalov, 4 vols., Moscow, 1967–9, vol. II, pp. 85, 120, 145–8, 162, 323; D.M. Lang, *A Modern History of Georgia*, London, 1962, pp. 120–1, 124, 139–40 and passim.

[8] *Aziatskaya Rossiya*, vol. I, p. 235; *Entsiklopedicheskiy slovar*, vol. XXIX, pp. 763, 807; vol. XXXI, pp. 377–84; vol. XLI, pp. 622, 626; A. Gieysztor et al., *History of Poland*, Warsaw, 1968, pp. 327, 463, 481–3, 533, 536; L.M. Goryushkin, ed., *Ssylka i katorga v Sibiri (XVIII–nachalo XX v.)*, Novosibirsk, 1975, pp. 40–4, 153–60; *Istoriya Sibiri*, vol. II, pp. 189–90, 314, 474–6; vol. III, pp. 114–22; Kennan, *Siberia*, vol. I, pp. 76–7, 81, 87–98, 114, 299, 311–20, 387–8; vol. II, pp. 368, 544–55; *Narody Sibiri*, pp. 138, 167, 176–7, 277; Solovyov, *Istoriya Rossii*, vol. VII, pp. 111, 240; vol. XI, p. 405; Yadrintsev, *Sibir kak koloniya*, p. 84.

favourite, Prince Menshikov, who, after the Tsar's death, was despatched to Berezov in 1728, and soon died there. Many other members of the nobility were exiled to various remote parts of Yakutsk district. One of the most notable of these was F.I. Soymonov who, after being flogged and sentenced to twenty years at the salt-works at Okhotsk for opposition to von Bühren, was freed by Empress Elizabeth and eventually appointed governor of Siberia – a duty he performed with exceptional probity from 1757 to 1763.

In the reign of Catherine the Great the first of a new type of enemy of the state was exiled to Siberia – A.N. Radishchev, whose humanitarian attack on autocracy and serfdom, published the year after the French Revolution, made him a dangerous criminal in the eyes of the Empress. Radishchev spent six years in exile at Ilimsk. One result of his sojourn in Tobolsk on his way there was a courageous denunciation of the violence and injustice of the Russian state system made by the Orthodox priest P.A. Slovtsov in his sermons in Tobolsk cathedral. Arrested in 1794, Slovtsov was taken to St Petersburg and incarcerated for a time in Valaam monastery on Lake Ladoga. Subsequently he became one of the first historians of Siberia. The nineteenth century brought many more political prisoners to Siberia, including participants in the 1825 Decembrist revolt, 105 of whom were sentenced to periods of up to twenty years of hard labour in the silver mines of Nerchinsk district, followed by enforced settlement for life in various towns and villages of Siberia, and 22 men of Petrashevskiy's circle arrested in 1849. Among these was the writer F.M. Dostoyevskiy, who spent four years in the convict prison at Omsk, followed by seven years of enforced service in the ranks of the Semipalatinsk garrison. Such cases of suppression of political opposition were particularly numerous in the 1870s and 1880s, during the reigns of Alexander II and Alexander III, when the Populist revolutionary movement was at its height. The writer N.G. Chernyshevskiy was one of those who suffered lengthy exile at this time.

Although the use of exile to Siberia as a punishment for common criminals was stopped in 1900, it was still applied to offenders against religious and political regulations. As a result, up to 1917 many people continued to be sent to Siberia as convicts, especially in the reactionary aftermath to the 1905 Revolution when almost 100,000 people were put into the prison of the Russian Empire because of their political activities. Among the members of revolutionary parties who suffered exile at this time were some, like the SR Socialists V.G. Bogoraz and V.I. Iokhelson, who participated in geographical and ethnographical expeditions in north-east Siberia and left important published works on the native peoples.[9]

---

[9] *Entsiklopedicheskiy slovar*, vol. XXXI, pp. 380–3; Goryushkin, *Ssylka i katorga*, pp. 15–37; Hrushevsky, *History of Ukraine*, pp. 333, 344; *Istoriya Yakutskoy ASSR*, vol. II, pp. 226–7; Kennan, *Siberia*, vol. I, pp. 81, 256–8; vol. II, pp. 223–74; *Istoriya Sibiri*, vol. II, pp. 312, 449, 465–74; vol. III, pp. 121–7; Slovtsov, *Istoricheskoye obozreniye*, pp. 5–14; Yadrintsev, *Sibir kak koloniya*, pp. 184–5.

THE RUSSIANS OF SIBERIA

After three centuries of occupation and immigration, the non-indigenous population of Siberia was composed of many different elements and was in many respects unstable. Agricultural settlement had brought not only Russian peasants but also Ukrainians, Belorussians and people from the Baltic and Middle Volga, while the urban population included a proportion of two nationalities characteristic of Russian town life in the late nineteenth century: Jews and Tatars. Until the 1830s Jews had reached Siberia only as convicts or exiles, and they were specifically forbidden to settle there by the laws restricting Jews to residence within the Pale of Settlement. Under the contradictory legislation of Nicholas I's reign some Jews were first encouraged to move to Siberia as agricultural settlers, then forbidden to remain. Thereafter their residence was subject to the same discriminatory regulations and arbitrary administrative actions that prevailed in European Russia. Despite these hazards, however, by the end of the century there were some 34,500 Jews living in Siberia, the largest communities being in Yekaterinburg, Chelyabinsk, Tobolsk, Omsk, Tomsk, Irkutsk, Kainsk, Verkhneudinsk and Chita. The great majority of Jews settled in towns, where they fulfilled their characteristic functions in crafts and commerce, thus making a significant contribution to the economic development of the colony.[10]

Volga Tatars from the rural region around Kazan had been moving to Siberia in small numbers since the seventeenth century, either as exiles or as voluntary settlers, but many more went east during the nineteenth century because of over-population and poverty, so that by 1900 over 27,000 Kazan Tatars lived east of the Urals. Western Siberia with its population of indigenous Tatars provided an obvious refuge for many Kazan Tatars, who could readily assimilate to (and give a cultural leavening to) the local communities around Tobolsk and Tyumen, along the Irtysh, and in the Baraba steppe and Tomsk; but at least as many found their way beyond the Ob into Central and Eastern Siberia. As a result, in 1897 over 6,500 Tatars lived in Irkutsk and its surroundings, and 2,600 in Transbaikalia. Even in the remoteness of Yakutia there were about 1,500 Tatars – some of them, no doubt, exiles. Like many of their compatriots in European Russia, Kazan Tatar migrants in Siberia found employment in towns as craftsmen, factory workers and carters, or as labourers, while some achieved prosperity as merchants specialising in the grain, salt or leather trade.[11]

[10] *Aziatskaya Rossiya*, vol. I, p. 85; *Encyclopaedia Judaica*, vol. XIV, cols. 1486–8; *Entsiklopedicheskiy slovar*, vols. VI, p. 67; XI, pp. 646, 657; XIII, pp. 324–5, 328, 331, 939; XVI, pp. 554–5; XXI, pp. 46, 48, 938–9; XXXIII, pp. 384, 487, 490; XXXVIII, pp. 492, 880; XLI, pp. 622, 628–9; *Sibirskaya Sovetskaya Entsiklopediya*, vol. I, cols. 869–71.

[11] *Aziatskaya Rossiya*, vol. I, p. 83; *Entsiklopedicheskiy slovar*, vol. XXXIV, p. 349; *Narody yevropeyskoy chasti SSSR*, vol. II, pp. 634, 640; Tumasheva, *Dialekty sibirskikh tatar*, pp. 16–24.

Although the dominant population was clearly Russian, and nearly all the essential elements of Russian society and government had been imported into Siberia and taken root there, its status as a colony or possession was still ambiguous. It was not yet plausible to assert – as the Soviet government would claim fifty years later – that Siberia was an integral part of Russia. The colonial status of Siberia – not to mention the steppe regions of Kazakstan and Central Asia – was an obvious fact to Russians at this time, and the question of migration (*pereseleniye*) – the eastward movement of masses of people to colonise the unsettled lands – was a living issue, one of the obsessions of Russian society, on which a host of books and articles appeared in the final decade of the nineteenth century and the first of the twentieth.[12] The social and political strains involved in this mass migration were considerable. Within the Russian community the interests of the new raw settlers had to be reconciled with those of the Russian Old Siberians; the old interests of the state – mining and punitive exile – conflicted with the bustling urban development which had produced a middle class with a sense of civic pride; and the interests of the colonisers clashed with, and generally overrode, those of the native peoples.

As in any empire, relations between the metropolis and the residents of the colony were often perceived by the latter as unnecessary, and their meaningfulness was less clear the farther they lived from administrative centres. For the citizens of European Russia, on the other hand, much of the vast colony came within the category of 'backwoods' – primitive lands devoid of the fruits of civilisation. Thus Governor-General Speranskiy, after his investigative tour of Siberia in 1819–21, wrote: 'It's terrible to spend two years without meeting a single cultured person or hearing one intelligent word!'[13] The farther north and east one went, the less enlightenment had penetrated, and the total absence of any centres of culture in the remote provinces, where mail might be delivered only three times a year, was notorious. Even along the main southern highway, however, the level of culture in the towns was, in Chekhov's experience (1890) little better:

The local intelligentsia ... drinks vodka from morning till night ... After the very first phrases of conversation your local intellectual never fails to ask – 'What about a drop of vodka?' And out of boredom the exile drinks along with him ... So far as drunkenness is concerned, it's not the exiles that corrupt the old Siberian population, but the old Siberians that corrupt the exiles ... leaving aside the bad restaurants, the family bathhouses and the numerous brothels, open or clandestine, to which the Siberian is so addicted, there is no form of recreation whatever in the towns.[14]

Not everyone took such a pessimistic view of Siberia, which did have its cultured people who were concerned both about the present state of the

---

[12] *Aziatskaya Rossiya*, vol. I, maps between pp. 490 and 491; vol. III, pp. lxxiii–xcviii.
[13] *Entsiklopedicheskiy slovar*, vol. XXIX, p. 812.
[14] Chekhov, 'Iz Sibiri', ch. 7; *Polnoye sobraniye sochineniy i pisem*, Moscow, 1974–83, vol. XIV–XV, p. 27.

colony and its future. One of the main problems of practical politics was that, although Siberian municipalities enjoyed the same degree of self-government as those in European Russia, rural districts did not. When in 1864 the elected rural government councils or *zemstvos* were created, they were restricted to the provinces of European Russia where land-owners could play the leading role in the councils. Since Siberia had no privately owned estates, the *zemstvos* were not extended to the colony, with the result that no mechanism existed for local initiative in the fields of education, hospitals or the promotion of the economy. In the early years of the twentieth century three views of Siberia's future needs were current among its Russian inhabitants. Most believed that the introduction of *zemstvos* was essential, and would permit local communities to exercise the necessary degree of self-government. The right wing, on the other hand, held with the government's view that without an upper class the Siberians were incapable of governing themselves. The third and most radical view was that Siberia required semi-independent status under its own government.[15]

It was a fact that to most of its 'old Siberian' inhabitants Siberia was not Russia. They referred to people from beyond the Urals as 'Russians' (*rossiyskiye*), asked 'Are you from Russia?', and were not particularly interested in what was happening in that distant land.[16] The many differences between the colony and European Russia were inescapable, especially in the Far East, as Chekhov found:

my God, how far removed life here is from Russia! . . . While I was sailing down the Amur I really felt I wasn't in Russia at all, but somewhere in Patagonia or Texas. Quite apart from the strange, un-Russian scenery, I constantly got the impression that our Russian way of life is completely alien to the old settlers on the Amur . . . and that we who come from Russia appear as foreigners.[17]

Apart from the geographical distance separating Siberia from European Russia, the ethnic differences between the people of the two regions were used as an argument for autonomy. The ethnic elements introduced to Siberia by the Russian conquest undoubtedly left a deep mark upon the racial features of the native peoples, and vice versa. From the beginning of Russian penetration beyond the Urals thousands of native women became slaves, concubines or wives of the incomers of all social categories from *voyevodas* to peasants. As a result, the population of Siberia includes a large component of half-breeds, whose mixed origin is reflected in their physical features and language. In most places the Russian 'Old Siberian' population which developed in isolation from centres of compact Russian settlement,

---

[15] Nansen, *Through Siberia*, pp. 288–9; Treadgold, *Great Siberian Migration*, pp. 21–2; Yadrintsev, *Sibir kak koloniya*, pp. 47–8.
[16] Yadrintsev, *Sibir kak koloniya*, pp. 62–3.
[17] Chekhov, *Ostrov Sakhalin, Polnoye sobraniye sochineniy i pisem*, vol. XIV–XV, ch. 1, pp. 42–3.

possessed many Asiatic features, however Russian their names might be. Not only did they have the wide, prominent cheekbones, more or less 'slanting' eyes, sparse beard and black straight hair of their Samoyed, Ugrian, Tungus, Yakut or Buryat Mongol ancestors, but they had adopted the behaviour of the local natives. For instance, those in the Far North ate raw meat, wore the costume of the native people, and frequently believed as much in the powers of shamans as in Orthodox Christianity.[18]

The view of Siberia as a separate entity no doubt emerged at quite an early stage of its conquest by the Russians, as a natural result of its remoteness from European Russia. This factor encouraged not only Cossack mutineers, but in some cases *voyevodas* and governors, to act in disregard of the central government, treating parts of Siberia as if they were independent of Russia. Even a certain degree of official encouragement was given to the notion of autonomy in the 1760s, when Catherine the Great instituted the 'Siberian kingdom' (*Sibirskoye tsarstvo*) on the grounds that it should not be merely a dependency of Russia but a kind of self-supporting dominion with its own currency. After 1781, however, the idea of the Siberian kingdom was abandoned and no Russian government ever gave any encouragement to the federal concept or 'regionalism' (*oblastnichestvo*) as it came to be called. Neither the *zemstvo* reform nor the full juridical reform of 1864 were extended to Siberia, and when as a result of the 1905 Revolution the State Duma was created, there were only 21 deputies (out of the total 524) for the whole of Siberia, and this number was reduced to 14 (out of 442) in the Third Duma. From the point of view of Nicholas II's government this small number of deputies was no doubt justified in view of the relatively radical 1907 election results in Siberia, which produced no deputies farther to the right than the Constitutional Democrats with six seats, along with three SD-socialists and three SR-socialists or 'Labourists'.[19]

There was reason for the central government's apprehensiveness about the radicalism of the relatively democratic Siberian 'periphery', since the possibility of the colony separating itself from Russia, as the USA had gained independence from Britain, had been an obvious and commonly expressed idea since the first half of the nineteenth century. Constitutional projects formulated by the Decembrists were influenced by American federalism, and some of the Slavophiles envisaged Siberia as one distinct element in a

---

[18] *Aziatskaya Rossiya*, vol. I, pp. 185–6; *Istoriya Sibiri*, vol. II, p. 14; Kozlov, *Natsionalnosti*, p. 228; Tokarev, *Etnografiya*, p. 33; Yadrintsev, *Sibir kak koloniya*, pp. 11, 14–19, 33–8, 42, 50.

[19] *Istoriya Sibiri*, vol. II, p. 233; L. Martov et al., *Obshchestvennoye dvizheniye v Rossii v nachale XX-go veka*, St Petersburg, 4 vols, 1909–14, vol. IV, pt. 2, pp. 143–4; D. von Mohrenschildt, *Toward a United States of Russia: Plans and Projects of Federal Reconstruction of Russia in the Nineteenth Century*, London, 1981, p. 91; C.J. Smith, 'The Russian Third State Duma: an analytical profile', *The Russian Review*, 1958, vol. XVII, pp. 208–9; Treadgold, *Great Siberian Migration*, pp. 20, 197.

Slavic federation uniting the various Slavic lands of Eastern Europe and Russia. By the 1860s the idea of Siberian autonomy was popular among St Petersburg students hailing from Siberia, who formed an association under the characteristically nationalist title of 'Young Siberia'. The leaders of this circle were G.N. Potanin and N.M. Yadrintsev, both of whom had attended school in Omsk. Among their aims were the economic development of Siberia as an entity independent of European Russia, the establishment of a university in Siberia to avert the drift of gifted young people to the metropolis, and improvements in the conditions of the native peoples. Some members of the Young Siberia circle were radical revolutionaries, and the discovery in Omsk and Irkutsk of proclamations calling for the secession of Siberia from Russia as an autonomous republic led to the arrest of many of them in 1865. Potanin and Yadrintsev both received long sentences to hard labour. The discussion of radical views on the future of Siberia was thus silenced, but the question of the colony's distinctiveness and possible autonomy – perhaps with a status like that of the Dominion of Canada, created in 1867 – did not disappear, but continued to engage the minds of Siberian intellectuals. When revolution came in 1917, therefore, it was not surprising that the Russian Siberians, although they could scarcely claim to be a separate nationality like the Tatars or Ukrainians, nevertheless reasserted their demands for autonomy.[20]

[20] *Istoriya Sibiri*, vol. II, p. 14; von Mohrenschildt, *United States of Russia*, pp. 18–30, 43, 62, 92–130; A. Wood, 'Chernyshevskii, Siberian exile and oblastnichestvo', in R. Bartlett, ed., *Russian Thought and Society 1800–1917: Essays in Honour of Eugene Lampert*, Keele, 1984, pp. 50–61.

10

THE FAR EAST IN THE NINETEENTH CENTURY

SAKHALIN AND THE KURIL ISLANDS

RUSSIA'S trans-Pacific venture was relatively short-lived, but at the same time as the government was being forced to the conclusion that Alaska was more of a liability than an asset, new compensatory possibilities for expansion were opening up for the Russians on their own side of the Pacific.

When the Russians' brief occupation of parts of the Amur basin had been brought to an end by the Treaty of Nerchinsk in 1689, they were pushed back north of the watershed in the Stanovoy mountains. Thereafter the Russians respected this as the frontier and did not make any official incursions into what they recognised as Chinese territory. A Russian request for permission to sail on the Amur in 1758 was rejected by China, and this deterred Russia for half a century, during which time it concentrated its attention on the Japanese domain, of which Sakhalin was an important feature.[1]

Sakhalin forms part of the noose of islands which enclose the Sea of Okhotsk and partially separate it from the Pacific Ocean. Its proximity to the southern part of Russia's Siberian coastline on the one hand, and the Kuril Islands on the other, made it inevitable that it would attract the attention of the Russian mariners who explored these waters in the eighteenth century. Coming into contact with the Japanese of Hokkaido, these voyagers sighted the south-eastern end of Sakhalin, and the first Russian landing there was made in 1783. The Japanese themselves had been visitors to the southern end of the island since at least the beginning of the seventeenth century. Their fishermen came there from Hokkaido every summer, and in 1806 a Japanese explorer, Mimiya Rinzo, sailed north up the Tatar Strait and into the mouth of the Amur. The Chinese too knew something of Sakhalin. As early as the fourteenth century the realm of the Ming dynasty extended

[1] Alekseyev, *Osvoyeniye*, pp. 49–50, 52–3; Solovyov, *Istoriya Rossii*, vol. XIII, p. 352.

northwards to Nurkan at the mouth of the Amur, and the native tribes living in the northern part of the island paid regular tribute to the Ch'ing authorities up to the late eighteenth century. Consequently the first Russian explorers were cautious in their approach, because they had reason to believe that Sakhalin belonged either to China or Japan.[2] In fact at the beginning of the nineteenth century Sakhalin did not clearly 'belong' to any organised state, although it was the home of several ethnic groups, some of whom were tributaries of China or Japan. At that time even the northernmost island of present-day Japan – Hokkaido – had not yet been intensively colonised by the Japanese, and, as in southern Sakhalin and the Kuril Islands, most of its inhabitants were Ainus.

It was the Russias who first demonstrated the determination of the European powers to force their way into Japan and China at all costs. The Tsar's envoy Rezanov, infuriated at the receipt of yet another rebuff when he tried to establish direct trading relations with Japan in 1804–5, decided to use force. As a result, piratical raids were carried out by ships of the Russian navy against Japanese fishing posts in southern Sakhalin. While a Samurai of the time fulminated against these murderous forays by 'barbarians', a typical modern Russian account presents this aggression in a heroic light: 'The officers performed with honour the mission assigned to them ... they ... visited Aniwa Bay in 1806, raised the Russian flag, compiled a description of all the places they visited, threw out the Japanese and sent them back to Hokkaido.'[3] Thereafter the Russian ships proceeded to make raids on the Japanese Kuril island of Etorofu (Iturup) and on Hokkaido itself.[4]

It was for strategic reasons that the Russian government, seeing the increasing intrusion of Britain and the USA into the affairs of the Far East, decided on the occupation of Sakhalin in 1853. Ignoring the presence of Japanese posts at Tomari and Kushunnai, the Russians claimed the whole of the island for the Russian Empire. Diplomatic negotiations led to a treaty whereby the Kuril Islands were divided between Japan and Russia, while Sakhalin was to be undivided but shared jointly by the two countries. This situation was maintained during the ensuing twenty years, and colonisation by both Russians and Japanese proceeded apace, but the rival claims of

---

[2] Alekseyev, *Osvoyeniye*, pp. 66, 70, 171; Bai Shouyi, *Outline History of China*, pp. 298, 333; Lee, *Manchurian Frontier*, pp. 15, 43–5, 48; G.A. Lensen, *The Russian Push toward Japan: Russo-Japanese Relations, 1697–1875*, Princeton, 1959, pp. 94n., 132, 247–8, 271–3, 425, 427; J.J. Stephan, *Sakhalin: a History*, Oxford, 1971, pp. 19–23, 32–3; Twitchett and Fairbank, *Cambridge History of China*, vol. X, pt. 1, p. 334.

[3] Alekseyev, *Osvoyeniye*, p. 74.

[4] Lensen, *Russian Push toward Japan*, pp. 103–16, 121–2, 158, 168, 171, 178–93, 247–8, 272; G. Sansom, *A History of Japan 1615–1867*, London, 1964, pp. 181–2; Stephan, *Kuril Islands*, pp. 73–7, *Sakhalin*, pp. 45–7.

Japan and Russia were resolved in 1876 in a new treaty according to which Japan relinquished entirely its rights to Sakhalin in exchange for the surrender of the whole of the Kuril Islands to Japan.[5]

THE AMUR BORDERLANDS OF MANCHURIA

Between the Treaty of Nerchinsk (1689) and the late eighteenth century, Chinese and Russian interest in the Amur basin had been minimal. Officially the Manchu rulers of the Ch'ing dynasty retained Manchuria as their own preserve, from which the other inhabitants of China, chiefly the predominant Han population, were excluded. In fact, however, as the Manchus became assimilated to Chinese culture they lost their links with the tribal past of their homeland, while, notwithstanding the laws which excluded them, the Han Chinese began to move into Manchuria. As a result, by 1800 not only were the southern parts of Manchuria proper full of Chinese settlers, but even in the northern Heilungchiang province nine-tenths of the population of the towns were Hans. The Manchu military system of 'banners' still constituted the nominal élite of this north-eastern corner of the Chinese Empire, but its original composition of Manchus, Mongols and Chinese had been augmented by units composed of local Dahurs, Tungus (Orochons and Solons) and Nanai tribesmen. The motley nature of its population was further increased by the fact that Manchuria was used by Peking during the eighteenth century as a kind of Chinese Siberia – a place of banishment for disgraced state officials, and for convicted criminals who became part of the floating population of the region. In any case Manchuria had become a natural haven for Chinese outlaws, who engaged in such illegal activities as poaching game, seeking ginseng (which was a government monopoly), prospecting for gold or simply operating as bands of robbers – the notorious *hunghutzŭ* or 'red-beards'.

So far as the Manchus and Chinese were concerned, for most purposes their territory stopped at the Heilung river (Amur). Where it was feasible to establish contact with the 'barbarian' peoples who lived along the Amur and the Ussuri, such as the Nanais and Nivkhs, these had nominally been subjected to the Emperor and were required to give an annual tribute of furs in the same way as other native peoples of Siberia had to give *yasak* for the Tsar, but apart from the garrison and market towns of Aihun and Deren, there were few Chinese on the river at the beginning of the nineteenth century. The first Russians to take advantage of the ill-defined limits of China here were hunter-trappers and Cossacks who ventured to cross the Stanovoy range and descend the valleys of the Zeya and Bureya in quest of prey, and Yakuts also began to hunt in the northern parts of the Amur basin.

---

[5] Lensen, *Russian Push toward Japan*, pp. 337, 426–7, 442–5; Alekseyev, *Osvoyeniye*, pp. 58, 78–9; Stephan, *Kuril Islands*, pp. 86–95, *Sakhalin*, pp. 49–64.

Proposals for the annexation of the Amur were made in St Petersburg from as early as 1756, and it was only the desirability of maintaining good trading relations with China through Kiakhta, and fear of China's strength as a military adversary, that prevented the Russian imperial authorities from embarking on such an adventure at that time. Thus, apart from occasional visits by Russian hunters, Cossacks or escaped convicts from Nerchinsk, the indigenous peoples of the Amur basin were left to their own devices from 1689 to the nineteenth century.[6]

Officially the Russian government respected China's refusal to open up the 'question' of the Amur territories, which clearly belonged to China by the Treaty of Nerchinsk, but exploration or reconnaissance of the region went ahead under the flag of the Russo-American Company and with the tacit approval of the Russian government. The most important Russian explorations were carried out by Captain G. Nevelskoy, an ardent empire-builder enjoying the patronage of the Siberian governor-general, Count N. N. Muravyov. In 1850 Nevelskoy, having ascertained that the Chinese government had no army in the lower Amur region, set up two military posts, including the future town of Nikolayevsk, near the mouth of the river. Three years later, during the same expedition which claimed Sakhalin for the Russian Empire, Nevelskoy founded two Russian posts on the Chinese coast of the Sea of Japan. By then China was in the throes of the T'aip'ing Rebellion (1850–64), during which Britain and France launched the 'Second Opium War' against her.[7] Faced with the fact of Russian occupation of the lands beyond the Amur, where villages had been founded, forest land cleared for agriculture, and military garrisons installed, the Chinese government was obliged to sign the Treaty of Aihun (1858), whereby all territory north of the Amur was ceded to Russia. The supplementary Treaty of Peking in 1860 recognised the annexation by Russia of the territory between the Ussuri and the Sea of Japan – which the Russians in any case had already designated at their Maritime Province (*Primorskaya oblast*) as early as 1856! The southern part of the territory seized from China embraced most of Lake Hsingk'ai (Hanka) and the lower reaches of the Suifen river, on the very doorstep of Korea. Here, on a promontory projecting into the bay to which the Russians gave the name of Peter the Great, the strategic seaport of Vladivostok – 'Power-in-the East' – was quickly established. Thus Russia's exploitation of a beleaguered China's weakness resulted in the latter being

---

[6] *Aziatskaya Rossiya*, vol. I, pp. 21, 515–16; *Entsiklopedicheskiy slovar*, vol. XVIII, pp. 557, 580; Lee, *Manchurian Frontier*, pp. 2–6, 20–3, 32, 42–51, 70–115; Twitchett and Fairbank, *Cambridge History of China*, vol. X, pt. 1, pp. 38–47, 331, 343.

[7] Alekseyev, *Osvoyeniye*, pp. 52, 56–60, 76; Bancroft, *History of Alaska*, pp. 570–2; Golder, *Russian Expansion*, pp. 264–5, Lensen, *Russian Push toward Japan*, pp. 273, 284; Twitchett and Fairbank, *Cambridge History of China*, vol. X, pt. 1, pp. 334–43.

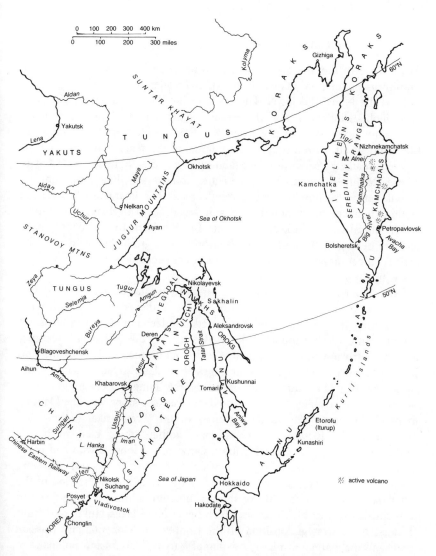

Map 8 The Far East in the nineteenth century

despoiled of 'a country as large as France and Germany put together, and of a river as large as the Danube', as Engels wrote.[8]

THE INDIGENOUS PEOPLES OF THE AMUR AND SAKHALIN

At the time of the annexation of the Amur–Ussuri region by the Russian Empire its population was composed of a considerable number of peoples, such as the Nanai, Ulchi, Nivkh and Udeghe. The most widespread, and most mobile, inhabitants of the Amur region were the Ewenki Tungus. Before the nineteenth century, when no effective state frontiers existed here (the Amur itself, frozen over for six months of the year, is no obstacle) the Ewenkis roamed freely from the Stanovoy mountains to the Great Hsingan. These Reindeer-Tungus (known to the Chinese as Olunch'un from the Ewenki term Orochon 'possessing reindeer') in their characteristic deerskin clothing followed the traditional nomadic way of life with their herds, camping in conical skin or bark-covered tents. In Manchuria the Orochons, many of them belonging to the Birar or Manegir clans, gradually lost or gave up their reindeer, adopted horse-riding, and were pressed into service with the Manchu banner armies.

Other Ewenki clans of the upper Amur and Zeya had been associated with the Mongolian-speaking Dahur settlers or, farther downriver, with the Manchurian Juchers, and had abandoned reindeer nomadism in favour of fishing, cattle-rearing and agriculture. When, after the seventeenth-century Russian intrusion into this region, the Manchus forced the Dahurs and Juchers to move away from the Amur, these Ewenkis also moved south to the river Nonni in Manchuria. Here these 'Horse Tungus' became known as Solons, and were obliged to enter the banner armies along with the Dahurs, in much the same way as the Ewenkis of the Transbaikal region were enlisted by the Russians as Cossacks. Another ethnic element in the Manchus' Amur province of Heilungchiang were Mongols who had come over either from the Baikal region or from Outer Mongolia, and who were designated collectively as the Barga. After the Manchus' subjection of the Khalkha Mongols at the end of the seventeenth century they annexed to Manchuria the part of Mongolia which lies around lakes Hulun and Buir. Because of its strategic position on the frontiers of Mongolia and Russian Transbaikalia, banner armies consisting of Bargas, Dahurs and Solons were

---

[8] F. Engels, 'Russia's successes in the Far East', in K. Marx and F. Engels, *Collected Works*, London [Moscow], 1975–, vol. XVI, p. 83, quoted in Bai Shouyi, *Outline History of China*, p. 445. A Soviet Russian account cites Marx in implied *approval* of Russia's actions in China, and rejects the idea that any international problem might exist concerning the 'natural boundaries' of Russian territory in the Far East, Alekseyev, *Osvoyeniye*, pp. 58–62.

sent to garrison the Hulun-Buir district, which thus came to have a very mixed population.[9]

The Tungus also made a specific contribution to the population of the lower Amur and neighbouring seaboard. On the Amgun, the left-bank tributary nearest the mouth of the Amur, lived people known as Negidals (from Ewenki *ngegida* 'shoreside'), the descendants of Ewenkis who had settled down to a way of life in which the hunting of forest animals was combined with fishing and sealing. They adopted many of the common elements of Amur life – heated winter houses, wrap-over robes of fishskin, and plank boats – while preserving, along with their Tungus language, some other features of Ewenki life, such as conical teepees, broad skis, the use of reindeer for riding, the open-fronted deerskin coat with apron, birchbark canoes etc. The Negidals were a small community of less than 500 people in the nineteenth century.

Reindeer-herding Tungus had also penetrated the Pacific coastal region south of the Amur estuary. Some indeed had migrated across the straits to Sakhalin, forming a small ethnic group (no more than 750 people) known as Oroks. Like the Negidals, they combined traditional Ewenki reindeer culture with the less typical occupations of fishing and seal-hunting, but their language is closely related to that of the Ulchi. On the mainland, east of the Amur, lived yet another small community, the Oroches. They spoke a Manchurian language close to that of their neighbours the Udeghe; they harnessed their dog-teams in the Nivkh manner; and they wore either wrap-over robes of the general Amur type or open-fronted Ewenki coats and aprons of deerskin.[10]

THE NIVKH, ULCHI AND OTHER PEOPLES OF THE LOWER AMUR

At one geographical and ethnic extreme of the Amur population were the Nivkh people, who lived around the Amur estuary and in the northern half of Sakhalin island, where they had contacts with the Ainus. The Nivkhs (formerly called by the Russians 'Gilyaks') were essentially a maritime people who stood out from their neighbours by their almost total dependence on fishing and the hunting of sea-mammals, like the Chukchis and Eskimos of the north. Fish was preserved, chiefly by drying, for consumption in winter, and their diet was supplemented by wild fruits gathered in summer and

---

[9] Gurvich, *Etnicheskaya istoriya*, pp. 129–43; Lee, *Manchurian Frontier*, pp. 15–16, 32–34, 48–51, 64–5, 122–4; Qiu Pu, *The Oroqens – China's Nomadic Hunters*, Beijing, 1983, pp. 31–3, 41–5, 75–8; Shirokogorov, *Social Organization*, pp. 62–3, 67–8, 74, 77–8.

[10] A.F. Majewicz, 'The Oroks: past and present', in Wood and French, *The Development of Siberia*, pp. 124–31; *Narody Sibiri*, pp. 776–82, 844–60.

autumn. They were unrelated to any of their neighbours in language, and their way of life had features in common with the Ainus, Itelmens and other North Pacific peoples. Their most usual winter dwelling, for instance, was a timber lodge sunk into the ground and covered with earth, while in summer they lived in huts raised above the ground on stilts. Dogs played a central part in the life of the Nivkhs, not only for pulling sleds, but also in their religion and their diet. For mobility on river and sea the Nivkhs had various types of boat, ranging from light canoes made out of bark or dug-out poplar trunks, to larger vessels of the kind common to all the Amur peoples, constructed of planks. Untypically, the Nivkhs cremated their dead, breaking the sled on which the body was brought to the pyre, and killing and eating dogs as a sacrifice. The ashes were gathered for preservation in a specially constructed little house, along with a wooden effigy incorporating bone and hair from the deceased, and a series of memorial feasts were held there over a period of up to three years. Nivkh decorative art, chiefly patterns carved on wooden implements and ritual objects, differed from that of other Siberian peoples in using motifs of twisted and interlaced ribbons. Being located within the cultural orbit of China, the Nivkhs, like the other Amur peoples, had advanced beyond the stage of stone and bone implements and were able to work in iron which they received from the Chinese or Japanese, and in olden times some of them possessed coats of armour made with iron plates. Silver and copper were used for the ornamentation of spear-tips. In the religion of the Nivkhs various 'masters' of natural phenomena were revered, including the killer-whale, as the master of all animals. The cult of the bear was highly developed, the most important religious event of the year being the clan bear feast in honour of a deceased relative. For this purpose a family would nurture a bear in captivity for several years, and when the time came it was tethered between posts and shot with arrows. Fixed rituals dictated the manner in which the bear was then skinned, dismembered, cooked and eaten, being treated all the time with respect so that it would not seek vengeance when it was resurrected, and its skull was added to the collection in the clan sanctuary. The festivities, which lasted several days, included dog-sled races, archery contests, dances and the sacrifice of dogs.

Because of the uniqueness of their culture, the Nivkhs are considered by Russian historians to be the descendants of an original Neolithic population on the lower Amur, which has left many remnants of clay vessels decorated with patterns of spirals and human faces. These, along with many rock-carvings, testify to the existence of a relatively advanced civilisation here in the fourth to third millennia BC. (In the nineteenth century none of the native peoples of the Amur region made pottery.) Whatever their origins, the Nivkhs, who numbered about 5,000 in the middle of the nineteenth century, suffered less direct interference from the Russians than their neighbours, and so preserved their original culture – including an exogamic clan system, mutual aid, blood vengeance and a kind of group marriage – more or less intact until the end of the nineteenth century.[11]

Linguistically, while Nivkh is not related in basic vocabulary or structure to any of its neighbours, nor to Chinese, Japanese or any other language, all the other indigenous peoples of the Amur and maritime region belong to the same Manchu-Tungus family as the Ewenkis. The words in Table 4 demonstrate these linguistic similarities and differences.[12]

Table 4

	Manchu	Nanai	Ulchi	Udeghe	Nivkh
man	haha	bey	bey	bey	utku
father	ama	ama	ama	ami(n)	ytyk
mother	eme	enie	enie	eni(n)	ymyk
home	dyog	dyo(g)	ju	jugdi	ryf, tyf
fish	nimakha	sogdata	sugdata	sugjegä	cho
big	amba	dai	dai	sagdi	pil
I	bi	mi	bi	mi	nyi
one	emu	emun	um(un)	omo	n–
two	juwe	dyuer	juel(i)	ju	m–
three	ilan	ilan	ila(n)	ila	t–
five	sunja	toinga	tunja	tunga	t'–
ten	juwan	dyoan	jua(n)	ja	mkho
to be	bi–	bi–	bi–	bi–	had
to kill	va–	ma–	ma–	va–	kud

The Manchus, Nanais, Udeghes and Ulchis are descendants of the Tungus tribes of Ilou, Mohe and Pohai, which played a considerable part in Chinese history from the first century BC to the tenth century AD, and of the once powerful Jurchens who gave rise to the Manchus in the sixteenth century.[13]

The stretch of the Amur basin immediately upstream from the Nivkh territory, and eastward as far as the sea-coast opposite Sakhalin, was the home of the Ulchi people, who in the nineteenth century numbered about 1,500. Their main source of food was the river with its rich harvest of fish – principally the salmon which came up the Amur from the ocean to spawn

[11] *Entsiklopedicheskiy slovar*, vol. VIII, pp. 686–8; Gurvich, *Etnicheskaya istoriya*, pp. 222–39, and *Semeynaya obryadnost*, pp. 195–9; *Narody Sibiri*, pp. 783, 861–76; A.P. Okladnikov, ed., *Ancient Art of the Amur Region: Rock Drawings, Sculpture, Pottery*, Leningrad, 1981, plates 18–19, 25–6, 44–7, 84–97, 106–12, and passim; L.Ya. Shternberg, *Gilyaki, orochi, goldy, negidaltsy, ayny. Statyi i materialy*, ed. Ya.P. Alkor, Khabarovsk, 1933, pp. 11–388; Ch.M. Taksami, *Nivkhi (sovremennoye khozyaystvo, kultura i byt)*, Leningrad, 1967, pp. 6–7; Tokarev, *Etnografiya narodov SSSR*, pp. 513–22.

[12] *Yazyki narodov SSSR*, vol. V.

[13] *Istoriya Sibiri*, vol. I, p. 408; E.V. Shavkunov, *Kultura chzhurchzheney-udige XII–XIII vv. i problema proiskhozhdeniya tungusskikh narodov Dalnego Vostoka*, Moscow, 1990.

each summer. Not only did fish provide them with food but, like the Nivkh and all other native peoples of the Amur and maritime region, they used the skins of large fish, suitably treated, to make outer garments. For this reason the Chinese called the Amur tribes 'fishskin Tatars' – *yüp'itatzŭ*. For the Ulchi, in contrast with the Nivkh, the hunting of elk, deer and other forest animals was also an important activity. In costume all the Amur–Ussuri peoples conformed to the general cultural complex of Mongolia and Manchuria in wearing over their trousers a robe which was always wrapped over to the right, with a band of coloured ornament around the collarless neck, down the edge of the wrap-over and around the sleeves. This band, and frequently also the front and back of the robe, was richly decorated with appliqué or painted designs, and women wore shells and tinkling metal ornaments around the hem. In summer wide conical sun-hats of birch-bark were worn, and in winter fur caps and overcoats. Two male garments were characteristic of all the Amur peoples: a fish-skin over-skirt worn in winter for hunting expeditions on skis or sleds, and summer headgear consisting of skull-cap of dog or seal-skin with a veil which hung over the neck and shoulders as a protection against the gnats and mosquitoes which swarmed in the forest.

The Ulchis were a semi-sedentary people, who readily shifted the location of their villages if need arose, but whose only regular movements were between their summer dwellings, which stood above the ground on stilts, and their winter homes. Sometimes the latter were semi-subterranean lodges like those of the Nivkh, but the most characteristic Ulchi winter house was of the centrally-heated type standard throughout Manchuria, which probably originated in northern China. The walls were made of a wooden framework covered with clay, or sometimes planks, and there were windows made of fishskin or Chinese waxed paper. Clay stoves inside the house were connected to ducts running underneath raised sleeping plat-forms around the walls, before being led outside to a free-standing chimney. Unlike the Nivkhs, who disposed of their dead by cremation, the Ulchis placed the body in a board coffin and left it, above ground, in a small wooden house.[14]

Although the various areas where the Amur peoples lived can be indi-cated, by the middle of the nineteenth century these were not in any sense exclusive tribal or clan territories. In the area of Nivkh settlement, for instance, there were also Ulchis, Negidals, Nanais, Oroks and Ainus, and occasional Yakuts, Ewenkis and Koreans. Similarly the Ulchis shared their territory with Oroches, Udeghes, Nivkhs, Negidals, Nanais, Ewenkis and Ainus. So mobile and open to incomers were the lower Amur peoples that even their clan affiliations quite frequently underwent changes. Among the

---

[14] *Entsiklopedicheskiy slovar*, vol. XXXI, p. 924; *Narody Sibiri*, pp. 817–30.

Nivkhs in particular, practically every settlement included families belonging to various clans and nationalities, and several clans having Nivkh names and speaking the Nivkh language were in fact composed of people whose recent ancestors were Ainus, Negidals, Ulchis, Nanais or Oroks. It was the special geographical features of the Amur river system which led to this mixing of ethnic stocks through the migration of individuals and families. While the Amur–Ussuri valley offers considerable attractions to human settlers – fertile soil, a relatively mild climate with moderate snowfall and hot summers, abundance of fish and good forests for game – it also has its hazards. Its middle section is fed from the north by the river systems of the Zeya and Bureya, draining a large area enclosed by the Stanovoy Mountains, while below this it receives the waters of the Sungari, fed by the Hsingan and Changp'ai ranges, and the Ussuri whose waters come from the Sikhote-Alin. When one or more of these basins receives unusually heavy rainfall during the summer monsoon, this results in a sudden rise of the water level in the Amur valley by as much as 50 feet, producing devastating floods which carried away many a settlement.[15]

THE UDEGHES AND NANAIS

In contrast with the peoples of the lower Amur, those who lived further upriver – the Nanais, and in the Ussuri maritime region, the Udeghes – were ethnically more homogeneous.

Of all the Manchu-Tungus peoples, the Udeghes of the Sikhote-Alin Mountains and the Sea of Japan coast lived in the greatest isolation until the nineteenth century. Essentially hunters, they were less sedentary than the Amur peoples. They roamed the forest in individual families during the summer, living in bark-covered cabins or teepees, and their winter homes were somewhat more substantial structures of the same types. The Udeghes had no draught animals, but they travelled swiftly on their long skis and when necessary pulled their sledges themselves. In this and in their costume they betrayed affiliations with the Ewenkis, as did their neighbours the Oroches, whose culture was very similar to that of the Udeghes. A sign of their relative isolation from and independence of the Manchus was the fact that Udeghe men wore their hair in two plaits and not in a single pigtail. Traditional clan organisation was still strong among the Udeghes in the nineteenth century, with defined clan hunting grounds, mutual aid, blood vengeance, and the conduct of inter-clan wars according to recognised rules, including the inviolability of women and children. In common with all Siberian peoples, they held ritual feasts whenever a bear was killed, but unlike the Ulchi and Nivkh, did not nurture bears in captivity for ritual

[15] *Entsiklopedicheskiy slovar*, vol. I, p. 68; Gurvich, *Etnicheskaya istoriya*, pp. 227–9, 232–41; Kalesnik, *Dalniy Vostok*, p. 35.

killing. As an element of their tribal religion the Udeghes carved simple but artistically effective effigies and amulets in the form of people and animals, which were considered to be embodiments of spirit guardians. Shamans, male and female, played an essential part in curing the sick and in funeral rites, and they had sacred trees, carved with symbols and with effigies fixed to the branches, as well as tall spirit figures holding swords or spears standing before the shaman's house. None of the Amur–Ussuri peoples had elaborate shaman accoutrements, satisfying themselves with figures of human beings, dragons, serpents and animals painted on the shaman's fishskin robe. At the end of the nineteenth century the total number of Udeghes and Oroches was about 2,400.[16]

The most numerous nationality living on the middle Amur region were the Nanais (about 5,400 in 1861) whose territory began about 250 miles upriver from its mouth and extended 500 miles to the south-west along the banks of the Amur and its tributaries the Ussuri and Sungari. Like the other peoples of the region they had no sense of nationality and no name for themselves except 'local people', *nanai* – a general designation used also by the Ulchis and Oroches to describe themselves. A variety of other names have been applied to the Nanais. Downriver Nanais called those living farther upstream Goldi, while the latter referred to their downriver cousins as Hejenai. Like the Ulchis, the Nanais combined fishing with hunting for deer, elk, wild pigs, bear and other animals. In fact the differences between the way of life of the Nanais and that of the Ulchis were not inherently great, but the Nanais used dogs less for transport than for hunting, and they kept domestic animals (pigs and hens) and to some extent cultivated crops of millet and maize. Otherwise, their homes, boats and costume were similar to those of the Ulchis, as was their social organisation, with exogamic clans, polygamy, levirate, cross-cousin marriage, extended family, mutual aid and clan fire.

The Nanais revered the same 'master' spirits of forest, fire, river, mountains, etc. as the other Amur peoples, and the cult of the bear was an element in their religion. Living as they did within the territory of another even more formidable predator – the tiger – the Nanais, like the Udeghes and Oroches, treated it with even greater respect than the bear, and avoided killing the sacred animal if at all possible. (A likely portrait of a Nanai hunter, Dersu Uzala, and his animistic beliefs, is given in the works of V.K. Arsenyev.)

The cultural influences of the Chinese impinged to some extent upon all the peoples of the Amur and maritime region, but had their most profound effect on the Nanais, whose territory originally extended to the south beyond the Amur–Sungari confluence as far as the borders of the Manchu home-

[16] V.K. Arsenyev, *Po Ussuriyskomu Krayu. Dersu Uzala*, Leningrad, 1978, pp. 175, 230, 405–6; Gurvich, *Etnicheskaya istoriya*, pp. 229, 233; *Narody Sibiri*, pp. 831–43; Okladnikov, *Ancient Art*, pls. 28–31, 35–8, 48, 69–74.

8 Nanais of the Amur. A studio group portrait, early twentieth century. Most are wearing Mongolian-style wrap-over coats (some of fish-skin) with bands of Nanai decoration. The 'Chinese' hats are made of birch-bark, and the men at the front have hunters' veils covering the back of the head and neck. Like many Siberian peoples, by the nineteenth century the Nanais were much given to pipe-smoking. AMNH neg. no. 41614.

land. Trading links with China had existed from at least the fourteenth century AD, since the land of the 'fishskin Tatars' was the source of several products greatly desired by the Chinese, such as furs, the antlers of tufted deer (reputed to have aphrodisiac qualities) and ginseng root which was also believed to have remarkable powers as a panacea. In exchange for these commodities the Nanais obtained Chinese textiles, padded coats, guns, iron, furniture, flour, rice, tea, tobacco etc. From the Chinese government's point of view the things received from the northern barbarians were considered to be tribute, so that the Amur peoples who participated in the official trade were nominally subjects of the Emperor even though these distant lands were never fully subjugated.

From the viewpoint of the Manchus, the Amur was a part of their exclusive realm, and they asserted their rule by appointing representatives of the Ulchis, Nivkhs and Nanais as clan and village chiefs, and by arranging marriages between daughters of Manchu nobles and Nanai, Nivkh and Ainu chiefs. The process of subjection had gone farthest with the Nanais. The most southerly of these, called Hurka (like the river in whose valley they lived) had formed a powerful tribal federation in the seventeenth century when, under their leader Sosoku, they fought against Nurhachi, thus hindering Manchu expansion towards the Amur. But in 1631 they submitted to Abahai, and thereafter, like some of the more southerly Udeghes, the Hurkas became assimilated to the Manchus as an element in their banner armies. The Nanai living downriver from the Hurkas were known to the Manchus as Heje. Most men of the Amur region, like the Manchus themselves, wore their hair in a single plait or pigtail, but the mark of subjugation to the Manchus – obligatory for all subject nations, including the Han Chinese – was shaving the front of the head. Those Nanai who lived upstream from the confluence of the Amur and Ussuri conformed to this rule and were called the Shaven Heje, while those living farther north, including the Ulchis, disregarded it and were known as the Unshaven Heje.

Undoubtedly the material and spiritual culture of the Nanais, Ulchis, Udeghes and other Amur peoples came under the prolonged influence of China, which gave them, among other things, the heated house, iron cooking-pots, cotton and silk materials and rudimentary agriculture and animal husbandry. The same influence is clear in the remarkably accomplished decorative art of these peoples, applied to clothing, bed-covers and birch-bark baskets and boxes. This incorporated symmetrical designs derived largely from ancient Chinese motifs such as stylised monster masks and birds in the form of scrolls and spirals, while some of their ceremonial robes combined their own versions of the Chinese dragon with indigenous fish-scale designs. Chinese Buddhist religion also had some effect in modifying the shamanist beliefs of the northern peoples, some of whom celebrated the Chinese New Year and said they 'believed in the Chinese god'.[17]

RUSSIAN COLONISATION OF THE FAR EAST

From the beginning of Russia's annexation of the Amur–Ussuri lands, military considerations were dominant in the process of colonisation. While the Amur basin had attracted some Russian settlers from other parts of Siberia, the hazards of its climate and its remoteness did not make settlement there an attractive prospect. The journey itself was daunting: at least 3,500 miles

[17] *Entsiklopedicheskiy slovar*, vol. IX, pp. 138–9; Lee, *Manchurian Frontier*, pp. 17–18, 34, 42–9, 121; I.S. Vdovin, *Priroda i chelovek v religioznykh predstavleniyakh narodov Sibiri i Severa*, Leningrad, 1976, pp. 145–52; Okladnikov, *Ancient Art*, pls. 23, 50, 53–5, 60–1, 66–8, 104, 113–17. In contrast with the collective work *Narody Sibiri*, 1956, which gives due recognition at many points to the cultural influence of China in the Amur region, Okladnikov's book contrives to ignore this altogether, while asserting entirely local, Jurchen-Manchu, origins for the whole cultural complex of the region, thus conforming to the prevailing anti-Chinese spirit in Russia during the 1960s and 1970s.

from the Volga, which could take between two and four years to cover by horse transport. Governor-general Muravyov, the instigator of Russia's Amur venture, therefore resorted to forced settlement in order to create quickly the beginnings of a Russian population. Between 1851 and 1862 some 16,000 men and women of the Transbaikal Cossack Host were transported to the Amur and planted in small settlements spaced out along the post-road. In this way two new Cossack communities arose in the Far East – the Amur and Ussuri Hosts – which were subsequently augmented by peasant volunteers and by the transfer of Cossack families from the Don, Kuban and other Hosts. Both the Amur and the Ussuri Hosts remained comparatively small, numbering 19,700 and 7,000 respectively in 1894, compared with some 190,000 in the Transbaikal Host. By 1914, in addition to these Cossack Hosts, capable of putting some 6,500 men in the field, there were probably more than 50,000 regular soldiers in the two Far Eastern provinces, so that the region was highly militarised. The first Russian military headquarters to be established (in 1851) was Nikolayevsk near the mouth of the Amur, but in 1856, another town, Blagoveshchensk, was founded much farther upstream, and two years later Khabarovsk – named after the seventeenth-century adventurer – appeared near the confluence of the Amur and Ussuri. In the 1880s Khabarovsk became the administrative centre of the whole Amur and the seat of the governor-general, with a population which grew from 15,000 in 1897 to 60,000 in 1914. Blagoveshchensk grew more quickly to a population of 64,400 in 1911, while Vladivostok, founded as a port and fortress in 1860, became the unrivalled metropolis of the Far East with almost 120,000 inhabitants in 1914.

After the official annexation of the Far Eastern territories to the Russian Empire, non-military colonisation was encouraged by offering peasant settlers exemption from poll-tax, military service and other obligations. As a result, during the last four decades of the nineteenth century some 100,000 people from European Russia and other parts of Siberia were induced to migrate to the new Amur and Ussuri colonies. Migration to the Far East by the long and arduous land route proceeded slowly until 1882, when the transportation of emigrants by sea from Odessa to Vladivostok began. Over 62 per cent of the migrants in this movement were drawn from the Ukraine and Bessarabia – 275,000 out of the 436,395 immigrants in the period 1883–1914. The majority of these settled in the South Ussuri district, so that by 1898 Ukrainians comprised over 96 per cent of its civilian population. In general the more northerly districts of the Amur valley attracted fewer immigrants. So far as the Russian authorities were concerned the number of immigrants to the Far East was still insufficient, and on the eve of the First World War they were greatly concerned to increase the rate of colonisation for strategic reasons in view of the continuing militancy of Japan and the internal developments in China which followed the 1911 revolution there.[18]

During the last quarter of the nineteenth century Russians began to be drawn to the Far East by another magnet which took the place of sable fur in the popular imagination: gold seeking. The first find in the Far East was in the basin of the Zeya in 1868, and within a year 1,350 men were at work on various sites. Subsequently many other deposits were discovered on other rivers of the Amur system – principally the Selemja and Bureya – as well as on the Okhotsk coast, and the placers, employing thousands of workers, were by 1910 producing amounts of gold second only to the production of the Lena field.[19]

One province of the Russian Far East remained an exception so far as colonisation was concerned: the island of Sakhalin. After the Russian government obtained possession of the island they found little practical use for it except as a penal colony. Some convicts had been taken there as early as 1858, but it was not until after Alexander II's decree shifting the area for punitive exile entirely to Eastern Siberia, that a batch of 800 prisoners were sent to Sakhalin to build prisons in 1873. Nine years later it was decided that henceforth only the Nerchinsk mines and Sakhalin would be used for violent criminals and political prisoners. Some attempt to colonise the island with free agricultural settlers had been made in 1868–86, but this failed, and the only inhabitants of the island, apart from 4,000–5,000 Ainus, Nivkhs, Oroks and Tunguses and some miners at the coal-mines of the west coast, were the inmates and staff of the penal settlements. In 1897 the free Russian population was about 7,000, while the 13,500 convicts and exiles consisted of over 11,000 'Russians' (including Ukrainians and Belorussians), 371 'Finns', 132 Jews, 1,500 'Tatars' and some 320 people from the Caucasus and Turkestan.[20]

THE EFFECTS OF RUSSIAN AND CHINESE COLONISATION ON THE NATIVE PEOPLES

By the second half of the nineteenth century the indigenous Amur–Ussuri peoples found themselves between the hammer and the anvil. The Russians

[18] Alekseyev, *Osvoyeniye*, pp. 137, 143, 146; *Aziatskaya Rossiya*, vol. I, pp. 259, 311–12, 315–16, 346, 350, 369, 520–4; vol. II, pp. 526–8, 531–40; *Entsiklopedicheskiy slovar*, vol. XIII, pp. 888–893; vol. XXIII, pp. 275–6; vol. XXIX, p. 813; vol. XXXV, pp. 28–31; vol. XXXVI, p. 946; V.M. Kabuzan, *Dalnevostochnyy kray v XVII – nachale XXvv.: istoriko-demograficheskiy ocherk*, Moscow, 1985, pp. 59, 61, 96–8, 106–23, 200–5, 214–17, 224.

[19] *Aziatskaya Rossiya*, vol. II, p. 186; Kabuzan, *Dalnevostochnyy kray*, pp. 129–30, 170, 242; Kalesnik, *Dalniy Vostok*, p. 87.

[20] N.B. Arkhipov, *SSSR po rayonam. Dalnevostochnaya oblast*, Moscow, 1926, pp. 13, 24; *Aziatskaya Rossiya*, vol. I, pp. 52, 82–6; vol. II, p. 191; Chekhov, *Ostrov Sakhalin*; *Entsiklopedicheskiy slovar*, vol. XXVIII, p. 483; Kolarz, *The Peoples*, p. 52; *Sibirskaya Sovetskaya Entsiklopediya*, Moscow, 1929–35, vol. II, cols. 582–4; Stephan, *Sakhalin*, pp. 84–95.

were entering their homeland from the north, ousting the Nanais from their fishing grounds and pushing them southward, while the Chinese were infiltrating from the south, establishing themselves in the Ussuri and Sikhote-Alin regions, and pushing northwards into the Amur valley. Many Chinese had settled among the Nanais and created farms, with the result that here too the native people abandoned their homes and moved deeper into the forest. While some of the Nanais themselves gradually adopted Chinese horticulture and agriculture, the hunting Udeghes on the whole did not adjust so easily to the new conditions which were being created around them. They were, however, often obliged to do so by the Chinese settler–traders who, like the Russians in Siberia, were adept at the deceitful exploitation of naive indigenous people. Thus, many Udeghes were induced, often by means of alcohol or opium, to enter into debtor contracts with Chinese merchants, mortgaging next season's catch in advance. In this way they became hopelessly entangled and enslaved, so that they eventually gave up hunting and were reduced to labouring on the Chinese farmers' fields for a pittance.

In the case of the Nanais, the closer relationship between the 'Shaven Hejes' and the Manchu-Chinese authorities, with clan and village headmen responsible for the collection of tribute, allowed them to preserve their independent culture to a greater extent, but still their society experienced assimilation to the Chinese. Many of them also fell prey to the rapacity of Chinese traders and became perpetual debtors and slaves. As in Russian Siberia, there was no redress for the unfortunate natives who lost their personal freedom in this way and, to complete the parallel, the ultimate stage in the process of ruthless exploitation was that the Chinese creditors took the wives and daughters of his Nanai or Udeghe debtors as concubines for themselves or to be sold to others. Since many of the Chinese settlers were outlaws who had connections with the *hunghutzŭ* robber organisations, they maintained their system of oppression by terrorising the natives with sadistic punishments in the case of default or rebellion.

Oppressed by remorseless foreign invaders and decimated by famine and smallpox epidemics, the Nanais and Udeghes were helpless to preserve their independent culture and way of life, and were generally reduced to a demoralised and impoverished condition. Many of them became assimilated to the Chinese through intermarriage, and lost not only their traditional culture and costume but even their native languages. By the beginning of the twentieth century only a few pockets of Nanais, totalling about 3,000, remained as a distinct group in the Sungari-Ussuri region of China. At the same time the Nanais and Udeghes were undergoing the assault of immigration by Russians and Ukrainians, which reached massive proportions from 1907 onwards, so that the native peoples were swamped by incomers in a proportion of almost ninety to one. Here too the ultimate tendency was towards assimilation to the imported culture with its mixture of blessings and vices.[21]

According to Soviet Russian historians the effects produced on the native inhabitants of the Amur–Ussuri lands by Russian colonisers were wholly beneficial, since they brought technological innovations, better communications and new commodities such as kerosene, potatoes, flour and sugar. On the other hand, the Russians' method of clearing land for agriculture by slashing and burning, and their use of wood as fuel and for the construction of dwellings and fortifications, destroyed large areas of forest. In Nanai territory, as in other parts of Siberia, the Russian settlers quickly exterminated the sable, grabbed the best fishing grounds, and exploited the Nanais as labourers. On the lower Amur too, the way of life of the Nivkhs was undermined, particularly by the invasion of their fishing grounds by Russian commercial fisheries. The more mobile Udeghe people of the Sikhote-Alin mountains avoided contact with Russian culture by withdrawing to remote areas. So far as administration was concerned, the Russians introduced their usual system of village chiefs and police officers, but in the Maritime province this had little effect on the lives of the natives because of the ambiguous situation whereby Russian officials exercised nominal authority, but the native peoples thought little of them and respected only the local Chinese officials.[22]

On Sakhalin island the lives of the native peoples were inevitably affected not only by the usual results of Russian occupation, but more specifically by the presence of the convict settlements. While most of the Nivkhs lived on the eastern side of the island, away from direct contact with the Russians, and the Ainus lived in the south, the prisoners were mainly violent criminals, desperate and reckless when they made a run for freedom. In such cases the mildness and openness of the natives conferred no immunity – the Russian desperadoes frequently murdered the men of a Nivkh or Ainu village and raped the women. Some Nivkhs unfortunately became directly involved in the institutions of civilisation imported to their land by the Russians. A few were employed as prison warders, while in general they learned to be ruthless in hunting runaway convicts, because of the money paid by the Russian authorities for each one caught or killed. Apart from this form of moral corruption, the Nivkhs were subject to the temptation of vodka offered by

[21] Arsenyev, *Po Ussuriyskomu krayu*, pp. 65, 89–90, 94, 114, 149, 153–4, 175, 194, 211, 222–6, 230, 253–4, 263, 298–9, 345, 348, 404–5; Bai Shouyi, *Outline History of China*, p. 9; Lee, *Manchurian Frontier*, pp. 110–11, 120–1; *Narody Sibiri*, pp. 785, 789–90, 802, 831–2, 834, 836; V.A. Shvarev, ed., *Dalniy Vostok za 40 let Sovetskoy vlasti*, Komsomolsk, 1958, pp. 432–4; Taksami, *Nivkhi*, pp. 19–20, 27–28.

[22] Arsenyev, *Po Ussuriyskomu krayu*, pp. 90, 154; *Entsiklopedicheskiy slovar*, vol. IX, p. 140; Lee, *Manchurian Frontier*, pp. 125–6; Nansen, *Through Siberia*, pp. 327–31, 340–1; *Narody Sibiri*, pp. 791, 825–6, 832, 836; Shirokogorov, *Social Organization*, p. 92; Twitchett and Fairbank, *Cambridge History of China*, vol. X, pt. 1, pp. 343, 347.

Russian traders as a means of obtaining furs at low prices. Indeed, so arbitrary and lawless was life under the Russians that, as Chekhov records, one merchant of Nikolayevsk regularly crossed to Sakhalin like a seventeenth-century 'boyar's son' to extort fur tribute from the Nivkhs, whom he tortured or even hanged if they did not satisfy his demands. That other legacy of Russian conquest – epidemic diseases – also took its toll of native lives on Sakhalin. From whatever cause, the number of Nivkhs living on the island fell considerably from some 3,270 in 1856 to 2,000 in 1897. The Ainu inhabitants of southern Sakhalin also dwindled from about 2,000 in 1856 to 1,500 at the end of the century. Here one cause was the affinity the Ainus felt towards the Japanese, and their dependence upon rice as their staple food. When the Japanese were ousted from the island in 1875, 800 Ainus accompanied them across the strait to Hokkaido, and for all practical purposes the Ainus had no further contact with the Russians during the next forty years. In the Russian half of the island the small community of Oroks avoided the Russians by nomadising with their reindeer in the inaccessible forests, despite the fact that they had been nominally converted to Christianity and had abandoned many of their traditions in favour of Russian culture.[23]

THE 'YELLOW PEOPLES' IN THE RUSSIAN FAR EAST

While the Russians were establishing themselves in the Amur–Ussuri region, the whittling down of the Chinese Empire by western countries, including Russia, continued. The multiple pressures directed against Peking, combined with astute diplomacy on the part of the Russians, gained the latter important concessions: the peninsula of Liaotung was leased to them, and there they built the ports of Dairen and Port Arthur. Even before this, in 1896, the Chinese government had granted Russia a concession to build a railway across Manchuria, linking Vladivostok with Chita. This Chinese Eastern Railway was built in 1897–1904, along with a branch line joining Harbin to Port Arthur. On the territory of these railroads the Russians exercised complete control, while they also had an increasing presence and influence in Harbin and other towns along the routes. The Japanese government, realising that Russia's occupation of Manchuria in 1900 heralded a further expansion of the Russian Empire, launched a surprise attack on Port Arthur in February 1904, defeated the Russian army on the river Yalu, cut rail communication with Harbin, and took Port Arthur after a five-month siege. In Manchuria huge Japanese and Russian armies confronted each other at Mukden until February 1905, when the Russians were finally forced

[23] *Aziatskaya Rossiya*, vol. I, p. 80; Chekhov, *Ostrov Sakhalin*; *Entsiklopedicheskiy slovar*, vol. VIII, p. 686; vol. XXVIII, p. 483; Kolarz, *The Peoples*, 87; Majewicz, 'The Oroks', pp. 132–7; Stephan, *Sakhalin*, pp. 65–77.

to retreat to Harbin. Their army having been completely vanquished, the Russian government had to accept the peace treaty of Portsmouth (New Hampshire) by which it surrendered to Japan the Liaotung peninsula, the southern branch of the Manchurian railway and the southern half of Sakhalin.

Among the manifestations of Russian chauvinism which became prominent in the first decades of the twentieth century, racial prejudice against the 'yellow peoples' came second only to anti-semitism. It was no doubt the humiliation which the Russians suffered at the hands of the Japanese in 1904–5 that engendered a self-defensive attitude combining contempt and fear in relation to their Far Eastern neighbours. A further reason for such feelings was the ever-increasing number of Chinese and other 'yellow people' in the recently annexed Amur–Ussuri region, where by the end of the century it was they, and not the Nanai and other indigenous peoples, who formed the largest non-Russian element in the population.

The presence of the Chinese in the Russian Far Eastern provinces was one manifestation of the great emigration of people from central China which took place in the nineteenth century as a result of over-population and political turmoil. This migration spilled over spontaneously into the Russian-occupied Amur–Ussuri territories where because of new economic developments (principally gold-mining) and the later Russian occupation of Manchuria, not only farmers, but large numbers of Chinese labourers appeared each spring, seeking employment until the onset of winter. As a result, by 1885 there were over 10,500 Chinese in Amur province, while in Maritime province, in addition to 9,500 settled Chinese, there were some 30,000 seasonal workers. At the same time a movement of Korean peasants was taking place into the Tumen valley of northern China and the Suifen valley in the south of the Russian Ussuri province, where some 8,800 Koreans settled in the early 1880s, while several hundred founded the village of Blagoslovennaya on the Amur.

By 1897 over 65,000 Chinese and Koreans were living in the Ussuri–Amur region and about 2,400 in Trans-Baikal province, and thirteen years later these numbers had more than doubled. Such numbers were not great, but within the relatively small population of the Russian Far East they formed a considerable proportion – 12 per cent in Amur province and 21 per cent in Ussuri in 1911. Even more significant was the large number of non-Russians in Vladivostok – the bastion of Russian power in the Far East. In 1902 it had 39.4 per cent 'yellow people' among its inhabitants, a total preponderance of Chinese (of whom there were 15,000) over Russians (about 11,500 civilians) only being avoided thanks to the presence of 13,000 Russian military personnel. By 1914, when the city's population had increased to 120,000, the Chinese, at 24,770, still accounted for 20.7 per cent.[24] Apart from the inescapable fact of its oriental population, the Chinese affinity of the southern Ussuri region was evident in the place-names recorded on Russian maps of the region.[25]

Economically, the degree of Russia's dependence upon the Chinese and other orientals was great. The Chinese, well known for their industry and frugality, provided much of the labour force for railway construction, dock-yards, works and mines throughout the Far Eastern provinces. In Khabarovsk, for instance, it was a fact that the Russian citizen

lives in a house built by Chinese labour with Manchurian timber, the stove is made of Chinese bricks ... In the kitchen the Chinese boy gets the Tula samovar ready. The master of the house drinks his Chinese tea, with bread made of Manchurian flour, from a Chinese bakery ... The mistress of the house wears a dress made by a Chinese tailor ... In [the] yard a Korean is at work chopping wood.[26]

Despite – or because of – this dependence, the Russians indulged in racial discrimination against Chinese workers in the same spirit as the USA ban-ned their immigration in 1882, and British Australia from the 1860s severely restricted Chinese immigration so that the new dominion would be all 'white'. In the Russian Far East labour was badly needed, Russian workers were in short supply and Chinese labour plentiful and cheap; nevertheless after 1910 it became official policy not to permit any Asian labourers to take part in the construction of the Amur railway or any other state project. This 'fight against yellow labour'[27] made no sense economically, but was con-ceived entirely in Russian nationalist terms of security in the face of the supposed 'Yellow peril' – a concept which Tsar Nicholas II may have adop-ted from Wilhelm II of Germany. It was expressed (in an anti-semitic context!) by one of Russia's most virulent racists, in these words: 'The Sanhedrin [the imaginary international Jewish council which had supposedly instigated the Russo-Japanese War by 'hypnotising' the Japanese into believ-ing they were one of the tribes of Israel!] prepared to set a distraught Russia awash with blood and to inundate it, and then Europe, with the yellow hordes of a resurgent China guided by Japan.'[28] As a practical application of

[24] *Aziatskaya Rossiya*, vol. I, pp. 41–52, 82–5; 369; vol. II, pp. 527–8; *Entsiklopedicheskiy slovar*, vol. XIII, pp. 888, 893; vol. XXXV, pp. 28–9; J.F. Fraser, *The Real Siberia, together with an Account of a Dash through Manchuria*, London, 1902, pp. 159–60, 191, 202; Kabuzan, *Dalnevostochnyy kray*, pp. 94, 162, 182–5, 224, 229; Kolarz, *The Peoples*, pp. 43–4; Lee, *Manchurian Frontier*, pp. 90, 122–4, 127, 168–9; Nansen, *Through Siberia*, pp. 365–7; Twitchett and Fairbank, *Cambridge History of China*, vol. X, pt. 1, p. 348.

[25] J. Forsyth, 'Chinese place-names in the Russian Far East', in W. Ritchie et al., eds., *Essays for Professor R.E.H. Mellor*, Aberdeen, 1986, pp. 133–9.

[26] Quoted in Nansen, *Through Siberia*, pp. 369–70.

[27] *Aziatskaya Rossiya*, vol. I, p. 468.

[28] S.A. Nilus, *Velikoye v malom i Antikhrist, kak blizkaya politicheskaya vozmozhnost*, 2nd edn, Tsarskoye Selo, 1905, p. 415.

such ideas it was known in 1914 that the Russian governor-general of the Far East was waging 'a war of extermination' against the Chinese in order to drive them out of his domain.[29] Instead of employing coolies, some 150,000 Russian workers were introduced to the Far East during 1911–13, and a contemporary writer could state with satisfaction that the Amur railway 'would be built exclusively by Russian labour without the least participation of yellow people'.[30] Naturally, such attitudes on the part of the ruling class could only encourage rank-and-file Russians to be equally arrogant in their dealings with Chinese people, unceremoniously deporting those whose papers were not in order, and feeling at liberty to rob and shoot Chinese travellers in the forest. Foreign visitors to the Far East in the early years of the twentieth century were struck by the colonial attitude of the Russians, for instance at Khabarovsk railway station:

The scene was one that had a close comparison to that you see in India. Instead, however, of British officers walking up and down with the confident stride of superiority while the Hindus and Mohammedans gave way ... there were Russian officers clean and smart promenading the platform while the ... cowering Chinese and the cringing, frightened Koreans made room for them ... The Russian ... is the white, civilised Westerner, whose stride is that of a conqueror.[31]

Beneath the surface of Russian arrogance towards the 'yellow race' lay a potential for actual genocide which had exploded as early as July 1900 (at the time of the 'Boxer' Rebellion in China) in a notorious massacre at Blagoveshchensk. Here all the local Chinese and Manchus were herded by Cossacks on to the banks of the Amur and forced at bayonet-point to swim across the river to the Chinese side. As many as 5,000, including women and children, were drowned.[32]

People of oriental nationalities other than Chinese suffered somewhat less discrimination. By 1910 there were over 51,000 Koreans in the Ussuri province, and about 1,500 on the Amur. Their placidity, stamina and conscientiousness earned them the reputation of good settlers, whether as farmers or gold-miners, especially as many of them became converted to Russian Orthodox religion. Consequently, even after the ban on Chinese labour, Korean workers were still accepted for work on the Amur railway. As farmers the Koreans were much more effective than the Russian Cossacks who held much of the agricultural land in the Far East. The greatest concentration of Korean settlers was in southern Ussuri province, from Posyet near the Korean border to the region of Vladivostok, where there were twenty or more Korean villages. Of the 57,290 Koreans in the Ussuri

[29] Nansen, *Through Siberia*, pp. 339–40.
[30] *Aziatskaya Rossiya*, vol. II, p. 541.
[31] Fraser, *The Real Siberia*, pp. 195–6.
[32] Ibid., pp. 177–80; *Sibirskaya Sovetskaya entsiklopediya*, vol. II, col. 687.

province in 1912, almost 17,500 were Christian converts officially registered as Russian citizens.[33]

The Japanese enjoyed a special status in the Russian Far East, thanks to the terms of the Treaty of Portsmouth. They had the right of fishing in all coastal waters of the Okhotsk and Bering Seas, and established operations on such a large scale – with 8,890 Japanese in residence in Kamchatka during the fishing season – that the stocks of salmon on which the Kamchadals and Koraks relied for their survival were soon depleted. In addition, the Japanese had freedom of movement in Russia's Maritime province, with the result that in 1910 there were 4,000 of them in Vladivostok alone. Despite the official attitude of toleration towards them, in the Russian popular imagination the suspicion that all Japanese were 'spies' was already widespread at that time.[34]

CHINA'S MONGOLIAN BORDERLANDS

In the early twentieth century the political and economic breakdown of China in the face of foreign intrusion had led to much unrest and to attempts at internal reform. This culminated in the Young China movement and the anti-Ch'ing revolution of 1911, which deposed the last emperor and created a republic. At this time of increasing turbulence it was impossible for Peking to exercise control over its own borderlands, threatened as they were by Russian and Japanese expansionism. The proponents of Russian imperialism were as presumptuous as those of the British Empire of the day. Among the opinions expressed by government ministers under Nicholas II was the view that no frontiers could or should limit the expansion of Russia's interests in Asia, and that the only logical future frontier between the Russians and the 'yellow race' was the Gobi desert. The first major check to Russia's ambitions in the Far East was its defeat in the war against Japan in 1904–5, but subsequently Russia, far from avoiding contact with the Japanese, actually had continuous diplomatic contacts and came to four separate agreements with Japan between 1907 and 1916. As the presence of strong British, German, French and American influences in China hindered Japanese and Russian plans there, these two rival states agreed to act in unison, dividing

---

[33] Arsenyev, *Po Ussuriyskomu krayu*, p. 26; *Aziatskaya Rossiya*, vol. I, p. 531; vol. II, p. 541; Chekhov, *Ostrov Sakhalin*; D.J. Dallin, *The Rise of Russia in Asia*, London, 1950, pp. 13, 35–6, 43–4; *Entsiklopedicheskiy slovar*, vol. XXV, p. 217; Fraser, *The Real Siberia*, p. 175; Kabuzan, *Dalnevostochnyy kray*, pp. 94, 182–5, 201–5, 224, 228; Kolarz, *The Peoples*, pp. 32–4; Nansen, *Through Siberia*, pp. 339–40, 343, 346, 362–3, 381–2; Shirokogorov, *Social Organization*, p. 91; Shvarev, *Dalniy Vostok*, p. 149.

[34] *Aziatskaya Rossiya*, vol. I, p. 509; Kabuzan, *Dalnevostochnyy kray*, pp. 223–4, 227–9 shows considerably fewer Japanese – 1,660 in Vladivostok in 1912 and 2,498 in South Ussuri district; Kolarz, *The Peoples*, pp. 50–1n., 59; Nansen, *Through Siberia*, p. 340; *Narody Sibiri*, p. 984.

the Chinese Empire between them in terms of 'spheres of interest'. So in 1907 Japan agreed that Outer Mongolia lay in the Russian sphere, whereas Japan had a free hand in Korea, and in 1912 they resolved to divide Inner Mongolia between them.

In Mongolia the last years of Ch'ing rule, with its encouragement of large-scale settlement of Chinese farmers there, led to the emergence of a movement for national independence, and many riots took place against the presence of Chinese officials, merchants and settlers. When the old régime in China was overthrown the Mongols saw this as their opportunity and, with rather cautious and sparing support from St Petersburg, the Chief Lama declared independence. However, Russia agreed with China that the Mongols should not be permitted full political independence but only autonomy, while remaining within the Chinese Empire. Moreover, even this did not permit the unification of all Mongols, but applied only to Outer Mongolia, while Inner Mongolia remained an integral part of China. The most easterly Mongol territory of Barga (Hulun-Buir), which had been annexed to Manchuria by the Ch'ing, was also prevented from uniting with Outer Mongolia by the Russians, who had infiltrated it to a considerable extent.[35] The probability of Russia's intention of annexing Barga to Siberia is suggested by the actual fate of the analogous territory of Tuva.

In the nineteenth century the Russo-Chinese frontier from the Altai to Lake Baikal ran along the ridge of the Western Sayan mountains, but here too, as in the Far East, a certain ambiguity prevailed. South of this line the basin of the Yenisey's twin sources Kaa Khem and Biy Khem forms a roughly pear-shaped region between the Sayan and the more southerly range of the Tannu Ola. From the Mongols' point of view this region – present-day Tuva – was, like the Altai, populated by 'Uriyangkhai' – Turkic-speaking nomads who herded reindeer and had been subjects of the Altan Khans, and subsequently of the Oirats. At the time of the Manchu-Chinese wars against Galdan and his successors, the Uriyangkhai territories were annexed to the Chinese Empire as part of Outer Mongolia, and placed under the administration of Khalkha officials. Although Russian exploring bands from Krasnoyarsk and Irkutsk had occasionally extorted *yasak* from Soyot and Kaisot tribes who lived on the margin of Tuva during the seventeenth century, it could not by any means be said to have 'belonged' to Russia, as Russian historians, both tsarist and Soviet, have claimed, but was clearly a vassal territory of Mongolia. However, because of equal ignorance of the geography of the region on the part of the Russians and the Chinese, after the subjugation of Mongolia by the latter they established their guard posts not along the Russian frontier in the Sayan mountain range, but much

---

[35] Bai Shouyi, *Outline History of China*, pp. 475–83, 492–505; Bawden, *Modern History of Mongolia*, pp. 184, 189–200; Dallin, *Rise of Russia in Asia*, pp. 13, 35–6, 43–6, 53, 87–8, 90, 103–4, 110–11, 117, 123–30.

farther south in the Tannu-Ola. Through this mistake the Manchu-Chinese practically relegated the Uriyangkhai, or Tuvans, to the status of a somewhat isolated appendage of Outer Mongolia.[36]

Nevertheless, the Chinese government required fur-tribute from its Uriyangkhai subjects, just as the Russians did. In northern Tuva the clans who had formerly roamed freely on both sides of the Sayan mountains now found themselves being forced to give *yasak* to two masters, and in order to escape from this situation they moved out of the frontier area. Some went south to join other Chinese subjects in the upper Yenisey basin, while others found themselves on the Russian side of the border – either to the west of Tuva in the Abakan valley, where they merged with Beltir clans, or to the east, where they formed a small self-contained community of hunters and reindeer-herders. The latter, known to the Russians as the Karagas, and later the Tofalar (i.e. Tubalar) were much oppressed and exploited by the Russians and Buryat Mongols of Irkutsk province, and by the late nineteenth century were reduced to a very low level of existence based on dwindling reindeer-herds and shrinking hunting-grounds. Within Tuva itself the native people were forbidden by the Chinese to move south of the Tannu-Ola where the imperial guard-posts were. As a whole, Tuva was subject to Manchu officials based in the town of Uliasutai in northern Mongolia, but local administration was in the hands of the rulers of the five Uriyangkhai tribes, the senior of whom was the *noyon* of Khemchik. As in the rest of Mongolia under the Manchus, a kind of feudal system existed in which the ruling minority enjoyed great privilege while the rank-and-file clan members were practically serfs, obliged to fulfil crippling demands for tribute and transport animals. Their lot was thus similar to that of the native tribespeople in Russian Siberia.

As well as the clan rulers, the Uriyangkhai herdsmen had to support a large number of lamas, especially in the south of the country where, as in the rest of Mongolia, Tibetan Buddhism of the Yellow church was well established. While it was the ambition of every Tuvan father to have one of his sons become a lama, to outsiders it appeared that the thousands of monks who did no productive work also played a considerable part in draining the resources of their compatriots. Buddhism was a relatively recent innovation among the Uriyangkhai, and the old shamanist religion of Siberia continued to exist side by side with it. As among the Mongols, the great leader Chingis Khan was an object of religious veneration.

The different racial elements which went to the making of the Uriyang-khai of Tuva – Samoyedic, Turkic and Mongolian – were reflected in the physical appearance and way of life of various regional groups, known to the Russians as Soyots, Darkhats and Soyons. Their general name for them-

---

[36] *Aziatskaya Rossiya*, vol. I, p. 21; Gurevich, *Mezhdunarodnye otnosheniya*, pp. 17, 55, 66, 87, 89, 91, 93, 100; Twitchett and Fairbank, *Cambridge History of China*, vol. X, pt. 1, p. 55.

selves was Tuba or Tuva – a name which in slightly varying form occurs over a wide area from the Tubalar of the Altai to the Tofalar of the eastern Sayan. Living in a region transitional between the Siberian coniferous forest and the grasslands of Mongolia, the Tuvans followed different ways of life ranging from hunting and fishing in the forests to cattle-herding and rudimentary agriculture in the open valleys and mountain steppes of the south. Their modes of transport showed a corresponding variety: the horse was ubiquitous, but reindeer, yaks, camels and oxen were also used. The homes of the forest-dwellers were teepees covered with bark or deerskin, while the cattle-herders lived in felt-covered yurts.[37]

RUSSIA AND TUVA UP TO 1914

While the Ch'ing government kept their Uriyangkhai territory segregated from Mongolia by guarding its southern limits in the Tannu Ola, along the real Sino-Russian frontier farther to the north little appears to have been done to keep intruders out. As a result, the Russians, ready as ever to take advantage of an unguarded frontier, began an informal penetration of Tuva during the first half of the nineteenth century. Coming among the isolated and primitive Tuvans, Russian peasants, trappers and traders found the same conditions for making quick and easy profit as had prevailed in Siberia at the beginning of the Russian conquest two centuries before. Valuable furs, livestock, labour and other services could be obtained from the Uriyangkhais in exchange for cheap trinkets, tobacco or tea, and, of course, alcohol. As a result, many Tuvans were drawn into the net of colonial exploitation, while considerable wealth was amassed by the Russian colonialists. By the 1860s Russian merchants, assisted by Abakan 'Tatar' interpreters, were setting up trading-posts in Tuva, competing successfully with the Chinese commercial firms which now operated throughout Mongolia and Sinkiang. A treaty which Russia forced the Ch'ing government to sign in 1860 included among its numerous concessions to the Russians the right to visit Tuva for purposes of trade, although no construction of permanent premises nor settlement by Russians was sanctioned. While in practice the Russians ignored the Chinese rules during the next twenty years, officially their settlement in Tuva continued to be forbidden until 1881. In that year the terms of the Treaty of St Petersburg included further concessions on Russian trading in Mongolia, and permitted the building of Russian settlements in Tuva.

---

[37] Bawden, *Modern History of Mongolia*, pp. 148–70, 417; Carruthers, *Unknown Mongolia*, vol. I, pp. 172, 179, 192–3, 200–6, 214, 222, 245–50, end-map; *Entsiklopedicheskiy slovar*, vol. XXX, pp. 718–20; *Narody Sibiri*, pp. 420, 424–5, 430–42, 530–5; Radlov, *Aus Sibirien*, vol. I, pp. 191, 207, 218, 221, 366; Reclus, *Earth and Its Inhabitants*, vol. I, pp. 357–8; S.I. Vaynshteyn, *Nomads of South Siberia: the Pastoral Economies of Tuva*, Cambridge, 1980, pp. 42–3, 53–83.

From that time onward the expansion of Russian interests in Tuva proceeded almost unhindered. The number of Russian residents grew enormously, amounting to 64,000 in 1913, thus equalling, if not exceeding, the number of native Tuvan people. So ineffectual was the jurisdiction of the Peking government in this remote region that by the early years of the twentieth-century Tuva was to all intents and purposes already a protectorate of Russia. The attitude of the Russians towards the Uriyangkhais, as conveyed by the English explorer Carruthers, was typical of colonialists of the day in its thoughtless assumption of the cultural superiority of European commercial endeavour. As in so many European colonial possessions, the natives were said to be lazy and devoid of ambition to better themselves, so that they preferred to 'run wild in the forest' and live in comparative poverty, instead of working for the Russian colonialists.[38]

Being a more primitive society than Mongolia, Tuva could scarcely produce a nationalist movement, but since the 1880s there had been stirrings of revolt among the tribespeople against their rulers, the Mongol or native *noyons*. As the privileged position of the latter derived its support from the existing Manchu-Chinese government system, they naturally tended to be pro-Chinese, and attempted to prevent contact between their subjects and Russian or other foreign visitors. After 1911 the *noyons'* intention was that Tuva should be a part of the new Mongolian republic. The ordinary herdsmen, on the other hand, are said by Russian historians to have found the Russians more congenial than the Chinese, and therefore tended towards union with Russia. Whatever the truth of this, the fate of the Uriyangkhai had become a matter of power politics, as Carruthers predicted at the time: 'it is certain that Russian protection would be welcomed by the natives, and in view of recent advances made by Mongol princes to Russia, and in consideration of the preference for Russian rule over Chinese rule, it would be strange indeed if these regions do not, some day, fall under the protectorship of the Russian Empire'.[39] This opinion no doubt echoed that of many contemporary Russian empire builders, such as those who pretended that a historical justification existed for Russia's possessing the whole course of the Yenisey. In the prevailing climate of unashamed colonialism such people could assert (like officially inspired writers under the later Communist Party régime) that Tuva was a 'natural appendage' of Siberia, and that, since the separation of Mongolia from China, the Uriyangkhai territory was 'gravitating towards Russia'.[40] And indeed, in 1913, two years after the beginning of the Chinese revolution, the *noyons* of two of the

---

[38] Bai Shouyi, *History of China*, pp. 446–7, 466–7; Carruthers, *Unknown Mongolia*, vol. I, pp. 163–71, 180, 220–1; Kolarz, *The Peoples*, pp. 161–2; *Narody Sibiri*, p. 426; Radlov, *Aus Sibirien*, vol. I, pp. 366–7.

[39] Carruthers, *Unknown Mongolia*, vol. I, p. 166.

[40] *Aziatskaya Rossiya*, vol. I, pp. 21, 40, 493.

Tuvan tribes were induced to offer allegiance to the Tsar, and in the following year the chief *noyon* followed suit by requesting a Russian protectorate. Despite the pronouncements of Russian empire builders, however, the people of Tuva were on the whole pro-Mongol, since their cultural ties had for centuries been primarily with Mongolia. By 1916 the denial of this natural bond of culture (including the Buddhist religion) had led to considerable unrest, which was suppressed by the use of Cossacks. However, the Russian annexation of Tuva proved to be only a short-lived episode at this time. The Russian Revolution of 1917 and the ensuing Civil War led to the collapse of central government in the Empire, and in 1918 Tuva was once again brought under nominal Chinese control, as Mongolia itself had been two years previously.[41]

---

[41] Dallin, *The Rise of Russia*, pp. 137–45. *Entsiklopedicheskiy slovar*, vol. XXX, p. 720; Kolarz, *The Peoples*, pp. 162–3; *Narody Sibiri*, pp. 426–7; Radlov, *Aus Sibirien*, vol. I, p. 220.

II

THE RUSSIAN REVOLUTION AND CIVIL WAR IN SIBERIA

POLITICAL FORCES IN SIBERIA, 1917–1918

IN Siberia the onset of the February Revolution followed the same general pattern as in other parts of the Empire. Large numbers of men (excluding the indigenous peoples) were forced to go and fight in the 'German war' far to the west of Siberian horizons, and the second year of war brought not only ever-growing lists of men killed and wounded, but food shortages. By 1916 this led to strikes in the principal cities.

In 1917, as news of the February Revolution in Petrograd and the formation of the Russian Provisional Government began to reach Siberia, politically aware people – principally Russians in the towns situated on the Trans-Siberian railway – created local 'Committees of social organisations' to maintain order and reform institutions. The members of these committees included Constitutional Democrats, socialists of the SR party, Menshevik SDs, and some Bolshevik SDs. In addition to the general programme of reforms introduced by the Provisional Government in Petrograd, the extension to Siberia, after long delay, of *zemstvo* and other local government bodies provided a more democratic form of administration. However, the policies of the Petrograd government were unwelcome to many Siberians in at least two respects: its determination to continue the war against Germany, and its opposition to the idea of regional autonomy. A desire for the latter had the strong support of much of the Siberian intelligentsia, and movements in this direction culminated in the meeting in Tomsk on 1 October 1917 of the first Siberian Regional Council for an autonomous Siberia, presided over by the veteran *oblastnik* G.N. Potanin.[1]

The other political development which followed the general Russian pattern in the spring of 1917 was the formation of councils (*soviets*) of workers'

---

[1] P. Dotsenko. *The Struggle for a Democracy in Siberia, 1917–1920*, Stanford, 1983, pp. 6, 20; *Istoriya Sibiri*, vol. III, pp. 460–9, 475–8; vol. IV, pp. 28, 38–9, 49.

and soldiers' deputies in the main centres of Russian settlement where there was a considerable industrial population, such as Krasnoyarsk, Tomsk and Barnaul. The most popular revolutionary party throughout Siberia was neither the Bolshevik nor the Menshevik faction of the Marxist SDs, but the peasant-orientated SR party led by V.M. Chernov and B.V. Savinkov. As there were no big landowners east of the Urals, no such anarchic movement by peasants to seize land took place as had occurred in European Russia; but in September a coordinating Committee of West Siberian Peasants' Soviets was formed, in which SR influence was supreme. After the October coup in central Russia the peasant soviets in Siberia gave as little support to the Bolsheviks as those in the rest of the Empire, and the outcome of the democratic elections for the Constituent Assembly in November 1917 was a large SR majority, only 10 per cent of votes being cast for the Bolsheviks in Siberia.

During the months following Lenin's coup, local power was claimed in the industrial regions of Siberia by the workers' and soldiers' soviets. In many places the date of the Soviet take-over is far from clear, since the situation was fluid and it took some time to squeeze out Menshevik and SR delegates and ensure the domination of the soviets by the Bolsheviks. In fact, in Siberia the latter were obliged – and in most cases were at first quite willing – to go on sharing political power in the soviets with the majority SRs, the Mensheviks and the Jewish Bund. Indeed, up to February 1918 the Siberian soviets not only supported the 'bourgeois' idea of an autonomous 'Siberian Socialist Republic', but opposed the conclusion of a peace treaty with Germany which was a central feature of Lenin's policy.

As a result of such ambiguities the process of imposing Leninist domination took a whole month in Omsk. In Irkutsk 'Soviet power' only became a reality after several days of severe fighting early in December. Similarly, in Tomsk, the democratic centre of Siberia, where it is claimed that the soviet assumed power on 6 December, the Bolshevik government was in fact repudiated next day by an All-Siberian Provisional Council which stood for the autonomy of Siberia and underlined its belief in a federal structure for Russia by establishing contact with the independent Ukrainian government. Preparations went ahead for the convocation of a Siberian Regional Duma in Tomsk on 7 January 1918. It was only on 26 January, after the receipt of an order from Bolsheviks, that the Tomsk Soviet usurped the Duma. Some of the members of the latter were arrested, while many leading SR politicians fled to the Far East in order to carry on the anti-Bolshevik struggle from there.[2]

While the Bolshevik take-over was proceeding in the towns of Western

[2] Dotsenko, The Struggle, pp. 6–7, 12–18, 21–2; G.Z. Ioffe, Kolchakovskaya avantyura i yeye krakh, Moscow 1983, p. 26; Istoriya Sibiri, vol. IV, pp. 30–2, 36, 42, 47–55, 58, 60, 95; P.T. Khaptayev et al. eds., Istoriya Buryatskoy ASSR, vol. II, Ulan-Ude, 1959, pp. 28–9.

Siberia, other political forces were forming in the steppe lands south of the railway. Here in the Altai region and northern Kazakstan the agricultural population consisted mainly of relatively new settlers from European Russia and the Ukraine. Independent, relatively efficient and prosperous, these farmers had much to lose in any political transformation. Many of them had returned from the front where they had been fighting against the Austrians and Germans, and they strongly resisted the only agricultural policy of the Bolsheviks at that time – the requisitioning of grain to supply the towns. As grain procurements from Siberia were essential to the survival of the Bolshevik régime in Moscow and Petrograd, numbers of industrial workers and communists were sent east to 'help' the Siberian farmers. These incomers (giving a foretaste of methods to be used a decade later during collectivisation) had the task of creating the first agricultural communes based on the village poor, whose animosity towards the more prosperous farmers was incited.[3]

At the same time opposition to the Bolshevik régime was crystallising among the other important element in the Russian population of the Siberian steppe frontier – the Cossack communities. The largest of these, the Orenburg Host, with a total population of 553,000 people, had a great vested interest in its province, since it owned 70 per cent of all the arable land. Similar conditions prevailed in the Ural River Host, with a population of 235,000, and the Siberian Host, centred on Omsk, which had 164,000 members. Two days after the October Revolution began, the ataman of the Orenburg Cossacks, A.I. Dutov, agreed with Kaledin and the leaders of the Ural Host on the formation of a South-East Cossack Union to fight the Bolsheviks.[4]

In the Far East of Siberia too, anti-Bolshevik forces coalesced around the Cossacks. In October 1917 at Blagoveshchensk, the centre of the 50,000 strong Amur Cossack community, a 'Committee of Public Salvation' was formed, uniting Constitutional Democrats, Menshevik SDs, and SRs. As democratic forces in the region became organised, they adopted a policy of complete autonomy for 'Great Siberia' under the banner of the Union of Siberian Federalists, which was formed on 22 December. By then, however, the Bolsheviks in Blagoveshchensk had created a Red Guard detachment and gained control of the local soviet, so that the forces of the Committee of Public Salvation were defeated and the Bolshevik régime was installed.[5] The concept of Siberian autonomy within a federal Russia enjoyed widespread support, but it was asserted most decisively in Eastern Siberia, where, after the October coup in European Russia, the Yakut nationalists, Russian

---

[3] *Istoriya Sibiri*, vol. IV, pp. 79–83.
[4] A.P. Yermolin, *Revolyutsiya i kazachestvo (1917–1920 gg.)*, Moscow, 1982, pp. 18–21, 26–7, 32–3, 37, 39, 45, 49, 52, 55, 81, 95, 98–103.
[5] *Istoriya Sibiri*, vol. IV, p. 55; Yermolin, *Revolyutsiya*, pp. 18, 55–6.

federalists, SR socialists, and members of the Yakutsk city council and the *zemstvos* combined in February 1918 to declare the independence of Yakutia from Soviet Russia. However, the town was taken over by the Bolsheviks on 1 July, and all political activities were for a time suppressed.[6] Meanwhile anti-Bolshevik ('White') political forces were reorganising themselves in underground movements based chiefly in Moscow. East of the Volga the White underground was particularly active in Omsk and Novonikolayevsk, and in May 1918 the SRs made their headquarters at Samara on the Volga.

Another strong base for the Whites lay in the Far East. Here one of Russia's most important strategic assets was the Chinese Eastern Railway, which ran across Chinese Manchuria, via Harbin, to link Chita with Vladivostok. By March 1918 Harbin was, apart from the isolated federalist government in Yakutsk, the seat of the only officially constituted independent Russian authority in Northern Asia, since both Vladivostok and Khabarovsk had been taken by the Bolsheviks in December 1917, and Chita in February 1918. Although only the narrow strip of the railway line was legally within Russian jurisdiction, during the next few years the Whites enjoyed the sanction of the Chinese government to range at will over the frontier areas of Manchuria and Outer Mongolia. This was the area of operations of the Cossack ataman G.M. Semyonov, a native of Buryatia who had built up a Cossack force in the Barga Mongol (Hulunbuir) region of Northern Manchuria, with which he harassed the Bolsheviks from January 1918.

Little could have been done by the isolated representatives of anti-Bolshevik groups in the Far East if foreign powers had not intervened to assist them. In April 1918 the British and Japanese landed small bodies of troops at Vladivostok, and the Allied intervention on behalf of anti-Bolshevik forces in Siberia began.[7]

CIVIL WAR AND FOREIGN INTERVENTION IN SIBERIA, 1918–1925

The outbreak of full-scale civil war in Siberia arose from an unexpected quarter – the Czech Legion, consisting of Czech and Slovak soldiers of the Russian Army and deserters and prisoners-of-war from the Austro-Hungarian Army who, with the cooperation of the Soviet government, were making their way to the Far East in order to be shipped to France as reinforcements for the continuing war against Germany. Trotskiy, as

---

[6] *Istoriya Sibiri*, vol. IV, pp. 59–63.
[7] W.H. Chamberlin, *The Russian Revolution, 1917–1921*, London, 1935, vol. II, pp. 1, 8, 14; Dotsenko, *The Struggle*, p. 21; Ioffe, *Kolchakovskaya avantyura*, pp. 25–7, 30–2, 36–59; *Istoriya Sibiri*, vol. IV, pp. 59, 87–9; J.A. White, *The Siberian Intervention*, New York, 1950, pp. 97, 189–90, 195–7; Yermolin, *Revolyutsiya i kazachestvo*, pp. 60–1, 83–4.

People's Commissar of the Red Army, had organised propaganda among the Czechs and Slovaks in the hope of inducing them to join its ranks, and now that few showed any desire to do so, he ordered the Soviets to disarm them. It was as a result of ineffectual attempts to carry out these orders in May 1918 that the Czechs, led by Colonel Gajda, decided to fight their way through to Vladivostok, for which purpose they required to gain control of the whole of the Trans-Siberian Railway. Their action was a godsend to the Russian anti-Bolshevik forces, who came out of hiding to overthrow the Soviet régime as the Czechs took command of one town after another, often after intense fighting with the Red Army.

The British and French governments, already engaged in military operations against the Bolsheviks in the north of European Russia, seized upon the 'Czech revolt' as the beginning of an Allied eastern front against the Bolsheviks. Several thousand Czecho-Slovaks reached Vladivostok, and at the end of June they overthrew the local Soviet, thus leaving the field open for anti-Bolshevik politicians to extend their activities there. It was then that the United States decided to join the British, French and Japanese in direct military intervention in the Far East, where the Civil War was to last for four years or more.[8] Whatever the real aims of the various interventionist powers may have been, there was a contrast between those of the Western Allies, who desired the defeat of the Bolsheviks and the establishment of a stable Russian government, and that of the Japanese, whose aim was the permanent conquest of Siberian territory. While Britain landed some 800 troops at Vladivostok, and the USA 7,000, the Japanese had put ashore at least 80,000 by the end of 1918. With the Cossack atamans Semyonov and Kalmykov as their allies, the Japanese armies occupied the whole of Amur Province and Transbaikalia, treating Russian Whites and Bolsheviks with equal ruthlessness and contempt and instituting 'a campaign of cruelty which must rarely have been exceeded'.[9] This inhumanity gave rise to some of the most widespread guerrilla warfare of the Civil War period.[10]

In Western Siberia the defeat of the Soviets by the Czecho-Slovaks did not resolve the problems of the Russian anti-Bolshevik forces, but rather permitted their mutual antagonisms and intrigues to burgeon. When Samara was taken by the Czechs in June 1918, the SRs, led by Chernov, set up a government consisting of members of the Constituent Assembly, which was

[8] The conventional view that the Civil War ended in 1922 (or even 1920!) only applies to European Russia, and ignores the fighting against the Bolsheviks in Siberia and Turkestan, which continued until about 1924. Chamberlin, *Russian Revolution*, vol. II, pp. 1–15; Dotsenko, *The Struggle*, pp. 25–33, 42–3; Ioffe, *Kolchakovskaya avantyura*, pp. 33–5, 60, 74, 147; *Istoriya Sibiri*, vol. IV, pp. 91–4, 97; White, *Siberian Intervention*, pp. 92, 184–8, 211–12, 217, 224, 228, 236–52, 255–9, 277; Yermolin, *Revolyutsiya i kazachestvo*, p. 113.

[9] White, *Siberian Intervention*, p. 263.

[10] Chamberlin, *The Russian Revolution*, vol. II, pp. 10–11, 173–81; *Istoriya Sibiri*, vol. IV, p. 94; Shvarev, *Dalniy Vostok*, pp. 148–71, 175, 236–59; White, *Siberian Intervention*, pp. 83–4, 112–13, 173–7, 181–8, 194–210, 215–16, 223–4, 254, 263–7, 276–8, 422.

abbreviated in Russian to 'Komuch'. From the start this 'government' was subject to conspiracies by the right-wing elements on which it was obliged to rely for support, but whose real aim was to institute a military dictatorship. One rival seat of power was in Orenburg, where, under the aegis of Dutov's Cossacks, an Ural Regional Government was created in July 1918. The most important centre of power, however, was Omsk, from 7 June the seat of the Provisional Government of Siberia – a body with strong right-wing tendencies directed as much against the SRs as against the Bolsheviks. As the Omsk government also rejected the concept of regional autonomy and stood for the Whites' idea of 'Russia one and indivisible', it immediately came into conflict with the supporters of the disbanded Provisional Government of Autonomous Siberia and the Regional Duma, which was resurrected in Tomsk in August. In fact, by September 1918 ten separate anti-Bolshevik 'governments' existed east of the Volga between Samara and Vladivostok.

By this time the Red Army had begun its counter-attack in the Volga-Ural region, taking Kazan, Samara and Ufa; in the northern steppes of Kazakstan Dutov's Orenburg Cossacks were defeated, and Orenburg itself occupied by the Bolsheviks in January 1919. The SR Komuch government, having been chased out of Samara by the Bolsheviks, now found itself threatened equally by the right-wing Whites, while in Omsk the Siberian Provisional Government began to suppress all rivals, and in mid-November, when British and French military units arrived in Omsk, Admiral Kolchak was proclaimed Supreme Ruler of Russia.[11] Kolchak devoted himself with zeal to his task of defeating the Red Army, while in rural areas his men resorted to violent means to exact grain for the towns and to conscript peasants for service in the White Army, terrorising the population and burning villages as mercilessly as the Japanese and Cossack atamans were doing in the Far East. As a result, the Siberian peasants, who until the summer of 1918 had been largely passive towards the revolution, were now forced to protect themselves against the Whites by organising guerrilla bands. On the whole, peasant sympathies continued to lie chiefly with the SRs. In Irkutsk province, for instance, much of the Russian peasantry rallied to the colours of an SR anarchist leader, the Georgian Nestor Kalandarashvili, to form a partisan army which caused considerable trouble to Kolchak's forces in Central Siberia.[12]

[11] Chamberlin, *Russian Revolution*, vol. II, pp. 13–16, 20–2, 173–88; Dotsenko, *The Struggle*, pp. 28–9, 38–9, 44–6, 51, 54, 57–9, 62, 71–2; Ioffe, *Kolchakovskaya avantyura*, pp. 10, 34–5, 60–77, 81–6, 90, 96–7, 100–4, 120–2, 129–47, 160–6; *Istoriya Sibiri*, vol. IV, pp. 92–3, 97–8, 112; Samsonov, ed., *Kratkaya istoriya SSSR*, vol. II, p. 89; Yermolin, *Revolyutsiya i kazachestvo*, pp. 9–11, 132, 141–6, 150–1, 161, 171, 177–8.

[12] Chamberlin, *Russian Revolution*, vol. II, pp. 194–5; Dotsenko, *Struggle*, pp. 76–7, 83–8, 90–4; Ioffe, *Kolchakovskaya avantyura*, pp. 96–7, 193–5, 221–4; *Istoriya Sibiri*, vol. IV, pp. 92, 107, 110, 115–21, 160; Khaptayev, *Istoriya Buryatskoy ASSR*, vol. II, pp. 170–7; White, *Siberian Intervention*, pp. 267–8; Yermolin, *Revolyutsiya i kazachestvo*, p. 143.

By June the Red Army had launched its final campaign against Kolchak, and the Ural cities were all taken by the end of July. Farther south in the Orenburg steppe the situation of Dutov's Cossacks had now become desperate, and in August they began their long retreat across northern Kazakstan, until their eventual regrouping in the region of Semirechye and Chinese Turkestan. After the last big battles in Western Siberia, the Red Army's advance was swift, and the refugee population in Omsk fled in panic to the east. The retinue of Kolchak abandoned Omsk on 10–12 November 1919, and the Bolsheviks entered the city. Kolchak's flight to the east ended in a confused series of events. In Irkutsk a successful uprising against the Whites was organised by a 'Political Centre' consisting of SRs and Mensheviks, but this body was forced to hand Kolchak over to the Bolsheviks, and on 7 February 1920 he was shot.[13]

The Soviet conquest of Western Siberia was not welcomed unanimously, and it was some time before all opposition was crushed. In accordance with Lenin's policy in every region where the Bolsheviks gained control – to crush opposition and force farmers to hand over every ounce of 'surplus' produce – the Soviet government in July 1920 issued an order for grain requisitioning in Siberia. This decree could not but evoke antagonism in south-west Siberia and northern Kazakstan – the region with the largest concentration of recent settlers owning prosperous farms. In anticipation of Bolshevik 'war communism' practices, a Siberian Peasant Union had been formed in June 1920 at Omsk, and its network soon extended from the southern Urals to the Altai. The first Peasant Union revolts held up the operations of Bolshevik requisitioning gangs in the black-earth regions of the Altai and northern Kazakstan, and by February 1921 a huge territory extending some 700 miles from Yekaterinburg to the Kulunda steppe was in anti-Bolshevik hands, as were the middle and lower reaches of the Ob from Narym to Obdorsk. A 'People's Army' was formed from armed peasants and Cossacks, while politicians, among whom the SR Party played the major part, attempted to set up a West Siberian government.

The generally expressed aim of the farmers' movement in Siberia – 'Soviets without communists!' – was the same as that of the other anti-Bolshevik revolts which were taking place all over Russia, culminating in the Kronstadt uprising of sailors of the Baltic Fleet in March 1921. Although these events forced Lenin to suspend the predatory practices of 'war communism' in favour of the so-called New Economic Policy, the turmoil in West Siberia, in which as many as 60,000 armed peasants and Cossacks took

---

[13] Chamberlin, *Russian Revolution*, vol. II, pp. 188–92, 200–3, 423; Dotsenko, *Struggle*, pp. 106, 112–18; Ioffe, *Kolchakovskaya avantyura*, pp. 97, 219, 232–3, 249, 253–6, 260–3; *Istoriya Sibiri*, vol. IV, pp. 111–14, 122–3, 128, 131, 134; Khaptayev, *Istoriya Buryatskoy ASSR*, vol. II, pp. 83–4, 100; *Sibirskaya Sovetskaya Entsiklopediya*, vol. II, col. 454; White, *Siberian Intervention*, pp. 268, 329, 344–5; Yermolin, *Revolyutsiya i kazachestvo*, pp. 139–40, 147, 152.

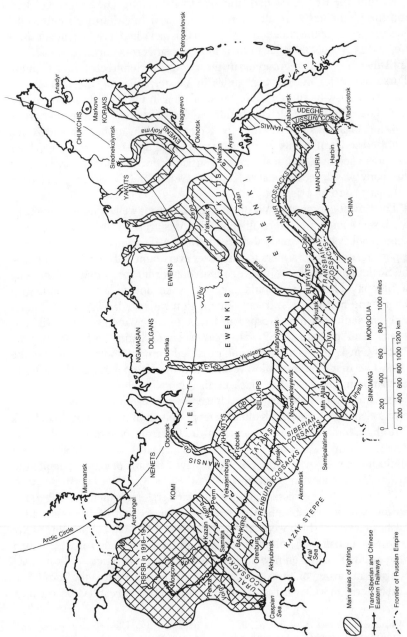

Map 9 The native peoples of Siberia during the Russian Civil War, 1918–1923

part, caused him great concern. Red Army troops and units of the Communist Party's political police (Cheka) were sent in, and the rebellion was crushed. One result was a further exodus of Cossacks of Omsk province who left their base in the Ishim steppe to join the White forces of Bakich in north-western China. Many guerrilla groups continued to operate for some time after the defeat of the main rebellion. In the Altai region in particular, anti-Bolshevik partisan operations continued both in the agricultural steppe-land of the north and among the 'Oirot' native people of the mountains.[14]

In Eastern Siberia too, warfare and instability continued after 1919 – in some places for one year, in others for as long as three or four years.

The collapse of Kolchak's régime robbed the Western Allies of their reason for having troops in Siberia, and they were glad to extricate themselves from the tangled web of the Russian Civil War. The Japanese, however, were reluctant to relinquish their hold on Russian territory and began to settle in for a much longer stay. Because of their influence, the White Russian forces in the Far East were also encouraged to prolong their desperate struggle against the Soviets. Only three days after the departure of the last American troops from Vladivostok, the Japanese launched an attack on the Bolsheviks all over the Far East from Vladivostok to the Amur. They stormed Khabarovsk, and made themselves masters of the Maritime region, where they remained in occupation for a year and a half.[15]

As this renewal of the Japanese threat came just at the time when a war with Poland had started in the Ukraine, Lenin's government resorted to a devious stratagem. Tactically exploiting the democratic aims of the remaining liberal and SR politicians in Eastern Siberia, Moscow in April 1920 sanctioned the creation of a nominally independent Far Eastern Republic. This puppet state had the pretence of a Political Centre government in Verkhneudinsk, but was in practice ruled by the communist Krasno-shchekov, and its 'people's revolutionary army' under the command of V.K. Blyukher of the Red Army was actively engaged in warfare against the Whites and the Japanese. The Far Eastern Republic's communist army

---

[14] Communist Party of the Soviet Union, Altai kraykom, *Altay v vosstanovitelnyy period. Sbornik dokumentov*, Barnaul, 1960, pp. 7–8, 12, 67, 76, 82, 96–100; M.S. Bogdanov, *Razgrom zapadnosibirskogo kulatsko-eserovskogo myatezha 1921g.*, Tyumen, 1961; Dotsenko, *Struggle*, p. 119; V.S. Flerov, ed., *Krestyanstvo i selskoye khozyaystvo Sibiri v 1917–1961 gg.*, Novosibirsk, 1965, pp. 59–61; *Istoriya Sibiri*, vol. IV, pp. 154–5; V.I. Lenin, *Sochineniya*, 3rd edn, 1935, vol. XXIX, pp. 489–91; J.M. Meijer, ed., *The Trotsky Papers 1917–1922*, The Hague, 1971, vol. II, pp. 384–7, 430–1 (I am grateful to Professor G. Hosking for this reference); O.H. Radkey, *The Unknown Civil War in Soviet Russia: a Study of the Green Movement in the Tambov Region 1920–1921*, Stanford, 1976; *Sibirskaya Sovetskaya Entsiklopediya*, vol. I, cols. 533–4; vol. II, cols. 428, 1010.

[15] Chamberlin, *Russian Revolution*, vol. II, pp. 164, 201; Ioffe, *Kolchakovskaya avantyura*, pp. 238–41, 262; *Istoriya Sibiri*, vol. IV, pp. 126, 133, 139, 42, 162; White, *Siberian Intervention*, pp. 285–9, 351–67, 423.

captured Chita in October 1920, and Semyonov's forces were driven into Manchuria a month later.

The main thorn in the flesh of the Soviet government in Buryatia during 1921 was another White ataman – the Baltic German Baron von Ungern-Sternberg – who led his Cossacks across the Mongolian frontier and in February 1921 took possession of the capital Örgöö, where his troops earned a reputation for brutality at least as bad as that of Semyonov's. Soviet soldiers sent into Mongolia destroyed him and his marauders at the end of August, and the installation of a pro-Bolshevik government in Örgöö in 1921 was the first step towards the subordination of Mongolia to Soviet Russia as a satellite state.[16]

Although the Japanese had been forced to evacuate Transbaikalia and the Amur in 1920, they continued to hold on to the Ussuri region and northern Sakhalin. Under the auspices of the Japanese the Whites launched an offensive against the Soviet army and partisans in the Ussuri–Amur region. It was during this period that the Whites made another desperate effort to establish a foothold to the north of the Amur by invading Yakutia, where anti-Soviet forces regrouped, and in September 1921 a coalition of Yakut nationalists, KDs and SRs overcame the Soviets in northern Yakutia and besieged Yakutsk itself. It was Kalandarashvili who led a Soviet army from Irkutsk to relieve Yakutsk, and although he himself was killed, the Bolsheviks succeeded in driving the insurgents back towards the Okhotsk coast. In order to lend support to these beleaguered White forces, an expedition was sent by sea from Vladivostok in September 1922. Landing at Ayan, the Whites advanced through the Jugjur Mountains, driving the Bolsheviks before them as far as Amga. Once again Irkutsk was called upon to send Red Army units down the Lena, and early in 1923 the Whites were again beaten back to the coast and defeated.[17]

While these last episodes of the Russian Civil War were taking place, pressure was being put upon the Japanese to abandon their military adventure on the Siberian mainland. On 25 October 1922 the last Japanese soldiers left Vladivostok by ship, and the only part of the old Russian Empire which remained under their occupation was the northern half of Sakhalin. From then until 1945 the island was divided between Soviet Russia and Japan, the latter holding the southern half in accordance with the terms of the 1905 Treaty of Portsmouth. Units of the Red Army made their entry into Vladivostok as the Japanese moved out, and as the Maritime Province was

[16] Bawden, *Mongolia*, pp. 188, 215–18, 232–6; Dotsenko, *The Struggle*, pp. 119–20; Ioffe, *Kolchakovskaya avantyura*, pp. 263–4; *Istoriya Sibiri*, vol. IV, pp. 161–73, 282; Kolarz, *Peoples*, pp. 2–3; *Sibirskaya Sovetskaya Entsiklopediya*, vol. II, cols. 454–5; White, *Siberian Intervention*, pp. 367–71, 378–81.

[17] Ioffe, *Kolchakovskaya avantyura*, pp. 264–5; *Istoriya Sibiri*, vol. IV, pp. 164–8, 280–2; *Istoriya Yakutskoy ASSR*, vol. III, p. 59; *Sibirskaya Sovetskaya Entsiklopediya*, vol. II, col. 455; White, *Siberian Intervention*, pp. 366, 387–90.

finally united with the rest of Siberia under the Soviet flag, the Far Eastern Republic, having outlived its usefulness to Moscow, was absorbed into the Russian Republic.

At the same time another mass exodus took place when thousands of Russians fled before the Soviet occupation forces to join the Russian community already living in Manchuria. Altogether the White Russian diaspora in the Far East amounted to 250,000 at this time. Over 60 per cent of these settled in Manchuria, chiefly in the city of Harbin, where out of 485,000 inhabitants 120,000 were Russians. The prevailing mood of these émigrés was understandably anti-Bolshevik, and patriotic societies were formed in Harbin, out of which a Russian Fascist Organisation developed in 1925.[18]

[18] Ioffe, *Kolchakovskaya avantyura*, pp. 264–5; *Istoriya Sibiri*, vol. IV, pp. 170–3, 288; Kolarz, *The Peoples*, pp. 52–3; Shvarev, *Dalniy Vostok*, p. 335; J.J. Stephan, *The Russian Fascists: Tragedy and Farce in Exile, 1925–1945*, London, 1978, pp. 33–47, 51–9, 117–18; White, *Siberian Intervention*, pp. 289–92, 391–405, 413–15.

12

THE NATIVE PEOPLES, 1917–1929

THE lives of all the native peoples of Siberia were eventually affected profoundly by the Revolution and Civil War, but those in the most northerly regions at first only experienced the indirect effects of the general breakdown of the economy and administration. Russians were relatively few and far between in these parts of the colony, and it had little economic value for the immediate purposes of their political struggle. On the whole, therefore, the Samoyeds, Tunguses, Yakuts, Chukchis, Koraks and others were left to their own devices. On the other hand, those native communities which lived farther south, near the principal areas of Russian settlement, came directly into contact with the fighting. From July 1919 the Red Army advanced against Kolchak on a relatively narrow front extending from the Ob Khanty lands in the north to the Kazak steppe in the south. The settlements of the West Siberian Tatars in particular lay close to the main zone of fighting – the Trans-Siberian railway between Tyumen and Tomsk – so that, although information is scarce, it can be assumed that they experienced hardships under the Kolchak régime and later, similar to those of the Russian and other settlers in the same region. For the Turkic native peoples of the Altai region the confusion of the Red–White conflict was further complicated by the widespread activities of Russian guerrilla bands consisting either of industrial workers fighting for the Bolshevik cause, or of peasants with SR sympathies who opposed the Reds here until 1921. Farther east, around the southern end of Lake Baikal, many of the Buryat Mongols and Ewenki Tunguses became involved in the war between the White forces of Ataman Semyonov and the Red partisans and soldiers, which lasted from early 1918 to the end of 1920. Similarly, in the Far East, fighting between the White armies and the Bolshevik guerrillas raged through the territories of the Tungus, Nivkh, Nanai and Ulchi peoples of the lower Amur and the Udeghes in the mountains of the Maritime region.

For the people of Siberia, as for all the subject peoples of the Russian Empire, the policy of any post-civil-war government towards the non-Russian peoples was a matter of great importance. Most Russian politicians, even if their views were liberal, could conceive no other possibility than the maintenance of Russia within its previous boundaries – a view expressed by the formulation 'Russia one and indivisible'. The Provisional Government, pending the Constituent Assembly, made no formal concession to the separatist movements which existed among many of the non-Russian nationalities such as the Poles, Finns, Ukrainians and Tatars, and it was only in September 1917 that it was forced to recognise the principle of self-determination for the peoples of Russia. On these matters the Bolsheviks had a more clearly formulated policy. As early as 1903 the SD socialists had committed themselves to the right of self-determination for every nation in the Russian Empire, and Lenin's subsequent theorising led him to a tactical view that granting autonomy to every nationality which had a definable territory would help to undermine the Empire and the wide spectrum of its 'bourgeois' politicians. While the aspirations of each nationality would be satisfied in terms of freedom to use its national language and have its own schools, this 'autonomy' would not amount to real self-government as a unit in a federal state. In Lenin's theoretical view differences of nationality were trivial compared with class divisions and allegiances, so that autonomy was simply a transitional stage towards centralisation, the ultimate aim being 'the closest drawing together and eventual merging of all nations'.[1] The first step towards this which the Bolshevik Party took when it came to power was to publish in November 1917 the 'Declaration of the Rights of the Peoples of Russia', which proclaimed the equality and sovereignty of all nationalities, the abolition of all national and religious discrimination, and the right of every nationality to free self-determination including secession from Russia – nominal rights which were subsequently incorporated into the Constitution of the USSR.

THE PEOPLES OF NORTHERN SIBERIA

To most Russians at the beginning of the twentieth century the peoples of the North scarcely existed. Pushed back as they were from the intensively colonised zone of the railway, hardly ever seen in the Russian towns, and generally referred to by the blanket term *yasashnye* (*yasak*-payers), the native peoples lived as separately from the 'white men' as did the Indians of North America. In this vast land the horizons of the Russian Siberians did not extend far beyond their own settlements, as Chekhov reported in the 1890s:

they hesitate to give a rough estimate of the extent of the forest, and in answer to our question they reply – 'It's endless'. All they know is that during the winter people of

[1] Lenin, *Sochineniya*, vol. XXIX, p. 261, quoted in T. Davletshin, *Sovetskiy Tatarstan*, Munich, 1974, p. 182.

some kind come on reindeer through the forest from the far north to buy grain, but what people they are or where they come from even the old men don't know.[2]

All those who did come into contact with the peoples of the northern forest and tundra in the early years of the twentieth century concurred that most of them lived in a state of near-destitution and apathy, and that they were destined to extinction in the near future.

After the February Revolution the Russian Provisional Government had little opportunity to do anything specific for the peoples of the North, but the Soviet government's Declaration of the Rights of the Peoples of Russia signified the end of the old colonial régime which had existed since Speranskiy's Regulations of 1822. *Yasak* was abolished, as was the supervision of the life of the native communities by the Russian police. Although the northern peoples were not in the main battle zone during the Civil War, they suffered greatly from its indirect effects – the interruption of supplies of grain, gunpowder, etc., and the breakdown of the fur trade on which their economy had become so dependent. The peoples of the North meanwhile kept themselves apart, as far as possible, from the savage and unedifying war between the Russians' warring factions.

In general the way of life of the peoples of the North changed little between 1917 and the late 1920s, with clan organisation wherever this had survived, and traditional institutions such as mutual aid, sharing of spoils, fostering and care of the aged. The activities of traders also continued to some extent during and after the Civil War, but in most places these were bad years for the hunters and reindeer herders. The latter in particular suffered disastrous losses not only from anthrax epidemics but also from unscrupulous raiding by participants in the Russian Civil War, and the necessity of killing deer in order to survive. As a result, by 1920 herds were severely depleted and many native communities faced famine. A typical report of the time was that 'The Ostyaks are completely destitute. They lack both outer and inner garments . . . and footwear . . . There is a great shortage of skins for bedding and clothes.'[3] As long-standing victims of a European colonial régime, the Siberian natives in most places displayed a deep-rooted and often fearful distrust and dislike of the Russians who came among them, and of whose unwanted and increasingly intrusive presence there seemed no possibility of ridding themselves.[4]

The early stages of Soviet government activity among the native peoples of the North was motivated by a philanthropic spirit. Between 1920 and 1923

[2] Chekhov, *Iz Sibiri*, ch. 9.

[3] I.S. Gurvich, ed., *Osushchestvleniye leninskoy natsionalnoy politiki u narodov Kraynego Severa*, Moscow, 1971, p. 280.

[4] Gurvich, *Osushchestvleniye*, pp. 15, 250–1; *Istoriya Sibiri*, vol. IV, pp. 64, 288, 296; *Narody Sibiri*, p. 547; M.A. Sergeyev, *Nekapitalisticheskiy put razvitiya malykh narodov Severa*, Moscow, 1955, pp. 210, 213, 226.

thousands of tons of grain are said to have been distributed to many communities, thus saving thousands of lives which were threatened by famine. As the same time work began on the provision of medical services in regions of Siberia where before 1917 little or nothing of this kind had existed. For instance, in the 97,000 square miles of Narym region on the middle Ob there had been only three very small hospitals and six medical stations; the vast region of the lower Ob and Yamal peninsula had similar provision; while the whole of the far north-east had only two first-aid stations. Indeed very little was known to the Russians about the state of health of the northern peoples, so that the first activities of the Red Cross after the Civil War were largely fact-finding expeditions. The traditional, and often effective, cures of folk medicine were practised by the shamans, but some of their methods of treatment were positively harmful, and in general the prevailing belief in the evil eye and various taboos frequently prevented the natives from accepting medical assistance even during epidemics.[5]

From the time of its seizure of power the Bolshevik party gave much thought to the 'native question' (*tuzemnyy vopros*) as one aspect of their nationalities policy and, since it was recognised that the small and primitive peoples of the North could do little to help themselves out of their 'backward' conditions, a succession of government measures were introduced to ameliorate the material conditions of their life. One of the worst legacies of the old régime – the entanglement of the native hunters in perpetual debt – was dealt with in 1920 by decrees cancelling all such debts to traders. Further special legislation for the peoples of the North followed in 1923–25, when the sale of alcohol in their territories was prohibited (not for the first – or the last – time) and they were absolved, for the time being, from all state taxes and labour obligations. At the same time as steps were taken to curb the activities of private traders in Siberia, the first consumers' cooperatives were introduced to provide a new and fairer basis for trade. However, despite these well-intentioned measures, after the end of the Russian Civil War economic life in Soviet Russia as a whole was at a low ebb, so that in practice the authorities were unable to make much of a positive impression upon the lives of the northern peoples. Indeed the defeat of the Kolchak régime was followed by a period of 'Red banditry' during which many of the Bolsheviks not only murdered any Russians who were unsympathetic to the new régime, but also seized reindeer arbitrarily and exploited the native people without compunction. In fact most of the latter remained beyond the influence of Soviet society, their conditions of life as primitive and precarious as before, throughout the 1920s.

[5] V.S. Flerov, *Stroitelstvo Sovetskoy vlasti i borba s inostrannoy ekspansiey na Kamchatke (1922–1926 gg.)*, Tomsk, 1964, pp. 251–4; Gurvich, *Osushchestvleniye*, pp. 16, 159–61, 250, 280–1; *Istoriya Sibiri*, vol. IV, p. 292; *Narody Sibiri*, p. 639; Sergeyev, *Nekapitalisticheskiy put*, pp. 290–3; Vdovin, *Priroda i chelovek*, pp. 35–6.

Meanwhile their future was the subject of discussion in Russian ruling circles. Some of the revolutionary socialists who had lived among the northern peoples and come to know and respect their way of life, such as V.G. Bogoraz, believed that they should be left to their traditional ways with as little interference from outside as possible. As the rightful occupiers of their vast, sparsely inhabited territories, they should have the integrity of their lands guaranteed by the establishment of native reservations. This view received little consideration from the Bolsheviks, who had as little doubt as any tsarist empire builders of Russia's right to possess the whole of northern Asia. Moreover, they were imbued with the spirit of Marxist historicism, which assured them that they indubitably represented progress and the highest human values, which it was their mission to propagate among the backward and ignorant peoples of Siberia. The most direct impingement of the new Russian government on the native peoples at this time was in the realm of tribal or clan institutions. Although the first courts under the Soviets were based upon existing clan gatherings, and judged disputes in accordance with local custom, in 1926 a law came into effect which defined 'crimes constituting relics of the tribal way of life', such as clan vengeance and blood-money, payment of bride-price (*kalym*), and marriages between minors. Here the new state authorities had no qualms about declaring such age-old practices illegal, and imposing Russian laws irrespective of the wishes of the people themselves.

So far as the organs of local government were concerned, attempts were made in the early 1920s to create soviets even among some of the nomadic Samoyed peoples of the North, but such endeavours were scarcely a reality in view of the extremely small numbers of political agents available: for instance, there were only four to cover the whole of the northern part of Yenisey province, where administrative centres and native settlements or encampments might be 1,000 miles apart. Where representatives of Soviet power did exist, the artificiality of their function among the primitive peoples, who neither understood nor wanted the 'white man's' new way of life, was made obvious by the fact that some of the conferences held to discuss the future of various regions were conducted without the participation of any natives.[6]

The greater degree of stability and prosperity attained by the Soviet Union in the second half of the 1920s permitted the government to devote more attention and more funds to Siberia, and in 1924 a Committee for Assistance to the Peoples of the Outlying Districts of the North (generally known as the

[6] B. Chichlo, 'La Collectivisation en Sibérie: un problème de nationalités', Centre d'études russes et soviétiques, *Colloque sur l'expérience soviétique et le problème national dans le monde (1920–1939)*, Paris, 1981, pp. 286, 291–3; Flerov, *Stroitelstvo*, p. 9; Gurvich, *Osushchestvleniye*, pp. 17, 19, 251, 280–6; *Istoriya Sibiri*, vol. IV, pp. 292–5, 300; Khomich, *Nentsy*, p. 233; Kolarz, *The Peoples*, pp. 65–6; *Narody Sibiri*, pp. 544, 547, 551–4, 629, 657, 754, 826; Sergeyev, *Nekapitalisticheskiy put*, pp. 216, 221, 241–7; Shvarev, *Dalniy vostok*, p. 75.

Committee of the North) was created with the aim of 'promoting the planned organisation of the small peoples of the North in respect of economic, judicial–administrative and cultural–medical matters'. Many of the members of the Committee of the North were Communist Party functionaries, but it also included scholarly ethnographers and geographers with first-hand knowledge of Siberia, such as V.G. Bogoraz and L. Ya Shternberg. Such men saw the Committee's task as helping the native peoples to preserve their own culture during the socio-political 'transformations' envisaged for Siberia, but as it possessed no administrative powers its practical influence was limited, and it was unable to challenge the policies and actions of the Communist Party. The aim of the ethnographic expeditions which it sent out was not to study the way of life and the needs of various ethnic communities objectively, but in order to bring about changes. One of the most important activities undertaken by the Committee of the North was the establishment in certain remote areas of 'cultural bases' which provided the local population with such services as a medical station, a veterinary station, a shop and a school. As the languages of the peoples of the North had never been committed to written form, the language of instruction in the few schools which could be set up in the 1920s was almost without exception Russian. For further development of such services it was essential to produce literate staff for administration offices and teachers for schools. To this end special 'northern departments' were opened in the colleges in Tomsk, Tobolsk, Irkutsk, Khabarovsk and other Siberian towns, and in 1925 the first group of nineteen students belonging to northern nationalities were sent to study at Leningrad University, where subsequently the Institute of Peoples of the North was founded. Thus Leningrad became the educational metropolis for the peoples of Siberia, especially after 1948, when the Northern Department of the Herzen Pedagogical Institute was created.

The cultural activities of the Committee of the North were, of course, not conceived in a political vacuum. Their aim was explicitly to 'draw all the natives (*tuzemtsy*) into socialist construction' and to 'create conditions for the development of organised self-help (*samodeyatelnost*) among the small nationalities of the outlying regions of the North on the new political and economic basis'.[7] For this purpose the Communist Party considered it necessary to involve the natives in the Soviet system, but as there were no industrial workers or proletariat, and no class consciousness or revolutionary feelings among them, a great deal of Marxist theorising and practical experimentation was required in order to decide upon the appropriate form for native Soviets by 'adapting them to pre-capitalist conditions'. This indeed became the principal theme of Soviet ethnographic studies of Siberia in the 1930s. The first piece of legislation in this field was the 'Provisional Statute

[7] Gurvich, *Osushchestvleniye*, p. 18; *Narody Sibiri*, p. 555.

9 Khanty woman of the Ob with her grandchild. Her cloth coat is decorated with coloured appliqué designs. The large shawl over a woman's head and shoulders was used to cover her face when she encountered an elder male relative on her husband's side – a practice reflecting the Islamic influence of the Siberian Tatars. In the background is a pole-tent covered with bark. (Early twentieth century.)

on the Administration of the Natives of Outlying Regions of the North of the RSFSR' (1926), which instituted the election of 'clan soviets' at traditional clan gathering places, and a structure of regional native congresses and executive committees. As clan organisation had all but disappeared from the lives of many ethnic groups, such as the Tungus and the peoples of the Amur, these were instead to form soviets on a territorial basis. In fact, within a few years, when it became clear that clan soviets with the participation of all members, rich or poor, did not provide the required subordination of the native communities to Communist Party policies, clan soviets were abolished in favour of territorial soviets.

From the very beginning of the Soviet period the Russian state had not only political, but economic plans for the Siberian peoples. Although *yasak* had been abolished, and a decree of 1927 nominally relieved the northern peoples from all taxes, in reality the new communist state was no less inclined than the old tsarist one to make the colonial natives pay for the privilege of being ruled by the Russians. The Soviet government instituted a trading system whereby the Siberian natives supplied furs and other commodities through cooperatives to state procurement agencies, receiving in exchange money credits, with which they could purchase various goods.

Instead of the spirits and trinkets which formed much of the stock-in-trade of pre-revolutionary traders, the state-organised stores now made available such wares as flour, cereals, salt, sugar, tools and raw materials. From the point of view of the Communist Party, the replacement of the former barter trade by this essentially commercial system not only satisfied practical requirements, but also conformed to Marxist ideological preconceptions. The traditional institutions of tribal society which existed everywhere in Siberia, such as mutual assistance and equal sharing of spoils, may have represented a kind of 'primitive communism', but they did not satisfy the formula of socialism: 'from each according to his capabilities, to each according to his work'. So far from respecting and building upon the old communal institutions, therefore, the Soviet authorities set out to destroy them, so that the natives would become involved in market relations and a money economy (which, ironically, were quite contrary to the deepest convictions of many of the idealistic Russian Marxists of the time). Thus the natives could be subordinated to the type of social and economic development deemed universally desirable by the Russian Communist Party.[8]

In Northern and Eastern Siberia hunting was the most lucrative occupation of the native peoples, since their chief saleable commodity continued to be, as it had been for more than four centuries, furs. From the beginning of the Civil War the Soviet government (as well as the Whites) had a great interest in exploiting the resources of the Siberian colony in order to make international payments for armaments and industrial equipment. Because of the total lack of control over hunting and trapping during the period 1916–23 in the Far East – the only significant source of sables remaining – that most valuable animal had suffered catastrophic destruction. Other animals too were subjected to ruthless extermination, such as the brown bear in Kamchatka, where hunters, Russian and foreign, killed thousands for their skins. The temptation to deal in furs was all the stronger because at this time no money existed in the Okhotsk–Kamchatka–Chukchi territory, so that until the 1930s all goods were bartered for furs or gold (or alcohol). In order to counteract the activities of foreign traders and establish a Soviet state monopoly over the fur trade, various official agencies were then created, such as the Okhotsk–Kamchatka Joint-Stock Fisheries Company (known in Russian as *OKARO*) and the Far East State Trading Company (*Dalgostorg*). In the post-civil war period furs once again became one of Russia's most important export commodities, along with grain, oil and timber. During the period 1924–29 furs accounted for between 10 and 15.3 per cent of the total value of Soviet Russian exports, worth from 295 to 523 million roubles per

[8] Chichlo, 'La Collectivisation', pp. 293–5; Gurvich, *Osushchestvleniye*, pp. 17–28, 50–65, 142–3, 172, 180, 252–4, 282; *Istoriya Sibiri*, vol. IV, pp. 293, 304, 472; *Narody Sibiri*, pp. 547–8, 551–2, 555, 826; Sergeyev, *Nekapitalisticheskiy put*, pp. 262–3, 281, 329–35; Shiroko-gorov, *Social Organization*, pp. 97, 296; Shvarev, *Dalniy Vostok*, p. 76.

annum. Given the great importance of fur exports, it is not surprising that one of the main concerns of the Soviet Russian government in Siberia during the 1920s was the creation of a network of trading posts to ensure regular deliveries by hunters, and that in order to encourage the peoples of the North to increase their kill of fur-bearing animals, the state offered credits to native cooperatives for the purchase of weapons, ammunition, and other equipment.[9]

THE UGRIANS AND SAMOYEDS

Among the first aboriginal communities to feel the effects of the Revolution and Civil War were those living in the Far North of the Ural and West Siberian regions. Here the names of two Nenets have earned a place in Soviet legend: G. Khatanzeiskiy, a sawmill worker on the Pechora who organised strike action as early as February 1917 and was later imprisoned and shot by the White Russians; and M. Yadobchev, a member of the Soviet at Obdorsk who, as one of the few Nenets to fight with the Red Guards, was executed by the Whites in the summer of 1918. From that time until late 1919 the whole of the North of European Russia and Western Siberia was under the control of the Whites who, with help from British, American and French troops based on the Murmansk–Arkhangelsk region, maintained a presence on the lower Ob and Yenisey by using the northern sea-route. Fighting between Reds and Whites took place around Obdorsk and Dudinka, the latter – one of the last refuges of the Whites on the Yenisey – falling under Soviet control in 1920, and the former only in 1921. By then on the western side of the Urals the first Nenets soviet had been created on the Pechora, and some of the earliest clan soviets were created during 1921–22 among the Selkups and Khanty on the middle Ob. Farther north, even in 1926 few of the Nenets, Enets and Nganasan had been drawn into 'nomad soviets'. Here, in the tundra, local chiefs still retained their power, and large groups of Samoyeds remained practically beyond the influence of the Soviet Russian authorities. Even in a district where a Nenets clan soviet had been elected as required, the people immediately held a second, secret meeting to select a regional prince, explaining that while the Russians needed a soviet, the Nenets needed a chief. However, in general the new Russian authorities

[9] T. Armstrong, *Russian Settlement in the North*, Cambridge, 1965, p. 60; A. Baykov, *Soviet Foreign Trade*, Princeton, 1946, tables IV–V; *Bolshaya Sovetskaya Entsiklopediya*, 3rd edn, vol. XXI, col. 744; R.A. Clarke, *Soviet Economic Facts 1917–1970*, London 1972, p. 46; Flerov, *Stroitelstvo*, pp. 45, 91, 119, 126, 145–6, 149, 164–78; Gurvich, *Osushchestvleniye*, p. 76; *Istoriya Sibiri*, vol. IV, p. 296; U.G. Popova, *Eveny Magadanskoy oblasti; ocherki istorii, khozyaystva i kultury evenov Okhotskogo poberezhya, 1917–1977gg.*, Moscow, 1981, pp. 81–2, 234; O. Swenson, *Northwest of the World: Forty Years Trading and Hunting in Northern Siberia*, London, 1951, pp. 56–7, 135–7, 143–6, 210–19; N.A. Zhikharev, *Ocherki istorii Severo-Vostoka RSFSR (1917–1953)*, Magadan, 1961, pp. 72–3, 131, 139–40.

succeeded in imposing their administrative system throughout north-west Siberia by 1928.[10]

After several years of civil war, many of the native peoples of the middle Yenisey and Ob – Selkups, Kets and Khanty – were almost destitute and in need of famine relief, as were some of the Ewenkis and Dolgans of the Far North. The first practical step taken towards self-help was the creation of consumer cooperatives, and in 1923 medical services began under the auspices of the Red Cross Society in the northern Yenisey district, with the aim of combatting high infant mortality, endemic diseases such as tuberculosis and trachoma, and epidemics of influenza and measles. All of these ethnic groups were illiterate, and the 1920s saw only the first small steps towards their education, with the foundation of primary schools among the Nenets of the Pechora and the Khanty on the lower Ob. A Nenets National Region was created west of the Urals in 1930 by separating off the northern part of the Komi–Zyrian Autonomous Region. Soon after this a large area around the estuary of the Ob was designated the Yamal Nenets National Region, while the territory from the lower Yenisey to the east became the Taimyr National Region, embracing a mixed population of Arctic nomads – Nenets, Enets, Dolgans, Nganasans, Ewenki Tungus and Yakuts. South of Yamal the region around the lower Ob became the Ostyak–Vogul National Region, with a native population of Mansi and Khanty. At the time of the 1926 census the Nenets on both sides of the Urals totalled about 16,500, the Enets 378, the Nganasan 867, and the Dolgan 1,445, while farther south there were some 17,800 Khanty, 5,700 Mansi, 6,000 Selkups, and 1,225 Kets. In the Far North at this time the native peoples still outnumbered the Russians by a ratio of 56:44.[11]

THE TUNGUS

By the time of the Russian Revolution and Civil War the Tungus, the most widely dispersed of all the native peoples of Siberia, were also among the most demoralised and in many areas denationalised. Because of their cultural conservatism and nomadic way of life they were an easy prey for their more aggressive neighbours, whether Russians, Buryats or Yakuts, and although some of the Reindeer Tungus of the taiga succeeded in maintain-

---

[10] T. Armstrong, *The Northern Sea Route: Soviet Exploitation of the North East Passage*, Cambridge, 1952, pp. 17–18; Gurvich, *Osushchestvleniye*, pp. 250–1, 279–82; *Istoriya Sibiri*, vol. IV, pp. 291–2; Khomich, *Nentsy*, pp. 225–9; *Narody Sibiri*, pp. 629, 657, 754; Sergeyev, *Nekapitalisticheskiy put*, pp. 219, 297; I.M. Suslov, 'Shamanstvo i borba s nim', *Sovietskiy Sever*, 1931, no. 3–4, p. 140.

[11] Chichlo, 'La Collectivisation', p. 292; Gurvich, *Osushchestvleniye*, pp. 16, 250–1, 255, 280–1, 285, 293–4; *Istoriya Sibiri*, vol. IV, pp. 292, 294–5, 465; Khomich, *Nentsy*, pp. 233, 308; *Narody Sibiri*, pp. 558–9, 570, 594, 603, 608, 629, 648, 661, 665, 687, 699, 742, 754; Sergeyev, *Nekapitalisticheskiy put*, pp. 314–15.

ing their traditional way of life by keeping themselves apart, many had lost their independence and become hired labourers. In Transbaikalia those of the Ingoda basin near Chita had become assimilated to Russian peasant settlers, some of them even belonging to the Old Believer community. Farther south, near the Mongolian frontier, the Horse Tungus were thoroughly Buryatised and so in places absorbed into the Transbaikal Cossack Host. Similarly, most of the Tungus living to the north-west of Lake Baikal were Russified or Buryatised by the 1920s, having lost most, if not all, of their reindeer, and they conformed to the agricultural and cattle-rearing economy of their neighbours. The more northerly Tungus of the forests east of Baikal, in the basins of the Barguzin, Vitim and Olokma, as well as those of the Amur and Okhotsk coast, still lived by reindeer-herding and hunting, as did the many groups that lived in Central Siberia north of Lake Baikal and in Yakutia. Those Tungus who lived in the basins of the Angara and Mountain Tunguska were particularly vulnerable to exploitation by Russian 'Tungusniks' – traders from Irkutsk who specialised in visiting the areas where the Reindeer-Tungus roamed, in order to obtain furs. In exchange they gave the native people cheap goods and vodka, thus contributing largely to the decline of their traditional way of life and morale. So notorious were the effects of this predatory trading by 'Tungusniks' that the government of Nicholas II took steps to prohibit their activities in 1912.[12]

Lacking any tribal cohesion or even effective clan allegiance, and having had their communal way of life undermined by Russian commercial interests, the Tungus were on the whole incapable of developing new initiatives or skills in competition with other peoples. In 1917, therefore, when so many ethnic communities in the Siberian colony were stirred into political activity, the Tungus remained almost without exception passive, only those in Transbaikalia showing any political awareness, which they expressed by attaching themselves to the deliberations of the Buryat National Committee. During the Russian Civil War too, the Tungus, having learned through long experience to be submissive or elusive in relation to the more masterful nations of Siberia, played almost no part. In Central Siberia some of the nomadic Tungus of the region between Lake Baikal and the upper Lena fled from the Russian theatre of war into more remote territory near the headwaters of the Lower Tunguska, while those in the Mountain Tunguska basin sought refuge in the forest between that river and the Chunya. An indication of the small extent to which the Tungus of Central Siberia and Yakutia were involved in the Russian Civil War is the fact that during the 1921–2 Yakut rebellion against the Soviet government, out of 726 Bolshevik sympathisers

[12] S. Patkanov, *Opyt geografii i statistiki tungusskikh plemen Sibiri, Zapiski Imperatorskogo geograficheskogo obshchestva po otdeleniyu etnografii*, vol. XXXI, St Petersburg, 1906, ch. 1, vyp. 1, pp. 11, 68; Shirokogorov, *Social Organization*, pp. 60–2, 88, 111, 125; Tugolukov, *Tungusy*, pp. 18–22, 54–6, 76–9, 103.

killed by the Whites only 2 were Tungus, as compared with 300 each Russians and Yakuts, and even 7 Koreans. However, even if the Tungus did attempt to keep out of the way in the taiga, their small isolated bands were extremely vulnerable to predation by guerrilla groups of whatever political persuasion, and in many cases their small herds of reindeer were badly depleted by the commandeering of animals for transport and food. Some Tungus helped the Russian anti-White partisans in their traditional role of pathfinders, and in 1924–5 those in the Okhotsk region were induced – in their ignorance, as they subsequently pleaded – to throw in their lot with Artemyev's Yakut nationalists and the White Russian expeditionary force.[13]

The induction of the Tungus into the Soviet Russian system began in different regions at different times, depending on when the Civil War ceased. In the lower Yenisey region, for instance, the first Tungus clan soviet was nominally created in 1921, but its practical activity was almost non-existent for several years. The first Tungus national districts were designated at Baikit on the Mountain Tunguska and on the Ilimpeya, a tributary of the Lower Tunguska. The gradual introduction of medical services and schools by the Committee of the North began to bring some benefits to the Tungus of Central Siberia, and the creation of cooperatives to compensate for the abolition of private trading (the 'Tungusniks' had renewed their operations during the Civil War) gave their economy, in terms of fur-trapping, a sounder financial basis. However, in the Lena basin and east of Baikal the nationalism of the Yakuts and Buryats made little concession to their weaker neighbours. In the basins of the Vitim and Olokma, for instance, the first schools, medical stations and veterinary services were set up on the local initiative of enthusiastic Russian cooperative organisers (who had to overcome the Ewenkis' tendency to hide from Russian officials) while the Yakutsk Committee of the North took no steps to provide such services until 1929. Meanwhile many Yakuts were moving into the lower Vitim–Olokma Tungus territory and settling there. In Transbaikalia the Buryat nationalism of the early 1920s discriminated against the Tungus, some of whom migrated across the border into Mongolia.

The provision of a national homeland for the Tungus in conformity with the nationalities policy of the Bolshevik Party raised many problems. As compared with some 75,000 people in 1911, the Tungus (Ewenkis and Ewens together) in 1926 totalled only about 41,000, the decrease being accounted for partly by the assimilation of the Horse Tungus in Transbaikalia to the Buryats or Russians. Similarly, many of the settled and semi-settled Tungus of the upper Lena and Angara region registered as

[13] *Istoriya Sibiri*, vol. IV, pp. 59–60; *Istoriya Yakutskoy ASSR*, vol. III, pp. 57, 101–2; *Narody Sibiri*, p. 732; Popova, *Eveny*, pp. 207–10; Patkanov, *Opyt geografii*, vol. I, vyp. 2, p. 67; Sergeyev, *Nekapitalisticheskiy put*, p. 210; Tugolukov, *Tungusy*, pp. 19, 78, 146, 200–1, 211–12.

Russians or Buryats after the abolition of the *yasak* system. The Reindeer-Tungus were, however, scattered over an enormous territory, parts of which came within several different provinces and republics. The solution adopted by the Soviet government in 1930–1 was that a large area of Central Siberia (roughly as big as Turkey or Texas) was designated the Ewenki National Region, as was a smaller, but still very substantial region in the Vitim and Olokma basins, carved out of the Yakut Autonomous Republic, the Siberian Territory (*kray*) and the Far Eastern Territory. Within the Yakut ASSR itself, where the Tungus formed the largest non-Yakut minority, fourteen smaller areas were designated Tungus national districts, and for the first time an attempt was made to distinguish between the Ewenki and Ewen Tungus. Two more Ewenki districts were created within the Buryat ASSR, near the northern end of Lake Baikal and Lake Baunt respectively; while in the Okhotsk coastal region a large area of mixed Ewenki and Ewen population was designated the Okhotsk–Ewen National Region. Some of these Tungus national territories subsequently underwent changes or, as in the case of the Okhotsk–Ewen district, were abolished.[14]

By the end of the 1920s some progress had been made by the Soviet Russian authorities in their self-appointed task of modernising the life of the Tungus people. The prohibition of 'bride-price' in 1925 eventually led to changes in the life of Tungus women, but the cases quoted in Soviet accounts are usually extreme ones, such as that of the prosperous Ewenki herd-owner Yakuni Gayul of Baikit district, whose two young wives were persuaded to leave him in 1930. One of them, to whom he had allotted 100 reindeer, handed these over to the local 'soviet farm', joined the Young Communists' League and was sent to be educated in Yeniseysk. As a result of investing Tungus women with equal civil rights it is said that they gradually began to be accepted as full members of the collectives and of clan and territorial soviets. If the opinion of the leading non-Bolshevik expert on the Tungus is to be believed, however, the simple clichés of 'bride-price' and 'inferior status of women' were alien constructs imposed upon traditional practices by Europeans, and bore no relation to the perceptions of Tungus women and men themselves. Women, acting as heads of families in the absence of a man, and as shamans, were on an equal footing with men, even if taboos associated with their sexual functions excluded them from certain social activities.[15]

---

[14] *Aziatskaya Rossiya*, vol. I, p. 82; Gurvich, *Osushchestvleniye*, pp. 250, 282, 285–6, 293–5; *Istoriya Sibiri*, vol. IV, pp. 292, 295, 300; *Istoriya Yakutii*, vol. III, p. 99; Khaptayev, *Istoriya Buryatskoy ASSR*, vol. II, p. 252 (in fact Ewenkis are scarcely mentioned in this book); Kolarz, *The Peoples*, p. 102; *Narody Sibiri*, pp. 559, 702, 732, 737, 754, 761; Popova, *Eveny*, p. 235; Sergeyev, *Nekapitalisticheskiy put*, pp. 219, 266; Shirokogorov, *Social Organization*, pp. 94, 111–12; Tokarev, *Etnografiya*, p. 513; Tugolukov, *Tungusy*, pp. 19, 21, 78; G. Vasilevich, 'Vitimo-Tungir-Olekminskiye Tungusy: geograficheskaya kharakteristika', *Sovetskiy Sever*, 1930, no. 3, pp. 103, 111–13.

[15] Shirokogorov, *Social Organization*, pp. 190, 218, 224–6, 259–61, 271.

One fundamental feature of Tungus life – their nomadism – came under attack by the Soviet state from the late 1920s onward. In 1927 the first Congress of small nations of the Yakut ASSR discussed among other matters the transition of the Tungus and others to a sedentary way of life. However, the political sovietisation of the nomadic clans made little progress before 1930, when the first 'cultural bases' were established in various parts of Central and Eastern Siberia – Tura on the Lower Tunguska, Ust-Kalakan on the Vitim, Ust-Maya in eastern Yakutia, and Chumikan on the Okhotsk coast. Combining the functions of cultural enlightenment, medical services and political propaganda with the economic role of fur-trading posts, the 'cultural bases' were intended as the first step in the process of subordinating the Tungus to the economic system of the Soviet Russian state. Gradually they also became the nuclei of settlements and assumed the role of administrative centres for the native territories.

Of all the peoples of Siberia, the Ewenki and Ewen Tungus with their mobile way of life, absence of hierarchical organisation or fixed tribal territory, and traditions of egalitarianism in the distribution of hunting spoils, were perhaps the nation least capable of adapting, or being moulded, to the social preconceptions of the Russian communists. However, the relatively limited penetration of Central and Eastern Siberian forest-lands by Russian state influence even as late as the 1940s gave some of the Reindeer-Tungus a respite from the inexorable advance of European civilisation.[16]

YAKUTIA

East of the Yenisey the dominant administrative area of the Russian Empire in terms of area was Yakut Province, which covered some 1,445,000 square miles – almost as big as European Russia, or more than one third the size of Europe or the USA. In this vast region of coniferous forest and tundra only some 275,000 people lived, at a density of one person to every five square miles. The most significant difference between this province and any of the other divisions of Siberia was that here in 1917 the native population of Yakuts and others far outnumbered the Russians, who amounted to only 26,000, or 10.5 per cent of the total. Since the Yakuts had a relatively developed educated class, who were active in the administration and commerce of their country, and had a strong desire for independence from Russian rule, the effects of the Russian Revolution and Civil War could not but be rather specific, especially as Yakutia was so remote from the rest of Russia. Only two routes were available for regular communication. One was a road, or cart-track, which led from Irkutsk to the upper reaches of the Lena, but which came to an end for practical purposes at Zhigalovo after only 280 miles, leaving almost 1,600 miles still to be covered – in summer by

[16] Gurvich, *Osushchestvleniye*, pp. 207–10; *Istoriya Yakutskoy ASSR*, vol. III, pp. 141–3, 146; *Narody Sibiri*, pp. 555–6; Sergeyev, *Nekapitalisticheskiy put*, pp. 262–3.

boat, in winter by sledge on the frozen surface of the Lena – in order to reach the city of Yakutsk. The other route linked Yakutsk by way of the valleys of the Aldan and Maya to Ayan on the Okhotsk coast, but much of this road was passable only by pack-horse or reindeer, as it had been two centuries before.

However, telegraph communication extended to Yakutsk, and it was by this means that news of the revolution in Russia was received in February 1917. Immediately a Committee of Public Safety was organised with representatives of all social groups, and the Russian vice-governor of the province was obliged to recognise its authority. While most of the members of the Committee were SR socialists, Mensheviks, or Yakut nationalists, its chairman was G.I. Petrovskiy, one of a number of Bolsheviks serving terms of exile in Yakutia. There were over 500 political exiles living in Yakutia at this time. After the amnesty in March 1917 many of these converged upon Yakutsk, augmenting the small Russian community in a city of only some 8,000 inhabitants, most of whom were Yakuts, and local trade unions and soviets of soldiers' and workers' deputies were formed. However, the Bolsheviks were unable to achieve the support of more than a small number of Russian and Yakut labourers, since the majority of the population – peasants and reindeer-herders – favoured the SRs, so far as they had any political views. Consequently, these Bolshevik politicians – Petrovskiy, Orjonikidze, Yaroslavskiy and Kirsanova – all set out for Petrograd at the end of May, leaving the situation in Yakutia to develop in its own way. In August the Yakutsk Committee of Public Safety purged itself of the remaining Bolsheviks and joined forces with the SR socialists and Yakut federalists, the nationalist association *Sakha aimakh* (Yakut kindred), the Yakutsk city council and the Council of Military Deputies.[17]

When news of the Bolsheviks' October coup reached Yakutsk, this 'United Democracy' (referred to in the official Communist Party history of Yakutia as a 'mob of counter-revolutionaries') refused to recognise Lenin's government, and in view of subsequent events created an anti-Bolshevik 'Committee to Safeguard the Revolution'. In February 1918, following the Bolshevik putsch against the Constituent Assembly in Petrograd, the acting government of Yakutia proclaimed the independence of Yakutia from the Russian Republic. The sporadic Bolshevik-inspired strikes against this 'bourgeois' government were now turned into a general strike which lasted for three weeks in March–April 1918. These events were, of course, on a small scale, in direct proportion to the small number of Russians who worked in Yakutia. Consequently, the pretensions of a fifty-strong Yakutsk Soviet to 'seize power' in the province were in the realm of fantasy, and it was only through armed intervention by troops sent from Irkutsk that the

---

[17] *Aziatskaya Rossiya*, vol. I, p. 310; vol. II, p. 504; *Istoriya Sibiri*, vol. IV, pp. 59–60; *Istoriya Yakutskoy ASSR*, vol. II, pp. 396–7, 407–14; vol. III, pp. 11–14, 119.

independent Yakutian government was overthrown and the Bolshevik régime imposed in July 1918. During its brief period in power the Bolshevik revolutionary committee imprisoned many 'counter-revolutionaries', abolished the *zemstvo* organisations, set up soviets wherever they could and, in quest of funds to support their venture, imposed punitive taxes on the most prosperous members of Yakutsk society. However, within ten days of the imposition of the Bolshevik régime, Irkutsk itself, the main base of Soviet power in Eastern Siberia, had fallen to the Whites and Czecho-Slovaks. The Yakutsk Soviet too was obliged to surrender on 5 August and a less liberal régime than before took over. This White Russian government sent many of the participants in the Soviet revolt to prison in Irkutsk and executed about twenty-four of them. In Yakutia, former institutions, including the *zemstvos*, were reinstated, and the Socialist Revolutionary V.N. Solovyov returned to his post as Provincial Commissar of the Siberian Provisional Government.

A year after this the Bolsheviks had turned the tide in the Urals region and the Red Army began its conquest of Siberia. In December 1919 as Kolchak retreated towards Irkutsk, a Bolshevik uprising broke out in Yakutsk and a Soviet executive committee was again installed. Once again all 'bourgeois' institutions were abolished, and the communists sentenced thirteen anti-Bolshevik leaders, including Solovyov and the Mayor of Yakutsk, to death by firing squad. Under the Soviet régime of 'war communism' produce was requisitioned from the peasants and class strife was fomented in the countryside.[18]

By the end of January 1920 opposition to the Bolsheviks in all parts of Yakutia had been overcome or forced underground, but this was only a breathing-space. Because of its importance to the Yakut patriotic movement, the *Sakha aimakh* organisation was suppressed by the Bolsheviks late in 1920. However, opposition to the latter revived in March 1921 when the SR leader of the Okhotsk coast regional government rebelled against the Bolshevik representatives of the Far Eastern Republic. Later in the year this revolt received reinforcements in the form of a White Cossack detachment under Bochkaryov, which arrived by sea from Vladivostok. By this time a number of men who were disaffected with the Soviet régime in Yakutia had congregated at various points in the east of the province and on the Okhotsk coast. These included the SR politician P. Kulikovskiy, the Tatar merchant Yusup Galibarov and the turncoat provincial commander of the Red Army, Tolstoukhov. Yakut nationalist leaders at this time conceived the idea of combining with part of Eastern Siberia to form a separate state under the protection of the Japanese – who were, of course, willing to support any military adventure having this as its aim. So in August 1921 a 'Yakut insurgent movement' established its headquarters at Nelkan and with an

---

[18] *Istoriya Sibiri*, vol. IV, pp. 62, 144–5, 148; *Istoriya Yakutskoy ASSR*, vol. III, pp. 14–41, 46.

army of about 200 men, including local Tungus and assisted by Boch-karyov's White Cossacks, launched an uprising against the Bolsheviks. The insurgents advanced deep into Yakutia, and by the spring of 1922 they had formed a 'Provisional Yakut provincial people's administration' at Churap-cha, while in the Far North their detachments occupied Verkhoyansk and Srednekolymsk, and in the west advanced far up the Lena and the Vilui. However, the main towns in central Yakutia, including Yakutsk itself, were defended staunchly by very mixed Bolshevik forces including not only Rus-sians and Yakuts but many other nationalities. By the middle of the year the Soviet army had reoccupied central Yakutia, and the nationalist and White Russian army was again driven towards the Okhotsk coast and the north-east.

This was not the final attempt by the Whites to maintain a foothold in Eastern Siberia. The remnants of Bochkaryov's band were still in control of the northern part of the Okhotsk coast and Gizhiga, where they survived by killing the reindeer herds on which the livelihood of the Ewens and Koryaks depended. In September 1922 this White presence in the Okhotsk region was reinforced by an expeditionary force of 700 men, mainly officers, which was brought by sea from Vladivostok and landed at Ayan. This 'Siberian Volunteer Militia' under General A.N. Pepelyayev, augmented by several hundred Yakuts and Tungus, had some success at first in penetrating as far as the river Amga, before being repulsed and chased back to the inhospitable Okhotsk coast, with their escape route cut off by the fall of Vladivostok to the Bolsheviks. In April 1923 the Bolsheviks in their turn sent an expeditionary force from Vladivostok to annihilate the remnants. Even after this, several bands of White soldiers contrived to survive in the sparsely populated wilderness of north-east Siberia, mainly by preying upon reindeer belonging to the natives, and kept up desperate attacks on representatives of the Soviet régime. Accordingly, in autumn 1923 a further Soviet expedition was landed at the mouth of the Kolyma to destroy the last pockets of White resistance.

Another rebellion against Soviet Russia occurred in 1924. At Nelkan, remnants of the Yakut nationalists led by M.K. Artemyev and Y. Galibarov succeeded in mobilising the support of the local Tungus for a campaign which gained control of the Okhotsk coast and penetrated northwards along the Indigirka to the Arctic coast, reaching as far west as Bulun on the lower Lena. An 'All-Tungus congress of the Okhotsk coast' proclaimed its autonomy under a Provisional Tungus National Government led by A. Ammosov. This apparently unique manifestation of Tungus nationalism was in fact mainly inspired by the Yakuts, who formed 65 per cent of the 'Tungus' army. Like its predecessors, this anti-Russian uprising, which involved only about 500 men at its height, suffered defeat at the hands of the Red Army, and in August 1925 the insurgent Tungus Committee was suppressed and clan soviets introduced. It was now only a matter of time

10 Yakut revolutionaries. An exiled Russian Bolshevik, Ye. M. Yaroslavskiy (second left) in Yakutsk in February–March 1917 with Yakut socialist leaders including (left to right) S.V. Vasilyev, S.F. Gogolev, M.K. Ammosov and S.M. Arzhakov – all of whom were killed twenty years later in the Communist Party terror.

before the last remnants of White Russian resistance – always referred to in Soviet accounts as 'bandits' – were mopped up by Bolshevik forces, but the situation remained so unstable in many districts that the creation of soviets was delayed until after 1928.[19]

After being used for seven years as a battlefield in the struggle between Russian Reds and Whites, parts of Yakutia and the far north-east were left in a state of devastation. Some native communities, such as the Yukagirs and many of the Ewen Tungus, had survived by withdrawing into remote districts, where they remained in ignorance of the political issues at stake in the struggle among the white men until the late 1920s. In the more accessible regions, however, the peoples of the North suffered severely from ruthless

[19] Flerov, *Stroitelstvo*, pp. 10–11, 27–8, 59–60, 90–4, 180–26; *Istoriya Sibiri*, vol. IV, pp. 153, 280–2, 291; *Istoriya Yakutskoy ASSR*, vol. III, pp. 40–1, 46–50, 57–64, 72–5, 101–3; Kolarz, *The Peoples*, p. 104; *Narody Sibiri*, p. 307; Popova, *Eveny*, pp. 51–4, 207–10. The difficulty of distinguishing between Tungus groups is shown by the fact that in the last-mentioned work the participants of the 1924–5 uprising are treated as Ewens, whereas in *Istoriya Yakutskoy ASSR* and Flerov's book they are considered to be Ewenkis.

raiding and requisitioning of their herds. The Ewenkis and Ewens of Okhotsk region lost two-thirds of their reindeer, the herds of the Kolyma Ewens and Yakuts were reduced by 80 per cent, some bands being left entirely without deer, while farther west in Verkhoyansk and Bulun districts over 39,000 reindeer were destroyed.

Meanwhile in central Yakutia the government was putting into effect such economic and political measures as were possible in this vast heterogeneous colonial territory. Since the Yakut Autonomous Soviet Socialist Republic, officially founded in February 1922,[20] was so large, its government had to create its own Committee for Aid to the Peoples of the Outlying Regions of the North, which established grain stores, distributed cattle, reindeer, guns etc. to those in need, and organised the first cooperatives. Other important aspects of social development in Soviet Yakutia included the revival and extension of medical services and schools (of which there had been 173 in 1917).[21]

From the point of view of Soviet Russia the most important economic factor in Yakutia was gold. Although the Lena goldfield at Bodaibo came within the boundary of Yakutsk province before 1917, in 1922 the border of the Yakut ASSR was moved to the east so that this rich resource fell within the Russian Republic. However, the close proximity of the Bodaibo gold-workings to Yakutia created a large demand not only for labour, but also for grain, meat, butter, fish, hay and horses. In such an under-developed and isolated region as the Yakut Republic, this caused very unstable market conditions, while the development of trade with other parts of the Soviet Union was hampered by extremely high overheads on transport, which could add 149 per cent to the cost of flour and 267 per cent to that of kerosene.

Yakutia's only exportable resource at the beginning of the Soviet period was furs: the total value of furs taken in the Yakut ASSR in 1925–6 was over 3 million roubles; in 1927 it produced 30 per cent of all furs in Siberia and 15 per cent of the total Soviet export. The other mainstay of Yakutia's economy was a new gold-field discovered in 1923 on the Aldan. As a result of the gold rush that developed, within two years the seasonal labour-force in this hitherto almost uninhabited region was over 13,000, of whom Russians made up 58 per cent, Chinese and Koreans 33.5 per cent, and Yakuts only 3.2 per cent. In 1925 state organisations moved in, gradually replacing primitive manual equipment with steam dredges, and within a few years the

---

[20] Its Constitution, drawn up in 1926, remained unratified until 1936 because the Moscow government disliked the strongly Yakut character of the republic: B. Chichlo, 'Histoire de la formation des territoires autonomes chez les peuples turco-mongols de Sibérie', *Cahiers du monde russe et soviétique*, vol. XXVIII, 1987, p. 372.

[21] V.I. Boyko and N.V. Vasilyev, *Sotsialno-professionalnaya mobilnost evenkov i evenov Yakutii*, Novosibirsk, 1981, pp. 8–9; *Istoriya Sibiri*, vol. IV, pp. 285, 292, 295, 297, 300; *Istoriya Yakutskoy ASSR*, vol. III, pp. 64–7, 75–9, 103–4, 110, 144–6, 158; *Narody Sibiri*, pp. 322, 894; Sergeyev, *Nekapitalisticheskiy put*, p. 210.

new gold-field was producing one-third of all gold in the USSR. As always in Siberia, transport remained the biggest problem, and in winter supplies for the Aldan field had to be carried by pack-horses, reindeer or camels.[22]

In the cultural domain it was difficult for the Soviet Russian authorities to push through measures directed against shamans, nomadism, and the traditional social role of women, because the number of communists was very small, especially in outlying areas. In 1926 there were 820 Communist Party members in Yakutia, which had a population of 288,000; by 1929 the number had increased to 1,443. As in all parts of the Soviet Union much emphasis was placed on the involvement of young people in social-political work, and the ranks of the Young Communist League swelled quickly, 62.3 per cent of its members in the republic in 1926 being Yakuts. Under the new Russian régime as under the old, the Yakuts continued to demonstrate their adaptability and initiative, so that in 1924 native Yakuts constituted three-quarters of the membership of district Soviet committees in the republic, and 82 per cent in the city of Yakutsk. At this time Yakuts were still by far the largest ethnic group in their republic – accounting for 235,926 out of the total population of 285,471 in 1926, while Russians only amounted to 30,156 – and their Turkic language was the dominant one, essential as the lingua franca. Nevertheless, the other nationalities which formed minorities within Yakutia also had the right to autonomy. This right was recognised in 1931 by the creation within the Yakut ASSR of a number of national districts for the Ewen Tungus (6,526 in nine districts), the Ewenki Tungus (5,772 in five national districts), the Yukagirs (321) and the Chukchis (351). However, once again the dominant role of the Yakuts was shown by the fact that in most of these districts the soviet chairmen were not members of the designated nationality, or Russians, but Yakuts.

Nor were the Yakuts willing to be dominated by the Russians during the first period of the existence of their Autonomous Republic. National self-awareness was stimulated by the introduction of the Latin alphabet for Yakut in 1922; instruction in schools in all districts where Yakut population predominated was in their native language, and this was used everywhere on a par with Russian as the official language. In 1926 a Yakut publishing house was founded, and the first works in the Yakut language – *The Red Shaman* (*Kyhyl oyuun*), *The Bolshevik*, and *Songs* (*Yrya khohoon*) by the communist writer P.A. Sleptsov-Oyunskiy were hailed as the beginnings of native Yakut Soviet literature. The focus of Yakut nationalism, however, was the cultural society Sakha Omuk (The Yakut People) founded in 1922 as a successor to Sakha aimakh. Its periodical, *Cholbon* (Morning Star), published material of exclusively Yakut interest, the spirit of which ranged from the apolitical to the frankly anti-Soviet. Thus the leading writer A. Kulakovskiy in his poem

---

[22] *Istoriya Sibiri*, vol. IV, p. 280; *Istoriya Yakutskoy ASSR*, vol. III, pp. 46, 80–4, 95–6, 104, 108, 116, 119–22, 131–2, 148.

The Shaman's Dream described Russian immigrants as bringers of doom and slavery to the Yakuts, while Altan Saryn published the anti-Soviet story *One Who Recalls the Past* and propounded a pan-Turkic doctrine aimed, among another things, at purifying the Yakut language by discarding Russian borrowings in favour of words derived from common Turkic roots. So strong and unanimous was the support enjoyed by Sakha Omuk that attempts made by the Russian communist authorities to infiltrate it had little success. Even at the fourth Congress of Soviets of Yakutia in 1926 many delegates expressed an openly anti-Russian line in opposition to Bolshevik policies, believing, it seems, that real autonomy would be permitted by the Soviet Russian government. They particularly opposed further immigration of Russians into Yakutia, and posited a special governmental role for the Yakut intelligentsia as intermediaries between the Soviet Russian authorities and the mass of the native people. In the following year the nationalists, led by M.K. Artemyev, went so far as to revive the Yakut 'federalist' (i.e. separatist) party under the title of 'Young Yakuts', and once again attempted to raise a rebellion in the countryside, using the familiar slogan 'socialism without communists'. The local communists were quick to organise armed bands to fight the Young Yakut movement, the leaders of which were forced to surrender at the beginning of 1928. The conclusion drawn from this revolt by the Central Committee of the Communist Party in Moscow was that the Yakut provincial committee had been too tolerant towards the national intelligentsia, and must in future maintain a more consistent policy of class conflict by cultivating the support of the rural poor and squeezing the upper and middle class out of positions of authority, as well as depriving them of their lands. In order to prevent the recurrence of Yakut nationalist insurgency the Communist Party suppressed the Sakha Omuk society, placed the periodical *Cholbon* (later renamed *Kyhyl yllyk* – Red Path) under the control of the People's Commissariat of Enlightenment and Public Health, and exiled some of the most active leaders of the patriotic movement from Yakutia. Thus the Russian Communist Party's policy of crushing all manifestations of local nationalism and misguided aspirations towards genuine autonomy was applied with as much force in this remote province of Siberia as it was in the Caucasus, the Ukraine, or Belorussia.[23]

THE FAR NORTH-EAST

Even in the most remote and primitive of all regions of the Russian Empire – the Far Eastern territories of the Okhotsk coast, the Kamchatka peninsula, Chukchi-land and the Commander Islands – the Russian Civil War produ-

---

[23] Flerov, *Stroitelstvo*, p. 204; *Istoriya Sibiri*, vol. IV, pp. 291, 300; *Istoriya Yakutskoy ASSR*, vol. III, pp. 103–5, 109–14, 117–19, 122–8, 141, 146, 159–63, 184–5; Kolarz, *The Peoples*, pp. 102, 107–8, 111; *Narody Sibiri*, pp. 894–5.

ced profound effects. Constituting one province – Kamchatka territory – of the four which since 1909 formed the governor-generalship of the Amur, this arctic and sub-arctic region covered more than 500,000 square miles, but had a total population of only about 36,000, giving an average density of 1 person per 14 square miles (the lowest of all in Russia except for Turukhansk territory). The governor was based at Gizhiga, the population of which was only 700, and the few other towns in the region were also small: Okhotsk had about 600 inhabitants and Petropavlovsk-in-Kamchatka 1,100, while the post of Anadyr had no permanent population at all, only being visited at the end of the winter by Russian merchants for the collection of furs from the natives. Other northern towns within 1,000 miles of Gizhiga were similarly tiny: Srednekolymsk, 650, Verkhoyansk, 450 and only at the mouth of the Amur, far to the south, was there a substantial town, Nikolayevsk, with a population of over 16,000. The total Russian population of this north-eastern territory amounted to 4,200 – a small minority among the 31,000 native Tungus, Koraks, Chukchis and others. (In fact many of the 'Russians' were half-Yakuts.) In effect this region was as isolated from the rest of Russia as an island, contact between the metropolis of the Far East, Vladivostok, and these far-flung outposts being maintained, at infrequent intervals, by sea. Consequently, Russian settlement did not extend far beyond the coastal areas around the ports of Petropavlovsk, Ayan, Okhotsk, Gizhiga, and Nizhnekolymsk on the Arctic Ocean, which received two ships per year. There were practically no roads, and the interior of the whole region remained almost unexplored so far as the Russians were concerned.[24]

After the February Revolution local Committees of Public Safety were formed even by the small Russian urban communities in Kamchatka territory. As in all parts of the Empire these committees took a liberal line, supporting the Russian Provisional government and the introduction of zemstvo institutions, and the political left was represented chiefly by the SRs. One of the earliest acts of the Provisional Government was the abolition of yasak, but otherwise the general idea was that everyday life should continue normally pending the decisions of the Constituent Assembly. However, Bolshevik agitation reached Petropavlovsk with agents sent from Vladivostok, while workers in the Okhotsk gold-mines, many of whom were Koreans, also formed a soviet to campaign for improvements in their working conditions. According to Soviet Russian accounts, by April 1918 'Soviet power' was established in Kamchatka and the Okhotsk coast by soldiers, and all the old organs of government were abolished. However, considering the small number of Russian inhabitants, the almost total absence of an industrial proletariat, the primitive condition of the native peoples, the huge

---

[24] *Aziatskaya Rossiya*, vol. I, pp. 44, 82–5, 88–90, 317, 342, 350; Bogoraz, *The Chukchee*, p. 709; Flerov, *Stroitelstvo*, p. 15; Popova, *Eveny*, pp. 43–4.

distances and poor communications, this can have been only a declarative gesture. Indeed the Bolshevik minority was soon ousted, the Petropavlovsk Committee of Public Safety proclaimed the autonomy of Kamchatka province, and (with the exception of the Okhotsk gold-mines, where the soviet survived until July 1919) Soviet power was not heard of again in the whole of the north-east until the end of 1919.

During this period, when United States and Japanese interventionist troops poured into Vladivostok, the far north-east of Siberia was left open to the operations of commercial entrepreneurs of these and other countries. Because of its proximity to Alaska, Chukchi-land during the nineteenth century had developed closer economic relations with the Americans than with the Russians. The latter were represented at infrequent intervals by visiting merchants and officials known for their dishonesty, whereas the Americans – albeit often equally inclined to cheat the unsophisticated Eskimos and Chukchis – were a regular source of useful wares, weapons and luxuries. The reason for relatively frequent contacts with Americans, and for the fact that a number of Eskimos and Chukchis learned a smattering of English, was the great development of whale-killing in the Bering and Okhotsk Seas. By the middle of the nineteenth century between 300 and 400 United States and Canadian whaling ships were operating in Alaskan (Russian) waters, and later in the century as many as 250 in the Sea of Okhotsk. In the late 1860s, as a result of the sale of Alaska to the United States a big increase in American whaling occurred, so that by 1900 the grey whale and Greenland whale were near the point of extinction. While Russian government-sponsored whaling enterprises did exist, they restricted their operations to the Sea of Japan and the southern part of the Okhotsk Sea, and it was only foreign whalers that operated in the northern Okhotsk Sea, the Bering Sea and the Arctic Ocean. From the late nineteenth century, American, Canadian, British, Norwegian and Japanese freebooters, defying inadequate Russian attempts to patrol these waters, caused havoc not only by ruthless whaling, but also by wholesale killing of fur-seals, and indiscriminate slaughter of walrus for their tusks – discarding the carcasses and thus creating a direct and disastrous effect on the main food supply of the Eskimos and coastal Chukchis. The foreign sailors, coming ashore to obtain from the native people polar-bear and arctic-fox skins and walrus ivory, were also responsible for giving them the taste for alcohol, with the usual disastrous effects.

Not all of the commercial activity by foreign companies was illegal. From 1871 onward the Commander Islands with their population of Aleuts were leased by the Russian government to various American fur-hunting companies, and between 1902 and 1912 the American North-East Siberia Company was granted a concession in Chukchi-land to prospect for gold, iron-ore and graphite. Indeed, the Russian government encouraged such ventures by offering *porto franco* facilities to all foreign traders in fur, fish or gold. The Japanese in particular availed themselves of this and other agreements for the extension of their fishing industry, so that by 1917 they dominated sea-fisheries in the Sea of Okhotsk and around Kamchatka.[25]

After the Revolution the operations of non-Russians in north-east Siberia became more aggressive and unrestrained. Seizing the opportunity presented by the collapse of authority, British, American and Japanese entrepreneurs moved in to the Okhotsk and Bering Sea coasts for whaling, sealing, fishing, and the purchase of furs, gold and walrus and mammoth ivory. Some Japanese and American freebooters simply raided the coast and offshore islands, particularly the Commanders, slaughtering walrus, seals and arctic fox at will. Soviet accounts say that financial assistance was given to the military expeditions of Bochkaryov and Pepelyayev by such firms as the Hudson's Bay Company, the Japanese Fukuda-Gumi and Arai-Gumi, and Olaf Swenson. The latter schooner operator, indeed, is presented as a villain of deepest dye, closely in league with the White 'bandits' in anti-Soviet operations, although Swenson himself denies any political involvement.[26]

After the fall of Kolchak and the creation of the Far Eastern Republic, Bolshevik forces again became active in north-east Siberia, initially on a small scale. In Chukchi-land in December 1919 it was two young ex-soldiers, one a Latvian, the other a Belorussian, who after escaping from Vladivostok, arrived in Anadyr to 'proclaim Soviet power'. These young and naïve Bolsheviks, totally isolated and lacking any real basis of power, proceeded to declare the nationalisation of fisheries, the confiscation of the property of foreign entrepreneurs, and the cancellation of the natives' debts to local traders. The latter murdered the two Bolsheviks five weeks later. Thereafter, Soviet power in Chukchi-land existed only at the village of Markovo, where the local Chukchis were persuaded to give their support to the extent of providing the Soviet Russian representatives with meat during the winter. Relief for the few Bolsheviks in the far north-east came only in the summer of 1920, when reinforcements were brought in by ship from Kamchatka. There an anti-White revolt had occurred in Petropavlovsk in

[25] Bogoraz, *The Chukchee*, pp. 12–13, 61, 708–14, 730–2; *Entsiklopedicheskiy slovar*, vol. XXV, p. 218; vol. XXVII, pp. 261–2; Flerov, *Stroitelstvo*, pp. 15–17, 61; I.V. Gushchin and A.I. Afanasyev, *Chukotskiy natsionalnyy okrug: kratkiy istoriko-geograficheskiy ocherk*, Magadan, 1956, p. 24; C.C. Hughes, 'Under four flags: recent culture change among the Eskimos', *Current Anthropology*, 1965, vol. VI, no. 1, p. 29; *Istoriya Sibiri*, vol. III, pp. 194, 439; vol. IV, p. 56; Kolarz, *The Peoples*, p. 91; *Narody Sibiri*, pp. 901–2, 971, 987; A.E. Nordenskiöld, *The Voyage of the Vega round Asia and Europe*, London, 1881, vol. I, p. 431; Popova, *Eveny*, pp. 45, 50, 102–3; Swenson, *Northwest of the World*, pp. 12–14, 21, 123; N.V. Yeliseyev, ed., *Krasnaya kniga RSFSR: zhivotnyye*, Moscow, 1983, pp. 89, 91, 93; Zhikharev, *Ocherki istorii*, pp. 9–27.
[26] Flerov, *Stroitelstvo*, pp. 21–33, 59–60, 82–5, 129–34; *Istoriya Sibiri*, vol. IV, p. 145; *Narody Sibiri*, pp. 921, 971, 987; Popova, *Eveny*, pp. 45, 50; Swenson, *Northwest*, pp. 81, 137; Sergeyev, *Nekapitalisticheskiy put*, pp. 211, 221.

January 1920, and a revolutionary committee was formed – initially a somewhat illusory triumph, as Japanese warships and troops moved in to dominate Kamchatka and the Kuril Islands. It was under their protection that a detachment of Bochkaryov's troops landed at Petropavlovsk in October 1921 and drove the soviet into the forest. In November 1922 Bolshevik partisans recaptured Petropavlovsk, the Japanese ships left, and a force of some 300 men arrived by ship to consolidate Soviet control over the peninsula.

The treatment which the native people received at the hands of the White Russian soldiers appears to have been unceremonious and often cruel, so that the latter, on the whole, antagonised the natives. The Bolsheviks, on the other hand, were sometimes able to obtain local support. In Kamchatka, for instance, following their reoccupation of Petropavlovsk in 1922 they recruited some Koraks for the two detachments – consisting of only nineteen Russians! – which drove the fleeing remnants of Bochkaryov's troops out of the peninsula and annihilated most of them near Korf and Gizhiga. In the spring of the following year Koraks and Ewens took part in the Soviet operation against Pepelyayev at Ayan, while the White fugitives who succeeded in reaching the Kolyma were run to earth by the Red Army with the assistance of Chukchis and Eskimos from Uelen and Naukan.

Even after the defeat of the Whites in the North-east it was not easy to establish the power of the Soviet Russian government in a vast territory where in 1924 there were only 100 communists, including 31 in Petropavlovsk and only two at Anadyr. The central government might issue eloquent proclamations, sometimes translated into native languages, prohibiting alcohol and foreign traders, or requiring the conservation of fur-bearing animals, but these could not be enforced because of the lack of police officers. Similarly, the inadequacy of the coastguard service permitted foreign ships to come and go with impunity – and here the view presented by Soviet Russian historians is ambiguous. On the one hand, foreign traders (along with Christian missionaries) are presented as the predatory, if not piratical, agents of the imperial powers, while on the other hand it was a fact that the economy of the Soviet Far East was in such chaos that the settlements in the north-east could not have survived without the supplies brought in by foreign ships. Consequently, in 1923 the Soviet government, so far from completely banning foreign traders, in fact made concessionary contracts with the supposedly notorious O. Swenson and the Hudson's Bay Company to bring in essential supplies in exchange for furs.[27]

[27] Flerov, Stroitelstvo, pp. 7, 17–18, 22–9, 49–53, 61–79, 89–94, 98–104, 124–42, 150–66, 171–3, 179; Gurvich, Osushchestvleniye, p. 16; Gushchin and Afanasyev, Chukotskiy natsionalnyy okrug, pp. 28–9; Istoriya Sibiri, vol. IV, pp. 288, 292–4; Istoriya Yakutskoy ASSR, vol. III, pp. 101–2; Narody Sibiri, pp. 921, 943, 971, 987; Popova, Eveny, pp. 45–6, 204, 213, 218; M.A. Sergeyev, Koryakskiy natsionalnyy okrug, Leningrad, 1934, p. 64; Sergeyev, Nekapitalisticheskiy put, p. 212; Swenson, Northwest, pp. 143–6, 185; Zhikharev, Ocherki istorii, pp. 34–59, 70–80, 83–7, 91–100, 106, 110–13, 117.

11 Chukchis trading with an American ship. In exchange for carcases of reindeer, taken from the herd by the man with the lasso, the Chukchis receive guns, with alcohol to seal the bargain (the legs bottom right belong to a drunk Chukchi). Above is a *yaranga* with thongs weighted with stones to keep the covering down, and a walrus-hide boat parked on a whale-rib rack. Engraving on walrus tusk by Ichel, 1930s.

THE PEOPLES OF THE FAR NORTH-EAST

The second half of the 1920s saw the gradual sovietisation of the Siberian North-east despite native resistance, active or passive, to the innovations of the Russian communists. The guiding principles for this process as set out in the 'Provisional Regulations for the Government of the Native Tribes of the Far East' (1924) were that the established way of life of the native peoples should be disrupted as little as possible, that separate clans should be united by giving them common tasks which would require cooperation, and that the central authorities should make contact with the native population in order to give them help and guidance for the defence of their interests, the development of their spiritual life and the improvement of their material well-being. No doubt an attempt was made to fulfil these requirements, so far as conditions allowed, during the early years of the Soviet Russian régime when the Committee of the North was active. At the same time, a proclamation was conveyed to all the nomadic, and illiterate, communities of Koraks, Ewens, Chukchis, Eskimos and Aleuts, in which the Russian Revolution was explained in the following simplistic terms:

There were bad people in Russia. They killed and robbed many other people; they wanted to become rich that way . . . Then the poor folk got together, took up weapons

265

and started driving out the bad people. A terrible war began. The people suffered. There was a shortage of goods – tea, tobacco, flour, guns and gunpowder. The ships stopped bringing goods ... But the poor folk defeated the bad ones ... All working people gathered together and created a strong Soviet republic. Goods again appeared ... Ships started running. The Russian people now hold congresses to speak about their needs ... Now they want to help you too, so that you, nomadizing over the hills and tundra, should more often come together at clan gatherings and speak about what you need ... The government of the Soviet republic now consists of the best people chosen by the whole nation. It will be to you like a father to a son, but you too must obey laws and obligations ... If you don't know what you should do and what you should not, go to the clan or district Soviet and they will tell you everything. You will find out when you may hunt fur animals and when you must not, so that the animals will multiply. If you need a school or a hospital, tell them about that too. A great man – comrade Lenin – has said that the Lamut and Korak and Chukchi should obtain much knowledge – he must study. When he has studied he will return to his own people and work there ... He will find out what they need and tell us and then we shall help you.[28]

Such sentiments, however philanthropic in intention, demonstrate the paternalistic attitude of the Soviet Russian government which – like other imperial governments – offered 'help' to long subjugated 'native tribes' on its own terms and in accordance with its own assumptions. In fact, the Russians were to act as the masters, while the 'natives' were to be recipients of the new culture.

During the 1920s Bolshevik influence on the native population was severely limited by the extremely small number of Communist Party workers in the Far North-east and the fact that they were, typically, urban Russians. They came to the task of administering the enormous territories over which they claimed authority, with dedication but also with a naïveté and lack of experience of anything except fighting, which made them incompetent to deal with the everyday realities which faced them. So the Revolutionary Committee in Petropavlovsk, which was responsible for the whole vast Okhotsk–Kamchatka–Chukchi-land territory, formed dozens of sub-committees and commissions to look into specific problems, but in fact was almost impotent to cope with them. The 'noble mission' of organising local soviets – which had been initiated by Red Army detachments in the first place – bore little fruit in the 1920s, because of the colonial legacy: a general distrust of all Russians, who had brought devastation to the reindeer herds. Despite the non-participation of many of the native people, soviet elections were held from 1925 onward, and clan soviets were created for the Tungus, Korak and Chukchi communities, and rural soviets for the Russian or Kamchadal peasants. However, the institution of the Soviet system did not go

---

[28] Quoted in Zhikharev, *Ocherki istorii*, pp. 131–2.

beyond these local soviets. Because of the instability of the situation in the north-east, and the lack of any real political base, no district soviets or congresses were convened, and the whole Kamchatka territory in fact remained under emergency rule, administered as a distant and isolated colony by Russian officials sent from the metropolis. In the native territories it was clear that the Reds who had driven out the Whites also came as strangers offering political concepts which were incomprehensible and unnecessary to the Chukchis, Eskimos, Koraks or Tungus.

One of the main features of the old life which the Bolsheviks wished to abolish was religion. In Kamchatka the anti-religious campaign began in 1923 when the Orthodox Church was deprived of its function as registrar of births, marriages and deaths, and church buildings and their furnishings were taken over as state property. As elsewhere in the USSR, the supposed iniquity and worldly greed of the clergy was made the subject of public lectures, ikons were burned in the street, anti-religious shows were presented, believers were taunted and many churches were closed. The attack on the primal religion of the native peoples was undertaken more circumspectly, in the first place in connection with the propagation of scientific knowledge about natural phenomena, health and hygiene. In fact, among the Ewens of the Okhotsk district, all of whom had been Christianised before 1917, the shamans emerged to take up a more active and public role after the closure of the Christian churches. Shamanism, indeed, became the principal guardian of Christian standards, especially among the nomadic reindeer-herding Ewens of the taiga.

Whatever success the representatives of the Communist Party may have had in putting their message over to the natives living in coastal settlements to which the Russians had access by sea, it was much more difficult to influence the nomadic reindeer-people of the interior, who made up almost half of the population. In fact, much of the Chukchi, Korak and Tungus population withdrew from contact with Russian settlements and remained practically independent until the end of the 1920s, since the soviets in the tundra and *taiga* had only a nominal existence. One of the few opportunities the Soviet authorities had of making contact with the nomads was at the annual markets where clan gatherings took place. Another means of spreading Soviet influence was by the foundation of cultural bases: two for the Chukchis and Eskimos at St Lawrence Bay and on the river Chaun, one for the Koraks on the Penzhina, and one for the Ewens at Nagayevo. About the same time, in the late 1920s, clan soviets in the North-east (as in other parts of Siberia) were replaced by those based on the territorial principle, at least among the settled Chukchis, Eskimos and Koraks of the coast and the Aleuts of the Commander Islands. In addition, with the aim of encouraging both a sense of ethnic cohesion and adherence to the Soviet administrative system, 'autonomous' territorial units were designated from 1928 onward as the

A HISTORY OF THE PEOPLES OF SIBERIA

national districts of the Chukchis, the Koraks and the (Ewen) Tungus of the Okhotsk coast.[29]

Amid these, on the whole philanthropic, attitudes towards the native peoples during the 1920s, in one case at least the Soviet Russian government's potential for eliminating small nationalities by decree was demonstrated in the case of the Itelmens of Kamchatka. Because so many of them, having lost their native language and adopted Russian, shared the way of life of the Russian peasants of the peninsula, they were, so far as the authorities were concerned, identical with the latter. They were accordingly lumped with them under the name of 'Kamchadals', who numbered about 4,000 at the end of the nineteenth century. In 1926 it was decided that no Kamchadal nationality existed and that all those who did not speak Itelmen were Russians. As a result, the Russophone Itelmens were at the stroke of a pen deprived of their nationality, while the name Itelmen was restricted to the 814 natives of the Tigil valley who did speak their own language.[30]

THE PEOPLES OF THE AMUR–USSURI REGION

Among the non-Russian peoples who suffered the longest and most destructive exposure to the effects of the Russian Civil War were the inhabitants of the lower Amur, Maritime and Sakhalin regions – that is, the Nanais, Negidals, Nivkhs, Oroks, Udeghes and Ulchis, and also the Koreans and Chinese. Between the first seizure of power by the Bolsheviks in the winter of 1917–18 and their occupation of Vladivostok in 1922, the Amur region changed hands half a dozen times. On the other hand, the Maritime region with its metropolis, Vladivostok, remained the headquarters of the Whites and interventionists (in particular the Japanese) throughout that time, while northern Sakhalin, after being taken by the Whites and retaken by the Reds, was invaded by the Japanese in 1920 and was occupied by them for the next five years.

In the Amur region, where the settlements of the native peoples were frequently in the direct path of the White Cossacks, the Red Army and forest partisans, or the Japanese army of occupation, their inhabitants were reduced to poverty by the war years. In particular, the Japanese soldiers imposed a brutal régime of terror on Russians and non-Russians alike – robbing, raping and killing the population and devastating forests, wild animals and fisheries. The activities of Kalmykov's White Cossacks were little better. As

[29] Flerov, *Stroitelstvo*, pp. 9, 15, 117–23, 186–7, 207–10, 215, 218, 221–6, 231, 239, 244–7, 252–5, 265–8, 271–6; Gushchin and Afanasyev, *Chukotskiy natsionalnyy okrug*, p. 33; *Istoriya Sibiri*, vol. IV, p. 291; *Istoriya Yakutskoy ASSR*, vol. III, pp. 103, 142; Kolarz, *The Peoples*, pp. 92–3; *Narody Sibiri*, pp. 555, 559, 771, 943, 987; Popova, *Eveny*, pp. 44, 172, 204–5, 212–20, 229, 235, 240; Sergeyev, *Nekapitalisticheskiy put*, pp. 238–9, 262–3, 314; Zhikharev, *Ocherki istorii*, pp. 7, 111, 125, 130–6, 140–2, 151.
[30] S. Vakhrin, 'Liniya ili oshibka?', *Severnye prostory*, 1988, no. 6, p. 15.

a result, some Nanais, Ulchis, Nivkhs and Udeghes cooperated with the Soviet Russian partisans in the role of pathfinders and scouts, and in ski detachments for winter operations. Many Chinese and Korean workers were also drawn into the Red guerrilla bands in the Amur–Ussuri region, and their detachments played a significant part in the war. October 1922 brought an end to the main warfare in the Far East, but mopping-up operations against residual groups of Whites and Japanese soldiers continued until 1926 in the Sikhote-Alin mountains, which were the home of the Udeghes. It was only in 1925, too, that the Japanese at last agreed to remove their troops from northern Sakhalin and restrict themselves to the southern half of the island. Information about the native peoples of northern Sakhalin under Japanese occupation – the Nivkhs, Tunguses and Oroks – is scarce, but Soviet Russian accounts assert that they suffered violence and intimidation.[31]

One of the first tasks of the Soviet Russian authorities was the introduction of a cooperative system as a means for restoring the disrupted native economy. It is said that by the end of the 1920s practically the whole population of the lower Amur had joined cooperatives, and individual hunters and fishers had almost disappeared. At the same time the administrative integration of the Amur peoples into the Soviet Russian system was taking place. Although relics of exogamic clans were relatively strong among the Nanais, Ulchis and Nivkhs, their settlements had for long been ethnically mixed, and the Russians decided that their village Soviets should from the start be formed on the territorial and not the clan principle. (Because of the almost universal illiteracy of the native peoples, the secretaries of these Soviets were Russians.) Despite the difficulties, here too attempts were made from 1926 onwards to create national districts for the Nanais, Ewenki Tungus, Ulchis and even the scattered and elusive Udeghes.

The Maritime region provided the Soviet Russian authorities with a unique problem because of its very mixed population and its proximity to China and Japan. The fertile Ussuri basin was inhabited in 1926 by Russians, a large number of Ukrainians, some 90,000 Chinese, and between 170,000 and 300,000 Koreans. The Chinese provided a high proportion of the labour force in the principal Russian industrial enterprises, such as the Suchang coal-mines east of Vladivostok, the Zeya gold-mines and the engineering works in Vladivostok and Khabarovsk. The Koreans also provided some industrial labour (in 1921, for instance, 1,000 Koreans were

---

[31] I. Babichev, 'Uchastiye kitayshikh i koreyskikh trudyashchikhsya v borbe protiv interventov i belogvardeytsev na Sovetskom Dalnem Vostoke', in Shvarev, *Dalniy Vostok*, pp. 148–71; A.A. Belyayev, 'Uchastiye nanaytsev v borbe za vlast Sovetov', in Shvarev, *Dalniy Vostok*, pp. 172–83; Gurvich, *Osushchestvleniye*, pp. 314–15; *Istoriya Sibiri*, vol. IV, pp. 162, 288; Kolarz, *The Peoples*, p. 35; *Narody Sibiri*, pp. 806, 832, 855, 876; *Narody Sredney Azii i Kazakhstana*, S.P. Tolstov et al., ed., Moscow, 1963, vol. II, p. 565; Sergeyev, *Nekapitalisticheskiy put*, pp. 211–12; White, *Siberian Intervention*, pp. 263–4, 280–6.

working far to the north, in the gold-mines of the Okhotsk coast), but most were farmers, and because of the different roles they played in the economy, the two oriental nationalities were treated differently by the Russian government. The Chinese continued to be looked upon as aliens 'harmful from the political point of view', and indeed they not only kept to themselves, preserving their own social institutions, but maintained strong cultural links with the motherland, as did other Chinese expatriates throughout the Far East. So far as the Russians were concerned, the Chinese had no right to be there, so that they were continually being ousted from the best land by Russian and Ukrainian settlers, and were faced with the choice of either going back to China or paying rent to the new landowners. Despite the usefulness of the Chinese, they became victims of Russian racial prejudice, especially at times of international tension, such as the crisis about the Chinese Eastern Railway, over which the Chinese government claimed control in 1929. At that time, when the ending of the 'New Economic Policy' stopped free commercial enterprise in the USSR, many Chinese traders left the Maritime region.[32]

Unlike the Chinese, the Korean settlers had shown a tendency to conform to the ways of the Russians, who had provided a refuge for them at the time of the Japanese occupation of their country in 1910. They were accepted as Russian subjects, and most of the Russian Koreans embraced the Orthodox religion. The willingness of the Korean settlers to play their part as citizens of the Russian Empire was shown during the First World War, when some 4,000 of them served in the Russian army. They also participated in the general assertion of national rights after the February Revolution: in May 1917 a congress of Korean revolutionary organisations (mostly SR socialists) meeting at Nikolsk, expressed itself against Russification, for better schools for Korean children, and for national representation in the Constituent Assembly. A second Korean congress, held in 1918, aligned itself with Russian *zemstvo* organisations, but declared the neutrality of the Koreans in the Russian Civil War. This body kept itself in being as the Korean National Council until 1920 when, under the Far Eastern Republic, it was disbanded. In 1925 nearly all the Koreans of the Russian Far East – amounting to at least 167,400 people – took Soviet citizenship. In the district of Vladivostok they constituted about 25 per cent of the population and, while they still manifested nationalist sentiments, they provided almost 80 per cent of the city's Young Communist League membership. There was, therefore, no doubt about the loyalty and even enthusiasm of the Korean minority in the period of reconstruction immediately following the Civil War. In recognition

[32] *Aziatskaya Rossiya*, vol. I, pp. 82, 296; *Entsiklopedicheskiy slovar*, vol. XXV, p. 217; vol. XXXV, pp. 28–30; Gurvich, *Osushchestvleniye*, pp. 314–15; *Istoriya Sibiri*, vol. IV, pp. 162, 292, 295; Kolarz, *The Peoples*, pp. 13, 43–9; R.K.I. Quested, *Sino-Russian Relations: a short history*, Sydney, 1984, pp. 98–9; Sergeyev, *Nekapitalisticheskiy put*, pp. 211, 294; Shvarev, *Dalniy Vostok*, pp. 75, 174, 418–20, 435–7; Swenson, *Northwest*, p. 123.

of this the Soviet Russian government, in the first flush of wholesale creation of autonomous districts in the late 1920s, designated a Korean National District around Posyet on the Korean border, where 95 per cent of the population were Koreans.[33]

THE BURYAT-MONGOLS

The Buryat-Mongols were the largest indigenous ethnic community in Siberia, amounting to some 332,000 people in 1911, and although settlers from European Russia already far outnumbered the Buryats and Ewenki Tungus in the region around and to the east of Lake Baikal, these natives still formed a ubiquitous element in the population outside the (Russian) towns. In certain regions, e.g. around Verkhneudinsk, the Buryats still constituted as much as 80 per cent of the population. Moreover, the Buryats were a distinctive ethnic community consolidated by a long cultural history and, especially east of Baikal, by the common religion of Buddhism. Most significantly, their culture and history was closely connected with that of the Khalkha Mongols, whose territory in Chinese Outer Mongolia and Manchuria was involved in the internal strife in China and the rival interventions of Japanese and Russian imperialisms.

The Buryats had much at stake when the Russian Revolution began in February 1917. As a result of the great increase in the number of Russian settlers in both Irkutsk province and Transbaikal region during the preceding twenty years, the Buryats had suffered considerable encroachment on their pastures. A further cause of resentment was the mobilisation of some 12,000 Buryat–Mongol men for pioneer duties in European Russia during the First World War. (Like all Asiatic nationalities, the Buryats were not generally liable for combatant service, except for those communities which formed a part of the Transbaikal Cossack Host.) It was natural, therefore, that the February Revolution led to a renewal of the demand for autonomy by leaders of the Buryat intelligentsia. From March 1917 onward many Buryat conferences took place in Irkutsk, Verkhneudinsk and Chita, culminating in an All-Buryat Congress in April. This called for Buryat autonomy within a single, continuous territory, under the administration of a Buryat National Duma (*Buryaad Ologun Tsogulgan*), a complete system of education in the native language, which at that time was considered to be literary Mongolian, and land reform. In Buryatia the political influence of

---

[33] *Entsiklopedicheskiy slovar*, vol. XXV, p. 217; Kolarz, *The Peoples*, pp. 33–6; *Narody Sredney Azii*, vol. II, pp. 564–5. So far as the number of Koreans in the Soviet Far East is concerned, the last-named work states that according to the 1926 census there were 167,400, while Kolarz, quoting a reliable Soviet source of 1929, says that unofficially their number was as high as 250,000; a recent Soviet work states the much lower total of only 87,000 for 1926 in a table which purports to show the continuous growth of the Korean population from that date: Kozlov, *Natsionalnosti SSSR*, p. 250; 2nd edn 1982, p. 287.

SR socialist ideas was as strong as in the rest of Siberia, and it was a Buryat of that persuasion, the outstanding historian M. N. Bogdanov, who was elected to be chairman of both the Transbaikal Committee of Social Organisations and the Regional Congress of Rural Deputies – the democratic bodies, of mixed ethnic and political complexion, which represented public opinion in the region until February 1918. After the SRs, who gained 50.2 per cent of votes in the Transbaikal elections for the All-Russian Constituent Assembly in November 1917, the next biggest vote went to the Buryat Nationalists, with 17.4 per cent. Their platform was essentially 'Buryatia for the Buryats', and one of their main political theses was that in traditional Buryat society there were no class divisions. In addition, they declared, vainly, that their land must not become involved in the Russians' revolution and civil war. The third-largest body of votes, 13.2 per cent, went to the Transbaikal Cossack Host, while the Bolshevik SDs received only 8.7 per cent, and the Constitutional Democrats 4.3 per cent.[34]

In contrast with the western part of Buryat territory – Irkutsk province, where Bolshevik influence was stronger and conflict between Russian political parties had resulted in the establishment of Soviet power in November–December 1917 – to the east of Baikal this outcome was not achieved until Bolshevik-controlled Cossack units returning from the war in Europe took over in Verkhneudinsk and Chita in February 1918. By that time the eastern Buryats were already embroiled in a tense and complex political situation created by Ataman Semyonov. As the influence of the Bolshevik Soviets grew in Irkutsk and Transbaikalia during December 1917, Semyonov moved his initially small force of Cossacks, who were drawn from Russian, Mongol and Buryat communities, to the town of Manchouli in the Hulunbuir district of Manchuria – the territory of the Barga Mongols where, because the Chinese Eastern Railway ran through it, Russian influence and settlement were considerable. From this base in Chinese territory Semyonov and his 'Special Manchurian Detachment' started raiding Transbaikal settlements. In order to combat this threat a Transbaikal People's Council was formed on 28 December by representatives of all political groups from Constitutional Democrats to SRs and SDs. This body, affiliated to the Tomsk Siberian Duma, governed the region until the Bolshevik coup took place in February 1918, and the Civil War began in earnest in Transbaikalia.[35]

Most Buryat leaders sought to continue the administration of their national territories according to the pre-revolutionary system, and some even

[34] *Aziatskaya Rossiya*, vol. I, pp. 82, 84; *Entsiklopedicheskiy slovar*, vol. XV, p. 904; *Istoriya Sibiri*, vol. III, pp. 303, 493–4; vol. IV, pp. 59–61; Khaptayev, *Istoriya Buryatskoy ASSR*, vol. II, pp. 17, 23, 27–8, 51–8, 142, 159, 242–3; R.E. Snow, 'The Russian Revolution of 1917–18 in Transbaikalia', *Soviet Studies*, 1971–2, vol. XXIII, pp. 205–10.

[35] *Bolshaya Sovetskaya entsiklopediya*, 1926–47, vol. LX, col. 278; Dallin, *The Rise of Russia*, pp. 143–5; *Istoriya Sibiri*, vol. IV, p. 56; Khaptayev, *Istoriya Buryatskoy ASSR*, vol. II, pp. 30–7; Shirokogorov, *Social Organization*, p. 88; Snow, 'Russian Revolution', pp. 214–15.

cherished hopes of returning to the dominance of Buryat and Cossack landowners through the nineteenth-century institution of steppe councils. However, in the face of local opposition and much sporadic violence, the Bolsheviks proceeded to organise Soviets, to agitate against 'bourgeois nationalism', to emphasise class conflict to the utmost, and to form local militias in order to apply the universally hated requisitioning of grain and cattle from the farmers. They also attempted to enforce a redistribution of land in a situation which was fraught with conflict not only between Buryats and Russians, but between Russian peasants and Cossacks. The concept of Buryat self-government was rejected by many members of the Irkutsk Soviet, but in Transbaikalia, where the Buryats were numerically strong, Soviet leaders had little choice but to sanction the operation of Buryat territorial units, the *aimaks* and *khoshuns*. On the White Russian side, Semyonov hoped to gain large-scale military support not only from the Transbaikal Cossack Host, but also from the Buryats. With this in mind, he formed in Hulunbuir a 'Government of the Transbaikal Region', one of whose departments was devoted to Buryat national affairs.

When in mid-1918 Semyonov's forces gained the upper hand in Transbaikalia and Irkutsk province, a Buryat People's Duma was formed to create the impression of national autonomy. The granting of political concessions to any of the Russian Empire's native, or 'alien' (*inorodets*) peoples – especially one of the 'yellow race' – was, of course, an incomprehensible idea to the Kolchak régime, but it was tactically useful to Semyonov (himself half-Mongolian) in gaining the support of the Buryats. It was also supported by the Japanese, who organised a 'Pan-Mongol' conference in Chita in February 1919. The delegates, who represented Buryat, Barga and Chahar (Inner Mongolian) Mongols, but not the Khalkha of Outer Mongolia, envisaged the creation of a Great Mongolian state to unify these regions, and elected a provisional 'Daurian' government headed by a 'reincarnated' lama Neisse-Gegeen. Thus encouraged, the Buryat national leaders collaborated with Semyonov in mobilising 1,800 young Buryats as cavalry for the White Army. When, however, he later proposed that the Buryat people as a whole should be transformed into Cossack communities – which would have been entirely at the disposal of the Russian rulers of Siberia – this was rejected by the Buryats. Moreover, because of the turmoil created in Transbaikalia by the Russian Civil War, large numbers of Buryats migrated across the border into Manchuria and Outer Mongolia, where they formed whole 'divisions' (*sumuns*) for administrative purposes. (After 1920 most of these refugees returned to Buryatia.) Meanwhile, west of Lake Baikal, the Bolshevik underground movement had gathered momentum, and its guerrilla bands, including some Buryats, were operating over a wide area, their campaign culminating in the capture of Irkutsk in December 1919. In Transbaikal region also, as many as 6,000 Soviet partisans were operating in 1920 against the Japanese and Semyonov's White Russian army, which included a 'Wild Division' of Chahar Mongols. Not until late 1920 did the long and bloody Civil War in Transbaikalia come to an end. A year later, when a pro-Soviet government had been established in Outer Mongolia – with the assistance of the revolutionary Buryats Tsyben Zhamtsarano and E.-D. Rinchino – the Bolshevik régime was firmly established throughout Buryatia.[36]

It was as a reaction against the involvement of young Buryats as soldiers in the Russians' Civil War that a new political movement appeared in Transbaikalia in 1919, among Buddhists of the Khori *aimak*. This movement combined the long-standing opposition of Buryat traditionalists to Russian institutions, with the concept of a theocratic state in which the chief lamas would enjoy a political status equal to that of the secular princes, as they did in Tibet and Mongolia. Thus the theocratic project put forward by the lama Sandan Tsyden was aimed not only against the conscription of recruits for Semyonov's army, but also against the Russified Buryat intelligentsia who formed the core of the nationalist movement, and the regular Buddhist church which conformed with the ideas of the latter. Tsyden and other theocratic leaders suffered imprisonment under both Semyonov's White Russian government and, after 1920, the Bolshevik-dominated government of the Far Eastern Republic.

Even after the formation of the latter, Buryat opposition to the Soviet régime continued, both in western Buryatia and Transbaikalia. In particular, the theocratic idea of the lamaist state – in the specific form of an administrative district separate from the Buryat–Mongol Autonomous Regions – continued to flourish in 1921–3 despite arrests and armed conflicts, and was not suppressed until 1924. However, dismissing objections from some Irkutsk Russian leaders that the Buryats were 'too uncivilised' to govern themselves and should be assimilated to the Russians, the central government insisted that plans for national autonomy, as conceived by the Communist Party, must go ahead. During 1921–3 two Buryat Autonomous Regions existed – one in the Far Eastern Republic and the other in Irkutsk province of the Russian Soviet Republic. When the war in the Far East came to an end and the Far Eastern Republic was absorbed into the Russian Republic, the two autonomous regions were united to form the Buryat–Mongolian ASSR, with M.N. Yerbanov as its prime minister. The main territory of the new Buryat republic, including Verkhneudinsk and the monastic centres of Tsongol and Goose Lake, almost completely surrounded Lake Baikal, except for its south-western end, which was within the

---

[36] Bawden, *History of Mongolia*, pp. 204, 210, 231, 264; *Bolshaya Sovetskaya Entsiklopediya*, 1926–47, vol. VIII, col. 241; *Istoriya Sibiri*, vol. IV, pp. 60–1, 65, 145–6; Khaptayev, *Istoriya Buryatskoy ASSR*, vol. II, pp. 35, 41–52, 58–62, 70, 80–2, 88, 95–105, 112–23; Kolarz, *The Peoples*, p. 119; White, *Siberian Intervention*, pp. 195, 200–6, 378; Yermolin, *Revolyutsiya i kazachestvo*, p. 96.

Russian province of Irkutsk. The republic stretched from the frontier of Tuva in the west to the river Vitim in the east (an area greater than that of Great Britain). In addition, two separate smaller areas, one to the west of the Angara and the other east of Baikal, including the Aga monastery, belonged to the Buryat–Mongol ASSR. Within this territory the Buryats in 1926 constituted 43.8 per cent of the population (some 215,000), while the Russians made up 52.7 per cent (258,000). It was therefore decreed that both Buryat–Mongolian and Russian were to be on an equal footing as official languages in the republic. The remainder of Transbaikal Region – the Ingoda-Shilka basin – was mainly inhabited by Russians, as indeed was much of the Selenga valley within the Buryat–Mongol republic, and its capital Verkhneudinsk (known after 1934 by the Buryat name Ulaan-Üde – 'Red Uda'). A significant innovation made in Buryatia by the Soviet Russian government was the extension of obligatory military service to the Buryats. Just as Semyonov had wanted to exploit the potential of the Buryats as cavalry, so in 1924 a cavalry school was founded and two years later a Buryat–Mongol squadron of the Red Army was created. By 1929 Buryat cavalry units were being used as part of the Far Eastern Army against the Chinese in Manchuria.[37]

The recovery of the shattered economy during the first few years after the Russian Civil War was helped in Buryatia, as in the rest of the Soviet Union, by the private trading which the government permitted under the 'New Economic Policy', so that the small-scale Russian industry of Transbaikal region was rebuilt, in the form of the pre-revolutionary engineering, glass and leather works and chemical industry at Verkhneudinsk, Selenginsk and other towns. On the land too the Civil War had taken a heavy toll, so that in the Transbaikal districts settled by Russian farmers the sown area had fallen by 34.5 per cent between 1916 and 1923, while the number of cattle was reduced by 38 per cent. A small beginning to agricultural and consumers' cooperatives was made after the war, and the number of livestock had regained the pre-1917 level by 1928. The fact that in the Buryat Mongolian national regions the ploughed area increased by only 4 per cent at this time shows that nomadic pastoralism maintained its place as the almost exclusive occupation of the Buryats.

The other traditional pillar of Buryat Mongol society, Buddhism, also survived practically unscathed up till the mid-1920s, as did the institutions of lama schools and Tibetan folk-medicine, which competed successfully with such services in the educational and medical fields as the Soviet Russian government was able to provide at that time (4,000 pupils were receiving

[37] Bawden, *History of Mongolia*, pp. 29–30, 33–4; Chichlo, 'Histoire de la formation', pp. 367–71; *Istoriya Sibiri*, vol. IV, pp. 282–3; Khaptayev, *Istoriya Buryatskoy ASSR*, vol. II, pp. 95–6, 141–61, 177–8, 182–7, 205–6, 248, 252; Kolarz, *The Peoples*, pp. 117, 121–3; Kozlov, *Natsionalnosti SSSR*, p. 108; Mantatov, ed., *Lamaizm v Buryatii*, p. 110.

instruction in the Buddhist *datsans* in 1922). As the first anti-religious campaign was already well under way in European Russia by then, the tolerance shown by the Soviet régime towards Buddhism in Buryatia indicates their awareness of the need to tread cautiously in an alien land where anti-Russian feeling ran high and the Russian Communist Party's organs of government and state coercion were not yet fully established. This situation changed radically from 1929 onward.[38]

THE ALTAI-SAYAN PEOPLES

After the Buryat Mongols, the largest ethnic group in southern Siberia were the Turkic tribes of the Altai-Sayan mountain regions, who numbered about 150,000 in 1911. Here, both in the Altai highlands and the Abakan steppe, intense antagonism between the native population and the Russians had developed as the imperial government took over more and more land for distribution to new colonisers from European Russia. Consequently the nationalism which had manifested itself among the Altaians around 1905 grew stronger up to the beginning of the First World War. So far as the influence of the Russian intelligentsia was concerned, here, as in the rest of Siberia, it was the ideas of the SR socialists, and not the Bolshevik SDs, that were dominant.

Like other south Siberian colonial peoples, the Altaians and 'Minusinsk Tatars' were mobilised by the central government for labour on the war front in 1916. This evoked resistance in the form of ignoring the summons to report, fleeing to remote areas, or in some places fighting off the Russian authorities with scythes and stones. The Altaians' resistance also expressed itself in a resurgence of their anti-Russian 'Burkhan' rituals. Feeling no debt of loyalty towards their conquerors, the Altaians saw no reason to become involved in their wars – an attitude which they maintained throughout the Russian Revolution and Civil War. In response to the February Revolution, in July 1917 they instituted their own Altai Mountain Duma, and in November this 'bourgeois nationalist' body rejected the Bolshevik take-over. Meanwhile in the Russian towns and districts of lowland Altai – Barnaul, Biysk, Slavgorod and Kuznetsk – Soviets of workers' and soldiers' deputies seized power during December 1917 and January 1918. Whether the Altaians liked it or not, their mountainous territory now became a refuge for some of the anti-Bolshevik Russians who fled from the Soviet régime in south-west Siberia. Some of these were democratic politicians of SR or Siberian autonomist allegiance, while others were military officers with rightist leanings. At the end of February 1918 all these anti-Bolshevik elements, along with

---

[38] *Istoriya Sibiri*, vol. IV, pp. 297–301; Khaptayev, *Istoriya Buryatskoy ASSR*, vol. II, pp. 191–3, 203, 356; Kolarz, *The Peoples*, p. 118; W. Kolarz, *Religion in the Soviet Union*, London, 1961, pp. 452–3.

native princes and landowners, held a Constitutional Congress of Mountain Altai at Ulalu, and in the prevailing spirit of national self-determination proclaimed the independence of Altai. In fact the Altaian nationalists had more ambitious aims than the mere autonomy of their own relatively small mountain region.

In the early years of the twentieth century the awareness of their former glory as a powerful nation provided the Turkic and Mongolian peoples of southern Siberia with a basis for a unifying ideology which can be compared with the Pan-Turkism of the Middle Volga and Central Asia. It may be recalled that the empire of Chingis Khan, which included the Altai-Sayan region, was Mongol–Turkic in its ethnic composition. In 1905 the Altaians had invoked the spirit of 'Oirot Khan', and now, in 1918, their Constitutional Congress declared itself for a separate state, under the name of Chingis Khan's capital, Karakorum, which would unite within its borders not only the territory of the tribes of Altai itself, but also those of the Abakan-Yenisey steppe (subsequently to be known as the Khakas tribes) and those of Tuva, which had been practically annexed to the Russian Empire in 1914. Along with neighbouring Turkic regions of Chinese Sinkiang and Mongolia, this project would have created a state of considerable size between these two countries and Russia.[39]

There was a price to be paid by the Altaian leaders for the support – or at least the suspended enmity – of the more right-wing Russian refugees who had come among them, and who were inherently antagonistic towards the nationalism of 'Tatars'. This was the provision of armed men to help in the fight against the Bolsheviks. In 1918 the White Russian officer Zalesskiy formed an 'Altai national guard', which he led in attacks on local Soviet forces. After the general resurgence of the Whites and the establishment of the Kolchak régime in Omsk, another White officer, Satunin, formed a 'native division' which became notorious for its savage punitive raids on settlements in Western Siberia and the Altai, inspiring an intense hatred which contributed to the fighting spirit of the anti-White guerrilla bands. For the benefit of the Altaian tribesmen this ataman was presented as the bringer of liberation, and it was even rumoured that he was the legendary Oirot Khan himself. However, when in 1919 Satunin led a mixed body of Russians, Altaians and Kazaks against the Bolshevik garrison at Biysk, the attack failed and he was killed. By then the peasant partisan movement in the Altai had reached large proportions, as had the Bolshevik offensive led by Mamontov and Gromov; the Whites suffered several defeats at their hands, and most of the region came under Soviet control in May 1920. However,

[39] *Aziatskaya Rossiya*, vol. I, p. 83; Chichlo, 'Histoire de la formation', pp. 373–7; Danilin, 'Burkhanizm', pp. 84–5; *Istoriya Sibiri*, vol. III, pp. 303, 402–3, 492–3; vol. IV, pp. 52, 56, 59–60, 144, 150; Kolarz, *The Peoples*, pp. 173–4; *Narody Sibiri*, pp. 351, 375; Potapov, *Ocherki po istorii altaytsev*, pp. 1, 233–5, 343–60.

determined resistance to the Russian Bolshevik régime was continued in the high Altai and the Abakan steppe by various elements, including tribal leaders, Russian peasants with SR or anarchist allegiance, and politicians of the SR and Menshevik parties. In their fight against these the Bolsheviks recruited as many of the native Altaians as they could. Remnants of various White Russian armies, led by atamans such as Bakich and Kaygorodov, also continued to range over a wide area of the Altai and Tuva until they were finally annihilated in the spring of 1922.

After four years of warfare in the Altai-Yenisey region, the living conditions of the native peoples were reduced to a low level. In the mountain Altai in particular, only about half the number of horses and cattle, and 30 per cent of the sheep which they possessed before 1917 had survived. One of the first tasks of the Soviet-Russian authorities was, therefore, the restoration of cattle-rearing. At this time the Turkic peoples were still in a rebellious anti-Russian and anti-Bolshevik mood, which expressed itself in the burning of school buildings and killing of Communist Party workers. Many of them cherished the idea of creating a united Turkic Soviet Republic embracing the Altai, the Abakan steppe, the territory of the Shors, and Tuva, but this was rejected by the Soviet Russian government. However, in June 1922, superficial autonomy was granted to the mountain Altai region, under the adopted national name of Oirotia, with its capital at Ulalu – and not a single native Altaian in any administrative post. Similarly, in 1923 part of Yenisey province was designated as the homeland of the various clans of 'Minusinsk Tatars', for whom the common ethnonym 'Khakas' was now created, with its regional centre capital at Khakassk.[40]

Under the permissive conditions of the 'New Economic Policy' the old institutions of pastoral nomadism continued to govern the lives of most of the population of the high Altai and the Abakan steppe – a patriarchal system which provided a livelihood for the poor tribesmen through mutual assistance, social care of the needy and usufruct of livestock.

Unlike the mountain Altai, the steppe homeland of the Khakas people was of economic importance to the Soviet Russian government on account of its coal-mines and gold-workings. Consequently, from the middle of the 1920s, when a new railway was built to link Abakan with the Trans-Siberian, a great influx took place of Russian officials and workers, most of whom settled in Abakan, Chernogorsk, Kommunar and Sarala. Clearly the Turkic population of 'autonomous' Khakasia was doomed to become an ever decreasing minority in its own land. In the original territory of the Shor people too,

---

[40] Danilin, 'Burkhanizm', pp. 85–6; V.A. Demidov, *K sotsializmu, minuya kapitalizm: ocherk sotsialisticheskogo stroitelstva v Gorno-Altayskoy avtonomnoy oblasti*, Novosibirsk, 1970, pp. 19–20, 26–7, 33–43, 49–68, 74–93, 100; *Istoriya Sibiri*, vol. IV, pp. 115–16, 123–5, 130–2, 144, 148, 154, 282–3, 286, 297, 306; Kolarz, *The Peoples*, pp. 174–7; *Narody Sibiri*, pp. 351–2, 405.

encroachment by Russian settlement and industry was far advanced even before 1917, but a small district in the mountains was marked out in 1929 as the Shor National District.[41]

TUVA AND MONGOLIA

Strictly speaking, the territory of the Turkic Uriyangkhai – Tuva – was no legitimate concern of Russia's during the period of the Revolution and Civil War. It had been annexed informally to the Russian Empire in 1914, when its chief settlement was named Belotsarsk – 'White Tsar's City', and within the next few years some 3,500 new Russian settlers moved in to take land. Nevertheless the Chinese government never renounced its sovereignty over Tuva as a part of Mongolia, and under the terms of the 1915 Treaty of Kiakhta a senior Chinese official was stationed there. In the power vacuum caused by the Russian Revolution the Chinese again deprived Outer Mongolia of its independence in 1918–19, and sent troops into Tuva to protect Chinese interests. By that time the Civil War had been exported to Tuva's substantial Russian colony in the form of a struggle between a small soviet of gold-miners (organised by Bolsheviks from Minusinsk) and the local merchants, peasants and Cossack garrison. Subsequently warfare between detachments of Kolchak's White army and Bolshevik guerrilla bands spread to Tuva. In 1921 Baron Ungern's activities also extended to Tuva, where the White army led by Kazantsev received the support of the native chieftains. After the Orenburg Cossack army of Dutov and Annenkov had been driven into Chinese Sinkiang, one White detachment under Bakich moved into western Mongolia, where they carried out raids into Tuva until their defeat late in 1921.[42]

By then Ungern's White band in eastern Mongolia had been annihilated by Soviet forces, while a Mongolian army led by Chagdarjav had routed the Chinese and, with the active intervention of Soviet Russia, declared the independence of Outer Mongolia under a 'People's Provisional Government'. Many of the most active leaders of the new Mongolian People's Party which seized control at this time were in fact citizens of Russia: Buryats and Kalmyks of the Red Army provided most of the troops and police for revolutionary Mongolia, and links with the Soviet Russian authorities were facilitated by two Buryats, Zhamtsarano and Rinchino. The former was a Buddhist scholar who played a leading part in establishing a modern school in Örgöö after the declaration of Mongolian independence in 1912. Zham-

---

[41] *Istoriya Sibiri*, vol. IV, pp. 298–300, 437, 443–5; Kolarz, *The Peoples*, pp. 169, 177; *Narody Sibiri*, p. 518.

[42] Yu.L. Aranchyn, *Istoricheskiy put tuvinskogo naroda k sotsializmu*, Novosibirsk, 1982, pp. 64–94; Bawden, *Modern History of Mongolia*, p. 201; Ioffe, *Kolchakovskaya avantyura*, pp. 263–4; *Istoriya Sibiri*, vol. IV, pp. 63–4, 146; Kolarz, *The Peoples*, p. 162; *Narody Sibiri*, p. 429.

tsarano, one of the principal authors of the programme of the Mongolian People's Party, was appointed deputy to the Minister of the Interior in 1921. At the same time he continued to be a fervent Buddhist and Mongol nationalist. Zhamtsarano's compatriot Rinchino, on the other hand, represented hard-line Soviet Russian policies in Mongolia, and as head of the internal security was largely responsible for the intrigues leading to the 'liquidation' of the first two prime ministers, Bodo and Danzan, in 1922 and 1924.

Although the Mongolian Provisional Government formed in 1921 is presented in official Soviet and Mongolian history as being pro-Bolshevik, all but two of its seven members were executed, under Russian auspices, between 1922 and 1939. What was set up at first was a kind of constitutional monarchy, still under the theocratic headship of the Chief Lama, and it was not until his death in 1924 that the Russian-inspired People's Revolutionary Party declared that there would be no further reincarnations of the Living Buddha to rule Mongolia, but that it would henceforth be a 'People's Republic'. Even then, however, the rulers of Mongolia contrived to maintain an independent national policy in which the unification of all Mongol peoples (including Buryats, Kalmyks and Chahars) under the rule of Örgöö played an important part. Not until 1928 was totalitarian rule on the Soviet Russian model definitively imposed upon Mongolia, with destruction of the feudal nobility, collectivisation, and communist domination by secret police methods, and the country became a puppet in the hands of Moscow.[43]

The same is true of Tuva, which in 1925 was 'recognised' by the Soviet Russian government as an independent People's Republic under the protection of the USSR – despite the fact that many of its inhabitants, including its first prime minister, Donduk, believed that it should be united with Mongolia. The 'independent' political status of Tuva in fact reflected Russian domination of Mongolian affairs as a whole. It was natural for the Mongols to look upon Tuva as an integral part of their land, but the Russian Communist Party had no intention of adding Tuva to the territory of Mongolia, and instead turned it into a separate puppet 'state'.

After the February Revolution the native people of Tuva had developed a national movement, and they expressed their wish to be independent in June 1918. During Kolchak's régime a Buddhist-inspired uprising against all Russians took place in the Khemchik region in western Tuva, but a few months later, when the Bolsheviks defeated the Whites at Belotsarsk, some Tuvan tribesmen were persuaded to join the Red partisan army in its march on Minusinsk. The Russians' use of Tuva as a Civil War battlefield consolidated their presence there, so that even before the final defeat of

---

[43] Bawden, *History of Mongolia*, pp. 190–1, 201–2, 210–17, 225–8, 231–5, 238–41, 254, 263–4, 274–88, 290, 294, 332–3, 336; *Bolshaya Sovetskaya Entsiklopediya*, 1926–47, vol. VIII, col. 241; Kolarz, *The Peoples*, pp. 133–5; Kolarz, *Religion*, p. 467.

Bakich's Whites the idea of turning it into a puppet buffer state similar to the newly founded Far Eastern Republic was conceived in Moscow, and in July 1921 a 'Soviet Colony of Russians' in Tuva was officially created. Nevertheless, the Soviet Commissar for Foreign Affairs declared in the same year that Russia's annexation of Tuva in 1914 had been illegal, and that Soviet Russia had no claims upon it. In this ambiguous situation the communists sought to strengthen their position by creating a Tuvan People's Revolutionary Party under the aegis of the Comintern, while the People's Republic of Tannu Tuva (Eastern Tuva), established under similar guidance in August 1921 (but led in fact by Prince Buyan-Badrakhu and other notables of the old régime) developed along nationalist lines as a nominally democratic state committed more to the maintenance of Buddhism and union with Mongolia than to the aims of international socialism. Some of the first legislation of the Great Khural (parliament) of the republic discriminated against Russian settlers, and in 1924 anti-Russian feeling expressed itself in another abortive uprising in Khemchik region. During the next five years the Tannu Tuva government under Prime Minister Donduk continued to pursue its own, non-Soviet, policies, which culminated in a decree of 1928 making anti-religious propaganda illegal and proclaiming Buddhism as the state religion.

Meanwhile the Soviet Russians were purposefully building up their influence, especially by propaganda among Tuvan youth. A 'Revolutionary Union of Youth' similar to that in Mongolia, was founded; young Tuvans were given military training; and others were sent to Moscow for ideological instruction at the Comintern school. The results of these preparations unfolded in 1928–30 in a series of events which closely paralleled those taking place in Mongolia at the same time. Congresses of the People's Revolutionary Party and the Revsomol attacked 'class enemies' and 'right opportunists' within their ranks, while anti-communist rebellions were suppressed by the 'people's army' assisted by Russian workers. In Tuva the culmination was a coup carried out by a small group of young Tuvans trained for the task in Moscow, who unleashed a cultural revolution aimed at the 'liquidation of feudal chiefs as a class' and the abolition of religion by the wholesale destruction of Buddhist monasteries and the victimisation of lamas and shamans. Thereafter Tuvan society was subjected to revolution from above by Soviet Russian agents, in the course of which the People's Revolutionary Party was purged and an attempt made to involve the masses in political work, while the bonds of friendship said to exist between the people of Tuva and the Soviet Union, uniting them against 'foreign imperialism', were extolled. On the other hand, the intention to weaken the age-old links with Mongolia as far as possible was shown in the replacement of Mongolian as the official and literary language by the Tuvan (Turkic) vernacular, for which a Roman alphabet was introduced in 1930. The recently created press then changed not only its alphabet but also the titles of newspapers, e.g. from Mongolian *Ünen* 'Truth' to Tuvan *Shyn*, and the names of administrative territories (*khoshuns*) underwent a similar change. The reality of subjection to Soviet Russia was underlined by the extension of full rights of citizenship in Tuva to the Russian ethnic minority. Despite land reform and pressure to collectivise, however, the People's Republic of Tannu Tuva continued to be almost exclusively a land of rather primitive cattle and reindeer herding, where 88 per cent of the population were nomadic, only a small proportion of livestock (6.5 per cent) was owned by collectives, and the great majority belonged to mainly illiterate herdsmen.[44]

THE LENINIST EMPIRE

At the end of the 1920s the general form of the USSR had been established in terms of national territories with varying degrees of nominal autonomy, under the control of the Russian Communist Party (as it was called until 1925) in Moscow. The Civil War with all its horrors was over, having swept away most of the old social and cultural norms of Russia, but the country's fate was left in the hands of a party dedicated to paper schemes for a totally new society which were based on a combination of humanism in words and ruthlessness in practice, of ostensible rationality and speculative theories, of revolutionary élan and ideological pedestrianism, of conspiratorial cunning and culpable naïveté. There was already cause for foreboding in the ruling party's reversion to the concept of total economic planning after the respite of the 'New Economic Policy', its preparation of enforced collectivisation of the peasantry, and its organisation of a brutal system of terror for the suppression of all opposition by depriving citizens of their freedom, herding them into prisons and concentration camps and breaking them in body and spirit. The Russians of Siberia, in particular the peasants, had experienced these methods of Communist Party rule for a decade, but their bearing upon the indigenous peoples of Siberia had not yet become clear, as it would during the 1930s.

[44] Aranchyn, *Istoricheskiy put*, pp. 64–173, 213, 218; Bawden, *History of Mongolia*, pp. 228–9, 243, 275, 298–300; Chichlo, 'Histoire de la formation', pp. 380–4; Kolarz, *The Peoples*, pp. 163–6; Kolarz, *Religion*, pp. 464–5; *Narody Sibiri*, pp. 429–32; R.A. Rupen, 'The absorption of Tuva', *Studies on the Soviet Union*, (ns), vol. XI, no. 4, pp. 145–62; S.I. Vaynshteyn, *Nomads of South Siberia*, Cambridge, 1980, p. 44.

13

SOVIET SIBERIA IN THE 1930s

NATIONAL AUTONOMY AND 'ENLIGHTENMENT'

LIFE in Siberia in the period from 1930 to 1940 was subordinated to the same political events as in European Russia: the ascendancy of Stalin in the Communist Party, the replacement of the relatively free economic and cultural conditions of the 1920s by an ideologically conceived social revolution with its five-year plans for industrialisation and collectivisation of both urban and rural life, and the accompanying intensification of coercive dictatorship by the Communist Party in a spirit of class antagonism and Soviet Russian nationalism. In this context, the life of the indigenous peoples of Siberia, despite the revolution, were still – and even, perhaps, increasingly – seen in the role of colonial natives whose interests were subordinated to those of the Soviet Russian state. The out-and-out totalitarianism of the Russian Communist Party under Stalin's leadership resulted in the abandonment of the spirit of philanthropic assistance to the native peoples of Siberia which had prevailed in the period immediately following the Civil War.

Up to the early 1930s there had been wide development of national autonomy, not only for the Buryats, Altaians and Yakuts, whose territories had been designated autonomous republics or regions in 1922–3, but also in the case of the smaller ethnic communities. In south-west Siberia and northern Kazakstan, for instance, soviets on a national basis were created in districts of compact settlement of Germans, Latvians, Estonians, Ukrainians and Belorussians. Similarly, in Omsk province thirty Kazak and eleven Tatar village soviets were founded. Between 1926 and 1932 national districts (*rayony*) were designated for the Nanais, Ulchis, Chukchis, Eskimos, Tofalar and Aleuts, while larger autonomous regions (*okruga*) were formed for the Samoyeds (one west of the Urals and one in Yamal peninsula for the Nenets, and one in Taimyr embracing the Dolgans and Nganasans), for the Khanty-

Mansis, the Selkups, the Ewenki Tungus (ten separate districts), the Ewens, the Chukchi and the Koraks.[1]

The intention behind the creation of these national territories was paternalistic and at first altruistic: as an unquestioned article of communist belief it was essential to bring the native peoples of Siberia into the twentieth century by telling them what was wrong with their traditional way of life and ultimately inducing them to abandon almost every aspect of it – nomadism, clan structure, tribal religion, polygamy, bride-price etc. This was in fact a kind of reforming missionarism without the Christian religion, but with an equally strong conviction of absolute enlightenment.

Apart from the Tatars, Buryat Mongols, Yakuts and Altaians, among whom education had made some progress before the Revolution and for whom more schools were opened after the Civil War, literacy was practically non-existent among the mainly nomadic native communities of Siberia in 1930. None of their languages had been given written form, so that, until alphabets and texts in the native languages were created, the language of the classroom had to be Russian. Considerable dedication was required on the part of the Russian teachers who undertook the work of 'liquidating illiteracy' among nomadic people, as did A.F. Anisimov in 1929:

Having reached the mouth of the Mountain Tunguska by steamship I had to make my way up-river in a small boat . . . Two months later I finally reached . . . the village of Baikit. Equipping myself here with reindeer and other essentials for the nomadic life, I rode off into the depths of the forest to wander with the Ewenkis . . . As I taught them, I learned myself, improving my knowledge of their language, studying their culture, and accustoming myself to practically all the burdens of nomadic life – the hard and demanding labour of the hunter and reindeer-herdsman.[2]

While the textbooks for elementary instruction in the North at this time were in the Russian language, the Committee of the North intended that eventually all primary education would be conducted in the vernacular. Textbooks were to be created in sixteen native languages ranging from that of the Saami (Lapps) in the west to the Aleuts on the Commander Islands, and in order to provide native teachers, a whole network of schools and teacher-training colleges was envisaged. In practice it proved impossible to fulfil this ambitious programme. A standard alphabet, based on Latin and not Cyrillic, was introduced in 1931 as a means of writing all the languages of the North, and school books and newspapers were produced in seven languages – Nenets, Mansi, Ewenki, Ewen, Chukchi, Eskimo and Nanai. However, for the Khanty, Selkup, Korak and Nivkh peoples, work did not progress beyond the compilation of primers, while in the case of other languages having widely differing dialects or a very small number of speakers

---

[1] Gurvich, *Osushchestvleniye*, p. 255; *Istoriya Sibiri*, vol. IV, pp. 287, 465–6; *Narody Sibiri*, p. 558.
[2] Anisimov, *Religiya evenkov*, pp. 10–11.

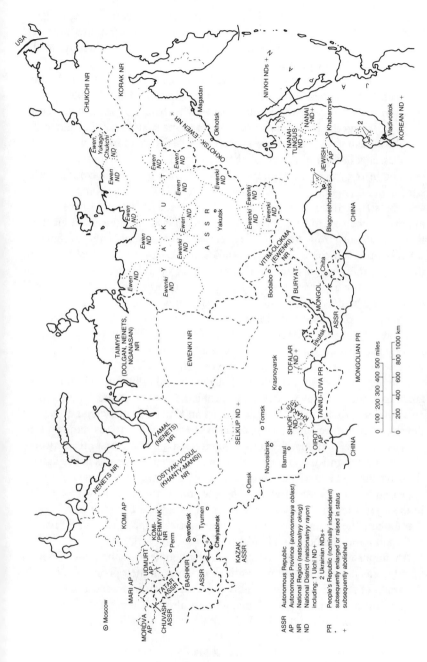

Map 10 National territories in Siberia and eastern Russia in 1934

ASSR   Autonomous Republic
AP   Autonomous Province (*avtonomnaya oblast*)
NR   National Region (*natsionalnyy okrug*)
ND   National District (*natsionalnyy rayon*)
        including: 1 Ulchi ND+
                   2 Ukrainian NDs+
PR   People's Republic (nominally independent)
.   subsequently enlarged or raised in status
+   subsequently abolished

0 100 200 300 400 500 miles
0 200 400 600 800 1000 km

and a lack of educated teachers – such as the Saami, Ket, Udeghe, Dolgan, Nganasan, Ulchi and Yukagir – up to 1940 not even a beginning had been made to the task of creating a written language and, consequently, to the introduction of education in the vernacular.

The problem was complicated by the fact that a knowledge of the Russian language was deemed to be essential for all citizens of the USSR, so that children had to cope with learning not only to read and write their native language, using the Latin alphabet, but also to speak and read Russian in the Cyrillic alphabet – all within the space of five years at primary school. Since the Russians had no intention of abandoning their national alphabet, it was decreed in 1937 that the languages of the Siberian peoples, in common with almost all others in the Soviet Union, must henceforth be written in Cyrillic, and the standard Latin alphabet was abandoned. At the same time as this important change, the Russian language itself was introduced in all non-Russian schools from the very first class. Thus, although the number of schools provided for non-Russian children increased considerably during the 1930s the general trend was towards greater influence of the Russian language at the expense of native languages. Nevertheless, in some national districts the 'nativisation' of the school system did gradually become a reality, as young people, educated either at regional colleges or in the Leningrad Institute of the North, returned to their own communities as teachers. Among the Ulchis, for instance, where at first all teachers were Russians, there were twelve native Ulchi teachers in 1935.[3]

The development of the native intelligentsia and of literature in the native languages was subject to the same problems. Some of the larger ethnic communities, such as the Buryats, Yakuts and Altaians, possessed quite well developed literatures in the vernacular by the end of the 1930s. However, in the case of small nationalities it was characteristic that the first literary works were published in Russian rather than the native language – as in the case of the Yukagir Teki Odulok, whose fine story *The Life of Imteurgin the Elder* appeared in 1934. Other northern peoples did write in their own languages in the 1930s, for instance the Ewenki and Ewen poets Lontogir and Nikolay Tarabukin, the Korak Ketsai Kekketin (stories *Khoyalkhot* and *Ernito the Herdsman*) and the Nenets Nikolay Vylka (the story *Marya*).[4]

An important aspect of spreading 'enlightenment' among the Siberian peoples was the emancipation of native women from their prescribed roles in the traditional social structure. This process, which had occurred sporadically in the late 1920s, gained momentum after a Communist Party conference on women's rights held in 1930. Apart from its inherent merits,

[3] Gurvich, *Osushchestvleniye*, pp. 143–8, 155; *Istoriya Yakutskoy ASSR*, vol. III, p. 224; Kolarz, *The Peoples*, p. 72; *Narody Sibiri*, pp. 826–7; Sergeyev, *Nekapitalisticheskiy put*, p. 286.
[4] Gurvich, *Osushchestvleniye*, pp. 184–8; *Istoriya Sibiri*, vol. IV, pp. 456–61; V. M. Sangi, compiler, *Vtoroye rozhdeniye*, Moscow, 1983, contains Russian translations of several of the earliest works of literature by peoples of the North and the Far East.

however, the women's movement contributed much to the sovietisation – and Russification – of native societies and their values. In addition to bride-price, other practices of clan society which the Soviet Russian authorities deemed to be reprehensible and therefore due for abolition, included polygamy, levirate, and arranged marriages involving young children. Another target of the reformers were the numerous taboos to which women, because of their sexual functions, were subjected, and which, by excluding them from clan councils, were considered to relegate them to an inferior position. One widespread taboo was the practice of putting a woman who was due to give birth out of the family tent, so that for several days she and her baby were exposed to the cold and discomfort of a rough temporary shelter. The generally subordinate position of women – which, of course, existed not only among Asiatic peoples but also in traditional Russian society – militated against their participation in soviet meetings as speakers and voters. From 1929, therefore, the Soviet authorities organised women's meetings and propaganda, and it was the assertion by these means of women's rights to a voice in clan soviets that set native women on the path to 'equality of rights'. This, in turn, created among native women in Siberia an important body of support for the Soviet systems, and led to the active participation of women in political life. As a result, by 1931 about one quarter of all deputies of soviets in the autonomous republics of Siberia were women.[5]

ANTI-SHAMANIST MEASURES

The religious beliefs and observances of the native peoples were an obvious target for the missionary zeal of the communists in Siberia. Shamanism had been officially banned since the 1920s, in the sense that shamans were forbidden to perform their rites in public and had their drums, special costumes and other attributes confiscated by the Soviet Russian authorities. (These coercive measures resembled those imposed by the Orthodox Church missionaries in tsarist times!) In some places instruction by communist propagandists is said to have led to the creation of an atheist cell, for instance, among the European Nenets, while one group of young Selkups was induced to expose the medical practices of their local shaman as trickery. However, in view of the fundamental incompatibility of outlook between atheist Russians and animist tribespeople, a general renunciation of ancient beliefs in favour of the new enlightenment could scarcely be expected to occur quickly. Not until much of the fabric of native society had been undermined by collectivisation and the abandonment of nomadism did a significant reduction in the influence of the shamans take place, so that in

[5] V.D. Diószegi, ed., *Popular Beliefs and Folklore Tradition in Siberia*, Bloomington, 1968, pp. 77–83; Gurvich, *Osushchestvleniye*, pp. 254, 290–1; *Istoriya Sibiri*, vol. IV, p. 436; *Narody Sibiri*, p. 558; Sergeyev, *Nekapitalisticheskiy put*, pp. 243–4; Vdovin, *Priroda i chelovek*, pp. 127–8.

the second half of the 1930s a considerable number of them were induced to forswear their activities.

From the beginning of the Soviet régime the shamans had incurred the displeasure of the Russian authorities by their opposition to the introduction of schools and medical services. As the recognised healers in their communities, the shamans opposed Western medicine as an offence to the spirits, and inspired distrust in it by the threat that those who accepted Russian medicine or entered a hospital would die. Shamans in the 1930s still commanded great respect in their own communities as practitioners of folk medicine – not all of which was a matter of magic rites, as it relied also upon accumulated lore about curative herbs and potions. Some shamans also moved with the times by learning to read and write, so that they could rival the authority of Russian officials. In Soviet Russian accounts of this period the shaman, like the Orthodox priest, is generally presented as a charlatan who consciously deceived and cheated his fellow men in order to live richly at their expense. However, if as in any field of human activity some predatory individuals no doubt existed, the evidence is that most of the shamans lived poorly, found their vocation a heavy burden, and accepted only small gifts or fees for the services they performed.[6]

In fact the Communist Party's assault on shamanism was largely ineffective at first because of their concentration on the externals – rituals and accoutrements – and their lack of understanding of the animist beliefs which were woven into every aspect of the life of the herding and hunting peoples. Another Russian teacher–ethnographer has described the difficulties of mutual comprehension which he encountered while working in a nomad school for Chukchis in 1932:

Once in December a young Chukchi came running . . . to tell me that Tameni the shaman would like to see me. I could not ignore such an invitation . . . as I approached I saw sixty or seventy Chukchis standing in a half-circle with Tameni facing them . . . For a while the women of the village danced to the sound of his drum. Then Tameni stopped and addressed the gathering, saying that as the Chukchis' life depended entirely on hunting, their children should not learn to read and write but should be training physically to become hardy hunters. The presence of the school, and even 'Russian smells' were frightening away the sea animals, and so on . . . Taking advantage of a pause in Tameni's speech, I said that all over our country the new life had now been established . . . as a result of the revolution led by Lenin . . . It was Lenin's will that all people should be equal and that all should be educated . . . After listening to me, Tameni asked: 'So Lenin came from the moon – its dark, western side?'[7]

---

[6] Chichlo, 'La Collectivisation', p. 300; Gurvich, *Osushchestvleniye*, p. 292; *Istoriya Sibiri*, vol. IV, p. 301; Kolarz, *The Peoples*, p. 75; *Narody Sibiri*, pp. 373, 557, 602; Popova, *Eveny*, pp. 173–4; Sergeyev, *Nekapitalisticheskiy put*, p. 357; I. Skachkov, 'Ob antireligioznoy rabote na Severe', *Revolyutsiya i natsionalnosti*, 1934, no. 7 (53), pp. 50–4; Suslov, 'Shamanstvo', pp. 128–32; Vdovin, *Priroda i chelovek*, p. 123.   [7] Vdovin, *Priroda i chelovek*, pp. 235–6.

Vdovin's reply that Lenin was of normal human birth did not satisfy the Chukchis, and he himself was perplexed by such an incongruous question until it was explained to him later that formerly the Tsar had been represented to them as the 'sun chief'. It was therefore logical that his overthrow could only have been brought about by the dark forces from the sun's antithesis – the moon. Similarly, the Chukchi phrase 'new life' – used by the Russian communists to translate 'Soviet power' – had an inherently mystical significance for the Chukchis, since its meanings covered not only 'way of life' and 'existence', but also 'deity'. Accordingly, the red flag of the socialist revolution was understood by them as a symbol of a new supernatural existence. In view of such profound semantic misunderstanding it is not surprising that the Siberian natives' cosmology, in which everything was related to the spirit world, was not to be undermined quickly by Soviet propaganda translated literally from Russian.[8]

The Russian Communist Party, in pursuit of a total monopoly of influence over the population, was determined to denigrate and persecute the shamans as ruthlessly as they did priests of other religions. It should not be forgotten too that many Siberian natives belonged in some degree to the Orthodox Church and suffered from its persecution in the 1920s and 1930s. For instance, there was a complaint in 1928 from some Khantys of the lower Ob that because the forest was full of demons they needed crosses and wanted to contribute to the upkeep of the local Orthodox Church and its priest, but the Soviet authorities had robbed them of the money they had given. Despite all the anti-religious measures employed by the Communist Party, shamans continued to operate in Siberia throughout the 1930s, and in places much later. For instance, a Russian doctor among the Nenets of the Ob estuary reported in 1934 that 'Here drums are beaten quite openly and the skins of sacrificed reindeer hang from trees for all to see', while among the Khantys one still came across sanctuaries with bear skulls. The mere fact of deprivation of their ritual accoutrements did not prevent shamans from performing their rites, more or less secretly.

One further fact of religious belief which angered the communists was that not infrequently even the official representatives of Soviet authority continued to believe in tribal religion and the powers of the shaman. Thus, more than a decade after the end of the Civil War, it was necessary for the Communist Party to admonish members of soviets, the Young Communist League, and the party itself, that they must be the first to demonstrate by their own example the virtue of renouncing the 'superstition' of tribal religion in favour of the 'scientific' ideology of Marxism–Leninism.[9]

[8] Ibid., pp. 5–9, 35–6.
[9] Gurvich, *Osushchestvleniye*, pp. 291–2; Skachkov, 'Ob antireligioznoy rabote'; Suslov, 'Shamanstvo', pp. 89–152.

12 The triumph of Enlightenment over Superstition: a propagandist painting in the Museum of the History of Religion and Atheism in Leningrad, depicting the expulsion by a Russian flying doctor of a shaman who had been called to treat a sick person. The cowering Ewenki shaman is an obvious copy from an exhibit in the State Museum of Ethnography.

COLLECTIVISATION IN SIBERIA

The most important aim of the Russian Communist Party's social policies in the 1930s was collectivisation, and it was imposed on the native peoples of Siberia with no less determination than, for instance, on the farmers of the Ukraine. The fact that reindeer-herders and hunters were also subjected to this radical social engineering shows how little collectivisation had to do with *agriculture* as an economic activity of the local community, since almost none of the Siberian natives cultivated crops, and even those who reared cattle, such as the Buryat Mongols and Yakuts, followed a nomadic way of life in which farms played little or no part. Still less were the primitive reindeer-herding peoples of any relevance from the point of view of agricultural production, since the main value of the peasantry to the Soviet system – providing food for the cities – was not a feature of the *native* economy. So far as help to the native Siberians in the pursuance of their herding, fishing and hunting was concerned, the cooperative system introduced in the 1920s by the Committee of the North already provided most of what they required, so that collectivisation as such could not increase their well-being. Perhaps the most valid arguments for collectivisation concerned the reindeer-herding peoples, whose almost exclusive dependence upon reindeer meat made it impossible for them ever to improve their standard of living, since the annual increase of their herds barely covered depletion by killing for food, so that, it has been argued, they were for ever doomed to a bare subsistence level. Collective farming, with the development of other sources of food – fishing, sea-mammal hunting and imported bread – would lead to a more healthy mixed diet. Linked to these arguments, however, was another consideration: the traditional way of life produced no surplus of reindeer meat and other 'valuable raw materials' which could be utilised by the Soviet Russian state as exportable commodities.[10]

Whatever economic arguments were adduced in the Communist Party's assertions of the need to collectivise the hunting, fishing and herding activities of the Siberian peoples, the real aim was to proletarianise them by binding them in collectives subordinated to the superstructure of the Soviet state. Just as the individualism and self-reliance of the peasants of European Russia had to be broken in order to bring them to the point of blind submission – however disastrous might be the effect upon the productivity of agriculture – so the Siberian native peoples also had to be disciplined, deprived of their leadership, and reduced to the level of serfs handing over their produce (especially furs) to the Soviet Russian state.

There were, of course, Russian, Ukrainian and other peasant farmers in Siberia, who during the first few years after the end of the Civil War had been subjected to the policy of war communism by which grain supplies were taken by force in order to feed the Bolshevik-controlled towns. From 1924 the 'New Economic Policy' gave the peasants a breathing-space, but 1928 brought a reversion to brute force in Western Siberia. Because of a shortfall in procurements of grain for the state during 1927, Stalin led a task force of Communist Party officials, supported by police units, to the Urals and Western Siberia, where local Soviet officials were stirred up to seize grain from farmers who were holding it in store, and punish them as 'kulaks'. Over 1,000 peasants were arrested and tried for sabotage during 1928. This first application of the 'Ural–Siberian method' – in effect an armed raid on the countryside by an alien government – created the pattern for subsequent treatment of the peasant farmers during mass collectivisation. From then onward the Communist Party incited the poor peasants and farm-labourers against the efficient farmers in order to procure grain and at the same time undermine their economic position. The farmers responded in many places by killing Communist Party and Young Communist League activists, setting fire to farm buildings and destroying their own grain stores. As early as

---

[10] Sergeyev, *Koryakskiy natsionalnyy okrug*, pp. 115–16.

December 1929, in anticipation of the campaign for mass collectivisation, the Siberian peasants everywhere began to slaughter their own livestock rather than be forced to hand them over to the collective farm.

When, at the beginning of 1930, the Communist Party launched its campaign of mass collectivisation, this followed the same course as in the rest of the Soviet Union. As a result of the zealous response of local authorities to the party's directives aimed at quick results, the statistics for 1930 show crazy fluctuations. Behind the statistics of fluctuating collective-farm membership in 1930–1 lay a continuing tale of violence as the peasant folk reacted to bureaucratic bungling, threats and naked coercion by themselves resorting to revolts and acts of sabotage and revenge against the communist authorities. Over the two years 1930–1 the total number of so-called 'kulak' families expropriated and exiled from the Siberian agricultural regions to the north – principally Turukhansk district on the lower Yenisey and Narym district on the middle Ob – amounted to about 330,000 people, according to the probably understated figures in Soviet publications.[11] In fact peasant resistance to collectivisation was far from being over in 1931. As the collectivised peasants were subjected to steeply increased demands for grain, punitive measures for non-fulfilment of quotas, and hunger as a result of poor harvests, retaliation against the Communist Party continued up to 1935, in the form of acts of sabotage and the murder of state officials.

With all the forces of the Soviet Russian state turned ruthlessly against them, the opposition of the so-called 'kulaks' was hopeless, and the percentage of the peasantry brought into the collective farms of Siberia increased to over 90 per cent by 1937. The scale on which peasants slaughtered their cattle before entering the collective was, however, even greater in Siberia than in European Russia, with the result that in 1937 the number of livestock was far below the 1916 level, and the formerly flourishing cattle and dairy-farming industry of Western Siberia was in a state of decline.[12]

---

[11] R.W. Davies, *The Industrialisation of Soviet Russia 1: the Socialist Offensive: The Collectivisation of Soviet Agriculture 1929–30*, London, 1980, pp. 56–63, 258; *Istoriya Sibiri*, vol. IV, pp. 178–9, 234–7, 330–40, 376, 384; N.Ya. Gushchin, *Sibirskaya derevnya na puti k sotsializmu*, Novosibirsk, 1973, pp. 288–91, 299–309, 427–36, 440–1; Nove, *Economic History*, pp. 148–54, 166–72; Shvarev, *Dalniy Vostok*, pp. 366–9; I.S. Stepichev, *Pobeda leninskogo kooperativnogo plana v vostochnosibirskoy derevne*, Irkutsk, 1966, pp. 441–52, 460–71, etc. Only some sixty years later did it become possible for the Russian press to publish accounts of the cold-blooded destruction of Siberian farmers and their families by the Communist Party, e.g. V. A. Novokshonov, 'Krestyanskaya ssylka v Sibiri. 30-e gody', *Sibirskiye ogni*, 1989, no. 12, pp. 100–17; V. Sapozhnikov, 'Khozhdeniye po Yeniseyu velikomu', *Sibirskiye ogni*, 1989, no. 9, pp. 48–9.

[12] *Aziatskaya Rossiya*, vol. I, pp. 235, 242; *Entsiklopedicheskiy slovar*, vol. VI, p. 67; Gushchin, *Sibirskaya derevnya*, pp. 431, 462–5, 478; *Istoriya Sibiri*, vol. IV, pp. 332–80, 389; Khaptayev, *Istoriya Buryatskoy ASSR*, vol. II, pp. 258, 271; Stepichev, *Pobeda*, pp. 327, 452–6.

COLLECTIVISATION OF SIBERIAN NATIVE COMMUNITIES

The imposition of collectivisation upon the native peoples of Siberia was a more protracted process than in the case of the Russian peasants, its pace varying according to the location of a given community in relation to centres of Soviet Russian control, according to its way of life as determined by the environment, and the relative importance of its economic activities to the interests of the Russian state. In the first stages of the campaign the usual manifestations of crude coercive zeal on the part of Russian officials occurred in many places, despite the cautious advice of the Committee of the North and some Politburo members that the date set for the completion of collectivisation should be staggered, so that Siberia and the North would reach that point last, in 1933 and not 1930. Consequently, in those national communities whose territories lay close to or overlapped the principal areas of Russian settlement, such as the West Siberian Tatars, Altaians, Khakases, Buryats and Yakuts, mass collectivisation was begun at the beginning of 1930, and gross 'mistakes' were made – that is, threats and force were used by local officials, the selection of farm sites was arbitrary and often inappropriate, so that violent retaliation by the natives occurred, and the initial flood of enforced entry to the collective farms was followed by a mass exodus. By the end of 1931, however, the core of efficient and prosperous community leaders had been 'liquidated' (not before they had slaughtered much of their cattle) and their compatriots were on the way towards total collectivisation, the percentages said to have enrolled in collective farms (*kolkhozy*) being: Khakas 72 per cent, Buryats 61 per cent, Altaians 50 per cent and Yakuts 42 per cent. By 1937 the degree of collectivisation ranged from 93.3 per cent in the case of the Khakas to only 71 per cent of Yakuts.

Collectivisation also progressed quickly in the settled fishing communities of the lower Ob, the Pacific coast and Amur regions, where the Soviet state was able to develop fisheries because the natives had already been drawn into the Russian commercial network before the Revolution. The various types of cooperative introduced here during the 1920s formed a convenient basis for the collectivisation of the native people. As the fur trade was still one of Russia's most important assets, hunting was also increasingly subordinated to collective control through local soviets. This was by no means easy to achieve, since the hunting peoples, from the Nenets west of the Urals to the Chukchi of the Far North-east, all conformed to one natural law which, one might have thought, would also command the respect of communists – that is *nimat*, according to which the spoils of the hunt must be shared out equally among all members of the community, and even those in neighbouring camps. This 'primitive communism', however, was not seen as a virtue by the communists, but on the contrary was considered to be a disguised form of exploitation and social parasitism. The Soviet authorities had to carry out a prolonged campaign for the abolition of equal shares, and it was only with collectivisation that the Siberian natives learned to abandon *nimat* in favour of a money economy and the 'socialist' system of payment by results. It became clear in the 1930s that the Russian communists, who saw the world in terms of 'the economy' and the human beings who worked in it, would not tolerate *nimat* or any other manifestations of primitive communism (such as mutual aid, communal grazing, fishing and hunting, adoption of orphans or care for the aged) but made it their aim to break down the 'patriarchal' clan institutions. So in the 1930s government policy towards the native peoples hardened, and the indulgent philanthropic attitude of the Committee of the North was gradually replaced by measures more in keeping with totalitarianism.

Most resistant to the wishes of the communist authorities were the reindeer herders of the taiga and tundra, whose nomadic way of life preserved them, at least temporarily, from direct interference by the state, and who, in any case, had less to offer to the Russian economy. Families collaborated in summer grazing irrespective of the relative size of their herds, and those who were impoverished through the loss of their reindeer were taken in by a more prosperous relative, who provided them with accommodation, clothing and food, while they lived and worked as part of the family. Their survival was thus ensured. In fact the rigours of the northern climate were a powerful equalising force, and the constant struggle for survival in unpredictable natural conditions generally deprived potential 'exploiters' of a lasting basis for self-enrichment. Where the traditional nomadic way of life remained in force up till the 1920s – for instance among the Nganasans of Taimyr – the relationship between rich and poor could not be reduced to a simple political formula:

The herdsmen were usually relatives of the big herd-owners. They used the reindeer for their own needs almost on equal terms with their employers, and received the same quantity of produce from the slaughter of domestic reindeer as the owners did ... In some cases the ownership of a certain number of animals by one family was purely nominal. In practice the reindeer were used by a whole group of families or even several groups in common.[13]

If there were nomadic reindeer-herders among whom the old communal system had been destroyed and stratification into prosperous and deprived classes had to some extent developed, this was a result of penetration by Russian commercialism.

By the late 1920s the grip of their own ideology upon the minds of the Russian communists committed them to the dogma that there could not be a classless society in the modern world – except as a result of Bolshevik revolution. Even in the primitive subsistence-level society of northern Asia,

[13] Gurvich, *Osushchestvleniye*, p. 249.

therefore, they set in motion the vicious process of singling out rich herd-owners who could be victimised as 'kulaks' in the interests of collectivisation and subjection to the state. Precise details of the 'administrative means' employed by the Russian authorities to make the Siberian natives combine in collectives are scarce, but some Soviet sources mention the use of threats that any uncooperative community would be deprived of its hunting or fishing grounds, that help for the needy would not be provided, and that essential supplies normally provided by the cooperative store would be withheld. As in the Ukraine or European Russia, it was the men with most initiative who tried to organize opposition to the collectivisers from the Russian towns, and it was such men – branded as 'big herd-owners and shamans' – who were by various means deprived of their influence, robbed of their possessions, and eventually 'liquidated as a class'. Few of the tyrannical acts carried out in Siberia in the name of collectivisation have been referred to in the Soviet Russian press, but one no doubt quite typical example demonstrates the high-handed treatment meted out to the Ewenki Tungus – a poor community without chiefs or large herd-owners – in what was nominally their own National Region in Central Siberia. Here in 1929 the Russian communist authorities, disregarding the 'voluntary principle' which is piously said to have existed, simply told the Ewenkis that they now belonged to collectives. On the Lower Tunguska all within a radius of 60 miles were forcibly brought from their forest encampments and put together in a single settlement which Communist Party officials designated as their 'commune'. This meant that apart from clothing, practically all their possessions (reindeer, traps, guns and domestic utensils) were made common property. Communes on similar lines were created in many places such as Turukhansk, Yakutia, the lower Ob and Yamal. When the destructive effects of these crude measures became apparent as a result of mass flight from the newly formed 'collective farms', the Communist Party beat a hasty retreat and prohibited the formation of communes. Instead the appropriate form of collective for most of the peoples of the North was declared to be the 'simplest production association' (*prosteysheye proizvodstvennoye obyedineniye* – PPO), in which pastures and hunting grounds were utilised collectively – if only at the appropriate season – but neither livestock nor personal possessions were to be communalised.

The passivity and submissiveness which had developed among many of the native communities in the Siberian colony during long subjection to their Russian masters no doubt made it relatively easy in many cases for local Communist Party workers to obtain compliance with their orders. Thus in the Maya-Okhotsk region two quite different Ewenki groups were forced to combine to form a fishing collective on a river that carried few fish, irrespective of their – presumably well-informed – objections to the site. In the case of reindeer-herding people, such as the Nenets Samoyeds or the Okhotsk

Tunguses, the formation of collective herds required either the purchase of reindeer from nomadic herd-owners – who usually refused to sell – or the commandeering of animals belonging to families subject to collectivisation. The Okhotsk Ewenkis, having been collectivised and forced to settle, were then obliged to undermine the well-being of their own reindeer by over-using them for transportation purposes – despite the fact that since 1925 the Siberian natives had supposedly been freed from all the old labour obligations which had helped to destroy their economy in tsarist times. Because of inappropriate and counter-productive measures, and the fierce resistance of the more independent reindeer nomads – who frequently slaughtered their animals rather than allow the Russian communists to confiscate them – only a very small number of people in the North had been collectivised by 1932 (roughly 12 per cent of all families). Two years later this number had increased threefold, but less than 19 per cent of the total herds of reindeer were held by collective or soviet farms, and even at the end of the 1930s about half of all reindeer still remained in private ownership.[14]

THE CLAN SYSTEM AND NOMADISM UNDER ATTACK

Collectivisation in Siberia was but one aspect of a comprehensive social revolution imposed upon the native peoples, which affected not only religion and the position of women, but the most fundamental features of traditional life – clan allegiance and nomadism. Despite the general breakdown of the old tribal organisation by the early twentieth century, it proved impossible for the Russian communists to ignore the fact of clan loyalties in the formation of collectives. Among the Ewenki Tungus, for instance, several were in practice clan collectives, where practically every member bore the same surname. Similarly, at least one Nenets collective in Yamal consisted entirely of members of the Okatetta clan. On the Kureyka in Central Siberia collectives were not only based upon nationality – Ewenkis or Kets – but in the latter case farms, and even 'brigade' work-teams had to be divided according to the exogamic phratries. Where clan structure was still strong enough for chiefs to enjoy some authority, they formed the focus of resistance to the imposition of collectivisation. However, it was relatively easy for the Soviet Russians to overcome such opposition by skilful manipulation of the 'poor',

[14] A. Andreyev, 'Iz opyta kollektivizatsii: korrespondentsiya iz Ayano-Mayskogo Evenskogo nats. rayona', *Sovetskiy Sever*, 1934, no. 4, pp. 96–8; P. Beskorsyy, 'Nekotorye itogi (materialy o sostoyanii kollektivizatsii na Kr. Severe)', *Sovetskiy Sever*, 1934, no. 2, pp. 57–61; M.M. Brodnev, 'Ot rodovogo stroya k sotsializmu (po materialam Yamalo-Nenetskogo natsionalnogo okruga)', *Sovetskaya etnografiya*, 1950, no. 1, pp. 93–9; Chichlo, 'La Collectivisation', p. 295; Gurvich, *Osushchestvleniye*, pp. 30–1, 203–4, 207, 249, 286; *Istoriya Sibiri*, vol. IV, pp. 440–53, 469; Kolarz, *The Peoples*, p. 71; A. Mikhalev, 'Uspekhi i tormozy kolkhoznogo stroitelstva (pismo iz Penzhinskogo rayona, Kamchatskogo okruga)', *Sovetskiy Sever*, 1931, no. 3–4, pp. 168–70; *Narody Sibiri*, pp. 485, 562; Popova, *Eveny*, pp. 75–6, 228; Sergeyev, *Nekapitalisticheskiy put*, pp. 246, 296, 330–5, 338, 341–6, 352–6, 359, 361.

and the exclusion of the 'rich' from local soviets during elections. At the same time, the clan as an institution capable of competing with the soviet for the allegiance of the native peoples was effectively undermined by the abolition of clan soviets in favour of territorial ones, and the prohibition of traditional clan gatherings.[15]

The campaign to make the nomadic and semi-nomadic peoples of Siberia give up their mobile way of life began at the same time as collectivisation and was closely bound up with it, since the collective farm headquarters provided a fixed centre around which people could gradually be persuaded to settle. The reasons usually mentioned to justify the Soviet Russian government's campaign against nomadism were philanthropic. Nomadising involved constant hardships and offered little security of shelter and nourishment; diseases, especially of the eyes and lungs, were associated with tent life and its cramped, often smoky conditions; personal hygiene was at a low level among the nomads; and they lived in isolation from human society and from that twentieth-century urban culture which the Russian communists considered to be without question the acme of human development. From the point of view of the 'enlighteners' it was certainly easier to provide schooling and medical services to communities settled in villages than to nomadic families. Where the Soviet Russians were unable to convince the Siberian natives of the benefits of civilisation as an inducement to settle down in a collective 'farm', they held another strong card as a means of persuasion: collectives received help in the form of credits, firearms, ammunition etc., and conversely, withholding such essential supplies from the nomadic hunters and herders could make their life much less tolerable.

Nevertheless the transition to a settled life was not easy for those brought up to nomadism. They missed the freedom of movement and contact with nature, and the absence of a camp-fire was felt so strongly by some that, it is said, they modified the small wooden huts which they received from the state, making a fireplace in the middle of the floor and cutting a smoke-hole in the roof. The nomadic way of life can be idealised as well as any other, and for many it was considered to be the right and eternal way, which it was sinful to abandon. Moreover, life in a wooden house in a village, which Russians automatically assumed to be superior to tent-life, was repugnant to many Siberian natives because of its stuffiness, dirty surroundings and, above all, static monotony. As a result, many resisted official pressure to settle, while some of those who were persuaded to do so thereafter returned to nomadism if conditions allowed.

In 1934 almost half of all Siberian natives were still nomadic, but the proportion was very much higher in some cases, such as the Nenets Samoyeds, of whom 96 per cent remained unsettled, the Ewens 91 per cent,

---

[15] Brodnev, 'Ot rodovogo stroya k sotsializmu', p. 94; Gurvich, *Osushchestvleniye*, pp. 203–6, 286; *Istoriya Sibiri*, vol. IV, pp. 466–8.

Ewenkis 87 per cent and the Chukchis 71 per cent. To the Bolshevik rulers of the Soviet Union the continuation of this primitive economy side by side with their grandiose plans for the 'conquest of nature' was intolerable. With the second five-year plan of industrial development under way, it was urged that the time was ripe for the 'liberation' of the northern peoples from nomadism, and indeed the movement towards settlement did gather some momentum in the late 1930s. In 1936, for instance, the small remnant of the Yukagir people near Verkhnekolymsk ceremonially burned their last tents to mark their final move into Russian houses. Up to 1940, however, significant success in the settlement of nomadic peoples could be claimed only for the larger nations of southern Siberia – the Altaians, Khakas and Buryats – and the small communities of Nanais, Ulchis, Negidals and Udeghes of the Amur region. Most of the northern peoples remained at least partly nomadic until the 1950s.[16]

While the welfare of the Siberian peoples themselves was one consideration in the Soviet Russian plan for settlement, other reasons of state were more potent. These included the organisation of the hunting and herding economy for higher productivity, the introduction of agriculture wherever possible in order to provide food for newly established industrial centres, and, in general, the possibility of utilising the labour of ex-nomads in 'socialist construction'. The exploration of Siberia's natural resources proceeded swiftly during the 1930s, and the imperatives of 'building socialism' made it inevitable that more and more Russian intrusion into native territories would take place, and that the lives of the native peoples would become increasingly subordinated to the industrial development of the Soviet Russian state. As large new enterprises were established under the administration of state industrial trusts, the rather benevolent activities of the Committee of the North on behalf of the native peoples became outmoded and incompatible with the outlook of the Stalinist Communist Party, so that the Committee was abolished in 1935.

Within the economic development of Siberia by the Soviet Russian state in the 1930s the native peoples performed the same functions as they had under the Tsars – subserving the activities of the Russians as pathfinders, carters and labourers, and providing profit for their masters by hunting and trapping fur-bearing animals. As the new industrial enterprises of the five-year plans required modern machinery and equipment from abroad, all products which could be used for barter on world markets were of great importance to the government. Animal skins were worth millions of roubles to the state, but the cost to the wild-life of the North was enormous. In the

---

[16] Gurvich, *Osushchestvleniye*, p. 287; *Istoriya Sibiri*, vol. IV, pp. 296, 443–4, 448, 452, 466; Ye. Kantor, 'Problema osedaniya malykh narodov Severa', *Sovetskiy Sever*, 1934, no. 3–4, pp. 3–9; *Narody Sibiri*, pp. 536–7, 567, 600, 629, 894–5, 925–6; Sergeyev, *Nekapitalisticheskiy put*, p. 457.

period 1930–5 between 14 and 16 million squirrels were killed in the Soviet Union each year; while about 2,000 sables could still be trapped annually in the few districts of Eastern Siberia where they still existed. The efforts made in the 1920s to control hunting and allow numbers of animals to increase again were continued in the next decade. Positive measures to this end included the creation of a sable reserve in the Barguzin region of the Buryat ASSR, so that surplus stock from its increasing sable population could be used for re-stocking other regions where sable had been exterminated. As an alternative to trapping, the breeding of such animals as silver fox in cages began in 1928 in fur-farms near Moscow, Arkhangelsk and Tyumen, and by the late 1930s there were many such establishments, the profitability of which was increased by the introduction of American mink.[17]

THE TURKIC PEOPLES OF WESTERN SIBERIA

The Siberian community least capable of standing out against collectivisation were the Turkic-speaking peoples of south-western Siberia – the Tobolsk, Tyumen, Tara and Baraba Tatars, and the Altai-Yenisey Turks, who had been exposed to increasing pressure by agricultural settlers from European Russia since the nineteenth century.

When the order for mass collectivisation came from Moscow in January 1930, the West Siberian Tatars found themselves – like the Bashkirs and northern Kazaks – in the zone of total collectivisation, and were swept up in the campaign as ruthlessly as the farmers of Russian, Ukrainian and other origins who lived in the south Siberian steppe. As a result, by the end of 1931 some three-quarters of the farms in the region had undergone collectivisation, resulting in farms with either exclusively Tatar or mixed Tatar and Russian membership. The most backward communities – those of the marshy region west of Tobolsk, and the bleak Baraba steppe – continued to eke out a living with fishing and hunting. From the 1920s the traditional culture of the Siberian Tatars changed greatly under the impact of schools and Soviet Russian ideology, and Islamic beliefs were gradually ousted. Tatar women began to play a greater public role, many of them being trained as teachers at the colleges for Tatars in Tobolsk, Tyumen and Tomsk. An important factor in the spread of literacy among the West Siberian Tatars was their use of Kazan Tatar as their literary language. In a region of isolated small communities lacking a single national territory and speaking several dialects, this lingua franca helped to create a sense of cultural unity shared with the Tatars of Kazan and distinct from that of the Russians. The first

---

[17] *Bolshaya Sovetskaya entsiklopediya*, 3rd edn, vol. IX, p. 430; vol. XXI, p. 252; A. Baykov, *Soviet Foreign Trade*, Princeton, 1946, pp. 17–18, 58, 65–6; *Istoriya Sibiri*, vol. IV, pp. 296, 448, 471; Kantor, 'Problema osedaniya', pp. 3–4, 8; Kolarz, *The Peoples*, pp. 67, 69; *Narody Sibiri*, pp. 250, 314–15, 596, 634, 734–5; Popova, *Eveny*, p. 232.

teachers in Siberian Tatar schools were from Kazan, as were the textbooks, and the Kazan Tatar language was also used for the newspaper *Azat Seber* (Free Siberia), published from 1931 onward. In any case this linguistic and cultural influence was already strong, as considerable numbers of Tatar peasants from the Volga had emigrated to the east during the nineteenth century and the beginning of the twentieth, and many of these had settled in Western Siberia.[18]

The native clans of the Minusinsk steppe, officially known as Khakas since 1923, were still partly nomadic up to the time of collectivisation. By the end of 1932 some 72 per cent of Khakas people had been engulfed by this process, and five years later 93 per cent were gathered into collectives and the nomads settled in villages of wooden houses. This social revolution was carried out with the usual coercion and arbitrariness and resulted in the slaughter of many cattle. Although the territory of the Khakas people had been upgraded to a 'National Province' in 1930, the reality of their dwindling presence in it (from 51 per cent in 1926 to 28 per cent in 1932) was reflected in the reversion of the name of its 'capital' from Khakassk to the neutral river name Abakan. At the same time the traditional culture of the Khakases was being eroded, as the influence of Soviet Russian education spread. An important positive factor in this was the creation of a written language for this formerly illiterate people. This went through three stages: in 1924 the first Khakas-language schoolbooks were printed in the Russian alphabet, but five years later this was dropped in the general movement to adopt the Roman alphabet for the new literary languages of the USSR, and in 1939 the reverse movement took place. By then the beginnings of a Khakas literature in the native language had been made. However, any embers of a Khakas nationalist movement were stamped out in 1935–6, when a project for a Turkic Soviet republic, uniting Khakases, Altaians and Kazaks, was discovered by the OGPU, and its creators punished. During the 1930s the Khakas community increased from some 46,000 to 53,000.[19]

The neighbours of the Khakas to the west, the Shor highlanders (who numbered about 13,000 in 1926) had the misfortune to live in a land rich in coal and iron ore which were of extreme importance to Soviet Russia for the development of the Kuznetsk industrial complex in the 1930s. Although the Shors were chiefly poor hunters living in the taiga, during and after the Russian Civil War they were obliged to confront Russian racism with their own nationalism. A Shor National District was recognised in 1925, but in it the Shors themselves constituted only 39 per cent of the total population,

[18] Gushchin, *Sibirskaya derevnya*, pp. 289, 291, 307; *Istoriya Sibiri*, vol. IV, pp. 287, 304–5; *Narody Sibiri*, pp. 476–8, 485–6, 488–9; Ponomarev, *Istoriya SSSR*, vol. VIII, map pp. 598–9; Tumasheva, *Dialekty sibirskikh tatar*, pp. 18–19, 273–4.
[19] *Istoriya Sibiri*, vol. IV, pp. 435, 441–2, 450, 452; Kolarz, *The Peoples*, p. 177; *Narody Sibiri*, pp. 414–16.

along with a long-established Russian colony. In 1929 a modified Roman alphabet was created for writing the Shor language, in which school-books and a newspaper *Kyzyl Shor* (Red Shor) were printed, and some native poets and prose writers appeared. However, by 1938, when the Roman alphabet was replaced by the Russian one, the cause of an independent Shor literary culture was practically lost. The exploitation of the coal resources of the Kuznetsk Basin was one of the major developments of the first two five-year plans (the main city of the region, Kuznetsk, was renamed Stalinsk in 1932) and this brought an influx of tens of thousands of workers from European Russia. As a result, by 1938 the Shors were in a minority of one to seven in their own land. In conformity with the overriding needs of the Soviet Russian state, the Kuzbass region was restructured in 1939 and the Shor National District abolished. Thereafter the number of Shors remained very stable, at about 16,000, while the number of immigrants from Russia continued to grow. One result of the Shors' reduction to the status of a small minority in their own land was that for written purposes their language fell into disuse, and Russian, or sometimes Khakas, was used instead.[20]

For the third large Turkic community in the Ob–Yenisey region, the Altaians, the late 1920s and 1930s was a time of turmoil. Although there were fewer Altaians than Khakases in 1926 (28,000 as compared with 46,000) the Altaians occupied a more compact and isolated territory and had a greater sense of national identity. From their mountainous autonomous province of Oirotia they looked down over the Kulunda steppe and Kuznetsk uplands – now dominated by Russian agriculture and industry – and still cherished their dream of a Turkic nomadic khanate independent of Russia. Consequently the Russian Communist Party's campaign of enforced collectivisation, denomadisation and destruction of the clan system met with intense and prolonged opposition. The national religious cult of 'Burkhanism', with its songs about 'Russian communists with their deceitful eyes', still had considerable influence and was therefore subjected to an intensive campaign to force the priests of the faith (called *yarlyks*) to renounce their calling, with the alternative of arrest and 'corrective labour'. As in all parts of the Soviet Union, the communists exploited the younger generation for the aggravation of conflicts within the community, organising members of the Young Communist League to persuade older men to shear off the pigtail which was the symbol of being a true Oirot. The Communist Party's collectivisation and anti-'kulak' operation in the Altai was vicious, with much use of force, deportation and false promises to induce both Russian peasants and Altaian semi-nomadic cattle-herders to form communes. Between 1929 and 1932 almost 56 per cent of all cattle in the Altai had been destroyed by their owners as a protest against collectivisation, while some Altaian groups joined

[20] A. Chudoyakov, 'Tragediya Shorii', *Sibirskiye ogni*, 1989, no. 8, p. 164; *Narody Sibiri*, pp. 518–19, 526–7; *Yazyki narodov SSSR*, vol. II, p. 467.

the Kazaks in migrating with their herds into Chinese Sinkiang. Those Altaians who were arbitrarily exiled 400 miles north to the Chulym taiga suffered not only the common hardships of deportation and concentration-camp life but also victimisation because of their ignorance of the Russian language and Russian ways.

The Soviet Russian attack on Oirot nationalism and clan institutions was renewed in 1933, when the Burkhan religion was prohibited (as, supposedly, a creation of the Chinese) and three years later the leaders of the Oirot Communist Party were dismissed and, presumably, imprisoned. By then the economic and social subjection of the Altaian people to Moscow had been largely achieved, with 87.4 per cent of farms collectivised, and herds partly built up again to 61 per cent of pre-collectivisation numbers.[21]

To the east of the Altai–Yenisey region only one other small Turkic community lived in the Sayan region of the Soviet Union (apart from the semi-independent republic of Tannu-Tuva). These were the Tofalar or Karagases – 400 nomadic hunters and reindeer-herders of the taiga, who were closely akin to the Toja tribe of Tuva. Having been thoroughly cowed, not only by the Russian state's exaction of *yasak*, but also by traders known as 'karagasniks' who specialised in exploiting them systematically, the Tofalar were very poor by the time of the Revolution. They were, moreover, so habituated to submissiveness towards their Russian masters that when *yasak* was abolished by the Bolsheviks, they could not believe this and continued to bring furs to the new Russian officials at the local soviet, until the latter persuaded them that this was no longer required. Nevertheless their potential value to the Soviet Russian state as producers of fur was not neglected, and they were brought into the network of soviets and cooperatives. The latter provided the means for the 'reconstruction of the Tofalars' economy' – which meant primarily the organisation of hunting, but also help in the restoration of their sadly depleted reindeer herds. Such a small community had little choice but to accept what the Russians presented to them, so that they began to forsake their skin or bark-covered wigwams for wooden huts with Russian stoves as early as 1927, and had become entirely settled within five years. Under these new conditions they took to cattle-rearing and the cultivation of hay, potatoes and vegetables under the instruction of their Russian neighbours. The collectivisation of the Tofalar was carried out at the same time, so that 90 per cent of them were gathered into three collective farms by 1932. At that time they formed a single native soviet for the Tofalar National District, the headquarters of which was the village of Alygjer on the northern side of the Eastern Sayan mountains. While they benefited from

---

[21] Chichlo, 'La Collectivisation', pp. 297–8; Danilin, 'Burkhanizm', pp. 75, 87–90; Gushchin, *Sibirskaya derevnya*, pp. 296–7, 428–9; *Istoriya Sibiri*, vol. IV, pp. 335, 444, 450, 453; Kolarz, *The Peoples*, pp. 173–5; *Narody Sibiri*, pp. 360, 366–7; Novokshonov, 'Krestyanskaya ssylka', p. 112; Stepichev, *Pobeda*, p. 499.

various aspects of Russian material culture, such as medical service and a boarding school, the Tofalar were so remote from large centres of population in the 1930s that they preserved their (unwritten) language to a high degree.[22]

THE SELKUPS AND KETS

North of the broad belt of Russian colonisation in Western Siberia, the marshy forests stretching towards the Arctic Circle were still in 1930 a very sparsely populated land where Russians were few and far between except in the valleys of the big rivers, and where the aboriginal peoples still pursued their primitive occupations of hunting, fishing and reindeer-herding.

Just north of the Russian cities of Novosibirsk and Tomsk began the country of the Selkups. One of their two communities inhabited the valley of the Taz near the Arctic Circle, while the territory of the more southerly group lay to both sides of the Ob in the valleys of its tributaries. Through prolonged contact with the Russians these southern Selkups were already largely assimilated to them in their way of life. In their Ob homeland the Selkups numbered only about 4,000, while the 'Old Russian' colonials who lived there amounted to some 119,000. The main effect of the first stages of collectivisation upon these 'earth-people' (*chumyl-kup*) or 'taiga people' (*shösh-kum*) as the southern Selkups called themselves, was a sudden, massive inundation of their land by new Russian settlers. These were 195,000 peasants from southern Siberia and European Russia and the Ukraine, whom the Communist Party had condemned as 'kulaks' to be deported to 'remote districts'. That the remote districts chosen for these 'special settlers' – the valley of the Ob and its tributaries the Ket, Tym, Chunya, Parabel and Vasyugan – happened to be the home of the Selkups or their Khanty neighbours, was irrelevant to the Soviet Russian authorities. Like tsarist officials, they felt no need to consult the wishes of indigenous people before designating an expanse of 'empty' land as a place of exile, and parcelling it out for settlement. To the Russians this region with its old Russian centre of Narym (the very name of which in the Khanty language means 'marsh') was notorious as a god-forsaken place to which the tsarist authorities in their day had consigned political prisoners. The mass of new political exiles in the 1930s – stripped of all their possessions apart from the barest essentials and provided with a minimum of money, provisions, seed-corn and livestock – had to build a new life from nothing in this land, 50 per cent of which was marsh. This meant in the first place felling trees, clearing ground and somehow building a log-cabin or other shelter before the onset of a harsh

---

[22] *Istoriya Sibiri*, vol. IV, p. 469; Kantor, 'Problema osedaniya', p. 5; *Narody Sibiri*, pp. 530, 535–8; Sergeyev, *Nekapitalisticheskiy put*, p. 235.

winter. In fact many of the deported families perished, and in 1932, after two winters, many of the survivors still had only temporary dwellings.[23]

As Narym region was only marginally suitable for agriculture, the new Russian exile colony had to support itself chiefly by hunting, fishing and timber-felling. This was in conformity with the intention of the Communist Party leadership that 'kulaks' should be dumped on the worst land. In fact, the reason for the choice of the Narym region for the settlement of exiles seems to have been the Communist Party's decision to exploit its natural resources, and the importation of dispossessed farmers provided some of the labour needed for this purpose. The principal objective at this time was the forest timber of the Ob basin and the creation of the chemical industry based upon it. For the sake of this development of the Soviet Russian economy the Committee of the North had to modify its attitude towards the native people. In the words of a contemporary report,

Only two or three years ago it seemed ... perfectly right and obvious that territory which had been used by the native population from time immemorial should be allotted to them for their practical needs, and that not only should unauthorised settlers be kept out of it, but that it should be excluded from the stock of land available for planned colonization.

Now that the exploitation and industrialisation of the North had become a priority, however, 'It would be quite impermissible to isolate the native from the common life of the country, to leave him in an artificial solitude using territory on the fantastic scale of the North so that he could roam with his picturesquely primitive trap as he did hundreds of years ago.'[24] It was essential to create more Russian settlements in order to supply the new extractive industries with labour, agricultural produce and fish, and those natives who were unable or unwilling to adapt themselves to the new life would have to move away to other territory where they could continue to pursue their traditional way of life. By 1938 some 488 square miles of virgin forest in Narym district had been cleared for settlements and farms, and the most populous village, Kolpashevo, was upgraded to the status of a town.

Inevitably the life of the Narym Selkups was profoundly affected by this invasion of their territory, which coincided with the beginning of their own subjection to the collectivisation and denomadisation policies of the Soviet Russian government. At the same time the valley of the river Tym was designated as the Selkup National District, to which those living further south were moved. While it was piously asserted that such resettlement must be carefully planned in order to avoid harming the life of the natives, it

---

[23] Gushchin, *Sibirskaya derevnya*, pp. 422, 440, 448–51; Sapozhnikov, 'Khozhdeniye po Yeniseyu', pp. 48–9.
[24] L.N. Dobrova-Yadrintseva, 'Osvoyenie severnykh okrain', *Sovetskiy Sever*, 1930, no. 5, pp. 17–18.

appears that the arbitrary actions of the Soviet colonial authorities in Narym district in 1930 in fact had a disastrous effect on the Selkups and stirred them up to more violent opposition than had been anticipated. Secondary consequences of greater Russian penetration into Selkup territory included the violation of two of their fundamental taboos: the indiscriminate killing of bears (which were finding the new settlers' cattle a convenient prey) and the commercial cropping of cedar-pine nuts, which the Selkups held sacred. Gross disruption of their established life caused many of the southern Selkups to seek homes elsewhere in a series of migrations spread over twenty years. To the surprise of the Russians, even Selkups who appeared to be completely Russified in language and way of life joined in this exodus, demonstrating the persistence of their awareness of national identity and their dislike of Russians. The general direction of flight was from more southerly locations in the valleys of the Bachkara, Chaya, Kenga and Parabel, as well as the Ob itself, 'which offered the best soil for Russian farmers', northward into the valleys of the Ket and Tym. From there some even made the long journey north to swell the previously small Selkup community in the Taz basin where, because of remoteness from Russian settlements, there was more chance of preserving their own language and way of life. Even here, however, Soviet Russian agents were able to penetrate the marshy forests to reach the small Selkup groups scattered along the tributaries of the Taz, and to identify a few native 'kulaks'. These were men whose reindeer herds at the beginning of the collectivisation campaign were counted only in hundreds, but who enjoyed a certain authority among their compatriots because of their trading activities and obligation of assistance to members of their clan. It may be assumed that the northern Selkups were forced into the net of collectivisation along with their neighbours the forest Nenets. No national area was designated for them, but they were included in the large Yamal Nenets National Region, with a Soviet administrative centre bearing the Russian name Krasnoselkup (Red Selkup).[25]

The even smaller ethnic community of Kets – some 1,200 in 1926 – lived as neighbours of the Selkups and to some extent intermingled with them, in the valley of the middle and lower Yenisey. Here too the natives continued to distrust the Russians, since even the peasants, having as a rule little skill as hunters, had not entirely abandoned their colonial practice of exploiting the Kets and other natives. Moreover, the official Soviet fur-trading agencies – Sibtorg (Siberian Trade Agency), Vsekokhotsoyuz (All-Union Cooperative Hunting Union) and others, were, like seventeenth-century *voyevodas*,

[25] *Bolshaya Sovetskaya entsiklopediya*, 3rd edn, vol. XVII, p. 291; Davies, *Industrialisation*, I, pp. 233–4; *Entsiklopedicheskiy slovar*, vol. XXXIII, p. 487; Gurvich, *Etnicheskaya istoriya*, pp. 119–22; *Istoriya Sibiri*, vol. IV, pp. 340, 384, 465, 468; Kalesnik, ed., *Zapadnaya Sibir*, pp. 230–6; *Narody Sibiri*, pp. 669, 681–6; V. Skalon, 'V tundre Verkhnego Taza', *Sovetskiy Sever*, 1930, no. 3, pp. 129–39; Sokolova, *Puteshestviye v Yugru*, pp. 137–8; Stepichev, *Pobeda*, pp. 460, 470–1; Vdovin, *Priroda i chelovek*, p. 117.

frequently in conflict over their sole purpose – to seize immediate advantage from the forest without concern for conservation or the life of the native people. Shamanism was very strong among the Kets, providing, along with the exogamic clan system, a cohesive force in a community which lacked any chiefs or class divisions. Since the numerous shamans did not constitute a professional élite, but were ordinary members of many families, working normally as hunters and fishers, it was unconvincing to attribute any exploitational role to them. Nevertheless, the fact that the Kets respected their shamans made them the enemies of the Russian Communist Party. In 1928, for instance, the first attempt to organise a Ket collective fishing enterprise on the Yenisey was frustrated by a shaman's unfavourable augury: warned by him that spirits sent by a Samoyed shaman to the fishing grounds would make them ill, the men returned the fishing equipment to the Soviet cooperative and went back to their camp. In such cases the Russian authorities employed various means, ranging from persuasion to the impounding or destruction of the shamans' costumes and drums, in an attempt to overcome resistance to their innovations. On the other hand, the Communist Party's campaign against nomadism may have been to some extent welcomed by the Kets, who are said to have acknowledged the benefits of fixed dwellings for their families during the winter hunting season when, without reindeer, they had to traverse long distances on skis. By 1938 about one quarter of the Kets had settled in hunting and fishing collectives. Literacy also made some progress among the Kets, 13 per cent of whom had learned to read and write by 1936. However, as in the case of the southern Selkups, the small numbers of the Kets militated against the creation of a written language, and Russian became the medium of education and official communication.[26]

THE KHANTY AND MANSI PEOPLES

In 1930 the Khantys lived scattered over a huge territory extending about 150 miles to either side of the river Ob, and stretching westward over 600 miles from the source of the Vakh to the Irtysh. West of the Ob and Irtysh the territory of the Mansis stretched for a further 200 miles towards the Ural mountains. Despite the presence of a considerable Russian population in the lower Ob valley, particularly around the old towns of Tobolsk and Berezov, the Revolution, Civil War, and industrial developments of the 1930s left much of this region of forests and marshes almost untouched, and, considering its relatively westerly location, it remained remarkably remote and primeval. For instance, the Vakh river Khantys did not learn of the Bolshevik

---

[26] Alekseyenko, ed., *Ketskiy sbornik*, p. 86; Gurvich, *Osushchestvleniye*, pp. 288, 291–2; A.K. Lvov, 'Ekspeditsiya Pushnogostorga i Sibtorga v Yeloguyskiy rayon Turukhanskogo kraya', *Sovetskiy Sever*, 1930, no. 2, pp. 102–10; *Narody Sibiri*, pp. 685, 687, 698–700; Suslov, 'Shamanstvo', pp. 96–7; *Yazyki narodov SSSR*, vol. III, pp. 396, 415; vol. V, p. 453.

take-over until 1927, and among the Mansis the bear-feast with all its rituals continued to be celebrated up to the late 1930s. Even twenty-five years later, most of the Khantys still lived in birch-bark tents, and the administrative centre of their National Region, Khanty-Mansiysk, could be reached from the nearest city only by paddle-steamer or seaplane.

In 1926 there were about 17,700 Khantys and 6,000 Mansis. By then the Soviet Russian authorities had begun the organisation of cooperatives in the more accessible regions, and eventually cultural bases of the Committee of the North were established on the Kazym and Sosva. Collectivisation was carried out most quickly among the Khanty–Mansis on the lower Ob and Irtysh, who had already been drawn into commercial fisheries before 1917. Away from the banks of the great rivers, the scattered communities in the depths of the forest were less easily absorbed into the Soviet Russian system, and those units which were created for collective hunting and fishing remained very small until the late 1930s. For another two decades indeed, Soviet industrialisation had little or no impact upon the natural environment of the middle Ob, and the semi-nomadic life of the forest Khantys went on as before with minimal change. Among the most northerly Khantys, who were partly engaged in reindeer-herding, collectivisation presented greater problems. Here exploitation by 'kulaks', in the sense of prosperous herd-owners, was to some extent a reality, and class conflict could be stimulated by the communists. Such native leaders as there were resisted the under-mining of the clan system and tried to prevent the formation of communal herds by dividing their herds and often by mass slaughter of deer as a sacrifice to the spirits. Despite such obstacles, it is claimed that over half of the Khanty–Mansis were collectivised within the first five years of the campaign, and sovietisation had gone far enough to allow the communist authorities to proceed to the next stage: persuading the Khanty–Mansis to settle in collective farms in which the inhabitants of several small forest bands would be grouped together.

As a result of being drawn into the commercial relations of the Soviet Russian economy and being trained to work in the interests of the state rather than their own community, the Khanty–Mansi rapidly began to lose the remaining features of their traditional folk life. Their beautifully, but laboriously, fashioned garments with rich embroidery were replaced by mass-produced Russian clothing, and domestic vessels formed from wood and bark gave way to metal or ceramic kitchen ware. In the eyes of the Communist Party and its native converts the progress which came in the form of kerosene lamps (and later electricity), powered transport, personal hygiene and medical attention, was the more successful the more rapidly and irredeemably it consigned to oblivion all relics of the 'primitive' past. In order to further the 'enlightenment' of the Khanty–Mansi people it was essential to provide books, newspapers and other forms of information and propaganda, which they could read in their own languages. As with other peoples of Siberia, the creation of written languages passed through successive phases of the Roman alphabet (1931) then the Russian alphabet (1937). However, the languages of the Khantys and Mansis presented particularly great problems, since they varied a great deal in different districts. With about seven dialects of Khanty, and four of Mansi, a single standard language could not be formulated, and eventually no less than five forms of the Khanty language were developed.[27]

THE NENETS, NGANASANS AND DOLGANS

The vast arctic and sub-arctic zone on both sides of the Urals, inhabited by some 20,000 Samoyed people (Nenets, Enets and Nganasan) and 1,450 Dolgans, was one of the most difficult regions for the Soviet Russians to subordinate to their political-economic system. The first Nenets reindeer-herding collective was formed in 1929 in the European tundra at the mouth of the Pechora, at the same time as two Nenets national regions were designated – one west of the Urals and the other to the east, including the Yamal peninsula. Although the Soviet Russian authorities here adopted a policy of swift mass collectivisation in January 1930, this was quite unrealistic. In the European tundra herd-owners found a temporary respite in migration east of the Urals or north into Yamal, or herds could be saved by being split up and distributed among sons and other dependants. As collective herds were formed by commandeering reindeer from big herds, the independent Nenets proprietors retaliated by dispersing their herds or, as a last desperate resort, slaughtering their own deer. Life in the tundra could be violent, and the commandeering of reindeer by Soviet Russian agents assisted by poor clansmen led to more than one murder. Because of these difficulties, the pace of collectivisation in the Nenets regions was relatively slow. In the European tundra it rose to about 86 per cent in 1937. By then, in addition to collectives (*kolkhozy*), several state reindeer farms (*sovkhozy*) had been formed in the European tundra with a total of some 25,000 animals. In the Yamal National Region where some 'rich' Nenets, possessing herds of several thousand head, held out against the collectivisation campaign, only 8.5 per cent of families were collectivised in 1932, but this number rose to 69 per cent in 1937. The northern part of Yamal peninsula was the last refuge of the independent Nenets herd-owners, who resisted so obstinately that in 1936 there was still not a single collective.

[27] I.I. Avdeyev, 'Dramaticheskiye predstavleniya na medvezhyem prazdnike u mansi', *Sovetskiy Sever*, 1935, no. 3–4, p. 169; Chichlo, 'La Collectivisation', p. 296; Gurvich, *Etnokulturnye protsessy*, p. 94; *Istoriya Sibiri*, vol. IV, pp. 295, 469; *Narody Sibiri*, pp. 570–607; Sergeyev, *Nekapitalisticheskiy put*, pp. 238, 352n., 354–7, 359; Sokolova, *Puteshestviye v Yugru*, pp. 9, 17; *Yazyki narodov SSSR*, vol. III, pp. 320–1, 338–9, 343, 359.

Not only was it impossible to carry out the collectivisation of the Nenets swiftly, but little could be done to make them settle in permanent homes. Although some collectives had centres with a few houses, practically all the Nenets continued to nomadise, using reindeer-skin covered teepees. By 1939 the spread of education and medical services had no doubt alleviated to some extent the hardships and diseases associated with tent life, but continuing nomadism inevitably meant the use of reindeer-skin clothing, with the attendant lack of personal hygiene. Although health care was hindered by the shamans, who predicted evil for those who consulted Russian doctors, their influence was gradually overcome as the Nenets came to recognise the benefits of European medicine.

From the point of view of the Soviet Russian authorities, one of the benefits of the collectivisation of the reindeer-herding Nenets was that it 'freed labour' for use in other work – principally fishing. The wide waters of the Ob and its estuary offered great scope for the development of commercial fisheries, and several fish-processing and canning factories were established in Obdorsk, which in 1933 was given the Nenets name Salekhard (Cape-town). At the same time the European Nenets Region was also given a new administrative centre, Naryan-Mar (Red town), where fish and meat-processing factories were founded. Both of these towns had colleges for training young Nenets to become teachers and veterinary surgeons, after attending local schools in which Nenets was the language of instruction. The mid-1930s was the time when responsibility for the development of the whole of the Far North was handed over to the Chief Administration of the Northern Sea Route (*Glavsevmorputi*), which, by establishing new seaports and regular voyages, not only facilitated the extraction of raw materials, such as fur, fish and minerals, but also increased the supply of manufactured goods to the native peoples.[28]

If the Yamal Nenets Region was remote from Russian administrative centres, the nomadic communities of Taimyr peninsula were even more isolated, since the only Russian settlement of any size, Dudinka, was itself over 1,200 miles from the provincial capital, Krasnoyarsk. Some of the native inhabitants of Taimyr were Samoyeds – Nenets and their eastern cousins the Enets and Nganasan – who together numbered no more than 1,250 souls in 1926. To the south of these lived the Dolgans, a somewhat larger group of about 1,445 people. All of these communities preserved the archaic way of life of tundra nomadism almost unaltered during the first decades of the twentieth century. However, the small band of zealous com-

---

[28] Brodnev, 'Ot rodovogo stroya k sotsializmu', pp. 97–104; Gurvich, *Osushchestvleniye*, p. 31; *Istoriya Sibiri*, vol. IV, pp. 469, 471; Khomich, *Nentsy*, pp. 236–8, 241–3, 284–8, 312; *Narody Sibiri*, pp. 559n., 595, 629–47; P.N. Orlovskiy, 'Kollektivizatsiya na Severe', *Sovetskiy Sever*, 1930, no. 1, pp. 48–57; Sergeyev, *Nekapitalisticheskiy put*, pp. 300, 352–5, 358; Sokolova, *Puteshestviye v Yugru*, pp. 110–11.

munists who administered the Taimyr National Region in the 1920s carried Soviet influence as far as possible, and in 1930, despite the primitive level of the native peoples, the Taimyr tundra was declared a region of mass collectivisation. The Nganasan hunters resisted this order strongly and unanimously, since their society was governed by ways of primitive communism, and no division into rich and poor classes existed. They were, moreover, practically independent of the Russian commercial network, never having been subject to *yasak*. The Nganasans also had the advantage of living in an Arctic wilderness which in the 1930s was all but inaccessible to the Soviet Russian authorities, with the result that they had no soviets whatever before 1931. Attempts by communist missionaries to introduce the Nganasans to literacy and hygiene were also repulsed successfully until 1936, when a young Russian woman went to share the life of one group of nomads for three years, broke through their prejudices and set them on the path of assimilation to Soviet Russian culture.

The southern neighbours of the Nganasans – the Yakut-speaking Dolgans, were in a more difficult situation, since their territory began within seventy-five miles of Dudinka, while its eastern extremity, beyond the Khatanga, was accessible from Yakutia. As a result of their contact with the Russians, the Dolgans relied to a considerable extent upon fur-trapping. The same foreign influence had led to some degree of social stratification among the Dolgans, the reindeerless poor being dependent upon the owners of large herds. The latter were able to supplement their wealth by hiring out their reindeer to the Russians for the transportation of goods from Dudinka on the Yenisey to Popigai on the Anabar, 500 miles to the east. Despite their relative remoteness, the Dolgans, after a period of strife during which at least one chairman of a nomadic soviet was killed, are said to have been completely collectivised by 1938 – in contrast with the Nganasans, whose primitive deer-hunting life appears to have been almost unaffected by the Soviet Russian régime for at least another ten years after this.[29]

The most direct incursion of Soviet Russians into the Taimyr region during the early 1930s came with the creation of new settlements. Under the auspices of *Glavsevmorputi* several polar weather-stations were established, in particular Dikson at the northernmost point of the Yenisey estuary, and the large port of Igarka upriver from Dudinka, thus turning the lower Yenisey into a busy shipping lane. Even more fateful was the development of non-ferrous ore-mining east of Dudinka, which led to the construction of the new Russian city of Norilsk as an important nickel-processing centre. According to a historian of the Soviet North:

[29] Gurvich, *Osushchestvleniye*, pp. 247–9, 257; Hajdu, *Finno-Ugrian*, pp. 228–9; A. Khazanovich, *Druzya moi Nganasany: iz Taymyrskikh dnevnikov*, Moscow, 1986; *Narody Sibiri*, pp. 648, 657, 661, 742, 754–5; Sergeyev, *Nekapitalisticheskiy put*, pp. 238, 345, 353, 358.

The industrial enterprises of the Far North are destined to serve as models guiding the economic life of the peoples of the North towards socialist reconstruction; they must concern themselves not only with their own specifically industrial aims, but must use all means at their disposal to help the advancement and transformation of the native economy, contributing to the training of natives to fill administrative posts, and their involvement in industrial production, while avoiding anything which might in the slightest degree prejudice the interests of the local population.[30]

In fact an industrial development such as Norilsk was of economic importance only to the Soviet Russians, and could serve the native people only as an illustration of Russian ruthlessness, since it was one of the big construction and mining projects carried out by the forced labour of people arrested by the Soviet People's Commissariat of Internal Affairs (NKVD). From 1935 until the early 1950s, thousands of prisoners from all parts of the Soviet Union were sent to the concentration camps of Siblag near Norilsk, to labour in appalling conditions. One effect of Russian activity around the Yenisey estuary was that Nganasans who had formerly come to the west coast of Taimyr for summer grazing ceased to do this. Similarly the Enets families who had lived near the coast now moved away towards the interior of the peninsula, where they lived in close contact with the Nganasans.[31]

THE EWENKI TUNGUS

How was it possible to collectivise such a widely scattered people as the Ewenki Tungus? In 1926 there were about 38,000 of them living in small groups of families, dispersed over a discontinuous territory 1,800 miles in east–west extension and 1,000 miles from north to south. The mainstay of existence for most of them was subsistence fishing and commercial hunting – individually providing furs to trade at the government stores for manufactured goods. Differences in wealth were minimal, being based only on ownership of reindeer which, while essential for transport, were a secondary element in the livelihood of an Ewenki household. Any grouping of Ewenki households already functioned as a kind of cooperative, since grazing, fishing and hunting had involved a certain amount of collective activity long before the Soviet régime came into existence. The old institutions of mutual aid and *nimat* also continued to operate, providing support for families who had lost their breadwinners.

Soviet Russian collectivisation demanded 'kulaks' to be victimised, but in Ewenki society 'nobody had a clear idea which households were to be

---

[30] Sergeyev, *Nekapitalisticheskiy put*, p. 402.
[31] Armstrong, *Russian Settlement*, pp. 129, 150, 152; Conquest, *The Great Terror*, pp. 258–65, 444, 469, 491; Gurvich, *Etnokulturnye protsessy*, p. 86; *Istoriya Sibiri*, vol. IV, pp. 323, 374, 421–2; vol. V, pp. 26, 83; Solzhenitsyn, *Gulag Archipelago*, vol. II, pp. 131, 223, 480, 488, 517, 531; vol. III, pp. 8–10.

designated as "kulak" and which should be put in the category of "prosperous" '. In fact the obligatory Marxist concept of 'exploitation' was mythi-
cal in this context, as one Ewenki representative protested at a congress of
the Committee of the North in 1931: 'It's very difficult to classify the native
as "poor", "middling", or "kulak" ... One man may have [only] ten to
fifteen reindeer, but in fact he's richer than another who has lots of deer.'[32]
The Russian Communist Party of 1929–30 was indifferent to such facts, and
complacently invoked the specious theoretical criterion that the use of hired
labour was in itself a form of exploitation. In vain might members of the
Committee of the North, who knew something about the living conditions of
the Ewenkis, protest that the very nature of the northern environment and
mixed economy constantly created the necessity for even quite poor families
to employ labour, because of illness or lack of able-bodied members to cope
with urgent tasks. Political dogma simply required the collectivisation of
people and the transformation of their way of life in accordance with Lenin's
dictates.

When the collectivisation campaign began in Central Siberia it was
imposed on the Ewenkis in the arbitrary manner already described (p. 295).
Such a lack of realism on the part of Communist Party zealots is also
illustrated in the case of the Ewenkis of the Bureya tributary of the Amur,
where it was decreed that the collective farm would be agricultural, despite
two fundamental facts: the local Ewenkis were exclusively nomadic hunters
and fishers with no experience of farming, and in any case this permafrost
region of forest was unsuitable for agriculture. However, the Soviet Russian
officials in Central and Eastern Siberia were few and inexperienced, and
lacked native collaborators for the implementation of their policies, so that
the Ewenkis appear to have succeeded in working out ways of coping with
enforced collectivisation and avoiding its worst results, at least in the first few
years. The time-honoured expedient of migration out of troubled areas was
tried by some, such as those of the Ilimpeya in Central Siberia, who moved
away to Yakutia.

Clan loyalties were a powerful force in the early 1930s, many Ewenki
collectives being formed exclusively of members of one or another clan, such
as the Yastrikovs on the Chunya who excluded from their collective anyone
not bearing this surname. This was the reason why a large number of small
collective units were created at first. In fact it appears that up to 1933 the
seven collectives, uniting 254 households and 10,000 deer, which had been
formed in the Ewenki National Region were collective farms only in name.
They did not organise work collectively, they kept no accounts, and in
general, their members had no idea of the aims of the collective system
which had been imposed on them. It was perhaps at this stage that the

[32] Gurvich, *Osushchestvleniye*, pp. 204–5.

13 An Ewenki hunter of the 1930s exhibits his contribution to the Soviet Russian economy in the form of furs. His open coat, deerskin leggings and boots, and broad skis are typically Ewenki, as is the kerchief worn instead of a fur cap.

Ewenki leaders began to be penalized as 'kulaks'. Certainly in 1934 a large number of Ewenki 'kulaks' (variously reported as 244 or 667) were expelled from collectives in Yakutia – as a result, it appears, of a 'mistake'.[33]

As intolerable as the 'kulaks' in the eyes of Russian communists were the Ewenki shamans, who undoubtedly did wield considerable authority over their clansmen. In Soviet political mythology they have been inflated into a kind of nascent priesthood, gifted not only with considerable intelligence but with enormous cunning which they used in exploiting the labour of their simple compatriots and extorting large payments for healing. Thus the sporadic and rather pathetic attempts they made to maintain clan morale and resistance to collectivisation by performing anti-Russian spirit rites and boycotting schools, are presented as 'the social fusion of the shamanhood and the property-owning clan elite'.[34] The role of the shamans as defenders of Ewenki national identity is typically twisted into an entirely self-interested conspiracy in which they acted as accomplices of the 'kulaks', and it was supposedly this unholy alliance which incited the Ewenkis in some places to set fire to schools and slaughter collective reindeer herds. The tragedy of such actions was that for such small and unorganised native communities the struggle against the imperious power of the Russian Communist Party was hopeless. Once the unsophisticated institution of shamanism was destroyed, the Ewenkis were doomed to assimilation to the Soviet Russian system.

Up to the beginning of the Second World War, however, this fate had not yet overtaken the Ewenkis. It is claimed that 86 per cent of them were collectivised by 1937, despite various manifestations of opposition, and this may be true so far as their hunting, fishing and herding activities were concerned. However, the total social transformation implied by assimilation to the Soviet system could be achieved only when people were tied down to fixed locations, and this could not possibly have happened at this time because of the innate nomadic habits of the Ewenkis. Some of their most southerly collectives to the north and east of Lake Baikal in the Buryat ASSR are said to have possessed established centres with hospitals, schools and other services, and to have started growing vegetables and keeping cattle. Similarly in the Yakut ASSR a beginning was made to the settlement of the Ewenkis, especially in the vicinity of the Aldan gold-field. However, these developments (if true!) do not appear to have been typical of the majority of Ewenki groups, especially in the National Region, where per-suading the Ewenkis to settle was still a topical question forty years later! In these circumstances it is also unlikely that education made much progress among the Ewenkis before the Second World War, and indeed no great

---

[33] Beskorsyy, 'Nekotorye itogi', p. 59; Gurvich, *Osushchestvleniye*, pp. 201–7, 286; *Istoriya Yakutskoy ASSR*, vol. III, pp. 147, 184; *Narody Sibiri*, p. 733; Sergeyev, *Nekapitalistickeskiy put*, pp. 345–6, 355; Shvarev, *Dalniy Vostok*, pp. 425–6.

[34] Anisimov, *Religiya evenkov*, p. 234.

claims are made in this respect. The first (Roman) alphabet for Ewenki was created as early as 1928, and the first school, on the Mountain Tunguska in Central Siberia, opened in 1929. By the middle of the 1930s there were several schools in various parts of Siberia in which instruction was given in the Ewenki language. However, as this has a number of dialects, it was not easy to create a common written language which would be widely accepted, and the future of Ewenki as a literary language was not assured.[35]

YAKUTIA IN THE 1930S

The Yakut ASSR was unique among the regions of Siberia by virtue of its enormous size, the variety of nationalities and economic activities within it, and above all the presence of one dominant cultural community – the Yakut people. As a result, the events of the 1930s combined the experience of primitive reindeer-herders of the North with that of a peasantry and intelligentsia in some ways comparable with those of European Russia. The nucleus of the relatively advanced part of the Yakut nation was concentrated in Yakutsk and the agricultural districts in the basins of the Lena, Aldan, Amga and Vilui, while the periphery of the republic was the home of nomadic Tungus and Yakut reindeer-herders and hunters.

The Yakut republic as originally constituted covered a vast territory, approximately equal to that of the Indian subcontinent. From the administrative capital, Yakutsk, it was 750 miles to the boundary of Transbaikalia in the south-west, 990 miles to Taimyr in the north-west, almost 500 miles to the ridge of the coastal range above Okhotsk, and over 1,200 miles to the farthest point on the river Anadyr in the north-east. In 1931 this territory was reduced by about one third, the biggest area detached being in the north-east. Part of this was allotted to the newly formed Chukchi and Korak National Regions on the grounds of the nationality of its inhabitants. The more southerly part, in the upper basin of the Kolyma river, was similarly attributed to the Okhotsk-Even National Region, but it is probable that the main reason for transferring it from Yakutia to the Far Eastern Territory of the Russian Republic was one of economic strategy. Gold had been discovered in the upper Kolyma region in 1927, and instead of leaving such a valuable asset within the Yakut Republic, a new Soviet industrial trust – known generally as 'Dalstroy' – was created in 1931 to exploit this and other mineral resources of north-eastern Siberia under the direct supervision of Moscow. Even after these reductions the Yakut ASSR,

---

[35] Ibid., pp. 10, 217–18, 232–4; Boyko and Vasilyev, *Sotsialno-professionalnaya mobilnost*, p. 166; *Istoriya Yakutskoy ASSR*, vol. III, pp. 131, 184–5, 188; Khaptayev, *Istoriya Buryatskoy ASSR*, vol. II, p. 437; *Narody Sibiri*, pp. 733, 737; Sergeyev, *Nekapitalisticheskiy put*, p. 352n.; Sokolova, *Puteshestviye v Yugru*, p. 137; Suslov, 'Shamanstvo', pp. 91–4; *Yazyki narodov SSSR*, vol. V, pp. 68–9.

with an area of almost 1,200,000 square miles remained the largest of all the non-Russian administrative units in the USSR, exceeding in size even the Ukraine and Kazakstan.

Within its pre-1931 boundaries, Yakuts had formed 82.6 per cent of the population of the republic (235,926 out of 285,471 in 1926), and this percentage would be considerably increased after the detachment of the minority territories. Russians made up only 10.6 per cent of the population, over half of these being peasants. In view of their own small numbers, the Russians had to rely heavily upon the Yakuts for collaboration in governing the republic and subordinating the minority nationalities to the Soviet system. Agriculture was backward, being based mainly on small settlements of ten or twenty people cultivating scattered strips, although a small number of clans chiefs (*toyons*) held larger estates. Land reforms aimed at dispossessing the rich and redistributing their land to the poor were proclaimed in 1924, but it was not until five years later that the assault on the larger estates was begun in earnest by poor peasants incited by the Communist Party. At this time the political situation in Yakutia was far from quiet, as anti-Soviet rebellions flared up, first in the central Yakut districts in 1927–8, then in the northern districts of Anabar, Bulun and Ust-Yansk, where 'White bandits' are said to have seized power in November 1929. No regular units of the Red Army were located in Yakutia, but local communist militias were quickly formed and the rebellions were suppressed. Subsequently 125 of the participants had their property confiscated, resulting in the distribution of over 28,000 of their reindeer to collective farms.

The process of collectivisation followed a course similar to that in other regions. The way was prepared by various types of cooperative, committees of the poor were organised by the communists, and 'kulaks' were expelled from the local soviets. As in many other places, the ill-informed zeal of Soviet agents in arbitrarily allocating Yakuts to the categories of 'poor', 'middling' and 'kulak' led to much anger, and in some places Russian officials were killed. The rate of collectivisation was no more constant in Yakutia than anywhere else: after a first wave of enrolments early in 1930, the usual disastrous blunders by Communist Party agents led to mass departures from collectives, and the average degree of collectivisation of peasant farms in the Yakut ASSR in 1937 – 70 per cent – does not appear to show any advance on the 1933 position.[36]

In fact there was determined resistance to collectivisation in Yakutia right up to 1937, involving arson, sabotage and slaughter of cattle on a large scale.

---

[36] Armstrong, *Russian Settlement*, p. 132; R. Conquest, *Kolyma: the Arctic Death Camps*, Oxford, 1979, pp. 39, 110; *Istoriya Sibiri*, vol. IV, pp. 299, 440–2, 450, 467; *Istoriya Yakutskoy ASSR*, vol. III, pp. 88–92, 100–1 map, 117, 123–8, 136–9, 147–8, 153–5, 183, 190, 198, 323; Kalesnik, *Dalniy Vostock*, p. 332; Ponomarev, *Istoriya SSSR*, vol. VIII, maps pp. 116–17, 630–1; Zhikharev, *Ocherki istorii*, pp. 139, 149, 151, 159, 180–1.

One of the most violent incidents occurred in the central Yakut district of Kangalassy, where the collective farm chairman and manager were killed and the deputy chairman of the local soviet was wounded. Such actions were carried out in retaliation for the threats and violence frequently employed by communist activists in order to achieve a high degree of collectivisation in a short time, and for their desire to communise every aspect of peasants' lives. For instance, at Ust-Aldan a gang organised by the Communist Party set about destroying the old Yakut family dwellings because all members of the new commune were to share a single large hostel.

It should be noted, as an example of the way in which sovietisation among the non-Russian peoples was brought about, that in Yakutia the natives themselves played quite a large part in forcing Communist Party policy upon their compatriots. Yakuts made up 46.7 per cent of membership of the Yakut party organisation in 1933, Yakuts and Ewenkis together 49.7 per cent, so that only about 50 per cent were Russians. In the youth movement the proportion of local, chiefly Yakut, members would no doubt be even higher, and these were the 'shock-troops' of the collectivisation campaign. In the euphoric atmosphere of 'revolution from above' which dominated Communist Party theory and practice in the 1930s, grandiose ideas of changing the universe and even defying its scientifically ascertained laws in favour of absurd theories had their repercussions even in remote Yakutia. Under the delusion of pushing forward the frontiers of agriculture in the North, in accordance with the biological doctrines of Lysenko, collective farms spent large sums of money on futile attempts to grow crops beyond the Arctic Circle at such places as Zhigansk and Verkhoyansk. Even in the somewhat milder districts of central Yakutia, where the cultivation of potatoes, vegetables and even grain for local consumption was possible to a limited extent, the official planners often disregarded the most basic realities of local conditions – such as the severe climate and the shortage of labour – when setting ambitious targets for agricultural production. Fifty years later, even in central districts of European Russia, the difficulty of providing enough fodder to keep cattle alive over the winter was still a major problem. In the much more harsh and primitive conditions of Yakutia in the 1930s this problem was quite insurmountable, despite the extension of ploughed land to produce more hay, so that as many as 50–60 per cent of calves could be expected to die each winter.[37]

In northern and upland parts of Yakutia, where the native population consisted of Yakuts (54 per cent), Tungus (39 per cent), Yukagirs (2 per cent) and Chukchis (4.5 per cent), resistance to collectivisation of reindeer herds was as fierce as in other parts of the North, and the 'mistakes' committed by the communist authorities were just as bad. One problem

[37] *Istoriya Yakutskoy ASSR*, vol. III, pp. 139–40, 151, 171, 176–8, 220–2.

exacerbated by the development of Russian industry in the North was obligatory transportation by reindeer of large quantities of government freight, which placed a considerable burden upon the native population. Most of the 'simplest production associations' in northern Yakutia were still nomadic, and even as late as 1937 only 19 per cent of reindeer were collectivised. Although denomadisation had in general scarcely begun, in the three most southerly districts, around the upper Aldan, the Ewenkis had been induced to settle in 1932 and to cultivate vegetables and hay and keep cattle. The function of the collective farms thus created was to supply food and fodder to the Aldan gold-field.

Up to the second half of the 1930s, life in the remote regions of northern Yakutia still allowed considerable scope for private initiative. It was possible to employ hired labour, most reindeer and all horses and cattle were privately owned, and the distribution of earnings was not subject to the normal collective farm rules. As the Stalinist Communist Party and its organs of mass coercion tightened their grip on all aspects of life in the late 1930s, such laxity was no longer to be tolerated. In 1939 the Yakut Communist Party decreed that the 'simplest production associations' of the North must be transformed into the more formally constituted form of the *artel*. When this transformation was carried out in 1940 almost 94 per cent of households in the North had been brought into collective farms, and about one-third of all reindeer were public property.

The principal commodity of the northern economy of Yakutia continued to be furs. In 1937 about 20,000 hunters were at work in the republic, killing annually up to 1.5 million squirrels, 250,000 ermine and 35,000 arctic fox, which were worth around 16,000,000 roubles to the Soviet Russian state for foreign trade.

An important factor in the economic exploitation of northern Yakutia in the 1930s was the building of the seaport of Tiksi near the Lena delta, and the transfer of responsibility for trading and supplies to the Northern Sea Route administration *Glavsevmorputi*. In general, the weakest link in the economy of Yakutia was, as before, its remoteness from other industrial centres and the difficulty of communication between Yakutsk and other parts of the republic. In the early 1930s, for instance, instructions issued in Moscow could take up to ten months to reach outlying districts, half of which were practically cut off from Yakutsk for at least four months in the year. The nearest point on the railway was 580 miles away, and as no road linked Yakutsk with Irkutsk, an air-link was eventually established. In fact the only motor highway in the republic was the road, completed about 1933, which connected Yakutsk with the Trans-Siberian railway at Never. Apart from this, only one other main road came under construction in the late 1930s, which, when finished, would provide a 1,200 mile route eastward through mountainous terrain to the upper reaches of the Kolyma and the port of

Magadan on the Okhotsk coast – the centre of the NKVD colony of Dalstroy.

During the first five-year plans, gold from the Aldan gold-field was the main product of all-Union significance to be derived from Yakutia. In 1933 there were 38,000 gold-miners at Aldan (about 11 per cent of the total population of the republic), many of whom were Koreans and Chinese. The planners, the specialised engineers and most of the workers were Russians or others from western parts of the USSR. In view of the instability and absenteeism of the ex-peasant work-force throughout the USSR, the recruitment of over 1,000 Yakut peasants for work in the gold-mines was a significant step towards the emergence of a native industrial proletariat. As a result of the development of coal-mining it became possible to demonstrate the modernisation of Yakutia in the spirit of Lenin's dictum – 'Communism means Soviet power plus the electrification of the whole country' – when Yakutsk and other towns were electrified in the late 1930s.[38]

During the radical changes in the 1930s the Yakut people continued to show their determination to preserve their national culture. With the foundation of a teacher-training institute, and the publication of a growing number of textbooks, over three-quarters of schools in the republic had instruction in the Yakut language in 1937. Yet the aim of introducing universal seven-year education was hampered by a continuing shortage of qualified teachers. Moreover, the government decree of 1938 on the compulsory study of the Russian language in non-Russian schools, and the switch from the Roman alphabet to Cyrillic for Yakut in 1939, increased the influence of Russian as the language of the state. Yakut literature went on developing, despite the inhibiting effects of the purge of 1928 (the nationalist victims of which were serving sentences of 'corrective labour' on the White Sea canal in 1931–3). Several new decrees reinforced the Communist Party's call to Yakut writers to reject 'bourgeois' nationalist tendencies and propagandise Marxist–Leninist ideology, and in 1934, in parallel with events in Moscow and other republics, a Union of Writers of Yakutia was created as the guardian of conformity. Among the Yakut writers whose prose and drama enjoyed popularity were P.A. Oyunskiy-Sleptsov, S. Yefremov, Erilik Eristin, A. Ivanov-Künde and N. Mordinov. Other indications of the flourishing of Yakut culture – within the permitted limits – were the foundation in 1935 of the Institute for the Study of the Language, Literature and History of the Yakut ASSR, and the existence of twelve newspapers and a magazine in the Yakut language.

However, in the late 1930s a reign of terror was unleashed in Yakutia as

---

[38] Beskorsyy, 'Nekotorye itogi', p. 59; *Istoriya Sibiri*, vol. IV, pp. 437–9, 445–6, 469–70; *Istoriya Yakutskoy ASSR*, vol. III, pp. 117, 134, 140, 152, 166–8, 180–4, 221–3; Kantor, 'Problema osedaniya', pp. 5–6; Kolarz, *The Peoples*, pp. 104–8; *Narody Sibiri*, pp. 314, 317; Sergeyev, *Nekapitalisticheskiy put*, p. 353.

much as in every other corner of the land, and the thousand or more direct victims of imprisonment, torture and execution by the Soviet political police – often on the absurd charge of being Japanese spies – included many of the Yakut Bolsheviks who had first fought for the revolution, such as M.K. Ammosov, the first secretary of the Yakut Communist Party, S.M. Arzhakov, I.N. Barakhov and P.A. Oyunskiy-Sleptsov, the talented writer and first President of the Yakut ASSR.[39]

[39] *Istoriya Sibiri*, vol. IV, p. 461; *Istoriya Yakutskoy ASSR*, vol. III, pp. 162–3, 188–91, 223–4, 285; Kolarz, *The Peoples*, p. 107; G.G. Makarov, 'O nekotorykh voprosakh istorii Yakutii', *Polyarnaya zvezda*, 1989, no. 3, p. 126; *Narody SSSR*, pp. 323, 326; G. Syromyatnikov, 'Pervyy syezd pisateley Yakutii', *Polyarnaya zvezda*, 1989, no. 3, pp. 93–7.

14

SOVIET RUSSIA'S FAR EAST IN THE 1930s

INTERNATIONAL AND INTERNAL POLITICS

DURING the 1930s the life of the native peoples of the Far East was overshadowed not only by the policies and actions of the Russians, but also by the relations between the USSR and its neighbours, China and Japan.

After October 1917 Soviet Russia won the approval of China's national revolutionary party, the Kuomintang, whose leader, Sun Yatsen, saw the Soviet Union as an anti-imperialist state offering China the hope of expelling Western colonialists. In 1922 the Kuomintang decided to collaborate with the Chinese Communist Party in building the new China, but this alliance was an uneasy one, and during 1925–7 the nationalists annihilated the Chinese Communist Party in Shanghai and other cities. As civil war spread in China, Soviet Russia broke off relations with the nationalist régime and switched its support to the Chinese Red Army. From 1931 onward Japan re-entered the arena with the aim of conquering China and eventually dominating the whole of Eastern Asia. A Japanese army occupied Manchuria, and in the following year Tokyo proclaimed its separation from China as the state of Manchukuo – in reality a puppet of Japan. Japan's actions increased the Soviet Russian government's resolve to fortify its Far Eastern Territory against possible attack, and a build-up of industry and military power began. By 1937 the Special Far Eastern Army numbered some 300,000 men.

One direction of Japan's ambitions on the mainland of Asia was indicated by its creation within Manchukuo of a Mongolian Office. In Hulunbuir on the Russian frontier the Japanese sought to gain the favour of the native Barga Mongol population by making it a separate province under its own Mongol prince. Later, when the Japanese invaded the territory of the Chahar Mongols, they set up an 'autonomous government' of Inner Mongolia there. As a continuation of the Japanese-inspired Pan-Mongol movement of the 1910s, these measures did evoke some response in the Mongolian People's Republic, and indeed a pro-Japanese uprising took place there in

1932. For this reason Soviet Russia tightened its grip on Mongolia, where a disastrous collectivisation campaign in 1929–32 and an abortive five-year plan for industry, were followed by a 'New Course'. Plans for industrial development were suspended, while collective farms were dissolved and the herding of cattle and sheep was restored to its former status as the mainstay of Mongolia's economic life. However, active assistance to Mongolia in any significant measure was provided only in fields where the defence of the Soviet Union was concerned, that is, the equipment and training of the Mongolian army and the construction of a new railway line in 1938 to link the Chita–Manchuria line with Choibalsang in Eastern Mongolia.

The assault upon lamaist Buddhist institutions – the foundation of traditional Mongol society – was intensified in 1935, and as a result of military action by the Mongolian and Soviet Russian armies many monasteries were reduced to rubble and the Buddhist church was virtually destroyed. A Soviet Russian army had been stationed in Mongolia since 1936, and it is clear that by then power was effectively in the hands of the NKVD, since, in close parallel with events in Russia itself, many Mongolian political leaders and officials, including the prime minister Gendung and the commander-in-chief of the Mongolian army, Demid, were arrested and murdered in 1937. In fact the first purge of 'traitors' had occurred in 1934, and it was notable that out of thirty-two arrested twenty were Buryats – the remnants of the men of that nation who had helped to create communist Mongolia ten years before, but who were now treated as potential agents of the Whites and Japanese.[1]

The 'Japanese spy' fever which Stalin's Communist Party generated in the late 1930s as part of its campaign of terror against internal opposition, gained some credibility from the fact that the Japanese made several probing forays across Russia's border with Manchuria, the most publicised of which was their occupation, in July 1938, of a small area near Lake Khasan on the Korean border, which Russia claimed as its territory. A more serious war between Japanese and Soviet Russian forces took place in 1939 on the Mongolian frontier, where Japanese occupation of the Inner Mongolian province of Chahar had brought the easternmost corner of the Mongolian People's Republic under threat. The frontier lay near the river Khalkhin-Gol, and it was here that the Japanese launched their attack in an undeclared war which lasted three-and-a-half months before the Japanese army was repulsed. In the following year Mongolia, under a new constitution, was bound even more closely to the Soviet Union, and at the same time the

---

[1] Bawden, *History of Mongolia*, pp. 241, 293, 301–51, 359–78; *Bolshaya Sovetskaya Entsiklopediya*, 1926–47, vol. 60, cols. 278–80; S.D. Gusarevich and V.B. Seoyev, *Na strazhe Dalnevostochnykh rubezhey*, Moscow, 1982, pp. 41–4; *Istoriyaq Mongolskoy Narodnoy Respubliki*, pp. 369–87; Kolarz, *The Peoples*, pp. 15–18, 135–8, 146, 156; Kolarz, *Religion*, pp. 467–8; Shvarev, *Dalniy Vostok*, p. 23.

Soviet Union and Japan concluded a mutual non-aggression pact which temporarily suspended the inevitable conflict between them.[2]

The strategic importance to the USSR of its Far Eastern Territory required its development as a strong bastion of Soviet Russian power with a large population and strong industrial base, but on the other hand created the possibility that it might become a second centre of power capable of challenging that of Moscow. The Bolshevik leaders who made a name for themselves in the Far East during and after the Russian Civil War were men of character and independent mind, such as Ya.B. Gamarnik, chairman of the Far East Revolutionary Committee from 1923 to 1928, and the army commanders I.P. Uborevich and V.K. Blyukher. The Special Red Banner Far-Eastern Army was for over fifteen years under the command of Blyukher who, as a self-educated peasant's son and Old Bolshevik of relatively moderate views, was widely respected by the people. Because of his influential position he was able to speak out against forced collectivisation in the Far East, albeit from military considerations, and he was not the only Far Eastern leader who attempted to avert the follies of economic planning by a government which was ignorant of conditions in the territory.

The Stalinist Communist Party's reign of terror against potential opposition began as punctually in the Far East as in the west. Early in the spring of 1937 many civilian officials, especially on the overloaded Far Eastern railways, were arrested as 'Japanese spies' or 'Trotskyists', interrogated with torture and consigned to concentration camps or the grave. Shortly after this, army officers began to be arrested in great numbers and most of the Far Eastern high command were 'liquidated'. Marshal Blyukher was one of the last officers to be taken to Moscow, where he perished, having refused to sign a confession of spying for Japan.[3]

THE SOVIET CHINESE AND KOREANS

Of the non-Russian peoples of the Far Eastern Territory, the large minorities of Chinese and Koreans felt the most direct effects of the international and internal events of the 1930s. In 1926 Vladivostok had 22,000 Chinese inhabitants (21 per cent in a total population of about 104,600), and up to 1937 many Chinese and Korean labourers continued to work there and at other industrial locations such as the Suchang coal-mines and the gold-workings of Eastern Siberia. The total number of Chinese in the Soviet

---

[2] Bawden, *History of Mongolia*, pp. 241, 293, 301–51, 359–78; Conquest, *The Great Terror*, p. 618; Gusarevich and Seoyev, *Na strazhe*, pp. 34–48; Kolarz, *The Peoples*, pp. 8, 15–18, 37, 47, 135–46, 156; Kolarz, *Religion*, pp. 467–8; Quested, *Sino-Russian Relations*, pp. 96–9.
[3] Conquest, *The Great Terror*, pp. 198, 283–4, 403, 615–21; *Iz istorii organizatsiy KPSS na Dalnem Vostoke*, Khabarovsk, 1962, pp. 164–8; Kolarz, *The Peoples*, pp. 4–11, 13n., 19–20; B. Levytsky, *The Stalinist Terror in the Thirties: Documentation from the Soviet Press*, Stanford, 1974, pp. 104–13; Samsonov, *Kratkaya istoriya SSR*, vol. II, p. 89.

Union in 1926 was 92,000. As the civil war between the Chinese Communist Party and the Kuomintang developed, the Soviet Russian government encouraged the Chinese in the Far Eastern Territory by giving them a role in local government, by praising the conscientiousness of Chinese industrial workers and by establishing Chinese schools in Vladivostok, Khabarovsk and other towns, while an Oriental workers' faculty was created in the new university of Vladivostok. In this and other towns of the Russian Far East, traditional Chinese theatres flourished, and a Chinese newspaper was published from 1922 onward.

Despite this tolerance at the official and scholarly level, the Chinese minority suffered from abuse and persecution by Russian workers and petty officials, especially after the Chinese Eastern Railway incident in 1929, when Russian chauvinism ran rife. An article in *Pravda* in April 1938 about supposed Japanese spies and saboteurs among the Chinese and Korean citizens of the USSR was followed by the removal of the Chinese miners from the Suchang pits. No doubt the same happened at the Vladivostok shipyards, in Khabarovsk, and at numerous timber and gold-mining sites farther north. The Chinese theatre was closed, publication of Chinese newspapers and books ceased, Chinese schools were abolished, and the whole University of the Far East in Vladivostok was shut down and not reopened until after Stalin's death fifteen years later. About 63,000 Chinese then vanished, their fate never to be mentioned in official Soviet publications. According to Solzhenitsyn, they were all convicted as spies and sent to prison camps in the North, where they perished.[4]

The fate of the 167,400 Koreans who lived in Russia in 1926 was only slightly better than that of the Chinese minority. Like them, they had their own schools and colleges and a theatre in Vladivostok. Several newspapers were published in Korean, and there was a Korean National District around Posyet on the Korean border. As farmers, they were involved in collectivisation in 1930–1, and it would have been in character for them to submit to this without resistance. However, they were faced with the racial prejudice of the Russian and Ukrainian peasants of the Ussuri region – not to mention communist officials and members of the Young Communist League. Violent clashes occurred over the distribution of land and machinery, until the Communist Party headquarters in Khabarovsk intervened against these manifestations of 'Great-Russian chauvinism'. When the 'Japanese spy' mania was generated in 1937, most of the Korean community, unlike the Chinese, appear not to have been imprisoned, but they were deported in the mass to the totally alien environment of Kazakstan. There, amid the arid desert, according to a standard work on the peoples of Central Asia and Kazakstan, the state – which had just uprooted the Koreans from their

---

[4] Kolarz, *The Peoples*, pp. 38, 45–51; Shvarev, *Dalniy Vostok*, pp. 18–19; *Sibirskaya Sovetskaya Entsiklopediya*, vol. II, cols. 687–8; Solzhenitsyn, *Gulag Archipelago*, vol. I, p. 247.

homes and transported them over 4,000 miles in unimaginable discomfort – 'provided every possible support for the Korean collective farms organised in 1937–1938 on previously uncultivated land ... Thanks to the help of the state and the self-sacrificing labour of the collective farmers, desert places were quickly turned into cultivated land on which the Korean peasants began to raise good harvests of rice and other crops.'[5] Eventually, those who survived created a more or less tolerable life, and the younger generation of the 1950s, availing themselves of such educational facilities as were open to them, became, according to Solzhenitsyn, the main component of the educated stratum in the Kazak Republic.[6]

JEWS IN THE SOVIET FAR EAST

At the same time as the Soviet Russian government was expelling the Korean and Chinese inhabitants from the Far Eastern Territory it was introducing another new ethnic component into the region in the form of a Jewish Autonomous Province. The number of Jews who had reached the Far East along with Russian colonisers before 1917 was very small, as the local economy was too little developed and the way of life too primitive to attract them. During the 1920s, however, the question of a national homeland for the world's Jews was a matter of intense debate, as was the attitude of the Russian people and the Soviet régime towards them. From the point of view of the latter, the creation of a national territory for Jews within the Soviet Union would solve two problems. Firstly, according to Leninist dogma, a nationality based simply on culture but lacking a national territory could not be recognised: if the Jews were to be granted national status and autonomy, it was essential that they should have such a territory. Secondly, if Jews, inspired by Zionism, continually looked abroad towards the national homeland outside Russia – Palestine – their allegiance to the Soviet Union would be in doubt: the creation of a Jewish homeland within its borders would avoid this division of loyalty.

Accordingly, a sparsely populated territory in the basins of the Bira and Bijan – tributaries of the Amur to the west of Khabarovsk – was surveyed in 1927 and approved as the site of a potential Jewish homeland. It was characteristic of Soviet Marxist perceptions that in their new 'home' the Jews, instead of their traditional trading and handicraft functions, were expected to engage in the 'productive labour' of agriculture, in which they had little or no experience. The population of the region in 1928 consisted of 27,200 Russians (80 per cent), 2,856 Ukrainians and Belorussians (8.4 per cent), and

---

[5] *Narody Sredney Azii*, vol. II, p. 566.
[6] Kolarz, *The Peoples*, pp. 36–7, 41–2; A.M. Nekrich, *The Punished Peoples*, New York, 1978, pp. 98–9; Solzhenitsyn, *Gulag Archipelago*, vol. III, p. 387, 401; *Narody Sredney Azii*, vol. II, p. 581.

3,400 Koreans (10 per cent). According to projected figures for migration to Biro-Bijan, its Jewish population would reach about 120,000 in 1938, and eventually it would qualify for the status of an autonomous republic.

During the 1930s a certain degree of 'cultural autonomy' did exist in the Jewish Autonomous Province, as it was designated in 1934. Yiddish was recognised, along with Russian, as the official language, in which a small number of books were published, while a Jewish theatre and a library named after Sholom Aleykhem were founded in the administrative town of Birobidzhan. Several of the local Communist Party functionaries were Jews, such as the chairman of the district executive committee, Joseph Liberberg. However, in the prevailing spirit of anti-religious measures, no synagogue was permitted, so that prayer-houses had to be organised secretly, and Hebrew culture could be passed on only with great difficulty. In fact the number of Jewish immigrants to Biro-Bijan never reached anything like the projected figures. Only some 2,825 arrived in the first two years (1928 and 1929), and over 60 per cent of these did not remain. The peak of immigration was about 9,000 in 1932, but because of the continuing high rate of departure, this resulted in a total Jewish population of only 5,185. Between then and 1937, when a certain amount of pressure was applied to Jews in European Russia to go east, a further 25,000 made the journey – but the resident Jewish population still reached only 20,000. By then, Biro-Bijan, like the rest of the Far Eastern Territory and the Soviet Union as a whole, had become a prey to the paranoia of the Stalinist Communist Party, and many Jews, including Liberberg, were arrested as 'enemies of the people' and killed. Jewish organisations and schools were closed down, Yiddish books were removed from the libraries, and the newspaper *Birobijaner Shtern* (Birobijan Star) ceased publication.

Thus, despite a considerable amount of enthusiastic promotion by some Jewish politicians and intellectuals, the new 'homeland' was a fiasco. Of its 108,000 inhabitants in 1939, only about 18.5 per cent were Jewish.[7]

NATIVE PEOPLES OF THE LOWER AMUR AND SAKHALIN

Among the peoples of the Lower Amur and Northern Sakhalin, most of whom had a more or less sedentary way of life, the Russians had found it relatively easy to form local soviets in the mid-1920s. Cooperatives were created in practically every settlement, and through them a beginning was

[7] *Encyclopaedia Judaica*, vol. IV, col. 1044–8; vol. XIV, col. 1488; Frumkin et al., *Kniga o russkom yevreystve*, pp. 162, 164, 175–6, 185; Kochan, *The Jews in Soviet Russia*, pp. 64–77; Kolarz, *The Peoples*, p. 45; W. Kolarz, *Russia and her Colonies*, 3rd edn, London, 1953, pp. 169–74, 177; *Sibirskaya Sovetskaya Entsiklopediya*, vol. I, cols. 871–3. Forty years later Jews accounted for only 5.4 per cent of the population of the Jewish Autonomous Province, *Census 1979*, p. 84; and by 1989 only 4 per cent, S. Heitman, 'Jews in the 1989 USSR census', *Soviet Jewish Affairs*, 1990, vol. XV, no. 1, pp. 23–30.

made on the literacy campaign. As early as 1926 a group of young people from the lower Amur were sent to Leningrad to study at the Institute for Peoples of the North, while nearer home, facilities for the training of native teachers and clerks were provided at Nikolayevsk and Khabarovsk. As the native languages had not yet been committed to writing, the medium of instruction was Russian, and the inexorable process of alienating young people from their national culture began as soon as they left their villages to attend the new residential schools. By 1934 primary education was in force for all native children, with thirteen Nivkh schools, two for the Negidals, seven for the Ulchis, seventeen for the Nanais, six for the Udeghes and Oroches, and seven in Sakhalin for the Nivkhs and Ewenkis. As in other parts of Siberia, a certain amount of instruction in such fields as hygiene, women's rights and, of course, politics was carried out in the late 1920s by itinerant propagandists, and medical stations were gradually established. Recognition of nationality rights (within the Soviet Marxist understanding of this term) was confirmed by the creation of several small national districts, e.g. for the Nanai and the Ulchi on the Amur, and in north-western Sakhalin for the Nivkhs and Ewenkis.[8] In 1931, in accordance with the Committee of the North's idealistic fostering of the use of vernaculars as written languages, Roman alphabets were created for the Nanai, Udeghe and Nivkh. However, apart from Nanai, in which school-books and a modest literature were produced, the small numbers and dialectal divisions of these communities worked against the development of written vernaculars. As a result, Udeghe and Nivkh, like Ulchi, Negidal, Oroch and Orok, remained in practice unwritten languages, the speakers of which used Russian as the language of education and culture.[9]

After the Russian Civil War and five-year-long Japanese intervention, the Nivkhs – especially those in Sakhalin – were among the most downtrodden of all the peoples of the lower Amur. Their traditional communal system and clan organisation had been undermined by prolonged contact with the Russians, while social division into rich and poor had developed to a certain degree. At the time of collectivisation, therefore, the Soviet Russians were able to incite conflict by playing upon the emotions of young people. The religious foundations of Amur Nivkh society were shaken in the late 1930s by communist persecution of their shamans, and when the latter sought refuge with their kinsmen in Sakhalin, the League of Militant Atheists there took their anti-religious mission so far as to desecrate the Nivkh cemetery

---

[8] *Narody Sibiri*, pp. 558, 807; Sergeyev, *Nekapitalisticheskiy put*, p. 314; O.P. Sunik, *Ulchskiy yazyk*, Leningrad, 1985, p. 3.
[9] Gurvich, *Osushchestvleniye*, pp. 143, 314, 325–7, 329, 331; *Istoriya Sibiri*, vol. IV, pp. 291, 466, 472; *Narody Sibiri*, pp. 806–7, 812, 826–7, 880; Sergeyev, *Nekapitalisticheskiy put*, p. 314; Shvarev, *Dalniy Vostok*, pp. 425–6; *Yazyki narodov SSSR*, vol. V, pp. 109, 129, 172, 191, 210, 408.

and ancestral sanctuary. Not surprisingly, despite the benefits of civilisation offered by the Soviet Russians, the Nivkhs (of whom there were 4,076 in 1926) put up a fight against collectivisation, especially as this meant removal from their scattered villages to bigger settlements located nearer the fishing grounds which it was the wish of the Russian authorities to exploit. Collectivisation was carried out as arbitrarily on the Amur as in the rest of Siberia. Force was used to hasten the formation of collectives, to move people to larger villages, and to communalise their personal belongings. 'Kulaks' and 'wreckers' had to be found, and the primitive communal heresy of equal shares had to be stamped out. In fact Soviet Russian policies prevailed quite quickly, and by 1939 over 96 per cent of all Nivkhs had been collectivised and settled in villages in the Russian style.[10]

Events followed a similar course among the Nanais (of whom there were 5,757 in 1926). Class divisions here were perhaps even harder to perceive than among the Nivkhs, and the Soviet Russian authorities appear to have acted with slightly greater caution in order to avoid stimulating clan solidarity around the shamans. Nevertheless it is reported that by late 1932 in the Nanai National District 93 per cent of the natives had been collectivised. There may have been more active resistance to collectivisation among the Ulchis, where in 1933 'antagonistic elements' sabotaged the collective fisheries. During the collectivisation of the Nanais another of the aims of the Russian Communist Party was achieved: the reduction in the number of scattered, and mobile, Nanai settlements and their concentration into a smaller number of villages made it much easier to absorb them into the Soviet system. By 1939, instead of occupying 105 sites as in 1926, the Nanais were huddled into only 28 villages.[11]

By 1933 the native peoples of the lower Amur were already minorities in their 'national districts', as intensive immigration and settlement of people from European Russia proceeded in order to provide personnel for the industrial and strategic development of the Far East. The native fishing collectives, organised and provided with boats and gear through the 'Motor-fishing Stations' (the equivalent of MTS in agricultural regions) made a considerable contribution to the feeding of the builders of Russian industry on the Amur. The largest single new intrusion of Soviet economic development in the region was the foundation of the new town of Komsomolsk-on-Amur in 1932 in the heart of Nanai territory – an event which supposedly heralded 'the flowering of the material and spiritual culture of the small nationalities', and 'created the conditions for leading backward, semi-

[10] Gurvich, *Osushchestvleniye*, p. 317; Kolarz, *The Peoples*, p. 84; *Istoriya Sibiri*, vol. IV, p. 466; *Narody Sibiri*, pp. 872, 877–8; Sergeyev, *Nekapitalisticheskiy put*, p. 356; Shvarev, *Dalniy Vostok*, pp. 425–6; Taksami, *Nivkhi*, pp. 45, 62–6.

[11] Gurvich, *Osushchestvleniye*, p. 316; B.M. Rosugbu, *Malye narodnosti Priamurya v 1956–1965 gg.*, Khabarovsk, 1976, p. 93; Sergeyev, *Nekapitalisticheskiy put*, p. 356; Shvarev, *Dalniy Vostok*, pp. 424–5, 544.

nomadic peoples onto the path of socialism'. Some Nanais were trained for various trades, while others were drawn away from the traditional community life to join the ranks of Russian labourers in the felling of forest trees.[12]

Beyond the Amur in the Sikhote-Alin mountains, the Udeghe hunters (altogether 1,347 in 1926) were, because of their nomadic life and distrust of foreigners, more difficult to bring within the Soviet Russian fold than the Nanai and Nivkh. For a long time after the end of the Civil War they hid away in the forest and had to be sought out by Communist Party agents. The story of their introduction to the Soviet system indicates the relationship that existed between the authorities and native communities: in 1926 all the Udeghes of the Khor valley were *told* to congregate at the Kafen encampment in order to meet a Soviet Russian official. The latter *told* them they must form a 'native soviet' to protect their interests, and Sessili of the Kimonko clan was chosen as chairman, and a red flag was raised. Similar meetings were arranged on the Iman and Bikin rivers, and two years later the Udeghes of the Samarga valley on the eastern side of the mountains were also brought into a 'native soviet'. Since no Udeghes were literate, the secretaries of these native soviets were Russians. National districts for the Udeghes were designated, but because of the dispersed nature of the Udeghe community these were abolished in 1936. It was not until 1934 that an attempt was made to bring the Udeghe hunters into collectives, the composition of which was to a great extent dictated by clan allegiances. Those on the Khor were the most homogeneous, since this was largely Kimonko territory, but one of the four collectives consisted of members of the Kälunjuga clan. In 1937 the traditional antagonism between these two clans led to a feud in which a collective chairman was murdered. In the Bikin valley, where several clans were represented in the two collectives, the Soviet authorities decided to bring about a social transformation by making the Udeghes cultivate the land (which had formerly belonged to Chinese settlers). Only after fifteen years of unsuccessful, and no doubt unhappy, farming was the folly of this acknowledged, and the Udeghes were allowed to revert to the traditional occupation of hunting. Similarly on the Pacific side of the Sikhote-Alin, arbitrary 'social engineering' took the form of the enforced concentration of the Samarga Udeghes in one village, where they were given cattle and implements confiscated from 'kulaks', and told to become farmers. These Udeghes had to wait twenty years for permission from the colonial authorities to go back to hunting as their main source of income. However, the most southerly group of sinicised Udeghes or Tatzǔ, who were long accustomed to agriculture, formed a successful collective farm. Other Udeghe communities on the sea-coast were induced to form

[12] Gurvich, *Osushchestvleniye*, pp. 316, 318; Kolarz, *The Peoples*, pp. 16, 82; Shvarev, *Dalniy Vostok*, pp. 419, 428.

fishing collectives, as were the Oroches, whose small community (405 in 1926) eventually gravitated to the one village of Uska. Meanwhile in Sakhalin the small communities of Ewenkis and Oroks were brought into reindeer collectives, so that by 1937 nearly all of the native peoples of the Amur, Maritime Province and Sakhalin were organised in collectives and subordinated to Soviet Russian economic planning.[13]

THE BURYAT-MONGOLS, 1930–1940

Buryatia presented special problems to the Soviet Russian government in the 1930s on several counts. Not only was this a relatively large ethnic group (the most numerous indigenous nationality in Siberia, with 237,500 people in 1926), with a strongly developed national consciousness, but it was a frontier region linked ethnically with Mongolia, and culturally also with China. Moreover, the basis of its national culture, Buddhism, was a great world religion providing a certain affinity with the Japanese, who used this fact wherever possible to promote Asiatic solidarity in the face of the advance of the European powers in the Far East.

In the middle of the 1920s there were 47 monasteries (*datsans* and *dugans*) in Buryatia, with 15,000 lamas (all but 400 of them in Eastern Buryatia), and for the time being there was little state interference in their religious affairs. A new development at this time was the emergence of a kind of reformed or neo-Buddhism – analogous to the 'Living Church' in Orthodox Russia – which was propounded by the Chief Lama of Buryatia, Agvan Dorzhi, and also supported in Mongolia by such figures as Zhamtsarano. According to this idea, no conflict need arise between Soviet communism and Buddhism, since it was Buddha himself who had created communism.

The 1920s also saw the continuation of other aspects of Buryat national culture, including the publication under the auspices of the Banzarov Buryat-Mongol Learned Society of textbooks of the national language – which was at that time a general Mongolian language based upon the Khalkha dialect and preserving the old Mongol vertically written alphabet. The cultural conservatism of Buryat-Mongolia did not please the Russian Communist Party, which issued a declaration in May 1929 attacking Buryat nationalism and Pan-Mongolism, and calling for greater anti-religious activity. In the previous year a dispute between lamas and atheists had been staged at Verkhneudinsk and, as part of the ideological campaign throughout the USSR to accompany the launching of the first five-year plan, a League of Militant Godless was formed in Buryatia. This body of zealots indulged in the usual crude, and therefore counter-productive, kinds of violence and sacrilege against Buddhism, but even when the Buryatian League of Militant

---

[13] *Narody Sibiri*, pp. 839–42, 853, 860; Sergeyev, *Nekapitalisticheskiy put*, p. 352; Shvarev, *Dalniy Vostok*, pp. 435–41.

Godless was disbanded two years later because of the harm it had done to its own cause, the undermining of Buddhism went on in a more sober, calculated way. By 1929 the number of lamas in Buryatia was reduced by half. The first monastery to be closed (in 1929) was that of Alar in western Buryatia. In the following year the famous *datsan* at Goose Lake disappeared, as did the old Tsongol *datsan* in 1931. Three years later the Chief Lama Agvan Dorzhi was deported to Leningrad, where he was held in exile until 1937. At the same time a museum was created in Verkhneudinsk to house the rich collection of religious objects and Buddhist texts removed from the monasteries when they were closed down or demolished. Aga monastery, an important centre of Buddhist scholarship, was also closed (but, exceptionally, not destroyed), and in 1937 the temple in Leningrad suffered the same fate. By 1935 only 900 lamas were left, and soon many of these were to be arrested and despatched to the Communist Party's concentration camps. In western Buryatia, in addition to the closure of the few Buddhist monasteries, the Russified Buryats were no doubt deprived of their Orthodox priests and churches, while the shamans too were subject to persecution.

Not only monasteries, but secular institutions also were suppressed by the Russian Communist Party, starting in 1930 with the Buryat-Mongol Learned Society, which had concerned itself with the geography, history and ethnography of Buryatia. At least six Buryat periodicals were closed down between 1930 and 1934, including *Soyolyn khubiskhal* (The Cultural Revolution) and *Buryaadyn gegeerel* (Buryat Enlightenment), and Communist Party control of literature was ensured by the creation of a Union of Writers of Buryatia on the Russian model. At the same time the Buryat literary language was subjected to radical alterations. These may have brought it closer to the contemporary vernacular, but their main purpose was to make it less similar to the Khalkha Mongol language so that the latter could not become a common language unifying all Mongols. In 1931 the difference was accentuated by the decision to replace the Mongolian alphabet by the Roman as the medium for written Buryat – a change which Buryat nationalists only succeeded in postponing for two years. (In Mongolia itself the old Mongolian alphabet continued to be used until the 1940s, when it was replaced by a Cyrillic alphabet similar to that brought in for Buryat in 1939.) Meanwhile the Buryat Communist Party secretary M.N. Yerbanov assured the Moscow government that no problem of local nationalism existed in the Buryat-Mongol Republic.[14]

[14] Bawden, *History of Mongolia*, pp. 269, 287–8; C. Humphrey, *Karl Marx Collective: Economy, Society and Religion in a Siberian Collective Farm*, Cambridge, 1983, pp. 417–32; Khaptayev, *Istoriya Buryatskoy ASSR*, vol. II, pp. 14, 351–2, 356, 363, 370–4, 384; Kolarz, *The Peoples*, pp. 117–19, 125–6; Kolarz, *Religion*, pp. 450–8; Mantatov, *Lamaizm v Buryatii*, pp. 44–5; N.L. Zhukovskaya, 'Sovremennyy lamaizm (na materialakh Buryatskoy ASSR)', in *Voprosy nauchnogo ateizma*, Moscow, 1969, vyp. 7, p. 224.

Collectivisation in Buryatia was forced upon a highly traditional society in which class differences undoubtedly existed, but in which the concept of 'class struggle' was absent. Since the mid-1920s, it is true, the Russian Communist Party had carried its agitation to the Buryat pastures with the aim of setting the 'working peasantry' against the chiefs and big herd-owners, but as no land reform had been carried out, the enormous problem of dispossession remained to be tackled in the heat of the collectivisation campaign – a task which could not be carried out without considerable external force. As 90 per cent of Buryats were nomadic or semi-nomadic, the formation of collectives and allocation of pastures was also bound up with the Soviet Russian conviction that they must be made to give up their mobile way of life and settle in villages. At the same time it was intended that the Buryats would go over from their old extensive form of cattle-rearing to more modern methods, thus releasing labour for the development of grain-cultivation, in conformity with the Russian government's strategic plan to make Buryatia the main producer of food for the Far East. This required a big increase in the area ploughed for cultivation (which had been a sin under the old Mongol ideology of nomadism) at the expense of pasture-land.

Among the few available revelations about the coercive methods practised by the Communist Party in the collectivisation of Siberia is the following, relatively innocent, account by a British apologist for the communist system:

Instead of conducting propaganda among the Buryats and peasants, urging them to displace the rich men of the ulus encampment and the village, the Bolsheviks of Buryatia sometimes adopted the 'easier' method of what Stalin called the 'cavalry raid'; the 'propagandist' called a meeting of the ulus or village, slammed his revolver on the table and announced that the village or ulus was now 'collectivised' . . . The result was that the number of registered collective farms rose quite satisfactorily . . .[15]

While this method, in the eyes of its narrator and the Soviet sources from which it was derived, was simply a 'mistake' – to be swiftly corrected by the virtuous communist authorities – the people presented as the real villains of the collectivisation campaign were its opponents, the vicious 'kulaks, lamas and noyons'. It is difficult to imagine how such a powerful establishment – and its natural following of loyal clansmen – could have been overcome by individuals with revolvers and not by direct military action by bands of police, urban workers or soldiers. The Buryats' reaction to the first stage of the campaign – a decree of 1929 which claimed 780 square miles of land from clan chiefs for redistribution to collective farms – was, in fact, a violent general uprising. The rebellion was most determined in the Tunka, Mukhorshibir and Bichura *aimaks*, but many Communist Party officials, Soviet secretaries, and policemen were beaten or murdered in every Buryat district, both east and west of Lake Baikal. After the suppression of the

---

[15] G.D.R. Phillips, *Dawn in Siberia*, London, 1942, pp. 150–1.

revolt, according to unconfirmed reports, thousands of Buryats were executed and many more imprisoned by the Soviet Russian authorities. Once the main opposition had been crushed, the Buryat-Mongols, faced with the inescapable destruction of their whole way of life, took the only retaliatory measures available to them – mass slaughter of their own livestock.

In 1931 the Russian Communist Party sent out the order to proceed to the 'liquidation of the kulaks as a class'. Now those who refused to submit were, like their peasant counterparts throughout the Soviet Union, subject to expulsion from their lands and deportation to northern regions. This repression could not have reached the proportions it did, had it not been for the numerous urban workers, chiefly from Leningrad, who volunteered to 'help' by coercing peasants into collectives, and who often stayed on as alien chairmen of the 'farms' they created. The campaign against nomadism also went ahead, accompanied by the bribe of relief from state taxes for five years, so that by 1932 about 23,000 families had settled in villages. Here, as in Yakutia, Khakasia, the Mountain Altai and other regions, 'planned settlement' involved many distressing 'mistakes', as the sites selected for collective settlements by incompetent communist officials were all too often quite unsuitable because of lack of water, pastures, meadows or woods. Nevertheless the campaign of denomadisation went on inexorably, so that by the end of 1937 about 92 per cent of all Buryat households had been collectivised and practically all had moved into villages.

The principal result of the chaotic events in Buryatia between 1929 and 1932, apart from great human suffering, was that the number of cattle – the Buryat-Mongols' main economic asset – had fallen by 62.5 per cent. Although herds were built up again in the following years, the number of animals in 1937 was still only 51 per cent of the 1929 figure.[16]

Another factor which had a profound effect upon Buryat-Mongol society in the 1930s was the increase in immigration from European Russia, as workers were brought into build and run the new enterprises of the five-year plans, such as the railway repair works at Verkhneudinsk, to which over 5,000 workers were sent. A further wave of immigration occurred five years later, when special rates of pay for service in the Far East were introduced. While a few Buryats were also drawn into the Soviet Russian industrial enterprises, they remained predominantly a rural people, and the capital of 'their' autonomous republic, Ulaan-Üde ('Red South', as Verkhneudinsk was renamed in 1934) was essentially a Russian city where, out of 129,000

[16] N.Ya. Gushchin, *Rabochiy klass Sibiri v borbe za sozdaniye kolkhoznogo stroya*, Novosibirsk, 1965, pp. 66–7; *Istoriya Sibiri*, vol. IV, pp. 301, 440–4, 452–3; Khaptayev, *Istoriya Buryatskoy ASSR*, vol. II, pp. 234–5, 252, 254, 258, 263–4, 272–3, 286–7, 319, 437–8; Kolarz, *The Peoples*, p. 124; *Narody Sibiri*, pp. 245, 253–4; Phillips, *Dawn in Siberia*, pp. 149–52; Solzhenitsyn, *Gulag Archipelago*, vol. I, p. 51.

inhabitants in 1939, only about 20 per cent were Buryats. By that time over half of the inhabitants of the Buryat-Mongol ASSR were non-Buryats.

The Buryats are one of a relatively small number of nationalities of the USSR who are shown by official statistics to have declined between 1926 and 1939: from 237,500 to 224,700 – a decrease of 5.4 per cent. As no explanation for this is offered in the standard work on the demography of Soviet nationalities, it can only be assumed that, as in the case of the Ukrainians and Kazaks, who also experienced 'a reduction in natural growth in the early 1930s' – i.e. the period of collectivisation – it was this social cataclysm that caused drastic losses by violence, famine, deportation, and perhaps emigration to Mongolia (where, however, conditions were no better!). So far as Buryat 'autonomy' is concerned, the very large decrease in the native population of the Buryat-Mongol ASSR between 1926 and 1939 – from 215,000 (43.8 per cent of the total population of the republic) to 116,300 (only 21.3 per cent) was caused partly by the territorial changes made in 1937. The four West Buryat *aimaks* lying to the north of Irkutsk (Alar, Bokhan, Ehkirit-Bulagat and Olkhon) were detached from the Buryat republic and ascribed to Irkutsk province of the Russian Republic under the title 'Ust-Orda Buryat-Mongol National Region', while the two south-eastern *aimaks* of Ulaan Onon and Aga, which were already physically separate from the main territory of the Buryat republic, were now subordinated to Chita province of the Russian Republic as the 'Aga Buryat-Mongol National Region' (in Russian *Aginskiy Buryat-Mongolskiy natsionalnyy okrug*). The administrative justification for breaking up the Buryat territories was presumably a desire to integrate the two native enclaves into the economy of the surrounding Russian provinces.

Another, political, reason was, however, cited at the time: the Aga district, which is within 160 miles of the Manchurian frontier, was said to be riddled with enemy agents engaged in anti-Soviet sabotage on behalf of the Japanese. Both this region and the north-western Buryat *aimaks* were said by the Soviet press to be deeply involved in the conspiracy-ridden misrule imputed by Moscow to the native communist leadership of Buryatia. As the Communist Party's reign of terror reached its culmination throughout the USSR, the invective used to condemn the Buryat 'band of gangsters' was particularly violent and grotesque. The Communist Party secretary, M.N. Yerbanov, the President of the Buryat Republic, Dampilon, and the whole membership of the Council of People's Commissars of the Republic were arrested and accused of being wreckers, 'bourgeois' nationalists and fascist agents intent upon separating Buryatia from the Soviet Union and making it a vassal of Japan. After a show-trial staged in Ulaan-Üde in September 1937, Yerbanov and fifty-three other Buryats were executed, as were the Buryat architects of the puppet state of Mongolia, Zhamtsarano and Rinchino. Many other Buryats and local Russians of all stations in society also suffered arbitrary arrest and delivery to the concentration camps.[17] The venerable Chief Lama Agvan Dorzhi was brought from his Leningrad exile to Ulaan-Üde in 1937, accused of being a Japanese agent, and in the following year he 'died' in prison. While the much-reduced autonomous republic struggled on under new communist management, the cultural confusion in Buryatia was increased in 1939, when not only the alphabet was changed again – this time from Roman to Russian Cyrillic – but a different dialect – that of the Khori region instead of Selenga – was adopted as the basis of the Buryat-Mongol literary language.[18]

EWENS AND KORAKS

The north-eastern extremity of Siberia, including the peninsulas of Kamchatka and Chukchi-land, stretches from Okhotsk, roadless and without convenient arterial rivers, for about 1,500 miles as the crow flies. In the mid-1920s this wide-flung wing of the Russian Empire, with its rugged tundra and sparsely forested landscape of mountain ranges, gulfs and promontories, was inhabited by no more than 36,000 people, at an average density of one person per 14 square miles. One sixth of these were Russians and the remainder were aboriginal peoples: about 7,000 each Tungus and Koraks, 12,000 Chukchis, 1,300 Eskimos, and small remnants of the Yukagirs and Itelmens, numbering 443 and 814 respectively. In addition, a certain number of Yakuts had moved into Yukagir territory since the seventeenth century to settle in scattered groups (totalling about 425 people) along the upper reaches of the Kolyma. Because of the remoteness of the region and the sparseness of Russian settlements, in 1929 almost 40 per cent of the indigenous communities were still, in the eyes of the Communist Party, 'unorganised' – that is, not subordinated to the Soviet Russian administration – and the imposition of the collective system had scarcely begun before 1931.

The Tungus – Ewenkis in the vicinity of Okhotsk, Ewens to the north of this – had no coastal settlements apart from a few impoverished families completely deprived of reindeer. They roamed the larch forests and tundra of the mountains and uplands in the basins of the Kolyma and Omolon, avoiding contact with Russians. As a result, the first schools, medical stations

---

[17] The standard *History of the Buryat ASSR* contains one paragraph referring to 'illegal repressions' at the time of Stalin's 'cult of personality', without giving a single concrete detail, even about the fate of Yerbanov: Khaptayev, *Istoriya Buryatskoy ASSR*, vol. II, p. 343. Truthful accounts have appeared in the Buryat press since 1987, e.g. I. Boldogoyev, 'Pravda o gibeli pisatelya Ts. Dona', *Baykal*, 1990, no. 3, pp. 126–30.

[18] Khaptayev, *Istoriya Buryatskoy ASSR*, vol. II, pp. 277–82, 301, 305–8, 347, 373, 400, 582–3; *Istoriya Sibiri*, vol. IV, p. 438; Kolarz, *The Peoples*, pp. 120–4; Kolarz, *Religion*, p. 457; Kozlov, *Natsionalnosti SSSR*, pp. 250–2; *Narody Sibiri*, p. 258; Phillips, *Dawn in Siberia*, pp. 169–71, 180.

and other institutions established among the Russian colonists of the Okhotsk region in the 1920s made no impression upon the Ewenkis and Ewens. Where 'nomadic soviets' were created, they functioned only in summer when the Ewens came down to the coast. The first inept attempt to form a settled collective 'farm' among the Ewenkis near Ayan has already been mentioned (p. 295). Nevertheless the Russians gradually succeeded in bringing their influence to bear upon those Ewens with whom they could establish contact, notably near Ola on the coast of Taui Bay. Here in 1930 the Committee of the North founded a cultural base at Nagayevo, and some of the poorer Ola Ewens agreed to form collectives, most of which came to nothing. A similar episode occurred farther north in the following year, when, after listening to a harangue by a Communist Party representative, fifty Ewens put their names down as members of herding and fishing collectives, but again almost none of these became a reality. A more serious alienation of the Ewens, resulting from an attempt by the communist authorities to commandeer reindeer for transport during the winter of 1931–2, led to their withdrawal into the depths of the forest, so that practically none of the Ewens had been collectivised up to 1932.[19]

Four hundred miles farther to the north-east from Nagayevo, at the head of Penzhina Bay, lay Gizhiga, a Russian base on the edge of the territory of the Koraks, which extended from there across to the Pacific coast and down the isthmus of Kamchatka. Here too, because of bad experiences during the Russian Civil War, the natives – Korak and Ewen nomads – avoided contact with Russians. Unlike the Ewens, the Koraks were divided into two communities: more than half were reindeer nomads of the interior (Chauchywaw), while the others (Nymylu) lived in coastal settlements. Among the latter a beginning was made to collectivisation in 1929, when a fishing collective was formed at Gizhiga, but this proved a fiasco. Because of the lack of sea transport, for two years running the season's catch was not picked up for shipment, and was wasted. The unreliability of shipping to Gizhiga also resulted in a chronic shortage of essential supplies from the 'mainland', such as grain and gunpowder. While there was little differentiation in prosperity among the coastal Nymylu, the Reindeer Koraks presented a more complex social structure, with about 65 rich herd-owners (some of whom possessed as many as 10,000 head) and about 390 families owning an average of 100 reindeer each. The poorest families, with as few as ten or fifteen animals, were dependent upon the big herd-owners within the normal institutions of mutual aid – working for a rich relation in exchange for board and lodging in his tent. As they lived and migrated with their liveli-

---

[19] Flerov, *Stroitelstvo*, pp. 15, 268–9; *Narody Sibiri*, pp. 761, 885, 897, 934, 951, 978; Popova, *Eveny*, pp. 81, 206, 208, 212–14, 219–20, 229, 231–2, 242; Sergeyev, *Nekapitalisticheskiy put*, p. 238; N.I. Spiridonov, 'Oduly Kolymskogo okruga', *Sovetskiy Sever*, 1930, no. 9–12, pp. 176–9; Zhikharev, *Ocherki istorii*, pp. 7–8, 139, 200–1.

hood and wealth around them in the form of their herds, the nomadic Koraks had not been brought into any form of collective organisation by 1931, and showed no signs of interest. In any case, as one Soviet representative reported in that year in connection with the eleven existing fishing collectives in Penzhina district, six of them lacked a single literate person, and not one Russian could be found who had the slightest skill in such simple technical jobs as driving a motor-boat.

When, in 1932, the Russians began to press for the mass collectivisation of the Reindeer Koraks – a more unsubmissive and territorially conscious people than the Ewens – they encountered stiff resistance. Class conflict was induced by the communists in order to weaken the existing social structure, reindeer for collective herds were 'purchased' by force from herd-owners, and many deer were slaughtered by the latter as a protest against collectivisation. As a result, the number of reindeer in the Korak National Region fell from 264,000 in 1926 to 127,000 in 1934. Conflict also arose in the long-established Korak coastal settlements, where native fishing cooperatives had been formed under the guidance of the Committee of the North, but the large-scale state fishing organisation of AKO disregarded the natives' interests and, as in pre-revolutionary Russia, arbitrarily took over the fishing grounds on which their livelihood depended. Similar high-handedness was manifested by the managers of the state reindeer farms, who usurped the pastures used by Korak families. The motivation of big state enterprises in thus disregarding official resolutions aimed at safeguarding the interests of the native peoples, was identified as early as 1934 by a contemporary writer: it was their subjection to the inexorable obligation to fulfil and overfulfil the production plans set by the Communist Party authorities.

Collectivisation went slowly among the Koraks. By 1934 only 20 per cent of reindeer people and 47 per cent of maritime people were organised in collectives. Originally they lived in small clusters of substantial semi-subterranean houses on the sea-coast, but as a result of cooperative fishing, many of the inhabitants of these hamlets gravitated towards larger settlements such as Manily on the Penzhina. The development of education in the region was encouraged by the foundation of a teacher training college at Tigil in Kamchatka, and a number of Koraks proceeded to Khabarovsk or Leningrad for further education.[20]

[20] Gurvich, *Etnokulturnye protsessy*, pp. 144, 148, 150; Kolarz, *The Peoples*, p. 71; A. Mikhalev, 'Uspekhi i tormozy kolkhoznogo stroitelstva (pismo iz Penzhinskogo rayona, Kamchatskogo okruga)', *Sovetskiy Sever*, 1931, no. 3–4, pp. 168–70; *Narody Sibiri*, pp. 951, 964–6, 972; Sergeyev, *Koryakskiy natsionalnyy okrug*, pp. 107, 110–15; Sergeyev, *Nekapitalisticheskiy put*, pp. 286–7, 345, 352n., 355, 359–60; S.N. Stebnitskiy, 'Koryatskiye deti', *Sovetskiy Sever*, 1930, no. 4, p. 39.

CHUKCHIS AND ESKIMOS

Apart from four small Orthodox schools attended by Russian children, there were no schools in Chukchi-land (which the Russians call *Chukotka*) until the late 1920s, when eleven were founded. The coastal Chukchis and Eskimos appear to have shown a great interest in learning to read and write, probably because they had more contact with the world outside Russia than any other native people of northern Siberia. As a result, even in 1926 there were 72 literate Chukchis (in a population of 13,100), 10 of whom were women. Like the Eskimos, the coastal Chukchis showed great aptitude for carving and engraving walrus tusks, and, as in North America, this cottage industry became the basis for an expressive sculptural and pictorial art. Scope for progress in the general cultural development of the Chukchis and other peoples of the North-east was provided by the designation in 1930 of national regions for the Chukchis, Koraks and Okhotsk Ewens. In the following year a modified Roman alphabet was introduced for the Chukchi, Eskimo and Korak languages, and 'nomadic schools' began to be organised for the reindeer people in addition to those operating in coastal settlements. The shamans, as the guardians of traditional culture, are strongly condemned in Soviet Russian accounts for their attempts to prevent Chukchi and Eskimos from participating in cooperatives or allowing their children to attend school, and it was perhaps at their instigation that several village Soviet chairmen and literacy instructors were murdered in the late 1930s. During the campaign against the shamans young Chukchis and Eskimos who attended Russian schools were encouraged to report on the activities of their local shamans and to lampoon them in verses and plays.[21]

The Committee of the North's first cultural base was established at St Lawrence Bay in 1928, when ten motor-powered whale-boats were provided on credit, and some of the existing Chukchi and Eskimo boat crews came together to form seasonal hunting cooperatives. To encourage further enterprises of this kind, another cultural base was founded at Chaun Bay on the northern coast, as well as one inland near Markovo, where the reindeer pastures of Chukchis, Koraks and Ewens met on the Anadyr river.

The drive for collectivisation which the local communists set in motion in 1931 encountered intense resistance from the Chukchis, both the nomadic reindeer-herders of the interior and the settled sea-hunters of the coast. Among the latter, according to a Soviet account of the period, an elaborate conspiracy for exploitation and self-enrichment was maintained by the shamans. At the settlement of Uelen, for instance, the seven whale-boats were

---

[21] Gurvich, *Osushchestvleniye*, p. 155; *Narody Sibiri*, pp. 921, 928–9, 943; Sergeyev, *Nekapitalisticheskiy put*, pp. 288–90; Vdovin, *Priroda i chelovek*, pp. 234–6, 248–9; *Yazyki narodov SSR*, vol. V, pp. 248, 271; A.K. Yefimova and Y.N. Klitina, comps., *Chukotskoye i eskimosskoye iskusstvo*, Leningrad, 1981.

owned not by a cooperative, but by individuals, some of whom were shamans. As a result, there were 'rich' and 'poor' boat crews, and much injustice in the division of walrus meat between families. The intention of this account is obviously to discredit the traditional social relationships existing before collectivisation. A later Chukchi writer, however, transmits the recollections of compatriots who lived at that time and who not only recalled fairness in the sharing of meat, but also saw the justification for individual boat-ownership, since 'many Eskimos had equipped themselves with their own whale-boats or canoes. Much had been achieved by honest hard work and the success which comes to those who are most persistent.' The person to whom these words are attributed, the Eskimo Ashkamakin, who as a boy had collaborated with Soviet Russian officials in persuading the Eskimos and Chukchis to form the first hunting cooperatives, recalled that

we had to convince people that collective ownership of the whale-boat or canoe was to everybody's advantage. At the time I hadn't much idea of Marxist revolutionary theory, so what I emphasized was our ancient customs and the way Arctic people had always collaborated in the work of hunting. And this often had more effect than some of the slogans that I myself didn't really understand at the time.

However, where persuasion failed to overcome resistance to the self-confident resolution of the collectivisers, less gentle means were used. Ashkamakin tells of a defiant shaman whose family used guns to prevent Soviet agents from landing near their home on Arakamchechen island, until a seaplane swooping low over their *yarangas* terrified them into submission.[22]

The Reindeer Chukchi of the inland tundra were harder men than the coast-dwellers, and much less accessible to the attentions of the Russian collectivisers. Consequently the collectivisation of reindeer herds could at first only be attempted in districts having a considerable Russian population, such as the Little Anyui valley in the north-west, and the lowland region on the middle course of the river Anadyr, where a state farm (*sovkhoz*) was set up in 1929 by the Kamchatka Joint-Stock Company (AKO). This enterprise possessed initially 300 reindeer, obtained despite the taboo on the sale of live animals, and impoverished Chukchis were employed as herdsmen. Altogether over forty collectives were formed between 1931 and 1936 – half of them for reindeer-herding and half for sea-mammal hunting – as well as a few for fishing and fur-trapping. However, the collectives – or 'cooperative grazing associations' – formed among the Reindeer Chukchi by 1933 were very small and embraced only 3 per cent of the population (as compared with 60 per cent of the coastal people), and in 1939, when about 95 per cent of the latter had enrolled in Soviet collectives, the percentage of collectivised reindeer nomads had increased only to 11 per cent. Almost 90 per cent of all

[22] Yu. Rytkheu, *Sovremennye legendy*, Leningrad, 1980, pp. 256–60.

reindeer in Chukchi-land were still privately owned in 1941, so that the
great majority of Reindeer Chukchis remained entirely outside the collective
system, turning their backs on the benefits of modern civilisation offered by
the Russians and adhering to the traditional ways of nomadic life. Several
Chukchi 'reindeer kings' such as Venikano still possessed herds of up to
50,000 head in the 1930s and gave employment to a number of poor
herdsmen. The principal refuge of the Reindeer Chukchi lay in withdrawal
from the Anadyr basin to the great sea of upland tundra in the north between
Chaun Bay and the river Amguema – an inaccessible region where many so-
called kulaks roamed with their herds until the 1950s. Others moved away to
the forested hills and plain of the Big Anyui basin on the border of Yakutia.
The desire to escape from collectivisation also led to a complete change in
the way of life of some coastal Chukchis: one small community at Chaun Bay
abandoned their sea-mammal hunting and joined the more prosperous
nomadic reindeer-herders of the interior. Naturally, the Reindeer Chukchis
in these regions preserved their old beliefs in spirits of nature almost
unchanged, and their shamans had great influence. Much work of
'enlightenment' – or anti-religious propaganda – remained to be done by
Soviet Russian educators before they could be absorbed into the Soviet
system.[23]

One unique aspect of the life of the native peoples of the Far North-east
was that the frontier between the USSR and the USA in the Bering Strait
remained relatively open until 1945. Between Prince of Wales Cape in
Alaska and Dezhnyov Cape in Chukchi-land lie the two Diomede Islands,
the smaller of which, known as Inalik to the Eskimos, belongs to the USA,
while the larger, Ratman Island, belongs to the USSR. As the distance
between them is no more than three miles, and each is only about twenty-
two miles from the nearest point on the mainland, they form stepping-stones
between Asia and North America which the Eskimos had always used. Until
the late 1930s intercourse between the Eskimos on the two islands was fairly
common, especially for the traditional annual dance and song festivals.[24]

THE KOLYMA TRUST AND DALSTROY

While the collectivisation of the coastal hunters and some of the reindeer
nomads of the Far North-east proceeded gradually during the 1930s, Rus-

[23] N.N. Dikov, ed., *Ocherki istorii Chukotki s drevneyshikh vremen do nashikh dney*, Novosibirsk,
1974, pp. 179–80, 183, 236, 253, 404; Gurvich, *Etnokulturnye protsessy*, p. 145; Gushchin
and Afanasyev, *Chukotskiy natsionalnyy okrug*, p. 42; I.A., 'Usilim borbu protiv shamanstva!',
Sovetskaya Arktika, 1938, no. 10–11, pp. 109–11; *Narody Sibiri*, pp. 921, 943, 946; Rytkheu,
Sovremennye legendy, pp. 249, 258–9; E.Ye. Selitrennik, 'Nekotorye voprosy kolkhoznogo
stroitelstva v Chukotskom natsionalnom okruge', *Sovetskaya etnografiya*, 1965, no. 1, pp. 14–
16, 22–7; Sergeyev, *Nekapitalisticheskiy put*, pp. 355, 358, 407; Spiridonov, 'Oduly', p. 176;
Suslov, 'Shamanstvo', pp. 97–9.
[24] Rytkheu, *Sovremennye legendy*, pp. 177, 189, 242–4, 250, 264, 270.

sian intrusion into the region assumed a new form and an unprecedented scale with the opening of state mining enterprises. The ongoing exploitation of alluvial gold deposits in the Okhotsk region had led to further prospecting in the late 1920s under the aegis of the state enterprise Dalzoloto – 'Far [East] Gold'. Signs of platinum as well as gold had been discovered on the rivers Kolyma and Indigirka, and in 1928 the first official expedition, led by Yu.A. Bilibin, landed near Ola, and, with the assistance of Ewen and Yakut guides, made its way inland towards the upper reaches of the Kolyma. In the following year work began at the gold-field of Srednekan and soon the number of miners swelled to about 4,000, as expropriated peasants from other parts of Siberia were brought in to serve their terms of 'corrective labour' here. The heavy work of breaking up frozen sub-soil and transporting it to the rockers was performed with the most primitive tools: pick-axes, spades and wheelbarrows, methods which remained in use almost unchanged for the next twenty-five years of the Kolyma gold-field's existence.

Up till this time Soviet Russian exploitation of the Far Eastern colony had been carried out by a number of different agencies in a totally uncoordinated way. It was in order to provide over-all planning and control that the 'State Trust for the Development of Industry and Roads in the Upper Kolyma Region' was founded in December 1931. This Kolyma Trust was given a territory of over 190,000 square miles (larger than Poland or California) as a separate administrative unit cutting across the normal borders of the Yakut ASSR and the Okhotsk-Ewen National District from which it was composed, and its administration was subordinated directly to the Communist Party. Direction of the Kolyma territory was put in the hands of the Latvian Bolshevik Eduard Berzin, whose experience as a military commander in Moscow and industrial organiser in the Urals was used to drive along the Trust's project in the extremely difficult conditions of this inhospitable region.

An enterprise on this scale demanded a whole army of workers, but the austerity of conditions made it virtually impossible to recruit labourers, or indeed qualified mining engineers, especially in view of the lack of any special inducements. Consequently, almost from the start, the Kolyma gold-workings relied upon the involuntary labour of thousands of prisoners, and a close connection with the Soviet state's organs of oppression was established. Thus the upper Kolyma region was used by the Communist Party as a penal colony, just as Sakhalin had been under the Tsars – except that the numbers of political prisoners sent to the Kolyma was much greater and their treatment was incomparably more inhumane. One monument to the work of the Kolyma Trust is the city of Magadan, founded near Nagayevo harbour in 1933 as the administrative centre of the region. As a town – eventually stone-built, with colleges, a publishing-house, hospitals and other modern amenities – Magadan became a pleasant enough place for Soviet Rusian officials to live in, if they could close their minds to the sinister reality of slave-labour camps all around them.

During the first six years under the direction of Berzin, the project is said to have been well organised, and conditions for the convict workers reasonable. However, the whole project demanded the sacrifice of thousands of human lives for the sake of the gold which Stalin's Communist Party needed in order to buy machinery from Germany and other countries. The strategic importance of the North-east was further increased by the discovery of tin ore, the mining of which began in 1937. Stalin and the NKVD were fully in command of the Soviet Union by then, and although Berzin, as a dedicated communist, appears to have kept the work of the Kolyma Trust in step with Moscow's demands, he became a victim of his own party's tyranny and was shot in 1939.

Under Berzin's successors (one of whom, Garanin, was also shot in 1939!) the whole Kolyma enterprise, renamed the Chief Administration for the Development of the Far North – 'Dalstroy' – was placed under the exclusive control of the Communist Party and its organ of oppression, the NKVD. In the period of unbridled terror which had begun throughout the USSR, hundreds of thousands of political prisoners from Soviet Russia were shipped, under appalling conditions, to Magadan, for labour in the concentration camps of Dalstroy, the main aim of which, according to one Western writer, was no longer so much the extraction of gold as the destruction of the prisoners.[25] Such a view, naturally, clashes with the information offered in a Soviet work that 'At Dalstroy work also proceeded on the big, demanding task of re-education through socially useful labour of its complement of former criminals and other socially dangerous elements.'[26] The sufferings of these 'elements', which included, for instance, the famous poet Osip Mandelshtam, have been documented in many accounts by survivors. While this 'useful' work proceeded, the Kolyma Communist Party conference in 1939 pledged itself to further 'labour-intensive' (!) projects, including the construction of a road from Magadan to Yakutsk.[27]

[25] Conquest, *Kolyma*, p. 115.
[26] Zhikharev, *Ocherki istorii*, p. 212. Before 1987 most Soviet books made no reference whatever to the Kolyma concentration camps. For instance in the multi-volume *Istoriya Sibiri* edited by A.P. Okladnikov, this region is mentioned only twice, very briefly, in such terms as: 'Soviet people built roads and mines. New gold-fields, workers' settlements and towns with schools, hospitals and clubs appeared' (vol. IV, p. 363; also vol. V, p. 26). V.A. Shvarev's book on 'forty years of Soviet power in the Far East' mentions briefly on pp. 62–3 the 'mighty state Trust' which 'using high-speed methods began the construction of ... industrial installations and workers' settlements', but no hint is given about Dalstroy, prison-camps or forced labour.
[27] Armstrong, *The Northern Sea Route*, pp. 56–60; Conquest, *The Great Terror*, p. 55; Conquest, *Kolyma*, pp. 10–11, 17, 38–45, 50–7, 108, 111, 115, 122, Dikov, *Ocherki istorii*, pp. 222–3; T. Green, *The New World of Gold*, rev. edn, London, 1985, pp. 70–5; *Istoriya Yakutskoy ASSR*, vol. III, pp. 183, 264, 266; Kalesnik, *Dalniy Vostok*, p. 332; Nove, *Economic History*, p. 211;

DALSTROY AND THE INDIGENOUS POPULATION

The original territory of the Kolyma Trust lay mostly in the northern half of the Okhotsk Ewen National District, and from the start the interests of the Ewen and other natives were entirely subordinated to those of the Soviet Russian state and its industrial development. In 1931 the Committee of the North's cultural base, founded at Nagayevo for the benefit of the Ewens only four years previously, was requisitioned as one of the few existing buildings, for use by the Trust. At the same time, the influx of a substantial new alien population immediately created an urgent demand for food and transport which the Ewens were expected to satisfy. As very little accommodation existed and food supplies at the best of times were inadequate, the most primitive conditions prevailed among the Russian newcomers. This had serious repercussions on the native people, as desperadoes seeking food in the surrounding forest indiscriminately killed wild game and reindeer belonging to Ewen herds. Consequently, those Ewens who had been used to pasturing their deer near the Ola coast moved away from the Russian settlement into the depths of the forest. A serious conflict arose between the Ewens and Russians during the crisis at the gold-mines in the winter of 1931–2, when, in the absence of any other means of transport, the Soviet Russian authorities decided to 'mobilise' reindeer transport and obtain meat supplies by commandeering animals from the Ewens. On the basis of their total ignorance about, and no doubt contempt for the 'natives', the newly arrived communists designated as 'kulaks' many Ewens who possessed only 200 to 400 head – the minimum required to support a family of six – and imposed absurd fines (up to 30,000 roubles in some cases!) on those who refused to surrender their reindeer. Understandably, the Ewens, whose lives depended upon preserving their herds, moved away farther into the tundra. However, the presence of the Ewens and their deer was so indispensable to the Russians for the operation of the Kolyma Trust that they arranged that most of them were 'brought back' with the help of 'working Ewens', that is, some of the coastal poor who were incited by the Soviet Russians to betray their compatriots.[28]

For the Russian rulers of Kolyma, indeed, it was imperative to obtain the services of the Ewens as carriers, even though this meant training them to use their animals in an entirely unaccustomed way. Like all Tungus, they employed reindeer only for riding and pack-carrying, and never for drawing sledges. Now, however, they were to learn to harness deer to sledges in the way used by the local Yakuts. In fact, most of them could not or would not

Popova, *Eveny*, pp. 245–6; L. Schapiro, *The Communist Party of the Soviet Union*, London, 1960, pp. 392, 394, 396, 408; Zhikharev, *Ocherki istorii*, pp. 139, 148–52, 155–73, 177–81, 184, 187–9, 191–2, 202, 204–13, 219–22, 225.
[28] Zhikharev, *Ocherki istorii*, p. 166.

make this fundamental change, and only the Ewens of Talaya district allowed themselves to be diverted from their normal occupations and taken over by the Russians for the work of transporting freight to the gold-workings throughout the 1930s.

The delivery of their land into the hands of the Kolyma Trust put the natives of the Okhotsk Ewen National District into a different category from other northern peoples, since it took them out of the purview of the Committee of the North. A Soviet decree of October 1932, in fact, made the Trust responsible not only for economic matters in its territory, but for all aspects of political and cultural life as well. In response to Berzin's plea for a single, powerful Communist Party organisation on the Kolyma, various administrative changes were made, including the abolition of the Okhotsk Ewen National District. Clearly, in a region of intensive industrial exploitation, the Soviet Russian government was unlikely to leave the aboriginal inhabitants uncollectivised and unexploited for the aims of 'socialist construction'. A beginning to the recruitment of native youth for communist organisations had been made as early as 1928 at Ola, and now this Young Communist League stimulated class antagonism among the coastal Ewens, forcing 'rich' people to hand over increased quotas of fish and furs. As in other northern regions, however, the more numerous reindeer-herding nomads were less easy to locate and coerce, so that most of the collective activities were at first limited to the coastal Ewens (and local Russian settlers) of Ola and Taui, among whom a few fishing and fur-trapping collectives were organised in 1930. The conflict over reindeer in 1931 had made the Reindeer Ewens and other local people, including the small Yakut communities, very wary of Soviet Russians, and vindictive towards those herdsmen who became communist activists. Here and there, however, the Russians succeeded in having 'kulaks' and shamans expelled from the more accessible nomadic soviets, and cooperative herds were gradually formed. There was little to tempt the Ewens into the cooperative system, however, in this region where the Russians themselves received essential supplies so irregularly that the stores had little or nothing to offer as an inducement to rank-and-file herdsmen to forgo the protection of the herd chiefs. Resistance to collectivisation on the part of the reindeer-herders took the usual forms of flight to the forest and tundra and, when intolerable pressure was brought to bear upon them, the slaughter of their own herds. As a result, the number of reindeer in the Trust's territory was greatly reduced during the 1930s. The remote northern parts of the territory provided a refuge for some of the most important Ewen clan chiefs, such as the Khabarovs and Boldukhinovs, whose policy was that the Ewens might collaborate with the Russians in fishing, but must keep them out of the taiga, where some of the Reindeer Ewens were able to hold out till the 1950s.

The principal economic purpose behind the Soviet Russian authorities' creation of collectives was to provide food for their industrial sites and the officials who administered them (if not for the convict workers). Gradually some of the natives were drawn into the work of these farms. For instance, by 1936, the Yukagirs of Korkodon river were incorporated into a collective farm which not only herded reindeer, but had horses and cattle, and grew hay to feed them.

It is ironical, in view of the nature of Dalstroy's labour force and the inhuman ways in which it was used and abused, to read that the natives of the territory were helped to understand the benefits of disciplined, collective labour for society by the example of hard-working Russian peasants and the achievements of socialist industry, the new centres of which 'in far away Arctic regions served as beacons to the nomad, pointing the way to the new life'.[29] We may be sure that (apart from those who concealed themselves in the remote taiga) the native peoples of the Far North-east under the super-vision of the NKVD were subjected to the same excesses of 'labour disci-pline' and arbitrary rule as the working Russian population was. Nevertheless, some cultural benefits may be said to have accrued to the Ewens during the 1930s. One of these was the introduction of the alphabet – based at first (1932–6) on Roman, and thereafter Cyrillic – which permitted the publication of elementary school-books and a few literary works in a written language based on the dialect of Ola. A number of Ewen schools came into operation, staffed from 1937 onward by native teachers trained at the Magadan college of education.

Although at first Chukchi-land, like the Korak National District, did not come within the sphere of the Kolyma Trust, in 1939 the transfer of responsibility for geological exploration from Glavsevmorputi to Dalstroy led to the absorption of both regions into the NKVD empire. Tin ore had been discovered near Pevek on Chaun Bay – a district with even more severe climatic conditions than the Kolyma basin – and in 1940, when the start of the Second World War increased its strategic importance, mining began there, as work of equal priority to gold production. As Pevek became the centre of a new industrial region an influx of Russian workers took place, with a consequent demand for food. This in its turn made it imperative, from the Russians' point of view, to collectivise more of the reindeer-herding population, first by the amalgamation of several small cooperative herds around Chaun Bay and then, in 1943, by the creation of a reindeer state farm near Pevek.

Thus the 1930s brought to the North-East of Siberia the beginning of large-scale exploitation of natural resources by the Russian Communist Party régime, the impact of which upon the native inhabitants and the delicate natural environment was already profound, and would inevitably

---

[29] *Istoriya Yakutskoy ASSR*, vol. III, p. 183.

increase during subsequent decades in accordance with the economic and political imperatives of the Soviet state.[30]

[30] Dikov, *Ocherki istorii*, pp. 197, 223–4; *Istoriya Yakutskoy ASSR*, vol. III, p. 183; *Istoriya Sibiri*, vol. IV, p. 460; Kolarz, *The Peoples*, p. 88; *Narody Sibiri*, pp. 771, 775; Popova, *Eveny*, pp. 76, 178, 214, 222, 226–46, 250–1; Selitrennik, 'Nekotorye voprosy', p. 18; Sergeyev, *Nekapitalisticheskiy put*, p. 360; *Yazyki narodov SSSR*, vol. V, p. 88; Zhikharev, *Ocherki istorii*, pp. 154, 157, 162–3, 166, 174–7, 182, 184, 194, 197–8, 200–4.

15

SOVIET SIBERIA AFTER 1941

THE SECOND WORLD WAR AND THE SIBERIAN PEOPLES

IT was the Second World War that finally confirmed the long-standing assumption that Siberia was an integral part of Russia and that the lives of the native peoples were unquestionably subordinated to the paramount needs of the metropolis. From this time onward they were, like all other nationalities, absorbed into the mass of the 'Soviet people' in its ostensibly fraternal unity under the leadership of the predominantly Russian Communist Party.

The most important single factor in this process was probably military conscription. Until 1936 the Soviet Russian government had maintained a policy similar to that of the tsarist government in exempting most of the native peoples of Siberia from obligatory military service. While this regulation was intended to give special protection to the smaller, more primitive communities, it was also an indirect acknowledgement of the colonial status of the territories they inhabited. Of the Siberian peoples, only the Buryat-Mongols, the Altaians and the Khakases were subject to military service from the second half of the 1920s, as were the Kazaks. In 1936, however, the situation was altered by the new 'Stalin' Constitution. According to this and another law of 1939, universal military service in defence of the 'Motherland' was proclaimed the 'sacred duty' of every citizen of the USSR, and conscription was extended to all males without distinction of nationality. This, we are told, released the native peoples from a sense of inferiority and satisfied their long-cherished wish to share the honour of army service. At the same time the policy on ethnic military units was changed: shortly after the 1937 purge of Red Army officers, national units, such as those of the Buryats and Kazaks, were abolished and ethnically mixed units became the rule. The theoretical justification for this was the principle of internationalism, but the more obvious practical end was the integration and Russification of the armed forces through the universal use of the Russian language for instruction and commands. For recruits drawn from non-Russian communities, however, service in mixed units entailed an alien environment and lack of contact with compatriots.[1]

After the rout of the Soviet army in June 1941, when mass mobilisation of the armed forces took place throughout the Soviet Union, only certain categories of industrial workers and students were exempted from military service, while all other men, including peasants and non-Russians of all regions and all degrees of social development, were swept up into the army or industrial work. According to Communist Party propaganda, all, including those from the most remote corners of Siberia, were fired with the spirit of Soviet patriotism to defend the 'fatherland' against the German invaders. Powerful indeed must have been the political indoctrination which could lend to events in Europe and on Russia's distant western borders any relevance to the lives of hunters and herdsmen of Siberia, the Far North and Far East, most of whom had little conception of the world beyond Russia's frontiers. Nor could the native peoples have any appreciation of political systems apart from that imposed upon them by self-assured Russian communists. The political divisions and conflicts within the Europeanised world, and its ideological polarisation, must have been as remote and meaningless as they were to the Indians of the South American forests.

While the total number of Siberian natives was small in relation to the millions mobilised into the Soviet armed forces, they were of considerable use in certain specific functions for which their way of life qualified them – that is, as scouts, ski-troops and snipers. Many, including Tunguses, Yakuts, Nanais, Udeghes, Altaians and Nenets, earned medals for their service in these capacities, and not a few were killed or wounded. In one district of Yakutia, for instance, out of forty Ewenkis who were conscripted, twenty-two were killed in the war. Another field in which northern peoples such as the Nenets were employed was in transportation of military supplies by reindeer in the north-western parts of the USSR. The Buryat-Mongols with their Cossack traditions provided soldiers on a greater scale. After the German invasion when, in the interests of efficiency and *esprit de corps*, the 1938 commitment to ethnically mixed units was reversed and national military formations were once again created, a whole Buryat-Mongol Rifle Division was formed. This fought, under its Buryat commander I. Baldynov, not only on the German front but also against the Japanese in the brief Far East campaign in 1945.

---

[1] H.J. Berman and M. Kerner, *Soviet Military Law and Administration*, Cambridge (Mass.), 1955, p. 35; *Istoriya Buryatskoy SSR*, vol. II, pp. 205–6; T. Rakowska-Harmstone, 'The Soviet army as the instrument of national integration', in J. Erickson and E.J. Feuchtwanger, eds., *Soviet Military Power and Performance*, London, 1979, pp. 132–5; *Narody Sibiri*, p. 551; Sergeyev, *Nekapitalisticheskiy put*, pp. 411–12; *Sibirskaya Sovetskaya entsiklopediya*, vol. II, col. 1019; B. Ukachin, *Povesti*, Moscow, 1983, pp. 87, 117.

Thus the USSR involved men of its North Asian colonial territories in war service in the same way as, for instance, Britain used 'native' troops from Africa and India. However, while the latter were volunteers, indigenous Siberians were conscripted without choice on a par with Russians, Ukrainians and other nationalities of European Russia. (In the USA too, Indians were recruited on a voluntary basis, while the Eskimos of Alaska were organised voluntarily into a home defence force.) Induction into Russian army life, enforced association with large groups of alien men in training, and exposure to the horrors of twentieth-century warfare must inevitably have had a traumatic effect upon men from small 'primitive' communities, causing changes in social and ethical attitudes which could not easily be reversed when they returned to their own communities after the war. A secondary, but not negligible, effect of service in the Red Army upon members of non-Russian nationalities was an increase in their use of alcohol, in the Russian national form of vodka.[2]

In addition to the direct effects of obligatory military service, the total mobilisation of the male population of the Soviet Union placed an enormous strain upon the rural economy of every region, whatever its way of life. Only women, children and old men were left to carry on the work of farming, tending livestock, fishing and hunting, while tractors, lorries and horses were requisitioned for the war front. The effect of this upon the agricultural regions is well known: four years of all-out war effort in a country lacking a secure production and supply base, and now largely deprived of agricultural vehicles, in many regions resulted in a return to primitive manual methods of cultivating the land. After the German invasion most of the grain-producing lands of European Russia and the Ukraine were under enemy occupation, so that, as during the Civil War of 1918–22, the grain production of Western Siberia and northern Kazakstan became crucial for food supplies to the cities and industrial regions of the western USSR. Even before the war, however, Western Siberia suffered from a shortage of agricultural labour in comparison with other regions of the USSR, so that an ever-worsening labour crisis occurred during the war, and the West Siberian peasantry, including the Tatars, had to face superhuman tasks – much of the additional burden falling on the shoulders of women.

Some idea of the difficult conditions created by the Second World War in the non-Russian communities of Siberia can be gleaned from published accounts. In the Mountain Altai, for instance, the women and children of the

[2] Berman and Kerner, *Soviet Military Law*, pp. 35, 38, 95–7; C.H. Enloe, *Ethnic Soldiers*, Harmondsworth, 1980, pp. 192–3; Gurvich, *Osushchestvleniye*, p. 333; *Istoriya Yakutskoy ASSR*, vol. III, pp. 251–2; Khaptayev, *Istoriya Buryatskoy ASSR*, vol. II, pp. 484–97; Khomich, *Nentsy*, p. 244; Kolarz, *The Peoples*, p. 82; M.R. Marston, *Men of the Tundra: Alaska Eskimos at War*, New York, 1969; *Narody Sibiri*, pp. 809, 812; Phillips, *Dawn in Siberia*, p. 174; B. Ukachin, *Povesti*, Moscow, 1983, pp. 80, 174, 183–4.

Turkic population who were left to tend the herds of cattle and sheep, lived in primitive and dilapidated huts and teepees, and were frequently so near starvation that they ate moles and gophers and made 'tea' from plant-roots and barley husks. Their children went barefoot in inadequate clothing, so that among the Altaians one of the incidental consequences of the war was admiring envy of the good-quality clothing issued to soldiers. Despite the poverty of their life, the people of collectivised Altai settlements were required by the harsh decrees of the Soviet Russian state to fulfil rigid quotas for the production of milk, meat and eggs, risking financial penalties and accusations of sabotage if they fell short, or if livestock were lost because of severe weather, depredation by wolves or other accidents. A similar burden of unceasing labour was placed upon the Nenets women of the Far North, who took over the work of reindeer-herdsmen, fishermen and hunters. In the Far East too, the collectivised Nivkh and Nanai communities, whose menfolk had been taken away for army service or industrial labour, nevertheless had to satisfy the demands of the Russian state, so that the badly maintained fishing vessels had to be taken out in all weathers by crews of women and old men. The central part of Yakutia was particularly unfortunate during the Second World War, as its womenfolk, old men and children not only had to cope with the regular difficulties of farming in northern latitudes, but also with the additional disaster of drought in the years 1939–42. In a desperate attempt to save their cattle they made long migrations in quest of pastures, and the area of Yakutia under the plough fell by 20 per cent. There was also a big fall in the number of cattle in the Yakut Republic from about 475,600 in 1940 to perhaps 300,000 at the end of the war. Many Yakut peasants lost all of their privately owned cattle, and with them a degree of independence.

The overriding needs of the Soviet Russian war effort also had a disastrous effect upon the native communities of the North, as their reindeer herds were depleted by slaughter for meat. In the Nenets and Khanty-Mansi regions the most immediate requirement was food for the industrial workers of the Urals and Western Siberia, whose numbers had been greatly augmented by the evacuation of western enterprises. Herds in the Yamal Nenets Region were reduced by 37 per cent during the war, and a similar loss can be assumed for the Nenets National Region west of the Urals. Farther east, the Ewenki and Ewen reindeer-herders of Yakutia suffered the loss of 68 per cent of their animals during the first eighteen months of the war. Not only reindeer-herding, but also the hunting economy of Siberia was affected, since furs were urgently required for winter clothing for the army and over-hunting of many species of fur-bearing animals took place. In Siberia, as in the whole of the Soviet Union, the years of reconstruction following the end of fighting in 1945 did not bring immediate relief from hardships. The shortage of clothing and food continued for many years, so that for instance in the Mountain Altai Autonomous Province the people were glad to eat bran and cattle-cake.[3]

The overwhelming part played by the USSR in defeating Hitler's armies is universally recognised, as is the heroism of the Russian people in driving such a powerful and ruthless enemy from their soil. However, notwithstanding the fearful cost of the war to the Russians themselves, the cost of their single-minded war effort to the non-Russian communities of Siberia was disproportionately high. Their relatively small numbers can scarcely have made a significant contribution to the war, since they were counted in thousands as against the millions who made up the population of the Soviet Union. In 1939 there were about 829,000 indigenous, non-Russian inhabitants of Siberia, including the 'larger' nationalities such as the Yakuts (242,100) and Buryat Mongols (225,000). Of this total, men of military age (roughly 20 per cent) amounted to no more than 165,800. Compared with the total number of men in the 18–55 year old age group in the USSR: about 34.1 million – or the number of Russians eligible for war service: 20 million – the numerical contribution of the Siberian peoples was tiny: about 0.49 per cent of all men of military age. Considering not only the small numbers involved, but also the inefficiency of Soviet Russian organisation, which meant considerable wastage of man-power, it must be concluded that the value of the conscription of Siberian natives to the Soviet Russian and Allied cause could scarely justify the hardships imposed upon the native communities and the destruction of their way of life caused by the wholesale uprooting of their menfolk for use in the Red Army or the industrial labour-force.

The effects of the war on the peoples of Siberia are suggested by the census figures for 1939 and 1959. During this period, despite war casualties, the total number of Russians in the USSR increased by 13.7 per cent, and, for instance, that of the Tatars by 15.7 per cent, while some of the smaller peoples of European Russia such as the Mari, Udmurt and Chuvash increased by between 3.1 and 7.3 per cent. Of the Siberian peoples, however, only the Buryats, Khakases and Khantys increased over this period (by 12.6, 7.6 and 4.9 per cent respectively), while decrease was the rule for the others, as Table 5 shows:[4]

The biggest demographic factor in Siberia since the 1940s, however, has been the inundation of the native communities by a swiftly increasing contingent of people from the European part of the Soviet Union. By November 1941 the equipment of 1,360 factories had been moved by rail to the

---

[3] Flerov et al., *Krestyanstvo*, pp. 88–105, 112–15; *Istoriya Yakutskoy ASSR*, vol. III, pp. 220, 222, 230, 236–9; Khomich, *Nentsy*, pp. 244–5; Kolarz, *The Peoples*, pp. 72, 95; *Narody Sibiri*, pp. 486, 568, 809; Popova, *Eveny*, pp. 256–7, 264; Sergeyev, *Nekapitalisticheskiy put*, pp. 416–17; Shvarev, *Dalniy Vostok*, pp. 441–2; Taksami, *Nivkhi*, pp. 69–70; Ukachin, *Povesti*, pp. 3–6, 14–16, 21–2, 33–8, 49, 80–1, 98, 106, 108, 144, 148; Zhikharev, *Ocherki istorii*, p. 229.

[4] Figures from Kozlov, *Natsionalnosti SSR*, 2nd edn, pp. 285–7, 290–1.

Table 5

	1939	1959	Percentage decrease
Yakuts	242,100	236,700	2.2
Ewenkis	29,700	24,700	16.8
Ewens	9,700	9,100	6.2
Chukchis	13,900	11,700	15.8
Nenets	24,800	23,000	7.3
Altaians	47,900	45,300	5.4
Shors	16,300	15,300	6.1
Nanais	8,500	8,000	6.0

industrial regions of the southern Urals, south-western Siberia and Central Asia, where it was re-assembled and put into production. The workers and their families accompanying this movement caused a great increase in the population of Sverdlovsk, Magnitogorsk, Chelyabinsk and other towns in the Ural region, which became the main base of the armaments industry. A similar sudden expansion occurred in the Omsk, Novosibirsk, Kuzbass and Tomsk districts of Western Siberia, where in 1943 about 1 million evacuees from the west were working. In addition to the normal work-force of local residents and evacuees, industry east of the Urals swallowed up considerable numbers of prisoners-of-war and prisoners of the Communist Party's Gulag. The latter category continued to provide expendable labour for mining and industrial construction in Novosibirsk province (the Mariinsk camps), Krasnoyarsk province (the 'Kraslag' and Kansk camps), Norilsk, Kolyma and many other places all over Siberia and northern Kazakstan. Such a flood of newcomers, including Communist Party officials, NKVD troops, industrial workers and managers, all requiring to be housed and fed – albeit in some cases at the lowest possible level – inevitably had an effect upon the native communities living in the vicinity of Russian settlements. Another direct effect was that in the Kuzbass and Kemerovo coal-mining areas some of the native people – Shors and Altaians – were drawn into the labour force.[5]

THE WAR IN THE FAR EAST

In the Far East the last stages of the Second World War brought an unprecedented build-up of Russian presence and activity, both industrial and

[5] Flerov, ed., *Krestyanstvo*, p. 98; G. Hosking, *A History of the Soviet Union*, London, 1985, pp. 283–4; Kalesnik, *Sovetskiy Soyuz. Ural*, pp. 92–3; *Zapadnaya Sibir*, p. 98; Samsonov, *Kratkaya istoriya SSSR*, vol. II, pp. 309–10; Solzhenitsyn, *Gulag Archipelago*, vol. II, p. 124; Ukachin, *Povesti*, p. 116.

14 Buryat-Mongolian martial tradition. I.V. Baldynov, during the Second World War the colonel commanding the Buryat-Mongol Infantry Division from the Caucasus to Yugoslavia, and against the Japanese in Manchuria. For distinguished service Baldynov's Buryats were awarded the status of a Guards Division and he was promoted to Major-General.

military. Although the USSR and Japan refrained from attacking each other, the alliance between the USSR and USA after Japan's attack on Pearl Harbour led to the shipping to Vladivostok of over 9 million tons of American 'lend-lease' supplies, and the ferrying of nearly 8,000 aircraft from Alaska to Seimchan on the Kolyma. The Soviet Union's declaration of war on Japan on 8 August 1945, two days after the Americans dropped the atomic bomb, opened a new phase of Soviet Russian activity in the Far East. According to agreements made at the Yalta Conference, Russia's intervention in the war against Japan would gain recognition of its right to dominate Mongolia and Northern Manchuria and to occupy both the southern half of Sakhalin and the whole of the Kuril Islands. A huge army consisting of about 1,735,000 Soviet and Mongolian troops crossed the frontier into northern China and defeated the main Japanese army, and by the end of August Red Army units were within 120 miles of Peking. Meanwhile, on 11 August Soviet troops advanced from Northern Sakhalin into the Japanese southern half of the island and overran all of it. The assault on the Kurils began on 18 August with a landing on the northernmost island by troops from Kamchatka, and by 1 September the whole archipelago was in Russian hands. The Soviet Far Eastern campaign was a final blow to the Japanese, who lost 677,000 men in it – 34 per cent of the total military casualties sustained by Japan during the Second World War.[6]

The inhabitants of Sakhalin and the Kuril Islands were profoundly affected by Soviet Russian occupation. As a result of Japanese colonisation of Sakhalin after 1925, the Japanese population in 1944 was almost 448,000, some 300,000 of whom were captured by the Russians. After a transitional period, when local Japanese officials and businessmen were useful for the restoration of order and commerce, most of them were repatriated to Japan. In South Sakhalin almost every trace of Japanese occupation was erased, and place-names were changed: Toyohara, for instance, becoming Yuzhnosakhalinsk ('South Sakhalin town') and Otomari Korsakov.

Along with the Japanese, about 43,000 Koreans who had been imported by them as industrial labour fell into Soviet Russian hands, and these too were useful in keeping industry running. The situation of the Koreans was complicated by the Russian and American occupation of Korea in 1945–50, the ensuing Korean War, and the continuing partition of their country. Repatriation was difficult, with the result that about 67,450 Koreans remained in the Soviet Far East in 1959. Almost two-thirds of these were in southern Sakhalin, and the rest in the Amur–Ussuri and Kamchatka

[6] J.R. Deane, *The Strange Alliance: the Story of American Efforts at Wartime Co-operation with Russia*, London, 1947, pp. 87–103; Gusarevich and Seoyev, *Na strazhe*, pp. 59–85; R.H. Jones, *The Road to Russia: United States Lend-Lease to the Soviet Union*, Norman (Oklahoma), 1969, pp. 112–13, 155–60, 210–13, 277; Kolarz, *The Peoples*, p. 142; Samsonov, *Kratkaya istoriya SSSR*, vol. II, pp. 352, 357–9; Stephan, *Sakhalin*, pp. 111–55.

regions. Twenty years later Sakhalin had 35,000 Koreans, with a Korean-language publishing-house, a newspaper, radio broadcasts, libraries, and a number of schools in which the Korean language was used.[7]

The native peoples of southern Sakhalin were the Ainus (about 1,300 in 1941) and Oroks (about 300). Under Japanese rule the Ainus had been subjected to intensive Japanese cultural influence, and in 1947 approximately half of them, including a few hundred in the Kuril Islands, chose to emigrate along with the Japanese to Hokkaido. Those who remained in Sakhalin are said to have been absorbed into fishing collectives, but recent listings of the nationalities of Siberia make no reference whatever to Ainus. Until 1945 the Oroks were subjected to the pressures of collectivisation and sovietisation in the northern half of the island, while those who lived in the south underwent Japanese assimilative policies, including military conscription. Many of the Oroks, like the Ainus, moved to Hokkaido between 1947 and 1955, while those who remained under Soviet Russian rule either continued their nomadic reindeer-herding or lived in settlements near Poronaisk. Their cousins in northern Sakhalin belonged to a single reindeer collective on the east coast.[8]

SOVIET RUSSIAN EXPANSION IN INNER ASIA

The Far East was not the only region of northern Asia in which the Soviet Union made territorial gains during the Second World War. Mongolia and Tannu Tuva were nominally independent foreign countries, but their actual status as satellites of the USSR made it possible for the Russians to place heavy demands upon them as a traditional source of replenishment for their depleted herds of livestock. As a puppet of Moscow the government of the Mongolian People's Republic mobilised the whole country to subserve the Soviet Russian war effort. Even more direct pressure could be applied by the Soviet Russian government to the 'people's republic' of Tannu Tuva, whose small-scale industry was put on a war footing and whose by no means prosperous nomadic tribesmen were obliged to hand over 50,000 horses (over one-third of their stock) and tens of thousands of cattle, as well as 'gifts' of money, leather, skis, wool and other natural produce.

Although the army of Mongolia proper was enlarged greatly after 1941 by the introduction of conscription, it did not play a direct part in the war until 1945. In Tuva, however, obligatory military training was introduced at the end of 1941, and in response to Communist Party propaganda many young

---

[7] *Atlas narodov mira*, Moscow, 1964, p. 25; *Atlas SSSR* (3rd edn), Moscow, 1983, p. 129; Bawden, *History of Mongolia*, pp. 384–5; *Narody Sredney Azii*, vol. II, p. 564; Solzhenitsyn, *Gulag Archipelago*, vol. II, pp. 294–5; vol. III, pp. 35, 51; Stephan, *Sakhalin*, pp. 156–64, 194–5, 204–6.

[8] Kolarz, *The Peoples*, p. 87; Majewicz, 'The Oroks', pp. 141–3; *Narody Sibiri*, pp. 855, 860; Stephan, *Sakhalin*, pp. 116, 193.

Tuvans volunteered for service in the Red Army cavalry and tank corps – thus swelling the ranks of the Buryat, Kalmyk and Altai units which the Germans looked upon collectively as 'Mongolian troops'.[9]

Since 1930 the people of Tannu Tuva had passed through a bewildering cycle of political and social changes. The 'cultural revolution' of 1929–33 had deprived the tribal lords of their wealth and power, undermined the influence of the Buddhist monasteries, and resulted in the collectivisation of three-quarters of the Tuvan population – at the price of much violence. In 1933, perhaps because of an awareness of anti-communist revolts in Mongolia and the consequent abandonment of its five-year plan of industrialisation, a nationalist reaction against Soviet Russian influence emerged in Tuva, and the central committee of the People's Revolutionary Party declared that henceforth their country would be a 'bourgeois democracy' with a policy of native administration and reduction in the number of Russian residents. Tuvan herdsmen began to desert the collectives, and although the Russians hastened to re-establish their dominance and sent more Communist Party agents to purge the Tuvan party, it was impossible to impose upon most Tuvans anything beyond a cooperative system of cattle-rearing, so that in 1943 over 93 per cent of all livestock belonged not to collective farms but to individual families. By this time the 'right opportunists' in the Tuvan People's Revolutionary Party had been swept up by the Soviet NKVD in the 1937 reign of terror, after which Tuva fell under the same régime of bureaucratic tyranny as the Soviet Union itself. One development in the field of culture which was in line with practice in the national regions of the USSR at this time was that the Roman alphabet, which had been used for the Tuvan language since 1930, was abolished.

It was during the first years of Russia's 'Great Fatherland War' that the influence of Stalin's Communist Party in Tuva reached its peak, all remnants of political opposition being suppressed by the NKVD, and the whole economy of the country subordinated to the needs of Soviet Russia. In 1944, without any public announcement in Moscow (no proclamation of the fact was made until 1948) a 'request' from the puppet government of Tuva for union with the USSR was received and acceded to. Thus the last vestiges of Tuvan independence were annulled by a Russian take-over, and the Tannu Tuva People's Republic was reduced to the status of an 'autonomous' province of the RSFSR, its separate People's Revolutionary Party being incorporated into the Communist Party of the Soviet Union. Russia's decision to annexe Tuva was no doubt based above all on long-cherished strategic considerations, but the presence of minerals, including coal, copper, cobalt, mercury, lead, zinc, gold and asbestos, gave it considerable economic value. Ethnically, it brought into the Soviet Union the last of the

---

[9] Aranchyn, *Istoricheskiy put*, pp. 246–64; *Istoriya Mongolskoy Narodnoy Respubliki*, pp. 430–6.

Turkic-language peoples of the Altai-Sayan mountain region – a relatively large community of over 80,000 in 1944.[10]

While Tuva, the former vassal of Mongolia, was being incorporated into the Soviet Union, Mongolia itself remained ostensibly independent of Moscow. The reason for the Russians' restraint on this occasion was no doubt that 'Unilateral Soviet annexation of Mongolia ... would have torpedoed Stalin's expectations for American support in bringing Nationalist China to submit to the Yalta provisions, including recognition of Soviet rights in Manchuria, a strategic area highly desirable to the Russians. It would, therefore, have been foolish to annex Mongolia as well as Tuva...'[11] Cultural annexation, however, was carried out – one significant step towards this being, as in Tuva, the adoption of the Russian alphabet for the Mongol language. The final stage in the detachment of former Outer Mongolia from China – the establishment of its nominal independence as a puppet of the Soviet Union – was confirmed by a plebiscite held in 1945, in which an improbably unanimous vote demonstrated clearly the direct involvement of the Russian Communist Party in its organisation. Thereafter the imposition of Soviet institutions continued. In 1948 a five-year plan of industrial development was adopted and a Union of Mongolian Writers was created to control literary production, while the number of Buddhist monasteries was reduced to five. However, Mongol cultural traditions were not abandoned without a struggle. Between 1949 and 1952 the Mongolian government felt obliged to castigate writers for supposed idealisation of their 'feudal' past and of the historical role of Chingis Khan. The fact that this nationalistic tendency in the Mongolian People's Republic, and the Communist Party's attack on it, was paralleled in Soviet Buryat-Mongolia was an indication of the strength of the cultural affinities which continued to connect the Mongolian people on both sides of the frontier.

Meanwhile the very basis of traditional Mongol culture – pastoral nomadism – came under attack. In the early 1950s over 80 per cent of herds in Mongolia were still owned by the individual nomadic households which made up 61 per cent of the country's population. An intensive collectivisation campaign launched in 1955 quickly changed this. By methods of coercion familiar in the USSR practically all households were collectivised and many forced to settle. As in every other community subjected to this process by the Communist Party, the cattle-breeders' resentment against the enforced social revolution was reflected in a reduction in numbers of livestock by slaughter – from 23 million head in 1957 to 20 million in 1961.

[10] Aranchyn, *Istoricheskiy put*, pp. 125–6, 161–4, 188–94, 204, 207–9, 216, 240, 246–66, 271; *Aziatskaya Rossiya*, vol. I, p. 494; vol. II, pp. 613–14; *Istoriya Mongolskoy Narodnoy Respubliki*, p. 371; Kolarz, *The Peoples*, pp. 165–9; Kolarz, *Religion*, p. 465; *Narody Sibiri*, pp. 429–30; Rupen, 'Absorption of Tuva', *Studies on the Soviet Union*, Munich (ns), 1971, vol. XI, no. 4, pp. 147, 161; *Yazyki narodov SSSR*, vol. II, p. 387.

[11] Rupen, 'The absorption of Tuva', p. 147.

It was at this time that preparations began for a big celebration, both in the Mongolian People's Republic and Chinese Inner Mongolia, on the occasion of the 800th anniversary of the birth of the national hero (and near-deity) Chingis Khan. This manifestation of Mongolian nationalism was, however, nipped in the bud by the Russian Communist Party, which strongly disapproved both on ideological and historical grounds.[12]

THE CHINESE FRONTIER

Relations between the Soviet Union and China in the postwar period continued to have indirect effects upon the native communities of Eastern Siberia. By the end of 1949 the Chinese Communist Party held most of mainland China, and succeeded in establishing the 'People's Republic'. A period of close cooperation between the USSR and the People's Republic of China was inaugurated by a treaty of mutual assistance which led to plans for large-scale collaboration in numerous industrial development projects, including joint utilisation of the Amur valley for hydro-electric schemes. However, following the death of Stalin, Khrushchev's conciliatory doctrine of 'peaceful co-existence' with the capitalist system led to an ideological power struggle between China and the USSR. The latter withdrew its technical assistance from China in 1960, and four years later relations between the two countries worsened to the extent of an open break, which was to last for over twenty years. In this conflict both sides made exaggerated claims in terms of 'China's lost territories' (including Mongolia and Vladivostok) which had been taken by 'imperialism' – and on the other hand, of Russia's 'inalienable rights' to what had been 'Russian territory from time immemorial'.[13]

Because of this nationalistic enmity and border tension, the USSR maintained a large army in the Far East, and it became the region of the USSR with the highest rate of population growth, increasing by 48 per cent between 1959 and 1982. The pattern of ethnic distribution east of Lake Baikal has been reinforced since the war. East of the Onon-Ingoda confluence and the Aga Buryat National Region, a continuous band of territory

---

[12] Bawden, *History of Mongolia*, pp. 344, 378, 382–3, 390, 394, 397, 400, 413, 417–18, 422; *Istoriya Mongolskoy Narodnoy Respubliki*, p. 476; Kolarz, *The Peoples*, pp. 141–57; Kolarz, *Religion*, p. 468.

[13] V.F. Buturlinov et al., *O sovetsko-kitayskoy granitse*, pp. 61–7; Cheng Tien-fong, *A History of Sino-Russian relations*, Washington, 1957, pp. 316–32; V. Connolly, *Siberia Today and Tomorrow*, London, 1975, pp. 217–24; D.J. Doolin, *Territorial Claims in the Sino-Soviet Conflict: Documents and Analysis*, Stanford, 1965; Shvarev, *Dalniy Vostok*, pp. 18–19, 45. Examples of changing Soviet attitudes towards Chinese cultural influences occur, for instance, in the respectful expressions in *Narody Sibiri* (pp. 33, 58, 77, 101–5, 783–5, 796, 814–18) written before the rift, and the vituperative tone of various works edited in the period 1960–1980 by A.P. Okladnikov: *Istoriya Sibiri*, vol. I, pp. 340, 386, 402, 404–8, etc.; *Otkrytiye Sibiri*, 1979, pp. 19–20, 162, 166–7; *Ancient Art of the Amur Region*, 1981, p. 96.

along the Chinese frontier on the Amur, 100 to 200 miles wide, is populated exclusively by Russians and other nationalities from west of the Urals, and is practically devoid of native peoples. The latter – Ewenkis, Nanais, Nivkhs, Udeghes and others – are found in areas of Amur and Khabarovsk provinces farther from the frontier, while the Maritime (Ussuri) territory is almost entirely without aboriginal peoples.[14]

RUSSIAN INDUSTRIAL DEVELOPMENT IN SIBERIA

During Soviet Russia's participation in the Second World War, gold production might have been expected to decrease in importance compared to the mining of more essential metals, but in fact gold at all costs was still the prevailing spirit in the NKVD's empire of Dalstroy. The war did, of course, create a heavy demand for iron, lead, tin and other metals, and stimulated the exploitation of new sources. New coal-mines were opened by Dalstroy at Omsuchkan and other places on the Kolyma to provide fuel for the metallurgical plants at Magadan and Orotukan. Timber-felling and the construction of roads (particularly the one between Magadan and Yakutsk) continued, and as new geological discoveries were made, Dalstroy's territory was vastly increased until it embraced all of north-eastern Siberia east of 140° – some 926,640 square miles. Only the death of Stalin in 1953 made it possible for Khrushchev to expose the criminal inhumanity of the Soviet prison-camp system, and Dalstroy itself was finally disbanded in 1957.

After 1945 major developments took place in various parts of Siberia, which produced far-reaching effects upon its population and natural environment. The extension of the electric power network by the construction of hydro-electrical dams on several Siberian rivers between 1955 and 1974 resulted in the inundation of huge areas of the Angara valley upstream from Irkutsk, Bratsk and Ust-Ilimsk, and of a similar stretch of the upper Yenisey from Krasnoyarsk to the Sayan gorge, while other dams created lakes of considerable size on the Zeya in Amur Province and the Vilui in western Yakutia. The largest new mineral developments were the oil-field of the middle Ob basin, in the Khanty-Mansi National Region, and the big deposits of natural gas lying to the north of this in the Yamal-Nenets National Region. This involved large-scale tree-felling and earth-moving works which devastated considerable areas of West Siberian forest and tundra. Meanwhile, the discovery of large iron-ore deposits on the upper Lena, and coal, copper and nickel farther to the east, led to the construction of a second Trans-Siberian railway round the northern end of Lake Baikal, cutting across northern Buryatia and southern Yakutia (Ewenki territory) to

[14] *Atlas SSSR* (3rd edn), map 128–9; T.V. Ryabushkin et al., eds., *Naseleniye soyuznykh respublik*, Moscow, 1977, pp. 42, 48, 51; Shvarev, *Dalniy Vostok*, p. 28; D.I. Valentey et al., eds., *Naseleniye i trudovye resursy RSFSR*, Moscow, 1982, pp. 4–5, 107–10, 113.

Komsomolsk-on-Amur. Work on this Baikal–Amur Mainline (BAM), which had been planned in the 1930s but interrupted by the war, was resumed in 1974, and the completion of the track was officially (but prematurely) celebrated in 1984. The most notorious case of damage to the natural environment by industry was the pollution of the formerly pure waters of Lake Baikal by paper and cellulose works.

Much havoc was also caused by the extension of agriculture. The campaign for ploughing up 'virgin lands' in the 1960s deprived many species of their habitat in south-western Siberia and Transbaikalia, while here and in the Altai-Sayan region more intensive grazing and a campaign for the extermination of 'pests' – ranging from marmots to eagles – also caused permanent loss. The region where the greatest threat to wildlife existed was the Far East, where in the Amur–Ussuri region recent intensive settlement has brought more species of fauna near to extinction than in any other part of the RSFSR, including tiger, leopard, black bear and spotted deer.

While regulations restricting the hunting of certain animals were introduced by the Soviet government from the 1920s onwards, they were widely disregarded, and it was only in the late 1970s that the government began to pay serious attention to ecological problems and to introduce measures directed against wholesale destruction and pollution of the natural environment.[15]

To man and maintain the industrial development contemplated for Siberia would require a large influx of people from other parts of the USSR, and indeed in 1968–70 the population of the Far East increased by 111,500 through immigration, and Eastern Siberia by 23,400. Such nett figures, however, conceal the far greater numbers who went east for a limited period of work and returned to their permanent domicile with their earnings. The fact that migration figures are complicated by temporary settlement at sites of new developments, and by high turnover, demonstrates the continuing colonial status of Siberia as a strategically important but relatively under-developed territory still requiring pioneer settlers from the metropolis. In the oil and gas development region of north-western Siberia, the population of the Khanty-Mansi National Region increased by six times between 1959 and 1982, and that of the Yamal-Nenets Region by 3.7 times – most of this increase arising from immigration on a temporary basis. The overall increase in the population of Siberia in this period, however, was only about 25 per cent. The province with the largest increase was Magadan which, despite its

[15] Aganbegyan and Ibragimova, *Sibir ne ponaslyshke*; Armstrong, *Russian Settlement*, pp. 132–3; Conquest, *Kolyma*, pp. 16, 55, 107–14, 177; Deane, *Strange Alliance*, pp. 87–103; Dikov, *Ocherki istorii*, pp. 247–9, 294, 315; *Istoriya Sibiri*, vol. V, pp. 220, 301; Kalesnik, *Sovetskiy Soyuz. Dalniy Vostok*, pp. 27, 370–1; Kolarz, *The Peoples*, pp. 55–8; B. Komarov, *The Destruction of Nature in the Soviet Union*, London, n.d., pp. 3–16, 23–4, 112–19; Popova, *Eveny*, pp. 264–7; Shvarev, *Dalniy Vostok*, p. 28; N.V. Yeliseyev et al., eds., *Krasnaya Kniga RSFSR: zhivotnye*, Moscow, 1983; Zhikharev, *Ocherki istorii*, pp. 160, 228–33, 237–9, 248–9.

notoriety as a penal settlement, grew from 235,600 inhabitants in 1959 to 500,000 in 1982.

Siberia, with almost 57 per cent of the total territory of the USSR, remained a sparsely populated region, the average density in 1979 being about 5.7 inhabitants per square mile. Its share of the total population of the Soviet Union increased only moderately from 8.7 per cent in 1939 to 10.8 per cent in 1982. The most densely populated part of Siberia, with about 14 persons per square mile in 1982, corresponded to the main zone of Russian settlement – a wedge with its base in the Urals, dwindling to the apex at Irkutsk, and with 'ribbon development' from there to Vladivostok and along the courses of the main rivers. Apart from this there were vast sparsely populated 'islands' with less than 3 persons per square mile. This pattern of population distribution, reflecting the location of Russian settlements, was established before the twentieth century, and although the network of non-indigenous settlement has gradually extended, natural conditions of latitude, climate and soil, which limit the development of agriculture, make it improbable that Siberia north of 60° latitude will ever become as densely populated as even the corresponding northern part of European Russia.

Nevertheless, Siberia has become to an overwhelming degree a Russian land. Russians proper, who accounted for 52 per cent of the population of the USSR as a whole in 1979, made up 86 per cent of the population of Siberia, and along with Ukrainians and Belorussians constituted a Slav element of 89 per cent.[16] Despite the natural limitation on further dense settlement by Russians, the once sparsely populated, native regions of Siberia were gradually being pushed back at the edges, cut across by new roads and railways, eaten into by seaports and river ports, so that the ethnic map shows ever-shrinking islands of 'unassimilated' native Siberia.[17]

---

[16] The proportion of Russians in many provinces east of the Urals, including Sverdlovsk, Tomsk, Novosibirsk, Altai, Krasnoyarsk, Kemerovo, Irkutsk, Chita, Amur, Khabarovsk and Primorye (omitting the autonomous native territories) is between 87 and 92 per cent – comparable with several provinces of European Russia, e.g. Leningrad, Arkhangelsk, Penza, Saratov and Volgograd, while the central Russian provinces, such as Moscow, Tula, Kaluga, Kursk, Ryazan, Tambov, Vladimir and Novgorod have between 94 and 98 per cent Russians, according to figures in USSR. *Census 1979.*

[17] Aganbegyan and Ibragimova, *Sibir ne ponaslyshke,* pp. 29, 203–4; Conolly, *Siberia,* pp. 176–81; Gurvich, *Osushchestvleniye,* pp. 73–4, 78, 110; I.S. Gurvich and B.O. Dolgikh, eds., *Preobrazovaniya v khozyaystve i kulture i etnicheskiye protsessy u narodov Severa,* Moscow, 1970, pp. 221–4; *Istoriya Sibiri,* vol. IV, p. 364; vol. V, pp. 213, 363; P.T. Khaptayev, ed., *Sovremennyy byt i etnokulturnye protsessy v Buryatii,* Novosibirsk, 1984, pp. 123–30, 145–6, 162–4; Kolarz, *The Peoples,* pp. 19, 56; Ryabushkin, *Naseleniye,* pp. 42, 48, 51–2; Valentey, *Naseleniye,* pp. 48, 105–18; Volodarskiy, *Naseleniye SSSR,* pp. 45–7.

16

THE NATIVE PEOPLES OF SIBERIA AFTER 1945

THE native peoples of Siberia had no choice but to survive as they could in the economic, political and cultural context created in Siberia by the Soviet Russian authorities. During the Second World War the processes of collectivisation and denomadisation begun in the 1930s were interrupted, but after 1945 they were resumed, and in general collectivisation in Siberia is said to have been completed in the late 1950s. However, even those communities which had undergone collectivisation before the war were subjected to further crises when the policy of amalgamating collective farms to form larger units (*ukrupneniye*) was imposed in all parts of the USSR including Siberia, evoking the same resentful response as the original collectivisation, including widespread slaughter of livestock. A second wave of amalgamations began in the mid-1950s, reducing the number of collective farms (*kolkhozy*) still farther and transforming many of the larger units into state farms (*sovkhozy*). In Siberia this policy was combined with the continuation of the campaign against nomadism. Not only were the scattered hunting and reindeer-herding communities of the North induced to abandon their tents for Russian huts, but many of the settlements previously created were moved from their sites and concentrated together at new 'farm' centres – a process which in fact led to the depopulation of districts, for instance in remote valleys or coastal sites, where people had lived formerly. The dictates of the planners led in some cases to tragic consequences as small communities were forcibly uprooted and their lives dislocated.

One social problem which the amalgamation of collectives exacerbated was the increasing distaste of young people, educated away from home at a regional centre, for the demanding life of the herdsman or hunter. This reflection of a universal trend towards urban life and a contempt for rural pursuits gained particular force from Communist Party propaganda for urbanisation, Russian-style culture, and the transformation of nature rather than living with nature. The fact that living and working standards were low in northern communities, and that the needs and rights of native peoples had been neglected, was recognised by the publication in 1957 of a Soviet government decree 'On measures for further development of the economy and culture of peoples of the North.' This was to have inaugurated a programme of reforms aimed at raising the living standards of reindeer-herdsmen, hunters and fishermen, and improving medical and educational facilities. Among the experiments introduced were new, 'scientific' methods of collective herding – pasture rotation, veterinary services, a shift system and payment of wages in money, together with the improvement of facilities at the farm centre and use of aircraft to transport herdsmen to outlying pastures.[1] On the whole, the provisions of the 1957 decree and its sequel published in 1980 remained on paper only, so far as the improvement of social amenities was concerned, and the peoples of the Soviet North in fact continued to fall behind the standards of the rest of the country, while funds provided for the implementation of these decrees were often misappropriated for purposes quite unconnected with the indigenous peoples.[2]

So far as indigenous social institutions are concerned, the changes in the postwar period further undermined those elements of clan structure which had survived until then, such as mutual aid, *nimat*, and exogamy. However, as awareness of clan affiliation died out, consciousness of belonging to the wider nationality into which the formerly separate clans have been consolidated appears to have strengthened, so that individuals became aware of being, for instance, Ewenkis rather than members of the Chapogir or Lontogir clans. Obviously this was not entirely in accord with the supposedly universal growth of allegiance to the supranational 'Soviet people'. Similarly, in the Minusinsk steppes, the five Turkic groupings are said to have lost their sense of being Kachas, Sagais, Beltirs, Kyzyls or Koibals, and to consider themselves now to be Khakases – a name which was unknown to them before 1917. In the Altai mountains the seven formerly distinct Turkic tribes now acknowledge the single ethnonym Altaians. Many relics of their traditional customs and beliefs survive, however, including *personal* awareness of belonging to a certain clan, such as Tölös, Tirgesh, Kipchak or Kirgiz, and in the 1960s there was a resurgence of national pride among both the Altaians and the Khakases which manifested itself, among other things, in a tendency to give children native Turkic names (such as Bairam, Oirot or Soliko) after decades of accepting names of Russian origin. Both of these newly 'consolidated' nationalities occupy compact territories, but even in the case of a nationality as fragmented and dispersed as the 300,000

[1] I.S. Gurvich, ed., *Etnokulturnye protsessy u narodov Sibiri i Severa*, Moscow, 1985, pp. 150–1; Gurvich, *Osushchestvleniye*, pp. 73, 78, 81–7, 110–11, 114–15; Nove, *Economic History*, pp. 304, 336; Popova, *Eveny*, pp. 269–75, 283; Rytkheu, *Sovremennye legendy*, pp. 211, 263–5, 269–70, 286–90; Sergeyev, *Nekapitalisticheskiy put*, pp. 423, 455–9.
[2] A. Krivoshapkin, 'Boli i trevogi Severa – v serdtse moyem', *Polyarnaya zvezda*, 1989, no. 2, p. 64; A.I. Pika and B.B. Prokhorov, 'Bolshiye problemy malykh narodov', *Kommunist*, 1988, no. 16, p. 81; V. Sangi, 'Otchuzhdeniye', *Sovetskaya Rossiya*, 1988, no. 211, p. 2.

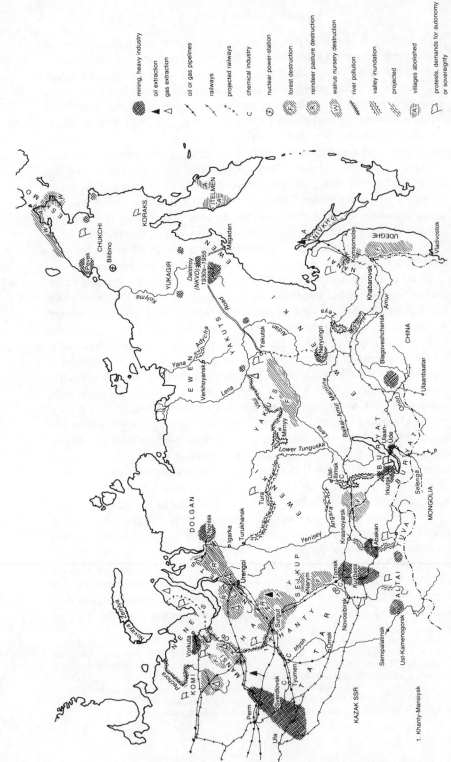

Map 15 The Russian economy and its effects on the peoples of Siberia

Siberian Tatars of Tyumen, Omsk and Tomsk provinces, the gradual erosion of contexts in which the native language is used, and assimilation to the Russians in costume and other elements of national culture, has not destroyed a strong sense of being Tatars.[3]

Traditional religion was also subject to further assault in the general postwar revival of anti-religious propaganda. If the world-view of young people thereby became more thoroughly imbued with Marxist–Leninist dogmas, among older people remnants of traditional beliefs persisted to a greater or lesser extent in all parts of Siberia. It was with the intention of consigning these to oblivion, while adding some colour to the drabness of Soviet life, that in the late 1950s Communist Party ideologists began to devise new atheist festivals and rituals. What replaced the old religious lore was in fact a highly Moscow-centric idealisation of the Soviet Russian state, the Communist Party and its youth organisations, and a militaristic glorification of armed struggle in the Bolshevik Revolution, the Civil War and the 'Great Fatherland War' of 1941–5. The revival of formerly suppressed traditional rituals was also encouraged, so long as no concession was made to religion – whether Shamanist, Christian, Islamic or Buddhist. While in agricultural regions of the USSR such occasions as spring ploughing or harvest festivals were promoted, in Siberia and the European North it was Reindeer-herdsman's Day or Fisherman's Day which were introduced. Among the Buryat-Mongols *sagaalgan*, a festival of spring, rebirth and abundance of milk was revived, with competitive horse-riding, archery and wrestling. Similarly in Yakutia the old fertility festival of *yhyakh* in June was given a new lease of life as a national holiday in which drinking *kumys* had its traditional function. In some parts of Siberia even the bear-feast was sometimes celebrated.

Among other things, the 'new secular rituals' allowed a certain revival of traditional dancing and singing, but as in other regions of the USSR, this led to the transformation of folk-dancing and music into an art-form within the Soviet Russian cultural conventions – balletic choreography, choirs trained according to European musical techniques and so on. The consequence of this denationalisation of indigenous culture was the degeneration of traditional costume to the level of fancy dress and of crafts to souvenirs. On the other hand, the growth of national intelligentsias led to the revival of interest and pride in the authentic material culture of their own peoples.[4]

---

[3] Gurvich, *Etnokulturnye protsessy*, pp. 6, 40–64; *Maadai-Kara. Ochy-Bala, altayskiye geroicheskiye skazaniya*, narr. by A. Kalkin, Moscow, 1983, p. 4; *Narody Sibiri*, pp. 329, 385; Superanskaya, *Spravochnik lichnykh imen*, pp. 46–65; Ukachin, *Povesti*, pp. 32, 67–9, 197.

[4] B. Chichlo, 'The cult of the bear and Soviet ideology in Siberia', in *Religion in Communist Lands*, 1985, vol. XIII, no. 2, pp. 171–4, 177–80; Gurvich, *Etnokulturnye protsessy*, pp. 30, 41, 194–202; Gurvich, *Osushchestvleniye*, pp. 206–7; Gurvich and Dolgikh, *Preobrazovaniya*, pp. 277–8; *Karmannyy slovar ateista*, Moscow, 1985, p. 261; Khaptayev, *Sovremennyy byt*, pp. 140–2; M.V. Khabarova, *Narodnoye iskusstvo Yakutii*, Leningrad, 1981, pp. 6–13; Z.P.

THE FAR NORTH-EAST

The Chukchis and Eskimos found their voice in one of the best-known writers to emerge among the indigenous peoples of the Soviet Union – Yuriy Rytkheu, whose autobiographical trilogy *The Time when the Snow Thaws* and other books describe the great cultural changes which have overtaken the peoples of the North-east in the twentieth century.

In the immediate postwar years the Soviet Russian government pressed on with further collectivisation in the Chukchi tundra, so that by the early 1950s practically all reindeer herds were state-owned. At the same time the number of collectives was reduced by amalgamation, and big state farms were created as subsidiaries of the industrial plants. Along the Arctic and Bering coasts the Communist Party also claimed success in its aim of ending nomadism by combining reindeer collectives with coastal sea-hunting settlements to form mixed 'farms'. While this was said to benefit the native people in commercial and social terms, the arbitrary abolition of small coastal settlements and relocation of their inhabitants brought much suffering, for instance to the small Eskimo community of Nevuqaq (or Naukan) near Cape Dezhnyov, whose members were dispersed when it was abolished.

The Eskimos were one of the Siberian communities worst affected by the operation of the Soviet system at this time. Pushed about ruthlessly from pillar to post, forced to move into Chukchi villages (where lack of housing led to friction between the two nationalities) or into still more alien Russian settlements, the scattered remnants of former Eskimo villages became disorientated and demoralised. As the Soviet Russians' exploitation of sea-mammals as raw materials increasingly monopolised eastern Arctic waters – often with appalling waste resulting from indiscriminate slaughter – walrus no longer came to many of the old breeding sites, and whaling was taken completely out of the hands of the Eskimos and Chukchis by fleets of big catcher ships. As a result, Eskimos became superfluous in their villages and either submitted to 'relocation' or remained in a state of poverty.[5] In this way many sea-hunters found themselves forced to move, in some cases more than once, to large settlements such as Lavrentiya, where their traditional skills were not required and they were reduced to the most menial jobs. Such compulsory relocation of people has been criticized by Rythkeu as 'economic experiments' made at the cost of their passive victims. Between

Sokolova, *Na prostorakh Sibiri*, Moscow, 1981, pp. 153–5; Sokolova, *Puteshestviye v Yugru*, pp. 33–4, 74–5, 106–7; L.A. Tultseva, *Sovremennye prazdniki i obryady narodov SSSR*, Moscow, 1985, pp. 52–8, 67, 78–80, 82–3, 104–6, 118–19.

[5] I.I. Krupnik, 'Demograficheskoye razvitiye aziatskikh eskimosov v 1970-e gody', in B.B. Prokhorov, ed., *Regionalnye problemy sotsialno-demograficheskogo razvitiya*, Moscow, 1987, pp. 106, 110; Yu. Rytkheu, 'Svet zvezd – bolshikh i malykh', *Pravda*, 1988, 31 Dec., p. 3; Rytkheu, *Sovremennye legendy*, p. 207; V. Sharov, 'Mala li zemlya dlya malykh narodov?', *Literaturnaya gazeta*, 1988, no. 33, p. 10.

1953 and 1967 the whole pattern of native settlement in the Chukchi 'National Region' was altered by this means, especially on the north-eastern promontory, where sea-mammal hunting had been the principal occupation. Over fifty settlements – centres of small collective enterprises – were reduced to a dozen, grouped into six 'farms', all but one of which were state administered.

Much has been written about the effect upon North American Eskimo communities of the construction of roads, pipe-lines, airfields and radar stations. Less is publicly known about similar events in the Soviet Union, but there are probably some 250 military installations in north-eastern Siberia, with a headquarters at Magadan and air-bases at Anadyr and Provideniya. The construction of radar stations, and the permanent military presence, must have had a damaging effect both upon the natural environment and the native peoples. Another major new intrusion of Soviet Russian industry into the Far North-east during the post-1945 period was the construction of a nuclear power-station in the Lesser Anyui basin at Bilibino to provide electricity for the gold and tin mines. Life in Chukchi-land was transformed by these new developments, with the consequent increase in air traffic and the large number of personnel stationed there. By 1979, Russians and other incomers from the west totalled 126,374 – 90 per cent of the population of the Chukchi National Region, the minority of native peoples being composed of 11,292 Chukchis, 1,278 Eskimos and 1,000 Ewens. In addition, the rest of Magadan Province and the neighbouring Korak National Region had 1,877 Chukchis, 5,660 Koraks and about 4,000 Ewens, who were also greatly outnumbered by incomers making up 93 per cent of the population.

The increasing use of Russian in the Far North-east as a result of this influx made inroads upon the native languages, in particular Korak and Itelmen. The Koraks also underwent arbitrary amalgamation of collective farms during the 1940s and 1950s, but as they were less unified, linguistically and culturally, than the Chukchis, the coastal and reindeer-herding Korak communities preserved their separate identities to a greater extent. However, their different dialects made it necessary to use Russian as the language of instruction in Korak National Region schools. The rate of bilingualism was therefore high: in 1979 over 90 per cent of all Koraks either claimed Russian as their native language or had a fluent command of it as a second language, while only 70 per cent claimed Korak as their native language. Moreover, the coastal Koraks showed a linguistic age-structure which was becoming common in Siberia: only those over 50 years of age were monolingual in their mother tongue, those between 30 and 50 were bilingual but claimed Korak as their native language, while those of 15 to 30 years were bilingual with Russian as their native language, and many younger children could speak only Russian.

Even less able to withstand the inexorable pressure of Russification were the Itelmens of Kamchatka. In the land which was their original home – the valley of the Kamchatka river – their remnants had long ago been absorbed into the half-breed Russian-speaking community known as Kamchadals. Small groups of Itelmen-speakers survived around Tigil on the marshy west coast of the peninsula, but by 1979 even here less than a quarter of the Itelmens claimed their mother tongue as their native language, while those having a fluent command of Russian or claiming it as their native language amounted to 96 per cent of the total. This was the highest degree of Russification of any Siberian nationality, equalled only by the 300 Aleuts who live on the Commander Islands. For the Itelmen people too, one of the main causes of social breakdown in the Soviet period was the enforced relocation of their settlements. This began in the 1950s with the amalgamation of some of the collectives in the Tigil region, and in the next decade half a dozen more villages were abolished. In the Kamchatka valley too several Itelmen villages were declared non-viable. As a result, hundreds of Itelmens were driven off the lands of their forefathers and reduced to the status of seasonal labourers – without the high rates of pay awarded to Russian incomers. By the 1980s the remaining communities of aboriginal inhabitants of Kamchatka were seen by some Soviet officials as simply '30,000 state welfare pensioners' who they would have been glad to be rid of.[6] However, while it might seem that the cultural and linguistic assimilation of the Itelmens had reached its final stages, and they were to all intents and purposes simply one of the regional variants of the Russian people, nevertheless they had not lost their national awareness, and the number of people claiming Itelmen as their nationality increased from 1,109 in 1959 to 1,370 in 1979.

Since the 1960s considerable changes have occurred in the ethnic consciousness of the native communities of the North-east. Most young Chukchis were said to be unaware whether their parents came from coastal hunting or tundra reindeer communities – formerly the most basic distinction in Chukchi life. In general, as a result of collectivisation, it was the Reindeer Chukchi culture which prevailed over that of the sea-mammal hunters, and the ethnonym *Chawchu* 'possessing reindeer' came to be accepted by nearly all Chukchis except those on the extreme peninsula. Another consequence of the economic exploitation of north-eastern Siberia by the Soviet Russians was the transition of many of the natives to urban life, so that in 1970 more than 10 per cent of the population of such towns as Anadyr and Provideniya were Chukchis and Eskimos. This tendency arose from the rejection by young people of traditional occupations, and a growing desire to take up 'modern' jobs and in general to conform as far as possible to the cultural norms of Soviet Russian society.

[6] Vakhrin, 'Liniya ili oshibka?', p. 14.

Not unnaturally, it was the older people who came to harbour doubts about the effects of 'progress' and 'civilisation' in their communities. Along with humane principles and social services they had witnessed the crude violence of the Communist Party's anti-religious campaigns, the forced relocation of communities, the new 'scientific' reindeer-herding methods introduced by outsiders unfamiliar with and unsympathetic to traditional ways, which destroyed the intimate bond between the herdsman and his animals. And if, since the Russian Revolution, the 'white man' brought to the native people better hygiene, intellectual enlightenment and protection from the elements, he also brought the vodka habit, idleness and the prevalence of suicide. Some Chukchis and Eskimos linked the increase in such social evils with the loss of identity and community, and this stemmed from collectivisation, denomadisation and the 'modernisation' of life in general. Historical perspective, in fact, brought to some natives of the North-east the realisation that

perhaps in that way of life which now seems so antiquated there was something real that we have lost? . . . A better life can't be imported from somewhere else but has to be created locally . . . To deprive us of the way of life which had become an integral part of us is to destroy the spiritual wholeness of the people of the North. People must be allowed to decide themselves how they should live.[7]

Given the austerity of their natural environment, their proud sense of the worth of their own culture, and that 'basis of morality which enabled people living at the very end of the earth to stand firm and proudly maintain their humanity',[8] it seems unlikely that the Chukchi people will vanish without trace into the amorphous mass of a quasi-Russian 'Soviet people'.[9]

THE PEOPLES OF THE LOWER AMUR

There is much less chance of survival for the native peoples of the lower Amur, Sikhote-Alin and Sakhalin. Most of these live in Khabarovsk Territory, where in 1979 (excluding the Ewenkis) they constituted only 1 per cent of the total population. Moreover, as Khabarovsk Territory is bordered to the west by Amur Province and to the south by Maritime Territory, in

[7] Rytkheu, Sovremennye legendy, p. 270.
[8] Ibid., p. 211.
[9] B. Chichlo, 'Les Nevuqaghmiit ou la fin d'une ethnie', Etudes Inuit, Quebec, 1981, vol. V, no. 2, pp. 29–47; Conquest, Kolyma, p. 110; Dikov, Ocherki istorii, pp. 240–8, 252–5, 263–5, 270, 280–3, 324, 376; Gurvich, Etnokulturnye protsessy, pp. 145–56; Gurvich and Dolgikh, Preobrazovaniya, pp. 198–213; Hughes, 'Under four flags'; Kolarz, The Peoples, pp. 92, 95–7; V.V. Leontyev, 'The indigenous peoples of Chukchi National Okrug: population and settlement', Polar Geography, Washington, 1977, vol. I, pp. 9–16; Narody Sibiri, pp. 925–6; Rytkheu, Sovremennye legendy, pp. 177–8, 183, 186, 189, 192, 194, 207, 217–18, 236, 242–50, 264, 268–74, 301; Selitrennik, 'Nekotorye voprosy', pp. 16–20; USSR. Census 1979, pp. 10, 13, 72–3, 86–9, 94.

both of which the population consists almost exclusively of settlers from European Russia, the small communities of Nanais, Ulchis, Udeghes, Oroches, Negidals and Nivkhs are completely isolated from any influence except that of Soviet Russians.

Like other Siberian communities, these peoples of the south-east were deprived of their menfolk during the Second World War, and the family members left behind had to carry out all the heavy work demanded by the collectivised organisation of the fisheries:

No-one who saw the Nivkh collective farms in those years will ever forget the heroic feats of labour performed by old men, women and adolescents. In storms, rain and frost they worked unremittingly to catch fish. As the collective farms had no self-propelled vessels, the fishers went out, however violent the gale, in their rowing-boats and canoes, paddling them dozens of kilometres each day ... At the height of the season they worked sixteen or eighteen hours a day.[10]

It was during the war that Russian industry began to recruit young natives, particularly Nanais, and this drift to urban employment continued in the postwar period, especially when another new town, Amursk, was built in their territory. By 1960 some 13 per cent of the lower Amur natives had forsaken their forest dwellings and taken up residence in Komsomolsk, Khabarovsk or other towns; ten years later a quarter of all Nanais and 13 per cent of Ulchis were living in towns.

In the native settlements themselves, while fishing became organised as a large-scale industry, Nivkhs, Nanais and others were drawn away from traditional occupations to become labourers in the expanding timber, mining and oil-drilling industries. The way of life of the Amur natives underwent further changes when the collectivisation policies of the Russian Communist Party in the 1960s demanded the concentration of people from scattered, mobile communities into larger, fixed villages. The settlements of the Nivkhs were thus reduced in number to nine on the Amur and three in Sakhalin, regardless of the wishes of their inhabitants, some of whom rebelled against joining the amalgamated 'farm' and remained in their old locality despite a total lack of amenities there. As a result of the disruption and relocation of communities and the drift to the towns, the social structure of the Amur peoples changed profoundly, the extended family, which had formerly been the rule, disappearing almost entirely. Mixed marriages were already common, since settlements were usually made up of people of various indigenous nationalities, but in the post-war period an admixture – often indeed a preponderance – of Russians and other incomers became common in the villages, so that marriages occurred not only between, for instance, a Nanai and a Russian, but (such is the mobility of individuals in the Soviet Union today) sometimes between a Nanai and a Kazak, a Bashkir, a Gypsy or even a

10 Taksami, *Nivkhi*, pp. 69–70.

Nganasan. In general, the reduced number of indigenous communities were so widely separated that there was more contact between a settlement and the surrounding Russian population than with other communities of the same nationality.

The process of settlement and concentration of the native communities on the lower Amur brought to a head the struggle between their traditional culture and twentieth-century European civilisation in its Soviet Russian version. The opportunities for education and professional training offered by the latter won young people over and created the generation gap on which the success of Communist Party indoctrination depends. Various cultural activities in the Russian mould were developed, including literature, so that by the 1970s a number of writers were having their works published either in their native language or in Russian, such as the Nanai Grigoriy Khojer, the Udeghe Jansi Kimonko, and the Nivkh Vladimir Sangi. Among older people, despite half a century of Soviet Russian 'enlightenment' and anti-religious propaganda, shamanist practices still persisted in the villages up to the 1970s. Shamans – some of them recent initiates – were sometimes called upon to treat sick people, to propitiate guardian spirits in connection with hunting, and for various rites of passage, including burial and the departure of young people to study or join the armed forces. Another tradition which persisted was the bear-feast, albeit in an attentuated version. A Soviet ethnographer gives the following interpretation of a Nanai bear-feast in the 1960s:

The feast occupied one evening. The old traditions connected with dividing the carcass and eating the bear-meat were observed, but otherwise it was rather like an ordinary party, with young people singing and dancing ... Ritual actions were performed, but it was only some of the old people who saw any religious significance in them. In general the ceremony was perceived as a festival of the hunt and a celebration of the successful hunter ...[11]

To whatever degree the ethnic awareness of the Amur peoples may survive in their present situation, the gradual extinction of their languages seems inevitable. In 1979 only about 56 per cent of Nanai people claimed this as their native language, while 44 per cent claimed Russian; for the Ulchi, Oroch and Negidal peoples the figures were approximately 40 per cent mother tongue and 60 per cent Russian; while almost 70 per cent of Nivkhs and Udeghes acknowledged Russian to be their native language. This is not surprising, considering that these nationalities number only a few thousand (in 1979 some 10,500 Nanais, 2,500 Ulchis, 2,200 Nivkhs, 1,550 Udeghes, 1,200 Oroches, 500 Negidals and perhaps 5,000 Ewenkis) scattered among 1.6 million people in Khabarovsk Territory. Their total number

[11] Rosugbu, *Malye narodnosti*, pp. 206–7.

of about 24,000 is many times less than even the population of one Russian city such as Komsomolsk or Khabarovsk.

The ascendancy of Russian over the native languages arose not so much from any explicit policy on the part of the Soviet authorities, nor from dialect differences or a lack of qualified native teachers, but mainly from the ethnically mixed character of settlements, where Nanai, Nivkh or Udeghe children quickly picked up the language of the Russian majority through playground games. As a result, while Nanai, the language of the largest native community, was established before the Second World War as the language of instruction in the first three years of school, it began to lose this role in the early 1950s, and was almost completely ousted from schools within the next ten years. Only in a few villages where Nanais, Ulchis or Nivkhs were still in the majority did the native language continue to be used, in the preparatory class only.

By the 1960s the general level of education and the development of a native intelligentsia in the towns of the lower Amur region had made some of its members aware of the impending disappearance of their languages as the basic element in their national cultures. As a result, it is reported that not only Nanais, Nivkhs and Ulchis, but even people of the smallest ethnic groups such as the Oroches and Negidals, began teaching their children to speak their native languages, and also collecting and recording their national folklore, in an attempt to preserve at least some remnants of their culture.[12]

TUVA IN THE SOVIET UNION

Before the complete annexation of their country to the USSR in 1944, the Tuvans had no indigenous industry, so that from the Soviet Russians' point of view the natural resources of Tuva were lying idle and 'unexploited'. In order to transform the country into a socialist republic integrated into the economic structure of the USSR, it was considered essential to develop industries based upon livestock breeding and on coal and other minerals, and to create an industrial proletariat which would eventually take over from the pastoral nomads who in 1944 made up 85 per cent of the population. Contrary to this design, those few Tuvans who had been drawn into the labour force of Russian mines and industrial works during the Second World War proved to be as little enamoured of the labouring life as they had

[12] Gurvich, *Etnokulturnye protsessy*, pp. 175–93; Gurvich, *Osushchestvleniye*, pp. 318–25, 329–37; Gurvich and Dolgikh, *Preobrazovaniya*, pp. 257–8, 276–8; *Istoriya Sibiri*, vol. V, p. 422; Kolarz, *The Peoples*, p. 83; *Narody Sibiri*, pp. 776, 781, 809, 812, 827–8; Rosugbu, *Malye narodnosti*, pp. 10, 94–5, 127, 152, 200–3, 206–7; Sangi, 'Otchuzhdeniye'; Shvarev, *Dalniy Vostok*, pp. 439–42, 544–6; O.P. Sunik, *Ulchskiy yazyk: issledovaniya i materialy*, Leningrad, 1985, pp. 4–5, 8; Taksami, *Nivkhi*, pp. 69–70; USSR. *Census 1959*, p. 334; *Census 1979*, pp. 72–3, 91.

been in the 1930s, and again drifted back to their herds in the late 1940s. In order to counteract this tendency the Russian government 'helped' the Tuvan economy by sending hundreds of Communist Party and Young Communist League organisers, economic specialists and technicians from European Russia, while residential schools were re-established for the training of tribesmen at state expense. As a basis for universal education, textbooks were translated into the Tuvan language, and a literacy rate of 90 per cent of the population was claimed by 1949. Special attention was, of course, paid to changing the role of women in Tuvan society through education and induction into industrial employment. As with other nationalities of Siberia the process of educating young Tuvans to be well-indoctrinated Soviet citizens was continued by the selection of the 'best' pupils for higher education in Leningrad, while in Kyzyl itself a teacher training college was founded in 1952. As the capital of Tuva was turned into a town on the Soviet Russian model and industrialisation began, hundreds of Tuvan natives were trained as builders, mechanics and drivers.

In 1944 the way of life of most Tuvans was nomadic pastoralism with herds of horses, cattle and sheep or, in the mountain forests, reindeer. By the late 1940s Tuvan cattle-rearing was in a state of decline. The number of livestock, which before 1917 and between 1932 and 1940 had averaged 1 to $1\frac{1}{2}$ million, was drastically reduced during and immediately after the Second World War by the Russian government's procurement practices, which were as arbitrary as they had been in the 'war communism' period of the Russian Civil War. In 1945 herds amounted to only 760,000 animals, of which over 60 per cent belonged to individual nomadic households which worked together as cooperatives but were neither collectivised nor settled. At this time Tuvan writers were criticised for their supposed idealisation of the old nomadic way of life – which was not surprising, as even in communist organisations the great majority of Tuvan members were individual herdsmen. Plans for a new collectivisation campaign were proclaimed in 1945, and in 1948 yet another campaign of mass collectivisation was launched upon the Tuvan people. Although this took place almost twenty years after the first collectivisation drive in Russia, the same 'excesses' – that is, crude mistakes and the use of naked force – which had been perpetrated by the Communist Party at that time, now occurred in Tuva. In the same way, too, the dictates of the Moscow government encountered determined resistance and those who defended their stock were dubbed 'landlords' and 'kulaks', and no doubt suffered arrest and incarceration in concentration camps. As in every part of the Soviet Union, the herdspeople of Tuva adopted the only method of protest against enforced collectivisation which lay in their hands – the slaughter of their own animals. Between 1948 and 1951 the Tuvans' livestock was cut down by 34 per cent in this way. Resistance to collectivisation continued in Tuva until 1954, by which time the number of livestock had begun to increase again from the nadir of 558,000 head (less than half of the 1916 figure!). The Tuvan collective farms were at first organised on the basis of traditional communities and clan pastures, but later the Soviet Russian authorities imposed new measures of amalgamation and denomadisation intended to break down clan-territorial allegiances and reduce the tribespeople to a single amorphous class of collectivised peasants. Little is known to the outside world about the means of coercion used in Tuva to bring about submission to these radical social changes, but it was claimed that by 1955 the collectivisation of practically all households and livestock was complete, and that three years later the last of the nomads moved out of their tents into permanent houses. At the same time a beginning was made to agriculture, which had been non-existent in Tuva. Areas of virgin steppe south of Kyzyl in the centre of the country, and around Ak-Dovurak in the west, were ploughed for wheat, oats, barley and fodder crops, and by 1955 Tuva is said to have become self-supporting in grain.

The achievement of a settled situation in Tuva and its assimilation to the administrative and economic system of the Russian Republic was marked by its upgrading in 1961 from the status of an Autonomous Province to that of an Autonomous Soviet Socialist Republic. After its annexation to the USSR the population of Tuva trebled from 95,400 in 1944 to 309,000 in 1989, but it remained one of the most sparsely populated regions of the USSR, with an average density of 3.5 persons per square mile. Of this population 65 per cent were Tuvans and most of the remainder Russians and Ukrainians. The Tuvans formed one of the most homogeneous communities in the Soviet Union, and one in which a very high proportion of its members claimed their mother tongue as their native language – 99 per cent in 1979. However, a large number also had a fluent command of Russian (59 per cent) and although only 16 per cent of Tuvans lived in towns in 1970, this number was bound to increase as the Moscow government stepped up the mining of coal, asbestos, cobalt and other minerals.

Tuva remained as a whole a remote region, cut off from Krasnoyarsk Territory and Irkutsk Province by the Western Sayan mountains. Only one motor road linked Kyzyl with the outside world, and there was no railway, so that the air connection between Kyzyl and Krasnoyarsk was vital. Within Tuva, apart from the main basin of the upper Yenisey, the mountainous fringe and all of the eastern region was without roads, so that the shepherds, reindeer-herders and hunters, although collectivised, maintained a way of life which did not differ greatly from that of their nomadic ancestors or their neighbours in eastern Buryatia and north-western Mongolia. Here, no doubt, despite intensive anti-religious campaigns, there also lingered on remnants of Buddhist and Shamanist beliefs, which by the 1970s had become an object of study for Tuvan scholars concerned with the future of their national culture.[13]

BURYATIA

Buryat-Mongol life changed considerably during the war. Although depletion of livestock had not been so disastrous as in some regions, the number of cattle had fallen considerably and only regained the pre-war level in 1953, while sheep-rearing greatly increased its share in the farming economy, and the number of horses – formerly the most characteristic animal in Buryat-Mongol life – decreased greatly. As a result of the ubiquitous amalgamation process, the number of farms and settlements was drastically reduced from the 1950s onwards, and this concentration of population around the head-quarters of collective and state farms signified the end, for all but a tiny fraction of the Buryat population, of life in small communities scattered over the steppes. However, while the old social structure of Buryat-Mongol society had by 1979 largely given way to Soviet Russian norms, in the countryside, where two-thirds of all Buryats lived, they tended to preserve the extended (three-generation) family to a greater degree than the Russian population, and despite the fading away of clan relations, the institution of mutual aid was still generally observed, as were traditional family celebrations and hospitality customs.[14]

The Buryats, the largest indigenous nationality in Siberia, increased in numbers from 252,959 in 1959 to 423,436 in 1989 – that is, by over 67 per cent. Of the three national territories, in 1959 the Buryat Autonomous Republic had more than half the total number of Buryats; Irkutsk Province, including the Ust-Orda Buryat National Region, had 28 per cent; and Chita Province, including the Aga Buryat National Region, 16 per cent. Within these nominally Buryat territories the proportion of Buryats varied considerably, the highest concentration being in Aga National Region, where Buryats made up almost half of the population, followed by Ust-Orda where they were about one-third of the total, while in the largest 'national' territory, the ASSR, only 20 per cent of the inhabitants were Buryats, most of the others being Russians. This distribution changed from the late 1960s onwards.

[13] Aranchyn, *Istoricheskiy put*, pp. 16–17, 27–8, 147, 165–6, 174, 200, 215, 220–1, 252, 275–8, 280, 284–98, 301–6, 310–24; Kalesnik, *Sovetskiy Soyuz. Vostochnaya Sibir*, pp. 237–49; Mongush Kenin-Lopsan, *Obryadovaya praktika i folkor tuvinskogo shamanstva: konets XIX – nachale XX v.*, Novosibirsk, 1987, pp. 3–5, 151; Kolarz, *Religion*, p. 465; Kozlov, *Natsionalnosti SSSR*, p. 100; *Narody Sibiri*, pp. 430, 446–9, 451–4, 464–5; Rupen, 'The absorption of Tuva', p. 146; USSR. *Census 1979*, pp. 72, 80–1.

[14] Humphrey, *Karl Marx Collective*, pp. 283–99, 333–47; Khaptayev, *Istoriya Buryatskoy ASSR*, vol. II, pp. 512–13, 519–20, 548–9; Khaptayev, *Sovremennyy byt*, pp. 26–7; *Narody Sibiri*, pp. 252–4.

While the Buryats east of Lake Baikal, in the ASSR and Aga Region, increased considerably in numbers, the Buryat population in the Ust-Orda Region and Irkutsk Province decreased, as thousands migrated beyond the lake, with the result that by 1979 almost 60 per cent of Buryats lived in the ASSR and over 10 per cent in the Aga National Region.[15] This migration may be explained partly by the attraction of the ASSR as the centre of Buryat national culture, but another factor in the exodus from Ust-Orda National Region was probably the construction of the Bratsk hydro-electric station. After the completion of the dam in 1967 an enormous lake was created by the flooding of the Angara valley. This left the westernmost district of the National Region, Alar *aimak*, cut off from the rest of western Buryatia by a wide stretch of water, while flooding of tributary valleys caused further fragmentation of Western Buryat territory. This also led to the loss of a considerable area of grazing and agricultural land, and doubtless the abandonment of a number of villages. Migration patterns are difficult to analyse, but it was probably such factors, along with the increase of Russian population in neighbouring industrial regions, that drove many Buryats to seek a more congenial home among their compatriots in the Autonomous Republic.

Although the Buryat Autonomous Republic was officially the main national territory, the Aga National District was in some ways the most essentially Buryat territory, since it had a more homogeneous native population, a high proportion of which was rural. Its significance was further enhanced by the fact that it contained one of the two surviving Buddhist monasteries. In the ASSR on the other hand, many Buryats were drawn into the towns – Ulaan-Üde, Selenginsk, Gusinoozersk, Severobaikalsk, and others – so that during the 1970s the number of urban Buryats doubled, with a corresponding growth in industrial workers and professionals.[16]

The cultural life of Buryatia was not without its ideological troubles in the period following 1945, when the Russian Communist Party reasserted its control over all aspects of Soviet life. In the campaign against 'manifestations of bourgeois nationalism' the first target of the Communist Party's vigilance was a new history of the Buryat-Mongol ASSR. Although its compilers had observed official warnings about the line to be followed in this work, when the first volume appeared in 1951 it did not satisfy the requirements of Russia's ideological dictators, and it was replaced three years later by a revised version. Another focus of Moscow's suspicion was the folk epic

---

[15] USSR. *Census 1959*, pp. 300–4, 332–3; *Census 1979*, pp. 72, 76–7, 84–7, 93, 101. The 1989 Census shows a similar distribution, but the proportion of Buryats in all three territories has increased because of a rate of demographic growth higher than that of the Russians (particularly in the ASSR and the Aga AR).

[16] Gurvich, *Etnokulturnye protsessy*, pp. 11–29; C. Humphrey, 'Population trends, ethnicity and religion among the Buryats', in A. Wood and R.A. French, *The Development of Siberia*, pp. 150–7.

about Geser Khan, which is part of the common oral tradition of the Tibetan, Turkic and Mongolian peoples. In 1948 a scholastic controversy broke out over the 'correct' interpretation of the Western Buryat versions of this legend: was it an original Buryat creation or an expression of pan-Mongol culture? was it an idealisation of 'the common people' or of 'the feudal khans'? did it glorify Chingis Khan, the great ogre of Russian history? did it have, as some said, an anti-Russian bias? For five years, study and publication of this ancient epic poem was prohibited until, after two ponderous 'discussions' organised by the Russian Communist Party, the official conclusion was that it had nothing to do with Chingis Khan, was not anti-Russian, and did express the spirit of 'the people'. Numerous scholars could breathe freely again, and the Buryat people were not obliged to reject an important element of their national culture. Nevertheless, Buryat writers in general were brought to heel at a Congress of Writers of the Buryat-Mongol ASSR in 1954, when – echoing similar events throughout the Soviet Union – various 'shortcomings' labelled 'bourgeois' and 'cosmopolitan' were pointed out, while budding poets were urged to write about such themes as the victorious Soviet Motherland and its ever greater achievements, the Communist Party, progress in the 'people's democracies' and the 'struggle for peace'.[17]

In the 1960s, festivals of art and literature were organised as manifestations of Buryat culture and also as occasions for cultural exchanges with other republics of the USSR. Contacts of this kind with the Mongolian People's Republic were also popular, despite the fact that the Soviet Russian government strove to minimise historical links between Buryatia and Mongolia, tending as they did towards the Pan-Mongol idea. It was for this reason that in 1958 the Buryat-Mongols and their republic were re-designated simply as 'Buryats' and the 'Buryat ASSR'.[18]

However, changes in the written language or ethnonym could not hide the undeniable fact of close affinities with the Mongols of the People's Republic. One of the major features of Buryat and Mongol national awareness up to 1930 had been the Buddhist religion. The war brought a halt to anti-religious propaganda and a reprieve for Buddhism, as for nearly all religions in the Soviet Union, and two *datsans* – at Aga and Ivolga – were reopened. In 1946, however, the Communist Party imposed new controls over the Buddhist Church, with a regulation to the effect that the spiritual hierarchy must be elected – subject to approval by the Russian Communist Party. The Chief

---

[17] Ts. Damdinsuren, *Istoricheskiye korni Geseriady*, Moscow, 1957, pp. 5, 13–14; Khaptayev, *Istoriya Buryatskoy ASSR*, vol. II, pp. 590, 593, 602–3; Kolarz, *The Peoples*, pp. 126–7; N.O. Sharakshinova, comp., *Geroicheskiy epos o Gesere: uchebnoye posobiye dlya studentov filologicheskogo fakulteta*, Irkutsk, 1969, pp. 3–5, 22–5; A.I. Ulanova, ed., *Abai Geser*, Ulan-Üde, 1960, pp. 3–5.
[18] Tokarev, *Etnografiya*, p. 445.

Lama appointed during the war, Lubsang Nipa Darma, was accordingly replaced in 1956 by Eshe Dorzho Sharapov, an entirely subservient figure who above all fulfilled the official role in contacts with Buddhists of other countries. While practising Buddhists were kept in a state of fear and uncertainty, academic respectability for an 'objective' interest in the religion was provided by the foundation at Ulaan-Üde of a centre for the Study of Buddhism.

The Soviet educational system and communist youth movement played their part in alienating young Buryats from Buddhist beliefs during the postwar anti-religious campaigns, and this was also one of the aims of the amalgamation of collectives and concentration of people into large villages, since it was considered that the old pattern of scattered farmsteads helped to perpetuate traditional beliefs and held back the process of secularisation.

According to a first-hand study by a British anthropologist, by the 1970s Lamaist Buddhism had few openly committed adherents among the Buryats, most of whom professed acceptance of the materialist world-view of the Communist Party. However, it is difficult for an outsider to define the latent significance of 'survivals' of religious beliefs in a given community. Lamas (often unofficial) appear to have retained important functions in rites connected with death, while a general adherence to the Buddhist system of marking the epochs in a person's life required at least occasional visits to one of the two functioning *datsans*. Moreover, a general belief in reincarnation persists widely, as does an apocalyptic conviction of the impending arrival of the Fifth Buddha.

During the Soviet period many of the Buryat folk ceremonials which predated Buddhism, especially those held at *oboo* cairns in the countryside, have lost their Lamaist overtones and reverted to their Shamanist nature. As a result, at the open-air community rituals celebrated at various seasons, blood-sacrifice of rams and horses to ancestor and nature spirits was still being performed. While attempts have been made by the authorities to substitute new socialist rituals for traditional ones, the latter preserve a life of their own.[19]

So far as the national language was concerned, in the 1970s Buryat was at a low ebb. Even in the Buryat ASSR it had lost ground to Russian in various social functions, since it was not used in scientific publications or official business. More critical was the reduction in the status of the Buryat language in education, since it had been abandoned as the language of instruction at any level, and Buryat schools had gone over entirely to a Russian curriculum,

---

[19] Humphrey, *Karl Marx Collective*, pp. 373–82, 402–32; Humphrey, 'Population trends', pp. 166–73; Khaptayev, *Sovremennyy byt*, pp. 137–8, 144–9; Kolarz, *Religion*, pp. 457–61; N.L. Zhukovskaya, 'Sovremennyy lamaizm (na materialakh Buryatskoy ASSR)', in USSR. Akademiya obshchestvennykh nauk, *Voprosy nauchnogo ateizma*, Moscow, 1969, vyp. 7, pp. 221–42.

Buryat being retained in schools only as an optional subject. (In any case Buryat had never been the language of instruction in the national 'capital' Ulaan-Üde,[20] even though the small Buryat contingent in its population – only 12 per cent – exercised the dominant cultural influence in the city.)[21] This development reflected parental concern that children should gain a good command of Russian with a view to higher education and a career, but perhaps it also expressed a misplaced confidence on the part of the Buryat people that the survival of their language was not in doubt. Most Buryats used their own language in everyday social intercourse, and it flourished as the medium of literature, drama, films, radio and journalism. Even in the scattered groups of Western Buryats in Irkutsk Province, where Russian influence and bilingualism had existed for many years, few of those who acknowledged Buryat nationality claimed Russian as their native language, and nearly all pre-school children spoke only Buryat. Thus, despite the general growth of bilingualism the Buryat language might appear to be flourishing as the medium of their national culture.[22]

THE YAKUTS

The Yakuts, who had slightly outnumbered the Buryats until the 1940s, were the second largest indigenous community in Siberia in 1989, with 382,255 people. Unlike the Buryats, the Yakuts were geographically isolated from the main zone of Russian exploitation and settlement by terrain, by latitude and by the lack of roads, and they had no cultural contiguity with any related people, such as the Buryats had with Mongolia.

In central Yakutia the rural majority of the native population experienced the general pattern of postwar reconstruction, Moscow's changing policies on agricultural organisation, and enforced amalgamation into large collectives and eventually state farms, while their main occupation continued to be the breeding of cattle and horses. Industrially, Yakutia was drawn into the Soviet Russian network by new developments beginning in the 1950s. The largest of these was the mining of diamonds on the upper Vilui and the building of the associated hydro-electric station and the new town of Mirnyy, which brought in a considerable contingent of workers of Russian and other nationalities. This development, along with the extraction of natural gas, coal and salt in various parts of the Lena–Vilui–Aldan basin, also drew some Yakuts into industrial work and urban life, and sometimes into mixed marriages with incomers.

As a result of immigration the place of the Yakuts in the population of 'their' ASSR was reduced from 46 per cent of the total in 1959 to 33 per

---

[20] D. Oshorov, 'Dvuyazychiye v buryatskoy shkole', *Baykal*, 1989, no. 6, pp. 66–70.
[21] Humphrey, 'Population trends', pp. 152, 158, 172.
[22] Khaptayev, *Sovremennyy byt*, pp. 153–62.

cent thirty years later, although they increased in absolute numbers by almost 62 per cent. The Russians in Yakutia accounted for half of the total population in 1979, but were very localised, principally on the upper Lena as far as Yakutsk, on the upper Vilui at Mirnyy, at the Arctic port of Tiksi, and at Verkhoyansk and other outposts of the north-east. Otherwise this vast republic remained very much a Yakut land, where the Yakuts played a dominant role. Consequently the Yakut language was able to hold its own in relation to Russian, and it was indeed almost the only Siberian native language in which self-instruction textbooks were produced to encourage Russians to learn it.[23] Another indication of the unusually secure status of the Yakut language is that in the 1970s it continued to be used as the medium of instruction throughout the first eight years of school, with text-books of history, geography, mathematics, biology and literature in Yakut.[24] It is also significant that Yakut itself is a dominant language. Many Yakuts live in regions of the Far North along with Ewenkis, Ewens and Yukagirs, and along with Ewenkis in the south-east of the ASSR. As a result of the strongly marked ethnic individuality and enterprise of the Yakuts the tendency had been for those other peoples to become 'Yakutized' in language, and this was further encouraged by the creation of large, ethnically mixed collective and state farms. Thus, in 1979, when 44 per cent of the 5,763 Ewens in the Yakut ASSR claimed Ewen as their native language, and 53 per cent had a fluent command of Russian as their first or second language, Yakut was used as first or second language by almost 70 per cent. Similarly, of all Ewenkis in the republic (11,584 in 1979) 85 per cent used Yakut as their native language, and only 11 per cent claimed the Ewenki language. Among the 526 strong Yukagir community also, while 30 per cent claimed Russian as their native language, 23 per cent claimed Yakut. Another subjective factor of significance in considering Yakut ethnic consciousness was that children of marriages with one Yakut parent nearly always chose to be registered as Yakuts at the age of first receiving an identity card. In general, therefore, to be a Yakut was considered a good thing, and Yakuts preserved a sense of their own worth in the face of the Russian majority.

The fervent national pride of the Yakuts impressed a Canadian writer who visited Siberia in the 1960s and found Yakut writers to be 'not anti-Russian' but 'unabashedly pro-Yakut'. They expressed the view that Yakutia could afford to welcome incomers without fearing they would take over, 'for we are so strong in ourselves'. However, the Yakuts he met were perhaps unrealistic in rejecting any suggestion that their country was a colony exploited economically by outsiders, and in believing that they could keep the leader-

---

[23] N.D. Dyachkovskiy et al., *Pogovorim po-yakutski: samouchitel yakutskogo yazyka*, Yakutsk, 1982, pp. 3–4.

[24] I am grateful to Frances Cooley for this first-hand information.

ship of their land themselves and avoid becoming subordinated to 'a stronger people'. It is improbable that a situation in which there was a great influx of Russians and others bent on developing mining and processing industries, while the Yakuts themselves continued to pursue rural occupations or work in consumer industries, could really represent 'a sensible division of labour' presenting no threat to the native culture.[25] It is in fact precisely such situations which in many parts of the world have led to cultural colonialism.

The national spirit of the Yakuts, which had been severely repressed by the Russian communist régime in the 1920s and 1930s, reasserted itself in the postwar period. In 1951 a Yakut historian, Georgiy Basharin, was taken to task for his vindication of the writers A. Kulakovskiy and A. Sofronov, who had suffered repression in the 1920s. This was part of a campaign to force Yakut writers to overcome 'ideological faults' and 'bourgeois national-ist tendencies'. However, after Khrushchev's denunciation of Stalin in 1956, many of the Yakut political and cultural figures who had been arrested and killed in the late 1930s were 'rehabilitated', including P. Oyunskiy-Sleptsov, S. Gogolev and M. Ammosov. The massive influx of Russians into Yakutia had begun to produce a strong national reaction in the 1970s. At that time the Ukrainian dissident V. Chornovil, exiled, like some of his nineteenth-century predecessors, to Yakutia, experienced the verbal abuse and physical violence by which Yakuts and Russians vented their mutual antagonism. So bad was the racial rioting in Yakutsk in 1979 that troops were called out to restore order. The repetition of such brawling on several occasions in the 1980s indicated that neither the arrogant attitudes of some Russians nor the resentment of the Yakuts to them as incomers had disappeared. Thus, despite the suppression of overt Yakut nationalism since the 1920s, this most original of Siberian peoples showed itself to be still capable of asserting its individuality in the face of constant Russian encroachment.[26]

THE EWENS AND EWENKIS

More than any other peoples of Siberia, the Tunguses – Ewenkis and Ewens – lack a national or geographical centre or boundary, because of their former nomadism and very wide territorial range.

On the Okhotsk coast a kind of centre was artificially imposed upon the Ewens in the 1930s, in the shape of Dalstroy and Magadan. Beyond this

---

[25] F. Mowat, *The Siberians*, London, 1970, pp. 91, 95, 100, 114, 125, 127, 130.
[26] *Istoriya Yakutskoy ASSR*, vol. III, pp. 238–9, 263–7, 285, 292, 322; Armstrong, *Russian Settlement*, p. 134; Gurvich, *Etnokulturnye protsessy*, pp. 7–8, 29–39, 139–40; Gurvich and Dolgikh, *Preobrazovaniya*, pp. 16, 218–19; Kolarz, *The Peoples*, pp. 106–11; Radio Free Europe/Radio Liberty, *Research*, n.p., 16 September 1983, RL 347/83; 1 July 1986, RL 251/86; Sokolova, *Na prostorakh Sibiri*, pp. 146–7; USSR. *Census 1959*, pp. 300–1, 334–5; *Census 1979*, pp. 72, 82–3.

region, however, the collectivisation of the Ewens remained far from complete until long after the war, as several of the biggest reindeer-herding clans were still at large in the upland forests and tundra.

Reindeer herding was the essential occupation and way of life of the Ewen people, but in this sphere Soviet Russian industrial priorities in the Magadan–Kolyma region had led to a drastic decline over the 1930s and 1940s in what was then regarded as an outmoded and unprofitable activity almost irrelevant to the socialist economy. Reindeer had been of use to the Russians as transport for geological expeditions and mining activities, and the available herds had been so overworked and neglected, from the veterinary point of view, that they had declined severely in numbers and physique, while many Ewen herdsmen had been diverted to the fisheries. After years of such administrative abuses, the Russian authorities began to realise in the middle of the 1950s that there was a danger that reindeer husbandry might disappear altogether as a branch of the regional economy. Subsequently, the introduction of modern mechanical means of transport made reindeer transport obsolete, and encouragement was given for a revival of reindeer-breeding in the Okhotsk region for purposes of meat-production. Meanwhile the final stages of collectivisation were taking place as the main body of Reindeer-Ewens were being induced to abandon their independent existence on the remote upland pastures to which they had fled in the 1940s. The last gathering of the Rassokha and Beryozov clans took place in 1959, and three years later all were collectivised. Finally, under the general policy of the 1970s, the collective farms of Okhotsk region were amalgamated and reorganised as state farms in which not only Ewens but also Ewenkis and Yakuts were combined. By then the industrial development of the Magadan–Kolyma region, and the accompanying influx of a multinational, but chiefly Russian, work-force had reduced the Ewens to a minority of only 1.3 per cent of the population of Magadan Province (excluding the Chukchi National District). Although most of the incomers were concentrated in the area around Magadan itself – a city of 121,250 inhabitants in 1979 – and the mining towns on the upper Kolyma, the impact of the ever-growing Russian population upon the native people was considerable. Bilingualism with Russian was very widespread, and the Ewen language was used as the medium of instruction in only a small number of primary schools.[27]

The territory of the Ewenkis falls into several different administrative divisions of Siberia. In the Far East it overlaps with that of the Ewens in the Okhotsk region, where indeed the distinction between the two peoples is

[27] Gurvich, *Etnokulturnye protsessy*, pp. 121–43; Gurvich and Dolgikh, *Preobrazovaniya*, p. 200; Kalesnik, *Dalniy Vostok*, p. 221; K.A. Novikova, *Ocherki dialektov evenskogo yazyka. Olskiy govor: glagol, sluzhebnye slova, teksty, glossariy*, Leningrad, 1980, p. 3; Popova, *Eveny*, pp. 137, 178, 214–15, 230, 247–9, 255–9, 263–6, 275–7, 287, 292; USSR. *Census 1979*, pp. 17, 88–9, 96.

somewhat unclear. More Ewenkis live in the Yakut ASSR than in any other territory – about 42 per cent of all, i.e. 11,584 out of the total number of 27,294 in 1979.[28] They mainly occupied parts of the north-west of the republic and the mountainous regions of the east and south, where their territory extended beyond the Stanovoy mountains into the Buryat ASSR, Chita and Amur Provinces, and Khabarovsk Territory – about 8,000 Ewenkis altogether lived in these regions east of Lake Baikal. Irkutsk Province also had 1,310 Ewenkis, and a large part of Krasnoyarsk Territory constituted their nominal homeland, the Ewenki National Region – a vast area of sparse population where in fact there were only 3,239 Ewenkis out of a population of 15,968, or about 20 per cent. The total number of Ewenkis in the USSR decreased from 32,800 in 1926 to 24,151 in 1959, but thereafter it increased. However, even with a relatively high birth rate they are unlikely ever to be more than a small minority even in the National Region that bears their name, where the proportion of Russians in 1989 was 68 per cent.

Although most of the Ewenkis in the National Region are said to have been collectivised before 1941, some of them were still nomadising in the 1960s, finding remote areas where they could live in their teepees (now covered with canvas as often as deerskin) free from interference by the Soviet authorities. In Amur Province too, many lived as before in small nomadic bands until the 1960s. One such band encountered by a Russian ethnographer consisted of the head of the family, an Ewenki called Pavel Yakovlev, his wives, four sons and four daughters. They lived by reindeer-herding and hunting and enjoyed perfect health on a diet consisting mainly of meat, without tea, sugar or salt, and they shunned the amenities of collective-farm settlements. This family was not alone in their conviction that settled life was both tedious and unhealthy: a few nomadic Ewenkis could still be found in the 1980s in various regions. Thus the 'problem' of nomadism – as it appeared to the Soviet Russian authorities – still existed, albeit on a small scale, after fifty years of collectivisation and denomadisation. For those Ewenkis who had settled in collectives, the postwar years brought amalgamations and relocations from outlying small settlements on rivers and lakes into the collective farm headquarters, and this in fact caused depopulation of areas which had formerly had their own scattered and mobile, but nevertheless local, population.

The life of some Ewenki communities was affected considerably by Soviet Russian industrial developments. As geologists conducted intensive surveys with a view to discovering new sources of minerals, and civil engineers began to construct hydro-electric dams and to lay the new Baikal–Amur Mainline railway (BAM), horse and reindeer transport was as indispensable as it had

---

[28] In addition over 15,000 Ewenkis and related Orochons lived in north-eastern China in 1978: Qiu Pu, *The Oroqens*, pp. 5, 18.

been in the eighteenth century, and Ewenkis were pressed into service in their traditional role as guides and reindeer-drivers. The main zone of BAM cut across what had been until then remote areas of the Stanovoy mountains inhabited almost exclusively by Ewenkis, for instance in the vicinity of Neryungri and Chara-Tonkin, and the North Baikal region where the new railway-track goes round the northern end of the lake. In quite a different region – north-western Yakutia – the opening of the diamond mines at Mirnyy and the creation of a huge lake on the river Vilui for a hydro-electric station certainly affected the lives of the Ewenkis whose territory began immediately to the west. It was found during the 1970s that Ewenkis were moving out of their former territories in western and southern Yakutia and into the central and northern regions of the republic, their reasons apparently being partly educational, but partly also withdrawal from areas of industrial development where there was a great influx of Russians, and where the Ewenkis' herding and hunting life was threatened. Those who were obliged to abandon their nomadic way of life and settle in villages in conformity with Soviet Russian socio-economic plans, inevitably succumbed to the common fate of demoralisation and alcoholism.[29]

Traditional practices and beliefs died hard among the Ewenkis. Even in the 1960s shamans still performed their rituals in places remote from the watchful eyes of the Russian Communist Party. The wolf and the bear still inspired a special respect, the spirit of the camp-fire had to be propitiated, and objects of use to the dead in the afterlife were left on graves. Although strict clan exogamy had largely given way to selection of a marriage partner from another collective farm, awareness of clan affiliation was still common even among young Ewenkis.

On the other hand, the abandonment of nomadism in favour of a settled, collectivised life undermined traditional Ewenki society by depriving children of the constant company of their parents. While men, and often also women, went out for the season at the pastures or hunting-grounds, it became usual to leave children in the care of a residential school, where they were exposed to common Soviet cultural norms. This affected first of all the child's command of its native language, as bilingualism in Russian became widespread. By the 1960s, even the sparsely populated Ewenki National Region was pervaded by Russians, and there were no exclusively Ewenki settlements. By 1979 over one-fifth of all Ewenkis acknowledged Russian as their native language. Nevertheless the National Region still had the highest proportion of Ewenkis claiming Ewenki as their native language – 86 per cent in 1979 (as compared with 92 per cent in 1970). The over-all numbers of Ewenkis in the whole of Siberia who claimed their own language was, however, low: only 43 per cent in 1979. Thus the use of the Ewenki

[29] Komarov, *Destruction of Nature*, pp. 123–4; V. Ogryzko, 'Sever stavit problemy', *Polyarnaya zvezda*, 1988, no. 6, p. 81.

language in Siberia was declining both in absolute number of speakers and as a percentage of the nationality. Apart from the extreme dispersion of the Ewenkis, and inundation by incomers, this decline is partly explained by dialect divisions. In the absence of a unifying form of written language, Ewenki writers wrote almost exclusively in Russian. However well Ewenki children knew their own language, therefore, the use of Ewenki as the medium of instruction in schools appears to have died out except in the preparatory class, and bilingualism with Russian was firmly established.[30]

THE WESTERN ARCTIC

The native population of the Arctic region from Arkhangelsk Province in the west to Taimyr in the east consisted in 1959 of some 27,000 Samoyeds (Nenets, Enets, Nganasans and Selkups), 10,000 Komis, 6,000 Khantys, 4,000 Dolgans, 1,000 Kets, and a few hundred Ewenkis and Yakuts. Much interaction had taken place between these peoples. The Komi people, whose original home lay to the west of the Urals, had moved north into the Nenets National Region in such numbers that they were as numerous as the Nenets, and many of the latter had in fact adopted Komi as their native language. Even in the Yamal National Region to the east, the Komis amounted to about a third of the number of Nenets. Here, too, in the northern fringe of the forest a considerable degree of mixing had occurred between the Nenets and Khantys and Selkups who moved in from the south as incoming Russian population encroached on their lands in the Ob and Yenisey basins. Despite these intrusions, the overwhelming majority of Nenets east of the Urals spoke Nenets as their native language. East of the Yenisey the small Samoyed people known as Enets, who had a long association with their Nganasan neighbours, had partly become assimilated to the latter or to the Nenets, to whom they were closely related in language and with whom intermarriage was common. As a result the Enets were not distinguished from the Nenets in census figures, and might have seemed to have disappeared entirely as a nationality. In fact, however, their small community (340 people all told) still preserved its own language and awareness of their ethnic distinctness in the 1970s. The Dolgans, who constitute an intrusion of Yakut–Ewenki culture and were alien to the Samoyed peoples as speakers of the Turkic Yakut language, had by the middle of the twentieth century advanced far into the Taimyr tundra. Dolgan territory stretched from Lake Pyasina and Norilsk in the south-west to the Khatanga estuary in the north-

---

[30] Boyko and Vasilyev, *Sotsialno-professionalnaya mobilnost*, pp. 5, 13, 42–3, 47, 57, 60–4, 160; Gurvich, *Osushchestvleniye*, p. 206; Gurvich and Dolgikh, *Preobrazovaniya*, pp. 179–94, 242–3, 250–5; Khaptayev, *Sovremennyy byt*, pp. 32–4, 165–9; *Narody Sibiri*, p. 733; Sokolova, *Na prostorakh Sibiri*, p. 102; Sokolova, *Puteshestviye v Yugru*, p. 137; Tugolukov, *Sledopyty*, pp. 9, 146–8, 153–62, 174, 188–95, 202.

east. Even in the 1970s very little racial mixing took place between the Dolgans and their northern neighbours the Nganasans, and as a rule neither nationality understood the language of the other.

Like the Far North-east, this was a region where the Soviet Russian authorities were unable to bring the native peoples completely within the collective farm system until the postwar period. Only the Dolgans appear to have been fully collectivised before the Second World War, during which their reindeer transport played an important part in communication between the lower Yenisey and the Khatanga region. However, many 'collectivised' Dolgans continued to lead a nomadic life in the 1950s and even later, as did their Samoyed neighbours. At that time, for instance, even west of the Urals the Nenets wandered in small family collectives without any fixed head-quarters, while two-thirds of Nenets in the Yamal National District were still unsettled, as were the Enets and Nganasans of Taimyr.

Even where the transition to settled life in Russian huts had taken place, many Nenets people found it hard to adjust to the domestic conventions of the Russians, so that, while some adopted European furniture and utensils, especially in urban settlements, others in more isolated places inhabited a wooden house as if it were a pole-tent, maintaining the traditional arrange-ment of the interior and sitting on deerskin mats on the floor to work and eat. Many Nenets, in fact, still lived in tents in the 1980s.

The process of collectivisation was resumed in the western Arctic after the war, and in most places the Nenets and other natives were collectivised by 1950. As in all other regions, the existing collectives in Taimyr National Region were subjected to amalgamation in the postwar period, so that the whole region was covered by eight collective farms and five state farms – most of the latter being in the Norilsk-Dudinka district. The Russian authorities' desire to achieve ethnic unification, or at least to overcome old antagonisms, led them to combine Nganasan and Dolgan collectives in mixed farms on the rivers Avam and Kheta. Even here, however, the two nationalities kept their own distinct customs, for instance in the arrangement of their encampments, and mixed marriages between Nganasans or Enets and Dolgans were very rare.

Russian influence became ubiquitous after the Second World War, even in the most remote corners of the Far North. Some of the industrial developments of the 1930s and 1940s had taken place within the territories of the northern Samoyeds, creating a big demand for transport, meat and fish. These were the Vorkuta coal-mines west of the Urals and the Norilsk nickel-mines in Taimyr – both projects being based on the forced labour of prisoners under the administration of the NKVD. Since those days the principal new development was the discovery and exploitation during the 1960s of the natural gas-fields in Yamal-Nenets National Region. Centred upon Urengoi on the lower reaches of the river Pur, it was linked with the

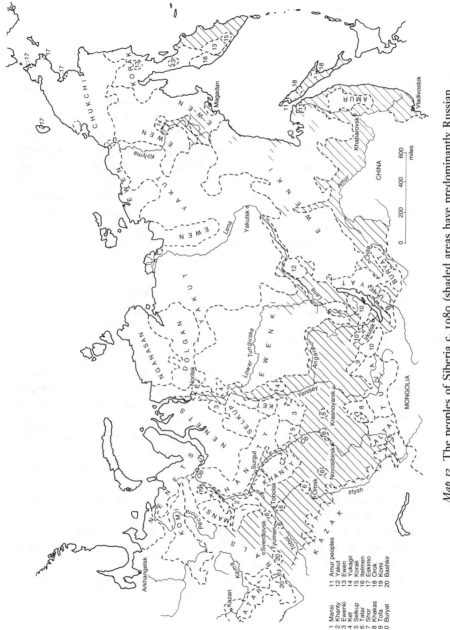

Map 12 The peoples of Siberia c. 1980 (shaded areas have predominantly Russian population)

1 Mansi
2 Khanty
3 Ewenki
4 Ket
5 Selkup
6 Tatar
7 Shor
8 Khakas
9 Tofa
10 Buryat
11 Amur peoples
12 Yakut
13 Ewen
14 Yukagir
15 Korak
16 Itelmen
17 Eskimo
18 Orok
19 Komi
20 Bashkir

industrial centres of the Urals by pipelines, and a railway was built from Nizhnevartovsk on the middle Ob to Urengoi. Other new railways projected for the western Arctic would extend beyond Urengoi to a gas-field at Yamburg on the Taz estuary, and from Labytnangi near the mouth of the Ob through the gas-field in Yamal peninsula to the Kara Sea coast.

In the Taimyr region the rapid growth of Norilsk to a city with 110,000 inhabitants (in 1959) had reduced the native peoples to less than 5 per cent of the population of the Nenets–Dolgan 'National' Region.[31] By 1979 this proportion had fallen to 3.5 per cent, the non-indigenous population of Taimyr amounting to 217,421 out of a total of 225,311. Over the same twenty-year period the proportion of native peoples in the Yamal–Nenets National Region had also decreased from 41 per cent to less than 20 per cent, while Russians and other incomers comprised 127,721 out of a total population of 158,844. Only in the western Nenets National Region did the Nenets and Komi slightly increase their share in the population from 22 to 24 per cent of the total, since the Russian element remained almost stable at about 36,000. Naturally the traditional cultures of these northern peoples underwent considerable change as a result of the high proportion of incomers in their territories.

Education also had its direct consequences, as native children, separated from their parents in September, spent the whole school year at some regional centre such as Salekhard. Here Nenets children were taught in their own language in the preparatory and first-year classes only, thereafter being taught in Russian. In the case of the Nganasans and Enets, for whose languages no standard written form had been developed, Russian was the language of instruction from the first day in school, while the Dolgans, because of the status of their language as a dialect of Yakut, were taught either in Yakut or in Russian.[32]

As a result of these factors the Russian language had obtained a firm foothold in the western Arctic by 1979. Only 57 per cent of the western Nenets claimed a good command of their own language, while 89 per cent knew Russian either as their first or second language, and Komi was the native language of 19 per cent. East of the Urals in Yamal National Region a much higher proportion (96 per cent) claimed Nenets as their native language, and only 3 per cent claimed Russian, but almost 68 per cent had a fluent command of Russian as their second language. The proportions of native and Russian languages were rather similar among the Nenets, Nganasans and Dolgans of Taimyr National Region. The peoples of the

---

[31] Official statements of the population of the Taimyr (Nenets–Dolgan) NR usually exclude Norilsk on the purely administrative grounds that the city does not belong to the National Region but is subordinated directly to the provincial capital Krasnoyarsk. Kalesnik, *Vostochnaya Sibir*, p. 214.

[32] In the 1959 and 1970 census figures no Dolgan nationality is mentioned, since they were counted as Yakuts, but they were distinguished in the 1979 census.

western Arctic were not threatened with extinction, since their absolute numbers increased considerably between 1959 and 1979: the Nenets, northern Selkups and Nganasans by almost 29 per cent, and the Dolgans by about 12 per cent. Ethnic awareness was still strong, as was the tradition of clan exogamy, especially among the Nenets, Enets and Nganasans in the east. So far as the material culture of these northern peoples was concerned, their austere environment and way of life dictated the continuing use of winter clothing made of deerskin and furs, although young people in settlements had largely adopted Russian dress for most occasions except journeys into the tundra or fishing expeditions.[33]

THE KHANTY-MANSI NATIONAL REGION

The administrative centre of the Khanty-Mansi National Region, Khanty-Mansiysk, lies within 1,200 miles of Moscow and only some 450 miles from the Trans-Siberian railway at Omsk or Kurgan, yet this region remained until the 1960s in many ways as remote as parts of Eastern Siberia or the Far North. This was because its known economic resources were slight compared with the obstacles to their utilisation by the Russians, in terms of dense forest, a multitude of rivers with low watersheds, and a huge area of marshland stretching from the Urals to Tomsk and from the Baraba steppe to the Arctic Circle. The whole region was without roads or railways, so that, apart from a slow journey by river, Khanty-Mansiysk could be reached from Tyumen, the capital of the province, only by seaplane.

In these circumstances the native peoples of Western Siberia, who in 1959 made up 17 per cent of the population of the Khanty-Mansi National Region, had been left, despite collectivisation, to follow more or less their old way of life. This was one of the regions of Siberia where relics of Shamanist religion persisted into the 1980s, where tree-spirits were propitiated and the bear-feast was celebrated. Primeval nature was relatively undisturbed, with dense coniferous forests where the Khantys, Mansis, Selkups and Kets on the whole still followed their traditional occupations of fishing and hunting. Their scattered family bands had been gathered into collectives in the 1930s and had to some extent been made to settle down, their collective settlements being subjected to the usual arbitrary amalgamation in the 1950s. However, the actual way of life of the Ob peoples up to the 1970s gave the lie to these decreed administrative changes. In fact it was essential

[33] S. Arutyunov, *U beregov Ledovitogo okeana*, Moscow, 1984, pp. 157–8; Brodnev, 'Ot rodovogo stroya k sotsializmu', p. 106; Gurvich, *Etnokulturnye protsessy*, pp. 84–8; Gurvich, *Osushchestvleniye*, pp. 150–1, 262–5; Gurvich and Dolgikh, *Preobrazovaniya*, pp. 42–4, 53, 155–61, 166–7, 175–8; Khomich, *Nentsy*, pp. 251–2, 260–5, 270–2, 279–80, 282–93, 300–1, 309; *Narody Sibiri*, pp. 631–9, 658–9, 664, 746, 754–9; Sokolova, *Puteshestviye v Yugru*, pp. 94–5, 99–102, 108, 111–12; Solzhenitsyn, *Gulag Archipelago*, vol. II, pp. 126, 568, 574; USSR. *Census 1959*; *Census 1970, Tom IV*; *Census 1979*.

for the Soviet Russian economy that they should continue to lead a semi-nomadic life – that is, that families should change their location with the seasons. The Ob and Irtysh produced two-thirds of all fish caught in Siberia's rivers, and the Khantys, Mansis and other native people played an essential part in this industry. Their 'expeditionary fishing' began in spring, when whole families left their scattered villages, embarking in boats – some of them traditional house-boats – to be towed by launches to fishing-grounds on the big rivers. There they might make several migrations from one summer settlement to another, their temporary dwellings often being the same types of primitive turf or bark-roofed huts which their ancestors had used. In autumn they would return to their permanent villages for the hunting season. In the north, reindeer-herding Khantys and Selkups were still nomadising, sleeping in pole-tents covered with skins or bark which no modern design of tent had superseded for warmth and convenience – just as nothing had proved to be better for moving around the waterways in summer than their light dug-out canoes made of aspen logs. The old division of labour in summer also continued – the men preparing wood, making boats, sledges and implements, while the women sewed winter clothing of reindeer skin – still considered to be the most practical and comfortable garments, although European town costume had gained a place for walking out in summer.

The 1960s brought a sudden massive intrusion of Soviet Russian industrial development into this hitherto neglected land. Up till then the major demand which the state made upon the Ob region had been for fish and timber. The new, much more extensive and fundamental industrial development was set in train in the 1950s in the form of geological explora-tion which discovered oil and natural gas fields extending over practically the whole of the Khanty-Mansi and Yamal-Nenets National Regions and the north of Tomsk Province. In 1960 the first oil flowed at Shaim on the river Konda near the Urals – in the main territory of the Mansis – and gas was tapped at Igrim. From the middle of the 1960s pipelines were laid to carry gas and oil to Perm and Tyumen, and a new railway between the Ob and the Urals cut across Mansi territory, thus creating a new ribbon of Russian settlement. The exploitation of oil deposits in Khanty territory on the middle Ob was on a greater scale. It began at a marshy lake known to the Khantys as Samotlor, and soon the two old, but hitherto insignificant Russian villages of Nizhnevartovsk and Surgut became centres of intensive oil-drilling opera-tions. To the east, in Tomsk Province, oil and gas-wells were drilled in the basin of the Vas-Yugan, and a new town of Strezhevoy appeared on the Ob. At the same time as the Ob oil-field was coming into production, so was natural gas at Urengoi, 350 miles to the north in the Yamal-Nenets National Region, and further discoveries were being made even farther north at Yamburg on the Taz Gulf, and in the Yamal peninsula. Apart from the immediate damage caused to forest and tundra by site clearing, heavy tracked vehicles, and oil spills, the extraction of gas and oil required the construction of long pipelines to link these sites with the Urals, Tyumen, Omsk, Tomsk and the Kuznetsk basin. There were also new roads and railways cutting through the landscape from Tyumen via Tobolsk to Surgut, and onward to Urengoi. Thus for the first time the territories of the Khanty, Selkup and Nenets peoples were deeply penetrated and cut up by the forces of modern industrialism.

In relation to the previous population of north-western Siberia the number of incomers was enormous. Surgut and Nizhnevartovsk mushroomed from a few thousand inhabitants in 1959 to over 100,000 each twenty years later, while the non-indigenous population of the Khanty-Mansi National Region as a whole increased from 98,000 to over half a million. While most of the native peoples made a modest increase in numbers during this period (the Khanty and Mansi increasing by 12 per cent to 28,497, and the Kets by 10 per cent to 1,122) their share in the population of 'their' National Region fell to less than 4 per cent in 1979. The newcomers – temporary residents attracted by good pay for short-term work in harsh conditions – came from all parts of the Soviet Union and, being brought in purely to serve in the exploitation of a region almost totally devoid of urban amenities or entertainments, they had little interest in it as a natural environment or as the homeland of the Khanty–Mansi and other indigenous peoples.

While a few of the native people were drawn into industrial occupations or into training for professions such as medicine and teaching, the proportion of town-dwellers among the natives of the middle Ob was still very low in 1970 (about 15 per cent of Khantys and 26 per cent of Mansis). Many Khantys, Mansis and Selkups, in fact, continued the movements of their peoples since the seventeenth century – away from the areas of Russian settlement. Some of the Ural Mansis moved east towards the Ob and Irtysh, while Khantys withdrew to the north-east, on to the northern tributaries of the Ob, or to the Taz, and into the tundra of the Yamal-Nenets National Region, or else eastward into Selkup country. The southern Selkups themselves – their National District on the river Tym having been abolished in 1950 – were faced with the choice of staying on to be inundated by Russian incomers, or moving away to join compatriots in the north. Those who remained on the upper reaches of the Ket – some 350 Selkups among several thousand Russians – seemed likely to become entirely lost through inter-marriage and cultural assimilation. Tomsk Province in general was the region with the lowest degree of survival of the languages of native peoples – in 1979 only 17 per cent of the Selkups and 22 per cent of the Khantys in the province claimed their mother tongue as their native language. In the Khanty-Mansi National Region the numbers of native people claiming their mother tongue was higher, ranging from 52 per cent of the Mansis to 65 per cent for the Khantys. The highest degree of preservation of native languages was in the Far North, where about 90 per cent of Khantys and northern Selkups in the Yamal National Region used their mother tongue – almost as high as the proportion for the Nenets themselves.

Under the changing conditions of the late twentieth century some elements of the old native culture of the peoples of the Khanty-Mansi National Region were lost, but others survived. Families were less commonly multigenerational, but much of their domestic property – houses, the larger boats and nets – were held in common, and food supplies, controlled as before by the oldest woman in the family, were shared freely with neighbours in need. For hunting and fishing, the old crafts were still practised, and awareness of the distinctive culture of the West Siberian forest peoples was still strong in those communities which succeeded in avoiding inundation by incomers.[34]

In many places on the Ob, however, where Soviet Russian intrusion was most marked, the 1970s brought demoralisation to some Khanty fishing collectives. In terms of subsistence they were quite well-off, since their fishing was in fact carried out on an individual basis, but drunkenness was rife and the general atmosphere was 'wild and violent'. This was partly the result of the use of the region as a place of punitive exile for young delinquents from other parts of the Soviet Union.[35]

---

[34] Conolly, *Siberia*, pp. 64–74; Gurvich, *Etnokulturnye protsessy*, pp. 108–15; Gurvich and Dolgikh, *Preobrazovaniya*, pp. 89–92; *Karmannyy slovar ateista*, p. 261; *Istoriya Sibiri*, vol. V, pp. 325, 329, 334, 337, 410; Komarov, *Destruction of Nature*, p. 127; Kozlov, *Natsionalnosti SSSR*, p. 100; *Narody Sibiri*, pp. 164, 582–3, 598–600, 681, 691–3; Nove, *Economic History*, p. 353; Sokolova, *Na prostorakh Sibiri*, pp. 47–61, 70–2, 97–8, 147; Sokolova, *Puteshestviye v Yugru*, pp. 36, 41, 43, 47, 54, 71–3, 81, 135–8; USSR. *Census 1959. RSFSR*, pp. 302, 312, 328, 330; *Census 1979*, pp. 72, 86–9, 92, 100.

[35] P. Lineton, first-hand account, quoted by Humphrey, *Karl Marx Collective*, p. 16.

17

SIBERIA IN THE 1980s

RUSSIAN SIBERIA

SOURCES for the history of the Siberian peoples under the Soviet régime were, until very recently, rather unsatisfactory. In ethnography and political, economic and social history the propagandist image presented in publications censored by the Communist Party let through only rare and ambiguous glimpses of reality. Only the assumption of leadership by M.S. Gorbachev in 1986 and the advent of greater truthfulness about the economic and moral state of the country permitted Soviet writers to refer openly to the inefficiency and corruption which had prevailed for over half a century. These enormous shortcomings – long apparent to many Western observers of the USSR but dismissed officially as 'anti-Soviet propaganda' – were as rife in Siberia as in the rest of the country, and in 1988, following Gorbachev's 'Murmansk Initiatives' speech,[1] a flood of candid articles began to appear in the official press concerning social, environmental and ethnic problems, especially among the peoples of the North.

The nationalities of Siberia, as a part of the Russian Republic, were in a somewhat different position from those in the fourteen other union republics of the Soviet Union, such as the Ukraine, Azerbaijan or Uzbekistan. In most of the latter the main indigenous nationality accounted for between 59 and 90 per cent of the population,[2] and they possessed a real, if strictly limited, degree of self-government. The RSFSR – by far the largest of the union republics – is, however, a firmly Russian land, even if its thirty-one nominally autonomous national republics, provinces and regions account for over half of its territory, and within the RSFSR Siberia is even more definitely Russian than European Russia is. The latter, for instance, contains

---

[1] D. Scrivener, *Gorbachev's Murmansk Speech: the Soviet Initiative and Western Responses*, Oslo, 1989.
[2] Exceptions are Kazakstan (which in some ways resembles Siberia, with Kazaks accounting for only 36 per cent of the population) Kirgizia and Latvia.

two compact regions – the northern Caucasus and the middle Volga – where non-Russian peoples constitute well over 50 per cent of the population. Siberia has no similar concentration of native peoples except the Tuva ASSR. In all other 'national' territories the proportion of indigenous inhabitants ranged in 1989 from as little as 1.4 per cent in the Khanty-Mansi Autonomous Region to 36 per cent in the Yakut ASSR, only the Aga Buryat Autonomous Region and Tuva ASSR having over 50 per cent. Despite all its racial variety, Siberia is in fact the part of the Soviet Union most completely integrated from the ethnic point of view with the central Russian lands around Moscow. So far as some parts of Siberia remain less thoroughly integrated into the Russian Republic, this is a matter of temporary postponement because of remoteness, forbidding climate, and lack of communications and readily exploitable resources.

In the postwar period the reforms and changes in the administration and economy proclaimed from time to time by Moscow were sometimes accompanied by resolutions specifically concerning the indigenous peoples of Siberia. This was at least an indication that here too there were faults in the system – even if the basic rightness of the 'Leninist nationalities policy' was continually asserted. Economic regionalisation and the creation of new 'territorial production complexes' gave a semblance of rational, programmed planning to the exploitation of the natural resources of Siberia, but the reality which was exposed from 1987 onward was often the irresponsible creation of vast projects by various ministries and other state bodies which were motivated more by self-interest than by real prospects of economic and social benefit, especially to the lives of the local inhabitants.

In Siberia conflict between the native peoples' traditional way of life and the aims of the imperial power was apparent from the very beginning of Russian occupation, and its effects had become critical in many parts of the colony by the end of the nineteenth century. However, it was only in the second half of the twentieth century that these effects reached truly annihilatory proportions. The most important factors in this were the development of twentieth-century technology which made access to and exploitation of natural resources even in the remotest parts of Siberia relatively easy; and the subordination of the whole colony to the industrial aims of Moscow, according to which it was seen simply as one of the regions of the USSR, the resources of which were to be utilised as part of the 'national economy'.[3] The needs, or demands, of central planning generated by the military and political interests of the state assumed an absolute priority against which consideration for the traditional way of life of the native peoples or the natural environment carried little weight.

Until 1987 state censorship suppressed all reference in the Soviet press to

---

[3] Officially it was divided in 1963 into three economic regions: Western Siberia, Eastern Siberia and the Far East.

ecological disasters perpetrated in the USSR, and official publications continued to extol the power of 'Soviet man' to change nature, reshaping it to his own ends – for instance, by the proposed diversion of the waters of the Irtysh and Ob south into Kazakstan. Recently, however, the large-scale environmental damage in every part of the Soviet Union caused by one grandiose scheme after another has been exposed in language far removed from the smug bombast of the past. In relation to nature in Siberia the prevailing attitudes and activities of industrial 'developers' are now frequently described as 'predatory', 'barbaric' or 'criminal', and the scale and pace of irremediable destruction of taiga and tundra has been compared with the 'colonial African way of development' or the destruction of the Amazon rain-forest.[4] One writer compared the irresponsible plundering of Siberia by ministries with the arbitrariness of medieval principalities, another with the Mafia,[5] while a third referred to it as 'the AIDS of the North'.[6]

Among the most harmful activities of state enterprises, gold-dredging, which destroys whole river-beds, proceeded without restraint for many years because the production of gold, as a 'strategic product', placed the industrial enterprises involved above the law.[7] More recently, the most notorious ecological disasters in Siberia have been the threat to the purity of the water in Lake Baikal; the construction of the Baikal–Amur railway (BAM) and associated mining towns; oil and gas extraction in Western Siberia with its spillage into lakes and rivers of a million tons of oil per year; and the huge hydro-electric dams on the Angara and Yenisey, inundating enormous areas of forest. Much forest has also been irreparably lost by felling, and by accidental fires which are said to have consumed as much timber as that cut down intentionally.[8]

The worst feature of these grandiose industrial projects in Siberia was that they proceeded without regard for the local people, whose whole livelihood could be destroyed by them. Not only had the Khantys and Nenets of Western Siberia, for instance, been ousted from their devastated homeland

[4] S.P. Danilov, 'Perestroyka i literatura. Doklad ... na XI syezde Soyuza Pisateley Yakutii', *Polyarnaya zvezda*, Yakutsk, 1988, no. 6, p. 98; D. Kravchenko and V. Chertkov, 'Ne splecha, a s golovoy', *Pravda*, 2 Dec. 1988, p. 3; Ye.A. Oborotova, 'Narody Severa v sovremonnom mire: vzglyady i pozitsii', *Sovetskaya etnografiya*, 1988, no. 5, p. 151; Pika and Prokhorov, 'Bolshiye problemy malykh narodov', p. 79; Pisateli Rossii, 'K rabochim geologicheskikh partiy; k stroitelyam nefte- i gazoprovodov ... osvaivayushchim promyshlennye rayony Severa, Sibiri, Dalnego Vostoka', *Severnye prostory*, 1989, no. 2, p. 5; R. Rugin, 'Dom. Eto khorosho!', *Severnye prostory*, 1988, no. 6, p. 3; S. Zalygin, 'Vozvrashchayas k vodnym problemam ...', *Kommunist*, 1988, no. 13, p. 53.

[5] V. Rasputin, 'Posluzhit' otechestvu Sibiryu', *Izvestiya*, 3 Nov. 1985, p. 3; F.Ya. Shipunov, 'Tsena kilovatta', *Severnye prostory*, 1989, no. 3, p. 5.

[6] V. Pervushin, 'Vsem mirom', *Severnye prostory*, 1988, no. 6, p. 5.

[7] Komarov, *Destruction of Nature*, p. 116.

[8] A. Khramtsov, 'Khodit Sever v pasynkakh', *Pravda*, 15 Nov. 1988, p. 6; Rasputin, 'Posluzhit'; Yu. Yermolenko, 'Po chernomu sledu "pokoritelya"', *Severnye prostory*, 1988, no. 5, p. 18; Zalygin, 'Vozvrashchayas k vodnym problemam', p. 54.

by the oil and gas industry, but they received no compensatory benefits from this 'development'.[9] Not only had the planners not consulted the natives' interests (some of them did not even know where the natives lived, and they frequently 'forgot' to invite their representatives to planning meetings) but in the long-term development plan for the Far East, compiled as recently as 1987, no mention whatever was made of the native peoples.[10]

At the local level it was Russian and other newcomers to Siberia who were blamed for the barbaric treatment of the environment and native peoples alike. These were geologists and workers attracted by specially high rates of pay, who were flown in to remote industrial sites on a rota system (*vakhta*) and who cared nothing for the 'wilderness' that they encountered, nor for its human and animal inhabitants.[11] Such 'transients' (*vremenshchiki*), not only on occasion destroyed all the fish in a lake or felled whole cedar trees in order to obtain a few nuts, but, for instance, desecrated the storehouses and burial places of the Khantys and Nenets, or simply robbed them of the clothes they wore. Some of the worst industrial damage to nature and the native economy occurred in the tundra, where large areas of reindeer pasture were turned into wasteland, and the number of reindeer was reduced to a lower level than at any previous time during the twentieth century.[12]

NATIVE SIBERIA UNDER SOVIET NATIONALITIES POLICY

Lenin's dictum that the Russian Empire was 'a prison of peoples' is much quoted in the Soviet Union with the aim of providing an antithesis to the Soviet 'multinational state' in which all nationalities are said to enjoy equality, and are united in harmonious fraternal cooperation. The constitutional rights of all citizens of the USSR to work, relaxation, health care, housing, education etc. are invoked in order to demonstrate that it is only thanks to the Bolshevik Revolution that the native Siberians – once oppressed and without rights – now enjoy a good life. Indeed it is to the Soviet régime that their very survival is attributed, since official Communist Party doctrine endorses literally the pessimistic forecasts of inevitable extinction which were current in Russia before 1917. For instance, the Chukchi writer Rytkheu wrote in 1981:

I shall never tire of repeating the truth, now self-evident, that the peoples of the North were saved by the Great October Socialist Revolution ... A complete change in the existing order, and the creation of a qualitatively new society founded upon

---

[9] B.B. Prokhorov, 'Kak sberech Yamal', *Znaniye – sila*, 1988, no. 7, p. 2.
[10] Sharov, 'Mala li zemlya'.
[11] O. Gusarevich, 'Vakhta za porogom', *Severnye prostory*, 1988, no. 5, pp. 28–30.
[12] Ye. Aipin, 'Not by oil alone', *Moscow News*, 1989, no. 2, pp. 8–9; Pika and Prokhorov, 'Bolshiye problemy', p. 78.

genuine humanism, was required before the peoples of the North could take heart, rise from their knees and discover a new historic future.[13]

Another contrast which is frequently expressed in Soviet and Western accounts is between the happy fate of the natives of Siberia and the miserable life of native minorities in capitalist countries, especially those of North America. The Canadian author Farley Mowat, for instance, wrote in the 1960s that, in contrast with the Indians and Eskimos of Canada, who were 'debilitated, disorientated islands of human flotsam, nearly devoid of hope and of ambition, surviving on charity – when they survived at all', the small peoples of Siberia have been 'treated with astonishing consideration', and have 'not only been enabled to survive as strong and viable segments of society but . . . have been permitted to retain their deep and subtle awareness of themselves as natural men. *Their* roots have not been severed. They remain a proud and integral part of the continuum of life.'[14] Sadly, this is untrue. Rytkheu also contrasted the supposed well-being and self-respect of his own people in Soviet Chukotka with the destructive effects of capitalist industry and commerce upon the Canadian Indians and Eskimos. As one of the most significant positive features of Soviet nationalities policy he cited the right to use the native language, contrasting this with the absence of Indian or Eskimo writers in North America and the punishment of children for using their native language in school during the 1940s and 1950s.

If the impact of mid-twentieth-century mining, oil-drilling and defence projects, and of ruthless commercial slaughter of caribou, walrus and other animals, was catastrophic for the Indians and Eskimos of the American North, it is also true that their medical services, educational facilities and employment opportunities improved in the 1960s. In the sphere of industrial development too, the contrast between the capitalist and communist systems is far from absolute, since the exploitation of the mineral resources of Siberia has been carried out by the Soviet Russian state just as relentlessly, and with as little regard for the traditional life of the native peoples. Here, as in Canada and Alaska, the latter have had to bear 'tremendous pressure from an apparently inexorable and invincible avalanche of incomers . . . the "conquerors of the North", with their mighty earth-moving machinery, all-shattering explosives and diamond-tipped drills'.[15]

[13] Yu. Rytkheu, 'Pod senyu volshebnoy gory', in *Izbrannoye v dvukh tomakh*, Leningrad, 1981, 2 vols., vol. I, p. 7; vol. II, pp. 432–3. Other typical statements in this vein include, e.g. *Istoriya Sibiri*, vol. IV, pp. 464, 473; vol. V, pp. 12, 46, 427; Pervushin, 'Vsem mirom', p. 4; V.N. Uvachan, *Perekhod k sotsializmu malykh narodov Severa (po materialam Evenkiyskogo i Taymyrskogo natsionalnykh okrugov)*, Moscow, 1958, pp. 181–2.

[14] Mowat, *The Siberians*, pp. 82–3, 90–1, 305.

[15] Rytkheu, *Izbrannoye*, vol. II, pp. 487–8, 500–5; *Sovremennye legendy*, pp. 197–8, 223, 226, 230, 272–3, 290, 327–8. This writer's opinions became much more outspoken after 1987, for instance in 'Svet zvezd – bolshikh i malykh', *Pravda*, 31 Dec. 1988, p. 3, and 'Beloye bezmolviya?', *Ogonyok*, 1989, no. 17, pp. 20–1.

Another Canadian writer's view of the inexorable expropriation by 'an expanding, internal imperialism' of native peoples 'who find themselves in the economic and political hinterlands of other people's nation states'[16] applied equally well to Siberia, despite superficial contrasts in politico-economic systems. Indeed the Siberian peoples had less chance than their North American counterparts of asserting their rights to land and the pursuit of their traditional occupations, since they have lacked until very recently the freedom of information, assembly and publication of their views which exists in Canada and the United States.

After 1987, in contrast with the assertion by writers of the past that Soviet nationalities policy had been a 'colossal success',[17] it became possible to write of the self-deception which had allowed the myth of progress and racial harmony to be maintained.[18] Rytkheu now stated that 'The true state of the northerners, which in the past was cloaked in the rosy mist of propaganda, is only now beginning to come to light' and related how individuals who sought to bring the plight of the Northern peoples to the notice of the central authorities during the 1950s were threatened with investigation by the KGB as 'nationalists'.[19]

According to some writers, indeed, from the 1960s to the 1980s the Soviet Russian government simply had *no* nationalities policy for the North,[20] so that the native peoples were left entirely at the mercy of random pressures from enterprises ruthlessly exploiting natural resources with the blessing of the moribund Communist Party leadership. Far from Soviet nationalities policy being a 'colossal success', indeed, one writer expressed the view that the Soviet Union's treatment of the natives of the North is comparable with the annihilation of the North American Indians by the white man.[21] Another result of *glasnost* has been that, after decades when only negative reports about the conditions of life of North American Indians and Eskimos were permitted in the Soviet press, favourable references are now frequently made to the positive developments which have occurred in the USA and Canada since native movements emerged there in the late 1950s.[22]

[16] H. Brody, *Living Arctic: Hunters of the Canadian North*, London, 1987, pp. 143, 181, 189, 213, 215, 227.
[17] V.B. Kozlov, 'O sochetanii traditsionnykh i novykh form zhiznedeyatelnosti narodnostey Severa v usloviyakh internatsionalizatsii obraza zhizni', in B.B. Prokhorov, ed., *Regionalnye problemy sotsialno-demograficheskogo razvitiya*, Moscow, 1987, p. 41.
[18] Sharov, 'Mala li zemlya'.
[19] Rytkheu, 'Beloye bezmolviye?', p. 21.
[20] Pervushin, 'Vsem mirom', p. 5; Pika and Prokhorov, 'Bolshiye problemy', p. 81.
[21] K. Hallik, Speech at the Congress of People's Deputies, 1989, quoted in K. Mihalisko, 'North American-style native reservations in the Soviet North?' in *Report on the USSR*, 1989, vol. I, no. 29, p. 33.
[22] L. Bogoslovskaya and others, 'Dom pod ugrozoy', *Severnye prostory*, 1988, no. 5, p. 4; Kravchenko and Chertkov, 'Ne splecha, a s golovoy'; Krupnik, *Arkticheskaya etnoekologiya*, pp. 230–1; Krupnik, 'Demograficheskoye razvitiye aziatskikh eskimosov', pp. 86–7; Pika and Prokhorov, 'Bolshiye problemy', pp. 78, 83; Shipunov, 'Tsena kilovatta'.

Racial discrimination and hardship have undoubtedly been a fact of life for North American Indians and Eskimos for a long time.[23] What was suppressed in Soviet publications was the fact that against a background of (perhaps ineffective) government measures dating back, in the case of the USA, to 1934, some North American Indian communities had been making successful claims for restitution of lands, or compensation for their loss, since the 1940s. In Alaska a native newspaper the *Tundra Times* was established in 1962, and four years later the Alaskan Federation of Natives succeeded in halting work on an oil project. In Canada too various organisations representing Indian and Inuit interests appeared in the late 1960s (such as the National Indian Brotherhood) and the first claims for compensation against industrial developers came in 1971. In the Soviet Union, however, admissions of the bad social conditions of the Siberian natives, and the first possibility of speaking out on their behalf, came only in the late 1980s, so that in this respect it was the Soviet Union which was twenty or thirty years behind the capitalist countries.

The picture of North Siberian native life which began to emerge in 1988[24] was shocking for those who had believed the official view presented by the Soviet Russian authorities. For instance, in contrast with oft-repeated assertions that nomadism had been eliminated by the 1960s, and that all Northern peoples resided comfortably in permanent settlements, it emerged that about one-tenth (15,000) still had no fixed abode and lived the year round in tents.[25] Where housing did exist for natives it was sub-standard and badly overcrowded, with as many as ten people living in a two-room hut.[26] The fate of native settlements was in any case dreadful: the amalgamation of small villages which began in the 1950s and 1960s – in practice the enforced deportation of people from their own home districts to newly created or expanded villages for the sake of administrative convenience – has been described as 'the most terrible' of the series of upheavals and ordeals affecting the Northern peoples.[27] This policy was continued in the 1970s as former collective farms (*kolkhozy*) were grouped together in state farms (*sovkhozy*), and outlying villages – Russian as well as indigenous – were 'liquidated' as non-viable.[28]

To the planners of the Soviet Russian state economy, people were simply

---

[23] N. A. Chance, 'Alaska Eskimo modernization', in D. Damas, ed., *Handbook of North American Indians*, vol. V, *Arctic*, Washington, 1984, pp. 650–1.

[24] For instance in Prokhorov, ed., *Regionalnye problemy*.

[25] O. Borodin and L. Shinkarev, 'Dayte slova yukagiru', *Izvestiya*, 7 Apr. 1989, p. 3; L. Nenyang, 'Pyatna v geografii', *Pravda*, 19 May 1988; Pika and Prokhorov, 'Bolshiye problemy', p. 77.

[26] Krivoshapkin, 'Boli i trevogi Severa – v serdtse moyem', p. 69; V. Ogryzko, 'Sever stavit problemy', *Polyarnaya zvezda*, 1988, no. 6, pp. 80, 87; Rugin, 'Dom. Eto khorosho!', p. 3.

[27] Sharov, 'Mala li zemlya'.

[28] Rasputin, 'Posluzhit' otechestvu Sibiryu'. His novel *Proshchaniye s Matyoroy*, Moscow, 1976, is on this theme.

'labour resources' which could be switched from one occupation, or one region, to another. According to this schematic view, the problems of the people of the North should be solved by depriving them of their traditional territories, occupations and 'outmoded' customs, and transferring them to 'the great world of industry' where a 'bright future' supposedly awaited them.[29] It was of no interest to the bureaucrats who imposed new rules on the native communities that their traditional pursuits were not just jobs like that of a clerk, but represented a whole way of life, a culture as valid as that of urban Russians, and that to destroy that way of life and the natural environment on which it depended was to deprive the native peoples of all hope for the future.[30] Huddled together in Russian-style villages and subjected to artificial work-schedules, more than half of the people of the North had become unemployed and aimless. Young people in particular had been systematically alienated from their own communities and traditional occupations by enforced residence at boarding-schools (*internaty*). As a result there was little chance of parents passing on skills to their children, who were brought up by strangers to see no prestige in the old way of life.[31] Opposition to the unnaturalness and cruelty of this system is expressed in one of Rytkheu's books by a Chukchi woman in a reindeer-herding camp:

Local education officials and doctors all press us to send our children to the crèche and the kindergarten ... to the *internat*. But we keep our children with us as long as we can ... for surely the most important thing people can do is to bring up their children to take over from them later. If not, what's the point of bearing children? To produce them and hand them over to the state? Do they think we're just animals?[32]

Only rarely did young people, after experience of town life, choose to return to the traditional occupations of their parents.[33]

Unemployment, or the possibility of obtaining only menial jobs, had reduced many Northern natives to apathy and a dependence on welfare benefits which added further to their pauperisation and very often ended in alcoholism. The ironical similarities to the condition of Alaskan and Canadian

---

[29] V.I. Boyko, quoted in V. Sangi, 'Otchuzhdeniye', *Sovetskaya Rossiya*, 11 Sept. 1988, n. 211, p. 2.

[30] Kravchenko and Chertkov, 'Ne splecha, a s golovoy'.

[31] G.I. Sukhomirov, 'Okhotnichye-promyslovoye khozyaystvo na Dalnem Vostoke', in V.L. Boyko et al., eds., *Problemy sovremennogo sotsialnogo razvitiya narodnostey Severa*, Novosibirsk, 1987, p. 136.

[32] Rytkheu, *Sovremennye legendy*, p. 265. Cf. Ye. Aipin, quoted in Ogryzko, 'Sever stavit problemy', p. 85; Borodin and Shinkarev, 'Dayte slovo yukagiru'; Kravchenko and Chertkov, 'Ne splecha, a s golovoy'; A. Nemtushkin, 'Bol moya, Evenkiya!', *Sovetskaya kultura*, 28 July 1988, p. 3; A. Nerkagi, 'Pered broskom', *Severnye prostory*, 1989, no. 1, pp. 6–7; T.A. Pechetegina, 'Ne otkladyvaya na zavtra', *Severnye prostory*, 1988, no. 5, pp. 2–3; Pika and Prokhorov, 'Bolshiye problemy', pp. 80–1.

[33] Nerkagi, 'Pered broskom'; Ch.M. Taksami, 'Sootnosheniye traditsionnogo i novogo v kulture narodnostey Severa', in V.I. Boyko et al., eds., *Problemy sovremennogo sotsialnogo razvitiya*, p. 171.

natives twenty years before were obvious, as were the health problems and inadequacies of medical care which were exposed.[34] Life expectancy for natives of the Soviet North in 1988 was only 45 years for men and 55 for women – eighteen years less than the USSR average. (Meanwhile the life expectancy of Canadian Inuit had increased by fifteen years.)[35] Infant mortality was high (two or three times the average for the RSFSR),[36] tuberculosis was still fairly common,[37] and the indigenous people of the North were generally more prone to disease than incomers with higher standards of living. Statistics linking deteriorating health standards and social conditions had been consistently suppressed by the Soviet authorities,[38] and in the case of one particular region, Chukchi-land, quite horrifying facts were revealed in 1989. It was reported on good evidence that, presumably as a result of nuclear tests in the atmosphere carried out during the 1950s and 1960s in Novaya Zemlya there was a high level of radiation contamination, especially of reindeer moss, which, passing from the deer to those who ate their flesh, produced a very high incidence of cancer and other diseases. As a result the native people had an extremely high infant mortality rate (70–100 per 1,000 births) and an average life expectancy of only forty-five years.[39] The high mortality rate among Siberian natives in general, however, arose chiefly from violent deaths: accidents, alcoholic poisoning, murder and suicide – social causes which reflected the insecurity of life in the native communities.[40] One Eweki writer states that 40 per cent of Ewenki school children were double orphans, and that this was attributable to Russian vodka.[41]

Family life also suffered severely from deteriorating social conditions and the influx of 'transients'. The resulting 'mixed marriages' of official statistics – in fact brief liaisons between native women and Russian men, which became a mass phenomenon in the 1960s – have been more appropriately

[34] Pechetegina, 'Ne otkladyvaya na zavtra'; A.I. Pika, 'Demograficheskaya politika v rayonakh prozhivaniya narodov Severa: problemy i perspektivy', in Prokhorov, ed., *Regionalnye problemy*, pp. 52–3.

[35] K. Mihalisko, 'SOS for native peoples of Soviet North', *Report on the USSR*, 1989, vol. I, no. 5, pp. 3–6; Pika and Prokhorov, 'Bolshiye problemy', p. 80; Rugin, 'Dom. Eto khorosho!', p. 3; R. Rugin, speech at Supreme Soviet, quoted in Mihalisko, 'North American-style native reservations', p. 34.

[36] Yu. Shestalov, speech at the Union of Writers of the RSFSR, *Literaturnaya Rossiya*, 23 Dec. 1988, quoted in Mihalisko, 'SOS for native peoples'. This gives an infant mortality rate of between 38 and 57 per 1,000 live births.

[37] Ogryzko, 'Sever stavit problemy', p. 87; Rytkheu, 'Beloye bezmolviye?', p. 21.

[38] Rytkheu, 'Beloye bezmolviye?'

[39] V. Lupandin and Ye. Gayer, 'Chernobyl na Chukotke: narody Severa rasplachivayutsya za yadernye ispytaniya', *Moskovskiye novosti*, 1989, no. 34, p. 5; 'O Novoy Zemle, mirnom i nemirnom atome', *Severnye prostory*, 1990, no. 2, pp. 1–4.

[40] Pika, 'Demograficheskaya politika', pp. 49–50; Pika and Prokhorov, 'Bolshiye problemy', p. 80.

[41] A. Nemtushkin, quoted in Ogryzko, 'Sever stavit problemy', p. 81.

described in terms of 'temporary wives' or 'provisional concubinage'.[42] Single-parent families – which were unheard-of in the traditional way of life – had become the rule in many northern communities, and the number of half-breed children in some Eskimo villages was as high as 50-70 per cent. Such children were usually registered as Eskimos, so that their mothers qualified for the welfare benefits provided for all native children in the north. Similarly, Nenets, Dolgan and Chukchi women during the 1960s frequently had seven or eight children, most of whom were by different 'white' fathers.[43] In recent years, however, the birth rate among Northern women has fallen, largely because of abortion.[44] The other side of the picture of the breakdown of traditional marriage was that, if only because of the isolation of herding and hunting men from the villages where the women generally remain, there were now many unmarried native men in the North who had no prospect of ever having families.[45] Thus for demographic and social reasons a situation had arisen where once again, after an interval of some sixty years, people in Russia were writing about the possibility that at least the smaller native communities in Siberia could die out if serious steps were not taken to help them.[46]

Of all the regions in Siberia it was perhaps in Taimyr that social conditions were at their worst in the 1980s. Once the most remote Arctic territory of the Soviet Union, the 'Dolgan–Nenets' (and Nganasan) Autonomous Region had become dominated by the industrial monster of Norilsk with its non-ferrous metallurgy plants. Vast areas of reindeer pasture near Norilsk had been turned into lifeless zones by the use of tracked vehicles, and formerly prosperous reindeer-herding collectives farther east had fallen into neglect as a result of amalgamation under a bureaucratic and corrupt state-farm management. While the latter made large profits from fur and fish production, thousands of domesticated reindeer reverted to the wild. In Ust-Avam district the nomadic Nganasans had no domestic amenities and no occupation except menial services for the Russians, who now had even taken over most of the hunting. Where natives did have accommodation other than tents, the overcrowding was on a third-world scale, with as many as thirteen people housed in one room. However poor the provision of medical and other facilities might be in other parts of Siberia, Taimyr, with a very high infant mortality rate, a high incidence of mentally retarded children and

[42] Chichlo, 'La Tchoukotka', p. 150; Krupnik, 'Demograficheskoye razvitiye', pp. 104, 109.
[43] Komarov, *Destruction of Nature*, p. 121; Krupnik, 'Demograficheskoye razvitiye', pp. 104, 109; Pika and Prokhorov, 'Bolshiye problemy', p. 80.
[44] One out of three pregnancies is terminated: Pika, 'Demograficheskaya politika', pp. 49–50.
[45] Krivoshapkin, 'Boli i trevogi Severa', p. 70; V.I. Zadorin, 'Sotsialno-ekonomicheskiye problemy optimizatsii severnogo olenevodstva', in Boyko et al., *Problemy sovremennogo sotsialnogo razvitiya*, pp. 147–8.
[46] Ye. Aipin, election manifesto quoted in *Moscow News*, 1989, no. 12, p. 6; Pika, 'Demograficheskaya politika', pp. 44–7; Pika and Prokhorov, 'Bolshiye problemy', p. 76; A. Chudoyakov, 'Tragediya Shorii', *Sibirskiye ogni*, 1989, no. 8, pp. 164–6.

much tuberculosis, was considered by one writer to be thirty years behind the rest of Siberia in social development. Meanwhile, modern amenities well above the norm for the Soviet Union were provided by the metallurgical combine for the 180,000 Russian inhabitants of Norilsk, whose authorities contributed nothing to the wellbeing of the people of the surrounding tundra. Thus what had been communities of hardy nomadic hunters and reindeer-herders, possessing a unique, highly developed culture, had been reduced to apathy and alcoholism, frequently resorting to fighting with knives, and having a cowed sense of inferiority reinforced by taunts and physical attacks by Russian chauvinist hooligans if they visited the administrative centre of 'their' autonomous region, Dudinka.[47]

NATIONAL CULTURES AT RISK

The preservation of national identity is difficult in any community which is swamped by an overwhelming preponderance of incomers. In Siberia this is true equally of the larger nationalities which have 'autonomous' republics – the Buryats and Yakuts – and of smaller ones, such as the Nenets, Khanty-Mansis, Altaians, Ewenkis and Koraks, who enjoy only the status of 'autonomous provinces' (*avtonomnye oblasti*) or 'national regions' (renamed in 1977 'autonomous regions' – *avtonomnye okruga*). It is, of course, particularly true in the case of those which were too small in numbers to be granted any nominal autonomy whatever, such as the peoples of the lower Amur and Sakhalin or the Yukagirs, or those who were at first allocated national territories, only to have them abolished subsequently, such as the Shors, Tofalar and Selkups. The inexorable growth of the Russian component in the population makes it appear possible that at least the smallest native peoples face inevitable assimilation and extinction as distinct communities. However, two factors perhaps justify a less pessimistic view. Firstly, the combination of a relatively high birth-rate among the indigenous peoples, and a lack of enthusiasm for migration to Siberia on the part of people in other regions of the USSR, apparently resulted in a halt in the proportional growth of the incomer element during the 1970s and 1980s, so that, as table 6 shows, while the total population continued to increase, the proportion of natives and 'Russians' (including incomers of all non-indigenous origins) stabilised at approximately 5 per cent and 95 per cent respectively.

Second, there are more native Siberians in the late twentieth century than there have ever been before. Far from 'dying out', as many people predicted at the turn of the century, their numbers have grown continuously ever since the seventeenth century – apart from a reduction in the period of revolution and civil war. During the years following the end of the Second World War

[47] Komarov, *Destruction of Nature*, p. 120; N. Menitskaya, 'Krichashchaya parallel'', *Severnye prostory*, 1988, no. 6, pp. 18–21; Nenyang, ' "Pyatna" v geografii'.

15 Aniko of the Nogo clan: an illustration to a story by the contemporary Nenets writer Anna Nerkagi, about a student whose return to her fur-clad tent-dwelling kin after fourteen years absence at Soviet boarding-school and college brings home to her her own alienation from them and the critical situation of her people in the modern world.

most Siberian nationalities increased in absolute numbers at a higher rate than the average for the Soviet Union as a whole or the Russian people in particular. For instance, while the whole population of the USSR increased in the thirty-year period 1959–89 by 37 per cent, and the Russian people by 27 per cent, the Siberian native peoples as a whole grew by 69 per cent. Of course, in relation to the Russians their total numbers range from small to tiny. The largest Siberian nation, the Buryat Mongols, increased during this period by 67 per cent, reaching a total of 421,700 – less than the size of one middling Russian city such as Ryazan or Murmansk. Similarly, the Yakuts increased by almost 61 per cent to 382,300, while the Altaians with an increase of 60 per cent reached a total of 71,300. Among the smaller peoples, up to 1979 the Nenets made a 28 per cent increase to 29,900, while the Ewenkis, with a low increase of 11.3 per cent, totalled 27,300. At the low end of the scale, a few very small communities declined in numbers, such as

Table 6 *Table of Population of Siberia*[48]

Year	Total population of Siberia	Native peoples		'Russians'	
		number	% of total	number	% of total
1897	5,730,000	861,900	14.4	4,814,000	80.7
1911	9,366,300	1,064,000	11.4	8,100,000	85.4
1926	12,309,000	788,000	6.4	11,519,000	93.6
1939	16,674,000	816,900	4.9	15,857,100	95.0
1959	22,559,000	957,500	4.2	21,601,500	95.8
1970	25,353,400	1,205,900	4.8	24,147,500	95.2
1979	28,615,000	1,378,600	4.8	27,236,400	95.2
1989	32,099,000	1,617,900	5.0	31,481,100	95.0

the Selkups, who fell by 6 per cent from 3,800 to 3,570. Others apparently made very large percentage increases in their tiny numbers, such as the Aleuts and the Eskimos, who grew by approximately 37 per cent (from 400 to 546, and from 1,100 to 1,510 respectively) while the Yukagirs made an increase of 109 per cent from about 400 in 1959 to 835 in 1979!

Although the proportion of indigenous Siberians in relation to the Russians and other non-indigenous peoples held its own in the 1960s and 1980s, the latter nevertheless amounted to 95 per cent of the population. Even in their own 'autonomous' territories, therefore, nearly all native peoples of Siberia constituted minorities, and it seems impossible that this imbalance could ever be corrected. Moreover, even if the nominal survival of a nationality may seem to be assured in terms of increasing numbers, the external pressures to which it is subjected, including an increasing proportion of half-breeds, tend towards the degeneration and eventual loss of the national culture. In the words of a writer who in 1988 visited one isolated Yukagir village in north-eastern Yakutia: 'A people which has lost its memory is doomed to die out; so is a people corrupted by idleness.'[49] Formerly the 200 Yukagirs in this community were relatively prosperous, until they were incorporated in a state farm which was too far away from their homes to provide any occupation for them. As a result many of them had nothing to do but sleep all day. Most of the young people were half Russian, and the national culture was already forgotten by all but a few old people.

For any nationality a crucial factor is the continuing use of the national language, and as we have seen, in Siberia most circumstances tended

[48] Calculated from *Aziatskaya Rossiya*, vol. I, pp. 82–5; V.I. Kozlov, *Natsionalnosti SSSR*, 2nd edn, 1982, pp. 285–7; *Narody Sibiri*; USSR, *Censuses*, 1959, 1970, 1979, and preliminary data for 1989 published in *Report on the USSR*, 1990, no. 201, pp. 15–19.
[49] L. Yefremova, 'Zyryanka i okrest', *Polyarnaya zvezda*, 1989, no. 1, p. 106.

towards a decline in the use of native languages in social intercourse in general, and more particularly in the educational system. As in any multinational state or empire, the common language of communication was inevitably that of the dominant nationality, so that in the school syllabus the native language was in competition with Russian as the language of instruction, and in higher education the use of Russian was almost inevitable. Census figures show a reduction in the percentage of non-Russian people claiming the language of their own nationality as their native language between 1959 and 1989: from 98 per cent of all Yakuts to 94 per cent, from 95 per cent to 86 per cent in the case of the Buryats, and, for all other nationalities of Siberia and the North grouped together, from 84 per cent to 72 per cent. (Tuvans are exceptional: 99 per cent consistently claim their own language.) At the same time, bilingualism in the native language and Russian increased, so that in 1989 a fluent command of Russian as second language was claimed by 65 per cent of Yakuts, 72 per cent of Buryats, and 60 per cent of all other Siberian peoples.

The status of national languages in Soviet schools was particularly affected by two pieces of legislation: the decree of 1938 'On the obligatory study of the Russian language in schools in the national republics and territories', and that of 1959 'On reinforcing the connection between school and life and the further development of the educational system in the RSFSR', which gave parents the right to choose in which language their children would be taught. These measures led to an increase in the use of the Russian language in schools, especially among the smaller nationalities of Siberia, and it was with the aim of improving children's command of Russian, not the native language, that the pre-school preparatory class in the native language was introduced for many nationalities in 1948. In the case of peoples having no standard written form of their native language, such as the Yukagirs, Ulchis, Udeghes, Nivkhs and Itelmens, the vernacular was dropped altogether in favour of Russian as the language of instruction from the first day in school.[50] It was also the small Far Eastern peoples who had the lowest degree of retention of their native languages in 1979, ranging from 41 per cent for the Oroches to only 18 per cent for the Aleuts. Some of these peoples seemed therefore to be doomed to lose their native languages altogether in favour of Russian. On the other hand, several other nationalities

[50] In a list of languages used in schools of the RSFSR in 1972 only the Altaians, Buryats, Tuvans, Khakas and Yakuts had the vernacular as the language of instruction beyond the preparatory class, while, apart from them, only the Nenets, Chukchis and Ewenkis had their native languages on the curriculum as a subject of study beyond the first class. The absence from the list of any mention of twelve languages: Aleut, Itelmen, Ket, Korak, Nanai, Nganasan, Nivkh, Oroch, Selkup, Udeghe, Ulchi and Yukagir, indicates that at that time these languages were not used in schools at all: Yu.V. Bromley et al., eds., Sovremennye etnicheskiye protsessy, pp. 271–3. See also Boytsova, 'Shkola narodov Kraynego Severa', pp. 150–1.

which were both small in number and without school-books in the vernacular showed a considerably higher degree of retention of the native language, e.g. the Dolgans and Nganasans (in both of which 90 per cent of the people claimed the native language), though this was not due to the educational system but, presumably, to the relative isolation of these communities from Russian influence.

By the late 1960s the decline in command of the native languages among young children of the North was causing concern in their communities, so that teachers' conferences proposed greater use of the native languages at pre-school and primary school levels.[51] As a result, the teaching of some languages, such as Nanai and Nivkh, in the first two years of school was reintroduced in the early 1980s.[52]

As recently as 1985 it was possible for a Soviet magazine to assert that the USSR was sixty years ahead of the United States in fostering the native languages of northern peoples,[53] and many people in the West have long expressed this view with admiration. However, Rytkheu has since acknowledged that in fact – quite apart from any incidental decline because of various causes – state support for native languages was consciously downgraded from the 1950s.[54] At that time an opinion became prevalent in some circles that under communism, when it was achieved, the minority languages would die out in any case, and this engendered a 'nihilistic' attitude towards them, even among some of the indigenous peoples themselves.[55] The prevalence of this attitude reflected the real, assimilative, nationalities policy of the Russian Communist Party. From Estonia to Yakutia, local patriots who asserted the need to promote their native languages, or insisted on using them, rather than Russian, at meetings where the indigenous people were in the majority, were quickly reported to the authorities for displaying 'nationalism'.[56] As it was understood that 'nationalism can only be bourgeois' in the Soviet context,[57] it was but a short step to the threat of an accusation of 'anti-Soviet' ideas, with potentially very serious consequences.[58]

The disastrous effect upon native culture of compulsory boarding-school attendance from the age of seven has already been mentioned, but it is clear that Russification began even before this, in the kindergarten, where most nurses and teachers were Russian speakers. Even where some of them were

---

[51] Boytsova, 'Shkola narodov kraynego Severa', pp. 153–5.
[52] Gurvich, *Narody Dalnego Vostoka*, p. 227.
[53] S. Norman, 'Rythkeu – a Chukchi voice in London', *Soviet Weekly*, 26 Jan. 1985, p. 12.
[54] Rytkheu, 'Svet zvezd'.
[55] Danilov, 'Perestroyka i literatura', pp. 101–2; also G.N. Kurilov (Uluro Ado), 'Pod severnymi zvezdami', *Polyarnaya zvezda*, 1988, no. 6, p. 107.
[56] Danilov, 'Perestroyka i literatura', p. 101; G.I. Kunitsuyn, 'Oblucheniye proshlym: istoki i preodoleniye', *Polyarnaya zvezda*, 1989, no. 2, p. 75; Tumarcha, 'Sprosi khozyaina', *Severnye prostory*, 1989, no. 3, p. 2.
[57] Kunitsyn, 'Oblucheniye proshlym', p. 76.
[58] Nemtushkin, 'Bol moya, Evenkiya!'

natives, however, there were cases when children or the nurses themselves were reprimanded for using their native language. Reference to this fact by several Siberian writers[59] inevitably recalls previous condemnation of similar discrimination against native children in Alaska.[60]

The result of neglect of and discrimination against native languages for some thirty years was that in Yakutia, for instance, not only was the younger generation largely incapable of writing in their own language, but they were frequently unable to converse with their own grandparents, being as monolingual in Russian as the old people were in Yakut.[61] It was therefore not entirely incredible that the native languages of Siberia were in danger of disappearing completely, depriving the national cultures of their very basis, so that in the end the native communities themselves would cease to exist.

On the positive side, the revival of interest in national cultural traditions which developed in all parts of the Soviet Union in the 1970s also occurred in Siberia among the emerging native intelligentsia. As early as 1981 Rytkheu had written about the need for Northern peoples to rediscover their cultural roots, ending a long period of collaboration in the disparagement of their own past, and to proclaim that not everything in their old way of life had been bad (as official Soviet ideology had been asserting since the 1920s). In addition to the practical achievements of the native peoples, who were the real 'conquerors of the North' long before the white man came, their institutions of communal and family life had had many positive virtues.[62] Rytkheu even came to regret the Communist Party's indiscriminate campaign against the primal religion of his people and to feel a new sympathy not only with its inherent respect for nature, but even with the shaman, whom he no longer saw, in the stereotype of anti-religious propaganda, as merely an ignorant, predatory charlatan, but in many cases as a highly gifted person with skill in healing, wisdom above the average, and the spiritual elevation of a poet.[63] Another Siberian writer, the Ewenki Alitet Nemtushkin, also spoke of the ethical values of his people – honesty, candour, conscientiousness and hospitality – now being swamped by the sordid realities of modern life and Russian bureaucracy.[64] Similarly, the Yukagir Uluro Ado wrote that if nothing was done to save native culture, future generations would lose the proud and generous nature of the northerner and find themselves 'stranded on the roadside of someone else's culture' as 'temporary guests in the land of

[59] Ye. Aipin, quoted in Ogryzko, 'Sever stavit problemy', p. 85; Ye.A. Gayer, 'Khotela by dobavit k skazannomu', *Pravda*, 26 June 1989, p. 2; Rytkheu, 'Svet zvezd'.
[60] Rytkheu, *Sovremennye legendy*, pp. 223–73.
[61] Danilov, 'Perestroyka i literatura', p. 101.
[62] Rytkheu, *Sovremennye legendy*.
[63] Yu. Rytkheu, *Magicheskiye chisla*, Leningrad, 1986.
[64] Nemtushkin, 'Bol moya, Evenkiya!'

their ancestors, deprived of the skills and knowledge which were built up over many centuries'.[65]

A NATIVE RIGHTS MOVEMENT?

There was no question of these northern writers indulging in romantic idealisation of the life led by their parents or grandparents, since its hardships were all too familiar to them. If the negative features of modern materialism had brought them to an appreciation of the spiritual and social values of the old life and even of the traditional occupations which were its economic basis, nevertheless they could not accept the practical exclusion of their compatriots from the benefits of civilisation which had long been promised them.[66] Consequently, in the late 1980s a kind of 'native rights movement', somewhat similar to that in North America, began to emerge in many parts of Siberia, drawing its leadership from native writers, and using the forum of a more liberal official press and of the new Congress of People's Deputies which met in 1989.

Important though the questions of education and native traditions were, the concern of the Siberian native intelligentsia went far beyond cultural matters, since problems of industrial development and ecology inevitably led them into the political field and the question of native rights, particularly with reference to territory. What did the nominal 'autonomy' of regions, provinces and republics in fact mean, if all parts of Siberia were treated in practice as colonial sources of raw materials, if the native inhabitants were never consulted about the effects of new projects,[67] and if their way of life and even their survival as communities was not taken into account? Now, at least, local and native public opinion in Siberia existed as a reality which might have some influence and could demand of ministries information and consultation in advance of industrial developments.[68]

The problems and opportunities of the post-Brezhnev period involved all the nations of Siberia, great or small. In Buryatia long-suppressed national sentiments again came to the surface, one sign of this revival being the decision taken in 1987 to reinstate Buryat as the language of instruction in schools where Buryats were in the majority. The need for remedial measures

[65] Kurilov, 'Pod severnymi zvezdami', pp. 109–10.
[66] L. Nenyang, 'Komandirovka na rodinu', *Druzhba narodov*, 1989, no. 8, p. 3.
[67] F. Kurchatova, letter to the director, *Severnye prostory*, 1989, no. 3, p. 6; Tumarcha, 'Sprosi khozyaina', p. 2; Shipunov, 'Tsena kilovatta', p. 6.
[68] Ye. Aipin, election manifesto; V. Bogachev, 'Nastupleniye na Yamal priostanovleno', *Severnye prostory*, 1989, no. 3, pp. 10–11; Bogoslovskaya et al., 'Dom pod ugrozoy'; Pika and Prokhorov, 'Bolshiye problemy', p. 82; Shipunov, 'Tsena kilovatta', p. 5.
[69] *Radio Liberty Research*, 1987, no. 355; A. Zhdanov, 'Ne vina, a beda', *Pravda*, 20 Feb. 1989, p. 2.

was illustrated by an incident during the election campaign for the new Supreme Soviet when a Buryat candidate in Ulan-Üde was unable to reply to a question put to him in his own language. Because this had become quite typical of Buryats living in the towns of the Buryat ASSR, indeed, the republic's Communist Party newspaper, in an attempt to improve the situation, began to print lessons in the Buryat language.[69] By 1989 Buryat had become the language of instruction in the great majority of schools, and pressure to extend it further continued.[70]

The Buryat press also launched a discussion about the suppression of national culture and the persecution of talented people during the Soviet period. Books previously banned as 'nationalist' were republished, and a new, and presumably less distorted, *History of the Buryat ASSR* was undertaken. A new impulse was given to pan-Mongolian sentiments in 1990 – the 750th anniversary of the epic chronicle *The Secret History of the Mongols*. In Buryatia, as in Mongolia, scholars used the occasion to praise this as an outstanding contribution of the Mongolian peoples to world civilisation and to affirm that its hero, Chingis Khan, was a great historical figure.[71] Such developments were tolerated by the communist government under conditions of more freedom of speech, but some of the demands made by the Buryat intelligentsia went beyond this to questions of autonomy, national territory and official language which, like similar movements in the Baltic republics and the Caucasus, raised acute political issues. While Buryat public opinion proposed the unification into one territory of the three separate 'autonomous' – and originally 'national' – areas (the Buryat ASSR and the Aga and Ust-Orda Autonomous Regions), the Soviet Russian government's opposition to claims to a special right to a territory on the part of any nationality was demonstrated by its turning the situation upside down and asserting that the interests of 'the great majority' of the population of these areas – that is the Russian 68 per cent – would be unfairly prejudiced if reunification of a greater Buryatia was permitted.[72] Undoubtedly, anti-Russian feelings exist among the Buryats, whose ethnic social structures are a closed book to the Russians, and these problems will not go away.[73]

In the Sayan-Altai borderlands of Siberia too, national feelings were stirring in the late 1980s. For the Mountain Altai Autonomous Province the crucial question was the threat of construction of a hydro-electric dam which would flood much of the valley of the Katun, one of the sources of the Ob, devastating the cattle-rearing economy of the native people and obliterating

[70] Oshorov, 'Dvuyazychiye v buryatskoy shkole', pp. 67–9.
[71] M. Khomonov, 'Istoriko-kulturnoye znacheniye literaturnogo pamyatnika "Sokrovennoye skazaniye"', *Baykal*, 1989, no. 6, pp. 97–100; D. Ulymzhiyev, '"Kruglyy stol" mongolovedov', *Baykal*, 1990, no. 3, pp. 141–4.
[72] Zhdanov, 'Ne vina, a beda'.
[73] Humphrey, 'Population trends', pp. 158–9, 163, 165.

their culture in this last remaining corner of their historical homeland. The Altaians succeeded in having the project shelved, and demanded a greater degree of autonomy for their province, which until now has been subordinated to the largely Russian Altai Territory.[74] Meanwhile their neighbours the Tuvans reached a point where an outburst of national feeling in 1990 led to almost ninety deaths and an exodus of Russian industrial workers from the republic.[75]

The huge Yakut ASSR, which had not been subjected to such intensive industrialisation and urban development as Buryatia (and had only about 50 per cent Russians in its population) continued to manifest the idiosyncratic national spirit which had given the Yakuts a reputation for nationalism.[76] The continuation of friction between natives and incomers was illustrated by a complaint from a Yakut writer that his native land was 'under the sway of transients, scroungers, poachers, alcoholics, and drug addicts, who are brought here from the central provinces of the country although we already have more than enough drunkards of our own to cope with'.[77] This refers to the fact that Siberia was still being used by Moscow as a dumping-ground for criminals, many of whom, after release from prison-camps, stayed on in Yakutia.[78]

Great concern was generated by the industrial exploitation of some areas of Yakutia, in particular the pollution of the Vilui river as a result of a hydro-electric dam providing power for the diamond mines.[79] Meanwhile plans were advanced for further catastrophic projects, such as the diversion of the waters of the river Amga, and the construction of a hydro-electric power station near Verkhoyansk, which would require the inundation of large areas of forest and the removal of many settlements.[80]

In the field of culture, the bitterness felt by the Yakut intelligentsia about the repression of writers and patriots in the 1930s was expressed by an official rebuttal of decrees of 1952 and 1960 which had imputed the crime of 'bourgeois nationalism' to such notable Yakuts as P.A. Oyunskiy, M.K. Ammosov and A.Ye. Kulakovskiy, and by attempts to find out the precise circumstances of their deaths.[81] Characteristically, the Yakuts were the first

[74] L. Sherstova, 'Katunskaya GES glazami etnografa', *Sibirskiye ogni*, 1990, no. 7, pp. 148–52; Moscow TV quoted in *SUPAR Report*, no. 8, 1990, pp. 72, 84.
[75] A. Sheehy, 'Russians the target of interethnic violence in Tuva', *Report on the USSR*, 1990, vol. II, no. 37, pp. 13–17.
[76] Kunitsyn, 'Oblucheniye proshlym', p. 76.
[77] Tumarcha, 'Sprosi khozyaina'.
[78] *Izvestiya*, 4 Aug. 1988, p. 3; *Izvestiya*, 11 May 1989, p. 6; Radio Petropavlovsk-Kamchatskiy, 21 Mar. 1989; *Sovetskaya Rossiya*, 19 Aug. 1988, p. 2, and 10 Mar. 1989, p. 6, all cited in *SUPAR Report*, no. 6, Jan. 1989, pp. 39, 45 and no. 7, July 1989, pp. 89–90.
[79] I. Danilov, 'Chelovek zhivet prirodoy', *Polyarnaya zvezda*, 1989, no. 3, p. 109.
[80] Bogoslavskaya, 'Dom pod ugrozoy', p. 4; Danilov, 'Chelovek zhivet prirodoy'; Tumarcha, 'Sprosi khozyaina'.
[81] 'Postanovleniye byuro Yakutskogo obkoma KPSS ot 10 maya 1989g.'; I.Ye. Fedoseyeva, 'Dokumenty rasskazyvayut', *Polyarnaya zvezda*, 1989, no. 4, pp. 126–8, 131–5.

nation in Siberia to push their demand for autonomy as far as a formal declaration that their republic would be a 'sovereign state' (the Yakut-Sakha Republic) within the RSFSR.[82]

Even among the very small and dispersed native communities of the lower Amur and Sakhalin, massively outnumbered by settlers and transients from European Russia, and lacking any autonomous national territories, public opinion emerged as a result of Gorbachev's new policies. The Nivkh writer Vladimir Sangi first brought the plight of his people to the notice of the public,[83] and in 1988 an enterprising Nanai woman, Yevdokiya Gayer, after election to the Supreme Soviet in Moscow made a passionate speech about the problems of the Nanai, Ulchi, Negidal and Nivkh peoples in terms of their disappearance or survival in the face of commercial exploitation of forest and river. In particular, the ruthless felling of virgin forest left little hope for the remnants of the Udeghe people, until the Supreme Soviet and the local soviet of the Maritime Region persuaded the USSR State Forestry Committee in March 1990 to hand over to the Udeghes the whole valley of the Samarga river. Similar rights to territories were granted to the Nivkhs, Nanais, Ulchis and other peoples of the Amur.[84]

One aspect of Gorbachev's reconstruction programme was to be the greater development of the Soviet Far East, and this brought a return to an ethnic situation which had prevailed before the Bolshevik revolution: as part of a general resumption of trade and joint economic ventures with China, agriculture in the Far East benefited from the efficient cultivation of vegetables by Chinese and Korean farmers, while the employment of cheap Chinese labour also began on various construction projects on Soviet territory.[85] With the extension of contacts with South Korea the Soviet government began to allow Koreans who had been held in Sakhalin since 1945 to return to Korea, and to consider the possibility of allowing the return of Koreans from their places of deportation in Kazakstan and Central Asia to their former home in the Soviet Far East.[86]

The most ravaged area of Siberia in the late 1980s was still the west, where large-scale oil extraction, accompanied by a drastic reduction of fish

---

[82] *Report on the USSR*, 1990, no. 32, p. 29; *Pravda*, 28 Sept. 1990, p. 2. In conformity with the general movement for independence among the nationalities of the USSR in 1990, declarations of 'sovereignty' and of higher administrative status were made or mooted by the Yakuts, Buryats, Tuvans, Khanty-Mansis, Yamal Nenets, Chukchis, Koraks and Altaians – *Report on the USSR*, 1990, vol. II, no. 44, p. 37; no. 45, pp. 23–5.

[83] Sangi, 'Otchuzhdeniye'.

[84] Gayer, 'Khotela by dobavit'; *SUPAR Report*. 1990, no. 9, pp. 135–6; Yu. Yefimenko, 'Posledniye iz Udege?', *Ogonyok*, 1990, no. 10, pp. 10–12.

[85] *SUPAR Report*, 1988, no. 6, *Chronicle*, p. 41; 1989, no. 7, pp. 18–21, 27; 1990, no. 8, p. 78; 1990, no. 9, pp. 25, 27–8, 30.

[86] S. Crowe, 'Progress in Repatriating Koreans on Sakhalin', *Report on the USSR*, 1989, vol. I, no. 33, pp. 19–20; *SUPAR Report*, 1988, no. 5, *Chronicle*, pp. 21–2; 1989, no. 6, *Chronicle*, pp. 43–5; no. 7, p. 91; 1989, no. 7, pp. 90–1; 1990, no. 8, pp. 45, 86–8; no. 9, pp. 125, 132–3.

catches as a result of the spillage of oil and chemicals, and the ruination of reindeer pastures by engineering works, had already had a catastrophic effect on the life of the native peoples.[87] When it became possible to speak out against this depredation it was the Khanty writer Yeremey Aipin who took the lead in the movement to protect the Ob – 'our common Ugrian homeland' – from total destruction. In support of his fear that the Khanty people themselves were threatened with extinction, he describes how the ubiquitous legacy of Russian domination – apathy and vodka – had claimed the lives of nearly all his male cousins before the age of forty.[88] A sensitive writer, still conscious of his ancestors' animistic respect for nature, Aipin expressed the hope that 'If we protect the Earth, there will be life'[89] – but already Soviet Russian industry had moved on voraciously from the Ob, the Pur and the Taz to a new region rich in natural gas deposits beyond the Arctic circle – Yamal.

Yamal, the 400-mile long peninsula forming the western shore of the Ob estuary, became one of the key cases in the struggle between environmentalists and industrialists in the late 1980s. While the continuing nomadism of the native Nenets people, at least in the absence of any modern amenities, was deplored by the Khanty writer Roman Rugin, it was the very existence of the reindeer economy which he saw to be at risk as a result of the plans of gas-extracting interests, involving the construction of a railway, roads and pipe-lines in Yamal: 'For wherever the modern "conqueror's" foot has trodden he leaves behind dead lakes and rivers, reindeer pastures that have been trampled and made useless, and degraded forest.'[90] This project, which as usual had been set in motion without consultation with the indigenous people, generated a considerable degree of public opposition, and early in 1989 it was indeed halted – at least for the time being – until the ministries concerned prepared a plan which would take account of nature conservation, the preservation of reindeer herding and compensation to the local inhabitants, including a realistic price for land.[91]

Problems of a slightly different kind faced the inhabitants of the Ewenki Autonomous Region in the valley of the Lower Tunguska, where it was proposed to build a high dam across the river at Great Rapids up-river from

---

[87] Ye. Aipin, election manifesto; Ogryzko, 'Sever stavit problemy', pp. 80–1; Pika and Prokhorov, 'Bolshiye problemy, p. 79.
[88] Aipin, 'Not by oil alone'.
[89] Aipin, election manifesto.
[90] Rugin, 'Dom. Eto khorosho!', p. 3.
[91] G. Britayev, 'Svedeniya dlya tov. Shapovalova', *Severnye prostory*, 1989, no. 2, p. 6; Yu. Chernov et al., 'Preduprezhdayut uchenye', *Severnye prostory*, 1989, no. 2, pp. 7–8; Kravchenko and Chertkov, 'Ne splecha a s golovoy'; Nerkagi, 'Pered broskom'; Pervushin, 'Vsem mirom'; 'Po chernomu sledu "pokoritelya" ', *Severnye prostory*, 1988, no. 5, pp. 16–19; Prokhorov, 'Kak sberech' Yamal'; V. Pryanishnikov, 'Khod na zhivoy zemle', *Severnye prostory*, 1989, no. 3, pp. 10–13.

its confluence with the Yenisey.[92] The ministries concerned showed no concern over the fact that this project, by raising the water-level by 650 feet and flooding 740 miles of the valley (covering an area of almost 4,000 square miles), would inundate the sites of all seven settlements in the Ewenki national territory, including its administrative centre Tura. The population of these villages, from the graphite-mining settlement of Noginsk to Yukte, numbered some 10,000 people, including 1,500 Ewenkis – almost half of the total Ewenki population of what in 1930 was designated as their 'national region'. These were no doubt small numbers compared with the grandiose figures of kilowatts to be generated, but the valley contained the pastures and hunting grounds upon which the livelihood and way of life of the Ewenkis depended. The justifiable conviction of the Ewenki writer Alitet Nemtush-kin was that 'technocrats don't care about ethics',[93] and in this case too a considerable campaign was waged to avert another ecological catastrophe. This involved a public-opinion poll, letters of protest to newspapers, articles in the press, speeches on behalf of the Ewenkis at the Congress of People's Deputies, and a charge of illegality in terms of the Constitution of the USSR if this, the only Ewenki autonomous region, were to be eliminated. The results of this unprecedented campaign were the rejection of the project by the regional Communist Party committee and the halting of work on it at least for the time being.[94]

RECONSTRUCTION AND INDIGENOUS SIBERIA

It was the small nations of the Siberian North whose future was most obviously threatened by the industrial developments of the 1980s, but remedies proposed in the course of widespread discussion echoed many of the opinions expressed about the economy, ecology, administration and autonomy throughout the USSR. There was, for instance, the democratic conviction that 'People will begin to take an interest in social concerns only when they cease to be mute performers of other people's will and get the feeling that they are partners.'[95] Another way of putting this was that the peoples of the North must feel themselves to be once again the true masters of the forest, the rivers, the reindeer herds and their pastures, and 'not day-labourers for the comrade with the brief-case'.[96] Industrial planners should

---

[92] S.S. Savoskul and V.V. Karlov, 'Turukhanskaya GES i sudba Evenkii', *Sovetskaya etnografiya*, 1988, no. 5, pp. 166–8. Geographically the term 'Turukhansk power-station' is rather misleading as the site is seventy-five miles away.

[93] Nemtushkin, 'Bol moya, Evenkiya!'

[94] Mihalisko, 'North American-style native reservations', p. 33; Nemtushkin, 'Bol moya, Evenkiya!'; S.S. Savoskul, 'Net! Turukhanskoy GES', *Severnye prostory*, 1988, no. 6, pp. 6–7; Savoskul and Karlov, 'Turukhanskaya GES', p. 168; Shipunov, 'Tsena kilovatta'.

[95] Borodin and Shinkarev, 'Dayte slovo Yukagiru'.

[96] Pika and Prokhorov, 'Bolshiye problemy', p. 83.

be obliged to take into account ecological problems and as compensation for any disturbance of the environment and way of life, to pay a percentage of profits to local communities for the improvement of their amenities.[97] Recognising the helplessness of local organisations – even of the Communist Party – in relation to the powerful ministries, many people called for the creation of a high-level governmental body directly responsible to the Central Committee of the Communist Party and the Council of Ministers – in effect a revival of the Committee of the North – as well as an Institute or University of Peoples of the North to assist in the revival of indigenous languages and cultures.[98] A need was also felt for unofficial pressure groups, and in May 1989 an Association of Peoples of the North was founded with V. Sangi as its chairman.[99]

Attention was also focused on local administration, in which many district committees and soviets had no representatives of native communities. At region level too, the necessity that native people should have some influence on industrial developments and social services gave rise to the conviction that not merely formal but real autonomy was essential.[100] When national regions (*natsionalyne okruga*) were first formed in Siberia in the 1930s they were indeed recognised as 'territories with the largest number of members of a single people or of several peoples sharing a similar culture and way of life', and the rights of representation in soviets and committees which they received gave them 'their own political organisation akin to that of provincial autonomy'.[101] Since the 1970s, however, as pressure on native territories from outside agencies became ever stronger, such autonomy as they had was disregarded in favour of the interests of the central government. At the same time the uncontrolled influx of outsiders tipped the demographic balance to the disadvantage of the natives who, being now a minority, might be said to deserve consideration only in proportion to their statistical weight in the total population. It was noticeable that, along with the change of title from 'national' regions to 'autonomous' regions, the central government had begun to refer to such territories as 'districts where northern peoples

---

[97] Ye. Aipin, election manifesto; V. Bogachev, 'Nastupleniye na Yamal priostanovleno', *Severnye prostory*, 1989, no. 3, pp. 10–11; Bogoslovskaya et al., 'Dom pod ugrozoy'; Nerkagi, 'Pered broskom'; Ogryzko, 'Sever stavit problemy', p. 87; Pechetegina, 'Ne otkladyvaya na zavtra'; Pika and Prohkorov, 'Bolshiye problemy', p. 83.

[98] Aipin, election manifesto; S. Gorokhov, 'Maksimum samoupravleniya', *Severnye prostory*, 1989, no. 2, p. 3; Krivoshapkin, 'Boli i trevogi Severa', pp. 64–5; Ogryzko, 'Sever stavit problemy', pp. 87–8.

[99] Krupnik, *Arkticheskaya etnoekologiya*, pp. 233–5; Mihalisko, 'North American-style reservations', p. 33; Pika and Prokhorov, 'Bolshiye problemy', pp. 82–3.

[100] Aipin, election manifesto; Menitskaya, 'Krichashchaya parallel', p. 21; Ogryzko 'Sever stavit problemy', p. 82; N.P. Otke, speech at Supreme Soviet, *Pravda*, 1 Dec. 1988, p. 4; Pervushin, 'Vsem mirom', p. 5; Pika 'Demograficheskaya politika', p. 54.

[101] Gurvich, *Osushchestvleniye*, p. 25.

---

reside',[102] as if these were not the age-old homelands of the indigenous Siberians, but merely areas where they now happened to live, but to which they possessed no particular rights. Contrary to this view it was argued by partisans of native rights that not only must the status of autonomous provinces and regions be raised by restoring effective autonomy to them, but that – since it is difficult for a culture to survive if the people have no territory of their own in which to maintain their distinctiveness – the category of national district (*natsionalnyy rayon*) which existed in the 1920s and 1930s should be revived.[103] By this means nineteen of the smallest Siberian peoples, who at present did not possess any official national territories – such as the Selkups, Kets, Tofalar, Yukagirs, Ewens, Eskimos and the small nationalities of the Amur – might obtain a new lease of life.[104]

An essential feature of increased local autonomy, in the eyes of some writers (who invoked the 1917 Bolshevik Decree on Land) was that there should be laws not only to protect traditional forms of land-use, but to confirm the rights of the indigenous population over its territory and the utilisation of its natural resources, so that, in the words of one Yakut writer, access to the North would be closed to 'undesirable' elements.[105] The next logical step was to propose the designation of territories for the exclusive use of native communities with legal barriers preventing intrusion by economic enterprises. Some spoke of 'national parks', but others went so far as to use the term 'reservations'. Despite the negative associations of this term, Aipin wrote that this was the only way to ensure the survival of the Siberian native peoples, while Nerkagi stated that she would gladly live on a reservation if its gates defended the Nenets people's land from domination and devastation by government ministries and departments.[106] Thus, after decades of vilification of North American Indian reservations in the Soviet press, they were now seen by some natives as a last resort to afford the natives at least some protection from the encroachment of the white man's aggressive world.

Just as important as the question of territories and administrative structures for the future of the native communities of Siberia was that of the basis of their traditional economy. As in every part of the USSR, the failure of

---

[102] '*rayony prozhivaniya narodnostey Severa*': for instance in the 1980 Decree of the Central Committee of the Communist Party and the Council of Ministers of the USSR, *Pravda*, 26 Feb. 1980, p. 1; see also Boyko et al., eds., *Problemy sovremennogo sotsialnogo razvitiya*, pp. 8, 99, 106, 185, and passim.

[103] In 1934 there were ninety-three national districts in Siberia: Gorokhov, 'Maksimum samoupravleniya', p. 2.

[104] Borodin and Shinkarev, 'Dayte slovo Yukagiru'; Krivoshapkin, 'Boli i trevogi Severa', p. 66.

[105] Tumarcha, 'Sprosi khozyaina'; also Bogoslovskaya et al., 'Dom pod ugrozoy'; Mihalisko, 'North American-style native reservations'; Nemtushkin, 'Bol moya, Evenkiya!'.

[106] Aipin, election manifesto; Borodin and Shinkarev, 'Dayte slovo yukagiru'; A. Nerkagi, quoted in *Izvestiya*, 15 June 1989; Ogryzko, 'Sever stavit problemy', pp. 82, 87–8. There is a useful survey of views in Mihalisko, 'North American-style native reservations'. Rytkheu, however, has consistently opposed the idea of reservations: 'Beloye bezmolviye?', p. 21.

collectivised agriculture to produce efficient husbandry or happy farmers led to an effort to counteract its evil effects by the incentive of contracts with the farm management, entered into by family or other small groups, who would regain personal ownership of livestock or of fishing and hunting enterprises.[107] Observation of the first rather cautious and half-hearted attempts at implementation of this reform among the cattle-herders of Tuva and the Ewen reindeer-herders of Yakutia did not suggest that decades of subordination to the dead hand of Russian communist bureaucracy would give way quickly to greater initiative and efficiency.[108] The obvious conclusion of such reforms, to which many Siberians, and others, aspire, would be the admission that ideologically inspired collectivisation had been a costly mistake, and the eventual decollectivisation of the whole rural population.[109]

Thus, despite the enormous changes in way of life which the twentieth century had brought to Siberia, in many ways the problems of fitting the Siberian native peoples into modern social patterns while allowing them to maintain their own cultures had come full circle and returned to the situation and ideas of the 1920s, when the transition from the Russian imperial system to that of the Soviet Union was just beginning. Now, as the dictatorship of the Russian Communist Party comes to an end and the Russian Empire which it grimly held on to breaks up (as so many of its subject nations desired after the Revolution of February 1917) the future of Siberia and its peoples also lies open. The economic chaos which prevails throughout the empire may begin to be overcome by the separate 'union' republics tackling their own problems, but within the gigantic 'Russian Republic' too, much more autonomy and federalism will be essential. On the one hand, this will have to offer real political autonomy to the other often forgotten republics below 'union' status, such as Tatarstan and Daghestan in European Russia – and to the communities of Siberia: the former ASSRs, 'autonomous regions' and others. On the other hand, 'Russian' Siberia itself may secede as a separate political entity or be divided into a number of regional units, such as the Far East. Whatever the future structure, the indigenous peoples of Siberia will have to be assured that their lands have ceased to be colonies exploited by Russian rulers, and now possess a form of statehood in which their sovereign rights are recognised.

[107] Nemtushkin, 'Bol moya, Evenkiya!'; Nerkagi, 'Pered broskom'; Pervushin, 'Vsem mirom', p. 7; Pika and Prokhorov, 'Bolshiye problemy', p. 83.
[108] C. Humphrey, 'Perestroyka and the pastoralists: the example of Mongun-Taiga in Tuva ASSR', *Anthropology Today*, 1989, vol. V, no. 3, pp. 6–10; P. Vitebsky, 'Reindeer herders of northern Yakutia: a report from the field', *Polar Record*, 1989, vol. XXV, pp. 213–18.
[109] Pervushin, 'Vsem mirom', pp. 4–5.

BIBLIOGRAPHY

Ackerknecht, E.H. *History and Geography of the Most Important Diseases*, New York, 1965.
Aganbegyan, A. and E. Ibragimova, *Sibir ne ponaslyshke*, 2nd edn, Moscow, 1984.
Aipin, Ye. (Election manifesto), *Moscow News*, 1989, no. 12, p. 6.
Inel lykhel sayny. V teni starogo kedra, Sverdlovsk, 1981.
'Not by oil alone', *Moscow News*, 1989, no. 2, pp. 8–9.
Alekseyenko, Ye.A. 'Categories of Ket shamans', in V. Diószegi and M. Hoppàl, eds., *Shamanism in Siberia*, 1978, pp. 255–64.
'Etnicheskiye protsessy na Turukhanskom Severe', in I.S. Gurvich and B.O. Dolgikh, eds., *Preobrazovaniya v khozyaystve i kulture* . . . pp. 62–84.
'Kety', in I.S. Gurvich, ed., *Etnicheskaya istoriya narodov Severa*, pp. 99–117.
'Nachalnyy etap sovetskogo stroitelstva na Turukhanskom Severe', in I.S. Gurvich, ed., *Osushchestvleniye leninskoy natsionalnoy politiki* . . ., pp. 276–96.
Alekseyenko, Ye.A. ed., *Ketskiy sbornik: antropologiya, etnografiya, mifologiya, lingvistika*, Leningrad, 1982.
Alekseyev, A. I. *Khozhdeniye ot Baykala do Amura*, Moscow, 1976.
Osvoyeniye russkimi lyudmi Dalnego Vostoka i Russkoy Ameriki do kontsa XIX veka, Moscow, 1982.
Andreyev, A. 'Iz opyta kollektivizatsii: korrespondentsiya iz Ayano-Mayskogo Evenskogo nats. rayona', *Sovetskiy Sever*, 1934, no. 4, pp. 96–8.
Andriyevich, V.K. *Sibir v XIX stoletii*, St Petersburg, 1889.
Anisimov, A.F. *Religiya Evenkov v istoriko-geneticheskom izuchenii i problemy pro-iskhozhdeniya pervobytnykh verovaniy*, Moscow, 1958.
Aniskov, V.T. 'Kolkhoznoye proizvodstvo Zapadnoy Sibiri v pervyy period Velikoy Otechestvennoy Voyny (1941–1942 gg.)', in V.S. Flerov et al., eds., *Krestyanstvo i selskoye khozyaystvo Sibiri*, pp. 87–116.
Antropova, V.V. 'Koryaki', 'Itelmeny', 'Aleuty', *Narody Sibiri*, pp. 950–90.
Antropova, V.V. and V.G. Kuznetsova, 'Chukchi', *Narody Sibiri*, pp. 896–933.
Aranchyn, Yu.L. *Istoricheskiy put tuvinskogo naroda k sotsializmu*, Novosibirsk, 1982.
Arkhipov, N.B. *SSSR po rayonam. Dalnevostochnaya oblast*, Moscow, 1926.

Armstrong, T. *The Northern Sea Route: Soviet Exploitation of the North East Passage*, Cambridge, 1952.

Russian Settlement in the North, Cambridge, 1965.

Armstrong, T. ed., *Yermak's Campaign in Siberia: a Selection of Documents*, trans. T. Minorsky and D. Wileman (Hakluyt Society, 2nd ser., vol. 146), London, 1975.

Arsenyev, V.K. *Po Ussuriyskomu Krayu. Dersu Uzala*, Leningrad, 1978.

Arutyunov, S.A. *U beregov Ledovitogo okeana*, Moscow, 1984.

et al., *'Kitovaya alleya': drevnosti ostrovov proliva Senyavina*, Moscow, 1982.

Atlas narodov mira, Moscow, 1964.

Atlas SSSR, 2nd edn, Moscow, 1969; [3rd edn], 1983.

Avdeyev, I.I. 'Dramaticheskiye predstavleniya na medvezhyem prazdnike u mansi', *Sovetskiy Sever*, 1935, no. 3–4, pp. 169–75.

Avrorin, V.A. 'Nanayskiy yazyk', in *Yazyki narodov SSSR*, vol. V, pp. 129–48.

and Ye.P. Lebedeva, 'Orochskiy yazyk', *Yazyki narodov SSSR*, vol. V, pp. 191–209.

Avvakum, *Zhitiye protopopa Avvakuma im samim napisannoye i drugie yego sochineniya*, ed. N.K. Gudziy, Moscow, 1960.

Aziatskaya Rossiya, ed., G.V. Glinka, 3 vols., St Petersburg, 1914.

Babichev, I. 'Uchastiye kitayskikh i koreyskikh trudyashchikhsya v borbe protiv interventov i belogvardeytsev na Sovetskom Dalnem Vostoke', in V.A. Shvarev, ed., *Dalniy Vostok za 40 let Sovetskoy vlasti*, pp. 148–71.

Babushkin G.F. and G.I. Donidze, 'Shorskiy yazyk', in *Yazyki narodov SSSR*, vol. II, pp. 467–81.

Baddeley, J.F. *Russia, Mongolia, China*, New York [1919].

Bai, Shouyi, ed., *An Outline History of China*, Peking, 1982.

Bakhrushin, S.V. *Ostyatskiye i vogulskiye knyazhestva v XVI–XVII vekakh*, Leningrad, 1935.

Nauchnye trudy, vol. III, *Izbrannye raboty po istorii Sibiri XVII–XVIII vv.*, part 1, *Voprosy russkoy kolonizatsii Sibiri v XVI–XVII vv.*; part 2, *Istoriya narodov Sibiri v XVI–XVII vv.*, Moscow, 1955.

Bancroft, H.H. *History of Alaska* (*Works*, vol. XXXIII), San Francisco, 1886.

Barthold, W. *Histoire des Turcs d'Asie Centrale*, Paris, 1945.

Basayeva K.D. and D.D. Nimayev, 'Sovremennyye etnicheskiye protsessy u buryat', in I.S. Gurvich, ed., *Etnokulturnyye protsessy ...*, pp. 11–29.

Baskakov, N.A. *Altayskaya semya yazykov i yeye izucheniye*, Moscow, 1981.

'Altayskiy yazyk', in *Yazyki narodov SSSR*, vol. II, pp. 506–22.

Batchelor, J. *The Ainu of Japan: The Religion, Superstitions, and General History of the Hairy Aborigines of Japan*, London, 1892.

Bawden, C.R. *The Modern History of Mongolia*, London, 1968.

Shamans, Lamas and Evangelicals: the English Missionaries in Siberia, London, 1985.

Baykov, A. *Soviet Foreign Trade*, Princeton, 1946.

Belenkin, I.F. 'Razvitiye pechati na yazykakh narodov Severa', in I. S. Gurvich, ed., *Osushchestvleniye leninskoy natsionalnoy politiki ...*, pp. 117–40.

Belov, M.I. 'Excavations of a Russian Arctic town', *Polar Geography and Geology*, 1977, vol. I, pp. 270–85.

Belov, M.I. et al., *Mangazeya. Mangazeyskiy morskoy khod*, pt. 1, Leningrad, 1980.

Belyayev, A.A. 'Uchastiye nanaytsev v borbe za vlast Sovetov', in V.A. Shvarev, ed., *Dalniy Vostok za 40 let Sovetskoy vlasti*, pp. 172–83.

Berman, H.J. and M. Kerner, *Soviet Military Law and Administration*, Cambridge (Mass.), 1955.

Bertagayev, T.A. 'Buryatskiy yazyk', in *Yazyki narodov SSSR*, vol. V, pp. 13–33.

Beskorsyy, P. 'Nekotorye itogi (materialy o sostoyanii kollektivizatsii na Kr. Severe)', *Sovetskiy Sever*, 1934, no. 2, pp. 57–61.

Bichurin N.Ya. (Iakinf), *Sobraniye svedeniy o narodakh, obitavshikh v Sredney Azii v drevniye vremena*, St Petersburg, 1851, revised and reprinted, Moscow, 1950.

Bogachev, V. 'Nastupleniye na Yamal priostanovleno', *Severnye prostory*, 1989, no. 3, pp. 10–11.

Bogdanov, M.N. *Ocherki istorii Buryat-mongolskogo naroda*, Verkhneudinsk, 1926.

Bogdanov, M.S. *Razgrom zapadnosibirskogo kulatsko-eserovskogo myatezha 1921g.*, Tyumen, 1961.

Bogoraz, V.G. *The Chukchee* (*Memoirs of the American Museum of Natural History*, vol. XI), Leiden, 1904–9.

Bogoslovskaya, L. et al., 'Dom pod ugrozoy', *Severnye prostory*, 1988, no. 5, pp. 4–5.

Bolshaya Sovetskaya Entsiklopediya, Moscow, 1926–47; 3rd edn, 1970–81.

Borodin O. and L. Shinkarev, 'Dayte slovo yukagiru', *Izvestiya*, 7 April 1989, p. 3.

Boyko, V.I. and N.V. Vasilyev, *Sotsialno-professionalnaya mobilnost evenkov i evenov Yakutii*, Novosibirsk, 1981.

Boyko V.I. et al., eds., *Problemy sovremennogo sotsialnogo razvitiya narodnostey Severa*, Novosibirsk, 1987.

Boytsova, A.F. 'Shkola narodov Kraynego Severa', in I.S. Gurvich, ed., *Osushchestvleniye leninskoy natsionalnoy politiki . . .*, pp. 141–58.

Boytsova A.F. et al., *[Evedy turen]. Evenkiyskiy yazyk: uchebnik dlya podgotovitelnogo klassa*, 2nd edn, Leningrad, 1981.

Bragina, D.G. 'O nekotorykh aspektakh sovremennykh etnicheskikh protsessov u yakutov v Tsentralnoy Yakutii', in I.S. Gurvich, ed., *Etnokulturnyye protsessy . . .*, pp. 29–40.

Britayev, G. 'Svedeniya dlya tov. Shapovalova', *Severnye prostory*, 1989, no. 2, p. 6.

British Museum, *Frozen Tombs: the Culture and Art of the Ancient Tribes of Siberia*, London, 1978.

Brodnev, M.M. 'Ot rodovogo stroya k sotsializmu (po materialam Yamalo-Nenetskogo natsionalnogo okruga)', *Sovetskaya etnografiya*, 1950, no. 1, pp. 92–106.

Brody, H. *Living Arctic: Hunters of the Canadian North*, London, 1987.

Bromley, Yu.V. et al., eds., *Sovremennye etnicheskiye protsessy v SSSR*, 2nd edn, Moscow, 1977.

Buturlinov, V.F. et al., *O Sovetsko-kitayskoy granitse: pravda i Pekinskiye vymysly*, Moscow, 1982.

Carlson, C. 'Kazak writers wistful about greater cultural autonomy in Yakutia', Radio Free Europe/Radio Liberty, *Research*, n.p., 16 September 1983, RL 347/83.

Carruthers, D. *Unknown Mongolia: a Record of Travel and Exploration in North-west Mongolia and Dzungaria*, 2 vols., London, 1913.

Chamberlin, W.H. *The Russian Revolution, 1917–1921*, 2 vols., London, 1935.

Chance, N.A. 'Alaska Eskimo modernization', in D. Damas, ed., *Handbook of North American Indians*, vol. V, *Arctic*, Washington, 1984.

Chanchibayeva, L. 'O sovremennykh religioznykh perezhitkakh u altaytsev', in A.P. Okladnikov, ed., *Etnografiya narodov Altaya i Zapadnoy Sibiri*, pp. 90–103.

Chekhov, A.P. *Iz Sibiri* and *Ostrov Sakhalin*, in *Polnoye sobraniye sochineniy i pisem*, Moscow, 1974–83, vol. XIV–XV.

Cheng, Tien-fong, *A History of Sino-Russian Relations*, Washington, 1957.

Chernetsov V.N. and W. Moszyńska, *Prehistory of Western Siberia*, ed. H.N. Michael, Montreal, 1974.

Chernov, Yu. 'Preduprezhdayut uchenye', *Severnye prostory*, 1989, no. 2, pp. 7–8.

Chichlo, B. 'La Collectivisation en Sibérie: un problème de nationalités' Centre d'études russes et sovietiques, *Colloque sur l'expérience soviétique et le problème national dans le monde (1920–1939)*, Paris, 1981, pp. 279–307.

'The cult of the bear and Soviet ideology in Siberia', *Religion in Communist Lands*, 1985, vol. XIII, no. 2, pp. 166–81.

'Histoire de la formation des territoires autonomes chez les peuples turco-mongols de Sibérie', *Cahiers du monde russe et soviétique*, vol. 38, 1987, pp. 361–402.

'Les Nevuqaghmiit, ou la fin d'une ethnie', *Études Inuit*, vol. V, no. 2, Quebec, 1981, pp. 29–47.

'La Tchoukotka: une autre civilisation obligatoire. Quelques observations sur le terrain', *Objets et Mondes*, vol. 25, Paris, 1988, pp. 149–58.

Chudoyakov, A. 'Tragediya Shorii', *Sibirskiye ogni*, 1989, no. 8, pp. 164–6.

Clarke, R.A. *Soviet Economic Facts 1917–1970*, London, 1972.

Collins, D.N. 'Russia's Conquest of Siberia: evolving Russian and Soviet Historical Interpretations', *European Studies Review*, 1982, vol. 12, no. 1, pp. 17–43.

'Colonialism and Siberian development: a case-study of the Orthodox Mission to the Altay, 1830–1913', in A. Wood and R.A. French, eds., *The Development of Siberia*, 1989, pp. 50–71.

Communist Party of the Soviet Union. Altai kraykom, *Altay v vosstanovitelnyy period. Sbornik dokumentov*, Barnaul, 1960.

Communist Party of the Soviet Union. Khabarovsk kraykom, *Iz istorii organizatsiy KPSS na Dalnem Vostoke*, Khabarovsk, 1962.

Comrie, B. *The Languages of the Soviet Union*, Cambridge, 1981.

Conolly, V. *Siberia Today and Tomorrow*, London, 1975.

Conquest, R. *The Great Terror: Stalin's Purge of the Thirties*, rev. edn, Harmondsworth, 1971.

Kolyma: the Arctic Death Camps, Oxford, 1979.

Current Digest of the Soviet Press, Columbus.

Czaplicka, M.A. *Aboriginal Siberia, a Study in Social Anthropology*, Oxford, 1914.

Dallin, D.J. *Soviet Russia and the Far East*, London, 1949.

The Rise of Russia in Asia, London, 1950.

Damdinsuren, Ts. *Istoricheskiye korni Geseriady*, Moscow, 1957.

Danilin, A.G. 'Burkhanizm na Altae i ego kontr-revolyutsionnaya rol', *Sovetskaya etnografiya*, 1932, no. 1, pp. 63–91.

Danilov, I. 'Chelovek zhivet prirodoy', *Polyarnaya zvezda*, 1989, no. 3, pp. 108–9.

Danilov, S.P. 'Perestroyka i literatura. Doklad ... na XI syezde Soyuza pisateley Yakutii', *Polyarnaya zvezda*, 1988, no. 6, pp. 95–105.

Davies, R.W. *The Industrialisation of Soviet Russia 1: the Socialist Offensive: The Collectivisation of Soviet Agriculture 1929–30*, London, 1980.

Dawson, R. *Imperial China*, London, 1972.

Deane, J.R. *The Strange Alliance: the Story of American Efforts at Wartime Co-operation with Russia*, London, 1947.

Demidov, V.A. *K sotsializmu, minuya kapitalizm: ocherk sotsialisticheskogo stroitelstva v Gorno-Altayskoy avtonomnoy oblasti*, Novosibirsk, 1970.

Deny, J. et al., eds., *Philologiae Turcicae Fundamenta*, vol. I, Wiesbaden, 1959.

Dikov, N.N. ed., *Ocherki istorii Chukotki s drevneyshikh vremen do nashikh dney*, Novosibirsk, 1974.

Diószegi, V. ed., *Popular Beliefs and Folklore Tradition in Siberia*, Bloomington, 1968.

Diószegi, V. and M. Hoppál, eds., *Shamanism in Siberia*, Budapest, 1978.

Dmitrieva, L.V. 'Yazyk barabinskikh tatar', in *Yazyki narodov SSSR*, vol. II, pp. 155–72.

Dmytryshyn, B. et al., *To Siberia and Russian America: Three Centuries of Russian Eastward Expansion: a Documentary Record*, 3 vols., Oregon, 1985–6.

Dobrova-Yadrintseva, L.N. 'Osvoyeniye severnykh okrain', *Sovetskiy Sever*, 1930, no. 5, pp. 17–26.

Dolgikh, B.O. *Rodovoy i plemennoy sostav narodov Sibiri v XIIIv.*, Moscow, 1960.

'Entsy', *Narody Sibiri*, pp. 661–4.

'Etnicheskiy sostav naseleniya Severa SSSR (voprosy chislennosti korennykh narodnostey i klassifikatsiya ikh yazykov v svete poslednikh statisticheskikh dannykh)', in I.S. Gurvich and B.O. Dolgikh, eds., *Preobrazovaniya v khozyaystve i kulture . . .*, pp. 11–27.

Doolin, D.J. *Territorial Claims in the Sino-Soviet Conflict: Documents and Analysis*, Stanford, 1965.

Dotsenko. P. *The Struggle for a Democracy in Siberia, 1917–1920*, Stanford, 1983.

Driver, H.E. *Indians of North America*, Chicago, 1961.

Dulzon, A.P. 'Chulymsko-tyurkskiy yazyk', in *Yazyki narodov SSSR*, vol. II, pp. 446–66.

Dyachkovskiy N.D. et. al., *Pogovorim po-yakutski: samouchitel yakutskogo yazyka*, Yakutsk, 1982.

Eccles, W.J. *The Canadian Frontier 1534–1760*, New York, 1969.

Encyclopaedia Judaica, 16 vols., Jerusalem, 1972.

Enloe, C.H. *Ethnic Soldiers*, Harmondsworth, 1980.

Entsiklopedicheskiy slovar, 43 vols., St Petersburg, 1890–1907.

Fisher, R.H. *The Russian Fur Trade 1550–1700*, Berkeley, 1943.

Bering's Voyages: Whither and Why, Seattle, 1977.

'Dezhnev's voyage of 1648 in the light of Soviet scholarship', in *Terrae incognitae*, vol. 5, pp. 7–26, Amsterdam, 1973.

Fitzhugh, W.W. and A. Crowell, eds., *Crossroads of Continents: Cultures of Siberia and Alaska*, Washington, 1988.

Flerov, V.S. *Stroitelstvo Sovetskoy vlasti i borba s inostrannoy ekspansiey na Kamchatke (1922–1926 gg.)*, Tomsk, 1964.

Flerov, V.S. et al., eds., *Krestyanstvo i selskoye khozyaystvo Sibiri v 1917–1961 gg.*, Novosibirsk, 1965.

Fletcher, G. *Of the Russe Commonwealth*, London, 1591, in L.E. Berry and R.O.

Crummey, eds., *Rude and Barbarous Kingdom: Russia in the Accounts of Sixteenth Century English Voyagers*, Madison, 1968.

Forbes, A.D.W. *Warlords and Muslims in Chinese Central Asia*, Cambridge, 1986.

Forsyth, J. 'Chinese place-names in the Russian Far East', in W. Ritchie et al., eds., *Essays for Professor R.E.H. Mellor*, Aberdeen, 1986, pp. 133–9.

Fraser, J.F. *The Real Siberia, together with an Account of a Dash through Manchuria*, London, 1902.

Fu, Lo-shu, *A Documentary Chronicle of Sino-Western Relations*, Tucson, 1966.

Gayer, Ye.A. 'Khotela by dobavit k skazannomu', *Pravda*, 26 June 1989, p. 2.

Gemuyev, I.N., A.M. Sagaleyev, A.I. Solovyov, *Legendy i byli tayozhnogo kraya*, Novosibirsk, 1989.

Gibson, J.R. *Feeding the Russian Fur Trade: Provisionment of the Okhotsk Seaboard and the Kamchatka Peninsula 1639–1856*, Madison, 1969.

Imperial Russia in Frontier America, New York, 1976.

Gieysztor, A. et al., *History of Poland*, Warsaw, 1968.

Golder, F.A. *Russian Expansion on the Pacific, 1641–1850*, Cleveland (Ohio), 1914.

Gorokhov, S. 'Maksimum samoupravleniya', *Severnye prostory*, 1989, no. 2, p. 3.

Goryushkin, L.M. ed., *Ssylka i katorga v Sibiri (XVIII – nachalo XX v.)*, Novosibirsk, 1975.

Green, T. *The New World of Gold*, rev. edn, London, 1985.

Grekov, B.D. ed., *Ocherki istorii SSSR. Period feodalizma*, 2 vols., Moscow, 1953.

Grevens, N. N. 'Kultovyye predmety khantov' in *Yezhegodnik Muzeya istorii religii i ateizma*, vol. IV, Moscow, 1960, pp. 427–38.

Gunn, G.P. *Po nizhney Pechore*, Moscow, 1979.

Gurevich, B.P. *Mezhdunarodnye otnosheniya v Tsentralnoy Azii v XVII – pervoy polovine XIX v.*, Moscow, 1979.

Gurvich, I.S., 'Etnicheskiye protsessy na Kraynem Severo-Vostoke Sibiri', in I.S. Gurvich and B.O. Dolgikh, eds., *Preobrazovaniya v khozyaystve i kulture . . . .*, pp. 195–225.

'Nekotoryye cherty sovremennogo etnicheskogo razvitiya chukchey i koryakov (izmeneniya v etnicheskoy i sotsialno-professionalnoy strukture)', in I.S. Gurvich, ed., *Etnokulturnyye protsessy . . .*, pp. 144–58.

'Severnyye yakuty i dolgany', 'Severo-vostochnyye paleoaziaty i eskimosy', 'Yukagiry', in I.S. Gurvich, ed., *Etnicheskaya istoriya narodov Severa*, pp. 168–222.

Gurvich, I.S ed., *Osushchestvleniye leninskoy natsionalnoy politiki u narodov Kraynego Severa*, Moscow, 1971.

ed., *Etnogenez narodov Severa*, Moscow, 1980.

ed., *Semeynaya obryadnost narodov Sibiri: opyt sravnitelnogo ucheniya*, Moscow, 1980.

ed., *Etnicheskaya istoriya narodov Severa*, Moscow, 1982.

ed., *Etnokulturnye protsessy u narodov Sibiri i Severa*, Moscow, 1985.

ed., *Narody Dalnego Vostoka SSSR v XVII–XX vv.: istoriko-etnograficheskiye ocherki*, Moscow, 1985.

Gurvich, I.S. and B.O. Dolgikh, eds., *Preobrazovaniya v khozyaystve i kulture i etnicheskiye protsessy u narodov Severa*, Moscow, 1970.

Gusarevich, O. 'Vakhta za porogom', *Severnye prostory*, 1988, no. 5, pp. 28–30.

Gusarevich S.D. and V.B. Seoyev, *Na strazhe Dalnevostochnykh rubezhey*, Moscow, 1982.

Gushchin, I.V. and A.I. Afanasyev, *Chukotskiy natsionalnyy okrug: kratkiy istoriko-geograficheskiy ocherk*, Magadan, 1956.

Gushchin, N.Ya. *Rabochiy klass Sibiri v borbe za sozdaniye kolkhoznogo stroya*, Novosibirsk, 1965.

Sibirskaya derevnya na puti k sotsializmu (sotsialno-ekonomicheskoye razvitiye sibirskoy derevni . . . 1926–1937 gg.), Novosibirsk, 1973.

'Kolkhoznoye stroitelstvo v Zapadnoy Sibiri v 1929–1932 gg.', in V.S. Flerov, et al., ed., *Krestyanstvo i selskoye khozyaystvo Sibiri*, 1965, pp. 73–86.

Hagan, W.T. *American Indians*, Chicago, 1961.

Hajdu, P. *Finno-Ugrian Languages and Peoples*, London, 1975.

Lidell Hart, B.H. *The Soviet Army*, London, 1956.

Herrmann, A. *An Historical Atlas of China*, new edn, Edinburgh, 1966.

Holmberg, U. (Harva), *The Mythology of all Races*, vol. IV, *Finno-Ugric, Siberian*, Boston, 1927.

Hosking, G. *A History of the Soviet Union*, London, 1985.

Hrushevsky, M. *A History of Ukraine*, Yale, 1941.

Hughes, C.C. 'Under four flags: recent culture change among the Eskimos', *Current Anthropology*, 1965, vol. 6, no. 1, pp. 3–69.

Humphrey, C. *Karl Marx Collective: Economy, Society and Religion in a Siberian Collective Farm*, Cambridge, 1983.

'Perestroyka and the pastoralists: the example of Mongun-Taiga in Tuva ASSR', *Anthropology Today*, 1989, vol. 5, no. 3, pp. 6–10.

'Population trends, ethnicity and religion among the Buryats', in A. Wood and R.A. French, *The Development of Siberia*, pp. 147–76.

'Theories of North Asian shamanism', in E. Gellner, ed., *Soviet and Western Anthropology*, London, 1980, pp. 243–54.

'The uses of genealogy: a historical study of the nomadic and sedentarised Buryat', *Proceedings of the International Meeting on Nomadic Pastoralism, Paris 1–3 Dec. 1976*, Cambridge and Paris, 1979, pp. 235–62.

I.A., 'Usilim borbu protiv shamanstva!', *Sovetskaya Arktika*, 1938, no. 10–11, pp. 107–11.

Innis, H.A. *The Fur Trade in Canada: an Introduction to Canadian Economic History*, New Haven, 1930.

Innokentiy, mitropolit (I.E. Venyaminov), *Zapiski ob ostrovakh Unalashkinskogo otdela*, 2 vols., St Petersburg, 1840.

Ioffe, G.Z. *Kolchakovskaya avantyura i yeye krakh*, Moscow, 1983.

Iokhelson, V. *The Koryak (The Jesup North Pacific Expedition*, ed. Frank Boas. *Memoir of the American Museum of Natural History*, vol. 6), New York, 1905–8.

Peoples of Asiatic Russia, New York, 1928.

'Kumiss festivals of the Yakut and the decoration of kumiss vessels', in *Boas Anniversary Volume: Anthropological Papers written in Honor of Franz Boas*, New York, 1906, pp. 257–71.

Istoriya Dagestana, ed. G. D. Daniyalov, 4 vols., Moscow, 1967–9.

Istoriya Mongolskoy Narodnoy Respubliki, eds. A.P. Okladnikov et al., 3rd edn, Moscow, 1983.

Istoriya Sibiri, ed. A.P. Okladnikov, 5 vols., Leningrad, 1968–9.

Istoriya Yakutskoy ASSR, 3 vols., Moscow, 1955–63.

Ivanov, S. V. 'Negidaltsy', 'Nanaytsy', 'Ulchi', 'Udegeytsy', 'Orochi', 'Oroki', 'Nivkhi', in *Narody Sibiri*, pp. 776–884.

Jian Bozan et al., *A Concise History of China*, Peking, 1981.

Joki, A.J. 'Notes on Selkup shamanism', in V. Diószegi and M. Hoppàl, eds., *Shamanism in Siberia*, pp. 373–86.

Jones, R.H. *The Road to Russia: United States Lend-lease to the Soviet Union*, Norman (Okla.), 1969.

Kabanova, I.K. 'Zdravookhraneniye v rayonakh Kraynego Severa', in I. S. Gurvich, ed., *Osushchestvleniye leninskoy natsionalnoy politiki . . .*, pp. 159–71.

Kabuzan, V.M. *Dalnevostochnyy kray v XVII – nachale XXvv: istoriko-demograficheskiy ocherk*, Moscow, 1985.

Kalesnik, S.V. ed., *Sovetskiy Soyuz: geograficheskoye opisaniye v 22-kh tomakh. Rossiyskaya federatsiya*, Moscow.

Ural, 1969

Vostochnaya Sibir, 1969

Dalniy Vostok, 1971

Zapadnaya Sibir, 1971.

Kantor Ye. 'Problema osedaniya malykh narodov Severa', *Sovetskiy Sever*, 1934, no. 3–4, pp. 3–10.

Karmannyy slovar ateista, Moscow, 1985.

Karpov, V.G. 'Khakasskiy yazyk', in *Yazyki narodov SSSR*, vol. II, pp. 428–46.

Kenin-Lopsan, M. *Obryadovaya praktika i folklor tuvinskogo shamanstva: konets XIX – nachalo XX v.*, Novosibirsk, 1987.

Kennan, G. *Siberia and the Exile System*, 2 vols., New York, 1891.

Khabarova, M.V. *Narodnoye iskusstvo Yakutii*, Leningrad, 1981.

Khaptayev, P.T. ed., *Sovremennyy byt i etnokulturnye protsessy v Buryatii*, Novosibirsk, 1984.

Khaptayev, P.T. et al., eds., *Istoriya Buryatskoy ASSR*, vol. II, Ulan-Üde, 1959.

Khazanovich, A. *Druzya moi Nganasany: iz Taymyrskikh dnevnikov*, Moscow, 1986.

Khlebnikov, K.T. *Russkaya Amerika v neopublikovannykh zapiskakh*, 2 vols., Moscow–Leningrad, 1979–85.

Khomich, L.V. *Nentsy: istoriko-etnograficheskiye ocherki*, Moscow, 1966.

'Sotsialisticheskoye stroitelstvo v Nenetskom natsionalnom okruge', in I.S. Gurvich, ed., *Osushchestvleniye leninskoy natsionalnoy politiki . . .*, pp. 229–44.

'Sovremennyye etnicheskiye protsessy na Severe yevropeyskoy chasti SSSR i Zapadnoy Sibiri', in I.S. Gurvich and B.O. Dolgikh, eds., *Preobrazovaniya v khozyaystve i kulture . . .*, pp. 28–61.

Khomonov, M. 'Istoriko-kulturnoye znacheniye literaturnogo pamyatnika "Sokrovennoye skazaniye" (Mongol-un nugutsa tobchiyan)', *Baykal*, 1989, no. 6, pp. 97–100.

Khramova, V.V. 'Zapadnosibirskiye tatary', *Narody Sibiri*, pp. 473–91.

Khramtsov, A. 'Khodit Sever v pasynkakh', *Pravda*, 1988, 15 November, p. 6.

Kirchner, W. ed., *A Siberian Journey: the Journal of Hans Jacob Fries, 1774–1776*, London, 1974.

Klyuchevskiy, V.O. *Sochineniya*, 8 vols., 1956–9.

Kocheshkov, N.V. *Etnicheskiye traditsii v dekorativnom iskusstve narodov Kraynego Severo-Vostoka SSSR (XVIII–XX vv.)*, Leningrad, 1989.

Kocheshkov, N.V. ed., *Istoriya i kultura itelmenov: istoriko-etnograficheskiye ocherki*, Leningrad, 1990.

Kolarz, W. *Russia and her Colonies*, 3rd edn, London, 1953.

The Peoples of the Soviet Far East, London, 1954.

Religion in the Soviet Union, London, 1961.

Kolesnikova, V.D. and O.A. Konstantinova, 'Negidalskiy yazyk', in *Yazyki narodov SSSR*, vol. V, pp. 109–28.

Kolonialnaya politika Moskovskogo gosudarstva v Yakutii XVII v., compiled by V.G. Geyman and I.M. Trotskiy, Leningrad, 1936.

Kolonialnaya politika tsarizma na Kamchatke i Chukotke v XVIII v., compiled by S.B. Okun, Leningrad, 1935.

Komarov, B. *The Destruction of Nature in the Soviet Union*, London, n.d.

Konstantinov, M. ed., 'K istorii "Soyuza Yakutov" ', *Krasnyy arkhiv*, Moscow, 1936, vol. 76, pp. 67–82.

Konstantinova, O.A. 'Evenkiyskiy yazyk', in *Yazyki narodov SSSR*, vol. V, pp. 68–87.

Kozlov, V.B. 'O sochetanii traditsionnykh i novykh form zhiznedeyatelnosti narodnostey Severa v usloviyakh internatsionalizatsii obraza zhizni', in V.V. Prokhorov, ed., *Regionalnye problemy sotsialno-demograficheskogo razvitiya*, pp. 33–43.

Kozlov, V.I. *Natsionalnosti SSSR: etnodemograficheskiy obzor*, Moscow, 1975; 2nd edn, rev., 1982.

Krasheninnikov, S.P. *Opisaniye zemli Kamchatki*, Moscow–Leningrad, 1949.

Exploration of Kamchatka, tr. with intro. and notes by E.A.P. Crownhart-Vaughan, Portland (Oregon), 1972.

Kravchenko, D. and V. Chertkov, 'Ne splecha, a s golovoy', *Pravda*, 2 December 1988, p. 3.

Kreynovich, Ye.A. 'Yukagirskiy yazyk', 'Ketskiy yazyk', in *Yazyki narodov SSSR*, vol. V, pp. 435–73.

Krivonogov, V.P. 'Izmeneniya v etnicheskom sostave khakasov v sovremennyy period', in I.S. Gurvich, ed., *Etnokulturnyye protsessy . . .*, pp. 54–65.

Krivoshapkin, A. 'Boli i trevogi Severa – v serdtse moyem', *Polyarnaya zvezda*, 1989, no. 2, pp. 64–71.

Krupnik, I.I. *Arkticheskaya etnoekologiya: modeli traditsionnogo prirodopolzovaniya morskikh okhotnikov i olenevodov Severnoy Yevrazii*, Moscow, 1989.

'Demograficheskoye razvitiye aziatskikh eskimosov v 1970-e gody', in B.B. Prokhorov, ed., *Regionalnye problemy sotsialno-demograficheskogo razvitiya*, pp. 85–110.

Krushanov, A.I. ed., *Istoriya i kultura Chukchey*, Leningrad, 1987.

Kunitsyn, G.I. 'Oblucheniye proshlym: istoki i preodoleniye', *Polyarnaya zvezda*, 1989, no. 2, pp. 72–7.

Kurilov, G.N. (Uluro Ado), 'Pod severnymi zvezdami', *Polyarnaya zvezda*, 1988, no. 6, pp. 105–11.

Kuzakov, K.G. 'Podyem ekonomiki i kultury korennogo naseleniya Koryakskogo natsionalnogo okruga', in I.S. Gurvich, ed., *Osushchestvleniye leninskoy natsionalnoy politiki ...*, pp. 297–313.

Lamb, A. *Asian Frontiers: Studies in a Continuing Problem*, London, 1968.

Lantzeff, G.V. *Siberia in the Seventeenth Century: a Study of the Colonial Administration*, Berkeley, 1943.

Lantzeff, G.V. and R.A. Pierce, *Eastward to Empire: Exploration and Conquest on the Russian open Frontier to 1750*, Montreal, 1973.

Lebedev, Ye. 'Reka Sob. Leto 1988', *Severnye prostory*, 1989, no. 2, pp. 22–3.

Lebedev, V.V. and Z.P. Sokolova, 'Selkupy', in I.S. Gurvich, ed., *Etnicheskaya istoriya narodov Severa*, pp. 118–29.

Lee, R.H.G. *The Manchurian Frontier in Ch'ing History*, Cambridge (Mass.) 1970.

Lensen, G.A. *The Russian Push toward Japan: Russo-Japanese Relations, 1697–1875*, Princeton, 1959.

Leontyev, V.V. 'The indigenous peoples of Chukchi national okrug: population and settlement', *Polar Geography*, Washington, 1977, vol. I, pp. 9–22.

Levin, M.G. 'Antropologicheskiye tipy Sibiri', *Narody Sibiri*, pp. 108–14.

'Eveny', in *Narody Sibiri*, pp. 760–75.

and L.P. Potapov, eds., *Istoriko-etnograficheskiy atlas Sibiri*, Moscow, 1961.

Levytsky, B. *The Stalinist Terror in the Thirties: Documentation from the Soviet Press*, Stanford, 1974.

Lobanov-Rostovsky, A. *Russia and Asia*, Ann Arbor, 1951.

Lupandin, V. and Ye. Gayer, 'Chernobyl na Chukotke: narody Severa rasplachivayutsya za yadernye ispytaniya', *Moskovskiye novosti*, 1989, no. 34, p. 5.

Lvov, A.K. 'Ekspeditsiya Pushnogostorga i Sibtorga v Yeloguyskiy rayon Turukhanskogo kraya', *Sovetskiy Sever*, 1930, no. 2, pp. 102–10.

Lvovskaya letopis (Polnoye sobraniye russkikh letopisey, t.20), St Petersburg, 1910.

Maadai-Kara. Ochy-Bala: altayskiye geroicheskiye skazaniya, narrated A. Kalkin, Moscow, 1983.

McLemore, S.D. *Racial and Ethnic Relations in America*, Boston, 1980.

Majewicz, A.F. 'The Oroks: past and present', in A. Wood and R.A. French, *The Development of Siberia*, pp. 124–46.

Malyavkin, A.G. *Istoricheskaya geografiya Tsentralnoy Azii: materialy i issledovaniya*, Novosibirsk, 1981.

Mancall, M. *Russia and China: their Diplomatic Relations to 1728*, Cambridge (Mass.), 1971.

Mantatov, V.V. ed., *Lamaizm v Buryatii, XVIII – nachala XX veka*, Novosibirsk, 1983.

Marston, M.R. *Men of the Tundra: Alaska Eskimos at War*, New York, 1969.

Martov, L. *Obshchestvennoye dvizheniye v Rossii v nachale XX-go veka*, St Petersburg, 1909–14, vol. IV, pt. 2.

Marx, K. and F. Engels, *Collected Works*, London [Moscow], 1980.

Meijer, J.M. ed., *The Trotsky Papers 1917–1922*, 2 vols., The Hague, 1971.

Menitskaya, N. 'Krichashchaya parallel', *Severnye prostory*, 1988, no. 6, p. 20.

Menovshchikov, G.A. 'Eskimossko-aleutskaya gruppa', 'Eskimosskiy yazyk', 'Aleutskiy yazyk', in *Yazyki narodov SSSR*, vol. V, pp. 352–406.

'Eskimosy', *Narody Sibiri*, pp. 934–49.

Michael, H.N. ed., *Studies in Siberian Shamanism*, Toronto, 1963.

Mihalisko, K. 'North American-style native reservations in the Soviet North?', *Report on the USSR*, 1989, vol. I, no. 29, pp. 31–4.

'SOS for native peoples of Soviet North', *Report on the USSR*, 1989, vol. I, no. 5, pp. 3–6.

Mikhalev, A. 'Uspekhi i tormozy kolkhoznogo stroitelstva (pismo iz Penzhinskogo rayona, Kamchatskogo okruga)', *Sovetskiy Sever*, 1931, no. 3–4, pp. 168–70.

Mikhaylov, T.M. *Etnokulturnye protsessy v yugo-vostochnoy Sibiri v Sredniye veka*, Novosibirsk, 1989.

Minenko, N.A. *Severo-zapadnaya Sibir v XVIII – pervoy polovine XIX v: istoriko-etnograficheskiy ocherk*, Novosibirsk, 1975.

Mohrenschildt, D. von *Toward a United States of Russia: Plans and Projects of Federal Reconstruction of Russia in the Nineteenth Century*, London, 1981.

Moszyńska, W. 'An ancient sacrificial site in the Lower Ob region', in V. Diószegi and M. Hoppál, *Shamanism in Siberia*, pp. 469–79.

Mowat, F. *The Siberians*, London, 1970.

Mueller, G.F. *Istoriya Sibiri*, 2 vols., Moscow, 1937–41.

Nansen, F. *Through Siberia: the Land of the Future*, London, 1914.

Narody Sibiri, eds. M.G. Levin and L.P. Potapov, Moscow–Leningrad, 1956.

Narody Sredney Azii i Kazakhstana, eds. S.P. Tolstov et al., vol. II, Moscow, 1963.

Narody yevropeyskoy chasti SSSR, eds. V.N. Belitser et al., vol. II, Moscow, 1964.

Nekrich, A.M. *The Punished Peoples*, New York, 1978.

Nemtushkin, A. 'Bol moya, Evenkiya!', in *Sovetskaya kultura*, 1988, 28 July, p. 3.

Nenyang, L. 'Pyatna v geografii', *Pravda*, 19 May 1988, p. 6.

'Komandirovka na rodinu', *Druzhba narodov*, 1989, no. 8, p. 3.

Nerkagi, A. *Severnye povesti*, Moscow, 1983.

'Pered broskom', *Severnye prostory*, 1989, no. 1, pp. 6–7.

Nilus, S. *Velikoye v malom i Antikhrist, kak blizkaya politicheskaya vozmozhnost: zapiski pravoslavnago*, 2nd edn, Tsarskoye Selo, 1905.

Nordenskiöld, A.E. *The Voyage of the Vega round Asia and Europe*, 2 vols., London, 1881.

Norman, S. 'Rytkheu – a Chukchi voice in London', *Soviet Weekly*, 26 Jan. 1985, p. 12.

Nove, A. *An Economic History of the USSR*, London, 1969.

Novgorodskaya pervaya letopis, Moscow, 1950.

Novikova, K.A. *Ocherki dialektov evenskogo yazyka. Olskiy govor: glagol, sluzhebnye slova, teksty, glossariy*, Leningrad, 1980.

'Evenskiy yazyk', *Yazyki narodov SSSR*, vol. V, pp. 88–108.

Nusupbekov, A.N. et al., eds., *Istoriya Kazakhskoy SSR v pyati tomakh*, Alma-Ata, 1979.

'O Novoy Zemle, mirnom i nemirnom atome', *Severnye prostory*, 1990, no. 2, pp. 1–4.

Oborotova, Ye.A. 'Narody Severa v sovremennom mire: vzglyady i pozitsii', *Sovetskaya etnografiya*, 1988, no. 5, pp. 146–51.

Ogorodnikov, V.I. *Ocherk istorii Sibiri do nachala XIX stoletiya*, vol. I, Irkutsk, 1920.

Ogryzko, V. 'Sever stavit problemy', *Polyarnaya zvezda*, 1988, no. 6, pp. 80–8.

Okladnikov, A.P. *Yakutia before its Incorporation into the Russian State*, ed. H.N. Michael (Arctic Institute of North America. *Anthropology of the North: Translations from Russian Sources*, no. 8), Montreal, 1970.

Otkrytiye Sibiri, Moscow, 1979.

Okladnikov, A.P. ed., *Itogi i zadachi izucheniya istorii Sibiri dosovetskogo perioda*, Novosibirsk, 1971.

ed., *Voprosy istorii Sibiri dosovetskogo perioda*, Novosibirsk, 1973.

ed., *Etnografiya narodov Altaya i Zapadnoy Sibiri*, Novosibirsk, 1978.

ed., *Ancient Art of the Amur Region: Rock Drawings, Sculpture, Pottery*, Leningrad, 1981.

ed., 'Drevneye naseleniye Sibiri i ego kultura', *Narody Sibiri*, pp. 21–107.

Okun, S.V. 'K istorii Buryatii v XVII v.', *Krasnyy arkhiv*, Moscow, 1936, vol. LXXVI, no. 3, pp. 156–91.

Onishchuk, N.T. *Sovetskoye stroitelstvo u malykh narodov Severa 1917–1941 gg. (po materialam Narymskogo kraya)*, Tomsk, 1973.

Opisaniye Irkutskogo namestnichestva 1792 goda, eds. D.N. Vilkov, A.D. Kolesnikov, M.P. Malysheva, Novosibirsk, 1988.

Opisaniye Tobolskogo namestnichestva [1784–90], compiled by A.D. Kolesnikov, Novosibirsk, 1982.

Orleans, L.A. *Every Fifth Child: the Population of China*, London, 1972.

Orlovskiy, P.N. 'Kollektivizatsiya na Severe', *Sovetskiy Sever*, 1930, no. 1, pp. 48–57.

Oshorov, D. 'Dvuyazychye v buryatskoy shkole', *Baykal*, 1989, no. 6, pp. 66–70.

Panfilov, V.Z. 'Nivkhskiy yazyk', in *Yazyki narodov SSSR*, vol. V, pp. 408–34.

Pankratova, A.M. ed., *Istoriya SSSR: uchebnik*, 3 vols., Moscow, 1957.

Pares, B. *A History of Russia*, rev. edn, London, 1947.

Parfenov, P.S. (Petr Altayskiy), *Grazhdanskaya voyna v Sibiri 1918–1920*, izd. 2-e, ispr. i dop., Moscow [1924].

Patkanov, S. *Opyt geografii i statistiki tungusskikh plemen Sibiri na osnovanii dannykh perepisi naseleniya 1897 g. i drugikh istochnikov (Zapiski imperatorskogo geograficheskogo obshchestva po otdeleniyu etnografii*, t. XXXI), St Petersburg, 1906.

Pechetegina, T.A. 'Ne otkladyvaya na zavtra', *Severnye prostory*, 1988, no. 5, pp. 2–3.

Pervushin, V. 'Vsem mirom', *Severnye prostory*, 1988, no. 6, p. 5.

Petrova, T.I. 'Orokskiy yazyk', in *Yazyki narodov SSSR*, vol. V, pp. 172–90.

Phillips, E.D. *The Royal Hordes: Nomad Peoples of the Steppes*, London, 1965.

Phillips, G.D.R. *Dawn in Siberia*, London, 1942.

Pika, A.I. 'Demograficheskaya politika v rayonakh prozhivaniya narodov Severa: problemy i perspektivy', in B.B. Prokhorov, ed., *Regionalnye problemy sotsialno-demograficheskogo razvitiya*, pp. 43–55.

Pika, A.I. and B.B. Prokhorov, 'Bolshiye problemy malykh narodov', *Kommunist*, 1988, no. 16, pp. 76–83.

Pilsudski, B. 'Der Schamanismus bei den Ainu-Stämmen von Sachalin', *Globus*, 1909, vol. 95, pp. 72–8.

'Das Bärenfest der Ajnen auf Sachalin', *Globus*, 1909, vol. 96, pp. 37–41, 53–60.

'Die Urbewohner von Sachalin', *Globus*, 1909, vol. 96, pp. 325–30.

Pisateli Rossii, 'K rabochim geologicheskikh partiy; k stroitelyam nefte- i gazoprovodov ... osvaivayushchim promyshlennye rayony Severa, Sibiri i Dalnego Vostoka', *Severnye prostory*, 1989, no. 2, pp. 4–5.

Pletneva, S.A. ed., *Stepi Yevrazii v epokhu srednevekovya (Arkheologiya SSSR)*, Moscow, 1981.

'Po chernomu sledu "pokoritelya" ', *Severnye prostory*, 1988, no. 5, pp. 16–19.

Podosenina, M. 'Pod koren', *Severnye prostory*, 1989, no. 2, p. 3.

Ponomarev, B.N. ed., *Istoriya SSSR s drevneyshikh vremen do nashikh dney*, Moscow, 1966–.

Popov, A.A. *Nganasany: sotsialnoye ustroystvo i verovaniya*, Leningrad, 1984.

'Nganasany', 'Kety', 'Dolgany', *Narody Sibiri*, pp. 648–60, 687–700, 742–59.

Popova, U.G. *Eveny Magadanskoy oblasti: ocherki istorii, khozyaystva i kultury evenov Okhotskogo poberezhya, 1917–1977gg.* Moscow, 1981.

Potapov, L.P. *Ocherki po istorii Shorii*, Moscow, 1936.
Ocherki po istorii altaytsev, 2nd edn, Moscow, 1953.
'Altaytsy', 'Khakasy', 'Tuvintsy', 'Shortsy', in *Narody Sibiri*, pp. 329–472, 492–529.
'Drevnetyurkskiye cherty pochitaniya neba u sayano-altayskikh narodov', in A.P. Okladnikov, ed., *Etnografiya narodov Altaya i Zapadnoy Sibiri*, pp. 50–64.
'Istoriko-etnograficheskiy ocherk russkogo naseleniya Sibiri v dorevolyutsionny period', *Narody Sibiri*, pp. 115–214.
Prokhorov, B.B. 'Kak sberech Yamal', in *Znaniye – sila*, 1988, no. 7, pp. 1–8.
ed., *Regionalnye problemy sotsialno-demograficheskogo razvitiya*, Moscow, 1987.
Prokofyeva, Ye.D. 'Khanty i mansi', 'Nentsy', 'Selkupy', *Narody Sibiri*, pp. 570–647, 665–86.
'Selkupskiy yazyk', *Yazyki narodov SSSR*, vol. III, pp. 396–415.
Pryanishnikov, V. 'Khod na zhivoy zemle', *Severnye prostory*, 1989, no. 3, pp. 10–13.
Qiu Pu, *The Oroqens – China's Nomadic Hunters*, Peking, 1983.
Quested, R.K.I. *Sino-Russian Relations: a Short History*, Sydney, 1984.
'Racial tensions in Yakutiya', *Soviet Analyst*, 1980, no. 25, pp. 6–8.
Radkey, O.H. *The Unknown Civil War in Soviet Russia: a Study of the Green Movement in the Tambov Region 1920–1921*, Stanford, 1976.
Radlov, V.V. *Aus Sibirien: lose Blätter aus dem Tagebuche eines reisenden Linguisten*, 2 vols., Leipzig, 1884.
Raeff, M. *Siberia and the Reforms of 1822*, Seattle, 1956.
Rakowska-Harmstone, T. 'The Soviet Army as the instrument of national integration' in J. Erickson and E.J. Feuchtwanger, eds., *Soviet Military Power and Performance*, London, 1979, pp. 129–54.
Rasputin, V. 'Posluzhit otechestvu Sibiryu', *Izvestiya*, 1985, 3 November, p. 3.
Rauch, G. von *A History of Soviet Russia*, 5th edn, London, 1967.
Reclus, E. *The Earth and Its Inhabitants*, London, 1876–94 [Asia], vol. I, *Asiatic Russia*.
Remezov, S.U. *The Atlas of Siberia*, facsimile edited with an introduction by Leo Bagrow (*Imago Mundi: A Review of Early Cartography. Supplement I*), The Hague, 1958.
Riasanovsky, N.V. *A History of Russia*, New York, 1963.
Rombandeyeva, Ye.I. 'Mansiyskiy yazyk', in *Yazyki Narodov SSSR*, vol. III, pp. 343–60.
Rosugbu, B.M. *Malye narodnosti Priamurya v 1959–1965 gg.*, Khabarovsk, 1976.
Rugin, R. 'Dom. Eto khorosho!', *Severnye prostory*, 1988, no. 6, p. 3.
Rupen, R.A. 'The absorption of Tuva', *Studies on the Soviet Union* (ns), Munich, 1971, vol. XI, no. 4, pp. 145–62.
Ryabushkin T.V. et al., eds., *Naseleniye soyuznykh respublik*, Moscow, 1977.
Rytkheu, Yu. *Vremya tayaniya snegov: roman*, Moscow, 1958–67.
Sovremennye legendy, Leningrad, 1980.
Magicheskiye chisla, Leningrad, 1986.
'Pod senyu volshebnoy gory' in *Izbrannoye v dvukh tomakh*, Leningrad, 1981, pp. 384–535.
'The shaping of identity', *Soviet Weekly*, 1988, 3 September, pp. 14–15.
'Svet zvezd – bolshikh i malykh', *Pravda*, 1988, 31 December, p. 3.
'Beloye bezmolviye?', *Ogonyok*, 1989, no. 17, pp. 20–1.

Safronov, F.G. *Russkiye na severo-vostoke Azii v XVII – seredine XIXv.*, Moscow, 1978.

Samsonov, A.N. ed., *Kratkaya istoriya SSSR*, Moscow, 1964, vol. II.

Sangi V. 'Otchuzhdeniye', *Sovetskaya Rossiya*, 1988, 11 September no. 211, p. 2.

Sangi, V.M. comp., *Vtoroye rozhdeniye: proizvedeniya zachinateley literatur narodnostey Severa i Dalnego Vostoka*, Moscow, 1983.

Sansom, G. *A History of Japan 1615–1867*, London, 1964.

Sat, Sh. Ch. 'Tuvinskiy yazyk', in *Yazyki narodov SSSR*, vol. II, pp. 387–402.

Savoskul, S.S. 'Etnichkeskiye izmeneniya v Evenkiyskom natsionalnom okruge', in L.S. Gurvich and B.O. Dolgikh, eds., *Preobrazovaniya v khozyaystve i kulture . . . .* pp. 179–94.

'Net! Turukhanskoy GES', *Severnye prostory*, 1988, no. 6, pp. 6–7.

Savoskul, S.S. and V.V. Karlov, 'Turukhanskaya GES i sudba Evenkii', *Sovetskaya etnografiya*, 1988, no. 5, pp. 166–8.

Schapiro, L. *The Communist Party of the Soviet Union*, London, 1960.

Scrivener, D. *Gorbachev's Murmansk Speech: the Soviet Initiative and Western Responses*, Oslo, 1989.

Selitrennik, E.Ye. 'Nekotorye voprosy kolkhoznogo stroitelstva v Chukotskom natsionalnom okruge'. *Sovetskaya etnografiya*, 1965, no. 1, pp. 13–27.

Sem, Yu.A. 'Sotsialisticheskoye stroitelstvo sredi nanaytsev', in V.A. Shvarev, ed., *Dalniy Vostok za 40 let Sovetskoy vlasti*, pp. 533–46.

Sergeyev, M.A. *Koryakskiy natsionalnyy okrug*, Leningrad, 1934.

Nekapitalisticheskiy put razvitiya malykh narodov Severa, Moscow 1955.

'Tofalary', *Narody Sibiri*, pp. 530–9.

Serkin, I.O. 'Kolkhoznoye stroitelstvo v Taymyrskom natsionalnom okruge', in *Sovetskaya Arktika*, 1936, no. 6, pp. 3–11.

Sgibnev, A.S. *Istoricheskiy ocherk glavneyshikh sobytiy v Kamchatke s 1650 po 1856*, St Petersburg, 1869.

Sharakshinova, N.O. comp., *Geroicheskiy epos o Gesere: uchebnoye posobiye dlya studentov filologicheskogo fakulteta*, Irkutsk, 1969.

Sharov, V. 'Mala li zemlya dlya malykh narodov?', in *Literaturnaya gazeta*, 1988, no. 33, p. 10.

Shashkov, S.S. *Istoricheskiye etyudy*, vol. II, St Petersburg, 1872.

Sheehy, A. 'Racial disturbances in Yakutsk', *Radio Liberty Research*, 1986, no. 251.

'Russians the target of interethnic violence in Tuva', *Report on the USSR*, 1990, vol. 2, no. 37, pp. 13–17.

Sherstova, L. 'Katunskaya GES glazami etnografa', *Sibirskiye ogni*, 1990, no. 7, pp. 148–52.

Shimkin, B.D. 'A sketch of the Ket, or Yenisei "Ostyak" ', *Ethos*, Stockholm, 1939, vol. 4, pp. 147–76.

Shipunov, F.Ya. 'Tsena kilovatta', *Severnye prostory*, 1989, no. 3, pp. 4–6.

Shirokogorov, S.M. *Social Organization of the Northern Tungus*, Shanghai, 1929.

Shternberg, L.Ya. *Gilyaki, orochi, goldy, negidaltsy, ayny. Statyi i materialy*, ed. Ya.P. Alkor, Khabarovsk, 1933.

Shunkov, V.I. *Voprosy agrarnoy istorii Rossii*, Moscow, 1974.

Shvarev, V.A., ed., *Dalniy Vostok za 40 let Sovetskoy vlasti*, Komsomolsk, 1958.

Sibirskaya Sovetskaya Entsiklopediya, vols. I–III, 1929–35.

Sibirskiya letopisi, St Petersburg, 1907.

Sieroszewski, W.L. (V.L. Seroshevskiy), *Yakuty: opyt etnograficheskogo izsledovaniya*, St Petersburg, 1896.

Simchenko, Yu.B. 'Nganasany', in I.S. Gurvich, ed., *Etnicheskaya istoriya narodov Severa*, pp. 81–99.

'Osnovnyye cherty sovremennykh etnicheskikh protsessov u korennogo naseleniya Avamskoy tundry Taymyrskogo natsionalnogo okruga', in I.S. Gurvich and B.O. Dolgikh, eds., *Preobrazovaniya v khozyaystve i kulture* . . ., pp. 164–78.

Simchenko, Yu.B. and V.V. Lebedev, 'Smeshannyye braki u yuzhnykh i vostochnykh chukchey', in I.S. Gurvich, ed., *Etnokulturnyye protsessy* . . ., pp. 158–75.

Skachkov, I. 'Ob antireligioznoy rabote na Severe', *Revolyutsiya i natsionalnosti*, 1934, no. 7 (53), pp. 50–4.

Skalon, V. 'V tundre verkhnego Taza', *Sovetskiy Sever*, 1930, no. 3, pp. 129–39.

Skorik, P.Ya. 'Paleoaziatskiye yazyki', 'Chukotsko-kamchatskiye yazyki', 'Chukotskiy yazyk', 'Kerekskiy yazyk', *Yazyki narodov SSSR*, vol. V, pp. 233–70, 310–33.

Skrynnikov, R.G. *Sibirskaya ekspeditsiya Yermaka*, 2nd edn, Novosibirsk, 1986.

Slovtsov, P.A. *Istoricheskoye obozreniye Sibiri*, St Petersburg, 1886.

Smith, C.J. 'The Russian Third State Duma: an analytical profile', *The Russian Review*, 1958, vol. 17, pp. 201–10.

Smolyak, A.V. 'Izmeneniya semeynogo stroya u narodov Nizhnego Amura s kontsa XIX v. do kontsa 1970-kh godov', in I.S. Gurvich, ed., *Etnokulturnyye protsessy*, pp. 175–94.

'Narody Nizhnego Amura i Sakhalina', in I.S. Gurvich, ed., *Etnicheskaya istoriya narodov Severa*, pp. 223–57.

'Osnovnyye puti razvitiya ekonomiki, kultury i byta za gody Sovetskoy vlasti u narodov basseyna nizhnego Amura i Sakhalina', in I.S. Gurvich, ed., *Osushchestvleniye leninskoy natsionalnoy politiki* . . ., pp. 314–41.

'Sovremennyye etnicheskiye protsessy u narodov basseyna Nizhnego Amura', in I.S. Gurvich and B. O. Dolgikh, eds., *Preobrazovaniya v khozyaystve i kulture* . . ., pp. 256–79.

Snow, R.E. 'The Russian Revolution of 1917–18 in Transbaikalia', *Soviet Studies*, 1971–72, vol. 23, pp. 201–15.

Sokolova, Z.P. *Na prostorakh Sibiri*, Moscow, 1981.

Puteshestviye v Yugru, Moscow, 1982.

'Obskiye ugry (khanty i mansi)', in I.S. Gurvich, ed., *Etnicheskaya istoriya narodov Severa*, pp. 8–47.

'Postanovleniya partii i pravitelstva o razvitii khozyaystva i kultury narodov Kraynego Severa (yuridicheskiye akty 1935–1968 gg.)', in I.S. Gurvich, ed., *Osushchestvleniye leninskoy natsionalnoy politiki* . . ., pp. 66–116.

'The representation of a female spirit from the Kazym river', in V. Diószegi and M. Hoppál, *Shamanism in Siberia*, pp. 491–501.

'Sovremennoye kulturnoye razvitiye i etnicheskiye protsessy u obskikh ugrov', in I.S. Gurvich, ed., *Etnokulturnyye protsessy* . . ., pp. 93–120.

'Sovremennyye etnicheskiye protsessy u obskikh ugrov', in I.S. Gurvich and B.O. Dolgikh, eds., *Preobrazovaniya v khozyaystve i kulture* . . ., pp. 85–105.

Solovyov, A.I. *Voyennoye delo korennogo naseleniya zapadnoy Sibiri: epokha srednevekovya*, Novosibirsk, 1987.

Solovyov, S.M. *Istoriya Rossii s drevneyshikh vremen*, 15 vols., St Petersburg, 1851–79, reprinted Moscow, 1962–6.

Solzhenitsyn, A.I. *Gulag Archipelago*, 3 vols., London, 1974–8.

Sobraniye sochineniy, Vermont, 1978, vol. IX.

Spiridonov, N.I. 'Oduly Kolymskogo okruga', *Sovetskiy Sever*, 1930, no. 9–12, pp. 167–214.

Stebnitskiy, S.N. 'Koryatskiye deti', *Sovetskiy Sever*, 1930, no. 4, pp. 39–47.

Stepanova, M.V. and I.S. Gurvich, 'Yukagiry', *Narody Sibiri*, pp. 885–95.

Stephan, J.J. *Sakhalin: a History*, Oxford, 1971.

The Kuril Islands: Russo-Japanese Frontier in the Pacific, Oxford, 1974.

The Russian Fascists: Tragedy and Farce in Exile, 1925–1945, London, 1978.

Stepichev, I.S. *Pobeda leninskogo kooperativnogo plana v vostochnosibirskoy derevne*, Irkutsk, 1966.

Sukhomirov, G.I. 'Okhotnichye-promyslovoye khozyaystvo na Dalnem Vostoke', in V.I. Boyko et al., *Problemy sovremennogo sotsialnogo razvitiya narodnostey Severa*, pp. 135–42.

Sunik, O.P. *Ulchskiy yazyk: issledovaniya i materialy*, Leningrad, 1985.

'Tunguso-manchzhurskiye yazyki', 'Ulchskiy yazyk', 'Udegeyskiy yazyk', in *Yazyki narodov SSSR*, vol. V, pp. 53–67, 149–71, 210–32.

SUPAR Report, Honolulu, 1987-

Superanskaya, A.V. ed., *Spravochnik lichnykh imen narodov RSFSR*, 2nd edn, Moscow, 1979.

Suslov, I.M. 'Shamanstvo i borba s nim', *Sovetskiy Sever*, 1931, no. 3–4, pp. 89–152.

Swenson, O. *Northwest of the World: Forty Years' Trading and Hunting in Northern Siberia*, London, 1951.

Taksami, Ch.M. *Nivkhi (sovremennoye khozyaystvo, kultura i byt)*, Leningrad, 1967.

'Podgotovka spetsialistov iz sredy narodov Severa', in I.S. Gurvich, *Osushchestvleniye*, pp. 172–87.

'Sootnosheniye traditsionnogo i novogo v kulture narodnostey Severa', in V.I. Boyko et al., *Problemy sovremennogo razvitiya narodnostey Severa*, pp. 169–74.

Terentyev, A. 'Pogromy nentsami yasachnoy kazny v 1641 i 1642 gg.', *Sovetskaya etnografiya*, 1933, no. 5–6, pp. 67–76.

Tereshchenko, N.M. 'Nenetskiy yazyk', 'Nganasanskiy yazyk', 'Enetskiy yazyk', in *Yazyki narodov SSSR*, vol. III, pp. 376–95, 416–57.

Tereshkin, N.I. 'Khantyyskiy yazyk', in *Yazyki narodov SSSR*, vol. III, pp. 319–42.

Timofeyev, A.I. ed., *Pamyatniki Sibirskoy istorii XVIII veka*, 2 vols., St Petersburg, 1882–5.

Tokarev, S.A. *Etnografiya narodov SSSR*, Moscow, 1958.

Tokarev, S.A. and I.S. Gurvich, 'Yakuty', *Narody Sibiri*, pp. 267–328.

Tomilov, N.A. 'Dinamika etnicheskikh protsessov u sibirskikh tatar v kontse 1960-kh – 1970-kh godakh (po materialam tomskikh tatar), in I S. Gurvich, ed., *Etnokulturnyye protsessy...*, pp. 40–54.

Toshchakova, Ye.M. 'Zametki o sovremennon semeynom byte u altaytsev', in A.P. Okladnikov, ed., *Etnografiya narodov Altaya i Zapadnoy Sibiri*, pp. 65–9.

Treadgold, D.W. *The Great Siberian Migration: Government and Peasant in Resettlement from Emancipation to the First World War*, Princeton, 1957.

Trotskiy, I.M. 'Nekotorye problemy istorii Yakutii XVII veka', in *Kolonialnaya politika Moskovskogo gosudarstva v Yakutii XVIIv.*, pp. xx–xxvii.

Tugolukov, V.A. *Tungusy (evenki i eveny) Sredney i Zapadnoy Sibiri*, Moscow, 1985. *Sledopyty verkhom na olenyakh*, Moscow, 1969.
'Evenki', 'Eveny', in I.S. Gurvich, ed., *Etnicheskaya istoriya narodov Severa*, pp. 129–68.
'Preobrazovaniya v khozyaystve i kulture u evenkov Amurskoy oblasti', in I.S. Gurvich, and B.O. Dolgikh, eds., *Preobrazovaniya v khozyaystve i kulture . . .*, pp. 226–55.
'Preodoleniye starogo v bytu i soznanii evenkov', in I.S. Gurvich, ed., *Osushchestvleniye leninskoy natsionalnoy politiki . . .*, pp. 200–12.
'Sotsialno-ekonomicheskiye i etnokulturnyye izmeneniya u evenov v sovetskoye vremya', in I.S. Gurvich, ed., *Etnokulturnyye protsessy . . .*, pp. 121–43.

Tultseva, L.A. *Sovremennye prazdniki i obryady narodov SSSR*, Moscow, 1985.

Tumarcha, 'Sprosi khozyaina', *Severnye prostory*, 1989, no. 3, p. 2.

Tumasheva, D.G. *Dialekty sibirskikh tatar: opyt sravnitelnogo issledovaniya*, Kazan, 1977.

Twitchett, D. and J.K. Fairbank, eds., *The Cambridge History of China*, vol. X, pts 1 and 2, Cambridge, 1978.

Ubryatova, Ye.I. 'Yakutskiy yazyk' in *Yazyki narodov SSSR*, vol. II, pp. 403–27.

Ugrin, M. 'Obraz Kamchatki v glazakh itelmenov', *Sibirskiye ogni*, 1989, no. 8, pp. 166–7.

Ukachin, B. *Povesti*, perevod s altayskogo, Moscow, 1983.

Ukrainska zagalna entsiklyopediya: kniga znaniya v 3-okh tomakh, Lviv [1935?].

Ulanova, A.I. ed., *Abai Geser*, Ulan-Üde, 1960.

Ulymzhiyev, D. ' "Krugly stol" mongolovedov', *Baykal*, 1990, no. 3, pp. 141–4.

Umanskiy, A.P. *Teleuty i russkiye v XVII–XVIIIvv.*, Novosibirsk, 1980.

USSR. Tsentralnoye statisticheskoye upravleniye [Census 1959] *Itogi Vsesoyuznoy perepisi naseleniya 1959 goda. RSFSR*, Moscow, 1963.
[Census 1970] *Itogi Vsesoyuznoy perepisi naseleniya 1970 goda.* vol. IV: *Natsionalnyy sostav naseleniya SSSR, soyuznykh i avtonomnykh respublik, krayev, oblastey i natsionalnykh okrugov*, Moscow, 1973.
[Census 1979] *Chislennost i sostav naseleniya SSSR po dannym Vsesoyuznoy perepisi naseleniya 1979 goda*, Moscow, 1984.
[Census 1989]
(a) 'O predvaritelnykh itogakh Vsesoyuznoy perepisi naseleniya 1989 goda', *Pravda*, 29 April 1989, p. 2.
(b) 'Demography', *Report on the USSR*, 1990, vol. II, no. 3, pp. 15–19.
(c) Gosudarstvennyy komitet SSSR po statistike, *Natsionalnyy sostav naseleniya*, ch. II, Moscow, 1989.

Uvachan, V.N. *Perekhod k sotsializmu malykh narodov Severa (po materialam Evenkiyskogo i Taymyrskogo natsionalnykh okrugov)*, Moscow, 1958.

Vakhrin, S. 'Liniya ili oshibka?', *Severnye prostory*, 1988, no. 6, pp. 14–15.

Valentey, D.I. et al., eds., *Naseleniye i trudovye resursy RSFSR*, Moscow, 1982.

Vasilevich, G.M. 'Evenki', *Narody Sibiri*, pp. 701–41.
'Tokminskiye tungusy', *Sovetskiy Sever*, 1930, no. 5, pp. 27–38.

'Vitimo-Tungir-Olekminskiye Tungusy: geograficheskaya kharakteristika', *Sovetskiy Sever*, 1930, no. 3, pp. 96–113.

Vasilyev, V. 'Ein tungusisches Schamanengrab', *Globus*, 1909, vol. 96, pp. 314–17.

Vasilyev, V.I. 'Nentsy i entsy', in I.S. Gurvich, ed., *Etnicheskaya istoriya narodov Severa*, pp. 48–81.

'Nentsy i entsy Taymyrskogo natsionalnogo okruga (Ocherk khozyaystva, byta i etnicheskikh protsessov, protekayushchikh na Yeniseyskom Severe)', in I.S. Gurvich and B.O. Dolgikh, eds., *Preobrazovaniya v khozyaystve i kulture* . . ., pp. 106–63.

'Osobennosti razvitiya etnicheskikh i yazykovykh protsessov v etnokontaktnykh zonakh Yevropeyskogo Severa i Severnoy Sibiri (po materialam . . . severosamodiyskikh narodov: nentsev, entsev i nganasan)', in I.S. Gurvich, ed., *Etnokulturnyye protsessy* . . ., pp. 65–93.

Vasilyev, V.I. and Yu.B. Simchenko, 'Pereustroystvo khozyaystva, byta i kultury korennogo naseleniya Taymyrskogo natsionalnogo okruga', in I.S. Gurvich, ed., *Osushchestvleniye leninskoy natsionalnoy politiki* . . ., pp. 245–75.

Vasilyev, V.I., Yu.B. Simchenko and Z.P. Sokolova, 'Problemy rekonstruktsii byta malykh narodov Kraynego Severa', *Sovetskaya etnografiya*, 1966, pt. 3, pp. 9–22.

Vasmer, M. *Russisches etymologisches Wörterbuch*, Heidelberg, 1953–8.

Vaynshteyn, S.I. *Nomads of South Siberia: the Pastoral Economies of Tuva*, Cambridge, 1980.

Vdovin, I.S. ed., *Priroda i chelovek v religioznykh predstavleniyakh narodov Sibiri i Severa*, Leningrad, 1976.

Veale, E.M. *The English Fur Trade in the Later Middle Ages*, Oxford, 1966.

Vitebsky, P. 'Perestroika among the reindeer herders', *Geographical Magazine*, 1989, June, pp. 22–5.

'Reindeer herders of northern Yakutia: a report from the field', *Polar Record*, 1989, vol. 25, pp. 213–18.

Volodarskiy, L.M. ed., *Naseleniye SSSR: spravochnik*, Moscow, 1983.

Volodin, A.P. and A.N. Zhukova, 'Itelmenskiy yazyk', *Yazyki narodov SSSR*, vol. V, pp. 334–51.

Vyatkina, K.V. 'Buryaty', *Narody Sibiri*, pp. 217–66.

Waxell, S. *The American Expedition*, London, 1952.

White, J.A. *The Siberian Intervention*, New York, 1950.

Wood, A. 'Chernyshevskii, Siberian exile and *oblastnichestvo*', in R. Bartlett, ed., *Russian Thought and Society, 1800–1917: Essays in Honour of Eugene Lampert*, Keele, 1984, pp. 42–66.

'Sex and violence in Siberia: aspects of the tsarist exile system', in J.M. Stewart and A. Wood, *Siberia: Two Historical Perspectives*, London, 1984, pp. 23–42.

'Crime and punishment in Imperial Russia', in O. Crisp and L. Edmundson, eds., *Civil Rights in Imperial Russia*, Oxford, 1989.

Wood, A. and R.A. French, *The Development of Siberia: People and Resources*, London, 1989.

Yadrinstev, N.M. *Sibir kak koloniya. K yubileyu trekhsotletiya: sovremennaya Sibir, yeya nuzhdy i potrebnosti, yeya proshloye i budushcheye*, St Petersburg, 1882.

Sibirskiye inorodtsy: ikh byt i sovremennoye polozheniye, St Petersburg, 1891.

Yakovlev, B. *Kontsentratsionnye lageri SSSR*, London (Ontario), 1983.

Yazyki narodov SSSR, ed. V.V. Vinogradov, vol. II, *Tyurkskiye yazyki*; vol. III, *Finno-ugorskiye i samodiyskiye yazyki*; vol. V, *Mongolskiye, tunguso-manchzhurskiye i paleoaziatskiye yazyki*, Moscow, 1966–8.

Yefimenko, Yu. 'Posledniye iz Udege?', *Ogonyok*, 1990, no. 10, pp. 10–12.

Yefimov, A.V. ed., *Atlas geograficheskikh otkrytiy v Sibiri i v severo-zapadnoy Amerike XVII–XVIII vv.*, Moscow, 1964.

Yefimova, A.K. and Y.N. Klitina, comps., *Chukotskoye i eskimosskoye iskusstvo*, Leningrad, 1981.

Yefremova, L. 'Zyryanka i okrest', *Polyarnaya zvezda*, 1989, no. 1, pp. 102–6.

Yegorov, G.M. comp., *Altayskiy kray (Turisticheskiye rayony SSSR)*, Moscow, 1987.

Yeliseyev, N.V. et al., eds., *Krasnaya kniga RSFSR: zhivotnye*, Moscow, 1983.

Yendin, A. 'Kolzhoznoye stroitelstvo v sele Bolchar Kondinskogo rayona', *Tayga i tundra*, 1933, vol. II, no. 5, p. 18.

Yepifaniy Premudryy, *Zhitiye Svyatago Stefana, yepiskopa Permskago*, St Petersburg, 1897.

Yermolenko, Yu. 'Po chernomu sledu "pokoritelya" ', *Severnye prostory*, 1988, no. 5, p. 18.

Yermolin, A.P. *Revolyutsiya i kazachestvo (1917–1920gg.)*, Moscow, 1982.

Zadorin, V.I. 'Sotsialno-ekonomicheskiye problemy optimizatsii severnogo olenevodstva', in V.I. Boyko et al., *Problemy sovremennogo sotsialnogo razvitiya narodnostey Severa*, pp. 142–50.

Zalkind, Ye.M. *Prisoyedineniye Buryatii k Rossii*, Ulan-Üde, 1958.

Zalygin, S. 'Vozvrashchayas k vodnym problemam', *Kommunist*, 1988, no. 13, pp. 52–61.

Zhdanov, A. 'Ne vina, a beda', *Pravda*, 20 February 1989, p. 2.

Zhikharev, N.A. *Ocherki istorii Severo-Vostoka RSFSR (1917–1953gg.)*, Magadan, 1961.

Zhornitskaya, M.Ya. 'Otrazheniye etnokulturnykh protsessov v khoreograficheskom iskusstve narodov Severo-Vostoka Sibiri', in Gurvich, ed., *Etnokulturnyye protsessy . . .*, pp. 194–202.

Zhukova, A.N. 'Koryakskiy yazyk', 'Alyutorskiy yazyk', *Yazyki narodov SSSR*, vol. V, pp. 271–309.

Zhukovskaya, N.L. 'Sovremennyy lamaizm (na materialakh Buryatskoy ASSR)', in *Voprosy nauchnogo ateizma*, Moscow, 1969, vol. VII, pp. 221–42.

Zoriktuyev, B. 'Bylo li vtorzheniye voyska Chingis-khana v Pribaykalye?', *Baykal*, 1990, no. 2, pp. 98–101.

INDEX

Page numbers grouped at the beginning of a reference to a nationality cover the indigenous material culture, way of life, social organisation beliefs, etc.

Numbers in italics refer to illustrations; those with M refer to maps.